PUBLICATIONS FOR THE NEW CHAUCER SOCIETY

THE NEW CHAUCER SOCIETY

Studies in the Age of Chaucer, the yearbook of The New Chaucer Society, is published annually. Each issue contains substantial articles on all aspects of Chaucer and his age, book reviews, and an annotated Chaucer bibliography. Manuscripts should follow the *Chicago Manual of Style,* 16th edition. Unsolicited reviews are not accepted. Authors receive twenty free offprints of articles and ten of reviews. All correspondence regarding manuscript submissions should be directed to the Editor, David Matthews, School of Arts, Histories and Cultures, University of Manchester, Oxford Road, Manchester M13 9PL, United Kingdom. Subscriptions to The New Chaucer Society and information about the Society's activities should be directed to David Lawton, Department of English, Washington University, CB 1122, One Brookings Drive, St. Louis, MO 63130. Back issues of the journal may be ordered from The University of Notre Dame Press, Chicago Distribution Center, 11030 South Langley Avenue, Chicago, IL 60628; phone: 800-621-2736; fax: 800-621-8476; from outside the United States, phone: 773-702-7000; fax: 773-702-7212.

Studies in the Age of Chaucer

Studies in the Age of Chaucer

Volume 33
2011

EDITOR

DAVID MATTHEWS

PUBLISHED ANNUALLY BY THE NEW CHAUCER SOCIETY

WASHINGTON UNIVERSITY IN ST. LOUIS

The frontispiece design, showing the Pilgrims at the Tabard Inn, is adapted from the woodcut in Caxton's second edition of the *Canterbury Tales*.

Copyright © 2011 by The New Chaucer Society, Washington University. First edition. Published by the University of Notre Dame Press for The New Chaucer Society.

ISBN-10 0-933784-35-X
ISBN-13 978-0-933784-35-2
ISSN 0190-2407

CONTENTS

CONTENTS

BOOKS RECEIVED

AN ANNOTATED CHAUCER BIBLIOGRAPHY, 2009

Mark Allen, Bege K. Bowers

Program, Seventeenth International Congress

INDEX

Studies in the Age of Chaucer

THE PRESIDENTIAL ADDRESS
The New Chaucer Society
Seventeenth International Congress
July 15–19, 2010
Università per Stranieri, Siena

The Presidential Address

Griselda in Siena

Richard Firth Green
The Ohio State University

THE GERM OF THIS ESSAY came to me as I was rereading Derek Brewer's *Symbolic Stories* in preparation for a commemorative session at the 2010 Kalamazoo Congress, and I hope that it may stand here as a modest tribute to one of the founding members of our New Chaucer Society and a standard-bearer for humane Chaucerian criticism throughout the world. We all miss Derek's genial presence, nowhere more so than here in Italy, a country he held particularly dear. Rereading *Symbolic Stories,*[1] I found myself wondering why it was that so few Chaucerians had followed Derek in keeping faith with the study of the traditional folktale through the long years of poststructuralism and new historicism. Since actual historians (particularly the French *annalistes* like Jacques Le Goff and Jean-Claude Schmitt and the British cultural materialists like E. P. Thompson and Eric Hobsbawm) had shown themselves far from indifferent to folklore, one might have thought that the historicist turn taken by Middle English studies would have fostered a similar interest. It was a historian, after all, Judith Bennett, who reprimanded delegates to the 2006 New Chaucer Society Meeting in New York for their lack of attention to popular ballads and carols.[2] Be that as it may, I should like to take this opportunity to pay homage to Derek Brewer's memory by attempting a Chaucerian reading that is both folkloric and historicist, and in deference to our charming surroundings I will take as my subject *The Clerk's Tale,* a story whose origins are rooted in the folklore of the Tuscan countryside, though in actuality I will be less con-

---

[1] Derek Brewer, *Symbolic Stories: Traditional Narratives of the Family Drama in English Literature* (Cambridge: D. S. Brewer, 1980).
[2] Judith M. Bennett, "The Curse of the Plowman," *YLS* 20 (2006): 221–23.

cerned here with *The Clerk's Tale* itself than with the generic story of Griselda, of which Chaucer's tale is but one early expression.

Almost everyone seems to agree that the story of Griselda began life as a folktale, but there is very little agreement as to what kind of folktale it was.[3] To my mind, genealogical debates about whether Griselda is to be traced back to a "Cupid and Psyche" archetype, or whether it is more closely related to the "Monstrous Husband" or the "Ogre Schoolmaster" subtype, are generally rather unproductive. However, I think it is rather more useful to imagine a forerunner of Boccaccio's story being told in a fourteenth-century equivalent of the Tuscan *veglia,* or evening gathering around the family hearth (Fig. 1), so vividly evoked for us by the Sienese scholar Alessandro Falassi (interestingly, Falassi's epigraphs for the chapters of his *Folklore by the Fireside* are taken from the *Decameron*).[4] The *veglie* attended by Falassi in the countryside around Siena in the 1970s proceeded in three stages, each concentrated on a different age group (first children, then those of marriageable age, and finally the elders). Here is his description of the final stage: "When at the end of the *veglia* the elders took the floor again, the tone and topic changed; the emphasis shifted to maintaining the family units, rather than the formation of couples. . . . In general, the elders liked and were more interested in the 'stories of married people,' in which the protagonists confronted situations with which the narrators or listeners who were 'old' (that is, 'adult' with positive connotation, deriving from age and experience) had to deal regularly at that stage of their life. Consequently, toward the end of the *veglia,* the narrators recounted pitiful cases, the events and vicissitudes of marriage" (148). One of the stories Falassi listened to in 1974 was the tale of *Pia de Tolomei,* the story of a falsely accused wife with obvious similarities to Griselda's; of course Dante alluded to Pia de Tolomei's story ("Siena made me, Maremma undid me"),[5] a fact perfectly well known to the *vegliatori* themselves, though there is no reason to suppose that the tale that Falassi heard had survived continuously and unchanged across more than six centuries. Nonetheless, the social dynamics of the *veglia,* as Falassi shows, reach deep into the traditions of the Tuscan countryside, and it is at least

[3] For a thorough overview, see William Bettridge and Francis Lee Utley, "New Light on the Origin of the Griselda Story," *TSLL* 13 (1971): 153–208.

[4] Alessandro Falassi, *Folklore by the Fireside: Text and Context of the Tuscan Veglia* (Austin: University of Texas Press, 1980).

[5] *"Siena mi fé, disfecemi Maremma"(Purgatorio,* V.134).

Fig. 1. "Getting Ready for the Veglia." From Alessandro Falassi, *Folklore by the Fireside: Text and Context of the Tuscan Veglia* (Austin: University of Texas Press, 1980). By permission of Alessandro Falassi.

arguable that they can tell us as much about the meaning of the story of Griselda for Petrarch's contemporaries as the far better-known remarks of his two humanist friends, the sentimentalist from Padua and the skeptic from Verona.[6]

When Giovanni Boccaccio took the folktale of Patient Griselda and adapted it as the last story in his *Decameron* in 1353, he planted a literary time bomb that would only be detonated two decades later with Francis Petrarch's Latin adaptation of it in his *Litterae seniles*. The explosion of Griselda texts over the next three decades is a phenomenon matched only in the medieval West by the more diffuse but, given the lower rates of lay literacy at the time, no less dramatic explosion of Arthurian texts in the half century or so following Geoffrey of Monmouth's *History of the Kings of Britain* (see Appendix I). Chaucerian scholarship, dependent as it has been on the solid, but outdated, work of Burke Severs,[7] and the more far-ranging, though equally outdated and rather less reliable, study by Elie Golenistcheff-Koutouzoff,[8] has scarcely begun to appreciate the scope of this explosion. The work of Raffaele Morabito in particular allows us to see Chaucer as only one piece in a puzzle of pan-European dimensions.[9] What was it about the story of Griselda that made it spread like wildfire from Italy, to Iberia, France, and England in a few short years at the end of the fourteenth century? Only the Germanic, Nordic, and Slavic countries were exempt, at least in the short term; there is no evidence, for example, that Petrarch's text was known in Germany before the Council of Constance (1414–18).[10] This essay will try to provide an answer.

"Within fairytales," wrote Brewer (citing Propp), "a function can only be correctly understood when its place in the sequence is established,"[11] and since, as any folklorist, including Propp,[12] will tell you,

[6] *Originals and Analogues of Some of Chaucer's Canterbury Tales,* pt. II, no. 10, ed. F. J. Furnivall (1875; London: Oxford University Press, 1895), 170–71.

[7] J. Burke Severs, *The Literary Relationships of Chaucer's Clerkes Tale* (New Haven: Yale University Press, 1942).

[8] Elie Golenistcheff-Koutouzoff, *L'histoire de Griseldis en France au XIVᵉ et au XVᵉ siècle* (Paris: Droz, 1933).

[9] Raffaele Morabito, "La diffusione della storia di Griselda dal XIV al XX secolo," *Studi sul Boccaccio* 17 (1988): 237–85.

[10] Joachim Knape, *De oboedientia et fide uxoris: Petrarcas humanistisch-moralisches Exempel "Griseldis" und seine frühe deutsche Rezeption* (Göttingen: Gratia, 1978), 21–22.

[11] Derek Brewer, "Towards a Chaucerian Poetic," *Publications of the British Academy* 60 (1974): 219–52 (238).

[12] V. Propp, *Morphology of the Folktale,* trans. Laurence Scott, 2nd ed. (Austin: University of Texas Press, 1968), 74.

things in the folktale tend to happen in threes, when we reach the third, it is always time to sit up and take notice: the third time Rumpelstiltskin visits the queen, for instance, he finds that she has discovered his name, and the third time Jack shinnies up the beanstalk, the giant smells him out. Something similar, I shall argue, happens with the story of Griselda, only here, of course, Marquis Walter submits his wife to *four* tests: (1) He has their infant daughter taken away, leaving Griselda with the impression that she is to be killed; (2) He has their infant son taken away under similar circumstances; (3) He produces a forged divorce document and sends Griselda home to her father; and (4) He brings Griselda back to the house to prepare it for the arrival of his new bride. Interestingly there is a tendency among readers to reduce these four to three, either by amalgamating the first two (thus the first test becomes "the removal of the children"),[13] or, more commonly, the last two (so that the third test becomes "the divorce and second marriage"—you'll find an example of this in the Wikipedia article on Griselda).[14] But regardless of how the tests are structured in the reader's imagination, one salient fact remains: the laws of the folktale mean that the crucial test, the one upon which Griselda's fate ultimately hangs, must be the last—her return to the house to prepare it for her replacement.

There is in fact textual evidence for such a progression. Boccaccio, for instance, describes Griselda as having "great grief in her heart" [*gran noia nel cuor*] when her daughter is taken from her, and "deeply griev[ing] within herself" [*forte in sé medesima si dolea*] at the news of the divorce, but when she learns she must prepare the palace for her successor, "all these words were a knife in Griselda's heart" [*queste parole fossero tutte coltella al cuor di Griselda*],[15] a phrase that evidently impressed itself upon Boccaccio's follower, Giovanni Sercambi.[16] Petrarch merely says that after the first two trials, Walter returned to testing Griselda "to the height of sorrow and shame" [*doloris ac pudoris ad cumulum*],[17] an ambiguous

[13] See, e.g., Bettridge and Utley, "New Light," 165–66; James Sledd, "The Clerk's Tale: The Monsters and Critics," *MP* 51 (1953): 73–82 (71).

[14] See, e.g., John P. McCall, " 'The Clerk's Tale' and the Theme of Obedience," *MLQ* 27 (1966): 260–69 (263); Brewer, *Symbolic Stories,* 97; Charlotte C. Morse, "The Exemplary Griselda," *Studies in the Age of Chaucer* 7 (1985): 51–86 (52); http://en.wikipedia .org/wiki/Griselda_(folklore).

[15] Giovanni Boccaccio, *Decameron,* ed. Vittorio Branca (Turin: Einaudi, 1984), 1244 (X.10:51).

[16] *Le Cronice,* ed. Salvatore Bongi, 3 vols., Fonti per la storia d'Italia (Lucca: Giusti, 1892), 3:223; *Il Novelle,* ed. Giovanni Sinicropi, 2 vols. (Florence: Casa editrice Le Lettere, 1995), 2:1303 (CLII:36).

[17] Severs, *The Literary Relationships of Chaucer's Clerkes Tale,* 278 (V:2).

phrase that might equally well refer to Walter himself as to the nature of his last tests, but one of his early French translators (the anonymous author of the *Le livre Griseldis*) removes this ambiguity: "Wishing to try and test his wife more than before" [*vueillant sa femme plus que devant essaier et tenter*],[18] and Thomas III of Saluce expands on this: Walter, he says, "wished to test his wife more strongly than before" [*vouloit essaier sa femme plus fort que devant*].[19] Chaucer's version is generally closer to the ambiguity of Petrarch's original, but even he suggests that Walter is bent on testing his wife "to the outtreste preeve of hir corage."[20]

A particularly graphic illustration of this progression is offered us by a series of three splendid *spallieri,* painted here in Siena by an anonymous artist (probably connected with the Ghirlandaio workshop) to celebrate the double wedding of the brothers Antonio and Giulio Spannocchi in January 1494. These paintings, now in the National Gallery in London, have recently been carefully restored and their provenance thoroughly investigated.[21] To the left of the first panel (Fig. 2), Marquis Walter's hunting party is seen encountering Griselda, who is carrying a water pot on her head; on the far right, Walter leads her back from her father's cottage, and in the right foreground she is shown being stripped naked and reclothed in courtly garments; the central tableau depicts their cere-monial betrothal. More interesting from our point of view are the second and third panels. In the center of the second one (Fig. 3), Walter is showing Griselda the supposed divorce document held by a figure in a red robe, presumably a canon lawyer; to the right she undresses to her shift and on the far right returns to her father's house; on the extreme left, and painted so small that at least one art historian missed it alto-gether,[22] Griselda hands a child to the sergeant, while in the back-ground and more centrally the same sergeant is shown carrying the

[18] Ibid., 279 (V:6–7). Earlier, he had added *et continue encors plus avant,* "and went even further," to the sentence, *mais en sa merancolie et dur ymaginacion de approuver sa femme proceda,* without any warrant from Petrarch (ibid., 277 [IV:39]).

[19] "A Critical Edition of Thomas III, marquis of Saluzzo's Le livre du Chevalier Er-rant," ed. Marvin J. Ward, Ph.D. diss. (University of North Carolina at Chapel Hill, 1984), 845 (383:26–27).

[20] *The Clerk's Tale,* IV.787; citations from Chaucer are from *The Riverside Chaucer,* gen. ed. Larry D. Benson (Boston: Houghton Mifflin, 1987).

[21] Jill Dunkerton, Carol Christensen, and Luke Syson, "The Master of the Story of Griselda and Paintings for Sienese Palaces," *National Gallery Technical Bulletin* 27: "Re-naissance Siena and Perugia" (2006): 4–71.

[22] "Although the birth and removal of the infants is omitted . . . ;" Ellen Callmann, "Subjects from Boccaccio in Italian Painting, 1375–1525," *Studi sul Boccaccio* 23 (1995): 19–78 (56) (no. 85).

Fig. 2. Master of the Story of Griselda, *The Story of Griselda, Part 1: Marriage*. Reproduced with permission of the National Gallery.

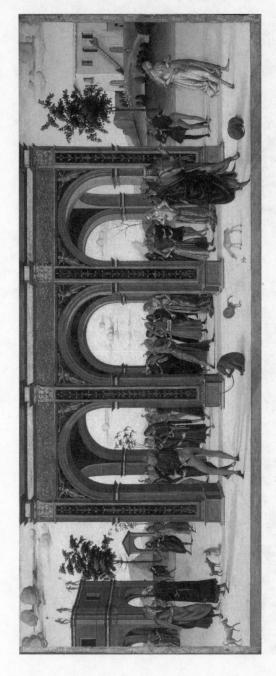

Fig. 3. Master of the Story of Griselda, *The Story of Griselda, Part 2: Exile*. Reproduced with permission of the National Gallery.

child away. By contrast, the final panel (Fig. 4) displays Griselda's servile role at the marriage feast prominently and in great detail. On the extreme right, Walter fetches her from her father's house, and on the extreme left she is shown sweeping the threshold of his palace; a little to the right of this, she instructs the servants, and on the right side of the panel she greets the supposed bride and her brother, while at the right-hand end of the table she waits upon them. There are, in other words, five depictions of Griselda in her role as servant, and only one, at the left-hand end of the table, of her final reconciliation with Walter (though even here she still wears her old clothes).

For the twenty-first-century reader, however, the idea that Walter's two last tests are more oppressive than the removal of the children is deeply counterintuitive. As Jean-Jacques Rousseau's heirs, we feel instinctively that the most barbarous thing Walter does is to separate Griselda from her daughter and son; anything done afterward may add insult to injury, but it cannot in any way match the gratuitous cruelty of this initial act. Without wishing to endorse Philippe Ariès's view of medieval attitudes to children,[23] I might, however, point out that well-born Tuscan mothers in the *trecento* were quite frequently separated from their infants: for one thing, they regularly put their babies out to wet-nurses, often wet-nurses who lived some distance from town, so that they saw them only intermittently in the first two years of their lives,[24] and for another, if a young Tuscan widow remarried (and she was often put under considerable pressure to do so by her parents), she was expected to leave her children, whatever their ages, behind with her first husband's family.[25] In what follows, I shall argue that not only is an overemphasis on Walter's cruelty in removing their children anachronistic, but that it distorts the real meaning that the tale held for fourteenth-century audiences. Only by restoring the motif of the woman's preparation of the house for her replacement to its proper place in the hierarchy of tests can we understand why this should be.

[23] *Centuries of Childhood: A Social History of Family Life,* trans. Robert Baldick (New York: Vintage, 1962); cf. Nicholas Orme, *Medieval Children* (New Haven: Yale University Press, 2001).

[24] See Christiane Klapisch-Zuber, *Women, Family, and Ritual in Renaissance Italy,* trans. Lydia Cochrane (Chicago: University of Chicago Press, 1985), chap. 7 ("Blood Parents and Milk Parents: Wet Nursing in Florence, 1300–1530"), 132–64.

[25] Klapisch-Zuber, *Women, Family, and Ritual,* chap. 6 ("The Cruel Mother: Maternity, Widowhood, and Dowry in Florence in the Fourteenth and Fifteenth Centuries"), 117–31.

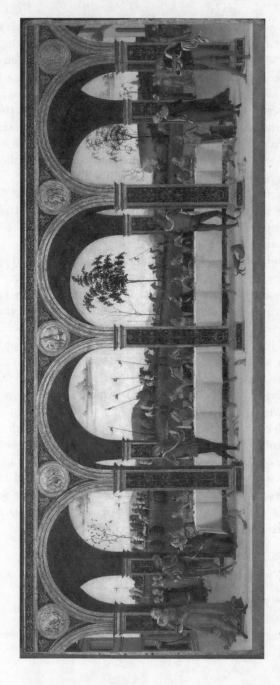

Fig. 4. Master of the Story of Griselda, *The Story of Griselda, Part 3: Reunion*. Reproduced with permission of the National Gallery.

Let us start with a twentieth-century example. Ruth Rendell, a writer who is as aware as anyone of the subversive potential of concealed folk-tale motifs, employs this one in her 1993 novel, *The Crocodile Bird*. Eve, a beautiful and talented young woman, traumatized by a brutal rape while away at college, takes a job as a housekeeper in a secluded country mansion whose owner spends much of his time traveling abroad. There, she works obsessively to bring up her daughter cocooned from the menace of the outside world. In a series of increasingly more desperate attempts to preserve this fragile sanctuary, she is driven not only to carry on a clandestine affair with the mansion's owner (less because she is attracted to him than because of her need to secure her claim on his house), but also to murder two men who, in different ways, threaten this asylum. By a clever use of the innocent eye, Rendell tells this story from the point of view of Eve's daughter, the Crocodile Bird of the title. At one point the owner writes to tell Eve that he is getting married.

On the Sunday morning while Liza was eating her breakfast, Mother said, "Mr. Tobias is getting married today. This is his wedding day."
"What's wedding?" said Liza.
So Mother explained about getting married. She turned it into a lesson. . . .
"Will they come and live here?" said Liza.
Mother didn't answer and Liza was going to repeat the question, but she didn't because Mother had gone a dark red and clenched her fists. Liza thought it best to say no more about it. . . .
And of course Mr. and Mrs. Tobias never did come to live at Shrove, though they stayed there from time to time, the first time being a fortnight after the wedding. Another letter came first. Mother read it, screwed it up, and looked cross.
"What does he mean, get a woman in to get the place ready? He knows I'll never do that. He knows that I'll clean it and that I'll clean it ready for his wife." And she said those final two words again. "His wife."[26]

From here, things go from bad to worse, and Eve eventually kills Mr. Tobias with a shotgun, though not directly as a result of this particular indignity.

Rendell could well have come across this motif in *The Clerk's Tale*

[26] Ruth Rendell, *The Crocodile Bird* (New York: Doubleday Dell, 1994), 114–15.

itself, but there are at least two other places where she might have encountered it. The more likely is the ballad of *Fair Annie*, where Annie, Lord Thomas's long-suffering mistress, who has borne him seven sons and is pregnant with the eighth, learns that she is to be replaced by a "braw bride" for entirely mercenary reasons:

> "It's narrow, make your bed,
> And learn to lie your lane;
> For I'm ga'n oer the sea, Fair Annie,
> A braw bride to bring hame.
> Wi her I will get gowd and gear;
> Wi you I neer got nane.
>
> "But wha will bake my bridal bread,
> Or brew my bridal ale?
> And wha will welcome my brisk bride,
> That I bring oer the dale?"
>
> "It's I will bake your bridal bread,
> And brew your bridal ale,
> And I will welcome your brisk bride,
> That you bring oer the dale."[27]

In performing this task, however, Fair Annie shows none of the stoic self-restraint of Griselda:

> And aye she served the lang tables,
> With white bread and with brown;
> And ay she turned her round about,
> Sae fast the tears fell down.
>   (62A.18)

And though the new-come bride eventually recognizes her as her long-lost sister and provides her with a marriage portion that enables her to marry Lord Thomas, it is not before the cast-off mistress has savagely cursed her own children:

> Gin my seven sons were seven young rats,
> Running on the castle wa,

[27] Francis James Child, ed., *The English and Scottish Popular Ballads,* 2nd ed. rev. by Mark F. Heiman and Laura Saxon Heiman (Northfield, Minn.: Loomis House Press, 2001–), 2:72–93 (no. 62A.1–3).

And I were a grew cat mysell,
I soon would worry them a'.

Gin my seven sons were seven young hares,
Running oer yon lilly lee,
And I were a grew hound mysell,
Soon worried they a' should be.
                                        (62A.23–24)

The final, and least likely, pattern for Rendell's Eve is Marie de France's
Le Freine.[28] Here, too, we have a mistress preparing the house for the
arrival of her lover's bride, but the atmosphere is far less menacing. The
groom, the Count of Dol, evidently still cherishes his old love but, like
Marquis Walter, is forced to take a wife merely to satisfy the demands
of his people; since Le Freine, a penniless orphan, can have no aspirations
to this position, she apparently dresses the bed chamber for the future
countess (who, like Fair Annie, will eventually turn out to be her long-
lost sister) in a spirit of loving and selfless generosity. There are no bitter
recriminations here, and no hints of violence. Interestingly, in Jean Re-
nart's retelling of Marie de France's tale, *Galéran de Bretagne,*[29] where
the heroine is far less passive, the motif is dropped altogether as entirely
inappropriate.

Each of these versions of this folktale motif has its own distinct character, but all four share one essential characteristic: the tension between
the woman's double role as loving bedfellow and dutiful servant. In the
three early instances, the social pathology of this situation is underlined
by its association with incest, and in the fourth by linking it with rape
(Liza believes, wrongly, that Mr. Tobias is her father). Le Freine apparently embraces this discordant situation willingly, but to varying degrees the other three are all forced into it by adverse circumstance—the
protection of their children, the maintenance of a roof over their heads,
the recognition that they lack any other means of support. Three of
the four are ex-mistresses of the prospective bridegroom, with all the
ambiguity of status that that role implies; only Griselda is, as she believes herself to be, an ex-wife, or, as the reader knows her to be, still
legally married. This paradox, I believe, is the key to the tale's power.
Walter systematically deprives his wife of everything that might give

[28] Marie de France, *Lais,* ed. Alfred Ewert (Oxford: Blackwell, 1963), 35–48.
[29] Ed. Lucien Foulet (Paris: Champion, 1925).

her a claim to something other than servile status—a consequential family to take her side, money and belongings of her own, the status acquired as mother of his children, and finally the legal protection of matrimony itself (or at least the appearance of such protection)—so that he is at liberty to test her willingness to serve him by casting her in the most menial and invidious of roles imaginable. The tale of Griselda, particularly in the hands of skilled storytellers like Boccaccio, Petrarch, and Chaucer, is of course about many other things,[30] but when we ask ourselves what made it a best-seller in late fourteenth-century Western Europe, why people found it a fascinating subject of conversation (as the Ménagier de Paris assures us that they did),[31] surely the answer must lie in this startling role reversal, from marchioness to chambermaid, and the fundamental questions about the marital relationship it so dramatically raises.

Many readers, including Brewer,[32] have noted the tension between the deeply "tradition centered" nature of the tale itself and Chaucer's own "naturalistic" rendering of it (Petrarch himself had termed these two poles *fabula* and *historia*),[33] but in one form or another this tension inheres in all early written versions of the story. Boccaccio's and Petrarch's renderings of the Griselda story, too, give a naturalistic cast to folk-tale material (after all, the marquisate of Saluce was real enough, and Thomas III, the man who held the title in Chaucer's day, was clearly convinced that Walter was one of his own ancestors),[34] but inevitably there are moments when such a "tradition centered" tale must frustrate normal mimetic expectations (Petrarch famously tells us that one of his readers, a man from Verona, was left unmoved by Griselda's plight because he believed that it was "only a story" (*nisi quod ficta*), an opinion

---

[30]See, for example, Robin Kirkpatrick, "The Griselda Story in Boccaccio, Petrarch, and Chaucer," in *Chaucer and the Italian Trecento,* ed. Piero Boitani (Cambridge: Cambridge University Press, 1983), 231–48.

[31]"Since others are familiar with it [the story of Griselda], I very much wish that you also may be familiar with it and be able to converse about such things as everyone else does." *The Good Wife's Guide: Le Ménagier de Paris, a Medieval Household Book,* trans. Gina L. Greco and Christine M. Rose (Ithaca: Cornell University Press, 2009), 119 (1.6:10).

[32]Brewer, "Towards a Chaucerian Poetic," 235.

[33]"Quis vel Portiam, vel Hipsicrateam, vel Alcestim & harum similes non *fabulas* fictas putet? Atqui *historiae* verae sunt" [italics mine], *Originals and Analogues,* ed. Furnivall, 171.

[34]He is told the story by Orosius, who begins, "certes, sire, et je vous veuil racompter ce que ceste Dame [Fortune] a fait a une bien vostre prouchaine," *A Critical Edition of Thomas III,* ed. Ward, 830.

apparently shared by the Ménagier de Paris.[35] A careful comparison of the various translations and adaptations of the tale reveals a number of pressure points, where early readers struggled to reconcile the details of the story with their knowledge of the way marquises and peasant girls behave in the real world. I am not thinking here of major shifts of emphasis—the way, for instance, the early fifteenth-century rhymed version, *Le roumant du Marquis de Saluce*,[36] apparently unable to accept the central premise of the folktale, turns Griselda into the daughter of a gentleman (named Jean-Colin) who has fallen on hard times—but rather with small troubling details that get reworked or omitted altogether. The stripping of Griselda before the wedding is one such moment. Can Walter really have exposed his future wife's naked body to the gaze of his own followers (*in presenza di tutta la sua compagnia*), as Boccaccio says?[37] Petrarch had evidently had difficulty with his original at this point,[38] while Francesco d'Amaretto Mannelli had written "that's crazy!" [*A' pazzi!*] in the margin of the manuscript of the *Decameron* that he himself copied in 1384.[39] *Le roumant du Marquis de Saluce* actually turns this shocking incident into the first of Walter's *five* trials of his wife (lines 215–22), while others, such as Petrus de Hailles, have Griselda returning to the decency of her father's cottage to change.[40] The forged letters from Rome constitute another pressure point: Can the pope really be implicated in such a shabby subterfuge? *L'estoire de Griseldis* certainly implies that he is, since he actually appears on stage,[41] but others, including Christine de Pisan, leave out the pope altogether.[42] A

---

[35] *Originals and Analogues,* ed. Furnivall, 170–71; Greco and Rose, trans., *The Good Wife's Guide,* 119 (1.6:10).

[36] Golenistcheff-Koutouzoff, *L'histoire de Griseldis,* 225–48.

[37] *Decameron,* ed. Branca, 1237 (X.10:17).

[38] See Ann Rosalind Jones and Peter Stallybrass, *Renaissance Clothing and the Materials of Memory* (Cambridge: Cambridge University Press, 2000), 222–23.

[39] K. P. Clarke, "Reading/Writing Griselda: A Fourteenth-Century Response (Florence, Biblioteca Medicea Laurenziana, MS Plut. 42,1)," in *On Allegory: Some Medieval Aspects and Approaches,* ed. Mary Carr, K. P. Clarke, and Marco Nievergelt (Newcastle: Cambridge Scholars Publishing, 2008), 183–208 (198); see also Guido Martellotti, "Momenti Narrativi del Petrarca," *Studi Petrarcheschi* 4 (1951): 5–33 (22 n. 1). I should like to thank here Christopher Kleinhenz of the University of Wisconsin–Madison and my colleague Janice Aski for their help with the difficult phrase "A' pazzi!"

[40] "Reclusum corpus tugurio"; Dieter Vetter, ed., *Die Griseldis des Petrus de Hailles: Ein philologischer Kommentar* (Hildesheim: G. Olms, 2009), 20–21 (lines 139–40).

[41] *L'estoire de Griseldis,* ed. Mario Roques (Geneva: Droz, 1957), 72–74 (lines 1874–1933).

[42] Maureen Cheney Curnow, "The 'Livre de la Cité des Dames' of Christine de Pisan: A Critical Edition," Ph.D. diss. (Vanderbilt University, Nashville, 1975), 904.

third (and my favorite) occurs when Griselda dons her old dress on her return to her father's house. Can we really believe that a woman who has borne two children (now twelve and eight) can still get into the dress she last wore when she was a slip of a girl? "The poor little dress," says *Le livre Griseldis,* "fitted her very badly, for the woman had put on weight and become plump" (*La povre robette . . . la couvry a grant mesaise, car la femme estoit devenue grande et embarnie*);[43] the margin of Mannelli's copy contains a similar observation.[44] One might have thought that Griselda's uncritical acceptance of Walter's final explanation of his reasons for testing her might have constituted another pressure point (in Boccaccio, after all, it had prompted her ladies to censure Walter for his unwarranted cruelty),[45] but the earliest versions all treat this scene unironically and only *Le roumant du Marquis de Saluce* echoes Boccaccio here.[46] For Francesco d'Amaretto Mannelli, by contrast, it provides the occasion for his most startling aside: "Go, piss on your hand, Walter!" storms his marginal Griselda, "Who'll give me back twelve years? The gallows?"[47]

The instance that I want to dwell on here, however, is when Griselda takes up a broom to sweep clean the palace for her replacement. Boccaccio doesn't mention the broom specifically (he merely says that Griselda sets her hand to every task just like one of the humblest maid-servants in the house—*e a ogni cosa, come se una piccola fanticella della casa fosse, porre le mani* [X.10:52])—but Petrarch, though unwilling to sully his humanist Latin with a vulgar word like *scopae,* says that she snatches up the "servile instrument" (*servilia instrumenta*) and begins to clean the house and to encourage the others to work (*ortarique alias*), just like a faithful retainer (*ancile in morem fidelissime*).[48] The problem here is one of

---

[43] Severs, *The Literary Relationships of Chaucer's Clerkes Tale,* 281 (V:60–62); so too Thomas III in *A Critical Edition,* ed. Ward, 848 (384:15–17).

[44] "Non le dovevan capere, essendo ella cresciuta ed ingrossata" (Martellotti, "Momenti Narrativi," 22 n. 1); Petrarch and, following him, Chaucer merely remark that the robe is old and worn.

[45] "Troppo reputassero agre e intollerabili l'esperienze prese della sua donna" (*Decameron,* ed. Branca, 1248 (X.10:66).

[46] Golenistcheff-Koutouzoff, *L'histoire de Griseldis,* 247 (lines 889–91).

[47] "Pisciarti in mano Gualtieri! Chi mi ristora di dodici anni? le forche?" (Clarke, "Reading/Writing Griselda," 200); the reference to the gallows is presumably meant to imply that only by suffering such a shameful death could Walter atone for all the suffering he has caused her.

[48] Severs, *The Literary Relationships of Chaucer's Clerkes Tale,* 282–4 (VI:14–17); *instrumenta* here clearly means "a broom"—the word is plural because the Latin word *scopae* is a plural noun with a singular sense (cf. English *scissors* or *trousers*).

social decorum: Are we really expected to believe that a marchioness would perform so menial a task in her own person? No wonder Philippe de Mézières remarks at this point, "What more can I say, to amaze the ladies of this world?"[49]

Of the two original fourteenth-century French translations based on Petrarch, *Le livre Griseldis* at this point is the more oblique; Griselda is not specifically said to take up a broom, though she does engage in sweeping; "[Elle] commence a besoingnier, *comme de baloier la maison* [my italics]."[50] Chaucer, however, is still more restrained (like the Catalan Bernat Metge, who was writing for the noblewoman Isabel de Guimera),[51] omitting all mention of the broom and leaving open the question of whether Griselda herself does any of the actual cleaning; he certainly implies that her main role is that of a supervisor who leaves the actual sweeping to her *chambereres*:

> And with that word she gan the hous to dighte,[52]
> And tables for to sette, and beddes make;
> And peyned hir to doon al that she myghte,
> Preyynge the chambereres, for Goddes sake,
> To hasten hem, and faste swepe and shake;
> And she, the mooste servysable of alle,
> Hath every chambre arrayed and his halle.
>
> (IV.974–80)

Although Chaucer's contemporary, Thomas III, Marquis of Saluce, follows *Le livre Griseldis* fairly closely as regards the cleaning of the house, he does respond to a second pressure point in the scene: the reason that Griselda must greet his guests in her old clothes, says Walter, is that he doesn't want to make his new bride suspicious of her.[53]

---

[49] "Que diray-je plus pour les dames du monde esmerveillier?" (Golenistcheff-Koutouzoff, *L'histoire de Griseldis,* 177, VI:48–49).

[50] Severs, *The Literary Relationships of Chaucer's Clerkes Tale,* 283–85 (V.83–84); cf. Remigi dei Ricci: "E'cciò detto premendo a servire, *incominciò a spazare la casa*" [my italics]. Raffaele Morabito, ed., *Una sacra rappresentazione profana: Fortune di Griselda nel Quattrocento italiano* (Tübingen: Max Niemeyer, 1993), 74.

[51] Bernat Metge: "E encontinent a manera de una seruenta comensa de endressar lo palau . . . e de amonestar les altres campanyes que li aiudassen." *Les obres d'en Bernat Metge,* ed. R. Miquel y Planas (Barcelona: Nova Bibliotheca Catalana, 1910), 74 (lines 527–30).

[52] Interestingly, three late *CT* MSS read "she gan the hous *do* dighte" here (instead of "to dighte"). See John M. Manly and Edith Rickert, *The Text of the Canterbury Tales,* 8 vols. (Chicago: University of Chicago Press, 1940), 6:357.

[53] *A Critical Edition of Thomas III,* ed. Ward, 849 (386:15–18).

The other French translation, that of Philippe de Mézières, *does* specifically mention the broom: he tells us that Griselda *prent les vilz instruments et commence à nestoyer le palays*.[54] Moreover, he omits all mention of other servants, though he does add a sentence that has no warrant in either Boccaccio or Petrarch: "And although Griselda was dressed like the poorest of maid-servants, it certainly seemed to all who saw her at her tasks that she was a woman of great honor and of marvelous prudence."[55] This remark is echoed in the play, *L'estoire de Griseldis,* thought by some to be the work of Philippe de Mézières himself,[56] but in other respects Griselda's role is quite different:

> la vierge qui vient a moy,
> Vueil que tu empregnes en toy
> Toute l'ordennance et la cure;
> Et tous, si comme c'est droiture,
> T'obeïront en ce faisant.[57]

["I wish you to take upon yourself all the supervision and care of the virgin who is coming to me; and everyone, as is proper, will obey you in this task"], says Walter to her, and immediately we see her taking charge of the household:

> Avant, mes amis! Labourez
> A ce que tout soit nettement
> Ordonné et que noblement
> Recevons l'espeuse nouvelle.
> (2363–66)

[Let's go, my friends! Work to get everything cleaned up so we can receive the new bride nobly!], though the stage directions do indicate that she is holding a broom in her hand at this point (*tenant un balay en sa main*). The Ménagier de Paris, also working from Philippe de Mézières, takes a similar line: "Then Griselda, like a poor servant girl, took

---

[54] Golenistcheff-Koutouzoff, *L'histoire de Griseldis,* 176 (VI.38–39).

[55] "Et combien que Griseldis fust en habit d'une très povre ancelle, si sambloit-il bien à tous ceulx qui le veoyent par ses euvres qu'elle fust une femme de grant honnour et de merveilleuse prudence." Ibid., 177 (VI:43–47).

[56] Grace Frank, "The Authorship of 'le mystère de Griseldis,'" *MLN* 51 (1936): 217–29.

[57] *L'estoire de Griseldis,* ed. Roques, 90 (lines 2345–49).

the humble implements *and gave them to the household* [my italics], ordering some to clean the palace and others the stables, urging the officers and the chambermaids, each to complete carefully his particular task."[58] Christine de Pisan, perhaps predictably, declines to describe the actual cleaning (though she does say that Walter puts Griselda in charge of it),[59] but perhaps the cleverest solution of all is the verse *Roumant du Marquis de Saluce*'s, where the "servile instruments" become the keys to the linen chest that Walter hands to his wife in order for her to have the chamber made ready.[60]

To put Walter's treatment of his wife in context here, we need only to compare it with the instructions of the Ménagier de Paris to his wife:

Next, my dear [*chere seur*], know that after your husband, you must be mistress of the house, giver of orders, inspector, ruler, and sovereign administrator over the servants. It is incumbent upon you to require submission and obedience to you, and to teach, reprove, and punish the staff. . . . Tell dame Agnes the Beguine with her own eyes to witness them starting the work that you want completed in short order. First she must assign the chambermaids early in the morning to sweep and keep clean the entrances to your house . . . and to dust and shake out the footrests, bench covers and cushions. Next, every day the other rooms should be similarly cleaned and tidied for the day, as befits our social position.[61]

Not the least interesting thing about this passage is its use of personal pronouns: not only does the Ménagier speak of "your" house (*vostre hostel*) and "our" social position (*nostre estat*), but, unlike Walter, he addresses his wife throughout as *vous*, not *tu*.

I will mention just one more detail. The speech that Petrarch puts into Griselda's mouth when she learns that she is to be sent back to her

---

[58] Greco and Rose, trans., *The Good Wife's Guide*, 116 (1.6:8); for the French see *Le Ménagier de Paris*, ed. Georgine E. Brereton and Janet M. Ferrier (Oxford: Clarendon Press, 1981), 333. The statement that Griselda gave the humble instruments to the chambermaids [*les bailla aux mesquines*] is a problem since chambermaids would not normally clean the stables (*estables*); evidently Greco and Rose's solution is to read *mesnage* for *mesquines*, while Brereton and Ferrier read *tables* for *estables*.

[59] "[J]e vueil que tu en ayes la charge et tous les offices t'obeyront." Curnow, ed., *The "Livre de la Cité des Dames"* 907.

[60] Golenistcheff-Koutouzoff, *L'histoire de Griseldis*, 242 (l. 7130). In Thomas III's version Griselda had handed him his keys before returning to her father's house. *A Critical Edition*, ed. Ard, 847 (383:70).

[61] Greco and Rose, trans., *The Good Wife's Guide*, 217–18 (2.3:6–7); *Le Ménagier de Paris*, ed. Brereton and Ferrier, 128–30.

father's house includes the sentence: "I have never held myself worthy to be your—I won't say wife, but—servant (*non dicam coniugio, sed servicio*), and in this house, of which you have made me lady, as God is my witness, I have always remained at heart a serving maid (*animo semper ancilla permansi*)."[62] In one form or another, almost every rendering of the Griselda story retains this speech,[63] and for good reason. Not only does Walter's treatment of his wife as a servant embody, to use a phrase coined by Tristram Coffin of the traditional ballad, the "emotional core" of the story of Patient Griselda,[64] but it encapsulates, I believe, its significance for contemporaries by throwing into stark contrast two competing models of marriage—the patriarchal and the cooperative,[65] or, to borrow David Wallace's terminology (since the personal is always political), the absolutist and the associational.[66] But having said this, we must at once acknowledge a historical irony that will surprise few modern feminists: that those Italian city-states where (male) associational political forms flourished most vigorously were also the ones least likely to allow a share of governance, whether civic or domestic, to women.[67]

The laws of the folktale are not those of naturalistic fiction, but it would be a mistake to suppose that they bear no relation to the material conditions from which they arise.[68] In the fourteenth century, as Wallace has reminded us so well, they did things differently in Italy, and readers in France and England, perhaps even in Piedmonte and Catalonia, confronted with the picture of marriage drawn by Petrarch, were clearly

---

[62] Severs, *The Literary Relationships of Chaucer's Clerkes Tale,* 278 (V.12–15).

[63] The *Roumant du Marquis de Saluce,* whose heroine is well born, omits it altogether (Golenistcheff-Koutouzoff, *L'histoire de Griseldis,* 238 [lines 543ff.]), and Christine de Pisan omits the second half [i.e. "I have always remained at heart a serving maid"] (Curnow, ed., "The 'Livre de la Cité des Dames,'" 904).

[64] Tristram P. Coffin, "'Mary Hamilton' and the Anglo-American Ballad as an Art Form," *Journal of American Folklore* 70 (1957): 208–14 (209).

[65] Other comparable terms are Lawrence Stone's "companionate marriage" (*Woman Is a Worthy Wight: Women in English Society, c. 1200–1500,* ed. P. J. P. Goldberg [Stroud: Sutton, 1992], x) and Barbara A. Hanawalt's "partnership marriage" (*The Wealth of Wives: Women, Law, and Economy in Late Medieval London* [Oxford: Oxford University Press, 2007], 9).

[66] David Wallace, *Chaucerian Polity: Absolutist Lineages and Associational Forms in England and Italy* (Stanford: Stanford University Press, 1997).

[67] David Herlihy, *Opera Muliebria: Women and Work in Medieval Europe* (New York: McGraw-Hill, 1990), 167.

[68] Eugene Weber, "Fairies and Hard Facts: The Reality of Folktales," *Journal of the History of Ideas* 42 (1981): 93–113; see also Robert Darnton, *The Great Cat Massacre: And Other Episodes in French Cultural History* (New York: Basic Books, 1984), 9–72 ("Peasants Tell Tales: The Meaning of Mother Goose").

startled. What kind of a world can it be, they must have asked themselves, where a marchioness must set her hand to a broomstick? Let me read two quotations that may help to encapsulate this gulf between north and south. The first is from Christine de Pisan's *Livre des trois vertus* (ca. 1405):

Because—like lords (though even more so)—knights, squires, and gentlemen travel and go to war, it is necessary for their wives to be sensible, and good managers, and have a clear head for business, because they spend most of their time in the household without their husbands (who are at court or abroad), so that they need to assume complete control in order to keep track of both income and possessions. It befits every woman in this position, if she has any sense, to know exactly what they take in each year and what the standard income from their lands is; and if she can, this sensible lady should speak to her husband with such sweet words and give such good advice, that they consult together and decide how to maintain a standard of living that is within their means, and certainly not one so excessive that at the year's end they find themselves owing money to their own servants or to other creditors.[69]

The second quotation comes from Leon Battista Alberti's *Della Famiglia* (ca. 1432)—Giannozzo, an elderly relative of Leon Battista's, is speaking of his early married life:

I kept none of my valuables hidden from my wife. I showed her all the treasures of my household. I kept only the ledgers and business papers, my ancestors' as well as mine, locked so that my wife could not read them or even see them then or at any time since. I never kept them in my pockets but always under lock and key in their proper place in my study, almost as if they were sacred or religious objects. I never allowed my wife to enter my study alone or in my company, and I ordered her to turn over to me at once any papers of mine she should find. To prevent her from ever wanting to see my papers or know about confidential matters, I often spoke against those bold impudent women who try so hard to find out their husband's or other men's affairs outside the home.[70]

[69] Christine de Pisan, *Le Livre des trois vertus,* ed. Charity Cannon Willard and Eric Hicks (Paris: Champion, 1989), 152–53 (my translation). See, further, Rowena E. Archer, "'How ladies . . . who live on their manors ought to manage their households and estates': Women as Landholders and Administrators in the Late Middle Ages," in *Woman Is a Worthy Wight,* ed. Goldberg, 149–81.

[70] *The Albertis of Florence: Leon Battista Alberti's Della Famiglia,* trans. Guido A. Guarino (Lewisburg: Bucknell University Press, 1971), 217.

Of course two isolated quotations, however dramatic, prove nothing by themselves, but many social historians would agree that in the fourteenth and fifteenth centuries the position enjoyed by women in general, and wives in particular, differed widely between London and Paris, on the one hand, and the cities of Tuscany, on the other. To read, for example, Barbara Hanawalt's *The Wealth of Wives: Women, Law, and Economy in Late Medieval London* alongside Christiane Klapisch-Zuber's *Women, Family, and Ritual in Renaissance Italy* is to find oneself moving between two radically distinct worlds.[71] In summary, well-to-do women in northwestern Europe married later than those in southern Europe and their age at first marriage was closer to that of their spouses; they were more likely to set up an independent establishment upon marriage (as opposed to moving in with their husband's family); their property rights within marriage (at least as regards real property) were more strongly protected in law, and their economic prospects in the event of widowhood were considerably brighter.[72]

It would be easy to attribute the manifestly lower status of Florentine wives around 1400 to the Tuscan dowry system since, as the economic historian Siwan Anderson succinctly puts it, "dowry payments . . . are consistent with a development process where women do not directly reap the benefits of modernization and men are the primary recipients of the new economic opportunities."[73] However, since wives were dowered in London and Paris too, things were evidently not quite this simple. One obvious difference was that London dowries were usually settled in the form of real estate (which as a consequence was far less easy for husbands to liquidate), whereas in Tuscan cities the preferred form was cash;[74] equally important, such dowries were frequently counterbalanced by real gifts from the husband to his bride, either in the form of dower lands or jointures,[75] both designed to guarantee her financial security in the event of widowhood. In the early Middle Ages,

[71] See notes 65 and 24 above.

[72] See Richard M. Smith, "Geographical Diversity in the Resort to Marriage in Late Medieval Europe: Work, Reputation, and Unmarried Females in the Household Formation Systems of Northern and Southern Europe," in *Woman Is a Worthy Wight,* ed. Goldberg, 16–59.

[73] "The Economics of Dowry and Brideprice," *Journal of Economic Perspectives* 21, no. 4 (2007): 151–74 (165).

[74] Hanawalt, *The Wealth of Wives,* 58; cf. Diane Owen Hughes, "From Brideprice to Dowry in Mediterranean Europe," *Journal of Family History* 3 (1978): 262–96 (281).

[75] On this distinction, see Hanawalt, *The Wealth of Wives,* 61–65.

Lombard brides too had been the recipients of a bride-price or *Morgengabe* from their husbands,[76] but long before the fourteenth century this custom had dwindled to a symbolic gift of clothing and jewelry—a gift that in actuality remained the property of the husband after the marriage. In London, a married woman's rights to chattels were if anything more circumscribed than in Tuscany, though in practice Florentine nondotal assets seem to have fallen *de facto*, if not *de iure*, under the husband's effective control.[77] For Tuscan widows, however, prospects were far bleaker than for those in London: in what looks very like a concerted campaign to channel family assets toward male heirs, civic laws from the twelfth century onward systematically restricted the amounts that widows could customarily expect to receive from their husbands' estates.[78] In the margin of a manuscript of Caffaro's chronicle for the year 1143, a vivid sketch of distraught women appears alongside an entry noting that the Genoese commune had abolished the customary right of widows to a third of their husband's household goods;[79] in London, by contrast, well into the sixteenth century a widow could expect to receive a third of her late husband's goods.[80] Where Alice of Bath is free to cast about for a sixth husband, many Florentine widows would have had little other than a cloister to look forward to. But women in late fourteenth-century London would have enjoyed other rights unavailable to their Tuscan sisters: they would have encountered far fewer barriers either to inheriting or bequeathing property, for instance, essentially enjoying "the same rights to lineal descent of property as did men."[81] While local customs varied in detail, by and large most of the towns of northwestern Europe, including Paris, were far closer to the London model than to anything in Tuscany.

A gulf in marital customs between southern and northwestern Eu-

---

[76] Hughes, "From Brideprice to Dowry in Mediterranean Europe," 268–72.

[77] Julius Kirshner, "Materials for a Gilded Cage: Non-Dotal Assets in Florence, 1300–1500," in *The Family in Italy from Antiquity to the Present*, ed. David I. Kertzer and Richard P. Saller (New Haven: Yale University Press, 1991), 184–207.

[78] David Herlihy, *Medieval Households* (Cambridge, Mass.: Harvard University Press, 1985), 98–99.

[79] *Annali Genovesi de Caffaro e de'suoi continuatori, dal MXCIX al MCCXCII,* ed. Luigi Tommaso Belgrano and Cesare Imperiale di Sant' Angelo, 5 vols. (Rome: Istituto Storico Italiano, 1890–1929), 1:31; see Hughes, "From Brideprice to Dowry in Mediterranean Europe," 277.

[80] Caroline Barron, "The 'Golden Age' of Women in Medieval London," *Reading Medieval Studies* 15 (1989): 35–58 (42–43).

[81] Hanawalt, *The Wealth of Wives,* 54.

rope helps explain why audiences in London or Paris were fascinated by the grotesque picture of marriage drawn by the tale of Griselda. Only the misogynistic Philippe de Mézières seems prepared to consider Griselda "a fine mirror" [biau miroir], in which married women [les dames mariées] "will easily be able to recognize their shortcomings and their advantages and the state of their marriages."[82] Others are clearly uncomfortable with such a reading: the Ménagier de Paris for one says that he has told his wife the story, "not to apply it to you, or because I expect the same obedience from you," and apologizes that "the story contains excessive accounts of cruelty, in my opinion more than was fitting, and I don't believe that it was ever true."[83] Chaucer, we will remember, chose to turn Petrarch's simple remark that Griselda's patience was scarcely imitable (vix imitabilis) into an assertion that it was totally unrealistic:

> This storie is seyd nat for that wyves sholde
> Folwen Griselde as in humylitee,
> For it were inportable, though they wolde.
>   (IV.1142–44)

Le livre Griseldis remarks that her patience and constancy "seem scarcely possible to follow" (a paine me semble ensuivable et possible), and Thomas III of Saluce calls her example "impossible to maintain" (comme impossible a porter); even Peter de Hailles adds that not only is it scarcely practical, but scarcely tolerable as well (vix sectanda michi pareat aut toleranda).[84] By contrast, such a gulf cannot account for the popularity of the story in its original homeland, for it is quite clear that, despite Anne Middleton's claim to the contrary,[85] Tuscans, like Parisians, read the tale of Griselda primarily as a story about marriage. To understand how this can be, we must appeal, not simply to relative differences between northern and southern Europe, but to a fundamental change in attitudes to women and marriage that, while it first began in fourteenth-century Italy, was

[82] "legierement porront cognoistre ou leurs deffaultes ou leurs bienfais et la condicion de leur mariage" (Golenistcheff-Koutouzoff, L'histoire de Griseldis, 155, Prologue, lines 64–67).
[83] Greco and Rose, trans., The Good Wife's Guide, 118–19 (1.6:10).
[84] Severs, The Literary Relationships of Chaucer's Clerkes Tale, 289 (VI.34–35); A Critical Edition of Thomas III, ed. Ward, 853 (389:5); Vetter, ed., Die Griseldis des Petrus de Hailles, 33 (III.506).
[85] "The Clerk and His Tale: Some Literary Contexts," SAC 2 (1980): 121–50 (138–41).

to spread inexorably northward over the course of the next two hundred years. Although many factors affected this change, its root cause clearly lay in the nascent capitalism of the Tuscan city-states.

It is not difficult to demonstrate this change. Throughout much of the fourteenth and fifteenth centuries, Florence experienced a period of dowry inflation. Dante comments on it in the early fourteenth century,[86] and though population losses in the wake of the Black Death may have slowed it somewhat, it evidently began to accelerate again early in the fifteenth century. This inflation placed a huge burden on well-to-do Florentine families and in 1425 the city set up a credit union, the *Monte delle doti,* whose ostensible purpose was to enable citizens to save for their daughters' weddings.[87] David Herlihy and Christiane Klapisch-Zuber have argued that the social consequences of this inflation were twofold: an increase in the age difference between bride and groom (men generally marrying women ten to fifteen years younger than themselves), and a widening of the social gap between couples (men tending to marry up and women to marry down).[88] Self-evidently, neither of these developments was likely to encourage harmonious matrimonial relationships. Even more important was the increasing commercialization of marriage as an institution; by the fifteenth century, Tuscan marriage contracts have taken on all the complexity of credit default swaps and mortgage-backed securities,[89] a situation that worried contemporary moralists like Bernardino of Siena, still wrestling

[86] In *Paradiso,* XV.102–5, Dante's ancestor Cacciaguida recalls a time when the birth of a daughter did not terrify the new father with the prospect of an immoderate future dowry: "Non faceva, nascendo, ancor paura / la figlia al padre, che 'l tempo e la dote / non fuggien quinci e quindi la misura."

[87] Anthony Molho, *Marriage Alliance in Late Medieval Florence* (Cambridge, Mass.: Harvard University Press, 1994).

[88] David Herlihy and Christiane Klapisch-Zuber, *Tuscans and Their Families: A Study of the Florentine Catasto of 1427* (New Haven: Yale University Press, 1985), 222–28; Molho, *Marriage Alliance in Late Medieval Florence,* while conceding that dowry inflation in late medieval Europe was often "accompanied by a greater frequency of 'out-marriage,' in which marriage partners were drawn increasingly from dissimilar social backgrounds" (324), disputes the wholesale application of this principle to medieval Florence.

[89] For translations of selected marriage documents of the period, see Thomas Kuehn, "Contracting Marriage in Renaissance Florence," in *To Have and to Hold: Marrying and Its Documentation in Western Christendom, 400–1600,* ed. Philip L. Reynolds and John Witte Jr. (Cambridge: Cambridge University Press, 2007), 411–20. For detailed records of the expenses of Tuscan marriages, see *The Society of Renaissance Florence: A Documentary Study,* ed. Gene Brucker (New York: Harper and Row, 1971), 29–40, and *Medieval Italy: Texts in Translation,* ed. Katherine L. Jansen, Joanna Drell, and Frances Andrews (Philadelphia: University of Pennsylvania Press, 2009), 446–50.

with the anachronistic notion that charging interest was a sin.[90] Another graphic demonstration may help to show the loss of status that this entailed for married women.

In the final act of the three-act drama that constituted a well-to-do Tuscan marriage in the *trecento* and *quattrocento* (the first two acts had constituted the marriage negotiations and the formal betrothal), the bride publicly processed from her own home to the house of the groom, or, more probably, of his parents. Prominent among the objects displayed in this procession were commonly a pair of chests, now generally referred to as *cassoni* (other contemporary terms were *cofani* and *forzieri*), destined to furnish the new bridal chamber. In the fourteenth century, these were generally simple coffers, decorated with chivalric or heraldic motifs, but by the beginning of the fifteenth they had evolved into handsome pieces of furniture, painted on the front and sides with mythical or historical scenes, and by the sixteenth, into monumental carved chests.[91] Just as interesting as this visual evolution, however, are the changes in the social function of these *cassoni*. In the fourteenth century, they were paid for by the bride's father and contained her trousseau— her clothes, linens, and jewelry (sometimes known as paraphernalia)— but by the fifteenth, the cost of providing them had begun to fall upon the groom's family and at this point their contents likewise changed.[92] They now contained, not the bride's trousseau, but something Christiane Klapisch-Zuber calls the counter-trousseau, in her view, a symbolic survival from the days of the bride-price or *Morgengabe*; this counter-trousseau also contained clothes, jewels, and finery (sometimes on a lavish scale), but there was one very significant difference. Unlike the trousseau, which was treated as a part of the dowry,[93] and over which the

---

[90] See, e.g., *Sermo XLII* (Quando licet ultra sortem), cap. 2: "Quod homo licite pacisci pro interesse damni emergentis de praesenti, ubi ostenditur quare pignus dotis uxoris marito non computatur in sortem" [That a man may legitimately be bound to pay interest on penalties arising from a marriage agreement, where it is shown how the pledge of a marital dowry to the husband is not counted in with the principal]; Bernardino of Siena, *Opera Omnia, studio et cura p.p. Collegii S. Bonaventurae*, 9 vols. (Florence: Quaracchi, 1950–65), 4:352–56.

[91] For a general introduction to these *cassoni*, see Caroline Campbell, *Love and Marriage in Renaissance Florence: The Courtauld Wedding Chests* (London: Courtauld Gallery, 2009).

[92] Christiane Klapisch-Zuber, "Les coffres de mariage et les plateaux d'accouchées à Florence: Archive, ethnologie, iconographie," *A travers l'image: Lecture iconographique et sens de l'oeuvre*, ed. Sylvie Deswarte-Rosa, Actes du Séminaire CNRS (GDR 712) (Paris: Klincksieck, 1994), 309–24 (310–15).

[93] Kirshner, "Materials for a Gilded Age," 186.

new wife thus retained some measure of personal control, the husband's gifts, which constituted the counter-trousseau, "were temporary. Once they had played their role the husband could repossess them."[94] The principle that Florentine husbands regained legal control of such pre-nuptial gifts after the wedding Klapisch-Zuber has astutely labeled "the Griselda complex."[95] It is not difficult to appreciate the symbolism of replacing *cassoni* paid for by the bride's father and containing her personal trousseau, with *cassoni* provided by the groom's family and containing finery that the bride could only enjoy temporarily and under sufferance—especially since in the public procession to her new home the bride's actual trousseau was now carried in two inconspicuous wicker baskets.[96] Where formerly brides had spent the first night of their marriage in a new bedchamber furnished with their own chests containing their own possessions, they were now provided with a forceful reminder that they owed the very clothes on their backs to their husbands. After this, do we need to be told that at least five surviving fifteenth-century *cassoni* are decorated with scenes from the story of Patient Griselda (Fig. 5)?[97] Imagine waking up after your wedding night to find yourself confronted with the image of Griselda on your bedroom furniture.[98]

The diminished status of Tuscan wives was noted by contemporaries. Where once, however circumscribed their position outside the home, wives had been undisputed rulers within it, they were now falling under the supervision of interfering husbands. "I kept for myself the tasks of going outside among men and earning money outside the home and left to my wife the care of lesser domestic matters," writes Leon Battista Alberti's spokesman, Giannozzo: "I do not know whether you will praise me for this, for I see many men who go around looking and searching in every corner of the house and allow nothing to remain hidden. There can be nothing so hidden that they do not find and touch it. They check everything, even seeing if the lamps have too thick a

---

[94] Klapisch-Zuber, *Women, Family, and Ritual,* 225.

[95] Ibid., chap. 10.

[96] Klapisch-Zuber, "Les coffres de mariage," 312.

[97] Callmann, "Subjects from Boccaccio in Italian Painting," 55–56 (nos. 79, 80, 81, 83, 84).

[98] Ellen Callmann, "The Growing Threat to Marital Bliss as Seen in Fifteenth-Century Florentine Paintings," *Studies in Iconography* 6 (1979): 73–92; Diane Owen Hughes, "Representing the Family: Portraits and Purposes in Early Modern Italy," *Journal of Interdisciplinary History* 17 (1986): 7–38; Cristelle L. Baskins, "Griselda, or The Renaissance Bride Stripped Bare by Her Bachelor in Tuscan *Cassone* Painting," *Stanford Review* 10 (1991): 153–75.

Fig. 5. The *cassone* illustrated here (Callmann, no. 83) was formerly in the Palazzo Serristori, Florence; it was sold at auction on May 9, 1977, and its current whereabouts are unknown. Photograph courtesy of Sotheby's.

wick. They say there is no shame in looking after one's own affairs and that they harm no one by establishing within their homes those rules of conduct which seem appropriate to them."[99] While conceding that "the diligent care of one's possessions [is] the mother of wealth," Giannozzo still can't quite bring himself to feel that this is the proper way for a man to behave. Equally striking is his insistence that his wife should keep a proper distance between herself and the servants, as if this, too, was an area where older proprieties were breaking down: "To seem very industrious, at times she would have done menial tasks, had I not immediately forbidden it," he writes (237); "'I do not want you to do everything yourself. There are many things which would not be proper for you when there are others to do them'" (235). Evidently Giannozzo's lesson is one that would have been lost on Marquis Walter. Even more telling is a passage from an earlier tract by Franciso Barbaro (Barbaro was a Venetian, but his *De re uxoria* was written as a wedding present for a Florentine friend): after attributing disorder in household affairs to

[99] Guarino, *The Albertis of Florence*, 215.

the capitalistic practice of buying and selling supplies in the market rather than raising them on the home farm ("this system of acquiring food, fuel, and wine one day at a time is more appropriate to the hectic life of a traveler or a soldier than a citizen or the head of a household"), he goes on to imply that such behavior has led to the devaluation of women: "I believe that the custom of the Romans should be followed in this, lest the noblest women should be set to the most ignoble tasks, for after a treaty was concluded with the Sabines, noblewomen were protected from having to work at milling, cooking, or such servile occupations."[100] Beneath the elegant humanist patina lurks an astute sense that the underlying cause for women's loss of status is to be sought in the vibrant commercial life of the city.

As I have said, with the relentless expansion of capitalism, the social changes first apparent in *trecento* and *quattrocento* Tuscany begin to be spread further north. When Ann Rosalind Jones and Peter Stallybrass seek to contextualize *The Pleasant Comodie of Patient Grissill,* staged in London by the Admiral's Men in early 1600, they draw on obvious parallels with Boccaccio's Italy.[101] But we must remember that Queen Elizabeth's London was a very different place from Richard II's. "The picture of the lifestyle of women in medieval London is quite a rosy one," writes Caroline Barron, "their range of options and prospects differed only slightly from those of the men who shared their level of prosperity. But it is clear that the situation began to change in the course of the sixteenth century."[102] It may be worth pointing out that (as Lawrence Stone has shown) in the late sixteenth century England experienced a period of dowry inflation comparable to that experienced in Tuscany a hundred and fifty years earlier.[103] Joan Kelly's argument, first floated almost forty years ago, that in the Renaissance "women as a group, especially among the classes that dominated Italian commercial life, experienced a contraction of social and commercial options that men of their classes . . . did not," no longer appears quite so revolution-

[100] Attilio Gnesotto, ed., "Francisci Barbari, *De Re Uxoria,*" *Atti e Memorie della R. Accademia di Scienze Lettere ed Arti in Padova,* n.s. 32 (1915–1916): 89 (1–9) [my translation].

[101] Jones and Stallybrass, *Renaissance Clothing and the Materials of Memory,* chap. 9.

[102] Barron, "The 'Golden Age' of Women in Medieval London," 47–48.

[103] Lawrence Stone, *The Crisis of the Aristocracy, 1558–1641* (Oxford: Clarendon Press, 1965), 640–48.

ary,[104] though as others, including David Herlihy,[105] have pointed out, a similar contraction was to be experienced all over Europe, merely occurring later in the less intensely capitalized north.

If the cooperative marriage was disappearing among the city elites of late fourteenth-century Tuscany, there was one place where it must still have maintained a foothold—in the surrounding countryside. This is shown by the much earlier age of first marriage for men in rural areas than in the towns and the explanation is purely economic: "The young peasant had first to marry before he undertook the cultivation of a farm; he needed the *help* of a wife and eventually children. In the city the merchant or artisan had first to achieve success in his trade before taking a wife and assuming the *burdens* of a family {my italics}."[106] At this social level, differences between north and south would have seemed far less marked. As Barbara Hanawalt has written of the partnership marriage of the English peasantry: "The coroner's inquests show husband and wife sitting down at table to eat together, and while the wife put food on the table, she was not acting as a servant and she did not stand behind her husband while he ate. Husband and wife walked side by side in fifteenth-century England."[107] Under the rule of what Ivan Illich has called "vernacular gender,"[108] wives may not have been able to claim equal status with their husbands, but they still enjoyed a well-defined, independent, and respected role.

Which brings us back finally to the Tuscan *veglia* with which we began. Alessandro Falassi has stressed the crucial role of the "housemother" in arranging and supervising the twentieth-century *veglia*,[109] and though we cannot know how her fourteenth-century counterparts might have behaved, we can at least feel fairly sure that the folktale of Patient Griselda would have done quite different cultural work in the rural farmhouses of *trecento* Tuscany than in its city palaces. Folktales frequently tell of fortunate young people who marry above their station, but in this case we are not dealing with a story about the rewards of courtship but about the trials of marriage; Philippe de Mézières may

---

[104] Joan Kelly, *Women, History, and Theory: The Essays of Joan Kelly* (Chicago: University of Chicago Press, 1984), 20.

[105] "The numbers of employed women in relation to men seem to have fallen all over Northern Europe throughout the late Middle Ages." Herlihy, *Opera Muliebria,* 173.

[106] Herlihy, *Medieval Households,* 142–43.

[107] Hanawalt, *The Ties That Bound* (Oxford: Oxford University Press, 1986), 218.

[108] Ivan Illich, *Gender* (New York: Pantheon Books, 1982).

[109] Falassi, *Folklore by the Fireside,* 7–17.

have seen it as a model for wives, but for the *vegliatori,* especially the younger ones, it must have looked very much more like a warning. Less wish-fulfillment than cautionary tale, the story of Griselda would clearly have belonged to those final stages of the *veglia* when "narrators recounted pitiful cases, the events and vicissitudes of marriage."

One of the very few theorists to take folklore seriously is the great Italian Marxist, Antonio Gramsci. For Gramsci, folklore is "a 'morality of the people,' understood as a determinate . . . set of principles for practical conduct and of customs that derive from them," and it is quite capable of standing "in opposition . . . to 'official' conceptions of the world."[110] It is from this perspective that I have been arguing for the tale of Griselda's being *about* a struggle between competing views of marriage (the patriarchal and the cooperative) in the late Middle Ages, despite the almost universal tendency of medieval authors themselves to treat it as an allegory of something else. As is well known, for Petrarch, and for many of his followers, the story of Griselda is really about the obedience of the good Christian to God's will, though this tendency to allegorize cannot be laid at Petrarch's door alone (Sercambi, who as far as we know had never read Petrarch's version, calls his heroine Constantina). Gramsci himself would have had no difficulty accounting for such allegorization—he would have regarded it as an expression of the kind of hegemonic thinking typically propagated by the representatives of civil society (and one could hardly ask for a better example of such a representative than Petrarch). In general, hegemonic thinking is not easy to penetrate, but its superimposition on a folkloric base here allows us a privileged point of view. I have tried to show how pressure points created by a contest between *historia* and *fabula,* between the mimetic and the symbolic, throw into sharp relief a set of deep-seated cultural anxieties in late medieval society—how, try as they might, Petrarch and his followers cannot quite paper over the brutal reality of forcing a broomstick into the hands of a marchioness.

[110] Antonio Gramsci, *Selections from Cultural Writings,* ed. David Forgacs and Geoffrey Nowell-Smith, trans. William Boelhower (Cambridge, Mass.: Harvard University Press, 1985), 189–90.

Appendix I:
The Early Dissemination of the Griselda Story[1]

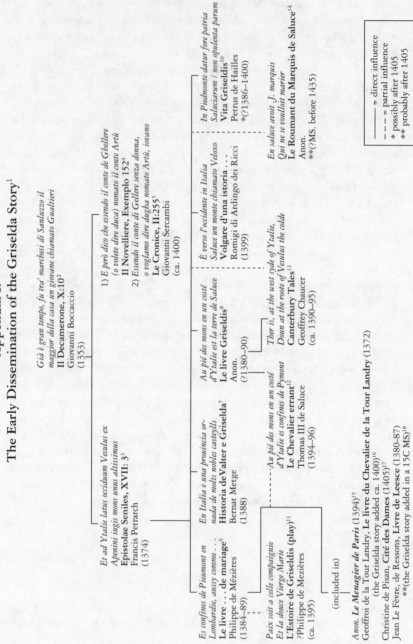

Già è gran tempo, fu tra' marchesi di Sanluzzo il
maggior della casa un giovane chiamato Gualtieri
Il Decamerone, X:10[2]
Giovanni Boccaccio
(1353)

Et ad Ytalie latus occiduum Vesulus ex
Apenini iugis mons unus altissimus
Epistolae Seniles, XVII: 3[3]
Francis Petrarch
(1374)

1) E però dico che essendo il conte de Ghellere
(o volete dire duca) nomato il conte Artù
Il Novelliere, Exemplo 152[4]
2) Essendo il conte di Gellere senza donna,
o voglamo dire dugha nomato Artù, iovano
Le Cronice, II:255[5]
Giovanni Sercambi
(ca. 1400)

Es confines de Piemont en
Lombardie, aussy comme . . .
Le livre . . . de mariage[6]
Philippe de Mézières
(1384–89)

En Italia e una prouincia or-
nada de molts nobles casteylls
Historia deValter e Griselda[7]
Bernat Metge
(1388)

Au pié des mons en un costé
d'Ytalie est la terre de Saluce
Le livre Griseldis[8]
Anon.
(?1380–90)

È verso l'occidente in Italia
Saluce un monte chiamato Veloxo
Volgare d'una istoria . . .
Romigi di Ardingo dei Ricci
(1399)

In Piedmonte datur fore patria
Salaciarum | non opulenta parum
Vita Griseldis[10]
Petrus de Hailles
*(?1386–1400)

Au pié des mons en un costé
d'Ytalie es confines de Pymont
Le Chevalier errant[12]
Thomas III de Saluce
(1394–96)

Ther is, at the west syde of Ytalie,
Doun at the roote of Vesulus the colde
Canterbury Tales[13]
Geoffrey Chaucer
(ca. 1390–95)

En saluce avoit .J. marquis
Qui ne se voulloit marier
Le Roumant du Marquis de Saluce[14]
Anon.
**(?MS. before 1435)

Paix soit a celle compaignie
Et la douce Vierge Marie
L'Estoire de Griseldis (play)[11]
?Philippe de Mézières
(ca. 1395)

(included in)

Anon. Le Menagier de Paris (1394)[15]
Geoffroi de la Tour Landry, Le livre du Chevalier de la Tour Landry (1372)
(the Griselda story added ca. 1400)[16]
Christine de Pisan, Cité des Dames (1405)[17]
Jean Le Fèvre, de Ressons, Livre de Leesce (1380–87)[18]
**(the Griselda story added in a 15C MS)

—— = direct influence
----- = partial influence
* possibly after 1405
** probably after 1405

References

1. See, in general, Elie Golenistcheff-Koutouzoff, *L'histoire de Griseldis en France au XIVe et au XVe siècle* (Paris: Droz, 1933), 115–50; Raffaele Morabito, "La diffusione della storia di Griselda dal XIV al XX secolo," *Studi sul Boccaccio* 17 (1988): 237–85; and Judith Bronfman, *Chaucer's "Clerk's Tale": The Griselda Story Received, Rewritten, Illustrated* (New York: Garland, 1994), 7–22.

2. Giovanni Boccaccio, *Decameron,* ed. Vittorio Branca (Torino: Einaudi, 1984), 1232–48 (X:10).

3. J. Burke Severs, *The Literary Relationships of Chaucer's Clerkes Tale* (New Haven: Yale University Press, 1942), 254–88 (even-numbered pages). Thomas J. Farrell's more recent edition is based on a text closer to Chaucer's; see *Sources and Analogues of the Canterbury Tales, I,* ed. Robert M. Correale and Mary Hamel (Cambridge: D.S. Brewer, 2002), 109–29 (odd-numbered pages).

4. Giovanni Sercambi, *Le Cronice,* ed. Salvatore Bongi, 3 vols., Fonti per la storia d'Italia (Lucca: Giusti, 1892), 3:216–26.

5. Giovanni Sercambi, *Il Novelle,* ed. Giovanni Sinicropi, 2 vols. (Firenze: Casa editrice Le Lettere, 1995), 2:1295–1306 (CLIII).

6. Golenistcheff-Koutouzoff, *L'histoire de Griseldis,* 153–82.

7. *Les obres d'en Bernat Metge,* ed. R. Miquel y Planas (Barcelona: Nova Bibliotheca Catalana, 1910), 51–79.

8. Burke Severs, *The Literary Relationships ,* 255–89 (odd-numbered pages).

9. Raffaele Morabito, *Una sacra rappresentazione profana: Fortune di Griselda nel Quattrocento italiano* (Tübingen: Max Niemeyer, 1993), 66–75.

10. Dieter Vetter, *Die Griseldis des Petrus de Hailles: Ein philologischer Kommentar* (Hildesheim: G. Olms, 2009), 16–33 (for the influence of Boccaccio see 12); see also Golenistcheff-Koutouzoff, *L'histoire de Griseldis,* 115–18.

11. *L'estoire de Griseldis,* ed. Barbara M. Craig, University of Kansas Publications, Humanistic Studies 31 (Lawrence, KA, 1954); *L'estoire de Griseldis,* ed. Mario Roques (Geneva: Droz, 1957); for Philippe de Mézières' possible authorship, see Grace Frank, "The Authorship of 'le mystère de Griseldis'," *MLN* 51 (1936): 217–29.

12. Marvin J. Ward, *A Critical Edition of Thomas III, marquis of Saluzzo's "Le livre du Chevalier Errant,"* PhD. diss. (University of North Carolina at Chapel Hill, 1984), 830–54 (a new edition by Dr. Robert Fajen, Julius-Maximilians-Universität Würzburg, is promised).

13. *The Riverside Chaucer,* ed. Larry D. Benson, *et al.* (Boston: Houghton Mifflin, 1987), 137–53.

14. Golenistcheff-Koutouzoff, *L'histoire de Griseldis,* 225–48. G.-K.'s evidence for the dependence of the *Roumant* on *Le livre Griseldis* (138) is weak; it seems rather to be an independent (third) translation.

15. *Le Ménagier de Paris,* ed. Georgine E. Brereton and Janet M. Ferrier; foreword by Beryl Smalley (Oxford: Clarendon Press, 1981) (Tale of Griselda omitted); *The Good Wife's Guide; Le Ménagier de Paris: A Medieval Household Book,* trans. Gina L. Greco and Christine M. Rose (Ithaca: Cornell University Press, 2009) (Tale of Griselda included).

16. *Le livre du chevalier de La Tour Landry pour l'enseignement de ses filles,* ed. M. Anatole de Montaiglon (Paris, Jannet, 1854) (Tale of Griselda omitted); see Golenistcheff-Koutouzoff, *L'histoire de Griseldis,* 131.

17. Maureen Cheney Curnow, *The "Livre de la Cité des Dames" of Christine de Pisan: A Critical Edition,* Ph.D. diss. (Vanderbilt University, Nashville, 1975), 900–910.

18. *Les Lamentations de Matheolus et le Livre de leesce de Jehan Le Fèvre, de Resson,* ed. A.-G. van Hamel, 2 vols. (Paris: Bouillon, 1892–1905) (Tale of Griselda omitted); see Golenistcheff-Koutouzoff, *L'histoire de Griseldis,* 132.

Appendix II:
Notes on the Dating of the Earliest Versions of the Griselda Story

While some early versions of the Griselda story—those of Bernat Metge (1388), Romigi di Ardingo dei Ricci (1399), and the play *L'Estoire de Griseldis* (evidently composed to celebrate the betrothal of Isabelle of France to Richard II in 1395)—can be assigned quite specific dates, the dating of others can only be deduced from manuscript evidence and internal allusions. Golenistcheff-Koutouzoff is probably right to date Philippe de Mézières's *Livre de la vertu du sacrament de mariage* to 1384–89 (53), but his placing of Thomas III of Saluce's version in the fifteenth century (134) is highly suspect, and in dating his so-called version B, *Le Livre Griseldis,* to early in the same century (83 n. 1), he is clearly wrong.

Since only one of the two surviving manuscripts of Thomas III of Saluce's *Chevalier Errant* (Paris, Bibliothèque Nationale, MS fonds français, 12559) contains the story of Griselda, Golenistcheff-Koutouzoff was able to argue that this story was a later insertion, but his argument ignores the fact that this manuscript can be reliably dated to the very earliest years of the fifteenth century (1401–4) and was evidently commissioned from a Paris workshop by Thomas III himself.[111] If the story of Griselda was indeed a later insertion, it must nevertheless have been both a very early and an authorially sanctioned one.[112] There are, however, perfectly good reasons for believing that the other manuscript (Turin, Bibliotheca Nazionale, MS L.V.6) represents the revised version, with the story of Griselda and Walter excised from an earlier draft; the Turin manuscript, for instance, is the only one to contain chapter headings (a feature, one might suppose, far more likely to be added than removed).[113] That Thomas shows clear signs of discomfort at the behavior of Walter, his imagined ancestor, offers an obvious motive for him, or one of his descendants, to have had second thoughts about including the story. If this is indeed the case, we can confidently date Thomas III's version of the Griselda story to the years 1394–96, when Thomas himself was being held prisoner in Turin.[114]

Golenistcheff-Koutouzoff was evidently unaware that his so-called B

[111] Ward, ed., *A Critical Edition of Thomas III,* xxvii–xxxi.

[112] N. Jorga, *Thomas III Marquis de Saluces: Étude historique et littéraire* (Paris: Champion, 1893), believes that the Paris manuscript contains a revised text, but nevertheless one prepared by Thomas himself (83).

[113] Ward, ed., *A Critical Edition of Thomas III,* xlv.

[114] Jorga, *Thomas III Marquis de Saluces,* 82–84; Ward, ed., *A Critical Edition of Thomas III,* xiii.

version, *Le livre Griseldis,* was used by Geoffrey Chaucer and thus must have been composed before the end of the fourteenth century. Since, however, it was also used by Thomas III of Saluce, we can safely push its *terminus ad quem* back to 1394. Unfortunately, *The Clerk's Tale* cannot be precisely dated, but given the prominence of Philippe de Mézières's version in the final years of the century, Chaucer's use of the less prestigious *Livre Griseldis* might possibly be taken to imply a date in the early 1390s or perhaps even earlier.[115]

Golenistcheff-Koutouzoff assigns the Latin verse translation of Peter de Hailles to the end of the fourteenth century (115) on the assumption that the translator is to be identified with the secretary of Guy II, Count of Blois, who is named in five documents dated between 1386 and 1390 (279–81). Even if the identification itself is correct, the grounds for associating the translation with this period of his life are slim, and the only certain *terminus ad quem* is the date of the actual manuscript (first half of the fifteenth century).[116]

By contrast, we can narrow somewhat the window in which the verse *Roumant du marquis de Saluce et de sa fame Grisilidys* was probably composed. Although Golenistcheff-Koutouzoff assigns its unique manuscript (Bodley, MS Douce 99) simply to "the fifteenth century" (137 n. 1), it was probably copied before 1435. Its final item (immediately following the *Roumant,* and in the same hand) is a short prose work entitled "La Prophetie de maistre Jehan de Baisseguy." This is said to have been composed in 1414 (fol. 98ʳ) but seems far more likely to have been constructed retrospectively in 1429/30. One of its prophecies in particular looks uncannily prescient: in 1435 [*sic*], it says, "une jouvencelle chetive" will come to the aid of the oppressed provinces of Touraine and Champagne, and "recouvra la coronne de la fleur de lix" (fol. 101ᵛ). It is surely not unduly cynical to suppose that this "prophecy" must have been composed after Joan of Arc's triumph at Orleans (in 1429), but before her capture by the Burgundians (in 1430) and her death at the hands of the English (in 1431). Indeed the "Prophetie" imagines that she is destined to rule the whole earth and will completely erase the

---

[115] For evidence (in my view inconclusive) that Philippe might have known *Le livre Griseldis* or (vice versa) that Chaucer may have known Philippe, see Amy Goodwin, in *Sources and Analogues of the Canterbury Tales,* I, ed. Robert M. Correale and Mary Hamel (Cambridge: D.S. Brewer, 2002), 130–34.

[116] Vetter, ed., *Die Griseldis des Petrus de Hailles,* 14.

English from living memory ("sera syre de tout le monde & destruyra le filz dou brut & toute lisle par telle maniere que de eulz ne sera jamays memoire"). Such a "prophecy" would have rung rather hollow after 1431, and it is difficult to see why anyone would have had any reason to copy it very much later in the century.

THE BIENNIAL CHAUCER LECTURE
The New Chaucer Society
Seventeenth International Congress
July 15–19, 2010
Università per Stranieri, Siena

The Biennial Chaucer Lecture

Living Chaucer

L. O. Aranye Fradenburg
University of California, Santa Barbara

Individual adaptability is not only of the greatest significance as a factor of evolution . . . but is itself perhaps the chief object of selection.

—Sewell Wright, 1932

I'VE BEEN LIVING WITH CHAUCER at least since high school. That makes him one of my oldest friends. True, he is a network of signifiers; but while the textuality of his companionship hardly reduces what is known to philosophers as "the problem of other minds," it does mean that, in some fashion—the fashion of the signifying process—his words really do live on and in my mind.[1] The literary friendship I feel for Chaucer is an attachment his work actively solicits, to a degree and in ways unique to his *corpus* but consistent both with premodern and contemporary understandings of the signifier and its role in intersubjective, hence also political and social, process.[2] The importance of signifying to human community was not lost on premodern thinkers. John of Salisbury defends "the sciences of speech" on the grounds that they ensure "the bond of human community."[3] Richard de Bury says that Boethius's

---

[1] A classic in this field is J. L. Austin's "Other Minds," in *Philosophical Papers*, ed. A. O. Wurmson and G. J. Warnock (Oxford: Oxford University Press, 1961). Stanley Cavell also addresses the problem of other minds in *Must We Mean What We Say? A Book of Essays* (1969; Cambridge: Cambridge University Press, 2002). Peter Fonagy's "On Tolerating Mental States: Theory of Mind in Borderline Personalities," *Bulletin of the Anna Freud Centre* 12 (1989): 91–115, considers the clinical implications of philosophy of mind.

[2] I do not mean to assert that Chaucer was an innocent, nice, or compassionate man. When I refer to "Chaucer's awareness" of this or "Chaucer's concern" for that, I am referring to textual Chaucer. His poetry can also be quite satirical and seems very familiar with the psychology of "sin." My focus in this essay is on his use of shared attention.

[3] Joan Cadden, "Science and Rhetoric in the Middle Ages: The Natural Philosophy of William of Conches," *Journal of the History of Ideas* 56 (1995): 1–24 (5).

41

narrator (one of Chaucer's most important textual companions) "beheld Philosophy bearing a sceptre in her left hand and books in her right" because "no one can rightly rule a commonwealth without books."[4] We share minds, and hence construct communities, primarily through speech, books, images—signifiers of all kinds. The argument of this essay is that intersubjectivity, and its transmission by the signifier, is central to the ways Chaucer's poetry thinks about change.

Historical and Methodological Considerations

Recent psychological research agrees that the "living on" of the signifier transforms its hosts' states of mind and body. Attachment theory, for example, links intergenerational transmission of "attachment styles" and theory of mind to the communicative practices of infants and their caregivers.[5] The now-famous "mirror neurons" are thought to be among the chief organic processors of imitative learning and empathy. (When we see another person perform an action, mirror neurons fire in the corresponding parts of the motor areas in our own brain; i.e., when we observe an action, our brains "do" much the same thing as they would if we were actually performing it.) The firings of mirror neurons, as Brian Boyd puts it, "form the basis for the simulations that underlie our rich social cognition, [which is in turn] so central to narrative."[6]

The idea of mirror neurons promises to enrich enormously our understanding of the psychology of reading and writing, affect-transmission, and the "embodied" nature of our responses to works of literature. Several studies have confirmed that verbal descriptions affect the motor areas of the brain in the same way that visual images do. The brains of Capuchin monkeys, for example, mirror the action of cracking open peanuts when they hear the sound thereof.[7] These days, neuroscience

---

[4] *The Love of Books: Richard de Bury's Philobiblon,* trans. E. C. Thomas, www.gutenberg .net, c. xiv.

[5] E.g., Fonagy, "On Tolerating Mental States," passim. John Bowlby's *Attachment and Loss: Volume I: Attachment* is a particularly influential early work in this tradition (London: Tavistock Institute, 1969); see also "Origins of Attachment Theory," in Bowlby, *A Secure Base: Clinical Applications of Attachment Theory* (New York: Brunner-Routledge, 2003), 20–38.

[6] Brian Boyd, *On the Origin of Stories: Evolution, Cognition, and Fiction* (Cambridge, Mass.: Harvard University Press, 2009), 156.

[7] Dr. Ellen Spolsky very kindly pointed me in this direction. See Evelyne Kohler, C. Keysers, M. A. Umiltà, L. Fogassi, V. Gallese, and V. Rizzolatti, "Hearing Sounds, Understanding Actions: Action Representation in Mirror Neurons," *Science* 297 (August 2002): 846–48. I am indebted to Dr. Fritz Breithaupt for this reference.

posits intimacy, not opposition, between "everyday" acts of imagination and motor activity in the material world. (The power of play to enrich experience rests on exactly this intimacy.) As Doidge suggests in *The Brain That Changes Itself,* the antinomy between fantasy and reality is thereby greatly reduced. If we couldn't create castles in the air, neither could we build them in Richmond.[8] Merlin Donald makes a similar point when he argues that our capacity to invent tools and fire depended in the first instance on our ability to imagine fictional situations.[9]

Contemporary scientists, then, regard the intersubjectivity of "signaling" as a verifiable, material phenomenon that can be mapped in a variety of ways. Does this scientific imprimatur mean that we can now finally be assured of the power of literature to make history? It is not, for me at least, a matter of scientific truth versus humanist intuitions and speculations. Rather, the broadening of interest in "plasticity" across almost all contemporary disciplines should inspire us to ask new (or at least renewed) questions about how literary traditions are made and evaluated. ("Neuroplasticity" refers to the brain's lifelong ability to sculpt itself through its interactions with the environment.) And if we seek, we readily find that ancient and medieval psychologies of reading and writing were highly interested in the sharing of mental experience.

Reading was, for Saint Augustine, a profoundly ethical activity, as *De Doctrina Christiana* amply attests. We all know that medieval educators took very seriously the persuasive power of rhetoric (hence also its power to shape minds and societies) and the moral-theological implications of memory training.[10] Classical and medieval physicians and philosophers believed in the power of the "talking cure"—for Plato, the use of reason and language to heal disorders represented a scientific advance over the use of charms and other magical devices.[11] Mary Carruthers underscores the intersubjectivity of reading in her book on memory. In the Middle Ages, she remarks, "Reading a book extends the process whereby one memory engages another in a continuing dialogue that approaches

[8] Norman Doidge, *The Brain That Changes Itself: Stories of Personal Triumph from the Frontiers of Brain Science* (London: Penguin, 2007), 207, 213–14.
[9] Merlin Donald, *Origins of the Modern Mind* (Cambridge, Mass.: Harvard University Press, 1991).
[10] Frances A. Yates, *The Art of Memory* (Chicago: University of Chicago Press, 1966); Rita C. Copeland, *Rhetoric, Hermeneutics, and Translation in the Middle Ages* (Cambridge: Cambridge University Press, 1995), e.g., 20, 35, 75.
[11] Stanley Jackson, *Care of the Psyche: A History of Psychological Healing* (New Haven: Yale University Press, 1999), 21–22.

Plato's ideal (expressed in *Phaedrus*) of two living minds engaged in learning."[12] As Milton wrote so powerfully in *Areopagitica*, "[B]ooks are not absolutely dead things, but do contain a potency of life in them to be as active as that soul whose progeny they are; nay, they do preserve as in a vial the purest efficacy and extraction of that living intellect that bred them."[13] Or, as Richard de Bury puts it in *Philobiblon*: "In books I find the dead as if they were alive."[14]

We have of course been through some changes on this question, via the Derridean critique of presence.[15] But undead life seems more apt a description of the signifier's mode of existence (as Derrida himself thought) than does simple absence or nonexistence. I wrote in *Sacrifice Your Love* about this form of "being-as-signifier":[16] given how susceptible we are to the signifier's designs, there is more connectedness than we think between living subjects and dead letters. Nature's signifiers vary in their realizations, but something, a shape, insists. The conceptual problem is not unlike the question of how genes can be said to duplicate themselves differently each time. Genes make "copies" of themselves, but the copies are never "perfect." Repetition in nature—"kynde"—fascinated premodern natural science and poetry (Alain de Lille, William of Conches, Jean de Meun, Chaucer, Spenser). Chaucer's own textual backgrounds and foregrounds contemplated the nature and naturalness of the signifier in the form of *forms,* and saw the combination of duplication and variation as the hallmark of living process. In our own time, we can expect more critical studies of literary intersubjectivities conceived as signifying networks, wherein relationships among writers and readers are understood to be somatic and affective as well as cognitive.[17] The implications for literary history are considerable.

[12] Mary Carruthers, *The Book of Memory: A Study of Memory in Medieval Culture* (Cambridge: Cambridge University Press, 1990), 211.

[13] John Milton, *Areopagitica* (http://www.dartmouth.edu/~milton/reading_room/areopagitica/index.shtml).

[14] *Philobiblon,* chap. 1.

[15] Jacques Derrida, *Of Grammatology,* trans. Gayatri Spivak (Baltimore: Johns Hopkins University Press, 1974): "We are dispossessed of the longed-for presence in the gesture of language by which we attempt to seize it" (141); and see L. O. Aranye Fradenburg, *Sacrifice Your Love: Psychoanalysis, Historicism, Chaucer* (Minneapolis: University of Minnesota Press, 2002): "The insentience of our works—including our techniques of living—is why we fear them" (14). The boundary between sentience and insentience, like that between presence and absence, is a moving target.

[16] Ibid., 23.

[17] A brilliant example is Julie Carlson, *England's First Family of Writers: Mary Wollstonecraft, William Godwin, Mary Shelley* (Baltimore: Johns Hopkins University Press, 2007).

Study of the experience of textual intersubjectivity is the study of how minds and bodies are changed, willy nilly, by the signifying process. It is difficult to understand other minds; but if it is difficult to understand the meanings of their transmissions, it is also a species of arrogance to think we could stop them from changing us. Arguably, then, Chaucer's words "live on" because the patterns they create really do change our minds and bodies. I believe this viewpoint to be a helpful alternative to our perennial question about whether we are representing the past rightly. Whatever representations of the English past we fashion, they are all in part the result of changes wrought in us, consciously and non-consciously, by living with Chaucer. The signifiers of the past are in us, whether we understand them "rightly" or not; we will never be certain what they mean, but we will certainly have been possessed by them. And our possession by (and of) past signifiers further transforms their range of meanings.[18]

Symbols transform living process; symbols *enable* living process. Or, to put it another way, living is an art. J. Z. Young in *The Study of Man* points out that art "has the most central of biological functions, 'of insisting that life be worthwhile, which, after all, is the final guarantee of its continuance.' "[19] All animals prefer enriched environments, grow bigger and stronger if they have lots of different toys, like to explore for the sake of exploring (lab rats and fish do not need the prospect of reward to run or swim mazes). It is impossible to distinguish striving to survive from striving to thrive. We cannot isolate what is "useful" or "necessary" to the animal, human or otherwise.[20] Plasticity, stylistics, enrichment are not embellishments of living process but are inherent in it.

In the life sciences, animal communications are no longer believed to be stereotyped, "instinctual," and unchanging.[21] Individuals of many species try to distinguish themselves from other potential mates through "performance display." One example is a chimpanzee named Mike, who

[18] Cf. Slavoj Žižek, "Plagiarizing from the Future," *Lacanian Ink* 36 (2010): 148–61.

[19] J. Z. Young, *Introduction to the Study of Man* (Oxford: Oxford University Press, 1971), 360; cited by Ellen Dissanayake, *What Is Art For?* (Seattle: University of Washington Press, 1990), 70.

[20] Georges Bataille, *Visions of Excess: Selected Writings, 1927–1939,* trans. Allan Stoekl (Minneapolis: University of Minnesota Press, 1985), 116.

[21] On "behavioral flexibility," see Marc Bekoff, *Minding Animals: Awareness, Emotions, and Heart* (Oxford: Oxford University Press, 2002), 96.

banged empty kerosene cans together to enhance his expressive reach.[22] Individuation and variation are inherent to living process; animals have traditions but are innovators, too. "Plasticity is a hallmark of [bird-]song," according to Healy and Rowe.[23] How is this possible? Among birds and mammals at least, much signal-recognition is learned, not genetically coded. Animals have aesthetics of repetition and invention, pattern-construction and recognition.[24]

In medieval natural science, the capacity of animals to reason and acquire knowledge was generally depreciated. Nonetheless, as in Bartholomaeus Anglicus's well-known *De Proprietatibus Rerum,* it was accepted that animals, even plants, and humans shared important states of mind. Late medieval philosophers and scientists were well acquainted with Avicenna's and Albertus Magnus's notion that animals and humans shared something like *estimativa,* "a power that could do what the five senses could not: recognize relationships and make value judgments not only of [intentions, e.g., of] benevolence and danger but also of filiation and maternity."[25] Awareness of filiation and maternity is noted throughout medieval animal lore: lambs and colts "know" their mothers, and use their voices to call to them. Moreover, "if one [mare] . . . dies and leaves her colt alive another mare feeds and nourishes him, "for the kynde of mares loves beasts of the same kind."[26]

I do not, by the way, think it is helpful to argue that these kinds of qualities are conventional and therefore virtually meaningless, or are "mere" allegories of human behavior or Christian truth. It is of course crucial to understand how much medieval animal lore is traditional and literary, passed on from one authority to the next, and crucial to understand also that this lore became rich material for typological exegesis. But these facts do not preclude medieval interest in, or knowledge of, actual animals. That there were scientists in the Middle Ages who re-

[22] Simon M. Reader and Kevin N. Laland, eds., *Animal Innovation* (Oxford: Oxford University Press, 2003), 5.

[23] Susan D. Healy and Candy Rowe, "Information Processing: The Ecology and Evolution of Cognitive Abilities," in *Evolutionary Behavioral Ecology,* ed. David Westneat and Charles Fox (Oxford: Oxford University Press, 2010), 162–74 (170).

[24] Magnus Enquist, Peter L. Hurd, and Stefano Ghirlanda, "Signaling," in *Evolutionary Ecology,* ed. Westneat and Fox, 266–284 (e.g., 284).

[25] See Peter G. Sobol, "The Shadow of Reason," in *The Medieval World of Nature: A Book of Essays,* ed. Joyce E. Salisbury (New York: Garland, 1993), 117, 119.

[26] John Trevisa, *On the Properties of Things: John Trevisa's Translation of Bartholomaeus Anglicus De Proprietatibus Rerum,* ed. M. C. Seymour et al., vol. 2 (Oxford: Clarendon Press, 1975), 1189.

spected and practiced observation and experimentation is incontrovertible (Roger Bacon, Arnold of Villanova, Guy de Chauliac). That there
were also plenty of animal lovers is attested by countless manuscript
illuminations that insist on the cute corporeality of all God's creatures,
however weighty the typological burdens they bear.[27] Chauntecleer's
and Pertelote's hybridity makes aesthetic sense only if the animality of
fable animals were thinkable in Chaucer's time, just as tales of Bikini
Bottom now spark children's interest in real oceanic lives. Chauntecleer
is unmistakeably a rooster. Nor are we ourselves exclusively "modern":
animals continue to fascinate us in ways that clearly have little to do
with "scientific method" or utilitarianism. Reynard has lost ground to
Spongebob, but themes of tricksterism and resistance to authority persist, while sponsoring compassion for those who cannot play. Perhaps
pigs can serve effectively as types of Christ in part because they are
capable of attachment and affection.

The assumptions that underlie my reading practices, then, include
the following: nothing is ever "merely" allegorical; as with metaphor,
"vehicle" always transforms "tenor." Both vehicle and tenor are signifiers; the vehicle does not simply serve to "represent" a concept or object.
Conventions become conventional because they continue somehow to
bear cultural meaning, and their meanings are not frozen in time; enduring signifiers engage in new interactions that change the ways they
can be used. We have never been purely "modern": scientific signifiers
have the same wayward intersubjective, intertextual, intergenerational
lives as do "literary" signifiers. We now know *in a new way* that "animals
can plan strategic futures," and "distinguish memory and future projection from perception."[28] But this new way is not unconnected to the
old.

Self/nonself distinction and the ability to detect degrees and kinds of
relationship (e.g., kinship) are capacities of even fairly simple life-forms,
like barnacles and tadpoles.[29] The mental activities that enable recogni-

[27] And of course there is the ever-popular ode to "Pangur Bán": "I and Pangur Bán,
my cat, / 'Tis a like task we are at; / Hunting mice is his delight, / Hunting words I sit
all night." See Lydia Cohen-Kreisberger, "The Creation of a Shared Space Through
Fantasy Between a Seven Year Old Child and His Therapist: A Case Study," *Clinical
Social Work Journal* 33 (2005): 259–70: "Like the interplay between the poet and his
cat, fantasy is intersubjective" (259).

[28] Boyd, *On the Origin of Stories*, 153.

[29] There is a vast literature on self/nonself distinction, for example, Yumi Izutsu and
Katsutoshi Yoshizato, "Metamorphosis-dependent Recognition of Larval Skin as Non-
self by Inbred Adult Frogs," *Journal of Experimental Zoology* 266 (1993): 163–67; and

tion of shared interests, as well as the absence thereof (prey/predator), are also widely shared abilities, expressed, for example, by both humans and chimpanzees, in the form of politics. Many animals have complex societies; both alterity and the commonweal are in Nature's jurisdiction.[30] If we have to continue worrying about whether we are imposing our own concerns on the past, we should at least consider the view of contemporary biologists that self-other distinction (a protein-based activity) must be flexible as well as reliable in order to support living process. Similarly, our ability to revise our memories actually supports our capacity for growth and therefore survival.[31] Our growing understanding of intersubjectivity is teaching us that there are many different kinds of relationships between past and future, selves and others, and they are always changing. For me, Chaucer is what self-psychology calls a "self-object" (an object "not experienced as separate and independent from the self," and yet known to be an other; family members, comrades, lovers, and pets are all examples).[32]

Playing Well with Others

Chaucer is centrally preoccupied with the role of language in enabling the sharing of attention. His poetry acknowledges how readily we misunderstand each other (e.g., the Man in Black and his interlocutor in *The Book of the Duchess*), but it is beyond question that a *we* of some

---

D. J. Crisp, "Gregariousness and Systematic Affinity in Some North Carolinian Barnacles," *Bulletin of Marine Science* 47 (1990): 516–25.

[30] David C. Queller and Joan E. Strassman, "The Evolution of Complex Societies," in *Evolutionary Ecology,* ed. Westneat and Fox, 326–40. Hence the power of the figure of territorial assemblage in Chaucer's poetry—from masses of singing birds startling the narrator out of sleep, to the parliament of fowls, the parliaments in *Troilus and Criseyde,* to the fox chase, Jack Straw's anti-Fleming rebels, the opening of the *General Prologue,* Melibee's counselors, and all the affects and appetites gathered together at the end of the *Canterbury Tales* under the sign of Justice.

[31] Daniel L. Schacter, *Searching for Memory: The Brain, the Mind, and the Past* (New York: Basic Books, 1996): "Memories are records of how we have experienced events, not replicas of the events themselves," and are "constructed from influences operating in the present as well as from information . . . stored about the past" (5–6, 8). For similar discussions of the plasticity of perception, see Thomas A. Stoffregen and Benoît G. Bardy, "On Specification and the Senses," *Behavioral and Brain Sciences* 24 (2001): 195–261; and Eli Brenner and Jeroen B. J. Smeets's commentary thereon, "We Are Better Off Without Perfect Perception," http://citeseerx.ist.psu.edu/viewdoc/summary?doi=10.1.1.37.9039.

[32] Heinz Kohut, *The Analysis of the Self* (Madison: University of Wisconsin Press, 1971), 3.

kind is trying to understand. Furthermore, whether or not, or what, we understand is almost irrelevant by comparison with the importance of the attempt itself. In Chaucer's poetry, intersubjectivity creates, and is created by, communication, irrespective of the accuracy of transmission. Communication *in and of itself* builds intersubjectivity and hence social bonds. The reasons for Chaucer's famed embrace of ambiguity lie here: interpretation is an intersubjective activity that *depends* on the ambiguity of signifiers. Chaucer's dream visions foreground ongoing attempts at (mutual) understanding (e.g., narratorial chitchat, varieties of diction), despite confusions and inconclusions. We leave his poems without tidings, but with the feeling that we have participated, intimately, in a search for meaning. In Chaucer's poetry, the sharing of attention is an end in itself. It is the *sine qua non* of intersubjectivity—hence, not just of the endless works of reading, storytelling, and listening, but also of the poetry's most important topics, like care, healing, conciliation, counsel, and parliamentary process.

Chaucer's awareness of the importance of shared attention is also responsible for his endless experimentation with the representation of textual influences and narratorial mediation. Old books return, ghostly, in the guise of friendly personifications. The Chaucerian narrator is a charmer, a good "felawe." But he is also a personification de-personified, as a "poppet," by Harry Bailey, who finds him mysterious ("elvish"). Geoffrey comes from another world, but he gets acquainted, tries to find his footing, to remember old rhymes, counsel patience, watch and listen, *pay attention*. He's fun to listen to, like Pandarus, but better (not quite as garrulous). Both characterizations draw on ancient and medieval discourses on friendship and the role of the consoler.[33]

Moreover, Geoffrey directly invites us to consider meanings, far more often and interestingly than any other medieval poet. It's just really too bad about that letter of Criseyde's, he says. He's afraid the conflicting messages about love at the portal to the dreamscape in *The Parliament of Fowls* apply to him, but maybe they don't. He thinks things over with

[33] The literature on these topics is vast and varied; see, for example, David Clark, *Between Medieval Men: Male Friendship and Desire in Early Medieval English Literature* (New York: Oxford University Press, 2009); Richard E. Zeikovitz, *Homoeroticism and Chivalry: Discourses of Male Same-Sex Desire in the Fourteenth Century* (New York: Palgrave Macmillan, 2003); and Anna Roberts, "Helpful Widows, Virgins in Distress: Women's Friendship in French Romance of the Thirteenth and Fourteenth Centuries," in *Constructions of Widowhood and Virginity in the Middle Ages,* ed. Cindy L. Carlson and Angela Jane Weisl (New York: St. Martin's Press, 1999), 25–48.

us; yes, we do know how language changes over the years. No, we weren't worrying about the "sodeyn love"; it feels like it takes Criseyde *forever* to fall in love with Troilus (we think things over with her, too). But okay, maybe we *should* be paying more attention to the real time of events in Troy. The construction of meaningful patterns is characteristic of living process; overinterpretation is by no means confined to the human animal. But human animals do love pondering what's going on in each other's minds. Chaucer distinctively invites us to accompany him in this highly psychological, yet highly social, activity.

It is above all affective companionship that Geoffrey seems to invite; anxiety followed by relief, joyful identification followed by disappointment, the happiness of companionship itself, as well as its risks. He's a narrator who almost always has a companion: the Man in Black, the eagle, "Affrykan." Alceste, in the Prologue to the *Legend of Good Women,* is a textual memory, retrieved from forgetfulness, restored to mind, herself the very type of the constant companion, made out of daisy-talk. There is enormous relish in Chaucer's poetry for conversation and debate, even internal conversation and debate. We can't be sure whether Geoffrey and the Man in Black share (are two parts of) the same mind, or whether they share an experience of intersubjectivity. But the point is precisely that we can't be sure, because the mind is always engaged with other minds. The role of the self-object in enabling shared attention, intersubjectivity, and transformation is central to Chaucerian art.

Chaucer, that is, has what I would call a clinical sensibility; he is at least as interested in how words, by creating shared experience, change us, as he is in what they mean. Meaning-making is "adaptive," enjoyable, for its own sake. I don't think we need despair just because a parliament of birds can't work it all out in one day. The point of radical democratic theory is that we never finish working things out, not that we never accomplish anything.[34] Lasting stability eludes intersubjective

---

[34] Marion Turner, *Chaucerian Conflict: Languages of Antagonism in Late Fourteenth-Century London* (Oxford: Oxford University Press, 2007), cites Ernesto Laclau and Chantal Mouffe, *Hegemony and Socialist Strategy: Towards a Radical Democratic Politics,* trans. Winston Moore and Paul Cammack, 2nd ed. (London: Verso, 2001), as evidence of discussion "of the idea that society is inevitably antagonistic" (5 n. 18). But Laclau and Mouffe's rejection of utopianism has very little to do with the political cynicism Turner claims to have objectively detected in Chaucer's poetry while the rest of us were merely putting all of our fears into it. (I find it just as likely that Marion Turner is channeling the late D. W. Robertson Jr.) Laclau and Mouffe's goal is to "redimension and do justice to workers' struggles" (167); if "Chaucer holds out no hope for social amelioration" (Turner, *Chaucerian Conflict,* 5), he is on a very different page indeed from radical democratic theorists.

communication, and therefore sociality, by definition. So does pure messaging: communication must always be crafted and performed. As the ethologists Enquist, Hurd, and Ghirlanda note, speaking of animal communication, "Signaling systems are likely to never reach equilibrium"; hence signaling and receiving behavior will "depart from the predictions of [for example] game theoretic models"; "new signals"—usually, because of their newness, "costly" but "more effective"—will "destabilize strategic equilibria."[35] Or, as Boyd puts it, "Play and art are non-zero-sum—that is, one side's gain is not another's loss—and that makes all the difference": both play and art depend on "the mutually amplifying effects of cooperation [and open-endedness]."[36]

Biopolitical theory cautions us, as it should, against getting too festive about living process; there can be no doubt that, as Foucault has argued so influentially, "life" is the business of power.[37] I stand, however, with Derrida's critique of the exclusive association of bio-power with modernity.[38] The powers of life and death, of care and punishment, are always co-constructed and constructing, however distinctive their styles of action. In the later volumes of *The History of Sexuality,* Foucault himself deliberately cuts across the divide between punishment and bio-power by taking "bodies and pleasures" back to Greek and Roman treatises on "care" (regimens, consolations, inspirations).[39] Boethius's *Consolatio Philosophiae* is one such treatise, focused in a properly (Neo-) Platonic way on the use of discourse and reason to *heal* (not simply get rid of) the narrator's dreadful misery. Though, looked at most ways, Chaucer's decision to translate the *Consolatio* was in no way odd, looked at another way, it was a more pointed choice than has often been recognized. Of Chaucer's prose treatises, three care for the "self": one aims

[35] Enquist, Hurd, and Ghirlanda, "Signaling," 274–75.

[36] Boyd, *On the Origin of Stories,* 87.

[37] Michel Foucault, *The History of Sexuality, vol. 1: An Introduction* (Harmondsworth: Penguin, 1978).

[38] Jacques Derrida, *The Beast and the Sovereign,* vol. 1, trans. Geoffrey Bennington (Chicago: University of Chicago Press, 2009), on "the linear history which . . . remains the common temptation of both Foucault and Agamben" (333).

[39] Foucault, *The Use of Pleasure: The History of Sexuality,* vol. 2, trans. Richard Hurley (New York: Vintage, 1990), and *The Care of the Self: The History of Sexuality,* vol. 3, trans. Richard Hurley (New York: Vintage, 1986). For two good translations of medieval consolations and discussions thereof, see Monika Otter's *Goscelin of St. Bertain: The Book of Encouragement and Consolation (Liber Confortatorius)* (Cambridge: D. S. Brewer, 2004), and Jean Gerson's *De consolatione theologiae,* ed. Clyde Lee Miller (Norwalk, Conn.: Abaris Books, 1998).

to cure melancholy; another, anger and violent "acting out"; yet another, guilt. The treatise on the Astrolabe aims to educate beginners:

as wel considre I thy besy praier in special to lerne the tretys of the Astrelabie. Than for as moche as a philosofre saith, "he wrappith him in his frend, that condescendith to the rightfulle praiers of his frend," therefore have I yeven the a suffisant Astrolabie as for oure orizonte, compowned after the latitude of Oxenforde . . .[40]

Treatise-making and teaching are also intersubjective activities because they must take into account the age and ability of the audience, as well as the novelty and difficulty of the knowledge being conveyed.

Whether as ideology of death or passionate utterance, consolations *accompany* misery.[41] In Chaucer's translation of Boethius's *Consolatio,* Lady Philosophy argues that all things require the "ferme stablenesse of perdurable duellynge, and eek the eschuynge of destruccion," "For the purveaunce of God hath yeven to thinges that ben creat of hym this, that is a ful grete cause to liven and to duren, for whiche they desiren naturely here lif as longe as evere thei mowen."[42]

There is no such thing as bare life, if all creatures desire. And our desire for life is itself the greatest cause of living and enduring—a powerful force indeed, if only under the sphere of the moon. *Boece* is well known for the beauty and affective power of its descriptions of earthly things as well as its preference for heavenly ones. (Matter longs for adornment, according to Aristotle [*Physics*] and Bernardus Silvestris [*Cosmographia*].)[43] Similarly, despite the fact that Saint Francis of Assisi's *Canticle of the Sun* ends with sobering lines about the unavoidability of Death and the woe that will come to those who die in mortal sin, it also lavishes lyric beauty on God's material creation and its capacity for af-

[40] The narrator famously excuses his "superfluite" on the grounds that repetition makes it easier "for . . . a child to lerne." *A Treatise on the Astrolabe,* ed. John Reidy, *The Riverside Chaucer,* gen. ed. Larry Benson (Boston: Houghton-Mifflin, 1987), 662, lines 3–10, 40–50 (all references to Chaucer are from this edition). See Richard Kieckhefer on Chaucer's special interest in science (alchemy, astronomy, automatons), in *Magic in the Middle Ages* (Cambridge: Cambridge University Press, 2000), 107.

[41] Herbert Marcuse, "The Ideology of Death," in *The Meaning of Death,* ed. Herman Feifel (New York: McGraw-Hill, 1959), 64; Stanley Cavell, "Performative and Passionate Utterance," in *Philosophy the Day After Tomorrow* (Cambridge, Mass.: Harvard University Press, 2005), 155–91.

[42] *Boece* 3.pr.11.178–87.

[43] See Winthrop Wetherbee, *The Cosmographia of Bernardus Silvestris* (1973; New York: Columbia University Press, 1990), 36.

finity: "Praised be you, my Lord, through brother Fire, through whom you light the night, and he is beautiful and playful, and robust, and strong."[44] The feelings of attachment sought by these aesthetic evocations of the material world are not easy to dispel. And they follow from assertions that all created things *share affects* of longing and aversion.

Attempts to define life and what is necessary to it became newly urgent when Catharism threatened both the goodness of matter and the power of the Vatican. Because the Franciscans both espoused the ideal of apostolic poverty and celebrated the beauty of created things, they seemed to Innocent III a perfect means of distracting dissenting ascetics from gross displays of temporal dominion.[45] Poverty was a charged issue in the thirteenth century, when the Vatican had to figure out how to show its contempt of the world (perhaps a treatise on the subject?) while retaining the right to dress up in it. The secular clergy's defamations of mendicancy were accompanied by debates about what was necessary to man, and whether necessity was a just defense for theft.[46] Matter also mattered in the form of natural science. Enlightened varieties of the history of science used to view scholasticism as an impediment to the elevation of practical knowledge and the common man who made it.[47] Others, Lynn White, for example, thought the schools played an important role in sheltering and supporting natural science, paving the way for—rather than obstructing—their more egalitarian, because mathematical and experimental, successors.[48] (The democratization of knowledge by means of mendicant preaching was itself of course a Franciscan mission.) White saw the *Poverello* as a change agent whose generous extensions of sentience to all the "things of nature" helped to legitimate study thereof. Those "things" were "fellow creatures placed on earth for God's inscrutable purposes, praising him in their proper ways as we do in ours." By preaching to them, the *Poverello* "imput[ed] moral personality" to birds and flowers, "forced man to abdicate his monarchy over the creation, and instituted a democracy of all of God's creatures" (433).

---

[44] *The Writings of St. Francis of Assisi,* trans. Father Paschal Robinson (Philadelphia: Dolphin Press, 1906), 153.

[45] See David L. Jeffrey, *The Early English Lyric and Franciscan Spirituality* (Lincoln: University of Nebraska Press, 1975).

[46] Louise O. Fradenburg, "Needful Things," in *Medieval Crime and Social Control,* ed. Barbara Hanawalt (Minneapolis: University of Minnesota Press, 1999), 49–69.

[47] For example, Edgar Zilsel, "The Sociological Roots of Science," *American Journal of Sociology* 47 (1942): 544–62; rpt. in *Social Studies of Science* 30 (2000): 935–49.

[48] Lynn White Jr., "Natural Science and Naturalistic Art in the Middle Ages," *American Historical Review* 52 (1947): 421–35.

White further linked Francis's communitarian leanings to his urban and mercantile roots. The son of a merchant, "reared in a thriving town, became the evangelist . . . of nature." This is a paradox perhaps intelligible because interest in "the properties of things" made sense in places where said things were made, sold, and conveyed. The notion of a valuable kind of knowledge more likely to be produced by scholars and commoners than by ruling elites was certainly thinkable in the Middle Ages. Arnold of Villanova—physician, teacher, and translator of Avicenna—writes that "since the properties of things cannot be discovered by reason but only by experiment or revelation, and experience and revelation are common to the ordinary man and to the scholar, it is possible that knowledge of properties may be attained by the common people sooner than by others."[49] It may well be that later medieval interest in natural science and experimentation was a corollary of the democratizing educational and pastoral (counter-heretical) programming launched by Lateran IV and transmitted by Franciscan evangelism. Mendicancy was a deterritorialization, never fully captured by the Vatican. These changing times also saw the establishment of poetry as an academic subject by the writers of the *artes poetriae,* including Geoffrey de Vinsauf—another of Chaucer's close textual companions, whose devotion to *renovatio* is well known: *"if a word is old, be its physician and give to the old a new vigour.* Do not let the word reside invariably on its native soil—such residence dishonours it. Let it avoid its natural location, travel about elsewhere, and take up a pleasant abode on the estate of another. There let it stay as a novel guest."[50] The Franciscan Order, likewise on the move, "attracted men who flung themselves into furthering the new natural science."[51] Much of this scientific ferment was centered on the Franciscan school at Oxford, home to Roger Bacon and likely to Bartholomaeus Anglicus as well as, in the fourteenth century, John Trevisa and John Wycliffe. The interplay between this environment and London was very rich. Scholars who have studied the geography of learning in the later fourteenth century have shown that

[49] Lynn Thorndike, "Roger Bacon and Experimental Method in the Middle Ages," *Philosophical Review* 23 (1914): 271–98 (289).

[50] My emphasis; Geoffrey de Vinsauf, *Poetria Nova,* trans. Margaret F. Nims (Toronto: PIMS, 1967), 43. The authoritative study of Geoffrey de Vinsauf's own textual afterlives is the marvelous Marjorie Curry Woods, *Classroom Commentaries: Teaching the Poetria Nova Across Medieval and Renaissance Europe* (Columbus: Ohio State University Press, 2010).

[51] White, "Natural Science and Naturalistic Art in the Middle Ages," 434.

intellectual trends were transmitted by Oxford-educated clerks who later sought position among the wordsmiths of London and Westminster—the secular, urban milieu that, Astell argues, was the true home ground of Chaucer's cultural experience, more than the court, more than the "civil service" per se, though developments in all these areas were highly interdependent at the time.[52] Directly or indirectly, Oxford exposed to natural science the intelligentsia, the arty types, the scribes, notaries, men of law, and civil servants who wrote parliamentary democracy into being.[53] This was also the time for translation: Chaucer's *Boece* and *Tale of Melibee*; John Trevisa's translations of the *Polychronicon* and *De Proprietatibus Rerum*; translations of Aegidius Romanus by Trevisa and Hoccleve; the Wycliffite Bible; and many, many almanacs, divination guides, astrological and medical treatises, and herbals, herbals, herbals! consequent on the plagues of the fourteenth century. Care of self was one of the primary textual symptoms of trauma in the "calamitous" fourteenth century: know how to do it yourself, care for yourself, poultice your children, choose a good day to begin a venture, because no one else will; the doctors and priests have died, or fled the countryside, along, perhaps, with divine *cura*.

The connection between "care" and textual intersubjectivity is clearly displayed by Chaucer's poetry. Glending Olson's book on premodern understandings of "the therapeutic value of literary entertainment" cites advice to melancholics to "associate with cheerful people and read pleasant and unusual things" ("hanter gens ioyeuses et lire ioyeuses choses et estranges").[54] When Pandarus tries to console Troilus in Book V, he recommends that he "hante" in just this way, that he go out and play with the cheerful people at Sarpedon's parties. Good cheer is Harry Bailey's business; he invites the pilgrims to play, for "confort" as well as "mirth." In *What Is Art For*, Dissanayake writes: "Perhaps the most salient and suggestive feature of play is its metaphorical nature. Something stands for something else—a ball of paper thrown along the floor releases prey-catching movements even when the cat is not hungry and when the object is not . . . prey. . . . A stick of wood is a doll or a boat

[52] Ann W. Astell, *Chaucer and the Universe of Learning* (Ithaca: Cornell University Press, 1996), 5–10.

[53] I do not intend this as an idealization of parliamentary democracy. Partly because they are self-organizing systems, parliaments are never predictable, and only occasionally are they "good."

[54] Glending Olson, *Literature as Recreation in the Later Middle Ages* (Ithaca: Cornell University Press, 1982), 57.

for a playing child."[55] Again, Geoffrey the Pilgrim is imagined as just such a doll or "poppet" by Harry Bailey, himself another of the narrator's chubby doubles. All non-Chaucerian *Galeottos*, eavesdroppers, and allegorical purveyors of wisdom aside, can you think of another poet of any age who more loved alter egos? Chaucer's poetry represents utterance as embedded in other utterances, in other words, intersubjectivity, with a relish and a playfulness unparalleled in late medieval poetry.

Of course it is not at all new to say that Chaucer is playful.[56] His comic sensibility has been asserted and adored by critics especially in the last two hundred years or so. I have argued that the lively, comical Chaucer of nineteenth- and early twentieth-century English criticism is something of a diversion of attention from the poetry's sensitive registrations of the affects associated with loss—grief, fear, anger, indifference—and I am far from recanting that position.[57] Of all medieval narrative poets, Chaucer is by far the most preoccupied with affective and cognitive states—with the state and nature of sentience as such. What I am arguing now is that Chaucer's wisdom about the nature of mourning actually helps us to make sense of his fondness for play. Mourning, first of all, is a process; it differs from melancholy by being a *work,* as Freud famously emphasizes—a process of (re)experiencing change rather than denying it: "Why do I feel so crabby this morning? Oh, I remember—I'm being sent to the Greek camp," as opposed to more melancholic formulations like "Well, in that case, I'll just have to come right back!" *The Book of the Duchess* says it all in advance: "Now maybe we can begin."[58]

The treatment for melancholic shortcuts, divagations, and megalomania is, in Chaucer, almost always some form of humor or play. When I read about the dark circles under Criseyde's eyes, I feel badly for her; she is *not* feeling well. By the time she has told Troilus all about how she would have killed herself had he been dead, and vice versa, I'm thinking, "This is getting kind of stupid." It's *Romeo and Juliet* manqué. (Chaucer was of course familiar with stories of suicidal lovers, if only prospectively with Romeo and Juliet.) The humor of this scene is slight,

---

[55] Dissanayake, *What Is Art For?,* 78.

[56] For example, Laura Kendrick, *Chaucerian Play: Comedy and Control in the "Canterbury Tales"* (Berkeley and Los Angeles: University of California Press, 1988).

[57] Louise O. Fradenburg, "Voice Memorial: Loss and Reparation in Chaucer's Poetry," *Exemplaria* 2 (1990): 169–202.

[58] The allusion is to the ending of Philip Roth's novel *Portnoy's Complaint.*

an echo of Chauntecleerian amplification, a bit of play, like an "I love you more" contest, with doom all around. It's the vanity of human wishes; the very presence of comedy, however muted, tells me that both Troilus and Criseyde have begun to "fall off the stage," as Lacan would put it.[59] The almost-comical uses to which Chaucer puts Boethius also indicate his awareness that healing is tricky and doesn't always work. People don't always want it, for one thing. Not right away anyway. Working through can't be rushed, and it never ends once and for all. Humor is, for Chaucer, counter-melancholic, posttraumatic. It's because he is so aware of our need to mourn—which means, among other things, to let go of our dreams of omnipotence—that he is by far the funniest of medieval poets. This is a distinctive feature of his sensibility that should never be forgotten in any analysis of his work.

Mourning and play are both counter-traumatic because they permit change, tolerate the frustrations of process, and therefore address anxiety. Chaucer's play with signifiers has enormous intersubjective appeal; he invites us to play with him, and usually we accept the invitation. Play is about signifying and thereby about becoming. It isn't so much about finishing. This is the import of Chaucerian unfinishedness, fascination with beginnings, resistance to forward propulsion. "Becoming" in turn is about process, in particular about processes of transformation of states of mind and body. Play lets us "become" doctor, princess, good yeoman of the greenwood. Play values experimentation. When we play, we are more open to the new, from within and without. We become "neophiles" and innovators, making active use of our imaginations. Playing and pretending are crucial to the becomings of living creatures, to adaptation and behavioral flexibility; "deception" is widespread in the world of flora and fauna.[60] Play teaches "vital skills"; it is transformative and transforming. We can neither thrive nor survive without it. And it is highly contagious, a powerful medium of affect transmission, as or in literature.

The psychoanalyst D. W. Winnicott suggests that the role of psycho-

---

[59] *The Seminar of Jacques Lacan, Book X: Anxiety,* trans. Cormac Gallagher (Eastbourne: Antony Rowe, 2002), chap. 25, 7. Cf. also Boyd, *On the Origin of Stories*: "Play often involves exaggerated or extreme behavior, like losing balance and then recovering, or risking defeat in play-fighting until attacker and defender swap roles. (Aptly, the name of the Japanese kabuki theater derives from the obsolete verb kabuku, 'to lose one's balance,' 'to be playful' " (93).

[60] On deception, see Enquist, Hurd, and Ghirlanda, "Signaling," 273–74.

therapy is to help the analysand become capable of play.[61] Chaucer's poetry tries to teach us to play, and to play better with (the) Ø/other(s), while it also teaches us how to mourn. His real interest is in the clinical power of the signifier, that is, the healing power of signifying process, whether the patient is the commonweal, or the realm of Nature, or a desperately distressed widower. I am speaking again of talking cures, "logotherapeutics," formalized by the pre-Platonic philosophers, by Plato himself, by Greek physicians, and on and on into the later Middle Ages, when, Olson writes, "A number of writers—physicians, philosophers, and poets . . . affirmed the very significant power of fiction and entertainment to revitalize. . . . [L]iterary delight makes something happen."[62] Communication, including language, extends and supports sentience; the arts foreground that function of the signifier. Chaucer's narrators and narrative stance are designed to provide us with enriched environments: friends, toys, and wheels (toy wheels, incidentally, being among the first crafted objects known to us).[63]

Playing and healing with the signifier are virtually identical for Chaucer. The point of the end of the *Canterbury Tales* is that the image or symbol of restitution (and symbol *as* restitution), that is, Libra, does a certain work: the image can't rival the hypervitality of heaven, but it can change states of mind into a certain readiness and attentiveness. In classical and medieval medicine, words help to create a safe, extraordinary and therefore potentially playful relationship between healer and sufferer.[64] It is axiomatic that the healer be "of" the sufferer's world but at the same time "disinterested"; the healer is always a liminal figure, in part because the healer is always a kind of self-object. Ideally disinterested, the healer should exercise great care when entering homes (lives, really); it is against the ethics of care, for example, to persuade wives out of their virtue when making house calls (this principle is articulated very early on).[65] In the classical tradition the healer is, or should be, a philanthropist, a lover of humankind, and a friend just personal enough to be able to keep the individual patient in mind, and prescribe the

---

[61] D. W. Winnicott, *Playing and Reality* (London: Tavistock, 1972; rpt. New York: Routledge, 1989–99): psychoanalysis is "a highly sophisticated form of playing," 41.

[62] Olson, *Literature as Recreation in the Later Middle Ages,* 232.

[63] Jane Jacobs, *Cities and the Wealth of Nations: Principles of Economic Life* (New York: Random House, 1984), 222.

[64] For example, by means of "pleasant" or "beguiling" speech; Jackson, *Care of the Psyche,* 20.

[65] Ibid., 26–27, 42.

proper remedies for her, but not personal enough to take part in her everyday life and concerns. Lady Philosophy is made out of these writings; she is an "extimate" figure, an "extraction" from interiority, a kind of self-object, an imaginary visitor who appears and disappears at will.

The liminal circumstances in which Chaucerian narrators so often find themselves derive from premodern writing on the ethics of healers and consolers. Friendly minds are always liminally situated—in homes not their own, woods and clearings, anonymous *thropes,* away from the main business of the day. Chaucer is not the only medieval poet to draw attention to the process of attending to others. But his narrators help by serving or seeking rather than knowing. They never understand what's just happened, but Langlandian frustration is bypassed by their willingness to keep on moving on, led, for example, by garrulous eagles or puppies so charming as to have real ears and enjoy having the tops of their soft heads patted by plump little poppets. It is charming to replace Pwyll's hounds of hell with a puppy. The narrator himself is of course similarly cute—harmless, a little lost, eager for friendship.[66] Even cuteness is about healing. Cuteness is inclusive, "generous"; it requires gestures that invite care and protection, hence the fantasy of intimacy without aggression. Like Woody Allen, with less anxiety, the Chaucerian narrator is so far from doing harm as to spend a good part of his time fearing it: "I don't want to achieve immortality through my work. I want to achieve it by not dying." His famous uncertainty is restorative *because* of its digressive and prolixifying formal qualities.[67] He accomplishes the easing of the Man in Black's heart by listening to him, trying to mirror his reflections back to him, misunderstanding him and generally engaging him in a *process* of intersubjective encounter, in *conversation.* Premodern psychologists, Chaucer among them, were perfectly aware that the relationship between healer and sufferer had therapeutic efficacy in its own right. Galen remarks on the paradoxical difficulty of attaining self-knowledge by oneself; because it is so difficult for us to understand our own problems clearly, we need the help of an other to articulate them.[68] Seneca cites Lucretius to the effect that "ever from

[66] For an introduction to the science of cuteness, see http://www.nytimes.com/2006/01/03/science/03cute.html.

[67] Chaucerian discourse shares with psychoanalysis the foregrounding of meaning-making as intersubjective process. Its point is made with the making of it. Or, to put it another way, analytical discourse is the Ø put and observed in action.

[68] Jackson, *Care of the Psyche,* 27–28, 40.

himself does each man flee"; each of us needs a friend "whose knowledge of us we fear less than our own."[69] Could there be a better description of the Chaucerian narrator/healer? Who knows better, despite and/or because of his own strangeness, that intersubjectivity itself is transformative, in large part because it undoes isolation and begins the rebuilding of fellowship?

The stated purpose of the Canterbury tale-telling contest is to provide "confort." When do we fear our fellow's knowledge of us more than our own? Harry Bailey's "myrthe" turns to anger when the Pardoner singles him out as particularly *envoluped* in sin. Sometimes words repair injury best when impersonal. When things get too personal, game is broken and healing stops. Getting personal, isolating the sinner, is the heart of the far-from-disinterested con the Pardoner describes in his prologue. Hate and the desire for revenge threaten peace, break play, and break apart intersubjectivity. By contrast, the Parson won't tell fables, but he'll knit up the *feste* with a penitential treatise designed to take "the sinner" from pain and suffering to the brilliance of a heaven in which the body is fully restored to joy—*per desperationem ad spem,* as Gerson puts it in *De Consolatione Theologiae.*[70] This consolation, like the *Melibee,* extols the *virtus patientiae.* In *Melibee,* wifely eloquence (about which David Wallace has written so eloquently) transforms the desire for violent revenge into a desire for reconciliation.[71] What enables us to risk change is the feeling that we are understood and (therefore) accompanied.

For the ideal image of disinterested pastoral care in Chaucer's time of abandoned parishes and roving entrepreneurial healers, we need only remember the Parson's portrait, and his penitential treatise, which addresses the sin and not the sinner. The forerunners of the literature on *caritas* include deliberations in pagan antiquity on the ethics of those who care for us, who come close enough to enter us, our homes, our minds, our families, whether by means of the knife or the drug or the consoling word, but always through the signifier, sometimes with honey on it. It is folly to disturb a mother grieving for her dead child, says Ovid, so Prudence allows Melibee time to grieve, and only after does she do her diligence "with amiable wordes . . . to reconforte" (VII.978).

[69] Ibid., 27.

[70] Gerson, *De consolatione theologiae,* x.

[71] David Wallace, *Chaucerian Polity: Absolutist Lineages in England and Italy* (Stanford: Stanford University Press, 1997), 212–46.

The doctors who advise Melibee should be rewarded, she argues, because they have done well and behaved as doctors should:

I seye yow that the surgiens and phisiciens han seyd yow in youre conseil discreetly, as hem oughte, / and in hire speche seyden ful wisely that to the office of hem aperteneth to doon to every wight honour and profit, and no wight for to anoye, / and after hir craft to doon greet diligence unto the cure of hem which that they han in hire governaunce.

(VII.1268–70)

Melibee could not be more aware of the vulnerability of the ear (and other portals) to counsel, and the pressing need therefore to ascertain the ethos of the counselor.

Chaucer's writing highlights the issue of healing, its basis in enriched intersubjectivity, and the vulnerability to the Other and others consequently entailed therein. Care means and creates the social, political, and economic dimensions of our experience; our lives depend on it, and (therefore) it cannot be accomplished without intersubjectivity, without attempts to articulate indescribable inner events. In premodern political theory, "community" was seen as the result of a " 'natural inclination to congregate' "; because of that inclination, moreover, it is in turn "natural" to reach out for help when we are suffering.[72] Persuasion was the means of awakening, in fallen man, recognition of that "natural inclination" and "its implications for [our] lives," including the paradoxical naturalness of the polis and its attempts to improve its citizens intellectually and morally.[73]

This is one of the reasons we must always ask of Chaucer's poems how and why they teach us to play. "Game" keeps people talking to each other. Hence Chaucer warns us not to read *The Miller's Tale* if we aren't ready for "game." This anticipates the tale's insistence that we stand unto our own harm. To share subjective experience with the Miller, we have to be willing to risk disgust, or even risk not feeling disgust when we should. (Disgust is a powerful social affect.) *Squaymousness* stands in the way of play because it is averse to reality, corporeality, and common-ness. (Play doesn't screen out reality; it plays with it.) The ways in which animals signal their intent to play, referred to by etholo-

[72] Cary J. Nederman, "Nature, Sin, and the Origins of Society: The Ciceronian Tradition in Medieval Political Thought," *Journal of the History of Ideas* 49 (1988): 3–26 (5).
[73] Ibid.

gists as "play markers," include cute "self-handicapping"—as when the Miller acknowledges he might himself be a cuckold, for all he knows, but whatever, he knows his limitations, and he certainly didn't mean to imply anything about the Reeve in particular.[74] But right away the Reeve takes things too personally—he can't play.

Absolon is too squeamish and pretentious to play. He's in fantasyland, which differs from the play world in having no elements from external reality—no wooden spoons pretending to be cudgels, no dolls at the tea party. Play demands an appreciation of the real world; it is directed toward it, fascinated with it, not (too) afraid of it. Nicolas loves to play, but in a manner that also pulls away from reality and intersubjectivity. For all his forwardness, it matters more to him to concoct elaborate plots and stage sets than it does to make it with Alisoun. John of course takes himself way too seriously, and isn't allowed to revenge his cuckolding, so the Reeve will try to do it for him, by tricking out another Miller in the same pretentiousness and snobbery the Miller had attributed to a carpenter prepared to believe he was chosen by God to renew humanity. The Miller-Reeve episode links the Oedipal plots of fabliau to questions of rank and protocol. Play is democratizing; anybody can be a princess. Whether play can democratize society is another question.

Chaucer is interested in the power of words and images to change people's minds; questions about the engagement of his poetry in social change and history can't be properly addressed in the absence of such an emphasis. Sociality is shared attention, and it is the novel, the de Vinsaufian, the creative signifier, to which we attend most. "Fiction, like art in general, can be explained in terms of cognitive play with pattern—. . . and in terms of the unique importance of human shared attention."[75] And shared attention is the consequence of attachment, of the intersubjective play that begins in our earliest moments of life. There comes a time, several months after birth, when a baby will no longer look at mother's pointing finger; instead the baby will follow the direction of the pointing finger to see what Mom wants her to notice. This is an absolutely crucial developmental moment; now the baby knows it has a mind that can attend to objects, and so does Mom, and they can notice things together; they can share a mental experience.

[74] Bekoff, *Minding Animals,* 124–26.
[75] Boyd, *On the Origin of Stories,* 130.

From here the infant's theory of mind will gallop forward. This is the kind of intersubjectivity that builds our complex social worlds and cultural practices (agreeing on and arguing over what is worthy of attention). "We come equipped to attend to, relate to, take our lead from, and understand other[s]."[76] I would add, and underscore, that we come equipped to care and be cared for by others; infants often try to return the favor by feeding their mothers, and our cuteness often takes the lead in encouraging others to take the lead in caring for us.

Current evolutionary theory proposes that "the pressure to understand others has been a major driving force in the growth of higher, especially primate, intelligence"; forgiveness and reconciliation are needed to repair social breaches and have been observed in many different species.[77] The pressure to understand others is what drives the tale-telling contest of the *Canterbury Tales*—that, and its corollary, the circumvention of violence, the defense of life and well-being. Rapprochement might well be taken to be the end point of most Chaucerian narratives, because the experience of narrative is itself a rapprochement with another mind. It is important for us to remember why play and shared attention are so important to so many species that they become ends in themselves.

Boyd notes that one important benefit of "advanced theory of mind" is "the capacity to handle multiple perspectives, multiple orders of belief or representation."[78] Expressive exchange between different life forms, however prone to misunderstanding, has real power of alteration. Fascination with extraordinary, or what the ethologists call "costly," communication is the hallmark of Chaucerian poetry. And the most consistent sign of that fascination is extraordinary intersubjective display across difference. Let us take the relation between predator and prey. This is usually understood as a relationship of minimal intersubjective exchange and minimal common interest. The animal fable foregrounds these basic matters of kill or be killed, of antipathy between species, or of how cooperation might come about (the Lion and the Mouse, for example). In *The Nun's Priest's Tale,* however, the accent is on learning, not on instinct; in it, predator and prey discover not just common interests but common foibles and frailties in the area of exaggerating one's importance to the world. We have not a single *moralitas* delivered by a dis-

[76] Ibid., 132.
[77] Ibid., 140–41.
[78] Ibid., 149.

tanced narrator, but two *moralitates* delivered by the freshly educated fox and cock, in dialogue form. The focus is on learning, on learning that even traditional enemies can discover shareable truths. This is, in my view, the best approach to the multiplicity of perspective characteristic of Chaucerian poetry—a multiplicity for which the narrator or one of his avatars is usually responsible. Turn over the leaf, choose another tale; men say, I don't, that Criseyde gave Diomede her heart; I know Blanche must seem the best to you; I didn't mean to insult women; I have to keep reading, this isn't finished for me yet. The capacity for multiple perspectives should be taken not only as poststructuralist *jeu d'esprit* but as crucial to living process and the representation and interpretation of expressions of life-states entailed therein.

The Account Book and the Treasure:

Gilbert Maghfeld's Textual Economy and the Poetics of Mercantile Accounting in Ricardian Literature

Andrew Galloway
Cornell University

I T WOULD BE HARD TO FIND A BETTER EXAMPLE of a single book standing as witness to the social and economic networks of late fourteenth-century London—and to the involvement of the region's major literary figures in them—than the account book for July 4, 1390–June 23, 1395, of Gilbert Maghfeld, ironmonger, credit broker, and money-lender.[1] The book is filled with "accomptes" of the transactions linking Maghfeld to numerous social spheres in London, Westminster, and Southwark, from silkwomen to the king, and to a number of known London writers—Chaucer, Gower, and Henry Scogan, and fleetingly, as can be shown for the first time, Thomas Usk as well. All were linked to Maghfeld by his professional roles as merchant, alderman, customs official, keeper of the sea, then royally appointed sheriff when the king took over London's administration in 1392. Predominantly, however, these individuals and their communities were connected to Maghfeld by his moneylending services, on which Maghfeld built his later career before his financial collapse and death in 1397.

This essay seeks to show that this unparalleled glimpse of Ricardian mercantile documentary culture can also reveal some central historical,

I am grateful for astute reports on an early version of this essay by two readers for *SAC,* and for deft and patient guidance by the editor of later ones.

[1] PRO (now TNA) E 101/509/19. See Edith Rickert, "Extracts from a Fourteenth-Century Account Book," *MP* 24 (1926): 111–19, 249–56. Quotations from Rickert's extracts are cited by her page number plus the manuscript's current foliation (rather than the original foliation she uses) and were checked against the original. Where foliation only is given, the quotation does not appear in Rickert. Translations throughout are mine.

ideological, and narrative features of Ricardian literature that would otherwise be far less visible, as Maghfeld's book itself has been in literary scholarship for more than eighty years. Maghfeld has gained some attention in economic history for his sprawling social affiliations, and most recently for illustrating the dangers of overextended credit in late medieval London.[2] But literary scholars' attention to his book flourished only long ago, in the work of Edith Rickert and John Manly, whose narrowly topical search for the "models" of Chaucer's characters among the denizens of late fourteenth-century London seems to have sunk wider literary-historical study of him.[3] For decades thereafter, the city and its mercantile culture generally receded from literary criticism's view; when the city reemerged, it has often been as a problem or erasure, summed up by David Wallace's assertion of an "absent city."[4]

There are good reasons for Wallace's bold phrase. The sense of an English mercantile world that is elusive or erased in the literature, and displaced or fragmented in its wider historical reality by partisan, religious, courtly, and authoritarian forces, is compelling, especially by comparison with the Italian contexts that Wallace invokes. The phrase also speaks for a number of trenchant studies over the last two decades stressing the inconsistent or elided role of London and mercantilism in the period's literature.[5] Indeed, a steady focus on the courtly centers of

[2] Margery K. James, "A London Merchant of the Fourteenth Century," *Economic History Review*, n.s. 8 (1956): 364–76; Pamela Nightingale, "Monetary Contraction and Mercantile Credit in Later Medieval England," *Economic History Review* 43 (1990): 560–75 (discussed below).

[3] As well as Rickert, "Extracts," see John Manly, *Some New Light on Chaucer* (New York: Henry Holt, 1926), esp. 193–200. F. R. H. du Boulay briefly mentions Maghfeld's book as a sign of the "small world" of Chaucer's literary associates (following Manly, ibid., 74–76): "The Historical Chaucer," in *Writers and Their Backgrounds: Geoffrey Chaucer,* ed. Derek Brewer (Athens: Ohio University Press, 1975), 33–57 (33–34); so too Derek Pearsall, *The Life of Geoffrey Chaucer* (Oxford: Blackwell, 1992), 222.

[4] David Wallace, "Absent City," in *Chaucerian Polity: Absolutist Lineages and Associational Forms in England and Italy* (Stanford: Stanford University Press, 1997), 156–81.

[5] Key instances include Lee Patterson, "Chaucerian Commerce: Bourgeois Ideology and Poetic Exchange in the *Merchant's* and *Shipman's Tales*," in *Chaucer and the Subject of History* (Madison: University of Wisconsin Press, 1991), 322–66; Derek Pearsall, "Langland's London," in *Written Work: Langland, Labor, and Authorship,* ed. Steven Justice and Kathryn Kerby-Fulton (Philadelphia: University of Pennsylvania Press, 1997), 185–207; and Robert Epstein, "London, Southwark, Westminster: Gower's Urban Contexts," in *A Companion to Gower,* ed. Siân Echard (Cambridge: D. S. Brewer, 2004), 43–60. These and others are discussed below. The views of Anne Middleton describing a "common voice" of "bourgeois moderation" among Ricardian London writers might have led in a different direction: see "The Idea of Public Poetry in the Reign of Richard II," *Speculum* 53 (1978): 94–114 (95); but as Patterson pointed out, such a "voice" is predicated on an effacement of particular social identity and origins, and this sense of

patronage and initial readership for the London writers we call "Ricardian" has led to their fulfilling that label not only by period but also insofar as they addressed the higher nobility and the king.[6] Yet whereas literary historians once followed the historians' view that London merchants typically framed their cultural ideals and identity in imitation of those of the nobility, more recent historical studies have unraveled this assumption.[7] Moreover, the basic reasons for literary attention to Maghfeld and his book should not be forgotten. Nearly forty of the figures mentioned in his book—far more than in any comparable courtly materials—are mentioned in Chaucer's life records, which Rickert was excavating from the then Public Record Office when she printed excerpts from Maghfeld's book (still almost the only portions in print). Manly used Rickert's results to suggest that Maghfeld was directly satirized in the portrait of Chaucer's Merchant. Such purposes tended to isolate Manly's and Rickert's inquiries both from postwar formalist and, later, wider historicist scholarship. Even Rickert, an immensely dedicated archivist, offered Maghfeld's text chiefly as a vehicle for revealing the minutiae of the "characters" of Chaucer's world. Concerning an entry where Maghfeld notes a loan given to mayor Adam Bamme to buy a hat in "silk of Tripoli," Rickert wonders, "was the goldsmith who made cups for John of Gaunt to give Philippa Chaucer a dandy?"[8]

Literary scholarship has, supposedly, left such "picturesque" uses of context behind, along with the concept of Chaucer's "realism" as simply

---

"effacement" of social particularity in that sense helped found rather than resist the later critical trend (*Chaucer and the Subject of History,* 331–32).

[6] Foundational studies here include Richard Firth Green, *Poets and Princepleasers: Literature and the English Court in the Late Middle Ages* (Toronto: University of Toronto Press, 1980); and V. J. Scattergood and J. W. Sherborne, eds., *English Court Culture in the Later Middle Ages* (New York: St. Martin's Press, 1983). A recent provocative contribution is Joyce Coleman, "'A bok for king Richardes sake': Royal Patronage, the *Confessio,* and *The Legend of Good Women,*" in *On John Gower: Essays at the Millennium,* ed. R. F. Yeager (Kalamazoo: Medieval Institute Publications, 2007), 104–23.

[7] For merchants' lack of a distinctive ideology and preferences for the trappings of noble culture, see Sylvia L. Thrupp, *The Merchant Class of Medieval London* (Ann Arbor: University of Michigan Press, 1948), 288–319. The claim was more qualified than some literary scholars have made of it; for counter-emphases by historians, see Pamela Nightingale's history of a single company, *A Medieval Mercantile Community: The Grocers' Company and the Politics and Trade of London, 1000–1485* (New Haven: Yale University Press, 1995); also Caroline Barron, "Political Culture of Medieval London," in *Political Culture in Late Medieval Britain: The Fifteenth Century IV,* ed. Linda Clark and Christine Carpenter (Woodbridge: Boydell, 2004), 111–34; W. Mark Ormrod, "The Origins of Tunnage and Poundage: Parliament and the Estate of Merchants in the Fourteenth Century," *Parliamentary History* 28 (2009): 209–27.

[8] Rickert, "Extracts," 115 n. 6.

"drawing . . . figures from the life."[9] But until recently, literary study has also left behind interest in the archive and, with it, the pursuit of Londonness. The turn to "documentary poetics," and the attention paid by Emily Steiner to the links between the period's literary productions and new literacies of all kinds (especially secular and vernacular religious texts and readers), has been re-foundational, as has Ethan Knapp's pursuit of the overlap of administrative and poetic presumptions and postures in the "bureaucratic muse" of the Westminster civil service shaping Thomas Hoccleve's poetry. Ralph Hanna's study of "London literature" to 1380, tracing London textual production from legal compilations and romances to *Piers Plowman,* has more directly shown that the archive and the idea of London can again be central in Ricardian literary scholarship.[10] Others have begun to pursue London's documentary and literary connections beyond Hanna's closing date, into the decades when vernacular English literature began to burgeon. Here, urban absence has begun to yield distinct outlines. Thus Marion Turner observes, "If London mattered less to Chaucer's poetry, it might be mentioned more." Turner proposes a set of motifs—prison, pubs, gossip, weaponry, and prostitution—as the impresses of "greater London" in Chaucer's narrative. Others have followed similar *viae negativae* into positive claims. C. David Benson, for instance, parallels Chaucer's intricate narrative stratagems with clever frauds recorded in the London Letter Books. Roger Ladd, noting that "no one has undertaken a comparative study of the position of merchants in late medieval English literature," pursues "antimercantile ideology" in works by Langland, Gower, Chaucer, and a range of writers in fifteenth-century England, finding a range of informed interest in and even direct literary address to the mercantile world. Although Ladd does not focus in detail on the merchants or mercantile practices themselves, his careful reading of the literary evidence suggests that these poets "who were not themselves merchants"

---

[9] Ibid., 256. For the "picturesque" resemblance of Maghfeld and Chaucer's Merchant, see Manly, *Some New Light on Chaucer,* 196. There is no need to rehearse here the history of critics' spurning anything that might make them a "Manly man" (J. A. W. Bennett, *Chaucer at Oxford and at Cambridge* [Toronto: University of Toronto Press, 1974], 9).

[10] Emily Steiner, *Documentary Culture and the Making of Medieval English Literature* (Cambridge: Cambridge University Press, 2003); Ethan Knapp, *The Bureaucratic Muse: Thomas Hoccleve and the Literature of Late Medieval England* (University Park: Pennsylvania State University Press, 2001); Ralph Hanna, *London Literature, 1300–1380* (Cambridge: Cambridge University Press, 2005).

were, in spite of their continued antitrade satire, able in some form "to give merchants a voice."[11]

Revisiting Maghfeld's book and social networks in the context of major London writers and their works offers the prospect of a further, and more historically integrated, exploration of the ways in which mercantile culture and the "new literacies" associated with credit and commerce contributed centrally to the development of Ricardian London literature. The history of what we may call late medieval documentary mercantilism has only rarely and indirectly been pursued. Maghfeld's book provides evidence that, though clearly less distinctive and self-possessed than its Continental parallels, such urban documentary culture in England possessed a creative dynamism in managing, defining, and transforming value that can explain the poets' exploitation of its features.[12] The inchoately consistent principles of Maghfeld's book had moreover the virtue of adaptability to the particularly varied social and economic spheres that a London merchant necessarily traversed, even if not always with success. Pursuit of the writers' and the literature's connections to Maghfeld's book and career can situate them more clearly in relation to one another and to mercantile London itself. For Maghfeld and the writers share what may be considered an array of "technologies," rather than simply social ideologies or literary conceits, as is suggested by the Ricardian London poets' term for their own textual production: "makyng."[13] That term alone might encourage us to

[11] Marion Turner, "Greater London," in *Chaucer and the City,* ed. Ardis Butterfield (Cambridge: D. S. Brewer, 2006), 25–40 (40); C. David Benson, "Literary Contests and London Records in the *Canterbury Tales,*" in ibid., 129–44; Roger A. Ladd, *Antimercantilism in Late Medieval English Literature* (New York: Palgrave Macmillan, 2010), 1, 160.

[12] Fundamental for study of medieval English textuality to 1307 (emphasizing royal and religious rather than civic contexts) is M. T. Clanchy, *From Memory to Written Record: England, 1066–1307,* 2nd ed. (Oxford: Blackwell, 1993). Some studies of English book-keeping (though not of this period) appear in *Accounting History: Some British Contributions,* ed. R. H. Parker and B. S. Yamey (Oxford: Clarendon Press, 1994).

[13] On this term in the context of the changing concept and status of labor, see Kellie Robertson, *The Laborer's Two Bodies: Labor and the "Work" of the Text in Medieval Britain, 1350–1500* (New York: Palgrave Macmillan, 2006), 13–50; for the notion of "technology," see Lee Patterson, "Perpetual Motion: Alchemy and the Technology of the Self," *SAC* 15 (1993): 25–57, rpt. in *Temporal Circumstances: Form and History in the "Canterbury Tales"* (New York: Palgrave Macmillan, 2006), 159–76. Accounting theory of the sixteenth century has been juxtaposed with the presentation of merchants and credit in Renaissance drama by Ceri Sullivan, though starkly separated from the discourse of "medieval avarice": *The Rhetoric of Credit: Merchants in Early Modern Writing* (Teaneck, N.J.: Fairleigh Dickinson University Press, 2002).

find ways to bridge London's poetic and commercial worlds at a point of rapid and creative development for both.

Maghfeld's Career and Book

Maghfeld's book was preserved at the Exchequer presumably because it was confiscated when Maghfeld died heavily indebted two years after its final entries. Its extant 55 paper folia (plus parchment cover) are only a part of his original documents: the book had at least two more leaves, and its opening summarizes debts carried over from a lost account book covering 1372–90. Written in London business patois—Anglo-French blended with Latin and English loanwords in a "mature" stage of maca-ronic language[14]—it shows the mobility between England's tongues that such writers as Gower and Langland further exploit. Maghfeld's surviving papers bespeak the emerging spheres of written English as well: folded into his book were found fragmentary pages of a private letter in English, the earliest known, written by an associate in Portugal. The second page (not mentioned by Rickert) apparently describes condi-tions for merchants in Lisbon.

Maghfeld's bankruptcy closed an otherwise prosperous and increas-ingly well-connected career. His house on the Thames at Billingsgate included a wharf that he had constructed in 1390 (a loose-leaf drawing of it was also found in his book). Although the area was less prestigious in the sixteenth century, it was still a place where (as John Stow says) "every great ship landing there paid for standage two-pence, every little ship with orelockes a penny, the lesser boat called a Battle a half-penny."[15] The variety of vessels suggests a place used for receiving and sending goods to local ports as well as those of Normandy, Portugal, Prussia, and beyond.

Maghfeld was the ironmongers' representative in the London com-mon council of 1376, assembled (in the spirit of the Good Parliament) by forty-one crafts demanding more participation in urban government; he later became alderman of Billingsgate. But much of his career was

[14] Laura Wright, "Mixed-Language Business Writing: Five Hundred Years of Code-Switching," in *Language Change: Advances in Historical Sociolinguistics,* ed. Ernst Håkon Jahr, Trends in Linguistics: Studies and Monographs 114 (Berlin: Mouton de Gruyter, 1999), 99–117, esp. 105–7.

[15] John Stow, *The Survey of London,* intro. by H. B. Wheatley (New York: Dutton, 1956, 1965), 185.

shaped by royal appointments, though these were brief and sometimes abruptly ended. After a shortened appointment as keeper of the sea in 1383 (his appointment in May was for more than a year, but he was removed by the King's Council after only seven months), the king appointed him customs collector at Southampton, a post he did not take up, instead serving as collector of the Boston customs (February 1386–November 1387)—the only nonlocal merchant to do so until 1390, when the king began routinely adding royal appointees to cities' customs staffs.[16] Reappointed to Southampton customs in September 1388, he took up the position but left the following May to serve as London customs collector.[17] From 1390 to 1392, he was collector of the London wool and petty custom; Chaucer, as clerk of the works (1389–91), would have received his customs.

In June 1392, the king, to punish the city for its long resistance to royal requests for loans and on vaguer grounds of social disorder, suspended the city's liberties, moved the central administration to York, and deposed the elected mayor and sheriffs, putting a royal warden in charge of the city and appointing two new sheriffs, one of them Maghfeld.[18] To Londoners, the crisis of 1392 was the most disruptive and expensive of Richard's crisis-ridden reign. Negotiations led finally to a settlement of the summer-long stalemate but compelled the city to pay enormous fines. The settlement was commemorated by the spectacular "Reconciliation" ceremony in August, complete with flowing wine in London's conduits and descending angels who offered the king and queen flattering speeches and exquisite gifts, all elegantly commemo-

[16] See S. H. Rigby, "The Customs Administration at Boston in the Reign of Richard II," *Bulletin of the Institute of Historical Research* 58 (1985): 12–24 (18).

[17] *Calendar of Fine Rolls, 1383–1391* (London: HMSO, 1929), 252–53, 288; *Calendar of Patent Rolls, 1385–1389* (London: HMSO, 1900), online at http://sdrc.lib.uiowa.edu/patentrolls/search.html, 425.

[18] See Caroline M. Barron, "The Quarrel of Richard II with London, 1392–97," in *The Reign of Richard II: Essays in Honour of May McKisack,* ed. F. R. H. du Boulay and Caroline M. Barron (London: Athlone Press, 1971), 173–210. On Maghfeld's life, see Elspeth Veale, "Maghfeld, Gilbert (d. 1397)," *Oxford Dictionary of National Biography* (Oxford: Oxford University Press, 2004), online at http://www.oxforddnb.com/view/article/52192, accessed September 21, 2010; *Chaucer Life-Records, From Materials Compiled by John M. Manly and Edith Rickert,* ed. Martin M. Crow and Clair C. Olson (Oxford: Clarendon Press, 1966), 501–3; and S. H. Rigby, *The Overseas Trade of Boston in the Reign of Richard II,* The Lincoln Record Society (Woodbridge: Boydell, 2005), 240–42. None, however, covers his career in full detail, for which recourse to various primary sources and calendars remains necessary.

rated in Latin by the Carmelite Richard Maidstone, then probably John of Gaunt's confessor.[19] In covering this period, Maghfeld's book serves to document his life's major transition. For the "day when the sheriffs went to the Tower" ("en le iour quant lez viscountz alont a tour") at the head of a four-mile long procession of guilds in the "Reconciliation," Maghfeld listed only the expenses of his co-sheriff, Thomas Newenton: a beaver hat and tun of wine, but presumably his own splendor was equivalent (perhaps indeed including, as Rickert suggests, the "Flaundryssh bever hat" that Chaucer has his Merchant wear).[20] When he describes Newenton as "one of the sheriffs of London" ("un des viscontes de Loundres"), he is by implication describing his own position as well; at least initially, however, this role, imposed by the king, was not necessarily one that London citizens would celebrate or that Maghfeld would complacently enjoy.[21] Indeed, Maghfeld's promotion marked the beginning of the end of his economic success, either because of resentment on the part of his London mercantile peers or from the excessive expenditures of cash that his position entailed (as in the many unsettled loans to Newenton, and even more his contributions to the king), or, more likely, both. His records of mercantile transactions nearly cease soon after his June 1392 promotion, when he turned almost exclusively to moneylending.[22]

An entry in John of Gaunt's register shows that Maghfeld's involvement with moneylending dated from at least 1374, when Gaunt paid Maghfeld 200 marks as the deputy ("attourne") of Benet Bodsawe, a merchant moneylender.[23] Perhaps this was Maghfeld's financial apprenticeship. By 1392, he was managing several agents, though in a far less centralized and high-volume system than the Italian and Flemish moneylending companies operating out of Bruges.[24] The ledger books

[19] See Richard Maidstone, *Concordia (The Reconciliation of Richard II with London)*, ed. and trans. A. G. Rigg and David R. Carlson (Kalamazoo: Medieval Institute Publications, 2003); Barron, "The Quarrel of Richard II with London"; Jenny Stratford, "Richard II's Treasure and London," in *London and the Kingdom: Essays in Honour of Caroline M. Barron,* ed. Matthew Davies and Andrew Prescott (Donington: Shaun Tyas, 2008), 212–29.

[20] Rickert, "Extracts," 256.

[21] Ibid., 249, fol. 31.

[22] Nightingale, "Monetary Contraction"; James M. Murray, *Bruges, Cradle of Capitalism, 1280–1390* (Cambridge: Cambridge University Press, 2005), 127.

[23] *John of Gaunt's Register, Part I: 1372–1375,* ed. Sydney Armitage-Smith, Camden Society 3rd Series 21 (London, 1911), 2:214, item 1400.

[24] On medieval theories of usury amid a wide intellectual frame for medieval mercantilism, see Joel Kaye, *Economy and Nature in the Fourteenth Century: Money, Market Exchange, and the Emergence of Scientific Thought* (Cambridge: Cambridge University Press,

of such Continental moneylenders differ as well: they clearly indicate profit and loss; Maghfeld's account book does not.[25] Maghfeld's loans must have profited him by fees silently included in the amounts due, or, where goods are involved, by repayment at a price above the market rate. Both kinds might be concealed in entries such as "John Maccles-field clericus doit por j hogeshed de vyn que prest a John Chillye: xxxiii s. iiij d" ("John Macclesfield, cleric, owes for a hogshead of wine that he received from John Chillye: 33s 4d" [fol. 11]; Chillye was one of Magh-feld's agents). But debt, not profit, is the exclusive language of the account book. Perhaps this bespeaks moral pressure: making money from money was by strict canon law the sin of usury, though on the Continent from the early fourteenth century on this was widely tolerated, even licensed, up to 43 percent interest per annum. But Maghfeld's exclusive focus on amounts due was probably also his and other English merchants' natural way to manage the social as well as economic obligations of English commerce, lacking the system of double-entry bookkeeping used by the Italians and others that would provide a constant calculation of available goods and capital, and dependent on a broad "economy of obligation" that persisted into the Renaissance.[26] The exclusive focus on debts smoothly merges his moneylending with his heavy use of credit in trade, up to perhaps 75 percent of the value of his transactions—a high but not unparalleled proportion in a period of scant bullion and coinage.[27]

Pamela Nightingale has emphasized that shortages of coinage due to Continental manipulations of bullion were the direct reason for Magh-

1998), 79–115. For overviews of merchant bankers' social functions, advancing different theories, see Raymond de Roover, *Money, Banking, and Credit in Mediaeval Bruges* (Cambridge, Mass.: Mediaeval Academy of America, 1948), and Murray, *Bruges, Cradle of Capitalism*.

[25] De Roover, *Money, Banking, and Credit*, 255, reproduces a leaf from Collard de Marke's ledger book.

[26] See B. S. Yamey, "Balancing and Closing the Ledger: The Italian Practice, 1300–1600," in *Accounting History*, ed. Parker and Yamey, 250–57. For an argument that Renaissance double-entry bookkeeping was created in order to justify profit morally as repayment of loss, see James Aho, "Rhetoric and the Invention of Double Entry Bookkeeping," *Rhetorica* 3 (1985): 21–43. Yamey rejects the idea that any mercantile accounting system was fashioned to suit morality: "a thief who keeps his books by double entry would have no difficulty in recording the proceeds of his enterprise" (257). But for the broader idea of an ethically defined "economy of obligation" in England, see Craig Muldrew, *The Economy of Obligation: The Culture of Credit and Social Relations in Early Modern England* (London: Macmillan, 1998).

[27] James, "A London Merchant of the Fourteenth Century," 373.

feld's fall. Initially at least, English royal policies may have exacerbated these. In order to bolster the royal stock of bullion, from December 1391 merchants were required to deposit an ounce of gold in the Tower for every sack of wool they exported. Indeed, the royal appointments of customs officers like Maghfeld at Boston and London served in part to ensure that this procedure was followed.[28] But the requirement was halved by 1392, then dropped in 1393.[29] General policy and available gold seem inadequate explanations for Maghfeld's fall. Margery James's earlier view that social isolation after his royal appointment to sheriff was the major reason for Maghfeld's fall is hard to rule out, especially in explaining Maghfeld's abrupt change of business plan in June 1392.[30]

That Maghfeld felt some need to repair relations with the civic community is suggested by his application for license on August 7, 1392, to donate land to the church of St. Botolph's in Billingsgate, "for making a cemetery for the burial of parishioners dying there and others wishing to be buried there." The date is exactly when the money for the king was being gathered, partly under Maghfeld's management, and two weeks before the public "Reconciliation." Stow notes that St. Botolph's church was famous for the aldermen and sheriffs buried there, a focus for parish and civic pride.[31] Finally, more conclusive evidence exists that from the early 1380s, a number of London merchants and civic figures regarded Maghfeld with enough antipathy to lodge continued complaints about his earlier service in "keeping the sea," as the materials in which Thomas Usk features show below.

Strictly "spiritual" expenditures like that of founding the cemetery are not recorded in the account book; Maghfeld's recorded transactions, however, increasingly involved luxury items, connoisseur goods, and prestigious clients, suggesting a movement toward more elite realms of cultural capital. He acted twice as a middleman for household furnishings for John Gower, "esquire"—clearly the poet, despite Rickert's caution on this point, since Gower was styled by that title in records from

[28] Nightingale, "Contraction and Mercantile Credit in Later Medieval England"; Rigby, "Customs Administration at Boston," 17–18; *Rotuli Parliamentorum*, 3:285, as reedited and translated in *The Parliament Rolls of Medieval England, 1275–1504*, gen. ed. Chris Given-Wilson (Leicester: Scholarly Digital Editions and The National Archives, 2005), CD-Rom.

[29] Rigby, "Customs Administration at Boston," 17.

[30] James, "A London Merchant of the Fourteenth Century."

[31] *Calendar of Patent Rolls, 1391–1396*, 141; Stow, *The Survey of London*, 186.

the 1390s, when he joined the Lancastrian affinity.[32] Maghfeld later lent money to Gower in 1395, as the book's final entry records. He helped settle debts for John of Gaunt's son Henry of Derby, later king of England and an extravagant bon vivant in these years. Maghfeld also loaned money to Chaucer, for just one week, under terms to be discussed below. He loaned money to Henry Scogan, wealthy East Anglian landowner and later royal tutor, to whom Chaucer wrote a witty "Envoy" complaining of the torrential rains—tears from Venus—that Scogan's failure to continue an unrequited love had brought forth (after Chaucer's death Scogan replied with the poem "The Moral Balade," which John Shirley says was read to the four English princes at a dinner in the Vintry, suggesting continued literary connections between the courtly and mercantile worlds).[33] Scogan was regularly in London from 1387 at the latest, when he sought protection from the notoriously violent Hugh Fastolf, then sheriff of London.[34] Maghfeld had loaned money to Fastolf earlier: the debt was carried over from the 1380s to his account book, where it was never cancelled (fol. 7v). Fastolf too found government service like Maghfeld: from 1382, he was receiver of subsidies at the port of London, where he would have reported to Chaucer, controller of the port customs, 1374–86; in 1385–86, Fastolf served with Chaucer on a commission of the peace for Kent.

Instances might be multiplied of links between Chaucer's and Maghfeld's "worlds," as well as between many of their London contemporaries. But this should not be understood as displaying a static and unvarying picture, with the account book simply "illustrat[ing] this close community."[35] Maghfeld's account book presents, and assisted, a volatile trajectory in which his increasing financial contracts with courtly figures and their more intermittently associated London affiliates opened major social and economic possibilities, but also new dangers, as he ascended higher into realms of prestige and "culture." A cluster of entries for December 22, 1392, suggests the financial risks from above:

[32] John H. Fisher, *John Gower: Moral Philosopher and Friend of Chaucer* (London: Methuen, 1965), 64; cf. Rickert, "Extracts," 119.

[33] See Derek Pearsall, "*The Canterbury Tales* and London Club Culture," in *Chaucer and the City*, ed. Butterfield, 95–108.

[34] *Calendar of Close Rolls, 1385–89* (London: HMSO, 1921), 443; Pamela Nightingale, "Fastolf, Hugh (d. 1392)," *Oxford Dictionary of National Biography* (Oxford: Oxford University Press, 2004); online at http://www.oxforddnb.com/view/article/52175, accessed September 22, 2010.

[35] Du Boulay, "The Historical Chaucer," 33.

the entries list Maghfeld's loan of 20 marks to the Guildhall as a corporation, 10 marks to the mayor to be given to the Earl of Huntingdon
(the king's half-brother), and 40 shillings to fund a Christmas "mumming" at Eltham for the king himself. The occasion—perhaps like the
princely banquet in the Vintry, where Scogan sent his poem praising
Chaucer—bespeaks artistic, dramatic, and social splendor, a celebration
of ties between the higher mercantile world and the royal court. But the
debts for the entire entry are not cancelled.[36]

Maghfeld's book and career reflect, and enabled, the increasing late
medieval convergence of mercantilism, moneylending, and lay literacy.
His own rapid charter hand (identifiable by loans to "Andrew nostre
vallet" [fol. 30] and "Esmond Willesthorp qe fuist mon clerke" [fol.
42v]) shows confidence in an up-to-date London administrative script.[37]
More significant as a sign of his respect for literacy is the long list of
payments for the schooling of two small boys, one his own son, the
other likely the son of a former ward (whose name the child shared).[38]

A more enigmatic indication of Maghfeld's increasing range of connections to intellectual and literary London is the mention of a book in
an entry for December 1393, three months after his service as sheriff.
Rickert notes that Maghfeld took objects as sureties for his debts, and
she briefly mentions this in a list of such objects, though she does not
provide any details or even a folio reference:[39]

Ffrauncyes Wynchester a Westminster ad engarde dapprest en lendemayn del
Echyphanie la lyvere appelle Tresor de Philosophie

[Francis Winchester at Westminster has entrusted on loan on the day after
Epiphany the book called *Tresor de Philosophie*.]

(fol. 35)

[36] Rickert, "Extracts," 117, fol. 35. Rickert suggests that Chaucer was present at this
mumming, since on January 10, 1393 he was issued a grant from the king of £10 "for
his good service" during the previous year (*Chaucer Life-Records,* ed. Crow and Olson,
120).

[37] Both the second entry in Figure 1, for Francis Winchester, and the third entry in
Figure 2, for Chaucer, are examples of his hand. Maghfeld, writing more freely than his
scribes, uses double-lobed "a," his "d" leans steeply back, and his capital letters are
flourished. The script can be compared to those used for proceedings in the King's
Bench (1383) and Common Pleas (1386), in L. C. Hector, *The Handwriting of English
Documents* (London: Edward Arnold, 1958), plates X (b) and XI (a).

[38] Rickert, "Extracts," 251–52, fol. 46.

[39] Ibid., 115.

The memorandum lacks any indication of a debt it might secure, though its lines are grouped together by a final bracket, as used throughout the account book to point to a sum in the margin (see Fig. 1). No other entry in the ledger lacks a sum in this way. Books could be precisely valued as sureties; in 1382, the fishmonger William Walworth, mayor of London 1374–75 and 1380–81, settled a loan to a merchant of Bruges by taking possession of a "book of Romance of King Alexander in verse, well and curiously illuminated," valued at £10.[40] Walworth's surviving will shows the wider interests that such a commercial transaction by a London merchant might indicate: Walworth's will mentions his "well-glossed" copy of the Pauline Epistles, a Latin Bible, a collection of saints' lives, the *Vitas patrum* (lives of the desert Fathers), and several volumes of canon and civil law and legal commentaries.[41]

If the *Tresor de Philosophie* was a surety for Maghfeld, it stood for an unspecified amount. Possibly, entrusting the book to him was Winches-

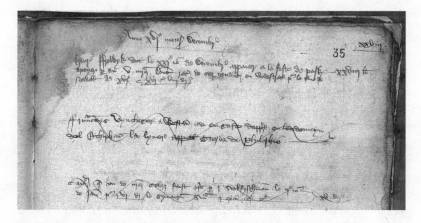

Fig. 1. National Archives, E 101/509/19, fol. 35 (by permission of TNA).

[40] Caroline Barron, "Chivalry, Pageantry, and Merchant Culture," in *Heraldry, Pageantry, and Social Display in Medieval England*, ed. Peter Coss and Maurice Keen (Woodbridge: Boydell, 2002), 219–42 (225). Could the magnificently illuminated mid-fourteenth-century Flemish copy of the *Roman d'Alexandre*, now Oxford, Bodleian Library MS Bodley 264, purchased in London in 1466 by Richard Woodville, Lord Rivers, into which an early fifteenth-century English scribe with a Midlands dialect copied the alliterative English debate poem *Alexander and Dindimus*, be the book Walworth acquired from the Flemish moneylender? On this book, see Thorlac Turville-Petre, *The Alliterative Revival* (Cambridge: D. S. Brewer, 1977), 43; Kathleen Scott, *Later Gothic Manuscripts, 1390–1490*, 2 vols. (London: Harvey Miller, 1996), 2:68–75.

[41] Dated December 20, 1385; TNA Canterbury Probate 11/1.

ter's way of opening an as yet unspecified credit line. If so, it would be a unique instance of that as well. Whatever its use, the absent valuation of the aptly named *Tresor de Philosophie* is puzzling amid the quantified goods and services in Maghfeld's accounts. As a bookish "treasure" from London's symbolic capital of multilingual literacy and elite social connections, it rests unquantifiably amid his transactions, briefly adding to his assets but perhaps also standing as a sign of his increasing economic vulnerability.

The Idea and the Literature of an Account Book:
Three London Poets

Although Maghfeld's book is a unique survival from London mercantile culture, an account book or register was becoming an essential idea as well as practical equipment for a successful and active manager of any complicated household, business, or expedition—well before the paeans of praise for accounting in the instructional manuals that appear in England in the sixteenth century. In 1543, the *Profitable Treatyce* by Hugh Oldcastle calls accounting "the glasse of a mannes state, wherin all men maie se clerely in what case thei stande, and other persones after theim maie perceive in what state thei wer in duryng their lifes, and how thei left al thynges at the houre of death."[42] Such sentiments were implicit earlier. Even late fourteenth-century London clerics used books to track prayers owed: friars used folding wax "tables" to record donations and hence the prayers owed to the donors, like the "peyre of tables al of yvory, / And a poyntel polysshed fetisly," as Chaucer's Summoner says, by which a friar's assistant "wroot the names alwey, as he stood, / Of alle folk that yaf hym any good, / Ascaunces that he wolde for hem preye."[43] So too Maghfeld's account book notes that 40 shillings loaned to Friar Walter Somerton in 1394 were secured by the friar's giving him "ij petitz tabulles dor" (two small golden tables).[44] A range of apparatus for reading, writing, and accounting, in religious and secular spheres, was increasingly common in the London area. Many ivory writing tablets, for instance, some with entirely secular motifs on them, presumably

[42] In B. S. Yamey, H. C. Edey, and Hugh W. Thomson, *Accounting in England and Scotland: 1543–1800* (London: Sweet and Maxwell, 1963), 7.

[43] *The Summoner's Tale*, III.1741–45. Quotations of Chaucer's writing (except for *The Equatorie of the Planetis*) are from *The Riverside Chaucer*, gen. ed. Larry D. Benson (Boston: Houghton Mifflin, 1987).

[44] Rickert, "Extracts," 115, fol. 42.

owned by laymen and women, are extant from the period.[45] Estimating "literacy" is always tricky both in kind and range, but further relevant evidence includes the ivory spectacle frames imported during this period (although of course eyeglasses could be used for other kinds of close work besides reading and writing). A single London tonnage and poundage roll of 1390 presents dozens of such frames, and thousands were imported in the following decades.[46]

Such accounting technology also enabled fraud, as London poets were quick to emphasize—with perhaps some competitive justification of their own "documentary poetics." Thus Chaucer's Summoner declares (against the Friar's vehement denial) that as soon as the friar collecting names in his small tables leaves a donor's house, the "sturdy harlot" accompanying him with a sack to collect the donations "planed awey the names everichon / That he biforn had writen in his tables" (III.1758–59). So too, Sloth in Langland's *Piers Plowman* confesses that he slips out of all sorts of financial obligations, either by not carefully noting them down in a record ("tailing" them), or, equally effectively, noting them inaccurately:

> "If I bigge and borwe auȝt, but if it be ytailed,
> I foryete it as yerne, and yif men me it axe
> Sixe sithes or sevene, I forsake it wiþ oþes;
> And þus tene I trewe men ten hundred tymes.
> And my servauntȝ somtyme, hir salarie is bihynde:
> Ruþe is to here rekenyng whan we shal rede acountes . . ."[47]

In a period of rapidly widening accounting literacies, the texts and tallies used to capture and effect economic transactions created unusual

---

[45] An ivory writing tablet depicting Mary and the Crucifixion from fourteenth-century London is presented and discussed in Geoff Egan et al., *Medieval Finds from Excavations in London: 6: The Medieval Household: Daily Living, c. 1150–c. 1450* (London: HMSO, 1998), 273–74; many writing tablets depicting secular love images are described and illustrated in Raymon Koechlin, *Les Ivoires gothiques français* (Paris: F. de Nobele, 1968), 2:116–29, items 1161–1222; vol. 3, plates 195–200. Several present love scenes near a tree or even the God of Love in a tree (items 1161, 1203, 1205), offering intriguing parallels to Chaucer's *Merchant's Tale* (with its casual presentation of May's literacy).

[46] Arthur MacGregor, "Bone, Antler, and Horn Industries in the Urban Context," in *Diet and Crafts in Towns: The Evidence of Animal Remains from the Roman to the Post-Medieval Periods,* ed. D. Serjeantson and T. Waldron (Oxford: B.A.R., 1989), 123.

[47] B V.423–28. Quotations are from *Piers Plowman: A Parallel-Text Edition of the A, B, C, and Z Versions,* 2 vols., ed. A. V. C. Schmidt (vol. 1: Harlow, Essex: Longman, 1995; vol. 2: Kalamazoo: Medieval Institute Publications, 2008).

dangers. Maghfeld's book amply illustrates this too: nearly two-thirds of his uncancelled entries turned out in inquests after his death to have been settled. The omissions might be oversights, but the consequences could be severe for those lacking receipts. A baker from the Billingsgate area whose debt from 1392 had been settled but not cancelled was committed to the Fleet prison and not pardoned until 1401.[48] Even if due to mere negligence, Maghfeld's omissions suggest the dangers of dying without careful settling of accounts, against which later writers passionately warn. The 1547 English translation of Jan Ympyn Christoffels' guide, for instance, laments the "incomodities and displeasures" that "maie come unto hym that diligently and perfightly kepeth not his boke": from "trouble in mynde and disquietnes of body" to death itself, partly produced by the torments of such poor record-keeping. Death in that condition creates further ills, both spiritual and social: survivors curse you, rather than pray for God's mercy on your soul, and executors "deny debtes, and claime more then was dewe," leaving your wife and children to the debilitating expenses of lawyers and courts to recover their goods, "for that nothyng was plainly kepte nor diligently written."[49] In Maghfeld's own time, some of the same warnings are offered by Langland's Ymaginatif, though his advice features the distribution of all one's goods before death, to avoid facing both God's dismissal of one's prayers and the depredations of executors on earth:

> Right so þe riche, if he his richesse kepeþ
> And deleþ it noȝt til his deeþ day, þe taille of alle is sorwe.
> Riȝt as þe pennes of þe pecok peneyþ hym in his fliȝte,
> So is possession peyne of pens and of nobles
> To alle hem þat it holdeþ til hir tail be plukked . . .
> Thouȝ he crye to Crist þanne wiþ kene wille,
> I leue his ledene be in Oure Lordes ere lik a pies. . . .
> By þe po feet is vnderstande, as I haue lerned in Auynet,
> Executours—false frendes þat fulfille noȝt his wille
> That was writen, and þei witnesse to werche riȝt as it wolde.
>
> (B XII.244–58)

Ymaginatif's brief beast-fable is further woven with warnings about the fragility of earthly accounting by the puns on "tail," "tale," and "tally,"

---

[48] James, "A London Merchant of the Fourteenth Century," 369 n. 1.
[49] In Yamey, Edey, and Thomson, *Accounting in England and Scotland*, 7.

and on "pennes" (feathers) and "pence," emphasizing, like Sloth's complacent "confession," the spiritual and social challenges of careful accounting.

In broad scope, London Ricardian literature both participated in and scrutinized documentary mercantilism; the literature presents forms of mercantile accounting, exploiting and extending this mode to wider ethical, social, psychological, rhetorical, and political ranges. As Maghfeld's accounting methods could be made to reach, with some strains, beyond a strictly mercantile world into wider and higher ones, so the London writers extended the technology to wider intellectual, cultural, and philosophical horizons. Langland explored the possibilities most fully; others who demonstrably dealt with Maghfeld—Chaucer, Gower, and finally Thomas Usk—used mercantile accounting to amplify in numerous dimensions their writings' analytical powers and claims to authority. Their work, along with Maghfeld's book and career, displays a range of ties between *lettrure* and *chevisaunce* that have been obscured more because of our historical and conceptual gaps than theirs.

Piers Plowman and the Invention of English Literary Accounting

William Langland does not appear in Maghfeld's surviving records. This is unsurprising, as by 1390 the poet was almost certainly dead. But his poem's connections to the city, though elusive, are undeniable and increasingly visible. A copy of the repeatedly revised *Piers Plowman* (ca. 1370–ca. 1388) is mentioned in the will of William Palmer (d. 1400), a London rector of St. Alphege from 1397, who bequeathed the book to one Agnes Eggesfeld; a later owner of a copy was Thomas Roos, a wealthy London mercer who died in 1433.[50] Possibly these were copies of the B-text, which show clear connections to London production, and sometimes indeed are written by the same scribes who produced works by Chaucer and Gower.[51] Copies of the final version, the C-text, from the 1380s—where the author included his most direct portrayal of his

[50] Caroline M. Barron, "William Langland: A London Poet," in *Chaucer's England: Literature in Historical Context,* ed. Barbara A. Hanawalt (Minneapolis: University of Minnesota Press, 1992), 91–109 (99).

[51] Simon Horobin and Linne R. Mooney, "A *Piers Plowman* Manuscript by the Hengwrt/Ellesmere Scribe and Its Implications for London Standard English," *SAC* 26 (2004): 65–112; Simon Horobin, "Adam Pinkhurst and the Copying of British Library, MS Additional 35287 of the B Version of *Piers Plowman,*" *YLS* 23 (2009): 1–84; Hanna, *London Literature,* 243–47.

own London life in a passage added between the first and second visions—consistently show traces of the dialect of the southwestern Worcestershire area where Langland's initial vision is set. This evidence has strongly contributed in recent decades to the view that the poet, ever agrarian or "manorial" in his basic outlook, retreated late in life from the intolerable and incomprehensible sins and practices of the metropolitan world to his native Malvern Hills. Yet new study of the distinct layers of scribal and inherited dialect, in relation to other features and affiliations of the copies, shows that the C-text copies, too, were almost certainly first released in London, their western dialect a sign of a shorter and perhaps more explicitly authorized London textual history than the A or B copies, and a demonstration in turn of a wider variety than had been assumed of socially prestigious "standard" dialects possible in the metropolis into the fifteenth century.[52] The C-text indeed shows even more direct address to the London world than the other versions. But all versions of the poem invoke and develop the diction, mode, and social and ethical capabilities of London mercantile accounting—evident in starker form in Maghfeld's book—as the central means for a new kind of ethical and social analysis, and a new and volatile kind of poetic production.

As both Sloth's and Ymaginatif's speeches quoted above suggest, accounting terms constantly offer possible puns in *Piers Plowman,* activated in numerous ways. Thus Conscience calls Lady Meed—that elusive yet central challenge to all accounting in *Piers* from the earliest version on— "tykil of hire tail, talewys of tunge" (A III.120; B III.131; C III.166), suggesting puns both on the "ticklish" and "fickle" nature of her intimacies and on her unreliable tally sticks or memory of debt and credit, capped by her daunting skill in rhetoric that seems to serve all of these. Such punning on "tail," "tally," and "tale," though Langland's is the earliest recorded, surely precedes him. The early sixteenth-century account book of the London draper Thomas Howell lists as its most frequent entry payments in credit to "my wyfe be taylle," and the usage was possibly a source of wit for Howell, and for merchants before and

---

[52] See Simon Horobin, "'In London and Opelond': The Dialect and Circulation of the C Version of *Piers Plowman,*" *MÆ* 74 (2005): 248–69, revising the influential view by M. L. Samuels, "Dialect and Grammar," in *A Companion to Piers Plowman,* ed. John A. Alford (Berkeley and Los Angeles: University of California Press, 1988), 201–22 (which was accepted, e.g., by Pearsall, "Langland's London," 108). On a parallel critique of Samuels's dialectology of London, see Hanna, *London Literature,* 26–31.

after.[53] But Langland's exploitations of such linguistic play are part of his serious emphases both on the difficulties in making distinctions between forms of reward and the need to make them.

In the scene with Lady Meed at the climax of the first vision, Conscience, notoriously, generates distinctions between different meanings of the word "meed," which expand with each version. Their debate marks a dramatic end to the vision and may indicate the first "finished" conception of the poem, though (if so) it was soon reconceived to contain the second vision, ending with the still more climactic Pardon. This episode, similarly expanded in each version, is similarly intent on an equivocation (what is "pardon"?) and similarly focused on fair and just reward.[54] "Meed" and "pardon" are both unfolded as ethical and social as well as lexical conundrums, in emphatic displays of the way in which textual accounting is both a potent tool—for allegory as well as analysis—and an intellectual aporia. The debate on "meed" begins with a broad consideration of politics and war, but soon focuses on issues of everyday exchange. Meed urges her universal and indeed indiscriminate utility and desirability; from kings down to merchant apprentices "no wiȝt, as I wene, wiþouten Mede may libbe!" (B III.227). Conscience, in reply, addressing the king in the Westminster "moot-halle" in the presence of the "commons," proposes to distinguish "two manere of medes" (B III.231), in increasingly complex grammatical, legal, and theological senses.[55]

Conscience's two-column accounting is generally clear enough, though its emphases are intricate and rather alien to modern views. Conscience distinguishes "mede mesureless" (the only thing Meed herself embodies, in his view), which particularly features payments made before a service is rendered (prostitutes, doctors, and—more obliquely mentioned—priests paid for masses are the examples named), from "mesurable hire," payments constituting the final and perfectly balanced closing of an arrangement. The positive term may seem to deny any legitimacy for mercantile profit—even, as Derek Pearsall declares,

---

[53] G. Connell-Smith, "The Ledger of Thomas Howell," *Economic History Review,* n.s. 3 (1951): 363–70 (367).

[54] For useful comments on the poem's genetic stages in terms of these units, although with attention to its development of *Winner and Waster* rather than the focus here, see Hanna, *London Literature,* esp. 260, 276.

[55] For discussion of this section, see Andrew Galloway, *The Penn Commentary on Piers Plowman: Volume I: C Prologue-Passus 4; B Prologue-Passus 4; A Prologue-Passus 4* (Philadelphia: University of Pennsylvania Press, 2006), 285–371.

in an influential argument claiming that Langland's social ideals always remain those of agrarian and manorial culture, revealing the poet's inability to approve of mercantilism in any form beyond "a primitive form of barter or exchange."[56] But Conscience's accounting is still more complex than this indicates. "Meed mesureless," in which an advance payment creates an open-ended contract, is opposed to mercantilism as a system of transaction based on transparency of comparative values. The payment of prostitutes, doctors, or anyone else in advance of the service leaves one side of the transaction unconstrained by full mutual knowledge, lacking final mutual assessment of fairness or consequences. It is in this sense a form of venture, but—unlike the other forms of venturing that Langland's poem pervasively praises—it relies on a more or less deliberate obscuring of the full terms and consequences of the transaction, a conscious acquiescence in deception that allows Conscience to claim that such transactions are intrinsically tied to further ethical and social deceptions: "Mede of mysdoeres makeþ manye lordes" (B III.207). "Mesurable hire" is, in contrast, equitable because mutually transparent: both parties ideally have as much information as possible about the values in the transaction before its completion.

Conscience's shifting analogies to account for payment preceding or following service are all designed to uphold the "commutative justice" defined by medieval scholastics, especially Albert the Great and Thomas Aquinas, as essential to the "just price": transparency and as full a mutual knowledge as possible in any transaction.[57] When Conscience declares, therefore, that "In marchaundise is no mede. . . . It is a permutacion apertly—a penyworþ for anoþer" (B III.257–58; also C)—which Pearsall picks out as epitomizing Conscience's naive view of mercantilism—in the context of Conscience's distinctions this claim succinctly defines a fully transparent, mutually informed transaction. "Permutation" (as A. V. C. Schmidt notes) can include profit beyond the material's most basic value, if the "penyworþ" that the merchant receives includes the value of the merchant's risk, labors, and basic necessities, as Aquinas allowed and as many mendicant friars—ever the guides for

---

[56] Pearsall, "Langland's London," 194.

[57] *Summa Theologiae,* 2a2ae q.77. For discussion and an argument that the "just price" was increasingly understood in terms of common market value, see Raymond de Roover, "The Concept of the Just Price: Theory and Economic Policy," *Journal of Economic History* 18 (1958): 418–34. For consideration of the wider dissemination of "just price" theory, see Martha C. Howell, *Commerce Before Capitalism in Europe, 1300–1600* (Cambridge: Cambridge University Press, 2010), 276–81.

urban piety—counseled merchants to ascertain.[58] The word "apertly," in turn, emphasizes the ideal transparency of such valuation of risks and needs. In such open, mutually conscious transactions there is no "mede" in the hidden, publicly unmeasured sense.

Such terms tend, however, to leave vague just what the "just price" *was* in a given instance, how much a "penyworþ" might be of the merchant's labors and needs: thus Langland can be condemned along with other, later urban religious writers who also tended to generate, as Odd Langholm notes, a "varied and confusing terminology" for determining the just price in the context of real commercial transactions.[59] Yet Meed's superficially simpler praise of monetary exchanges does not clarify these issues any better. Many of the uses of money that she sweepingly praises might fit Conscience's ideal category, but others clearly do not. The difference is that he offers a theory of contract, she one of collective social desires. His theories involve more difficulties in insisting on both individual venturing and on the answering (or "following") credit given by the recipient or creditor. Even when the analogies for this turn—as some do in the long and defiantly complex C expansion—to legal, grammatical, and manorial similes, they suggest the risk of bridging good-faith effort with repayment: "As a leel laborer, byleueth with his maister / In his pay and in his piete and in his puyr treuthe— / To pay hym yf he parforme and haue pite yf he faileth . . ." (C III.347–49). Given the likelihood of occasional failure, "pite" (or credit) on the part of the person who consumes the products and services is essential for the persistence of the economic system Conscience describes.

But apart from such hints, Conscience's discourse also leaves vague the faith that a community must have in a system of credit for it to function in general. That issue—the "public" credibility necessary for any monetary economy—is entirely made the purview of Meed, whose followers' unwavering "love" of her is the thrust of her argument: "Is no lede þat leueth þat he ne loueth mede / And glad for to grype here, gret lord oþer pore" (C III.281–82). In her presentation, such affect is

---

[58] Schmidt, *Piers Plowman,* 2:504; Odd Langholm, *The Merchant in the Confessional: Trade and Price in the Pre-Reformation Penitential Handbooks* (Leiden: Brill, 2003), 233–43. On earlier discussions of a wide range of ethical issues concerning prostitutes' earnings, elaborated by academics in Paris, where prostitution was common, see John Baldwin, *Masters, Princes, and Merchants: The Social Views of Peter the Chanter and His Circle,* 2 vols. (Princeton: Princeton University Press, 1970), 1:134–37.

[59] Langholm, *Merchant in the Confessional,* 239.

regularly given an erotic charge, rather than some sense of social "faith," but Conscience seems finally to concede that, in the more abstract social sense, her emphasis is crucial. When the king finally agrees simply to banish her from his kingdom, it is Conscience who doubts that this can be so easily accomplished: "Withoute þe comune helpe [B: But þe commune wole assente], / Hit is ful hard, by myn heued, herto to bryngen hit" (C III.176–77). In granting this fundamental aspect of her argument, he seems resigned finally to failure in realizing any of his criteria, or at least to restarting the entire debate.

This problem, of how to balance individual good- or bad-faith venturing with the answering credit, love, or "pardon" provided by some "comune" or other supra-individual creditor or auditor, haunts the poem. This does not mean, however, that the poem avoids or denounces the prospects of mercantilism. Although, as Pearsall correctly observes, *Piers Plowman* shows little sympathy with the idea of capital as a resource for further profit alone—in contrast to the way the merchant in Chaucer's *Shipman's Tale* blandly remarks of his estate, "hir moneie is hir plogh" (*Canterbury Tales,* VII.288)—this may be a difference in emphasis and ultimate purposes rather than flatly traditional antimercantilism.[60] The poem defines an ideal of the mercantile estate as comprised of those who faithfully and transparently perform their services before payment (or pardon), carefully remember their debts, and charitably reallocate their surplus wealth to the approving community as a whole. Such is the posture of the merchants who first fully appear in the Pardon scene, in response to Truth's temporary reprieve from judgment and extension of their credit:

> Marchauntʒ in þe margyne hadde manye yeres . . .
> Ac vnder his secret seel Truþe sente hem a lettre,
> And bad hem buggen boldely what hem best liked
> And siþenes selle it ayein and saue þe wynnynges,
> And amende mesondieux þerwiþ and myseisé folk helpe . . .
> "And I shal sende yow myselue Seint Michel myn angel,
> That no deuel shal yow dere ne drede in youre deying . . ."
> Thanne were marchauntʒ murie—manye wepten for ioye.
>   (B VII.18–37; also A and C)

---

[60] Pearsall, "Langland's London," 186.

The documentary emphasis of their appearance, with the marginal notations of time due, transforms the entire Pardon, at least briefly, into a merchant's credit and debit book. In this context, Truth's privately sealed "lettre" with its contractual terms arrives like a revised letter of obligation (like those found preserved amid Maghfeld's pages, fols. 20 and 36v, at least one of which has traces of a seal). In the A-text, the poet's direct role in such mercantile accounting is explicit when the merchants repay Will with woolen clothes "for he copiede þus here clause" (A VIII.44). That line is deleted from the longer versions, perhaps because of its awkwardly abrupt disclosure of the narrator as mercantile accountant ("a touch of ironic lightness . . . out of keeping with the solemn tone of the scene").[61] Yet it suggests that engagement with such documentary mercantile technologies was part of the poet's earliest conception of the Pardon scene, if not the entire poem.

To focus simply on debts to be settled or at least deferred, rather than profits reaped, may seem to us to take an implausibly incomplete view of commerce. Yet we should recall that this is also the exclusive focus of Maghfeld's account book, the practical as well as ethical basis for the "economy of obligation" that was just beginning, in the late fourteenth century, to accommodate notions of personal profit and self-interest as morally acceptable centers of economic activity.[62] Conscience's similar insistence in the poem's final passus on the stumbling block of debt, and on rendering what you owe (*Redde quod debes*), is the apotheosis of the ethic of obligation. As Ladd observes, merchants in that context are not excluded from the final select community that follows Conscience into the barn of Unity in flight from Pride.[63] Rather than those who hoard wealth for themselves (as the clergy are often seen to do), merchants are the poem's one professional group who have the potential to live out a commitment to faith, hope, and charity, with no signs of clerical mediation.[64] As D. Vance Smith observes, in the Pardon passus especially, mercantilism becomes a literal guide to salvation.[65]

Venturing, in this mindful, fully disclosing, yet self-consciously risky

---

[61] Schmidt, *Piers Plowman,* 2:562.

[62] See Muldrew, *Economy of Obligation.* For late medieval unraveling of the principle of economic "need," see Andrew Galloway, "The Economy of Need in Late Medieval English Literature," *Viator* 40 (2009): 309–31.

[63] Ladd, *Antimercantilism in Late Medieval English Literature,* 45.

[64] On their lack of need for clerical mediation for charity, see ibid., 40–41.

[65] D. Vance Smith, *Arts of Possession: The Middle English Household Imaginary* (Minneapolis: University of Minnesota Press, 2003), 108–53.

mode—the merchants do not know if they will be rewarded by either Truth or the vicissitudes of economic opportunity—is also a central value for the poem's poetic making and remaking. The city, for all its corruption, offers the prospect of transparent discourse, direct speech to the powerful, as well as financial exchanges. London's potential for both is sufficiently significant that the narrator of the C-text can interrupt the scene of Meed to demand directly that mayors not enroll any usurers or other profiteers as enfranchised "fremen" of the city, or anyone indeed without a close investigation of "what maner muster oþer marchandise he vsed" (C III.110)—once again, transparency and "apert" public consciousness define the ideal of mercantilism. Yet as that late plea suggests, the ethic of open and faithful venturing is surrounded by forces that threaten it. On the one side is the universally tempting power of Meed, whose desirability leads her followers to obscure their particular obligations. London's promise of transparency is undone by its "ravishing" opportunity for profit for its own sake, drawing "persons and parisshe preestes" away from care of their provincial parishioners "to haue a licence and leue at London to dwelle, / And syngen þer for symonie, for siluer is swete." So too, the central government tempts "bisshopes and bachelers" to leave their far-flung and needy flocks to "seruen þe King and his siluer tellen, / In þe Cheker and in þe Chauncelrie chalengen hise dettes" (B Prol.83–93). By the end of the poem, Westminster has become a place that obscures all private debts and profits, when, at the final coming of Antichrist, Covetousness overruns the central government "and boldeliche bar adoun wiþ many a bright noble / Muche of þe wit and wisdom of Westmynstre Halle" (B XX.133; also C).

Such is the setting for Conscience's final insistence that the whole "comune" must settle all debts. Once Antichrist is perceived to govern the central institutions of a documentary economy, the only way to preserve an entirely faithful and pardoning—creditable and credit-granting—community of exchange is by limiting its scope severely. The incredulous response by the community Conscience addresses shows that they take his demand as a retreat to a highly limited sphere indeed: "'How?' quod al þe comune; 'þow conseillest vs to yelde / Al þat we owen any wight er we go to housel?'" (B 19.395–96; also C). The careful accounting that Conscience finally insists on, in the face of Antichrist's overrunning of Westminster bureaucracy, chills all exchanges of credit with the wider spheres beyond the circle of those in Communion, destroying the ever-expanding venturing and transparent economy of obligation essential for urban mercantilism and urban poetics itself. A diminished group proceeds forward, and the poem ends with Conscience departing from Unity, alone.

The threat of private or hidden accounting is equally apparent in the portrayals of household or manorial lords, who exploit their dependent laborers in ways that evade higher auditing, along with any hope for credit and pardon. This is suggested by Sloth's maliciously negligent accounting, and still more by that of the manorial lord under Antichrist who, in a vicious reapplication of Conscience's demand to pay all debts, marshals the "spirit of intellect" and "spirit of strength" to extort violently and unforgivingly the debts his servants owe *him*:

> Thanne louʒ þer a lord, and "By þis light!" seide,
> "I holde it riʒt and reson of my reue to take
> Al þat myn auditour or ellis my styward
> Counseilleþ me bi hir aconte and my clerkes writynge.
> Wiþ *Spiritus Intellectus* þei toke þe reues rolles,
> And wiþ *Spiritus Fortitudinis* fecche it—wole he, nel he."
>
> (B XIX.463–68; also C)

The ideal of mercantile accounting, as good-faith and transparent venturing on behalf of a wide and forgiving community, is possible only tenuously and narrowly between these extremes of Meed's "ravishing" universalism and the manorial world's punctiliously exploitative feudal atomism. The C-text's mid-poem insertion of the narrator's "apologia" for a London life as a kind of merchant thus marks a dramatic late reendorsement of this ethic, applied to the elusive mode of production of the poet-narrator himself. To Reason and Conscience, coming upon the narrator in the Cornhill area of London, and demanding an account of his social and economic means, Will replies with a series of justifications of a vagrant life of uncertainly supported study, liturgical services, and poetry-making, "in London and opeland bothe" (C V.44); in his defense he ultimately figures himself as a merchant presenting his books, pleading, like the merchants in the Pardon episode, for temporary reprieve until he can "begin a time" to start repaying all debts:

> "That is soth," Y saide, "and so Y beknowe—
> That Y haue ytynt tyme, and tyme myspened;
> Ac ʒut, I hope—as he þat ofte hath ychafared

And ay loste and loste and the laste hym happed
A bouhte suche a bargayn he was the bet euere
And sette al his los at a leef at the laste ende . . .
So hope Y to haue of Hym þat is almyghty
A gobet of his grace, and bigynne a tyme
That alle tymes of my tyme to profit shal turne."

(C V.92–101)

In perhaps one of the final "leaves" added to the poem, Will's C-text self-defense is directly concerned with the legitimacy of his poetic labors and their "credit," but also with the poem's persistent dwelling on and in London's and mercantilism's problems and possibilities.[66] His accounting system is, accordingly, precise and up to date. A system for assessing overall net worth operates in only the clearest actual ledger books, and looks toward the principles of double-entry bookkeeping, used by Genoese banker merchants in England from the thirteenth century but not by any English merchants or institutions until the sixteenth century.[67] Even the notion of a "leef at the laste ende" to sum up gain and loss is rare until the seventeenth century—and discourse about it in any language novel indeed. Only with the 1569 (second) edition of James Peele's guide to accounting are there found in English "systematic instructions as to how to close the accounts when balancing and closing the whole ledger."[68]

The precariousness of this venture, however, is clear in the extreme tenuousness of the prospect Will is offering of his eventual restitution—a time to begin repayment—and in the incongruous use of a simile about the kingdom of heaven to describe the narrator's own hapless, and convincingly urbanely anonymous or isolated, pursuits, "lytel ylet by . . . Amonges lollares of Londone and lewede ermytes" (C V.3–4). His public London auditing closes with a plea not for reward but for credibility, for continuation of the much-extended faith of an audience—human as well as suprahuman—in him. Both Will's declaration and Conscience's, in the latter's final departure as a pilgrim pleading for

[66] For another London counterpoint for this passage, the reissued Statutes of Laborers of 1388, see the key essay by Anne Middleton, "Acts of Vagrancy: The C Version 'Autobiography' and the Statute of 1388," in *Written Work*, ed. Justice and Kerby-Fulton, 208–318.

[67] Yamey, "Balancing and Closing the Ledger"; Sullivan, *The Rhetoric of Credit*, 23–43.

[68] In Yamey, Edey, and Thomson, *Accounting in England and Scotland*, 165.

"grace" at the end of the poem, are thus endorsements of consummately risky ventures, and the momentous assertions of both seem amenable to what Martin Heidegger described, in a late essay on the purpose of poetry in a "destitute time," as the poet's "venturing into Being," which, unlike any other "venturing," is willing to expose the alienating and self-reifying dangers of the very technologies of venturing by which human beings turn everything into "self-assertive production."[69] Yet unlike Heidegger's views of isolated poetic "venturing" there, Will's late defense of venturing, with its focus on a supra-individual world's faith in *him,* serves as a much less solitary formulation of the plea for reprieve. It is certainly less isolated than Conscience's (earlier composed) plea at the conclusion of both the B- and C-texts where, fleeing Unity and without any visible community or auditor, Conscience cries out to an absent God for "grace" (B XX.387, also C). Will has at least Reason and Conscience as auditors, able to grant him credit to continue his way of life in central London in hope of some amendment, a temporary reprieve that allows the rest of the poem to constitute Will's attempt to make good on this extension of credit, for a community of auditors who are now allowed to be represented by Reason and Conscience themselves:[70]

> "Y rede the," quod Resoun tho, "rape the to bigynne
> The lyif þat is louable and leele to thy soule."
> "3e, and contynue!" quod Conscience; and to þe kyrke Y wente.
>
> (C V.102–4)

Mercantile accounting in its "true" and both publicly and spiritually "louable" form requires transparent and faithful venturing as well as continuous "pardon" or credit from a divine or human audience. Yet

---

[69] Martin Heidegger, "What Are Poets For?" in *Poetry, Language, Thought,* trans. Albert Hofstadter (New York: Harper and Row, 1975), 91–142 (111). Heidegger's views on humanity's relentlessly "self-assertive production" may carry some implications of his darker earlier political philosophy; in schematic form, however, these late views offer extensions of Marx's early thought (e.g., about "species-being") in terms that are suggestive for appreciating these key moments in Langland's poem. For adept use of Heidegger's (and other philosophers') ideas of "event" and contingency in relation to Ricardian (and later) literature, see J. Allan Mitchell, *Ethics and Eventfulness in Middle English Literature* (New York: Palgrave, 2009).

[70] For seminal comment on how the insertion of this late passage redefines the following poem, as "an act from which the actor is, in the nature of the case, never fully free, a work of which the maker can never take his leave, as a book he can never close," see Middleton, "Acts of Vagrancy," esp. 273.

overshadowed both by money's universal appetitiveness and by oppressively "private" and merciless accounting, transparent mercantile accounting, with its scope for an ever-expanding ethical, philosophical, and poetic venturing, constitutes only another "way between paired extremes" that "haunts *Piers Plowman* . . . more in the way of a bad dream than an achieved synthesis."[71] Langland's commitment to a lifetime of expanding and heroically endorsing the poetics of mercantile accounting also demonstrates its fragility and defeat.

Chaucer's Untimely Settlements

Among London poets, Langland's poetics of mercantile accounting constituted both the advance guard and the most ambitious exploration. Among later writers who demonstrably negotiated with Maghfeld, Chaucer, with his puns on accounting terms in *The Shipman's Tale* and elsewhere, suggests the most intensely ironic juxtapositions of mercantile and nonmercantile realms, by which, as Lee Patterson declares, the *Tale* "stimulates in its readers an unnatural alertness to the possibility of ambiguity," thus serving "as a textual version of the merchant's 'queynte world' of commerce." Indeed, for Patterson, Chaucer's mercantile figures and narratives extend this general "alertness" so broadly that they demonstrate mercantilism's capacity, in the form of "bourgeois liberalism," to stand as "life itself." Thus, the narrator of Chaucer's *Merchant's Tale,* Patterson argues, shows how a mercantile outlook can vanish into mere unsituated skepticism, "at once disillusioned and credulous, bereft of ideas and yet still clinging to the possibility of belief."[72] But another view of this process is to observe how Chaucer's poetics of mercantile accounting quantify and commodify increasingly wider realms of life. The most basic step in this process is the colonizing by a technology of time itself. To see this in succinct form, we may return to Maghfeld's book.

Chaucer's debt to Maghfeld listed on July 8, 1392, to be repaid the following Saturday, constitutes the only surviving record of a purely mercantile (rather than professional) transaction for Chaucer, apart from the lawsuits pursuing him for unpaid debts, which imply transactions we often know little about. The loan also concerns what appears to be

---

[71] Middleton, "The Idea of Public Poetry in the Reign of Richard II," 103.
[72] Patterson, *Chaucer and the Subject of History,* 360, 366, 340.

the smallest amount of his own money or monetary obligation among the hundreds of transactions in the *Life-Records*.[73] Equally distinctive is the loan's extremely short specified time frame:

Geffray Chauxcer doit dapprest en le xxviij jour de juyl a paier en le samedy proschein apres: xxvj s viij d.[74]

[Geoffrey Chaucer owes for a loan on July 28 to be paid the following Saturday: 26s 8d]

Many of Maghfeld's loans are time-marked, presumably to define the basis for the (always invisible) interest, possibly with some further penalties if the loan is not repaid on time. Typically, though not exclusively, due dates are religious festivals rather than secular days as here. None of Maghfeld's entries, however, is as short-term as this. Puzzlingly, the loan is dated only fifteen days after Chaucer had received the large sum of £13 6s 8d as partial payment on his salary in arrears as clerk of the king's works (a role he had surrendered in June 1391, but for which he was not fully compensated until May 22, 1393).[75] Whatever Chaucer's reasons for the small loan, its time frame suggests tight control. The entry is in Maghfeld's own hand, and emphatically cancelled in two (rather than, as often, one) pen strokes—as if Chaucer insisted on inspecting the cancelled entry or even on watching as it was struck out (see Fig. 2).

The larger timing of the loan might be relevant. July 1392 included the period when the king deprived London of its liberties and appointed Maghfeld sheriff. The occasion might well have been a time when any transaction with those involved in the events would be carefully defined and limited. But other debtors in this period did not control their terms of debts nearly so closely (Maghfeld's fellow sheriff Thomas Newenton and the royally appointed warden Sir Edward Dalynggrigg were both particularly profligate in their loans from him, sometimes with unsecured loans, "sans gauge").[76] Chaucer's loan shows structures of rhetorical control in disproportionate scale to the money and time involved;

---

[73] For the lawsuits, one of which may involve a loan of money (from 1393), see *Chaucer Life-Records,* ed. Crow and Olson, 384–401 (391–93).

[74] Rickert, "Excerpts," 119, fol. 31.

[75] Ibid., 119; *Chaucer Life-Records,* ed. Crow and Olson, 500–505, 469.

[76] Rickert, "Excerpts," 249–50.

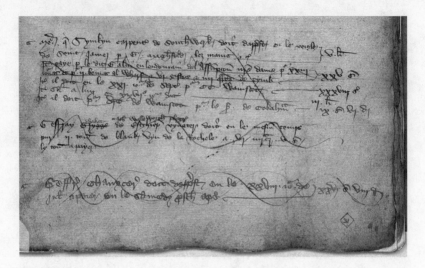

Fig. 2. National Archives, E 101/509/19, fol. 31 (by permission of TNA).

the exchange's terms, including its cancellation, loom larger than the loan.

For a layman, Chaucer was unusually sensitive to the technologies for the establishing and marking of dates. Early the following year, for example, someone—possibly Chaucer—completed the *Equatorie of the Planetis,* the preface of which says it was "compowned the yer of crist .1392. complet the laste meridie of decembre," and whose careful instructions in creating a sophisticated instrument for measuring the positions of all five planets plus the sun and moon required a single reference point, supplied in the sole existing manuscript by the note "Radix Chaucer" for 1392, in a hand like that of a 1378 memorandum quite likely by Chaucer himself.[77] Even if the *Equatorie* was not his work, a preoccupation with the powers of timing is obvious in Chaucer's writing, though displayed more efficaciously in mercantile contracts than by the movements of the planets.

Thus the Wife of Bath, who briefly but inconsequentially considers astrological powers over her life, more emphatically insists on mercantile terms for defining her social relations: "Why sholde men elles in hir bookes sette / That man shal yelde to his wyf hir dette?" (129–30). Her

[77] Kari Anne Rand Schmidt, *The Authorship of the "Equatorie of the Planetis"* (Cambridge: D. S. Brewer, 1993), 117.

referent for "hir bookes" is, in an irony she may or may not grasp, the Bible; like Langland's Will, she looks toward a final accounting. But hers will be the settlement of human, social debts that (she claims) she has already paid or collected, a state that often depends on her construction of the timing invoked in the formulation of her accounting:

> As helpe me verray God omnipotent,
> Though I right now sholde make my testament,
> I ne owe hem nat a word that it nys quit.
>
> (III.423–25)

A testament, as a final account book of a life, creates a perspective of credit and debts from which, with quasi-divine control, "alle tymes of my tyme" can be surveyed. Her imposition of a particular moment for closing the books imposes a form of control that can allow the relations to be shaped as she wishes. The "testament" of settled debts she mentions is, as she admits, premature and hypothetical—as her need to continue speaking shows that she is clearly not "quit" in all the words she feels she owes. Thus her counterfactual "testament" is consistent with a discourse that throughout presents folds of temporality in unpredictable memories she dallies in and relives, former interlocutors she continues to address, ancient stories of "wikked wyves" read by her fifth husband, whose lives she reawakens and in turn repays, by sympathetic retellings. She is acutely aware of how timing defines value in her life of negotiations: "unto this day it dooth myn herte boote / that I have had my world as in my tyme" (III.472–73), but her declarations of settlement are always themselves well timed, always further social negotiations. She chooses, for instance, to confirm her final "testament" and final cancellation of all debts at just the moment when she was about to describe her unsavory fourth husband. She imagines a final testament just when that can lift her above intrusive memories of irredeemably lost time, love, and hopeful innocence.[78]

Such application of accounting shows how mercantile principles, as Patterson argues, tend to obscure their literal social origins.[79] But the Wife is one of a number of Chaucerian figures who keep the mercantile

---

[78] For her evasions in discussing the fourth husband, see H. Marshall Leicester Jr., *The Disenchanted Self: Representing the Subject in the Canterbury Tales* (Berkeley and Los Angeles: University of California Press, 1990), 88–93.

[79] Patterson, *Chaucer and the Subject of History,* 366.

origins of such accounting emphatically in view. It is she who insists that "al is for to selle" (III.414), an ethic that led D. W. Robertson and those critics who followed him to locate her narrative almost entirely amid Augustinian views of *cupiditas,* until observations like Anne Kernan's shifted the issue to the ways in which Chaucer was exploring such theological "cupidity" more as a lived psychological state than an objective demonstration of sin.[80] Indeed, the Wife shows how mercantile accounting organizes consciousness itself, with all its capabilities of self-reflection or self-deception yet all its creative capacities to change its judgments by how it frames its temporal perspectives. This focus too has its theological and homiletic traditions, as in the tradition of the "book of conscience" with its record of accounts that will be opened on the Day of Judgment: as Alan of Lille stated in the twelfth century, a bad conscience is a book written by the devil, foully blotted by the pen of free choice using the ink of profound sin ("ubi calamus, libertas arbitrii, ubi incaustum, enormitas peccati"), and redeemable only when one scrapes it clean by confession, contrition, and satisfaction.[81] The Wife's accounting, however, is not simply a means for reading or misreading the self; it is also a construction of social relationships, living or imagined, and at least partly subject to her control by the rhetoric of temporality. The gains and losses of time and love, not contrition and sin, are the commodities that she can be seen to inscribe and scrape away from the account book of her memory and her Prologue.

The Wife's *Prologue* thus displays what H. Marshall Leicester calls "temporal indeterminacy," and Carolyn Dinshaw more generally describes as "queer temporality." For Dinshaw (quoting Roland Barthes), this produces a "generalized collapse of economies" by which "touch"—unexpected sympathies across time—can constitute ideal communities, just as making "untouchables" defines communities' scapegoats and boundaries.[82] But mercantile accounting in literature and account books offers its own "unnatural" manipulations not only of timing but also of

[80] Anne Kernan, "The Archwife and the Eunuch," *ELH* 41 (1974): 1–25; this essay offers a more nuanced integration of the "theological" and "psychoanalytic" methods canvassed by Lee Patterson, "Chaucer's Pardoner on the Couch: Psyche and Clio in Medieval Literary Studies," *Speculum* 76 (2001): 638–80, rpt. in *Temporal Circumstances,* 67–96.

[81] *Patrologia Latina,* 210:139.

[82] Leicester, *The Disenchanted Self,* 137; Carolyn Dinshaw, *Getting Medieval: Sexualities and Communities, Pre- and Postmodern* (Durham: Duke University Press, 1999), 42; see also 126–32.

a range of further resources that can be subjected to quantified negotiation and thus commodification, such as sexuality, friendship, and marital obligations. In Chaucer, this wider scope is most explicit not in the Wife's *Tale* but in the tale originally assigned to her, then transferred to the Shipman—perhaps because her *Prologue* ended up developing the point as well, or because a narrator familiar with the movements of sea trade was a better fit with the multiple and conflicting economies that *The Shipman's Tale* unfolds.

The Shipman's Tale begins with the merchant going "up into his countour-house" in a kind of retreat to secular self-examination and prayer, as if by economic self-scrutiny he might maintain control over the household and wife he officially manages:

> To rekene with hymself, wel may be,
> Of thilke yeer how that it with hym stood,
> And how that he despended hadde his good,
> And if that he encressed were or noon.
> His bookes and his bagges many oon
> He leith biforn hym on his countyng-bord . . .
>
> (VII.77–84)

His skills at monetary transactions are formidable, especially in his keen sense of how timing and perception govern value of any kind. He is aware, not only that for merchants "hir moneie is hir plogh," but also that the grounds and fruits of their labor depend on minute shifts of opportunity in exploiting a reputation. "We may creaunce whil we have a name" (VII.288–89)—words that might succinctly anatomize Maghfeld's fate.

The merchant's domestic standing, however, is more subject than he realizes to transactions in spheres that he does not consider as belonging within his commercial scope. Those manipulating the evidently non-commercialized elements of the household's resources and exchanges are his wife (who scolds him for spending all his time and energy accounting, while she plots to gain social prestige of her own) and her lover the monk (whose only need for money seems to be for the illicit sex he gains from the wife, which he obtains by pleading for a loan from the merchant). Their exchanges (the monk's of sex for money, the wife's of money for honor) take place without the merchant seeming to be aware of their nature as commodities subject to precise accounting. This status both the monk and the wife conceal from him even while they wittily exploit and traffic in these goods and resources. Whereas the monk neatly cloaks all his transactions as favors and gifts by claiming that the money he has given the wife is simply repaying the debt to the husband, the wife seems merely to invoke a well-worn joke when she says that her husband can regain the money she spent by her sexual services: "I am your wyf; score it upon my taille . . . By god, I wol nat paye yow but abedde!" (VII.416, 424).

The pun (narrower than its uses in Langland) shows how the wife indeed applies accounting to sex while seeming to keep it free within the realm of familiar jest. But the monk's skill at timing his "chaffare" with the wife, drawing from *fabliaux,* applies mercantile accounting more subtly over a much wider range of commodities and values. The monk shows a mastery of the quantifying of time in such a way as to produce desire; his ability to engage the merchant's wife in a deal depends on his encountering her at just the moment when she is regretting her husband's overlong preoccupation with account books, and wishing for the social standing that new clothing might give her. He fosters her interest in striking a deal by insisting on the fleeting time; she sharpens his desire by indicating a moment of fulfillment both tantalizingly vague yet "certeyn": the "plesance and service" he will get when "at a certeyn day I wol yow pay" (190–91). The monk's "chilyndre" (portable sundial), which he suddenly produces to close the negotiation, shows his constant readiness for seizing a moment ripe for a deal, as well as offering a visual double entendre as crude as her pun on "taillynge," with the chilendrum's stylus erectly protruding from its cap.[83] His "gift" of 100 francs to her, which he borrows from the merchant, requires his waiting until just the right moment for the merchant to be about to leave, and his final cheating of the wife of the money requires his perfectly timed mention to the merchant of how he has already sent to the wife the money in advance of the merchant's return.

So complex are the trades in sexuality, currency differences, gifts, and "honour" here that not even double-entry bookkeeping could accommodate them.[84] Elliot Kendall thus suggests that the economic modes in the tale include not mercantilism alone but also aristocratic gift-exchange, a mixture governing the great London household. For Kendall,

[83] J. D. North, *Chaucer's Universe* (Oxford: Clarendon Press, 1988), 112–16.
[84] See R. H. Parker, "Accounting in Chaucer's *Canterbury Tales,*" *Accounting, Auditing, and Accountability Journal* 12 (1999): 92–112.

the tale weaves together the mercantile and aristocratic "economic modes and social typing" in ways that are "intersectional, not polarising."[85] But even this may oversimplify. For the tale shows the extension of mercantilism on several fronts into realms not yet overtly commercialized. The monk's transaction with the wife is not a gift; instead, it refashions the aristocratic style of gifting into thinly veiled bargaining, sealed by the monk's clearly insinuating acceptance of an exchange of money for sex: " 'I wol delyvere yow out of this case; / For I wol brynge yow an hundred frankes.' / And with that word he caughte hire by the flankes, / and hire embraceth harde, and kiste hire ofte" (VII.200–3). It is the merchant, ironically, who errs by imagining a realm of sheer friendship and favor untouchable by mercantilism. Thus when the monk appeals for a loan of money from the merchant (supposedly to buy cattle for his monastery but in fact to pay the merchant's wife for sex), the merchant responds, "O cosyn myn, daun John, . . . My gold is youres, whan that it yow leste, / and nat oonly my gold, but my chaffare" (VII.282–85). The merchant knows only one sphere of accounting and credit, outside of which other exchanges like friendly gifting or spousal sexual services are off the books. The monk knows many modes of commerce, and he deploys them as opportunity allows, more subtly applying mercantile accounting to a wider range of temporality, desires, and relationships. Whereas the merchant seems to dedicate a religiously narrow reverence to his sacred records and the dealings that he thinks those govern, the monk is the consummate mercantile opportunist, for whom every value and situation is a chance for "chevisaunce." He deftly accommodates the styles of each realm, but his basic mercantile principles do not cease to colonize and ultimately govern what they contact.

Such consummate colonizing of new realms for mercantilism offers a parallel rather than an opposition to Maghfeld's mercantile venturing. That Maghfeld's negotiations could fail in a costly way when he accommodated the "gift-exchange" mentality and negligent repayments of the noble and royal world is clear from his funding of the Christmas celebrations discussed above. But many of his negotiations with higher nobility, though lacking the constraining terms visible in his loan to Chaucer, are presented as cancelled and thus successful transactions. In some of those, the rigid terms of "merchant's time" could be sus-

<hr />

[85] Elliot Kendall, "The Great Household in the City," in *Chaucer and the City*, ed. Butterfield, 145–61 (154).

pended—perhaps not by Maghfeld's choice so much as the other partici-pants'—in favor of something like "noble time," registered by a shift of style and sense of economic, social, and even narrative mode in his book.[86]

An example is an entry describing money loaned by John of Gaunt's son Henry of Derby to some clerks of Lynn while they were all in Prus-sia, conveyed to another individual who evidently served as Maghfeld's agent:

Johan Clerc de Botelston doit qe il ad receuz del Counte de Derby qe fuist appreste a luy en Pruce ouesqe autres gentz de Loundres de lynne & Botelston chescun x marcz desterling issint qe le dit Johan doit qe il ad recuz pour moy

[In margin: vj li. xiijs iiijd
R.de Blomvill
vj li. xijs vjd][87]

[John clerk of Botelston owes for what he received from the Earl of Derby what (the Earl) had loaned to him in Prussia with other individuals of London, Lynn, and Botelston, 10 marks sterling to each one there, for which the said John owes what he had received for me: £6 13s 4d; R. de Blomvill, £6 12s 6d]

Perhaps the small difference between the two sums in the margin (1s 2d) represents the commission, to Maghfeld or his agent, though as usual any profit in Maghfeld's moneylending remains unstated. Here that absence conforms to the particular cultural sphere that the entry encroaches on, where other things are unstated, too: the date and terms of the original loan are long lost in the chain of intermediaries. In other ways, however, the entry shows a discursive luxury rare in the book. Recapitulating Henry's other loans on the occasion, and evoking the specificity of a scene whose interest exceeds the single clerk's transaction entered, the entry tells more than seems strictly necessary. Its rhetoric

[86] Jacques Le Goff, "Merchant's Time and Church's Time in the Middle Ages," in *Time, Work, and Culture in the Middle Ages,* trans. Arthur Goldhammer (Chicago: University of Chicago Press, 1980), 29–42 (35, 42), defines salvation history and prayer hours as the counterpoint to mercantile time, but in the London world the more pertinent disparate temporalities seem to be mercantilism on the one side and noble conspicuous consumption and gift-exchange on the other. For compatible assessments of mercantile and noble culture, see Alexander Murray, *Reason and Society in the Middle Ages* (Oxford: Clarendon Press, 1978), e.g., 162–87, 355–82; see also Kaye, *Economy and Nature in the Fourteenth Century,* 37–55.

[87] Rickert, "Extracts," 116, fol. 22v.

of temporality is—as far as an account book allows—languidly retrospective. It even suggests imaginative lingering on a world of noble company and noble largesse, where the rich lend (and repay) money differently from you and me.

The particular context was perhaps familiar enough in London to attract such stories and memories. Henry's ten-mark distributions were part of his famously festive *Reyse* in Prussia in 1390; stocking two ships with thirty-two knights and a very large household, Henry planned the expedition as a crusade to Tunisia but, when passage there was blocked by the French king, met up instead with the Teutonic Knights, who were eager to attack the pagan Lithuanians of the Wilderness—the last European region that could justify holy war, whenever territorial needs or the zeal of the Teutonic Knights to find a "training ground" demanded (with recruitment rewards in pillaging and ransoming under papal sanction). After giving up on a long siege near Danzig, Henry spent a glorious winter in festivities that fill many leaves of his own account book; in 1407, he is recorded to have remarked that this journey was one of his life's greatest pleasures. His account book, drawn up by the treasurer of his father, who had sent the vast sum of £3488 7s $^{1}/_{2}$d in gold florins (the bounty of Gaunt's relinquishing of his claim to the Spanish throne) to fund his son's expedition, lists his chief expenses as lavish food, clothing, minstrels, heraldic painting, and, especially, gambling.[88] The last probably explains the playfully equal loans of ten marks to the various English clerks in Maghfeld's entry.

As might be expected from his tight control of temporality, in loans and narratives, Chaucer can also adapt his temporal framing to respond to the style of noble culture.[89] A tiny outline of the tour of Henry's *Reyse*—like a brilliant historiated initial—may be visible in the *General Prologue*'s résumé of the Knight (I.52–66), and the traveling community of Henry's quasi-religious expedition of 1390 hovers as an unstated background to Chaucer's entire frame: an incalculably lavish Continental version of Chaucer's wayward and ostentatiously "local" narrative pilgrimage. Yet even Chaucer's summary of the Knight's travels allows a quantifiable material world to encroach on the unquantified language

[88] F. R. H. du Boulay, "Henry of Derby's Expeditions to Prussia 1390–1 and 1392," in Du Boulay and Barron, *Reign of Richard II*, 153–72.

[89] See Paul Strohm, *Social Chaucer* (Cambridge, Mass.: Harvard University Press, 1989), 110–43, who uses Le Goff's terms but nevertheless (I think appropriately) tends to identify features of Le Goff's "church's time" with Chaucer's world of the nobility.

of noble values. The progressively opaque repetitions of the words "worthy" and "worthynesse" in the portrait, climaxed by the phrase "everemoore he hadde a sovereyn prys," suggest high monetary reward through the language of noble values, as visible as the equally available sense "exalted reputation."[90] The nostalgic retrospective of Chaucer's portrait as a whole parallels the suspended time and storytelling of Maghfeld's entry about Henry of Derby and the clerk of Botelston; and both Chaucer and Maghfeld display the rhetorical capacities of mercantile accounting to conform to and thus occupy even the highest social worlds. For both, though with varying final success, even seemingly timeless leisure and invaluable "high culture" may subtly be reframed within a more quantitative and negotiable material base.

Evidence of Chaucer's textual transactions with Henry of Derby's circle appears in his poetry—not with the directness that Gower displays in presenting his (rededicated) *Confessio Amantis* to Henry himself, but by way of intermediaries (reminiscent of Maghfeld's relation with Henry through R. de Blomfeld). At some date, Chaucer addressed an "Envoy" to Bukton. This is almost certainly Henry of Derby's steward Peter Bukton, who managed the provisioning of the first Prussian journey and traveled with Henry on a second (albeit one far less entertainingly protracted).[91] In his intimately Horatian epistle, Chaucer raises the question of whether he should offer counsel on Bukton's upcoming marriage, and he decides that he is not the one to do so—though he coyly comments that if he were, he would say that marriage is less fearful than being "take in Frise" (23). The Frisian coastal regions were the origins of many of the Teutonic Knights, and would serve as a plausible staging point (though not one Henry took) for the derailed crusade that ended up in Königsberg; thus Chaucer hints at his own membership in a splendid "companye" that might travel as Bukton did to the Continent on campaign. To close his fellow-courtly nonadvice, however, Chaucer also refers Bukton to the Wife of Bath—a text to "rede" (29) to make his assessment of marriage for himself. The invitation to apply mercantile accounting to the supposedly noncommercial noble world

---

[90] In an important "symposium" on Chaucer's audience in 1983, Patricia Eberle pointed to the traces of "commercial language" in the *General Prologue* to argue (uniquely in that symposium) for movement between the mercantile and noble worlds, though stressing Chaucer's central focus on the latter: "Commercial Language and the Commercial Outlook in the 'General Prologue,'" *ChauR* 18 (1983): 161–74.

[91] *Expeditions to Prussia and the Holy Land,* 126, 128, 133, 138, 265, 300n.

could not be more deft or more direct. The reference also constitutes Chaucer's own act of literary gift-exchange: the "Envoy to Bukton" may well have been accompanied by a copy of the work mentioned (as Hoccleve's short envoys to nobility mentioning his works generally were).[92] The invocation of the Wife applies her technologies of mercantile accounting more widely and simultaneously constitutes a gift in the covertly reciprocal spirit of noble culture: a double-dealing worthy of the Wife herself.

Gower's Everyday Mercantile Technologies and the Golden Treasury of Rhetoric

Perhaps thanks to mutual connections between Maghfeld and Henry of Derby, John Gower's patron, Gower used Maghfeld's financial services more than any other writer, almost more than any other client. Indeed, a sign of Maghfeld's decline in the years that his account book covers is that Gower was one of his few return customers (sharing this status with, for instance, Maghfeld's overextended fellow sheriff, Thomas Newenton). Maghfeld's book indicates that he procured for Gower a brass pot and a "cheste" in 1392, perhaps for Gower's house in Southwark, which his will indicates was large enough to include a hall.[93] Maghfeld also loaned Gower £3 6s 8d (or at least that was the amount due back to Maghfeld) for three weeks some time after 1395, though the entry is undated. It is the last entry in the book. All the entries concerning Gower—like those involving Chaucer and the book called the "treasure of philosophers"—are recorded in Maghfeld's hand, and all are cancelled.

Even more than other "London" writers who are marginal to the city, both in literary perspective and, so far as we can tell, profession and life, in his English poetry Gower is particularly unforthcoming on merchants or London. Robert Epstein suggests that we think of him more as a Southwark than a London writer, whose attention was in any case increasingly directed at the courtly world of Westminster.[94] At an early point he appears to have achieved financial independence, perhaps as a lawyer (certainly he made sharp dealings in real estate, as in the notorious "Septvauns affair," in which he purchased at a low price the prop-

---

[92] On an envoy Hoccleve sent with the poem mentioned in it, see J. A. Burrow, *Thomas Hoccleve: Authors of the Middle Ages* (Aldershot: Ashgate, 1994), 28.

[93] Rickert, "Extracts," 118–19, fol. 34; for the will, see Fisher, *John Gower,* 66.

[94] Epstein, "London, Southwark, Westminster."

erty of an indebted heir, who later turned out to be underage).[95] He accepted the livery of the Lancaster affinity in 1393, and presented the *Confessio Amantis* to Henry of Derby as well as King Richard II, who, he says in the first recension, commissioned it from Gower while he was on the royal barge as it floated "under the toun of newe Troye, / Which tok of Brut his ferste joye" (Prol.37–38*). It is the only overt appearance of London in the poem, and it disappears in the new dedication passage to Henry of Derby.

Decades of scholarship have explored how the *Confessio* addresses the nature and problems of rule and law, ideal princely behavior, and love as a center of secular ethics more broadly, but hardly Gower's relation to the city, much less mercantilism in particular, from which he seems, as Epstein says, "to stand at a remove."[96] Gower's Latin *Vox clamantis* presents a few glimpses of urban professions and urban culture, including, under Fraud, merchants and lawyers; but this work too was aimed at and read by the higher nobility and clergy rather than any urban community of readers, among whom Chaucer and Langland always claimed wider audiences.[97] Only in the French *Mirour de l'Omme* (ca. 1378) can Gower be said to use and address mercantile language and issues, albeit ultimately to lay out the sins to which merchants were particularly prone. Perhaps, as Roger Ladd suggests, Gower was writing this poem, whose survival in only a single copy does not suggest noble patronage, directly to them, by which Gower, "coopting promercantile ideology," sought to show merchants themselves how their own values condemn mercantile sins.[98]

Maghfeld's entries and Ladd's assessment of the *Mirour* suggest that a closer look at the English *Confessio*, finished in the 1390s—precisely the period of Gower's dealings with Maghfeld—is appropriate. Yet just

[95] Fisher, *John Gower*, 52–53; Matthew Giancarlo, *Parliament and Literature in Late Medieval England* (Cambridge: Cambridge University Press, 2007), 94–99.

[96] Epstein, "London, Southwark, Westminster," 43.

[97] In ibid., 49–51, Epstein notes the relevant sections of the *Mirour* and *Vox*. For the *Vox*'s noble readers, see M. B. Parkes, "Patterns of Scribal Activity and Revisions of the Text in Early Copies of Works by John Gower," in *New Science Out of Old Books: Studies in Manuscripts and Early Printed Books in Honour of A. I. Doyle*, ed. R. Beadle and A. J. Piper (Aldershot: Ashgate, 1995), 81–121. Quotations of the *Confessio* are from *The English Works of John Gower*, ed. G. C. Macaulay, EETS e.s. 81 and 82 (London: Oxford University Press, 1900–1901).

[98] Ladd, *Antimercantilism in Late Medieval English Literature*, 49–75 (74). For earlier notice of Gower's "mercantile" interests in the *Mirour* (especially his paean to wool, lines 25369–429), see Fisher, *John Gower*, 79–99.

as the *Confessio* avoids merchants, it also approaches the signature technologies of mercantilism—money and contracts—with few markings of Chaucer's or Langland's special interest or particular social origins. To be sure, Gower's Midas, exemplar of "avarice" and thus an obvious opportunity for denouncing money, declares that "Gold is the lord of man and beste, / And mai hem both beie and sell" (V.234).[99] The speech, with its personified presentation, draws on long traditions in Latin and some English poems on "Sir Penny," but may proximately rely on Langland's Lady Meed, with her speech on money's universal necessity and allure. But the differences are illuminating. For Langland, Meed's power is explicitly centered in urban, professional culture (as money is by Chaucer, as in *The Miller's Tale* [I.3380]) and marked as scandalous by rebuttals from numerous figures, including the narrator. In *Piers,* when money as such is considered, it at least seems to offer a distinct set of social locations and particular provocations (though both prove dizzyingly mercurial). In contrast, the powers of gold that Gower's Midas presents, unopposed, seem banal, the impersonal result of universally derivable thought. Gower spends more lines insisting that Midas's views are the product of reasoned and dispassionate thought than he does on the speech itself: "thus upon the pointz diverse / Diverseliche he gan rehearce / What point him thoghte for the beste" (V.217–19). Midas eventually learns to despise gold, and to understand that "mete and cloth sufficeth" (V.320), and the narrator then offers traditional praise for the time before gold was discovered, "Tho was the toun withoute wal, / Which nou is closed overal" (V.339–40). But cities' modern enclosures, a general condition, are a far cry from their imminent destruction.[100] Midas's calm reasoning leads merely to moderation of his "covetous" emphasis on gold, not to a rejection of the need for trade, manufacturing, and cities as such.

In Gower's presentation, mercantile contracts are similarly normalized, almost to the point where they disappear. As Brian Gastle notes, whereas Chaucer's *Wife of Bath's Tale* presents the "rash promise" motif of the Arthurian knight's contract with the Old Wife—Chaucer's knight agrees to let her name her price after rather than before she has

---

[99] For the traditions, see Galloway, *The Penn Commentary on Piers Plowman,* 216–24.

[100] For useful though brief comment on this speech, see Ethan Knapp, "The Place of Egypt in Gower's *Confessio Amantis,*" in *John Gower, Trilingual Poet: Language, Translation, and Tradition,* ed. Elisabeth Dutton with John Hines and R. F. Yeager (Woodbridge, Suffolk: D. S. Brewer, 2010), 26–34 (29).

told him the secret of what women all desire—Gower's parallel "Tale of Florent" proceeds through the negotiation "more as a traditional contractual obligation wherein the parties are privy to the terms and agree before executing the contract." Thus as Gower's Old Wife declares, "bot ferst . . . I wol have thi trowthe in honde / That thou schalt be myn housebonde" (I.1557–60). We may note that this confirms the shared mercantile literacy of Gower and Langland, whose Conscience insists on full disclosure of terms before payment. But Gastle goes on to point out that Gower almost never presents transactions with money; Florent's oath associates the "marriage contract with the social obligation of the individual," the principle where Gastle finds Gower's clearest modernity.[101]

Thus in contrast to the strategies of the other London writers so far considered, Gower's views of the basic technologies of mercantilism—money and contracts—appear so unpointed by rebuttal, so smoothly subordinated to other elements, and so familiar to our sense of their customary means and apparatus that they hardly draw attention in the way that Chaucer's disruptive and ironic reframing of timing in contracts and debts, or Langland's volatile presentations of credit and money, persistently do. Gower's unmarked and unemphatic absorption of money and mercantile contracts supports more easily than Chaucer's materials Patterson's claim that a "liberal bourgeois" mentality can obscure its history so completely that it seems like "life itself."[102] Yet that does not mean that all elements of mercantile technology in his world stand in this state, or are unprovocative for his poetics. Again, Maghfeld's book can help identify the terms and focuses where the shared technologies and energies of poetry and commerce are most traceable.

In seeking focuses where his poetry participates more dynamically in such technology, it is not whimsical to return to the "cheste" that Maghfeld procured for Gower. This was a late medieval prop directly involved in keeping and using wealth; as a tool for shipment as well as household security, it indicated the wide-ranging apparatus and capabil-

---

[101] Brian Gastle, "Gower's Business: Artistic Production of Cultural Capital and the Tale of Florent," in *John Gower, Trilingual Poet*, ed. Dutton, 182–95 (191–93); see also Andrew Galloway, "Gower's Quarrel with Chaucer, and the Origins of Bourgeois Didacticism in Fourteenth-Century London Poetry," in *Calliope's Classroom: Didactic Poetry from Antiquity to the Renaissance*, ed. Annette Harder, Geritt Reinink, and Alasdair MacDonald (Leuven, Paris, and Dudley, Virginia: Peeters, 2007), 245–68.

[102] Patterson, *Chaucer and the Subject of History*, 366.

ities of mercantilism, more fully indeed than gold or contracts.[103] Gower mentions chests and coffers twenty-two times in the *Confessio*. Sometimes he does so to treat, predictably, avaricious hoarding, as in the case where clerical promotion beyond pastoral duties to administrative positions causes spiritual as well as material blight: in such a case, "the stronge cofre hath al devoured" the "tresor of the benefice," as Gower says in his Prologue describing the decline of all estates, "under the keye of avarice," out of use of the poor whom it should "clothe / And ete and drinke and house bothe" (Prol.313–18; see also VII.2321). As that instance shows, the coffer brings out for Gower the contrasting sense of "use," whose dialectic with the idea of hoarding is explicated more generally in the book on avarice. There, Avarice never lets his many possessions escape his keeping: "Thus whanne he hath his cofre loken, / It schal noght after ben unstoken"—except, that is, when Avarice wishes to gaze on the gold, "hou that it schyneth brihte," but otherwise "he dar noght use / To take his part" (V.23–39). The placement of "use" at the line's end encourages the reader to dwell on the term in its technical economic sense, "consume."[104]

Although merchants as such are invisible, coffers and chests gain progressively wider implications in the English poem. Gower presents an entire tale, "The Two Coffers," in which a king, to prove that courtiers grumbling about lacking promotion should accept whatever God thinks they should have, offers two locked chests, one full of gold, one of stones and straw, and allows them to choose. A distinctly capitalist outlook emerges in the king's warning about the choice he offers them:

> Now ches and tak which you is levere:
> Bot be wal war, er that ye take;
> For of that on I undertake
> Ther is no maner good therinne,
> Wherof ye mighten profit winne.
>
> (V.2338–42)

Although the story appears in a section against avarice, the desired outcome here is to gain the capital not for itself but as something "wherof

[103] For evidence of chests in London, "probably the most widely used piece of furniture in the medieval period," see Jane Brennan, "Furnishings," in *Medieval Finds from Excavations in London: 6: The Medieval Household*, ed. Egan, 65–87 (65).

[104] *Middle English Dictionary* s.v., noun (1) (c); also at *Confessio* VI.547.

ye mighten profit winne." Evidently this is not opposed to a moral against avarice because the "profit" involves risk and venturing. There are two stages to this: first, the courtiers' risky choice of the unknown coffer, and second, the further investments possible but not certain from the correct choice. The protracted attention to the courtiers' indecision, like the protracted display of Midas's considerations (before both make the wrong choice), shows Gower's interest in venturing of nearly the kind that Langland pursues through debts and letters of obligation, and Chaucer achieves in the forays of commodification into time, friendship, and memories of innocence. The avaricious and grumbling courtiers are made into nervous merchant venturers, and almost at the same stroke failed ones, though they have been taught a new technology.

In a small way the courtiers' lesson is like that of the *Confessio*'s reader, and often focused on the same apparatus they encountered. In Gower's narratives, a coffer can offer the prospect of the "tresor" of capital, including its transport to new users and its potency as a resource "whereof ye mighten profit winne." The fullest instance of this trajectory appears in the story of Apollonius, the last tale of the *Confessio* and one with a heightened sense of the transportation of treasures in coffers around the world for increasingly wider use. Apollonius's wife and daughter are the focuses for this expansion: both are repeatedly closed up as if forever, then released miraculously for further profit and "use." When Apollonius, fleeing the incestuous tyrant Antiochus, marries the daughter of another king and thinks she has died in a sea storm, he laments his loss of her as "mi welthe and my recoverir" (VIII.1064). He puts her body to sea in a "cofre strong," the body wrapped "in cloth of gold," and then "Under hire heved in aventure / Of gold he leide Sommes grete." The treasure in the coffer is described as "in aventure" (emphasized at the end of the line) because Apollonius grants it (as he instructs in the letter accompanying this precious freight) to whoever finds her body and can fitly bury it and further reverence it. Even a treasure in a coffin has a use (VIII.1108–19).

The plot proliferates coffers and enclosures for both Apollonius's wife—revived in a distant land, she enters a nunnery, she thinks forever—and for his daughter. The daughter, left for dead and captured by pirates, is then enclosed in a prostitution house, the depraved opposite of the sacred enclosure for her mother, but equally "clos in a chambre be hireselve" (VIII.1425). That place too becomes a kind of sacred coffer when the daughter's holiness dampens the lust of all her would-be clients (VIII.1430–31). Feminine virginity, feminine marital fidelity, and heterosexual familial wholeness, when Apollonius and his wife and daughter are reunited, are the enclosed but circulating and continually reusable treasures that the story and the poem produce. Enclosures are important for preserving these treasures, yet the treasures must be opened and productively exploited. This economy thus stands doubly opposed to the incestuous rape by Antiochus of his daughter. She is deprived of her treasure—"and thus sche hath forlore / The flour which sche hath longe bore" (after which Antiochus himself stalks "out of the chambre" [VIII.303–4, 313]); and she is also left closed in forever, in suffocating isolation with her incestuous parent, removed from any productive "use" in the marriage market that circulates beyond them and forms the basis for properly civilized society.

Even these economies of protection, circulation, and use can be said to idealize and normalize the principles of mercantilism into "life itself." This is partly because they depend on repeated metaphoric and metonymic associations—treasures and women, coffers and economic circulation (VIII.1108, 1110, 1113, 1132, 1157, 1168, 1174, 1230), while the focus of the romance remains on the emotional investments of the human relationships. But the verbal tropes by which such economies are made to seem natural and inevitable emerge, when isolated as "rhetorik," as themselves an unnatural force. This is so even though the poem continually denies its use of rhetoric. Its implicit and explicit claims to safe transmission of one or another preexisting source text, marked as a "tale," or "matiere and the forme," or simply with "Lo!" introducing material translated from French, Latin, and even Italian, present its English contents as merely direct, rhetoric-free, goods, a principle asserted in the even more prosaic Latin glosses that presume to "summarize" the points of the tales, absent nearly all the frill of narrative interest.[105] However impossible such unchanging transmission, the pretense of commutability is pervasive, registered in its English narrator's earnest "plainness" of communicating, his avoidance of any elevated "Stile of my writinges" in order to "speke of thing [that] is noght so strange," fashioned "with rude wordes and with pleyne," free from "thilke scole of eloquence" (I.8–10, VIII.3122, 3115).

---

[105] For further contexts to explain their prosaic reductiveness, see Andrew Galloway, "Gower's *Confessio Amantis*, the *Prick of Conscience*, and the History of the Latin Gloss in Early English Literature," in *John Gower: Manuscripts, Readers, Contexts*, ed. Malte Urban (Turnhout: Brepols, 2009), 39–70.

Yet despite those claims to rude words and plain, the poet admits that rhetoric is necessary and unavoidable. Its ungovernable power, in spite of the poet's protestations, is patent throughout, from when "old" John Gower's narrator first becomes a lover at a stroke, "quasi in persona aliorum quos amor alligat" ("as if in the persona of those whom love binds," as the Latin gloss notes [I.60 gloss]), by mere declaration, lacking even any glimpse of a beloved. The power of how words mean is explored throughout Gower's ostentatiously "plain" style, as, for instance, when Amans the lover describes his presumed beloved in his confession of the book on Avarice, in terms showing how deeply he commodifies her and his own energies and objects by the language he uses. His speech uses a series of chiming "rimes riches" that turn his own language into a massy object of high value with constant images of wealth being heaped up and counted, wittily encrusting his denial that he has ever sinned in Avarice:

> If I hire hadde, I wolde hire kepe,
> And yit no Friday wolde I faste,
> Thogh I hire kepte and hielde faste.
> Fy on the bagges in the kiste!
> I hadde ynogh, if I hire kiste.
> For certes, if sche were myn,
> I hadde hir levere than a Myn
> Of Gold . . .
>
> (V.80–87)

Mercantilism's technologies of transformation, elsewhere so naturalized by their smooth metaphoric and metonymic presentations, reemerge explicitly in the exaggerated displays of rhetoric, whose role throughout is to carry out those commutations. Not only the Beloved but language itself becomes both the chief and least stable "good," more potent even than Midas's gold. Indeed, Gower's accounting of love's "wynnings" and losses—"Or forto lese or forto winne"—is so volatile a pursuit that it cannot be settled in its own terms, as shown in the way old "John Gower," returned to authorial form, must be exiled from the Court of Venus to return to where "vertu moral duelleth, / Wher ben this bokes, as men telleth, / Whiche of long time thou hast write" (VIII.2925–27), as if indeed those would somehow free him altogether from rhetoric's and love's powers. His ideal settlement can emerge only by taking a step beyond any narrative's actual experience, beyond narrative of any kind, in the creation of a narratively omniscient but fully human author.

The powers of such an author are visible in those forces he harnesses, as in Genius's discourse on kingship in Book VII, presenting rhetoric as capable of transforming the very facts of life:

> Above alle erthli creatures
> The hihe makere of natures
> The word to man have yove alone,
> So that the speche of his persone,
> Or forto lese or forto winne,
> The hertes thoght which is withinne
> Mai schewe, what it wolde mene . . .
> It hath Gramaire, it hath Logiqe,
> That serven bothe unto the speche. . . .
>   In Ston and gras vertu ther is,
> Bot yit the bokes tellen this,
> That word above alle erthli thinges
> Is vertuous in his doinges,
> Wher so it be to evele or goode.
> For if the wordes semen goode
> And ben wel spoke at mannes Ere,
> Whan that ther is no trouthe there,
> Thei don fulofte gret deceipte;
> For whan the word to the conceipte
> Descordeth in so double a wise,
> Such Rethorique is to despise
> In every place, and forto drede.
>
>   (VII.1507–57)

Language's "double" deceit is to betray the audience and the truth; but this itself doubles the sense of "descordeth." As J. Allan Mitchell notes, such self-referencing gestures show the potent unreliability of language at the very moment it is described. The passage constitutes one of the earliest descriptions of that "science" in English. Mitchell points out that Gower's presentation subordinates grammar and logic to rhetoric, rather than presenting them as equals as in his source here, *Li Livres dou Tresor* of Brunetto Latini (ca. 1280).[106]

That source, exotic as it is here, marks another point of contact with Maghfeld's economy: by way of the book that Maghfeld received from

---

[106] J. Allan Mitchell, "John Gower and John Lydgate: Forms and Norms of Rhetorical Culture," in *A Companion to Medieval English Literature and Culture,* ed. Peter Brown (Oxford: Blackwell, 2007), 569–82 (570).

Francis Winchester. At least it seems likely that Latini's *Tresor* is the book referred to in Maghfeld's entry as the *Tresor de Philosophie*. Latini's work is titled *Tresor de Philosophie* in some manuscripts, and it opens with phrases that would support this title:

Cis livres est apielés Tresors. Car si come li sires ki vuet en petit lieu amasser cose de grandisme vaillance, non pas pour son delit solement, mes pour acrois-tre son pooir et pour aseurer son estate en guerre et en pais, i met les plus chieres choses et les plus precieus joiaus k'il puet selonc sa bonne entencion; tout autresi est li cors de cest livre compilés de sapience, si come celui ki est estrais de tous les membres de philosophie en une sonme briement.[107]

[This book is called the Tresor. For so too a gentleman wishing to amass in a small place things of highest value—not only for his own pleasure, but to increase his power and keep secure his social estate in war and peace—puts there the most expensive things and most precious jewels he has, according to his best plan. In another way, the body of this book is compiled from wisdom, just as one succinctly puts into one summation all the limbs of philosophy.]

Latini's book, which spurred the tradition of calling any anthology a "treasury," circulated widely in late medieval European and English courtly and literary spheres, including London. A particularly splendid fourteenth-century copy, now Oxford, Bodleian Library MS Douce 319, has an inscription indicating that it was a gift from William de Mon-tague, earl of Salisbury, to John of Gaunt's brother, Thomas of Wood-stock, duke of Gloucester.[108] Latini's work was known to the early fourteenth-century London merchant-administrator Andrew Horn, whose compilations of London legal and historical materials include an excerpt of Latini's discussion of a mayor's ideal traits, including re-strained speech, since "he who speaks well and little is held wise" ("qi parle bien et poy len le tient a sage").[109]

[107] *Li Livres dou Tresor de Brunetto Latini,* ed. Francis Carmody (Berkeley and Los Angeles: University of California Press, 1948), 17.
[108] Otto Pächt and J. J. G. Alexander, *Illuminated Manuscripts in the Bodleian Library Oxford: 2: Italian School* (Oxford: Clarendon Press, 1970), 16 (#154). See Julia Bolton Holloway, "Brunetto Latini and England," *Manuscripta* 31 (1987): 11–21.
[109] Corporation of London, Records Office, *The Liber Custumarum,* fol. 6, printed in *Munimenta Gildhallae Londoniensis: Volume II, Part I, Liber Custumarum,* ed. Henry Thomas Riley, Rolls Series (London: Longman, 1860), 15–25; for description, see N. R. Ker, *Medieval Manuscripts in British Libraries: I: London* (Oxford: Clarendon Press, 1969), 20–21. Not mentioned by Holloway, "Brunetto Latini."

Latini's text enjoyed the kind of circulation and translatability traditionally reserved for Latin works. An Italian translation was made in the late thirteenth century, possibly by Latini himself, and in 1418 it was translated into Catalan.[110] The rare translations of medieval vernacular books into other vernaculars stand as instances of special status: the authority of having a "sentence" commutable to local secular tongues, like Latin writings, but unlike those, serving a transhistorical secular written culture just emerging in the fourteenth century.

Gower's work too was a unique member of this category. Around the time the *Tresor* was translated into Catalan, the *Confessio* was rendered into Portuguese prose by Robert Payn, a native of England but canon of Lisbon, probably working under the auspices of John of Gaunt's daughter, Philippa of Lancaster, who married the heir to the throne of Portugal. Shortly thereafter, perhaps due to the marriage of Gaunt's other daughter to the Castilian king, the Portuguese version of Gower's poem was turned into Castilian prose by Juan de Cuenca. A further copy of the Portuguese original was made about 1415 in Cuete, in northern Africa.[111]

As the only medieval English work translated into another European vernacular, Gower's *Confessio* became comparable to Latini's book. Gower's text's wrapping of its English in Latin makes both its powers of commutability and authorial control even more obvious than Latini's, suggesting a fully available machinery for the establishment of textual "value" and textual transformation. Such capability is confirmed by the Latin colophon accompanying many manuscripts of the *Confessio*, describing how in one book in French (the *Mirour de l'Omme*) Gower "discoursed about vices and virtues as well as the various social degrees of this world." In a second book in Latin (the *Vox clamantis*), he treated the various misfortunes "occurring in English during the period of King Richard II," and in a third treated "those things by which, according to Aristotle, King Alexander was taught both in his governance as in other matters"—and he adds, as if in an aside, that the main point of that

[110] See Julia Bolton Holloway, *Twice-Told Tales: Brunetto Latino and Dante Alighieri* (New York: Peter Lang, 1993), esp. 3–22; Brunetto Latini, *Llibre del tresor,* ed. C. J. Wittlin, 4 vols. (Barcelona: Editorial Barcino, 1971–89).

[111] R. F. Yeager, "Gower's Lancastrian Affinity: The Iberian Connection," *Viator* 35 (2004): 483–515; Joyce Coleman, "Philippa of Lancaster, Queen of Portugal—and Patron of the Gower Translations?" in *England and Iberia in the Middle Ages, 12th–15th Century: Cultural, Literary, and Political Exchanges,* ed. María Bullón-Fernández (New York: Palgrave Macmillan, 2007), 135–65.

third work "has its basis in love and lovers' infatuated passions."[112] However falsely this may seem to modern critics to characterize the *Confessio*'s lively and sensitively secular ethics,[113] the generic forms described here might roughly describe Latini's *Tresor,* with its division into ethics, history, and a mirror for princes.

Glossed and compendious, the *Confessio* is presented by Gower both as an account book of a long love's gains and losses and as itself the treasure—a "cheste" that contains within it everything one might need: Ovid, love poetry, sage wisdom, and Latin sermons, wrapped in a confessor's scheme that the English verse freely expands. Although the Latin glosses may not really be a "means to the understanding of the English poem but instructions on how to read it according to the conventions of a specific code of reading," their summaries of intellectual profit, reductive chains and bindings though they are, show with visual immediacy even to those unable to read them that his is a treasure to be guarded, transported to other shores, and commuted to other uses.[114]

Thomas Usk's Civic Ideals and the Politics of Accounting at Billingsgate Wharf

The many communities of Maghfeld's textual economy included not only the more socially and politically distant figures of the higher social castes—with whom Maghfeld, like Chaucer and Gower, sought so many negotiations and alignments—but also the many more intimately involved and partisan figures who remained within the walls of the London mercantile world. Many of these were clustered with or against— and in most cases, eventually both—the quintessentially London writer Thomas Usk. Although Usk appears nowhere in Maghfeld's book, his intersection with Maghfeld's career, not previously noted, illuminates the political and ethical impetus moving through and even helping to drive the technologies of mercantile accounting both within and beyond the city. Self-promoting though he has often seemed, Usk's writings and

---

[112] In *English Works of John Gower,* ed. Macaulay, 2:479–80.

[113] For secular love as the ethical center of the entire poem, see Peter Nicholson, *Love and Ethics in Gower's "Confessio Amantis"* (Ann Arbor: University of Michigan Press, 2005).

[114] Derek Pearsall, "Gower's Latin in the *Confessio Amantis,*" in *Latin and Vernacular: Studies in Late-Medieval Texts and Contexts* (Cambridge: D. S. Brewer, 1994), 13–25 (24); for the glosses as enabling uses by new audiences, see Siân Echard, "With Carmen's Help: Latin Authorities in the *Confessio Amantis,*" *SP* 95 (1998): 1–40.

life suggest that potent affective energies—such as the range of affect more deftly and ambitiously articulated in the wry, satiric, plangent, and hopeful elaborations of mercantile technologies by the Ricardian poets—powered the *poesis* of mercantile accounting at its urban core as well as through its furthest expansions.

Of all Ricardian writers, Usk seems to have had a calling for passionately promoting London's cliques and followings. Thus, earlier than any of the fifteenth-century followers who openly proclaimed Chaucer their guide and "father," Usk's *Testament of Love* created Chaucerianism.[115] Usk's Love praises Chaucer as "the noble philosophical poete in Englissh speche," for both extolling love and translating Boethius's ideas of providence and free will. "Wherfore," Love adds, "al that wyllen me good owe to do him worshyp and reverence both; trewly, his better ne his pere in schole of my rules coude I never fynde" (III.4.230–34).[116]

The specter of Chaucer here is neither the maker of experimental dream poetry nor of the *Canterbury Tales* (not yet written apart perhaps from a version of *The Knight's Tale*), but of *Troilus and Criseyde* (which must therefore have circulated in the mid-1380s) and Chaucer's *Boece*. Such works present the most direct communion with but also rivalry to ancient literary monumentality. Yet Usk's praise of these does not serve to monumentalize in turn his own Boethian dialogue in the *Testament*. On the contrary, Usk's praise of Chaucer as a classic allows Usk to elevate contemporary London culture to high prestige, and himself to its topical truth-teller. The urge for civic exaltation frames Usk's own direct address and petition, from the acrostic of its capital letters spelling out an appeal for "MERCI ON THIN VSK" to its direct address to some possible patron, literal or figural—"hertly, lady precious Margarit, have mynde on thy servaunt, and thynke on his disease" (I.I.18–20)— to, again, his general appeals to a London readership that Usk creates as much as assumes. "Let us shewe our fantasyes in suche wordes as we lerneden of our dames tonge," he proposes, a regional loyalty epitomized by his prayer to repair the city from earlier political errors (implicitly including his own): "by whiche cause the peace, that most in

---

[115] Cf. Scogan, "Moral Balade," in *Chaucerian and Other Pieces: Being a Supplement to the Complete Works of Geoffrey Chaucer,* ed. W. W. Skeat (Oxford: Clarendon Press, 1897), 7:237–44 (line 126); Thomas Hoccleve, *The Regiment of Princes,* ed. Charles R. Blyth (Kalamazoo: Medieval Institute Publications, 1999), line 1959.

[116] Citations are from Thomas Usk, *Testament of Love,* ed. Gary W. Shawver (Toronto: University of Toronto Press, 2002). Shawver's notes document Usk's many allusions to Chaucer's works (summarized on 27–28).

comunaltie shulde be desyred, was in poynte to be broken and adnulled, also the cytie of London, that is to me so dere and swete, in whiche I was forthe growen—and more kyndely love have I to that place than to any other in erthe" (I.6.85–89).

Usk's most politically active period began in 1384, when he helped foment London riots on behalf of the disappointed "populist" mayoral candidate and sometime Lancastrian client John Northampton, who could not tolerate a recent close defeat by his longtime opponent, the wealthy Grocer Nicholas Brembre. The latter had managed to resist the evidently charismatic Northampton's claims to break the monopolies of the wealthy guilds that Brembre stood for, in opposition to the pressures put on the city's independence by John of Gaunt, a threat that, as Pamela Nightingale shows, Northampton manipulated for his own purposes.[117] Usk, identified as Northampton's "scryveyn," was arrested but turned betrayer to Northampton by August, submitting to the king an elaborate "appeal" (a citizen's assertion of treason) in English. The king, probably to thwart his uncle, John of Gaunt, who had supported Northampton but was overseas during the riots, summarily condemned Northampton and his associate John More to death (they were later pardoned when John of Gaunt returned). Usk, remanded to Brembre's custody through the rest of 1384, was pardoned by the king and, under house arrest, evidently wrote the *Testament* the following year.

As Skeat first emphasized, the *Testament* is clearly designed to rehabilitate Usk's reputation, whose appearance of shifting loyalties Usk contradicts with what he calls in the *Testament* the pursuit of the "knotte" of "trouthe": an ideal of steady and close-knit loyalty that the work proposes as the means to aim at a general civic "peace."[118] Usk's quest

---

[117] For Usk's life, see *Testament of Love,* ed. Shawver, 7–24, some of whose details amend the fuller contextualizing in Paul Strohm, "Politics and Poetics: Usk and Chaucer in the 1380s," in *Literary Practice and Social Change in Britain, 1350–1530,* ed. Lee Patterson (Berkeley and Los Angeles: University of California Press, 1990), 83–112. For the text of Usk's "appeal," see *A Book of London English, 1384–1425,* ed. R. W. Chambers and Marjorie Daunt (Oxford: Clarendon Press, 1931; 1967), 22–31. The complex background to Brembre's and Northampton's politics and agendas is elucidated by Nightingale, *A Medieval Mercantile Community,* esp. 228–319, whose critical interpretation of Northampton's goals and style ("the politics of the mafia" [278]) is followed here. This departs from the older interpretation of Northampton as a popular liberator, with Brembre the proponent of oppressive mercantile monopolies (for the historiographic tradition, see ibid., 230). It may be noted that Nightingale's view fits what Usk says he came to believe.

[118] For further on this ideal, see Andrew Galloway, "Private Selves and the Intellectual Marketplace in Late Fourteenth-Century England: The Case of the Two Usks," *NLH* 28 (1997): 291–318; for an argument against that ideal's consistency or credi-

is also framed as seeking the Gospel's merchant's ideal: the pearl of great price, figured in his dedicatee, Marguerite. Both metaphors certainly allowed Usk to use his work to record his debts to the king, perhaps, as Marion Turner proposes, in the style of offering a "jewel" to the king in the mode of the many transactions that the Goldsmiths, whom Usk served as clerk, made with the king.[119] Love (in the role of Philosophia) praises the king's "for-yevenesse of [Usk's] mykel misdede" (II.4.107–12). But Usk in his own voice emphasizes his loyalty to "the cytie of London, that is to me so dere and swete, in whiche I was forthe growen—and more kyndely love have I to that place than to any other in erthe, as every kyndely creature hath ful appetyte to that place of his kyndly engendrure and wylne reste and peace in that stede to abyde" (I.6.86–90). Such peace "by angels voyce . . . confyrmed, our God entrynge in this worlde" is explicitly and topically political, meant to reconcile king and city, since "this God, by his comyn, made not peace alone betwene hevenly and erthly bodyes, but also amonge us on erthe; so he peace confyrmed that in one heed of love, one body we shulde perfourme." There is more than a hint of a monarchical ideal in his metaphor, but in the next breath Usk turns toward a fully civic model of elected and conciliar power: "Also, I remembre me wel, how the name of Athenes was rather after the god of peace, than of batayle, shewynge that peace moste is necessarye to comunalties and cytes" (I.6.90–102).

The *Testament* asserts that Usk followed the populist and nominally democratic Northampton only so long as he believed that Northampton sought civic reformation in service to "commen profyte in comynaltie" "with just governaunce" proceeding "from thylke profyte." For this, Usk joined Northampton's political conspiracies ("certain conjuracions and other great matters of ruling of cytezins"), although this subjected him both to "hate of the mighty senatours in thilke cyte" and "communes malyce." He turned against Northampton's group once his conscience alerted him to their true anti-communal purposes: "sythen, by counsayle of myne inwytte, me thought the firste paynted thynges malyce and yvel meanynge, withouten any good avaylyng to any people, and of tyrannye purposed" (I.6.48–61). Modern scholars, however, have

---

bility, see Marion Turner, *Chaucerian Conflict: Languages of Antagonism in Late Fourteenth-Century London* (Oxford: Clarendon Press, 2007), 93–126, esp. 103–4.

[119] Marion Turner, "Usk and the Goldsmiths," *NML* 9 (2007): 139–77.

tended to follow the cynical judgment of the Westminster Chronicler when that writer describes Usk's arrest in 1384:

About St. Margaret's Day [July 20, 1384] some Londoners arrested Thomas Usk, sometime clerk of the sheriff of London and secretary to John Northampton, many of whose projects for action in the city he had taken down in writing. He was lodged in prison and kept there for some time with the intention that he should disclose Northampton's secrets. Seeing that the way of escape was barred to him and that those to whom he had formerly clung had been clapped into prison and were unable at all to help him, he prudently bowed to the wishes of those whom he knew to be now in the ascendant, and set shrewdly and craftily to work to win the friendship of those whom earlier, without a doubt, he had clearly recognized to be his chief enemies.[120]

Although generally accepting these judgments of Usk's motives, scholars have rarely paused over the "sometime clerk of the sheriff of London," in whose office and personnel so many fourteenth-century tensions between civic and royal spheres were concentrated. The chronicle's editors note Usk's later appointment as undersheriff of London and Middlesex in October 1387, implying that the mention of this in 1384 is the chronicler's loose anticipation of events. It is true that Usk's royal promotion to undersheriff, which followed his release from Brembre's custody, and then several years of serving as a minor royal servant, must have marked him thereafter as a king's man (as Maghfeld's later promotion to sheriff perhaps did him). In the *Testament,* Usk indicates gratitude to King Richard only for the pardon, not the promotion, thus confirming that the *Testament* was finished before 1387, in a context of literary as much as political London partisanship, and indeed with a central focus on the "peace" of the city. As a result, however, of the assault on Richard's favorites by Richard's uncles, the Lords Appellant, during the "Merciless Parliament" of March to June 1388, when the Lords Appellant used a London parliament to arrest, convict, and execute many of the king's favorites both inside the city's governmental structure and in nearby Westminster, Usk was indicted as a "faux & malveise person de lour covyne" for having as undersheriff made "faux Arestes, Enditementz, & Atteindres . . . en Loundres, ou en Middlesex." He was grue-

---

[120] *The Westminster Chronicle, 1381–1394,* ed. and trans. L. C. Hector and Barbara F. Harvey (Oxford: Clarendon Press, 1982), 91.

somely executed.[121] His apparent siding against Northampton and with Richard and Brembre, the latter of whom the Appellants also executed, would be cause enough, even if nothing he did as undersheriff was.

It was probably necessary for the Appellants to define him as a traitor to remove a figure who presented a sign of the king's control over the city. Yet Usk's complex shifting alliances may in fact be explained as varying tactics in pursuit of some general ideal for the city, as his *Testament* insists. That ideal's nature is elusive and possibly always inchoate, but it may have been connected to the kind of moral "purity" that Northampton emphasized and from which Northampton evidently drew much of his initial popularity.[122] The mention of Athens suggests Usk's own peculiarly folded temporality, projecting a future goal from the ancient past. To be sure, Chaucer's account of Athens, in what became *The Knight's Tale* (perhaps already circulating among some readers in the final years of Usk's life), shows a city dominated by aristocrats and violence that can be knit up into "peace" only by a lord's or father's forcibly arranged marriage (garlanded with assurances that this is the cosmic order). Usk's outlook, a clear misreading of Chaucer, seems consistently aimed at a utopian civic community whose "love" would reach up and out from below rather than be imposed like the will of the "Firste Moevere" from on high (*Canterbury Tales,* I.2987). As Love in the *Testament of Love* insists, there are many paths of "grace" by which "shul men ben avaunced: ensample of David that from kepyng of shepe was drawen up into the order of kyngly governaunce, and Jupiter, from a bole, to be Europes fere, and Julius Cesar, from the lowest degre in Rome, to be mayser of al erthy princes, and Eneas, from hel, to be king of the country there Rome is nowe stondyng" (I.5.110–15). The work's political philosophy is thus antithetical to that of the courtly world in general, most clearly in suggesting that social opportunity for all would be a good, and moreover that civic renown should be supreme above any individual renown: "How shulde than the name of a synguler Londenoys," Love asks him, "passe the gloryous name of London, whiche by many it is commended, and by many it is lacked, and many mo places in erthe nat knowen than knowen?" (I.8.92–94).

These loyalties and ideals of social "advauncing" are clearly not mere Boethian postures, proclaiming the force of "true nobility" by a secure

---

[121] *Rotuli Parliamentorum,* 3:234; see *Testament of Love,* ed. Shawver, 21.

[122] See Frank Rexroth, *Deviance and Power in Late Medieval London* (Cambridge: Cambridge University Press, 2007).

member of the ruling class. Just how humble Usk's beginnings as an urban textual maker were and how rapidly he took his opportunities or found himself pulled into them has only begun to emerge. Caroline Barron, who recently discovered that Usk's least visible period as a "scryveyn" for Northampton included work as a clerk for the Goldsmiths in 1382, points out that Usk's low wages would not be enough to live on.[123] He must have had another job.

In fact, evidence of Usk's professional beginnings as a London textual worker may be found in the context of Maghfeld's own first royal appointment: as keeper of the sea. It was the echoes of this position in Chaucer's portrait of the Merchant—"He wolde the see were kept for any thyng / Bitwixe Middelburgh and Orewelle" (*Canterbury Tales,* I.276–77)[124]—on which Manly built much of his case for direct topical satire of Maghfeld. Maghfeld held the position with John Paris (with whom he had many financial dealings) until being abruptly dismissed by the King's Council in December 1383. Although the dismissal is unusual (Manly notes there is "no explanation"), a series of writs from London merchants and one knight, seeking parliamentary intervention in 1383 and again 1384, suggest why the council acted.[125] The complainants speak of losses from pirates, shipwreck, and other calamities, which Maghfeld and Paris are said to have allowed in spite of the wages they drew for their offices.

This confirms that coinage shortages alone cannot explain Maghfeld's downfall: many in the London mercantile world seem to have resented Maghfeld's failure in a royally appointed public duty—his first—where their export business was at stake. London shipping was a flashpoint in the struggles between the merchants and the king, who wished to circumvent London's massive importing and exporting business with the help of Genoese merchants who often significantly undersold the English. London merchants' anxieties from the 1370s over the threat to move the staple from Calais to an English port—where the London importers would become mere local middlemen and perhaps lose even that role to others—grew to a fervor against "aliens" in the 1380s, culminating in the murder of several Italian merchants. On the other side, price rises made attacks on London monopolies in imports (such as

---

[123] Caroline M. Barron, "New Light on Thomas Usk," *The Chaucer Newsletter* 26:2 (Fall 2004): 1.

[124] Manly, *Some New Light on Chaucer,* 196–200.

[125] *Rotuli Parliamentorum,* 3:168.

by the Fishmongers) a focus for the popular rioting that Northampton exploited against Brembre and the Grocers.[126] Maghfeld's actual fulfillment of his duties as keeper of the sea might not have been as lamentable as the complaints charge, but his association with the king's anti-London agenda might have roused deep distrust of his wholehearted effort to protect English shipping, and greater anger at incidents where he could be thought to have lapsed, even before London merchants had reason to resent his royal appointment to sheriff.

As often in the period, large political strands became entangled in an individual Londoner's career. Maghfeld's scandal of 1384 brought into focus a wide range of fears and ambitions circulating in the region. The efforts to bring Maghfeld and Paris before parliament to answer charges against their inadequate keeping of the seas continued through 1384, the year Usk was arrested; but another complaint reemerges as late as 1391, well after Maghfeld had left the position, thus likely serving simply as an antiroyalist protest. As often in medieval legal actions, all these writs were ignored or balked at by Maghfeld and Paris; no evidence shows that either man appeared before parliament or a civic court, though Maghfeld was indeed peremptorily dismissed from his post by the King's Council. But before that, the sheriffs, John More and Simon Wynchcombe, were unusually diligent in pursuing Maghfeld and Paris to answer the charges. Four writs, all dated December 6, 1383, show in their endorsements the multiple procedures used to bring the former keepers of the sea into court—up to ten steps. All the writs annotated in this way include the delivery of the writ by summons, declaring that the sheriffs had directly "informed Manfeld and Paris that they should appear before the court at the time and place contained in this writ." Each of the writs lists two bearers: on two John Gayton, on another, a man named Secchford, and on the other one, a man named Clare. On all four writs, however, the second summoner is Thomas Usk, noted in delivery "per Thomas Usk" or "per Usk."[127]

Simply in terms of institutional history, these writs provide a rare view of London's administrative textual production. Uniquely among English towns and cities, London regularly appointed two sheriffs, each

---

[126] See Nightingale, *A Medieval Mercantile Community,* esp. 228–319. Nightingale's acute unraveling of these issues does not discuss Maghfeld's position in them.

[127] SC 8/214/10702, SC 8/214/10703, SC 8/214/10704, and SC 8/214/10705. These (with thousands of others) are available, and to some extent searchable, under "Ancient Petitions" at http://www.nationalarchives.gov.uk/documentsonline/other.asp.

with his own staff: an undersheriff, a secondary, and a clerk of the papers, and below those "numerous other clerks known sometimes as
'clerks of the counters' or sheriffs' clerks, whose number fluctuated" (up
to nine).[128] Although the sheriffs' office (between Poultry and Bread
Streets) had one of the city's busiest courts, it has left no regular records
from this period, and only a few stray rolls from earlier. The writs from
1384 present the closest look at late fourteenth-century London sheriffs'
records that has so far been possible.[129]

The writs do still more in illuminating Usk's career. They confirm,
for instance, the precision of the Westminster Chronicler's description
of Usk as "clericus vicecomitis Londoniensis," which does not simply
anticipate his later role as undersheriff but describes him correctly as a
sheriff's clerk in 1384, hence in service to Northampton's associate
More, charged with delivering a summons to Maghfeld at just the point
when the largest political crises of the period in London were developing. Usk's role as a sheriff's clerk is consistent with his frequent employment as a public speaker and diplomat, as when he was hired in 1384
to denounce the "great men" of the city. His "Appeal," written eight
months later in August, displays a formidable knowledge of legal forms
and "genres" that Usk's hitherto documented career has not fully explained.[130] The "Appeal" also shows close knowledge of Northampton's
and More's attempt to gain endorsement of the mayor's power to pro-
secute usurers in London, an effort that Usk later says he regretted,
since "vnder colour ther-of [of arrest for usury] shulde . . . haue vndo
the worthy membres of the town that had be a-yens" Northampton and
his followers (lines 112–15). The effort to attack usurers—perhaps not
coincidentally echoed by Langland's address to mayors in the C-text
scene with Lady Meed noted above (C III.108–14)—would have directly targeted Maghfeld and his higher civic associates. Like Langland's
outburst on this to "mayres," the plan to denounce usurers was not an
antimercantile protest but an ideal of transparency in urban promotion,
which Usk may well have promoted until he realized it was itself a cover
for further personal ambition. The plan to indict urban usurers received

[128] Caroline Barron, *London in the Later Middle Ages: Government and People, 1200–
1500* (Oxford: Oxford University Press, 2004), 168–69.

[129] Penny Tucker, *Law Courts and Lawyers in the City of London, 1300–1530* (Cambridge: Cambridge University Press, 2007), 84–130.

[130] Paul Strohm, "The Textual Vicissitudes of Usk's 'Appeal,'" in *Hochon's Arrow: The
Social Imagination of Fourteenth-Century Texts* (Princeton: Princeton University Press,
1992), 145–60 (147–48).

no special help from the king or parliament (who simply endorsed the jurisdiction of holy church "as it used to have of old"),[131] but far more effective in causing urban change if not reform was Usk's unsolicited "Appeal," which did its work in bringing More and Northampton to account. By October 1387, both were exiled from London and Usk was elevated to undersheriff in the office where he had labored as a minor clerk.

Chaucer found a way to leave London shortly before the Merciless Parliament of 1388, in which, on March 3, Usk was convicted and immediately executed by the Lords Appellant, when they swept down on the city to put Richard's noble and civic supporters on trial. But there are no signs in Usk's writing or life that he was eager to depart. Even when he denounced his own earlier assistance to Northampton and More, he did so, he says in his "Appeal," because they acted "ayeins the Franchise of london for euer" (line 102). This need not be a trite formula or an attempt to address the king, for whom it would have had little force. As a sheriff's clerk, Usk might have thought he was furthering the ideals he initially saw in Northampton and More by summoning to justice such a wealthy guildsman and usurer as Maghfeld. Although he later repudiated any efforts to pit "the worthy persones" against "the smale people of the town" (line 73), it is possible that Usk indeed simply changed his view of how London might achieve the "peace" appropriate for the Athens of England, without changing his attachment to those fundamental goals.

Amid so many changing stratagems, it is impossible to know Usk's outlook on his service as civic summoner or anything else. But traveling to the imposing Billingsgate house with its butler, cook, four servants, clerks, and private wharf, arriving like Truth with a writ making an inexorable demand for just repayment, Usk would have delivered charges from a host of London merchants demanding due civic service from the wealthy Maghfeld, known usurer and client to nobility and the king. In the *Testament,* Love tells Thomas of the final social accounting that wealth and position receive: "Suche rychesse ben more worthy whan they ben in gatheryng: in departing gynneth his love of other mens praysyng. And avaryce gatheryng maketh be hated and nedy to many out-helpes ["outside helpers" *or perhaps* "those beyond help"]; and whan leveth the possessyuon of such goodes and they gynne vanyssh,

[131] *Rotuli Parliamentorum,* 3:143.

than entreth sorowe and tene in their hertes. O, badde and strayte ben thilke that at their departynge maketh men teneful and sory, and in the gatheryng of hem make men nedy!" (II.5.42–48). Advancement in his own London administrative and political career may well have been Usk's main motivation in serving the summons, but it is at least possible that other, equally potent impulses—at least representation of collective mercantile outrage at Maghfeld for negligence in civic duties, if not wider ideals of civic communalism or transparency—stirred him to his task of delivering the writs, on which, after all, his is the only name to appear all four times. To bring the great to account would dramatically sublimate to new uses the mercantile documentary culture by which Maghfeld so clearly was seeking his own enrichment. The promise of civic "peace" and a new Athens might even seem to be folded in the summons, fragments though they were of London's expanding documentary mercantile culture, just as in the *Testament* were "many privy thingȝ wimpled and folde" (III.9.68), amid the myriad obligations and profits that, as Maghfeld and all the Ricardian London writers knew, account books and literary treasures alike contained.

Unpleasures of the Flesh:

Medieval Marriage, Masochism, and the History of Heterosexuality

Sarah Salih
King's College London

T
WENTY-FIRST-CENTURY SCHOLARSHIP ON MEDIEVAL SEXUAL-
ITY has been much concerned with the fits and the misfits of the terms
in which these two periods conceptualize sexual matters. Historians of
sexuality have debated the utility of modern identity categories such as
"homosexual" in premodern contexts since Michel Foucault proclaimed
that "the sodomite had been a temporary aberration; the homosexual
was now a species."[1] More recent studies have extended the logic to
query the relevance of "heterosexuality" and its cognates to medieval
sexuality, for if homosexuality is a postmedieval concept, so too is heterosexuality, which has meaning only in relation to its twin. Judith Butler's analysis of the interdependence of homosexual "copy" and
heterosexual "original" dismantles the claims of heterosexuality to be
natural.[2] Jonathan Katz argues that heterosexuality has a history, and
that "an official, dominant, different-sex erotic ideal—a heterosexual
ethic—is . . . a modern invention."[3] While sexual contacts between men

Versions of this material were presented at the CMRS Ahmanson Conference,
"Medieval Sexuality 2009," UCLA, March 2009; at the Centre for Gender History,
University of Glasgow; to the Cambridge University Middle English Graduate Seminar;
to the Centre for Medieval and Early Modern Research, Swansea University. I am grateful to all concerned. Thanks also to Clare Lees and Bob Mills for encouragement and to
the anonymous readers for their detailed comments.

[1] Michel Foucault, *The History of Sexuality: An Introduction,* trans. Robert Hurley (Harmondsworth: Penguin, 1979), 43. On the problem of medieval "homosexuality," see
Robert Mills, "Homosexuality: Specters of Sodom," in *A Cultural History of Sexuality in
the Middle Ages,* ed. Ruth Evans (New York: Berg, 2011), 57–79.

[2] Judith Butler, "Imitation and Gender Subordination," in *The Lesbian and Gay Studies Reader,* ed. Henry Abelove, Michèle Aina Barale, and David Halperin (New York:
Routledge, 1993), 307–20 (313).

[3] Jonathan Ned Katz, *The Invention of Heterosexuality* (New York: Plume, 1996), 14.

and women have occurred throughout history, these actions were not necessarily conceptualized as manifestations of heterosexuality. Karma Lochrie's *Heterosyncrasies* and James Schultz's *Courtly Love, the Love of Courtliness, and the History of Sexuality* doubt that there was such a thing as medieval heterosexuality, or heteronormativity.[4] Lochrie and Schultz agree that "desire in medieval texts is not heterosexual: that is, it is not called into being by the sex of the object of desire."[5] Schultz thus argues for the elimination of the term from analyses of medieval sexuality: "If one refuses to abandon heterosexuality as a category of analysis, one refuses the effort to think outside the terms set by this regime. . . . Unless we are willing to make this effort, we will never be able to recognize the criteria according to which medieval people understood their intimate relations."[6] Lochrie, distinguishing heterosexuality from heteronormativity, argues that we need to "drive a methodological wedge between the modern identity formation we call heterosexuality, which is heteronormative, and past sexualities, which were not governed by heteronormativity."[7] Her formula leaves room to discover forms of heterosexuality other than modern heteronormativity: it does not prohibit the use of such terms but recommends an "epistemological humility" about the limits of their explanatory potential.[8]

Such humility liberates. It would hardly be practical to write criticism in an English innocent of all postmedieval language; most of the terms we use to discuss the Middle Ages, including the periodization itself, are anachronistic. Nevertheless, as Schultz warns, the unexamined use of terms such as "heterosexuality" risks producing misrecognitions. There are certainly moments in medieval literature when sexual difference is productive of desire, such as Troilus's admiration of Criseyde as a creature "nevere lasse mannyssh."[9] However, to assume that this moment is fully comprehensible once it has been labeled "heterosexuality" is to foreclose investigation into how it might relate to other motors of desire

---

[4] Karma Lochrie, *Heterosyncrasies: Female Sexuality When Normal Wasn't* (Minneapolis: University of Minnesota Press, 2005); James A. Schultz, *Courtly Love, the Love of Courtliness, and the History of Sexuality* (Chicago: University of Chicago Press, 2006); see also Ruth Mazo Karras, *Sexuality in Medieval Europe: Doing unto Others* (New York: Routledge, 2005).

[5] Lochrie, *Heterosyncrasies,* xiv.

[6] Schultz, *Courtly Love,* 57.

[7] Lochrie, *Heterosyncrasies,* xvi.

[8] Ibid., xvii.

[9] *Troilus and Criseyde,* I.284. Quotations from Chaucer are from *The Riverside Chaucer,* gen. ed. Larry D. Benson (Oxford: Oxford University Press, 1988).

in this poem; to obscure the complexity of Chaucer's anatomy of desire by seeing only what is already known. But although we should not expect a term such as "heterosexuality" fully to encompass medieval desires, the juxtaposition of the two may be informative. Marriage, a formulation that both Schultz and Lochrie identify as requiring scrutiny, insistently presents itself as a test case.[10] If medieval sexuality is not heteronormative, how do we understand that substantial body of legislation, narrative, rituals, images, and architecture that defined and supported the institution of marriage? What was marriage, and to what extent was its organization of gender, sex, difference, and power reliant on sexual difference?

Although there are numerous social and legal histories of medieval marriage, utilizing the rich records of the ecclesiastical courts, marriage was a relatively minor theme within the first wave of medieval sexuality studies. Such studies concentrated on the marginal, the saints or the sodomites, while skirting around the apparently more central topic of marriage. Vern Bullough and James Brundage's *Handbook of Medieval Sexuality,* for example, includes a chapter on chaste, that is, unconsummated, marriage but not one on the standard version.[11] Complementarily, Sue Niebrzydowski sites her study of literary wives, and by implication the whole topic of marriage, too, outwith the history of sexuality, differentiating it from "post modern critical practices that . . . interrogate lifestyles and sexualities other than normative, married heterosexuality."[12] However, studies of sexuality are becoming more interested in marriage, in part because controversy over gay marriage in the United States has made the history of the institution a question of current political import.[13] Medievalists such as Glenn Burger and Emma Lipton have taken the opportunity to show how marriage has varied through time and has answered to the needs of its moments.[14]

The importance of marriage to medieval culture can hardly be overstated:

[10] Schultz, *Courtly Love,* 60–61; Lochrie, *Heterosyncrasies,* xv.

[11] *Handbook of Medieval Sexuality,* ed. Vern L. Bullough and James A. Brundage (New York: Garland, 1996).

[12] Sue Niebrzydowski, *Bonoure and Buxum: A Study of Wives in Late Medieval English Literature* (Oxford: Peter Lang, 2006), 11.

[13] Emma Lipton, *Affections of the Mind: The Politics of Sacramental Marriage in Late Medieval English Literature* (Notre Dame: University of Notre Dame Press, 2007), 1.

[14] Glenn Burger, *Chaucer's Queer Nation* (Minneapolis: University of Minnesota Press, 2003); Lipton, *Affections of the Mind.*

> For Sposaylle es, als men may se,
> A state of grete auctorite,
> Of dignyte, and of halynesse.[15]

As Saint Augustine argued, "The first natural bond of human society is man and wife."[16] Both a sacrament and a contract, marriage secured the relations of individuals, families, and communities at all levels of society. As the only means of producing legitimate children, it was essential to the formation of dynasties and to the orderly transmission of property through the generations. Marriage was the culmination of romance plots, marking the achievement of adult masculinity. It was the subject of hundreds of sermons, both Latin and vernacular, and of a substantial literature of conduct books, which taught girls how to become wives. The gentry letter collections are full of news of the marriage market and marriage negotiations. Ecclesiastical courts did much of their business ruling on marital questions, and the late medieval laity understood the canonical status of marriage very well.[17] Medieval marriage was thus culturally privileged, but it was also a lesser good. In chastity literature, it was spiritually the lowest of the three states of virginity, widowhood, and marriage, which were to be rewarded in heaven, respectively, one hundredfold, sixtyfold and thirtyfold.[18] "[W]edlakes heuel bedd," the "mattress of wedlock," as the virginity treatise *Hali Meiðhad* puts it, catches the sexually active as they hurtle downward in their spiritual fall from the high tower of virginity, keeping them in a safe, but lowly, position.[19] In this image, marriage is the central point of a continuum, with virginity at one end and a mass of unregulated sexual activities— fornication, whoredom, sodomy—at the other, a scale moving from no sex through some regulated sex to uncontrolled forms and amounts of it. Marriage, to make a thoroughly anachronistic analogy, is like vacci-

[15] Ralph Hanna, ed., *Speculum Vitae: A Reading Edition,* 2 vols., EETS o.s. 331–32 (Oxford: Oxford University Press, 2008), vol. 2, lines 10991–93.

[16] Augustine, *On the Good of Marriage,* chap. 1, http://www.newadvent.org/fathers/1309.htm. Text from C. L. Cornish, trans., *From Nicene and Post-Nicene Fathers,* First Series, vol. 3, ed. Philip Schaff (Buffalo: Christian Literature Publishing Co., 1887); edited for New Advent by Kevin Knight.

[17] Frederik Pedersen, *Marriage Disputes in Medieval England* (London: Hambledon, 2000), 59–84.

[18] *Hali Meiðhad,* in *Middle English Prose for Women from the Katherine Group and Ancrene Wisse,* ed. Bella Millett and Jocelyn Wogan-Browne (Oxford: Clarendon Press, 1990), 20.

[19] *Hali Meiðhad,* 18.

nation: a weakened strain of that dangerously infective substance, sexual pleasure, is deliberately administered under controlled conditions in order to protect against the more virulent strains of sodomy and whoredom.

What is distinctive about marriage, as opposed either to chastity or to unregulated sexuality, is that its cultural work is to stabilize and reinforce the asymmetric coupling of man and woman, husband and wife, and that sex is one of its methods for doing so. Chastity and virginity may have gender-disturbing effects; chaste marriage often unravels husbandly authority and female virgins might be differentiated from women.[20] Mystical erotic devotion to Christ, often a key feature of chaste lives, destabilizes gender identities, for both men and women might adore him, in highly erotic terms, and his own gender is very slippery.[21] Unregulated sex, in the forms of sodomy or whoring, is effeminizing to the men who engage in it because it shows a failure to exert properly masculine self-control.[22] Marriage, however, ensures the stability of gender difference: hence considerable cultural energy is devoted to the task of doing marriage properly.

Michel Foucault argues that premodern marriage was not, as it was later to become, that which is unscrutinized because it is taken for granted: "The sex of husbands and wives was beset by rules and recommendations. The marriage relation was the most intense focus of constraints; it was spoken of more than anything else; more than any other relation, it was required to give a detailed accounting of itself."[23] There was indeed a substantial effort to examine and regulate marital behavior. Such regulation was not a top-down imposition: married and marriageable people actively participated in giving accounts of the state. Charles Donahue's study of marital cases in the ecclesiastical courts concludes that "the medieval canonical legal system could not operate for

---

[20] Dyan Elliott, *Spiritual Marriage: Sexual Abstinence in Medieval Wedlock* (Princeton: Princeton University Press, 1993), 252–24; Sarah Salih, *Versions of Virginity in Late Medieval England* (Cambridge: Brewer, 2001), 38.

[21] Karma Lochrie, "Mystical Acts, Queer Tendencies," in *Constructing Medieval Sexuality,* ed. Karma Lochrie, Peggy McCracken, and James A. Schultz (Minneapolis: University of Minnesota Press, 1999), 180–200.

[22] Karma Lochrie, *Covert Operations: The Medieval Uses of Secrecy* (Philadelphia: University of Pennsylvania Press, 1999), 186–92; Shannon McSheffrey, *Marriage, Sex, and Civic Culture in Late Medieval London* (Philadelphia: University of Pennsylvania Press, 2006), 175.

[23] Foucault, *History of Sexuality,* 37.

long without the cooperation of a large number of participants."[24] Disrupted and disputed marriages accounted for a significant proportion of the business of such courts: Donahue's figures show that matrimonial cases were the second most common category after ecclesiastical matters in the courts of York and of Ely, and that they demanded more court time, and generated more documentation, than other kinds of case.[25] The penitential text *Handlyng Synne* devotes its entire 446-line commentary on the sixth commandment, which it translates as "Þou shalt noun hordam do," to the regulation of marriage, including warnings that some apparently marital relationships are in fact versions of *hordam*, or illicit sex.[26] It seems actively designed to produce sexual anxiety in married people. Although the purpose of marriage was to secure gender stability and protect against sexual sin, it could not do so automatically. It required regulation because, left unexamined, it might become a site of disruption as married couples took advantage of their relative privacy to explore forbidden erotic possibilities such as nonmissionary positions or oral and anal sex. One medieval ghost story, for example, turns on the need to expose and correct marital sodomy, and hence on a fear that such behavior might easily go undetected.[27] In *Dives and Pauper*'s application of the Ten Commandments to fifteenth-century English life, the priest Pauper explained to the alarmed layman Dives that there are no fewer than eight forms of "synful medlyng togedere atwoxsyn housebounde & wif": sex remained live and unpredictable within marriage.[28] As Lochrie shows, improper marital sex constituted "an insurrection of gender categories and hierarchies."[29] Because all postlapsarian sex was a consequence and reenactment of human fallibility, the sexual pleasure admitted to marriage needed constant vigilance to protect it from corruption.

Medieval marriage, then, was not identical to heterosexuality as it

---

[24] Charles Donahue Jr., *Law, Marriage, and Society in the Later Middle Ages: Arguments About Marriage in Five Courts* (Cambridge: Cambridge University Press, 2007), 569.

[25] Ibid., 224–25; "matrimonial" includes two out of 117 cases of fornication.

[26] Frederick J. Furnivall, ed., *Robert of Brunne's "Handlyng Synne,"* EETS o.s. 119 (London: Kegan Paul, Trench, Trübner and Co., 1901), lines 1601–2046 (1654).

[27] Robert S. Sturges, "Purgatory in the Marriage Bed: Conjugal Sodomy in the *Gast of Gy*," in *Framing the Family: Narrative and Representation in the Medieval and Early Modern Periods,* ed. Rosalynn Voaden and Diane Wolfthal (Tempe: Arizona Center for Medieval and Renaissance Studies, 2005), 58–78.

[28] Priscilla Heath Barnum, ed., *Dives and Pauper,* vol. 1, pt. 2, EETS o.s. 280 (London: Oxford University Press, 1980), 58.

[29] Lochrie, *Covert Operations,* 185.

operates in the present-day West: crucially, it was not an unmarked category and did not have the heteronormative privilege of being unexamined. But it was *a* heterosexuality: a regulation of sexual activity organized around and securing gender difference. In this study, I examine marital sexuality—both the sexuality of marriage and the maritality of the sex—by focusing on a potentially distinctive feature of marital sex: that it has the capacity to be unpleasurable; that it may be endorsed despite or even because of that unpleasure; that this unpleasure may mark the difference between husband and wife's experience of marriage. Saint Paul's ruling, "Let the husband render the debt to his wife, and the wife also in like manner to the husband. The wife hath not power of her own body, but the husband. And in like manner the husband also hath not power of his own body, but the wife," elaborated and institutionalized by the canonists, obliged both husband and wife to satisfy their partner on demand.[30] The obligation to render the debt operated quite independently of procreation, the other legitimate function of marital sex: as Elizabeth M. Makowski points out, "Paul's purpose for marital union was not specifically procreative."[31] The debt meant that marital sex might be recommended or compulsory, and yet also that it was never an uncomplicated pleasure. Saint Augustine, in *On the Good of Marriage,* one of the founding texts of medieval marriage theory, argued that one virtue of the state was that it muted sexual pleasure: "[T]he lust of the flesh is repressed, and rages in a way more modestly, being tempered by parental affection. For there is interposed a certain gravity of glowing pleasure, when in that wherein husband and wife cleave to one another, they have in mind that they be father and mother."[32] To make sex less sexy, to make it an obligation rather than an indulgence, is hence a function of marriage. The laity was instructed in this concept of marriage: as Chaucer's Parson put it, "Man sholde loven hys wyf by discrecioun, paciently and atemprely, and thane is she as though it were his suster," and penitential texts taught that approaching a spouse for pleasure alone was a kind of adultery.[33] There are scant references to what must often have been the resulting unplea-

[30] 1 Corinthians 7:3–4; James A. Brundage, *Law, Sex, and Christian Society in Medieval Europe* (Chicago: University of Chicago Press, 1987), 241–42.

[31] Pierre J. Payer, *The Bridling of Desire: Views of Sex in the Later Middle Ages* (Toronto: University of Toronto Press, 1993), 84–86; Elizabeth M. Makowski, "The Conjugal Debt and Medieval Canon Law," *JMH* 3 (1977): 99–114 (100).

[32] Augustine, *On the Good of Marriage,* chap. 3.

[33] *Canterbury Tales,* X. 860; Payer, *The Bridling of Desire,* 122.

sures of marital sex. The marital sins listed in *Dives and Pauper,* for example, include excessive pleasures and matters such as sex in holy times and places, but the text has nothing to say about the absence of pleasure.[34] As David Aers remarks in relation to Margery Kempe, such sexual distress is a "common area of traditional female experience habitually blocked from literary record and exploration."[35] My aim here is to inquire further how people—most often women—understood and lived with the obligation to enact something that they may have experienced as boring, painful, humiliating, or disgusting.

I would suggest that there must surely have been a kind of pleasure in submission, in the awareness of one's conformity to an experience that was not in itself pleasant, and that response is what I am interested in examining here. The pleasure or unpleasure of sex is not necessarily located in the bodily act itself, but in the narrative framework of what it means. William Simon argues that the pleasures of sex may be largely social or narrative:

What has been neglected in the naturalization of the sexual is its capacity for and reliance upon a complex text, a script of the erotic. . . . Even within the context of overtly sexual acts, outside of the visible but indeterminate capacities of orgasm, pleasure or satisfaction is determined in critical ways by sociocultural meanings that occasion the sexual event and by the personal meanings occasioned by that event. The pleasuring capacities of the sexual event are the result of effective performance of the actor's interpersonal script and its embodiment of elements of the actor's intrapsychic script. In the necessary interplay between these two levels of scripting, the derived pleasure most often proves to be complex rather than pure.[36]

That is, people do not seek, have, and enjoy sex simply for sexual reasons, for the pleasure of the bodily act; they seek, have, and enjoy sex for reasons connected with their narratives of their selves. Bodily pleasure may be a minor consideration, or even entirely absent, yet sex still be entirely satisfactory. If we recognize the sexual motives of apparently nonsexual social behaviors, as Simon argues, we should also recognize the nonsexual motives in sexual behavior.[37] Simon assumes that such

[34] Barnum, *Dives and Pauper,* vol. 1, pt. 2, 58–59.
[35] David Aers, *Community, Gender, and Individual Identity: English Writing, 1360–1430* (London: Routledge, 1988), 90.
[36] William Simon, *Postmodern Sexualities* (London: Routledge, 1996), 29–30.
[37] Ibid., 47.

complexity is characteristic of postmodernism, and unavailable in traditional or "paradigmatic" societies, but attention to the social aspects of sexual pleasure in medieval texts indicates that this was a society rich in sexual narrative.[38]

In the context of medieval marriage, one such motive might be the pleasure derived from obedience and conformity. Enacting unpleasant sex would have permitted a form of agency that was enacted as self-denial and self-abnegation. Medieval marriage practices offered various opportunities for sexual obedience, for marital obligations were not easily evaded. The most numerous marital cases in the ecclesiastical courts were those brought by people seeking a judgment that their marriage was valid, often (though not inevitably) in the face of their putative spouse's denial of it.[39] There were, of course, good practical reasons why people might have sought to compel a reluctant spouse to live with them. The indissolubility of marriage left deserted partners, whether men or women, in an undesirable limbo, enjoying none of the benefits of marriage but not free to marry elsewhere. Women, in particular, would have an incentive to avoid the social disadvantage of living with a tainted reputation, and/or the financial struggle of single parenthood. Donahue finds that in both York and Ely in the fourteenth and fifteenth centuries "women valued marriage more than did men" and were more tenacious in their claims.[40] Nevertheless, successful plaintiffs would then be faced with the problem of reestablishing intimacy with a partner who might well have rejected them in word and deed, to the extent, in some cases, of marrying someone else, and who now required legal compulsion to persuade them to return to the marriage bed. Courts routinely instructed reconciling couples to live together amicably: "William . . . bishop of Lincoln . . . ordered Thomas Halys . . . and Agnes his wife . . . who for some time previously had separated from bed and board contrary to the rules of canon law, that they should forthwith live together as man and wife, that Thomas should treat Agnes in a proper way as his wife, and that Agnes should obey Thomas as her husband."[41] In some cases this remedy failed, and couples persisted in living apart: in

[38] Ibid., 8–9.
[39] R. H. Helmholz, *Marriage Litigation in Medieval England* (Cambridge: Cambridge University Press, 1974), 25.
[40] Donahue, *Law, Marriage, and Society*, 234.
[41] P. J. P. Goldberg, ed., *Women in England, c. 1275–1525: Documentary Sources* (Manchester: Manchester University Press, 1995), 136.

others, though, enforced intimacy must have reestablished the relation-ship.[42]

Although Christian sexual ethics limit the variety of possible sexual acts in marriage, they make available, as if in compensation, diverse narrative pleasures. The theory of marital debt obliges spouses to com-municate their desires to one another; Thomas Aquinas taught that hus-bands should be sufficiently attuned to their wives' sexual rhythms and signals to offer the debt to a wife too modest to make an explicit re-quest.[43] The canonists thought through the theory of marital debt by imagining scenarios, which pastoral instruction then obligingly con-veyed to the laity. Marital debt should not be requested during holy times: but if it were so requested, it should nevertheless be rendered.[44] It took precedence over other obligations: "a married serf whose wife demanded that he make love to her at the same time that his manorial lord required his services in the field ought to obey his lord, unless there was imminent danger that his wife might commit fornication. If the wife insisted, however, he was to comply with her demand."[45] The nar-ratives of marital debt, in which sex is subject to command, have a distinctly S and M flavor. Masochism, like heterosexuality, is a label picked from the nineteenth-century sexologists' toolkit, but it may never-theless illuminate some aspects of medieval marital relations. Criticism has discerned masochistic dynamics in the apparently more outré and culture-specific forms of medieval eros—courtly love and mystical desire—but the erotics of power, I would argue, are equally essential to mar-riage.[46] As Kristina Hildebrand argues, "Power, in a patriarchy, is sexy," and marriage is an institution fundamental to patriarchal power.[47] The interaction of sex and power, however, is rich and unpredictable. By eroticizing power, masochism turns it inside out. Masochism is "made

[42] Michael M. Sheehan, *Marriage, Family, and Law in Medieval Europe: Collected Studies,* ed. James K. Farge (Cardiff: University of Wales Press, 1996), 269.

[43] Payer, *Bridling of Desire,* 94; for further discussion, see Alcuin Blamires, *Chaucer, Ethics, and Gender* (Oxford: Oxford University Press, 2006), 81–83.

[44] Payer, *Bridling of Desire,* 100.

[45] Brundage, *Law, Sex, and Christian Society,* 359.

[46] See, e.g., Jeffrey Jerome Cohen, "Masoch/Lancelotism," *NLH* 28 (1997): 231–60; Julie B. Miller, "Eroticized Violence in Medieval Women's Mystical Literature: A Call for a Feminist Critique," *Journal of Feminist Studies in Religion* 15 (1999): 25–49.

[47] Kristina Hildebrand, "Her Desire and His: Letters Between Fifteenth-Century Lovers," in *The Erotic in the Literature of Medieval Britain,* ed. Amanda Hopkins and Cory James Rushton (Cambridge: D. S. Brewer, 2007), 132–41 (138).

to the measure of the victim"; it is the victim who takes responsibility for staging his or her domination.[48]

Marital debt means that power is never absent from marital sex, but pleasure is not thereby precluded: marital debt, indeed, resembles the "contractual relations" that Gilles Deleuze finds to be the defining feature of masochism.[49] Marital debt both reinforces and disrupts sexual differentiation. It sets up a utopian zone in which power is radically mobile. To marry is voluntarily to put one's body at the disposal of another. The ideal state of mind for the married person is that of the mystic, to have "no will at all that she has to will," because all volition has already been surrendered.[50] Marriage dissolves the boundaries of personhood as the partners become one flesh; marital debt enables the raptures of total control of the other and total emptying of the self. Gerard Loughlin argues that Paul's concept of marital debt was developed in a world where sexual slavery was a mundane reality: "Paul, at his most radical, imagines marriage as a partnership between sex slaves, where each disposes of his body for the use of the other, in imitation of their mutual master, who is the slave of all: a body entirely dispossessed for want of the other."[51] Its radicalism is that its slavery is not an inherent condition of the person, but a position that one must occupy for the duration of a partner's demand. The fact that both parties may demand and render the debt does not make this a relation of equality: it makes it two relations of supreme inequality. Power is exercised by the partner who demands and obeyed by the partner who renders: its full weight is at any one time on one side or the other. Marital debt gives rise to paradoxes: while requesting the debt might be sinful in some circumstances, it was generally considered that rendering it was innocent, and might even be meritorious.[52] The canonist Huguccio argued indeed that marital sex was free of sin only when performed out of obedience and

[48] Slavoj Žižek, "From Courtly Love to *The Crying Game*," *New Left Review* I/202 (1993): 1–9 (3).

[49] Gilles Deleuze, "Coldness and Cruelty," in *Masochism* (New York: Zone Books, 1991), 9–138 (20).

[50] Margaret Porette, *The Mirror of Simple Souls,* trans. Edmund Colledge, J. C. Marler, and Judith Grant (Notre Dame: University of Notre Dame Press, 1999), 27.

[51] Gerard Loughlin, *Alien Sex: The Body and Desire in Cinema and Theology* (Oxford: Blackwell, 2004), 182.

[52] James A. Brundage, "Implied Consent to Intercourse," in *Consent and Coercion to Sex and Marriage in Ancient and Medieval Societies,* ed. Angeliki E. Laiou (Washington, D.C.: Dumbarton Oaks Research Library and Collection, 1993), 245–56 (250–51).

without pleasure.[53] Only enforced sex, then, was untainted; physical and social rewards diverged.

Marital debt, in theory, was gender-neutral, and must indeed sometimes have been so in practice. It was a real obligation for husbands: pastoral literature instructed that they would be responsible should a sexually unsatisfied wife resort to adultery.[54] It is plausible that wives might have developed playful, seductive, and affectionate ways of invoking the debt, and authority would have been on their side. The debt is sometimes seen to counter sexual inequity; John W. Baldwin, for example, characterizes it as a "symmetrical relationship between spouses that resisted the imbalance of patriarchal society."[55] However, feminist analysis of medieval marriage is more skeptical, identifying marital debt as an enforcement of men's ownership of their wives' bodies. Dyan Elliott argues that "it is impossible that the debt alone should be free from all inequities built into the gender system."[56] The theoretical equality of marital debt must often have been outweighed by the obligation of wifely obedience. A bride might promise, while a bridegroom would not, to be "bonere and buxom in bedde and atte borde."[57] As we will see, husbands might use the debt to force sex on reluctant wives, but a wife would find it more difficult to force a reluctant husband.

Hence the debt must often have weighed more heavily on women. Some texts tell consoling narratives about how such wives' sexual misery might be evaded or ameliorated. There are plenty of stories, usually comic, about marital incompatibility: Chaucer's *Merchant's Tale,* for example, is quite specific about May's revulsion from sex with old January:

> The slakke skyn aboute his nekke shaketh,
> Whil that he sang, so chaunteth he and craketh.
> But God woot what that May thoughte in hir herte,
> Whan she hym saugh up sittynge in his sherte,
> In his nyght-cappe, and with his nekke lene;
> She preyseth nat his pleyyng worth a bene.[58]

[53] Makowski, "The Conjugal Debt and Medieval Canon Law," 103.

[54] Furnivall, *Robert of Brunne's "Handlyng Synne,"* lines 1877–86.

[55] John W. Baldwin, "Consent and the Marital Debt: Five Discourses in Northern France Around 1200," in *Consent and Coercion to Sex and Marriage,* ed. Laiou, 257–70 (259).

[56] Elliott, *Spiritual Marriage,* 148.

[57] W. G. Henderson, ed., *Manuale et Processionale ad Usum Insignis Ecclesiae Eboracensis,* Surtees Society LXIII (Durham: Andrews, 1875), 19*.

[58] *The Merchant's Tale,* IV.1849–54.

But this is fabliau, and so the resolution is comic: when May finds a more satisfactory lover, her obligations to her husband are allowed to fade out of the picture. Medical texts, such as the English "liber Trotularis," allude to the sufferings of women who find penetration painful, because they "mowe not suffer a mannes yerde for þe gretnesse þerof, & summe tyme þey be constreyned to suffer wyl they nyl they"; it then seeks to ameliorate the problem, either by prescribing ointments and medicines for the women, or administering antiaphrodisiacs to men.[59] *Hali Meiðhad* hints darkly at the horrors of the marriage bed, where the bride must "ȝeuest þin beare bodi to tukin swa to wundre, ant feare wið se scheomeliche" [give up your naked body to be so scandalously abused and treated so shamefully]: its proposed remedy is that the reader should commit herself to virginity to avoid being subjected to this licit nastiness.[60] These texts acknowledge sexual unpleasure as a problem for which there are remedies. However, neither virginity nor adultery was an option for an obedient wife, and medical remedies cannot always have been available and effective: there must have remained many women who could neither enjoy nor evade marital sex.

Although marital debt might oblige wives to have unpleasant sex, its narrative power compensated them with a framework for understanding their experiences. Wifely obedience enabled them to activate the masochistic potential of marital debt. I will now go on to reconsider three fairly well-known texts that concern women's obedience in the face of unpleasurable marital sex, and the rewards and pleasures that they extract from their obedience. The texts are of different genres—witness statement, private letter, and autohagiography—but more important is that all are presented as factual narratives, and that their efficacy depends on their being credible. The participants are members of the rural gentry and the urban elite: since these groups intermarried, we should not expect to find their expectations of marriage markedly divergent. In these social groups, almost all women married, some more than once; the contribution of wives to the family interests was acknowledged and respected, but they were nevertheless expected to make displays of deference and obedience. Lipton argues that the marital culture of these "middle strata" favored what she describes as "sacramental marriage," "a partnership between husband and wife," which modeled a "horizon-

---

[59] Beryl Rowland, ed., *Medieval Woman's Guide to Health: The First English Gynecological Handbook* (London: Croom Helm, 1981), 46, 166.

[60] *Hali Meiðhad*, 24.

tal" ideal of social relations.[61] She sees marital debt as a force that militates against such relationships:

Complicating the sacramental definition of marriage as consent, medieval theologians also taught the doctrine of the marital debt that required couples to engage in marital sex if the other partner required it. Another tension was between an understanding of marriage as a partnership based in love, a vision linked to the sacramental model, and a depiction of marriage as the rule of the husband over his wife. . . . Juxtaposition of conflicting marriage models without an acknowledgement of their seeming incompatibility is characteristic of late medieval marriage teachings.[62]

However, it may not be necessary to separate consent and debt, love and authority: it is quite possible that marriage was experienced as simultaneously consensual and contractual, affective and hierarchical, and that no incompatibility was perceived. I would argue that marriages may be companionate and mutually affectionate while still operating a specifically sexual inequality, and that such inequality may have been acceptable or indeed pleasurable to one or both partners. David Gary Shaw argues persuasively that burgesses' wives appeared to the world not as autonomous individuals, but as aspects of their husbands' social selves; sexual obedience might constitute the private face of this subordination.[63]

Three Examples

A case from the York consistory court shows the cultural normality of sexual unpleasure. Marrays c. de Rouclif is a suit for the restitution of conjugal rights, brought in 1365 by John Marrays, formally against his putative wife, Alice de Rouclif, but effectively against Sir Brian de Rouclif, her kinsman, guardian, or overlord, who had removed her from Marrays's sister's household.[64] The case depends on whether the mar-

---

[61] Lipton, *Affections of the Mind*, 9. "Sacramental marriage" is recognizable as what social historians know as "companionate marriage."

[62] Lipton, *Affections of the Mind*, 3.

[63] David Gary Shaw, *Necessary Conjunctions: The Social Self in Medieval England* (New York: Palgrave Macmillan, 2005), 201–2.

[64] York, Borthwick Institute for Historical Research, CP.E.89. There is no full edition of this document. Quotations are taken from the translated extracts in Goldberg, *Women in England*, 58–80: I am grateful to Professor Goldberg for confirming in a personal communication that these include all the substance of the witness statements. I am also

riage was valid, which in turn depends on whether Alice was of sufficient age to consent to it. That she did consent to marriage and consummation is not disputed: the question is whether she was almost eleven or almost twelve when she did so. Consummation, it is implied, was not a pleasurable experience. The court heard that John's niece Joan, who shared a room with Alice, had reported that "she saw John and Alice lying together in the same bed and heard a noise from them like they were making love together, and how two or three times Alice silently complained at the force on account of John's labour as if she had been hurt then as a result of this labour."[65] As Jeremy Goldberg cautions, this evidence should be read with an eye to its function. John Marrays's suit was for restitution of conjugal rights: his witness thus needed to prove that conjugal rights had in fact been established. The testimony is "designed to demonstrate not only that John Marrays and Alice de Rouclif shared a bed, not only that they had intended sex or even attempted sex, but that John had actually penetrated Alice."[66] Alice's complaint would be the sign that penetration had occurred; her silencing of it evidence that she obediently rendered her debt.

According to the witnesses, Alice, though she did not complain, negotiated. Two weeks later, as Anabilla Wascelyne, Marrays's sister, recalled, Alice said to John "Sir, I do not wish further to lie with you in bed before marriage is solemnised between us, for I am mature enough to be a true wife and not a mistress—in English 'leman.' "[67] Again, caution is necessary: Anabilla was proffering evidence of Alice's consent to the marriage. Nevertheless, the response had to be plausible and to fit an ecclesiastical court's conception of propriety; that John won his case indicates that it was and did. The court accepted that Alice made no complaint, despite the likelihood that her sexual experience had been painful, and that she wished the sexual relationship to continue, on condition that its status be clarified. Another witness understood Alice's

---

reliant on Goldberg's analysis of the legal and procedural issues. For interpretations of this case that differ in some respects, see Frederik Pedersen, "Marriage Contract and the Church Courts of Fourteenth-Century England," in *To Have and to Hold: Marriage and Its Documentation in Western Christendom, 400–1600,* ed. Philip L. Reynolds and John Witte (Cambridge: Cambridge University Press, 2007), 287–331 (303–6); and Pedersen, *Marriage Disputes,* 128–33.

[65] Goldberg, *Women in England,* 62.

[66] Jeremy Goldberg, *Communal Discord, Child Abduction, and Rape in the Later Middle Ages* (New York: Palgrave Macmillan, 2008), 106–7.

[67] Goldberg, *Women in England,* 61.

desire for John as a desire for obedience: "[Alice] was obedient to John as her husband because she lay with him in one bed alone and naked together and she would be obedient still if she were able."[68] If Alice had hoped that subsequent sexual activity would be more enjoyable, the thought goes unspoken; instead, witnesses report her repeatedly insisting that she was old enough, or adequate enough, to be a wife.[69] The sexual experience troubled her not, apparently, because it was physically unpleasant, but because the ambiguity of her marital status made her social identity uncertain: as Goldberg argues, her prime concern seems to have been her "sexual reputation."[70] Only marriage would give her the social reward of confirming her maturity. Whether she thought of sexual unpleasure as transient, or as inevitable, her prime concern was to ensure that she was appropriately rewarded for it with self-image and social position. She was, despite her youth, fully informed about its cultural value.

Another young woman spelled out in more detail the social rewards of sexual unpleasure. One of the best-known of the Paston letters, regularly cited to demonstrate the authoritarianism of medieval family values, concerns a proposed marriage between Elizabeth Paston and Stephen Scrope. In, probably, 1449, Elizabeth Clere, a cousin, wrote to John Paston I to alert him to the family's disharmony over the affair. Elizabeth Paston was at odds with her mother, Agnes, and was "betyn onys in þe weke or twyes, and som tyme twyes on o day, and hir hed broken in to or thre places."[71] However, she had managed to send a message to her cousin in which she outlined her thoughts on marriage to Scrope:

sche seith if ȝe may se be his evydences þat his childern and hire may enheryten, and sche to have resonable joynture, sche hath herd so mech of his birth and his condicions þat, and ȝe will, sche will have hym whethir þat hir moder wil or wil not, not-wythstandyng it is tolde hir his persone is simple, for sche seyth men shull haue þe more deynté of hire if sche rewle hire to hym as sche awte to do.

Of course, this may not be exactly what Elizabeth had said: however, I think it is likely to be accurate, at least in outline, and even if it is not,

[68] Ibid., 59.
[69] Ibid., 60, 70.
[70] Goldberg, *Communal Discord,* 122.
[71] Norman Davis, ed., *Paston Letters and Papers of the Fifteenth Century,* 2 vols. (Oxford: Clarendon Press, 1976), vol. 2, no. 446.

the important point is that this is a statement that could plausibly be attributed to a young woman in such a situation. In fact, the self-awareness and the sense of role-distance here ascribed to Elizabeth are not unlike the attitude Elizabeth herself displays in a later letter: having, eventually, married someone else, she cautiously feels her way into wifely attitudes and vocabulary: "And as for my mayster, my best-beloved that ye call, and I must nedes call hym so now, for I fynde noon oþer cause, and as I trust to Jesu neuer shall."[72]

Critical readings of Elizabeth Clere's letter are polarized. Clere, writing to a correspondent who was already aware of the situation, may have been less specific than we would like, but she does unambiguously report Elizabeth's conditional consent to the match. Nevertheless, the letter is often read to show that Agnes was trying to force her reluctant daughter to make a prestigious but personally repulsive marriage. Candace Gregory, for example, writes: "Agnes Paston began a long fight with her daughter Elizabeth over the latter's refusal to marry the man her mother had chosen for her. . . . The potential groom selected for Elizabeth was Stephen Scrope, step-son to Sir John Fastolf, but who was also thirty years older than she and disfigured by smallpox. For reasons that are fairly obvious, Elizabeth rejects what would have been a socially advantageous marriage offer."[73] For Gregory, Elizabeth's "obvious" priority was a marriage that offered personal gratifications that an unattractive older man was unlikely to provide. Kim Phillips, in a reading that makes better sense of the letter, argues that Elizabeth agreed to the marriage despite her mother's objections.[74] If Elizabeth Clere's report of her attention to her jointure is accurate, she was contemplating not only her future marriage but also her future widowhood. Marriage to Scrope thus presented itself to Elizabeth as an opportunity to become in due

[72] Ibid., vol. 1, no. 121.

[73] Candace Gregory, "Raising the Good Wife: Mother and Daughters in Fifteenth-Century England," in *Reputation and Representation in Fifteenth-Century Europe,* ed. Douglas L. Biggs, Sharon D. Michalove, and A. Compton-Reeves (Leiden: Brill, 2004), 145–67 (164). See also H. S. Bennett, *The Pastons and Their England,* 2nd ed. (1922; reprinted Cambridge: Canto, 1990), 30; and Ann Haskell, "The Paston Women on Marriage in Fifteenth-Century England," *Viator* 4 (1974): 459–71 (467), for readings based on the assumption that Elizabeth's refusal of Scrope was the problem; but see Diane Watt, *Medieval Women's Writing: Works by and for Women in England, 1100–1500* (Cambridge: Polity, 2007), 141–42, on the inconsistency of this letter with Agnes's own account.

[74] Kim M. Phillips, *Medieval Maidens: Young Women and Gender in England, 1270–1540* (Manchester: Manchester University Press, 2003), 185.

course one of the "rich old ladies" to whose hands numerous aristocratic and gentle estates stuck; to replicate, in fact, the life cycle of her own mother, who spent thirty-five years as the well-dowered widow of an older husband, managing her own property and wielding considerable authority over the family.[75]

To attain this position, Elizabeth was contemplating a marriage that she expected to be consummated, for she was making provision for future children, but from which she can have had no great hopes of sexual pleasure. Although she had not met Scrope, she was aware that he was sufficiently physically repulsive—"disfigured in my persone," as he himself acknowledged—for people to find it necessary to mention his condition as a possible hindrance to the match.[76] The lack of sexual interest was probably one-sided: Scrope had complained that he had been prevented from seeing Elizabeth, so he may well have thought, like January, that an old man "sholde . . . take a yong wyf and a feir, / On which he myghte engendren hym an heir, / And lede his lyf in joye and in solas."[77] For Elizabeth, however, Scrope's unattractiveness became, perversely, an attraction. Since submission to such a man would obviously not be a matter of personal gratification, her dutiful wifehood would ensure that "men shull have the more deynté of hire if sche rewle hire to hym as sche awte to do." She sketched a scenario in which observers would mark the mismatch between husband and wife and draw conclusions about the quality of their intimate relationship. Such a marriage was not likely to bring erotic satisfaction, but would—for that very reason—bring her instead the satisfactions of discipline, subordination, and conformity. The ostentatious performance of these virtues could be bartered into social power, producing the reputation for goodwifeliness, which would enhance her social standing. Marriage here is not a private zone but a theater, with a substantial audience among members of the Norfolk gentry, whom Elizabeth, quite rightly, presumes to be observing and passing comments on one another's success in maintaining proper marital relationships.

Elizabeth consented to marry Scrope under the considerable pressure

[75] Rowena Archer, "Rich Old Ladies: The Problem of Late Medieval Dowagers," in *Property and Politics: Essays in Later Medieval English History,* ed. Tony Pollard (Gloucester: Alan Sutton, 1984), 15–35; Colin Richmond, *The Paston Family in the Fifteenth Century: Fastolf's Will* (Cambridge: Cambridge University Press, 1996), 8.

[76] Richard Beadle and Colin Richmond, eds., *Paston Letters and Papers of the Fifteenth Century Part III,* EETS s.s. 22 (Oxford: Oxford University Press, 2005), no. 1012.

[77] *The Merchant's Tale,* IV.1271–73.

of familial disharmony and of the urgings of whoever had been telling her "so mech of his birth and his condicions." Elizabeth Clere endorsed her decision without enthusiasm: "me semeth he were good for my cosyn ʒowre sustyr wythowt þat ʒe myght gete here a bettyr," but that she wrote to John at all, risking Agnes's anger at her interference, shows how very undesirable the situation was. Elizabeth Paston coped with the pressure by exercising obedience, not to the immediate authority, her mother, but to her brother and, imaginatively, to her prospective husband. She was resourceful enough to use intermediaries to get a message to her brother; equally resourcefully, she found in the prospect of exercising obedience to Scrope a kind of ownership of her limited options.

The Book of Margery Kempe details a hagiographic variation, or extension, of Elizabeth's willed submission: Margery takes the pleasure of obedience and uses it not only as social but also spiritual credit. There are a few Continental hagiographies that treat the sexual martyrdom of unhappy marriages more explicitly, and to which this text has been compared.[78] However, Margery could equally well have developed her articulation of marital sexual unpleasantness from a starting point rather like that of Elizabeth Paston: the secular expectations of goodwifeliness. In 1436, recalling the events of maybe a quarter-century earlier, she gives a memorably intimate picture of her marriage. After hearing heavenly music:

sche had nevyr desyr to komown fleschly wyth hyre husbonde, for the dette of matrimony was so abhominabyl to hir that sche had levar, hir thowt, etyn or drynkyn the wose, the mukke in the chanel, than to consentyn to any fleschly comownyng, saf only for obedyens. And so sche seyd to hir husband: "I may not deny yow my body, but the lofe of myn hert and myn affeccyon is drawyn fro alle erdly creaturys and sett only in God." He wold have hys wylle, and sche obeyd wyth greet wepyng and sorwyng for that sche mygth not levyn chast. And oftyntymys this creatur cownseld hir husbond to levyn chast, and seyd that thei oftyntymes, sche wyst wel, had dysplesyd God be her inordynat lofe and the gret delectacyon that thei haddyn eythyr of hem in usyng of other, and now it wer good that thei schuld be her bothins wylle and consentyng of hem bothyn punschyn and chastysyn hemself wylfully be absteynyng fro her lust of her bodys.[79]

---

[78] Elliott, *Spiritual Marriage,* 228–30.
[79] Barry Windeatt, ed., *The Book of Margery Kempe: Annotated Edition* (Cambridge: Brewer, 2004), book 1, chap. 3, 62–63.

It has often been remarked that this passage shows that the apparent equality of marital debt subjected Margery in practice to "legal rape."[80] Margery's rejection of the narrative variety of marital debt leaves the Kempes with a single scenario, a narrative that has become so tedious with repetition that all that is left is the threadbare pleasure of the bodily act itself. Marital debt moves into a sadistic mode, exacted in violation of the other's will. However, that it is recorded as part of Margery's story shows that even this was of use to her. Margery reenergized the marital sex by throwing it into a different narrative; it may not have been enjoyable for her, but it certainly became a lot more interesting, and valuable, once she began to redefine it. Her unpleasure was the proof of her conversion, her rupture from the previous self that had enjoyed "inordynat lofe." She could not evade the unpleasing bodily experience, but she gained the awareness of performing obedience—and the worse the sex, the better the obedience. She displayed both the unpleasure and the obedience in her "greet wepyng and sorwyng," which vocalizing might have enlarged the audience by attracting the attention of the Kempes' servants and children. The experience enabled self-analysis: articulating her position, she distinguished between the actions of her body and the wishes of her heart. It provided an opportunity to practice the informal preaching that was to become an important component of her later piety. She took charge of the narrative of their shared marital life, retrospectively redefining what once must have seemed simple and licit pleasure into part of a more complex narrative of sin and redemption.

The pleasure of redefinition extends to considering the sex itself as being equivalent to the kind of penitential bodily behaviors practiced by other holy women, such as asceticisms based on eating unpleasant substances. Here we are on the verge of hagiographic territory, which occasionally mentions penitential resistance to marital sex, including practices such as self-wounding, to ensure that it did not risk being a source of pleasure. But only on the verge: Margery manages the situation in a conceptual rather than physical mode.[81] The equation she implies between taking filth into her body and taking in her husband's penis is none too subtle. The redefinition of her body as inherently pure,

[80] Sheila Delany, "Sexual Economics, Chaucer's Wife of Bath and *The Book of Margery Kempe*," in *Feminist Readings in Middle English Literature: The Wife of Bath and All Her Sect,* ed. Ruth Evans and Lesley Johnson (London: Routledge, 1994), 72–87 (82).

[81] Elliott, *Spiritual Marriage,* 229.

tainted only by the horrible foreign objects it is forced to ingest, is a powerful weapon in her psychological struggle with her husband. Suffering sexual unpleasure, Jesus assures her, is valuable. When she complains: "Lord, I am not worthy to heryn the spekyn and thus to comown wyth myn husbond. Nerthelesse it is to me gret peyn and gret dysese," he reassures her: "Therfor is it no synne to the, dowtyr, for it is to the rathar mede and meryte."[82] Jesus is both the target audience of this performance of conformity and its privileged interpreter. With that "therefore," he confirms that it is the unpleasure that has become the defining feature of this activity. This gives Margery, if anything, an incentive to continue to have unpleasant marital sex in order to transform it into meed and merit: her interests and John's curiously come to coincide. Eventually, of course, John agreed to a vow of chastity; but if he had remained unmovable, this equilibrium offered something for both of them.

Conclusion

The willingness of these medieval wives to use their own pain and degradation as the basis of their "intrapersonal script" bears analysis as a form of masochism. Masochism does not offer a total explanation of their behavior any more than does heterosexuality—since there are considerable differences of opinion between its theorists, this would hardly be possible—but some aspects of masochism, particularly those of practice-based accounts, do resonate with these situations. It may be, as Theodor Reik argues, that tolerance of sexual pain and humiliation is so useful to women living under patriarchal conditions that it barely registers as a peculiarity at all.[83] But these women are surely as heroic as the male masochist of whom Reik says, "By ordering his own punishment the masochist has made himself the master of his destiny."[84] Anticipating the worst that can be done to them, Alice, Elizabeth, and Margery step forward to take ownership of it. There are concrete social and material rewards for their obedience, but these texts show that the primary reward of obedience was a script of the erotic that could satisfy both personal and societal needs. Their performance of conformity is masochism

[82] Windeatt, *Margery Kempe,* book 1, chap. 21, p. 131.
[83] Theodor Reik, *Masochism in Modern Man,* trans. Margaret H. Beigel and Gertrud M. Kurth (New York: Farrar, Straus and Co., 1941), 214.
[84] Ibid., 161.

as theater, a "lived fiction" constructed by and starring the ostensibly dominated party.[85] The women invite observation of their sexual unpleasure, displaying it within the theater of the household, the family, and the neighbourhood in order to make use of it. Karmen MacKendrick argues that the masochistic experience exceeds the boundaries that demarcate the subject from the other, thus providing a glimpse of another way of being. The masochist (or the saint) finds that: "Under the intensification of impersonal desire provided by restraint, discontinuity is overcome. One loses a sense of the bounds of oneself. . . . In the loss of the discontinuous subject sense, paradoxically, is a touch of the loss of subjection: the emergence of the force of the will of the body under a quite different inscription, the body's freedom from its own unavoidable subjection under an other subjection fully sought."[86]

The examples cited here show that anticipation or endurance of marital sexual unpleasure may trigger self-examination and self-consciousness. These women ask fundamental questions about the relationship between interior and exterior, self and society. Am I wife or mistress, woman or child? Am I my heart or my body? What must I do to be respected? The breaching of the body's boundaries in sexual penetration provokes and models the breaching of the sense of unified selfhood. It is true, then, that unpleasure or the prospect of it brings on a dissolution of selfhood; but the crucial difference from MacKendrick's version is that the medieval examples show that self-dissolution may be preparatory to a conservative remaking. Elizabeth and Alice anatomize themselves in order to rebuild selves that conform to the requirements of their communities, and that gain the rewards of that conformity. By performing the operations upon themselves, they take ownership of what happens to them and find agency in conformity. Margery's case is a little more complicated, as part of the narrative of her transition from wife to saint, but it is the performance of dutiful and unpleasurable wifehood that gives her the leverage to make that transition.

These examples show conformity to be as interesting, complex, and difficult a form of agency as resistance, and as liable to produce excess in performance: these women carved out spaces for themselves in marriage by conforming to its terms. Their examples suggest that such development of a selfhood achieved through sexual unpleasure was quite

---

[85] Anita Phillips, *A Defence of Masochism* (London: Faber and Faber, 1998), 19.

[86] Karmen MacKendrick, *Counterpleasures* (New York: State University of New York Press, 1999), 118; thanks to Vicky Gunn for recommending this book.

a widespread operation, and its rewards mundane. If husbandhood is based on control and self-control, and wifehood on obedience, then marriage and marital sex offer both partners specifically gendered forms of ascesis.[87] Conformity and obedience in marriage offer women a sexuality with its own perverse pleasures, a masochism with social and individual rewards. This is a kind of heterosexuality: it is a sexual practice of which sexual difference is a key term, which works to produce gender differentiation, which was readily legible. Proper marital sex was performed on a very fine line: the prospect of its tipping over into perverse pleasures of one or the other kind, into indulgence in nonprocreative delights or into the theater of unpleasure, dominance and submission, could not be eliminated. This is heterosexuality, but not as we know it; or, rather, since modern heterosexuality is not a singular or coherent formation, this is not the face it prefers to show to the modern world.

[87] Derek Neal, *The Masculine Self in Late Medieval England* (Chicago: University of Chicago Press, 2008), 58.

Mutual Masochism and the Hermaphroditic Courtly Lady in Chaucer's *Franklin's Tale*

Tison Pugh
University of Central Florida

"THE BEST PART OF MARRIED LIFE is the fights. The rest is merely so-so," writes Thornton Wilder in *The Matchmaker*,[1] and his words capture a simple truth of narrative pleasure: in many instances, readers prefer depictions of conflict over companionship, of aggression over *amour,* and such is certainly the case throughout Chaucer's *Canterbury Tales*. Marriage recurs frequently as a subject during the Canterbury pilgrimage, but, as is readily apparent, often in problematic or unsettling ways. Cuckoldry and sexual aggression dominate the portrayals of marriage in *The Miller's Tale, Reeve's Tale, Merchant's Tale,* and *Shipman's Tale* (and even when cuckoldry is not surely depicted in Chaucer's fabliaux, its specter lingers, as in the flirtatious behavior between Thomas's wife and the friar of *The Summoner's Tale*). Domestic violence, both physical and emotional, disrupts marital harmony in *The Wife of Bath's Prologue, Clerk's Tale,* and *Manciple's Tale,* and marriage catalyzes religious conflict in *The Man of Law's Tale* (in which Custance's mothers-in-law embark on their murderous and duplicitous acts in response to their sons' unions) and *Second Nun's Tale* (in which Cecilia threatens Valerian with his imminent demise should he seek satisfaction for the marital debt). Due to the antagonism, pain, and humiliation associated with marriage in so many of the *Canterbury Tales, The Franklin's Tale,* with the apparently egalitarian relationship between Dorigen and Arveragus, stands as the strongest antidote to Chaucer's matrimonial satire.[2]

---

[1] Thornton Wilder, *The Matchmaker,* in *Three Plays: Our Town, The Skin of Our Teeth, and The Matchmaker* (New York: Harper Perennial, 1985), Act II, 299.

[2] It should be noted that additional companionate marriages appear in the *Canterbury Tales,* but Chauntecleer and Pertelote's union in *The Nun's Priest's Tale,* given Chaun-

149

But if Wilder is correct that the "best part of married life is the fights," then where is the pleasure of *The Franklin's Tale,* a narrative that, at least on the surface, doggedly refuses to depict marital disharmony? Numerous critics have analyzed *The Franklin's Tale* concerning its depiction of marital tribulations, pointing to subtle gradations of power and authority enacted in Dorigen and Arveragus's union. Notable voices in these discussions include Cathy Hume, who argues, "Having established an egalitarian marriage ideal at the beginning of the *Tale,* Chaucer goes on to explore how such an ideal would be tested by real world circumstances"; Craig Davis similarly observes, "Chaucer's *Franklin's Tale* shows us that perfect marriages can be just as fraught emotionally as any other kind, even when they are contracted with deliberate consideration of advantage and liability in social status, wealth, or political alliance."[3] These nuanced assessments of the marital dynamics depicted in *The Franklin's Tale,* along with those of Elizabeth Robertson, Conor McCarthy, David Raybin, Angela Lucas, and many others, enhance readers' understanding of a union that appears outwardly harmonious yet also hints at its inherent discontents.

The marital mutuality that stands at the core of *The Franklin's Tale* is not achieved easily, and Arveragus and Dorigen's mutual masochism enables their sharing of authority and submission in marriage. Numerous theoretical accounts of courtly love posit a sadistic/masochistic valence between the suffering suitor and his female beloved, but *The Franklin's Tale* subverts this binary relationship and invites readers to contemplate the possibility of a relationship founded upon oscillating positions of masochistic subservience, as well as the fruits of such a re-

---

tecleer's polygamous tendencies, can hardly be a model for human readers. Melibee and Prudence's marriage in Chaucer's *Tale of Melibee* exemplifies mutuality, yet their rich discussion of forgiveness is set within the context of the horrific violence against their family.

[3] Cathy Hume, "'The name of soveraynetee': The Private and Public Faces of Marriage in the *Franklin's Tale,*" *SP* 105.3 (2008): 284–303 (286); and Craig Davis, "A Perfect Marriage on the Rocks: Geoffrey and Philippa Chaucer and the *Franklin's Tale,*" *ChauR* 37.2 (2002): 129–44 (142). Additional studies focusing on marriage in *The Franklin's Tale* include Elizabeth Robertson, "Marriage, Mutual Consent, and the Affirmation of the Female Subject in the *Knight's Tale,* the *Wife of Bath's Tale,* and the *Franklin's Tale,*" in *Drama, Narrative, and Poetry in the "Canterbury Tales,"* ed. Wendy Harding (Toulouse: Presses Universitaires du Mirail, 2003), 175–93; Conor McCarthy, "Love, Marriage, and Law: Three *Canterbury Tales,*" *ES* 83.6 (2002): 504–18; David Raybin, "'Wommen, of kynde, desiren libertee': Rereading Dorigen, Rereading Marriage," *ChauR* 27.1 (1992): 65–86; and Angela Lucas, "The Presentation of Marriage and Love in Chaucer's *Franklin's Tale,*" *ES* 72.6 (1991): 501–12.

figuring of romance. Concomitant with the mutual masochism potential in courtly romance is the refiguring of gender roles within this archetypal dyad: the Courtly Lady need not be a lady when a relationship is defined through mutual masochism, and thus, when Arveragus assumes the mantle of this presumably feminine role, he models the latent hermaphroditism of ostensibly rigid gender hierarchies. The Franklin's mutually masochistic tale undermines standard structures of narrative as well, with the tale's focus on masochism paralleling that of the Franklin's performance of modesty for his fellow pilgrims, through which he likewise compels them to confront the fictions of gender.[4]

Mutual Masochism and the Hermaphroditic Courtly Lady, or Why Can't the Courtly Lady Be More Like a Man?

The logic of courtly love: such a phrase should be paradoxical, for under which epistemology (except perhaps its own) would its mores be considered logical? Slavoj Žižek nonetheless ponders the intransigence of courtly love in modern society, questioning its enduring legacy, its continued appeal despite its outmoded forms, and its persistently gendered tropes, all of which ostensibly assume an internal logic: "Why talk about courtly love [*l'amour courtois*] today, in an age of permissiveness when the sexual encounter is often nothing more than a 'quickie' in some dark corner of an office? The impression that courtly love is out of date, long superseded by modern manners, is a lure blinding us to how the logic of courtly love still defines the parameters within which the two sexes relate to each other."[5] The archetypal genders of courtly love endure in modern culture, but often these archetypes obscure more than reflect the gendered dynamics of the medieval texts, particularly romances and lyrics, from which they arise. Foremost among these para-

---

[4] In her *Chaucer and the Fictions of Gender* (Berkeley and Los Angeles: University of California Press, 1992), Elaine Tuttle Hansen explores the intersection of "the mutability of gender . . . and the instability of meaning" in Chaucer's canon, a pithy yet illuminating encapsulation of his play with gender, literary form, and social structure (60). Additional studies of gender and form in Chaucer's corpus that inform this analysis include Carolyn Dinshaw, *Chaucer's Sexual Poetics* (Madison: University of Wisconsin Press, 1989); Susan Crane, *Gender and Romance in Chaucer's "Canterbury Tales"* (Princeton: Princeton University Press, 1994); Angela Jane Weisl, *Conquering the Reign of Femeny: Gender and Genre in Chaucer's Romance* (Cambridge: D. S. Brewer, 1995); Jill Mann, *Feminizing Chaucer* (Cambridge: D. S. Brewer, 2002); and Holly Crocker, *Chaucer's Visions of Manhood* (New York: Palgrave Macmillan, 2007).

[5] Slavoj Žižek, *Metastases of Enjoyment: Six Essays on Women and Causality* (London: Verso, 1994), 89.

digms is the vision of the Courtly Lady, whose cruel and imperious command over her lover accords her absolute and arbitrary power over him. Jacques Lacan's excurses on the Courtly Lady have reified her standard features into a static entity, one who not only is eternal but is dehumanized as a reflection of unknown and untapped desires. For Lacan, courtly love in its entirety is a phantasy, a structure of imbuing meaning through elaborate images divorced from reality. His sense of *fin' amors* is of a complex poetic game, one with certain gendered tropes that are insistently uniform: "Courtly love was, in brief, a poetic exercise, a way of playing with a number of conventional, idealizing themes, which couldn't have any real concrete equivalent. Nevertheless, these ideals, first among which is that of the Lady, are to be found in subsequent periods, down to our own."[6] For Lacan, the Lady is ideal in her abstract yet recurrent features, and persistent through time: she survives the Middle Ages and courtly literature to flourish in the present day, yet she never existed other than as a phantastic formulation of desire's impossibility.[7]

Of course, the Lady need never have existed in order to function because her existence, in this instance, does not accord with her power. She is a psychological construct, one revealing the narcissistic desire of her suitor to assert his masculinity within the realm of a primarily homosocial grouping. Žižek discerns the Otherness that the Lady must embody and posits her as a reflection in which the knightly lover views himself narcissistically in response to her imperious commands: "This coincidence of absolute, inscrutable Otherness and pure machine is what confers on the Lady her uncanny, monstrous character—the Lady is the Other which is not our 'fellow-creature'; that is to say, she is someone with whom no relationship of empathy is possible. . . . Deprived of every real substance, the Lady functions as a mirror on to which the subject projects his narcissistic ideal."[8] Stripped of her humanity in Žižek's for-

---

[6] Jacques Lacan, *The Seminar of Jacques Lacan: Book VII: The Ethics of Psychoanalysis, 1959–1960,* ed. Jacques-Alain Miller, trans. Dennis Porter (New York: W. W. Norton, 1986), 148.

[7] Recent scholarship on modern theorists' debts to medieval literature, particularly that of Erin Felicia Labbie (*Lacan's Medievalisms* [Minneapolis: University of Minnesota Press, 2006]) and Bruce Holsinger (*The Premodern Condition: Medievalism and the Making of Theory* [Chicago: University of Chicago Press, 2005]), explores, in Labbie's words, "how the medieval is still dominant in our contemporary epistemological investigations" (34). Along these lines, this essay ponders how modern theory distorts the dynamics of medieval texts while nonetheless, in a cross-parallax of vision and insight, illuminating them.

[8] Žižek, *Metastases of Enjoyment,* 90.

mulation, the Lady is rendered inhuman and inhumane, serving merely to mirror masculine desire. In this paradigm, male narcissism transforms a woman into monstrosity: in needing and thus creating the cruel Lady as a means of ideal self-definition, the knight must metamorphose a woman into the Lady, must define himself through his relationship with her despite the fact that she has been rendered monstrous due to her presumed lack of humanity. In so doing, the knight's play with narcissistic desires reveals the inherent queerness of performing heterosexuality, for the narcissistic desire to be desired by a woman reveals the intransigence but ultimate superfluousness of the woman's role in the process. (As Narcissus himself showed, any mirror will serve this purpose.) The Courtly Lady becomes a mirror reflecting male desire for desirability who thus queerly reflects the knight's image: she highlights his failure to attain the standards of masculinity that she is coded to represent.[9]

In so doing, the Courtly Lady embodies a queer torquing of the knight's desires, despite their apparent sexual normativity. Queer theoreticians, including Lee Edelman, Tim Dean, and Simon Gaunt, have unpacked the convoluted workings of heterosexual desire by arguing for queer theory's necessity in interrogating social norms and their incoherencies. Edelman posits that "queerness attains its ethical value precisely insofar as it . . . accept[s] its figural status as resistance to the viability of the social while insisting on the inextricability of such resistance from every social structure."[10] Within this realm of inquiry, the aims of queer theory overlap with those of Lacanian examinations of desire. Tim Dean posits the unique conjunctions of analysis that are available by uniting queer theory with Lacanian thought. He suggests that "Lacanian psychoanalysis may provide handy ammunition for queer theory's critique of . . . heteronormativity." Certainly, as Dean points out, "By theorizing

---

[9] Regarding the potential solecism of discussing queerness and heterosexuality in the Middle Ages, in contrast with Karma Lochrie's and James Schultz's critiques of this practice, I use the rubric of hetero- and homosexuality simply to describe gendered object choices of desire but with no ensuing sense of a sexual, personal, or communal identity resulting therefrom; indeed, as I hope to demonstrate, the lability of ostensibly "straight" desires underscores the frequent obscurity of medieval sexuality, despite the plethora of prohibitions regulating it. For the limitations of this approach, see Karma Lochrie, *Heterosyncrasies: Female Sexuality When Normal Wasn't* (Minneapolis: University of Minnesota Press, 2005), esp. xi–xxviii; and James A. Schultz, *Courtly Love, the Love of Courtliness, and the History of Sexuality* (Chicago: University of Chicago Press, 2006), esp. 51–62.

[10] Lee Edelman, *No Future: Queer Theory and the Death Drive* (Durham: Duke University Press, 2004), 3. See also Edelman's *Homographesis* (New York: Routledge, 1994) for his earlier efforts to align queer theory with Lacanian psychoanalysis.

subjectivity in terms of language and culture, Lacan also denaturalizes sex."[11] In *Beyond Sexuality,* Dean also observes, "Lacan's response to normativity is not to produce alternative imaginaries, but to elaborate an alternative of a different order—that of the real, a conceptual category intended to designate everything that *resists* adaptation."[12] Furthermore, both psychoanalysis and queer theory frequently return to the question of love and its meanings. As Simon Gaunt summarizes, "Love, for Lacan, encourages the belief in a perfect and symmetrical union between a man and a woman . . . [b]ut this perfect union is a discursive lure, a myth, fantasy (in the strictly Lacanian sense of that which structures the symbolic order)." The utility of this myth for queer analysis, as Gaunt details, is that a "Lacanian framework may help us to understand . . . how courtly literature can be *both* profoundly homosocial *and yet* apparently attracted to the idea of a perfect union between a man and a woman."[13] From both psychoanalytic and queer perspectives, sex must be divorced from naturalistic discourses that establish it as a sacrosanct ideal of normativity and exposed for the contradictions of consciousness and culture that surface as inherent conditions in living as a sexual being.

At its core, *being* entails *being without,* and, for Lacan, the Lady signifies a lack, an absence that the knight seeks to fill through her position as the inscrutable Other: "The object involved, the feminine object, is introduced oddly enough through the door of privation or of inaccessibility."[14] The Lady can only be accessed through the knight's lack and thus becomes a cipher for the knight to decode, albeit an ultimately indecipherable code, one whose actions reflect not her desires but his refracted desires to project his identity through her. Lacan explains the ways in which the Lady must embody cruelty at its most arbitrary so that she represents both the knight's desire and the impossibility of comprehending desire:

By means of a form of sublimation specific to art, poetic creation consists in positing an object I can only describe as terrifying, an inhuman partner.

[11] Tim Dean, "Lacan and Queer Theory," in *The Cambridge Companion to Lacan,* ed. Jean-Michel Rabaté (Cambridge: Cambridge University Press, 2003), 238–52 (238, 243).

[12] Tim Dean, *Beyond Sexuality* (Chicago: University of Chicago Press, 2000), 230; italics in original.

[13] Simon Gaunt, *Love and Death in Medieval French and Occitan Courtly Literature: Martyrs to Love* (Oxford: Oxford University Press, 2006), 170–71; italics in original.

[14] Lacan, *The Seminar of Jacques Lacan,* 149.

The Lady is never characterized for any of her real, concrete virtues, for her wisdom, her prudence, or even her competence. If she is described as wise, it is not because she embodies an immaterial wisdom or because she represents its functions more than she exercises them. On the contrary, she is as arbitrary as possible in the tests she imposes on her servant.

The Lady is basically what was later to be called, with a childish echo of the original ideology, "cruel as the tigers of Ircania."[15]

Because of this cruelty, many readers see the Courtly Lady as the sadist to the knightly masochist, and Lacan cites the work of Chrétien de Troyes as a prime example of this dynamic (despite the paucity of evidence to support his claims).[16] Jeffrey Jerome Cohen memorably refers to Guinevere, in his Deleuzian reading of Chrétien's *Lancelot, ou Le Chevalier de la charrete,* as "Guinevere in Furs," a mordant yet nonetheless apropos assessment of her arbitrary power over an often hapless and suffering Lancelot.[17] Because the knight fails to prove his constant devotion by hesitating a mere two steps before debasing himself in the cart while attempting to rescue her, Guinevere asserts her amatory authority over him and unleashes much physical pain to punish him, notably in the tournament scenes in which she bids him to do his worst and thus to suffer mightily and physically.

It is nonetheless unclear in such scenes whether the Lady acts on her own volition or whether she is acted through in service of the knight's masochistic desires. Continuing his discussion of the Courtly Lady, Lacan describes her not as an agent but as a catalyst, one conscripted into her service as the Thing:

The idealized woman, the Lady, who is in the position of the Other and of the object, finds herself suddenly and brutally positing, in a place knowingly

---

[15] Ibid., 150–51.

[16] Ibid., 151. Other than Guinevere in *Lancelot, ou Le Chevalier de la charrete,* one might well wonder to which of Chrétien's female characters Lacan refers. As I discuss briefly at the end of this section, Enide more fits the role of the suffering suitor than the cruel Courtly Lady, and *Cliges* focuses more on the mutuality of suffering, first between Alexander and Soredamors and then between Cliges and Fenice, than on these women's supposed cruelties. Laudine's request that Yvain return to her after a year of knightly homosocial pastimes seems quite reasonable in its demands upon him, and Perceval's relationship with Blancheflor gives her little opportunity to dispense arbitrary or cruel tests of his knightly abilities.

[17] Cohen's rich reading of Guinevere and Lancelot's relationship pays particular attention to its inherently unstable dynamics and oscillating gendered inflections; see his "Masoch/Lancelotism," in *Medieval Identity Machines* (Minneapolis: University of Minnesota Press, 2003), 78–115.

constructed out of the most refined of signifiers, the emptiness of a thing in all its crudity, a thing that reveals itself in its nudity to be the thing, her thing, the one that is to be found at her very heart in its cruel emptiness. That Thing . . . is in a way unveiled with a cruel and insistent power.[18]

Lacan's passive descriptions of the Lady, who "finds herself" in the position of "brutally positing . . . the emptiness of a thing," establish her cruelty as incidental to her character (if she is granted any sense of character at all). If, for Lacan, *das Ding* is that which represents "the beyond-of-the-signified," whose function is that the subject is thereby "constituted in a kind of relationship characterized by primary affect, prior to any repression,"[19] the Lady's gender is ultimately unnecessary because, as she metamorphoses into *das Ding,* whose purpose is freed from her body, the knight grapples not with her corporeality but with his own interiority and his desires vis-à-vis his homosocial milieu. The Courtly Lady is thus also a Queer Thing, one by which the knight must confront the potential homoerotic desire inherent in the narcissistic mirroring that she performs for him. Furthermore, if the Lady is acted through rather than acting, she inhabits not a sadistic but a powerless position, one paradoxically staged by the knight through his own masochistic performance of subservience to and for her. Gilles Deleuze suggests that sadomasochism is primarily an illusion, positing instead that "the concurrence of sadism and masochism is fundamentally one of analogy only" and that the male masochist must "fashion the woman into a despot, . . . persuade her to cooperate and get her to 'sign.'"[20] Stripping away the facade of sadomasochism in medieval romance reveals the mutual masochism at its heart and the queer tensions inherent in a man defining and refining both his desire and his desirability through a woman acting as a Queer Thing, one who latently reflects the potential desirability of the knight among his homosocial affiliations rather than simply being a woman (if this possibility is available to her at all).

Accessing the power that the Courtly Lady purportedly wields, the knight seeks his narcissistic ideal by relying on the play of masochism, for masochism is often a performance. Žižek explains: "The next crucial

[18] Lacan, *The Seminar of Jacques Lacan,* 163.
[19] Ibid., 54.
[20] Gilles Deleuze, "Coldness and Cruelty," in Gilles Deleuze and Leopold von Sacher-Masoch, *Masochism* (New York: Zone, 1991), 9–138 (6 and 21). Deleuze dismisses the hypothetical union embodied in sadomasochism with such memorable turns of phrase as "pseudomasochism" (124) and as a "semiological howler" (134).

feature of courtly love is that it is thoroughly a matter of courtesy and etiquette; it has nothing to do with some elementary passion overflowing all barriers, immune to all social rules. We are dealing with a strict fictional formula, with a social game of 'as if,' where a man pretends that his sweetheart is the inaccessible Lady."[21] The knight engages in an elaborate theatrical ritual in which he shields his agency in service to his lady, but this subservience only masks his real power that is queerly designed to emasculate him. For in the patriarchal environs of the Middle Ages, when men wielded authority in virtually all realms of life, such performances are almost laughable in their farcelike enactments of male submission yet nonetheless transformatively effective in altering the gendered landscape of courtly society. One need only think of the rapist knight in Chaucer's *Wife of Bath's Tale* to see the severe penalties for forgoing the masochistic play of courtly love in favor of the violent sadism inherent in rape, yet these transgressions paradoxically encode further the masochistic ritual at the heart of knightly identity: the victim of Chaucer's rapist knight is forgotten by the tale's end, but he atones by embracing the passive queerness of submission to his wife in a masochistic performance of servility that ultimately redounds to his pleasure. Normative heterosexuality in marital bliss triumphs at this tale's conclusion, yet it is nonetheless a queered enactment of heterosexuality in which intercourse must be resignified into a pleasure so that it no longer signifies the violence or abjection that made it possible.

If the masochist stages the encounter with his cruel lady, then sadism itself is a ruse within the masochistic ritual, and the Courtly Lady may herself partake of the masochistic posturings frequent in the play of courtly love. Žižek investigates the tension between the masochist and his female partner, stressing the performative nature of their play:

Masochism . . . is made to the measure of the victim: it is the victim (the servant in the masochistic relationship) who initiates a contract with the Master (woman), authorizing her to humiliate him in any way she considers appropriate (within the terms defined by the contract) and binding himself to act "according to the whims of the sovereign lady." . . . It is the servant, therefore, who writes the screenplay—that is, who actually pulls the strings and dictates the activity of the woman [*dominatrix*]: he stages his own servitude. One further differential feature is that masochism, in contrast to sadism, is inherently theat-

---

[21] Žižek, *Metastases of Enjoyment,* 91.

rical: violence is for the most part feigned, and even when it is "real," it functions as a component of a scene, as part of a theatrical performance. Furthermore, violence is never carried out, brought to its conclusion; it always remains suspended, as the endless repeating of an interrupted gesture.[22]

Again the Courtly Lady wields little power: in Žižek's formulation, she follows the will of her masochistic lover, who "pulls the strings and dictates the activity of the woman." Feigning his lack of authority as he "stages his own servitude," the knight also stages the servitude of the Courtly Lady by directing her cruel behavior toward him so that he will be queered and so that the narrative will thus unfold on the expectation that he will somehow rehabilitate himself from this queering. Freedom from the gendered roles of male masochist and female sadist potentially emerges in this theatricality, for if the Courtly Lady is not a sadist because she responds to her suitor's masochistic contract, it is furthermore possible that she can stage her own complementary masochistic ritual in tandem and in response to her suitor's, to define herself narcissistically through him by likewise employing him as a Queer Thing.

For why must the Courtly Lady be a woman? If her function is to allow the knight to confront the impossibility of his subjectivity against the emptiness of signification, to see the emptiness of himself as a signifier as he narcissistically attempts to assert just such an identity, could not a man fulfill this role? If one is guided by the logic of the phallus, the answer must be no, since the phallus's role in signification adheres to a man's body, signifying the potential for signification even when such signifying is rendered incoherent. As Judith Butler argues in her deconstruction of phallologocentric "logic" and its insistent gendering of bodies, "The psychoanalytic critique succeeds in giving an account of the construction of 'the subject'—and perhaps also the illusion of substance—within the matrix of normative gender relations,"[23] and here the "logic" of courtly love sutures over Lacan's and Žižek's critiques

---

[22] Ibid., 91–92.

[23] Judith Butler, *Gender Trouble: Feminism and the Subversion of Identity* (New York: Routledge, 1990), 28–29. Butler's provocative troublings of psychoanalytic theories are relevant to the masochistic play of desire as well, as in her perceptive observation, "Desire will aim at unraveling the subject, but be thwarted by precisely the subject in whose name it operates. A vexation of desire, one that proves crucial to subjection, implies that for the subject to persist, the subject must thwart its own desire. And for desire to triumph, the subject must be threatened with dissolution" (*The Psychic Life of Power: Theories in Subjection* [Stanford: Stanford University Press, 1997], 9).

of Freud in terms of their own gendered arguments. Because the Lady is coded in and of absence, at least in Freudian terms, she better symbolizes the privations of identity and signification that stand at the heart of the encounter between her and her beloved, yet as Žižek also observes, relying on the body to distinguish the sexes obscures the symbolic processes at the heart of sexual identity: "It thus seems more productive to posit as the central enigma that of sexual difference—*not* as the already established symbolic difference (heterosexual normativity) but, precisely, as that which forever eludes the grasp of normative symbolization."[24] Affirming the gender of the Courtly Lady as female, however, succumbs to the logic of "established symbolic difference," while according the potential for the Courtly Lady to be a man, or to be a hermaphroditic figure capable of inhabiting masculine and feminine genders simultaneously, allows readers the freedom of "elud[ing] the grasp of normative symbolization." In the queer play of man and woman when heterosexuality falters at the point of desire, hermaphroditism emerges as a key tactic in ongoing power struggles in courtship and marriage.[25]

If readers grant the variability of the sexed body in relation to the identity of the Courtly Lady in medieval romances and courtly lyrics, numerous texts showcase her ultimately hermaphroditic cast. For example, Jane Burns notes the gender play inherent in courtly love, pointing out the "cross-gendered conundrum that lies at the very heart of courtly lyrics where a man's role (that of the feudal lord) is played by a woman who, while retaining the highly fetishized and desired female body, wields masculine abilities and male prerogative in love."[26] The polyvalent and hermaphroditic Courtly Lady is strikingly evident in Chrétien de Troyes's *Erec et Enide,* his account of the legend of "Gereint and Enid" as told in the *Mabinogion.* In brief, are not Erec/Gereint's stern com-

---

[24] Slavoj Žižek, *The Ticklish Subject: The Absent Centre of Political Ontology* (London: Verso, 1999), 324.

[25] As I discuss in *Sexuality and Its Queer Discontents in Middle English Literature* (New York: Palgrave Macmillan, 2008), conflicting models of hermaphroditism coexist: "Hermaphroditism can be envisioned in two complementary ways: either as the erasure of the dualistic construction of male/female through the embodiment of a merged, unified, and singular 'gender' or as the oscillation between male and female gender roles" (80–81). Given the inherent flux of hermaphroditic identities, their potential to signify in contradictory and complementary fashions disrupts gendered binaries by negating gender as an ostensibly stable referent.

[26] Jane Burns, "Courtly Love: Who Needs It? Recent Feminist Work in the Medieval French Tradition," *Signs* 27.1 (2001): 23–57 (27). Burns provides an excellent accounting of feminist readings of the courtly love tradition.

mands to Enide/Enid reminiscent of Guinevere's callous treatment of Lancelot in their virtually inexplicable cruelty, in their insistent punishments of trivial transgressions, in the ways in which the sadism apparently on display ultimately redounds the masochistic suffering of Lancelot and Enide to prove their virtue and desirability? Indeed, Gereint's motivations—why must he treat her so cruelly?—are so obscured in the texts of Chrétien and the *Mabinogion* that Alfred Tennyson provides a more credible explanation for this protagonist's inscrutable actions in *Idylls of the King,* positing Gereint's fear that Guinevere's adultery has tainted Enid: "and there fell / A horror on him, lest his gentle wife, / Thro' that great tenderness for Guinevere, / Had suffer'd, or should suffer any taint / In nature."[27] Without this hint of credible motivation, Erec/Gereint's actions appear merely arbitrary, designed to punish Enide/Enid and to force her to revel in masochistic abjection so that she may eventually triumph through her own masochistic ritual. In the lyric tradition, the Courtly Lady's hermaphroditic counterpart can be found in the figure who might be termed the Beautiful Monastic Boy, the object of desire in courtly love verses written by monastic authors who cast themselves as suffering masochistically when bereft of the ravishing boy's amorous attention.[28] Each of these texts and genres merits deeper investigation for their occluded hermaphroditic treatment of courtly identity, but I now turn to Chaucer's *Franklin's Tale,* in which these dynamics subvert the vision of companionate marriage by revealing the queer torsions of identity needed to achieve its peaceful resolution.

[27] Alfred, Lord Tennyson, *Idylls of the King,* ed. J. M. Gray (London: Penguin, 1983), 76, lines 28–32. In the *Mabinogion,* Enid merely declares, "Woe is me, if on my account these arms and chest are losing the fame and fighting ability they once possessed" (*The Mabinogion,* trans. Jeffrey Gantz [London: Penguin, 1976], 278), and in Chretien's *Erec et Enide,* she states, "Con mar I fus" (*Erec et Enide,* ed. Jean-Marie Fritz [Paris: Livre de Poche, 1992], 206, line 2503), a remarkably ambiguous phrase translated as divergently as "How disastrous for you" (trans. D. D. R. Owen, *Arthurian Romances* [London: Everyman, 1993], 33) and "Beloved, / How you've been wronged" (trans. Burton Raffel, *Erec and Enide* [New Haven: Yale University Press, 1997], 80, lines 2506–7). This obscure statement nonetheless instigates Erec's incessant testing of his wife. Tennyson's Enid, in contrast, states more clearly, "O me, I fear that I am no true wife" (78, line 108), a phrase misinterpreted within the context of the story, yet more damaging in terms of its apparent denotation. Tennyson frees his retelling of Gereint and Enid's relationship from the incoherency of desire frequent in medieval romance while nonetheless maintaining the mutual masochism at its heart.

[28] For a study of this dynamic in monastic verse, see Thomas Stehling, "To Love a Medieval Boy," in which he describes how monastic lyrics idealizing male beauty express a "casual indifference to female/male distinctions." *Journal of Homosexuality* 8 (1983): 151–70 (152).

Mutual Masochism and the Hermaphroditic
Courtly Lady in *The Franklin's Tale*

The opening lines of *The Franklin's Tale* stress its key theme of courtly love's masochistic edge in a knight's willingness to suffer for his beloved. In introducing Arveragus to the Canterbury pilgrims, the Franklin emphasizes his protagonist's love through his ready acceptance of pain and thus codes this character as a masochistic suitor who eagerly serves his lady according to the precepts of the courtly love tradition: "In Armorik, that called is Britayne, / Ther was a knyght that loved and dide his payne / To serve a lady in his beste wise" (V.729–31).[29] The Franklin's ambiguous description of Arveragus's love muddies attempts to read the knight's motivations: in particular, the object of his affections appears not to be Dorigen herself, who is as yet unnamed in the story and thus as yet indistinguishable from any other Courtly Lady, just as Arveragus is as yet indistinguishable from any other courtly lover.[30] Rather, the Franklin's words—that Arveragus "loved and dide his payne"—affirm not the knight's love for his lady but his love for the pain of serving her. Surely this passage contextually implies that Arveragus loves Dorigen and "dide his payne" to win her affections, but the grammatical construction of the sentence nonetheless establishes the painful service of Dorigen as Arveragus's objective. It is a telling example of the conflicted play of courtly love, in which desire for a beloved mutates into desire for the pain of courtly love rather than its solaces. The Franklin also soon comments, "Lerneth to suffre, or elles, so moot I goon, / Ye shul it lerne, wher so ye wole or noon" (V.777–78), thereby reaffirming the necessity of suffering in romance as a key theme throughout his depiction of an apparently ideal marriage.

The narrative moves quickly to Arveragus and Dorigen's marriage, but not before gesturing strongly to the standard tropes of the long-suffering courtier and his imperious beloved, whom he perceives as unattainable because of her high social status:

[29] All references to and citations of Chaucer are taken from *The Riverside Chaucer,* gen. ed. Larry D. Benson (Boston: Houghton Mifflin, 1987), and are noted parenthetically.

[30] In her *Naming and Namelessness in Medieval Romance* (Cambridge: D. S. Brewer, 2008), Jane Bliss notes the "performative function of name" in medieval romance in regard to "what it can do to characters in the story and what effect it can have on an audience" (15). In *The Franklin's Tale,* the delay in revealing Arveragus's and Dorigen's names first accentuates their status as stock literary characters—the courtly lover and his imperious beloved—before individualizing them and thus troubling their performances of these expected roles.

And many a labour, many a greet emprise,
He for his lady wroghte er she were wonne.
For she was oon the faireste under sonne,
And eek therto comen of so heigh kynrede
That wel unnethes dorste this knyght, for drede,
Telle hire his wo, his peyne, and his distresse.

(V.732–37)

Within the traditional tropes of romance courtship in which this scene is colored, to love a beautiful and high-born woman requires a knight to labor incessantly to break through her cold exterior to the love she hides underneath the surface. Arveragus's woe, pain, and distress are merely catalogued in these opening lines, rather than recounted in precise detail, because they are tropes that signal extensive suffering through their superficial mentioning. The brevity of the account, however, does not lessen the pain that has constituted his life in courting (and in suffering for) Dorigen.

In response to Arveragus's masochistic posturings, Dorigen confronts the shifting potential of courtly love, in which the ostensibly sadistic Courtly Lady may find herself bereft of the authority she purportedly wields. Deleuze posits that masochism "is animated by a dialectical spirit, . . . resulting in a scene being enacted simultaneously on several levels with reversals and reduplications in the allocation of roles and discourse,"[31] and this dialectical spirit circulates in the erotic tensions of their relationship. As encoded in the hierarchical gender roles of courtship, the Lady is granted power, in contrast to the man's submissiveness, yet the mutuality of masochism, which springs from its dialectical play, upsets typical expectations of feminine amatory authority. As she falls in love with Arveragus and accedes to her position as wife, Dorigen loses the power of the Courtly Lady while nonetheless maintaining the role:

But atte laste she, for his worthynesse,
And namely for his meke obeysaunce,
Hath swich a pitee caught of his penaunce
That pryvely she fil of his accord
To take hym for hir housbonde and hir lord.

(V.738–42)

---

[31] Deleuze, *Masochism*, 22.

162

Arveragus's worthiness and meek obedience define his character in this passage, but his agency emerges in these submissive performances, for it is through this play that Dorigen "fil of his accord." In accord with Žižek's theorization of masochism as a performance, Arveragus successfully performs his painful subservience so that Dorigen renounces her amatory authority. Intriguingly, Chaucer mentions Arveragus's "penance" in this passage, but readers see no evidence of any amorous (or spiritual) transgression for which he need atone; the suffering courtly lover, however, need not actually transgress against the dictates of love, for such transgressions are always and already the precondition of his pursuit and the basis of his performance.[32] From viewing Arveragus's performance of masochism, Dorigen realigns her role from imperious Courtly Lady to wife, one that further shifts the gendered inflections of their relationship. Both Courtly Ladies and wives are women of course, but the genders accorded to these vastly different feminine roles range widely, and thus the transience of gendered categories points to the hermaphroditic potential inherent in the Courtly Lady. If a woman can assume both the roles of Courtly Lady and of wife, so too may her suitor assume both the roles of husband and of Courtly Lady in what is ultimately a queering of gender.

After ceding her authority as Courtly Lady, Dorigen appears to be Arveragus's amatory equal, and the Franklin praises mutuality as love's key value. For courtly and marital relationships to prosper, the narrator argues, both a knight and his lady must embrace the mutuality inherent in their love:

> For o thyng, sires, saufly dar I seye,
> That freendes everych oother moot obeye,
> If they wol longe holden compaignye.
> Love wol nat been constreyned by maistrye.
>
> (V.761–64)

---

[32] *Penance* evokes a range of denotations and connotations, which, as registered in the *Middle English Dictionary,* include: "[t]he sacrament of penance or reconciliation"; "repentance, change of heart; compunction, contrition"; "penalty, punishment; a judicial sentence; also, divine chastisement"; "the practice of asceticism and self mortification as a penitential discipline"; and "[p]ain, suffering; affliction, hardship; also, a distasteful task or duty." The glosses of *penance* in *The Riverside Chaucer* (178, 1276) focus on the word's meaning as pain and suffering, yet given the hazy confluence of spiritual and amatory discourses in the play of courtly love, it seems likely that Chaucer encodes numerous connotations of *penance,* including its religious valences, in his descriptions of Arveragus's suffering for love.

The narrator's call for mutual obeisance stands as the ideal virtue espoused in the narrative, and the Franklin's vision of a successful marriage relies upon the impossibility of sadism through the renunciation of *maistrye*. Long-standing interpretations of *The Franklin's Tale* as the resolution of the marriage debate posit that, by declaring that "freendes everych oother moot obeye," the Franklin refutes the vision of husbandly sadism embodied by Walter in *The Clerk's Tale*.[33] Certainly, Arveragus's relationship with Dorigen evinces little of the cruelty evident in Walter's relationship with Griselda, but to view these marriages as opposite ends of a spectrum occludes their overlapping concern with the play of gender as a tactic in marital debates over authority and control.

Within the masochistic play of courtly love, such a paradigm shift as is evident in Arveragus and Dorigen's attempts to renounce *maistrye* would require not only that the Courtly Lady relinquish the veneer of sadism attributed to her, but also that her male suitor relinquish the play of masochism through which he orchestrates his lady's actions. But such a simplistic resolution merely camouflages the intertwined play of desire initiated in mutual masochism, in which cruelty can never be fully renounced because the masochistic play of both knight and lady now requires that each beloved demand his/her partner to instigate masochistically cruel rituals to test each other. Complementing their renunciation of *maistrye*, Arveragus and Dorigen vow sufferance to each other so that they may live together in harmony:

> And therfore hath this wise, worthy knyght,
> To lyve in ese, suffrance hire bihight,
> And she to hym ful wisly gan to swere
> That nevere sholde ther be defaute in here.
> (V.787–90)

How, though, can one promise *sufferance* without subjecting oneself to another's *maistrye*? The *Middle English Dictionary* includes among the definitions of *sufferance* the "willingness to be acted upon by an agent," which underscores the passivity inherent in Arveragus and Dorigen's

---

[33] Nearly one hundred years later, G. L. Kittredge's "Chaucer's Discussion of Marriage" (*MP* 9 [1912]: 435–67) remains relevant in exploring Chaucer's depiction of marriage. He concludes that *The Franklin's Tale* "ends an elaborate debate" and urges readers "to accept the solution which the Franklin offers" (467). Jill Mann, particularly in her chapter "The Surrender of *Maistrye*," offers a compelling evaluation of marriage and "maistrye" in *The Franklin's Tale*; see her *Feminizing Chaucer*, 70–99.

marriage through their joint adherence to this marital virtue.[34] As opposed to *maistrye,* mutual *sufferance* defines the parameters of conjugal harmony in this marriage, yet it is a virtue of masochistic passivity in which, paradoxically, Arveragus and Dorigen accept each other's *maistrye,* despite their purported rejection of it, through their mutual *sufferance.* Mutual masochism should not be envisioned as necessitating an on/off switch, in which one partner embraces the masochistic position of subservience to the other's Courtly Lady in rigid demarcations of performance and identity; on the contrary, these oscillating identities pulse erratically in Dorigen and Arveragus's relationship. Deleuze believes that masochism is characterized by its dialectical qualities, which, in this instance, emerge in the continuing return of *maistrye* to a marriage from which it has presumably been banished.

The hermaphroditism inherent in the Courtly Lady comes to the surface of the narrative as the Franklin subverts and reimagines gender roles throughout his romance. The Franklin exposes the contradictions at the heart of courtly love when he hints that women, who should enjoy the prerogatives of the Courtly Lady's authority, wield little real power: "Wommen, of kynde, desiren libertee, / And nat to been constreyned as a thral; / And so doon men, if I sooth seyen shal" (V.768–70). Both women and men desire liberty, but it is noteworthy that the Franklin emphasizes women's potential to be "constreyned as a thral" despite their supposedly superior positions in courtly love. The hazy relationship between courtly love and marriage, in that the two are often interrelated yet need not be so, could explain these lines in the latent suggestion that a woman cedes her power in courtship upon becoming a wife (which again underscores the variability in the gender roles of Courtly Lady and of wife).[35] Mark Taylor reads *The Franklin's Tale* as a dialectical assessment of courtly and marital love, in which

---

[34] The *Middle English Dictionary* also defines *sufferance* as "[t]he undergoing of hardship, affliction, punishment, etc."; "suffering"; "[t]he capacity to endure or manner of bearing up under pain"; and "[t]he patient endurance of hardship, affliction, etc."

[35] Distinctions between love in courtship and in marriage are encoded throughout Andreas Capellanus's foundational text *The Art of Courtly Love,* such as in this passage from the Eighth Dialogue between a man and woman of the higher nobility, in which the man declares: "I admit that I have a wife who is beautiful enough, and I do indeed feel such affection for her as a husband can. But since I know that there can be no love between husband and wife . . . and that there can be nothing good done in this life unless it grows out of love, I am naturally compelled to seek for love outside the bonds of wedlock" (Andreas Capellanus, *The Art of Courtly Love,* ed. John Jay Parry [New York: Columbia University Press, 1960], 116).

Chaucer "adopt[s] the ideal of the anti-adultery tradition and defend[s] it against the tradition of adulterous love."[36] Taylor's account of love's vagaries is persuasive, yet the ultimate impossibility of distinguishing between courtly and marital love once mutual masochism disrupts the expected parameters of this gendered paradigm muddies a dichotomous view either of Courtly Lady or of wife. For even when *The Franklin's Tale* most clearly endorses mutuality, the inherent imbalance of masochistic ritual remains in effect, as does the threat of serving "as a thral."

If the woman *qua* Courtly Lady faces the possibility of losing her authority in love and of thus sliding into a subservient position of thrall-dom when married, the Franklin's concomitant observation regarding men's desire "nat to been constreyned as a thral" is clearly linked to courtship rather than to marriage. Given medieval culture's assumption of masculine authority in marriage, men should not be expected to face thralldom in marriage after their masochistic performances during courtship have ceased.[37] The Franklin notes the distinction between men's gender roles in courtship and in marriage:

> Thus hath she take hir servant and hir lord—
> Servant in love, and lord in mariage.
> Thanne was he bothe in lordshipe and servage.
> Servage? Nay, but in lordshipe above,
> Sith he hath bothe his lady and his love.
>
> (V.792–96)

In common with the ways in which the biological sex of the lady masks two complementary yet discrete gender roles of Courtly Lady and wife, the knight's biological sex obscures the competing yet complementary versions of masculinity open for his performance: suffering suitor, au-

---

[36] Mark Taylor, "Servant and Lord/Lady and Wife: The *Franklin's Tale* and Traditions of Courtly and Conjugal Love," *ChauR* 32.1 (1997): 64–81 (77).

[37] Recent studies of medieval marriage and gender include D. L. D'Avray, *Medieval Marriage: Symbolism and Society* (Oxford: Oxford University Press, 2005); Conor Mc-Carthy, *Marriage in Medieval England: Law, Literature, and Practice* (Woodbridge: Boydell, 2004); and Christopher N. L. Brooke, *The Medieval Idea of Marriage* (Oxford: Oxford University Press, 1989). As studies of widowhood have shown, women often found greater freedoms after their husbands' deaths than during their marriages, which highlights the patriarchal gender dynamics of medieval marriage; see Louise Mirrer, ed., *Upon My Husband's Death: Widows in the Literature and Histories of Medieval Europe* (Ann Arbor: University of Michigan Press, 1992); and Sue Sheridan Walker, ed., *Wife and Widow in Medieval England* (Ann Arbor: University of Michigan Press, 1993).

thoritarian husband, and even, as Arveragus soon demonstrates, Courtly Lady. Here the knight's play of masochistic subservience in courtship is revealed as a ruse to gain control of his beloved in marriage, and even the egalitarian ideal of mutuality is merely a patriarchal facade, one by which Arveragus is able to maintain lordship over Dorigen in marriage because he wins her both as the Courtly Lady of romance and as his love in marriage. Both Courtly Ladies and wives, in their performance of gendered femininity, must accede to male prerogatives, yet nonetheless the man's potential position as Courtly Lady will reveal his willingness to perform for her narcissistic desires when she stages her own masochistic rituals.

Once married, Dorigen experiences the keen pain of suffering while awaiting her husband's return from England, and in these scenes she mirrors Arveragus's masochistic torments during their courtship.[38] Like her husband, who performed "many a labour" to win her, she snares the amatory attention of a suitor through the masochistic and public ritual of suffering without him. Deleuze theorizes that waiting enhances the masochist's experience of suffering, that the "masochist is morose," and this "moroseness should be related to the experience of waiting and delay."[39] After Arveragus departs, pain dominates Dorigen's life: "She moorneth, waketh, wayleth, fasteth, pleyneth; / Desir of his presence hire so destreyneth / That al this wyde world she sette at noght" (V.819–21). Her desire for Arveragus empties her life of meaning, and she sees herself as bound to Fortune's cruel vagaries: "Allas, . . . on thee, Fortune, I pleyne, / That unwar wrapped hast me in thy cheyne" (V.1355–56). Even the black rocks, emblematic of her emotional torment during Arveragus's absence, signify the performativity encoded in her suffering. On a surface level, they are concrete reminders of her loss and her fears for her husband's safety, yet Timothy Flake intriguingly

---

[38] Dorigen's status in a primarily masculine world has drawn the attention of numerous scholars, such as Alison Ganze, who sees her negotiating masculine values in her search for *trouthe* ("'My trouthe for to holde—allas, allas!': Dorigen and Honor in the *Franklin's Tale*," *ChauR* 42.3 [2008]: 312–29); Andrea Rossi-Reder, who describes the ways in which the tale establishes that "masculine mobility is grounded in female fixity" ("Male Movement and Female Fixity in the *Franklin's Tale* and *Il Filocolo*," in *Masculinities in Chaucer: Approaches to Maleness in the "Canterbury Tales" and "Troilus and Criseyde,"* ed. Peter Beidler [Cambridge: D. S. Brewer, 1998], 106–16 [115]); and Mary Bowman, who describes Dorigen as a possession traded between men rather than as an individual ("'Half as she were mad': Dorigen in the Male World of the *Franklin's Tale*," *ChauR* 27.3 [1993]: 239–51).

[39] Deleuze, *Masochism*, 70–71.

suggests that Dorigen needs these rocks, that she "really does not want the rocks to be removed. The rocks' presence . . . is the foundation of her sense of certainty, for it is on this certainty that she bases her defense against Aurelius's advances and her declaration of faithfulness to Arveragus."[40] The pain that readers witnessed in Arveragus's performance of masochism during courtship, which cracked when he could finally "Telle hire his wo, his peyne, and his distresse," now envelops Dorigen in marriage, but through such apparent passivity, she defines her own narcissistic image. Aurelius's desire for her—which he has hidden "[t]wo yeer and moore" (V.940) but can hide no longer—indicates her success in this regard.

The cause of Dorigen's suffering is at least somewhat arbitrary, for why, except to allow his wife to stage her masochistic ritual, does Arveragus depart for England? The Franklin mentions the knight's journey without explaining his motivation beyond a cursory reference to his knightly duties, and so here Arveragus enacts the arbitrary callousness of the Courtly Lady, as he compels Dorigen to experience his former suffering:

> A yeer and moore lasted this blisful lyf,
> Til that the knyght of which I speke of thus,
> That of Kayrrud was cleped Arveragus,
> Shoop hym to goon and dwelle a yeer or tweyne
> In Engelond, that cleped was eek Briteyne,
> To seke in armes worshipe and honour—
> For al his lust he sette in swich labour—
> And dwelled there two yeer; the book seith thus.
>
> (V.806–13)

From a conventional perspective, Arveragus is a knight and knights must engage in battle and fight in tournaments; it is simply an occupational obligation, one that reflects negatively neither upon him nor upon his devotion to Dorigen. Yet such a rationalization is based on establishing an internal logic to the machinations of courtly love, an amatory system almost immune to logic in its oscillating play of gender and

[40] Timothy Flake, "Love, *Trouthe,* and the Happy Ending of the *Franklin's Tale*," *ES* 77.3 (1996): 209–26 (219). Concerning these rocks, see also John Friedman, "Dorigen's 'Grisly rokkes blake' Again," *ChauR* 31.2 (1996): 133–44, who associates them with a "pre-Christian or actively anti-Christian point of view" (142).

amatory authority. Similar moments in other romances when knights fail to prioritize their ladies over their homosocial responsibilities and pleasures—such as in Chrétien de Troyes's *Yvain, ou Le Chevalier au lion,* when Yvain departs from Laudine to join Gawain in knightly tournaments, and in Marie de France's *Lanval,* when Lanval fails to adhere to his Lady's demand for silence regarding their relationship—highlight these knights' propensity to sabotage their love in order to replay the mutual masochism that should no longer be necessary due to love's fruition. Such scenes privilege the knight's homosocial relationships with his peers over his love for his lady, further positioning her as a narcissistic mirror of his performances for other men's pleasure. These plotlines also suggest that once the knight's relationship with her is so firmly established that he need no longer enact his masochistic ploys, he compels his beloved to experience the painful effects of his newly returned sense of agency, even to his own detriment, for by refusing his initial position of masochistic subservience, the knight paradoxically ensures that both he and his beloved will suffer more than previously by undermining the foundations of their love. At the very least, the Franklin's declaration that Arveragus prefers the worship and honor of arms to the sexual bliss of marriage—"For al his lust he sette in swich labour"—denigrates the love he so desperately sought but from which he seeks to escape after merely "[a] yeer and moore." The Franklin cites his textual source in this moment—"the book seith thus"—and this rhetorical flourish provides documentary evidence for a common trope of romance that makes little sense according to external logic but nonetheless profoundly affects the contours of courtly love and its perverse traditions. Fracturing the bliss of their marriage through his actions, Arveragus provides Dorigen with the opportunity to stage her own masochistic ritual, one that ensnares both her husband and her suitor in a new round of suffering. As she served as Queer Thing/Courtly Lady for Arveragus as suitor, so too will he serve this role for her by encouraging her to abandon the sadism to which she ostensibly had access in her role as Courtly Lady and to enjoy the suffering play of contractual masochism with both him and Aurelius.

Aurelius loves and fears Dorigen, and, like his rival Arveragus, he employs the standard tropes of masochistic disavowal in approaching her. "My righte lady, . . . / Whom I moost drede and love as I best kan, / And lothest were of al this world displese" (V.1311–13), he declares, performing his fear of her, and he also accords her the imperious position of the Courtly Lady by referring to her as "my sovereyn lady" before humbly placing his fate in her hands (V.1325, cf. V.1072). Readers learn that Aurelius has long loved Dorigen without seeking relief for his suffering: "But nevere dorste he tellen hire his grevaunce. / Withouten coppe he drank al his penaunce" (V.941–42). In these amatory posturings, complete with their tropes of suffering and penance, Aurelius mirrors Arveragus, and in this nascent conflict it appears that *The Franklin's Tale* will address the vexed (and often queer) negotiations of aggression and affection inherent in triangulations of desire.[41] The relationship between Arveragus, Dorigen, and Aurelius has the structure of an erotic triangle, and readers might expect the narrative, like *The Knight's Tale,* to end with Arveragus and Aurelius fighting in a tournament to ensure the winner's position as her beloved. In terms of the erotic choice before Dorigen, however, little distinguishes Arveragus and Aurelius from each other in terms of personality, appearance, or profession: like Palamon and Arcite in *The Knight's Tale,* the two men are nearly interchangeable in their performance of amatory ritual, yet within the logic of this romance, Arveragus's position as Dorigen's first lover, and thus as her husband, cannot be stripped from him.[42] Nor should it be: despite surface similarities between Arveragus and Aurelius, Arveragus's role as Dorigen's husband is sacrosanct within the erotic logic of this tale. *The Franklin's Tale* focuses on the pains and pleasures of abstention in courtship and marriage, not of action in adultery, and so this erotic triangle— unlike the violent enactment of triangulated desire in *The Knight's Tale*—concentrates on sharing masochistic ritual with Aurelius and thereby disciplining him into love's service. One does not need to defeat a masochist in an erotic rivalry; one need only encourage him to continue his masochistic subservience and to alienate him, to queer him, from a vision of masculinity predicated upon amatory success with women. He must be taught not to transcend masochism as the primary seductive tactic in a man's erotic repertoire but to languish in its painful pleasures.

[41] Eve Sedgwick's *Between Men: English Literature and Male Homosocial Desire* (New York: Columbia University Press, 1985) remains the theoretical foundation for analyzing the homoerotic cast of erotic triangles.

[42] Palamon and Arcite resemble each other in numerous qualities, but Catherine Rock, in her "Forsworn and Fordone: Arcite as Oath-Breaker in the *Knight's Tale*" (*ChauR* 40.4 [2006]: 416–32), explores how Arcite's actions after falling in love with Emily distinguish him morally from his sworn brother. In this instance, Chaucer's hesitance to distinguish between erotic rivals reflects the often inscrutable vagaries of Fortune in amatory affairs.

And so, rather than bolstering the aggression latent in triangulated desire, masochism infuses Arveragus and Aurelius's amatory competition with a mutually painful dynamic that strips away the aggression latent in love. Notably, Arveragus remains unaware of Aurelius's desire for his wife throughout most of the narrative, in which several years pass with little to advance the narrative. Time passes quickly yet slowly in *The Franklin's Tale,* which heightens the Franklin's rhetorical flourishes regarding love's suffering. For example, Aurelius suffers "[t]wo yeer and moore" after confessing his love for Dorigen (V.1102), and these lines regarding time's passage heighten the emotional pain of this scene, pointing to the long periods of suffering that the characters endure.[43] While pursuing another man's wife, Aurelius, rather than openly confronting his rival, publicly performs his masochistic suffering, and in this masterful performance he sings numerous songs of love ostensibly to hide yet paradoxically to announce his love:

> He was despeyred; no thyng dorste he seye,
> Save in his songes somwhat wolde he wreye
> His wo, as in a general compleynyng;
> He seyde he lovede and was biloved no thyng.
> Of swich matere made he manye layes,
> Songes, compleintes, roundels, virelayes,
> How that he dorste nat his sorwe telle,
> But langwissheth as a furye dooth in helle.
>
> (V.943–50)

Aurelius hides his amatory woe, only to reveal it in song in no less than five separate genres, as if it were a "general compleyning," not his personal lament. Both revealing and cloaking his pain, Aurelius transforms his private suffering into a public performance, one that occludes his masochism while it is nonetheless on full display for his audience.

When Dorigen confronts Aurelius about the impropriety of his desires, she focuses on the painful pleasure of forbearance, encouraging him to accept the queer regenderings of masochism available to him by renouncing the possibility of consummating his desires. In her rhetorical question to him—"What deyntee sholde a man han in his lyf / For to go love another mannes wyf, / That hath hir body whan so that hym

---

[43] Other such lines addressing time's passage in the tale include 806, 809, 813, 940, 1568, and 1582.

liketh?" (V.1003–5)—she emphasizes that he should disavow sexuality while simultaneously highlighting Arveragus's enjoyment of sexual pleasure with her. Michael Calabrese rightly points out the provocative nature of Dorigen's words, seeing them as "an inflammation of the male rivalry that Aurelius is conducting. . . . By reminding him in sexually suggestive terms that her body *is* freely enjoyed, but not by him, she only encourages Aurelius to commit himself to achieving the 'impossible' and to have what his rival freely enjoys."[44] I would only qualify Calabrese's perceptive observation by changing its verb tense: her body is not *currently* being freely enjoyed by Arveragus, who is in England pursuing homosocial knightly pastimes rather than sating his amatory desires when she speaks these words; rather, sexual pleasure, at the moment of this confrontation, is unavailable to Dorigen, Arveragus, and Aurelius, which leaves only the specter of sexuality behind. By so publicly performing her suffering during Arveragus's absence and by reminding Aurelius of the sexual pleasure of which she herself cannot partake, Dorigen accentuates love's pains as a renouncing rather than as a fulfilling of desire. In this passage she is both the Courtly Lady who enhances Aurelius's suffering through her cruel rejoinder while also serving as the masochist subservient to Arveragus, who, in his own role as Courtly Lady, disciplines her by denying her the sexual pleasure available to her in marriage (and, it appears from these lines, keenly missed).

In regard to the polymorphous gender play of masochism, Aurelius enacts the theatrical ploys of masochism not merely for Dorigen but for the magician who supernaturally obscures the black rocks so central to Dorigen's heartfelt performance of erotic suffering. These structural similarities of masochistic ritual in Aurelius's appeal to the magician do not suggest a latent homoeroticism in this scene but instead point to the queer and masochistic underbelly of desires circulating through both men and women and throughout their relationships; regardless of Dorigen's or of the magician's biological sex, Aurelius's narcissistic strategies reveal the ubiquity of masochism throughout virtually all encounters in this tale. He assumes the masochist's obsequious position vis-à-vis his superior, even threatening the magician with his suicide should his amatory pains be left unresolved:

---

[44] Michael Calabrese, "Chaucer's Dorigen and Boccaccio's Female Voices," *SAC* 29 (2007): 259–92 (264).

> Aurelius in al that evere he kan
> Dooth to this maister chiere and reverence,
> And preyeth hym to doon his diligence
> To bryngen hym out of his peynes smerte,
> Or with a swerd that he wolde slitte his herte.
> This subtil clerk swich routhe had of this man
> That nyght and day he spedde hym that he kan
> To wayten a tyme of his conclusioun.
>
> (V.1256–63)

Aurelius's relationship with the magician structurally mirrors his relationship with Dorigen, in which his masochism encourages these "masters" to act on his behalf, as Dorigen does in her rash promise to love him should he remove the black rocks. His ready embrace of death wins "swich routhe" from "this maister" that his plan to win Dorigen's affections proceeds apace. Deleuze believes that death intertwines with eroticism in masochism, such that "destruction is always presented as the other side of a construction, as an instinctual drive which is necessarily combined with Eros,"[45] and in this manner Aurelius pursues erotic satisfaction through his declared readiness for death.

From her relationship with Arveragus, Dorigen learned that masochistic suitors do not act except through their contractual performance of suffering, and so she is duly shocked when Aurelius informs her that he has successfully moved the black rocks from the coast. In a tale that emphasizes forbearance and inaction, Aurelius's apparent rejection of passivity shocks Dorigen:

> "Allas," quod she, "that evere this sholde happe!
> For wende I nevere by possibilitee
> That swich a monstre or merveille myghte be!
> It is agayns the proces of nature."
>
> (V.1342–45)

Dorigen refers to a "monstre" in Aurelius's successful removal of the black rocks, and this "monstre" could signify either the magical event or Aurelius himself. In at long last rising from his melancholic torpor and momentarily refusing the masochistic suffering that the suitor should continually perform, he metaphorically transforms himself into a

[45] Deleuze, *Masochism,* 116.

monster who abrogates the expected rituals of courtly love merely by acting. Surely the disappearance of the black rocks "is agayns the proces of nature," but so too is Aurelius, who disrupts the expected sexual roles of lover and beloved by disavowing the mutual masochism at the heart of their relationship in favor of activity rather than passivity. Like the Courtly Lady, he now acts as a Queer Thing in this passage, forcing Dorigen to confront the emptiness of her masochistic performances of forbearance and the possibility that the narcissistic image she created for herself is merely an antierotic facade, one that defined her virtue while awaiting Arveragus's return, but that can no longer withstand the pressures of an eroticism unconstrained by masochism.

The remainder of *The Franklin's Tale* must quell this disruption to its masochistic logic so that passivity will triumph as the defining feature of eroticism and its queer disruptions of gendered paradigms. When Dorigen contemplates suicide in a scene akin to Aurelius's threat of suicide to the magician, she again appears to be acting masochistically in pursuit of punishment, and Deleuze notes the "provocative fear" that sparks the masochist to "aggressively demand punishment since it resolves anxiety and allows him to enjoy the forbidden pleasure."[46] Because of Dorigen's multiple positions—as Courtly Lady, as Queer Thing, and as masochistic performer of her own suffering—gender can no longer guide her in her decisions, for gender is incapable of pinning down these oscillating roles to a singularly sexed body. When she catalogues virtuous wives and maidens who choose suicide over dishonor, she attempts to gird herself to act, to embrace the agency necessary to abrogate her suffering:

> "And with my deth I may be quyt, ywis.
> Hath ther nat many a noble wyf er this,
> And many a mayde, yslayn hirself, allas,
> Rather than with hir body doon trespas?"
> (V.1363–66)

Unlike the many heroines of Chaucer's *Legend of Good Women,* who prove their virtue by their willing deaths, Dorigen does not act; instead, she "pleyned . . . a day or tweye, / Purposynge evere that she wolde deye" (V.1457–58). Her masochism demands that such performances con-

---

[46] Ibid., 75.

tinue, for ending them would abrogate the oscillations at the core of her romance that define her pursuit of pleasure: although some might argue that suicide represents the logical end point of masochism in the disavowal of desire through death, suicide corrupts the performative nature of suffering and substitutes irrevocable action for momentary posturings designed to perpetuate the lovers' erotic play.

In his capricious and arbitrary reaction to Dorigen's amatory suffering, Arveragus again assumes the position of the hermaphroditic Courtly Lady, one whose actions deflect internal logic yet nonetheless compel Dorigen as masochist to embrace ever more suffering. Strangely, he initially seems pleased with Dorigen's plight: in response to her tears, he replies "with glad chiere, in freendly wyse" (V.1467), and his words to her, "Is ther oght elles, Dorigen, but this?" (V.1469), imply that the matter of her incipient unfaithfulness is a trifling concern, of little relevance to their continued happiness. Alcuin Blamires perceives in Arveragus's reaction "the Stoic ideal of the compassionate person, who relieves those who are in tears, but without weeping *with* them,"[47] and this image of reacting by not reacting captures the rigidity of the Courtly Lady's stance, in which the suitor must prove his devotion by acting against his own self-interest and privileging the beloved's inscrutable desires. In a swift reversal of his initial nonchalance, Arveragus then threatens Dorigen with her imminent death: "I yow forbede, up peyne of deeth, / That nevere, whil thee lasteth lyf ne breeth, / To no wight telle thou of this aventure" (V.1481–83). Raymond Tripp observes an "irony . . . emerg[ing] in the fact that Arveragus, in his attempt to escape his masculine role (and all of its attendant trials and complications), finds himself assuming an *absolute maistrye* over Dorigen, even to the point of threatening her with the 'peyne of deeth.'"[48] Whether the imperious Courtly Lady or the masochistic suitor, Arveragus acts through his inaction and thus paradoxically circulates masochistic desire throughout the triangulated affair. For in compelling Dorigen to degrade herself sexually in response to his arbitrary rulings as Courtly Lady/Queer Thing, Arveragus also showcases his impervious self-control by which he prepares himself for the pain of her cuckolding him, and

<hr />

[47] Alcuin Blamires, *Chaucer, Ethics, and Gender* (Oxford: Oxford University Press, 2006), 154–55; italics in original.

[48] Raymond Tripp, "The Franklin's Solution to the 'Marriage Debate'," in *New Views on Chaucer: Essays in Generative Criticism,* ed. William Johnson and Loren Gruber (Denver: Society for New Language Study, 1973), 35–41 (39).

consequently so too does he simultaneously reconfigure himself into yet another masochistic position as well. Deleuze observes the masochist's propensity to pander his wife: "the masochist persuades his wife, in her capacity as good mother, to give herself to other men."[49] The male masochist's ultimate humiliation in cuckoldry is thus the fullest pleasure available to him, but one to which he must coerce his wife to submit so that the queer pleasure of abjection will surface through the circulation of a woman among a male homosocial milieu.

The ending of *The Franklin's Tale* details the perfect stasis of masochism, in which none of the four primary characters sate their desires other than through the continued play of forbearance. The Franklin records Arveragus and Dorigen's "happily ever after" ending and then dismisses them from the narrative: "Of thise two folk ye gete of me namoore" (V.1556). It is intriguing to contemplate Arveragus's masochistic disappointment in his wife's failure to cuckold him, and readers see little evidence to suggest that the purportedly "happily ever after" ending concludes the mutually masochistic maneuverings that define their courtship and marriage. At the very least, the tale continues after its ostensible protagonists' departure from the narrative, which highlights that this husband and wife's marital adventures cannot circumscribe its thematic concerns, and instead posits masochism as a generative force within various human relationships. In light of Arveragus and Dorigen's mutual masochism, Aurelius purges himself of desire:

> And in his herte he caughte of this greet routhe,
> Considerynge the beste on every syde,
> That fro his lust yet were hym levere abyde
> Than doon so heigh a cherlyssh wrecchednesse
> Agayns franchise and alle gentillesse.
>
> (V.1520–24)

Furthermore, Aurelius is prepared to abase himself perpetually for their love: "I have wel levere evere to suffre wo / Than I departe the love bitwix yow two" (V.1531–32). Choosing perpetual woe, Aurelius emerges as an avatar of masochism, one rid of any desire other than to suffer for others so that he may be celebrated for such suffering. In a final scene of recuperating and reframing desire, the magician sacrifices

---

[49] Deleuze, *Masochism*, 63.

monetary gain and forgives Aurelius his debt. From the mutually masochistic play of courtly love and marriage, Dorigen, Arveragus, Aurelius, and the magician embody the emptiness of gender and the intransigence of the queer Courtly Lady, a hermaphroditic position that guides them to renounce desire for the sake of the painful pleasure at the heart of this renunciation and the narcissistic refashioning of desirability through the suffering and depredations incurred.

Epilogue: The Modest Franklin

I do not argue in this essay's concluding section that the Franklin engages in a mutually masochistic relationship with Harry Bailly and his fellow pilgrims by telling his tale. The relatively scant descriptions of the Franklin—his *General Prologue* portrait (I.331–60), his words with the Squire at the close of *The Squire's Tale* (V.673–708), and his *Prologue* (V.709–28)—do not offer sufficient evidence to warrant such an interpretation. The masochistic performances of amatory submission in the Franklin's tale and his performance of modesty in tale-telling are nonetheless analogous in their deployment of submission as an obfuscatory tool that camouflages desires circulating throughout interpersonal relationships. Power and gender dynamics resonate throughout the Canterbury pilgrimage, and the Franklin's modesty emerges as yet another tactic in the ongoing squabbling among the pilgrims, couched as it is under the guise of play and game.

The Franklin's relationship with his fellow pilgrims showcases the subtle power of modesty and etiquette, in which social pleasantries cloak his authority under a veneer of submission. In describing the Franklin in the *General Prologue*, Chaucer stresses this character's largesse and hospitality. He is compared to Saint Julian, patron saint of hospitality (I.340), and the abundance of food in his house establishes the character's ample generosity: "It snewed in his hous of mete and drynke" (I.345). Likewise, when the Franklin joins the narrative action of the pilgrimage by interrupting the Squire's rambling tale, readers witness the latent authority accessible to those who understand social ritual. "As to my doom, ther is noon that is heere / Of eloquence that shal be thy peere, / . . . / For of thy speche I have greet deyntee" (V.677–78, 681), the Franklin graciously declares to the Squire, but of course his deeper purpose is not to praise the young man but to silence him. Similarly, after Harry Bailly rudely interrupts the Franklin—"Straw for youre gen-

tillesse!" (V.695)—the Franklin employs eloquence to silence Harry
while promising to submit to him:

> "Gladly, sire Hoost," quod he, "I wole obeye
> Unto your wyl; now herkneth what I seye.
> I wol yow nat contrarien in no wyse
> As fer as that my wittes wol suffyse.
> I prey to God that it may plesen yow."
>
> (V.703–7)

Much like the Clerk, who earlier pledged his obedience to Harry's will
but then immediately qualified this submission—"And therfore wol I
do yow obeisance, / As fer as resoun axeth, hardily" (IV.24–25)—the
Franklin promises fidelity to Harry's rule while simultaneously excluding his full adherence to this authority. Like the masochist who performs
subservience for his imperious beloved, the Franklin plays his role in
submission to Harry's authority, but this performance only highlights
the potential emptiness of such playacting.

Chaucer continues his description of the Franklin's submissiveness
when, in his prologue, the Franklin introduces his tale through his modesty topos and deprecates his rhetorical skills:

> "I lerned nevere rethorik, certeyn;
> Thyng that I speke, it moot be bare and pleyn.
> I sleep nevere on the Mount of Pernaso,
> Ne lerned Marcus Tullius Scithero."
>
> (V.719–22)

Such proclamations of rhetorical modesty appear in other Chaucerian
narratives, and Donald Fritz posits that these instances of modesty reveal that Chaucer's characters "wrestl[e] with the problem of artistic
communication of deep and abiding truths."[50] The Franklin cannot
openly criticize the social structure of the Canterbury pilgrimage, but
he can employ his story to reimagine the gendered dynamics of the
pilgrimage that the blustering Harry Bailly controls. Tale-telling involves rhetorical choices that at times camouflage violent desires, as Sandra McEntire provocatively explains of *The Franklin's Tale*: "In taking

---

[50] Donald Fritz, "The Prioress's Avowal of Ineptitude," *ChauR* 9.2 (1974): 166–81
(179).

old stories, remaking them and interpreting them, Chaucer is in effect acting like Aurelius with the body of narrative. He takes a text and breaks it apart, rapes and dismembers it as it were, and puts it back together—remembers it—with his own insights, subtexts, interpretations."[51] McEntire's startling metaphors of rape and dismemberment for retelling narratives capture the aggressive dynamics latent throughout the Canterbury pilgrimage and point to the ways in which the Franklin engages in such aggression through rhetorical choices rather than through direct insults or bawdily allegorical narratives.

In regendering narrative through his mutually masochistic tale, the Franklin forecloses masculine pleasure in climax, and, in so doing, queers the meaning of normative gender for his fellow pilgrims. Numerous narratological theories posit that plotlines emulate the physiological pleasures of male orgasm, such as in Robert Scholes's (in)famous formulation:

The archetype of all fiction is the sexual act. In saying this I do not mean merely to remind the reader of the connection between all art and the erotic in human nature. . . . For what connects fiction—and music—with sex is the fundamental orgastic rhythm of tumescence and detumescence, of tension and resolution, of intensification to the point of climax and consummation. In the sophisticated forms of fiction, as in the sophisticated practice of sex, much of the art consists of delaying climax within the framework of desire in order to prolong the pleasurable act itself.[52]

But what of narratives without climaxes? Where is the narrative pleasure of orgasm in a tale that refuses its reader the pleasure of climax? One would be hard pressed to locate a climax in *The Franklin's Tale*: is it Dorigen's decision to commit suicide (which she then ignores), her confession to Arveragus of her commitment to Aurelius (which he then forgives), her meeting with Aurelius in which she is prepared to fulfill her obligations (of which he then absolves her)? One could argue that

[51] Sandra McEntire, "Illusions and Interpretation in the *Franklin's Tale*," *ChauR* 31.2 (1996): 145–63 (160).
[52] Robert Scholes, *Fabulation and Metafiction* (Urbana: University of Illinois Press, 1979), 26. See also Peter Brooks, "Freud's Masterplot: A Model for Narrative," in his *Reading for the Plot* (New York: Vintage, 1984), 90–112. For critiques of such narratological theories, see Teresa de Lauretis, *Alice Doesn't: Feminism, Semiotics, Cinema* (Bloomington: Indiana University Press, 1984), esp. 103–57, and Susan Winnett, "Coming Unstrung: Women, Men, Narrative, and Principles of Pleasure," *PMLA* 105.3 (1990): 505–18.

the tale's climax and its inconclusive conclusion unite in its closing *demande d'amour,* as the Franklin queries: "Which was the mooste fre, as thynketh yow? / Now telleth me, er that ye ferther wende. / I kan namoore; my tale is at an ende" (V.1622–24). To end a narrative with a *demande d'amour,* however, encodes a fundamentally different structure into its plotline, for in Chaucer's other narratives containing *demandes d'amour—The Knight's Tale* and *Wife of Bath's Tale*—these amatory rhetorical questions occur early in the plot and are at least implicitly resolved. *The Knight's Tale* queries, "Who hath the worse, Arcite or Palamoun?" (I.1348), and although the debate over whether the imprisoned lover who can see his beloved fares better or worse than the emancipated lover who cannot see her is not definitively resolved, the narrative concludes in favor of Palamon as he wins Emily in marriage and thus settles any unresolved aspects of the lovers' fates. The provocative query at the heart of *The Wife of Bath's Tale*—"What thyng is it that wommen moost desiren" (III.905)—is conclusively answered: "Wommen desiren to have sovereynetee / As wel over hir housbond as hir love, / And for to been in maistrie hym above" (III.1038–40).

The Franklin, in contrast, ends his tale with a question that refuses a pat answer and thus rejects the narrative rhythms of male desire and masculinist plotlines. As his play of modesty invites his fellow pilgrims to dismiss him as an inept storyteller before he commences his narrative, the Franklin reveals his sophisticated technique throughout his tale, which culminates without a climax or definitive conclusion. In so doing, he asks his fellow pilgrims to consider the possibility of a form of narrative pleasure distinct from those that have come before, one in which recalcitrant inaction trumps action.

The Franklin's refusal to end his story conclusively encodes an absence in his narrative, and as Elizabeth Scala argues, such absences in many instances constitute a narrative's core: "In these complex medieval stories themselves, and through their indications of what is *not* the subject of the story, the absent narrative is revealed as an unconscious subject of narrative."[53] Because Chaucer did not depict the pilgrims' reactions to *The Franklin's Tale,* it is impossible to gauge their response to it and its narrative ploys. Nonetheless, in reconfiguring the narratological expectations of pleasure in climax, the Franklin effectively asks

---

[53] Elizabeth Scala, *Absent Narratives, Manuscript Textuality, and Literary Structure in Late Medieval England* (New York: Palgrave Macmillan, 2002), 12.

his audience to experience female narrative pleasure. The Franklin does not address narratology when he declares, "Pacience is an heigh vertu, certeyn / For it venquysseth, as thise clerkes seyn, / Thynges that rigour sholde nevere atteyne" (V.773–75), but these words are nonetheless intriguing in their dismissal of masculine rigor in favor of endless patience and suffering and in their rewriting of mutually masochistic forbearance into the rules of courtly love and of narrative. As Dorigen, Arveragus, and Aurelius queer the foundations of gender and reveal the inherently convoluted play of masochistic desire in *The Franklin's Tale,* so too does the Franklin coerce his fellow pilgrims to embrace such patience, even if this narrative strategy refuses them the pleasure of climax in favor of patiently waiting for an ending that will never arrive.

The Anxiety of Exclusion:

Speech, Power, and Chaucer's Manciple

Craig E. Bertolet
Auburn University

I

SCHOLARS HAVE SEEN CHAUCER'S MANCIPLE as a critic of un-restricted tongues and dangerous language, even as a pilgrim who re-grets his one speech in the *Canterbury Tales*.[1] In the words of Louise Fradenburg, "Language—its uses and abuses—has seemed to so many critics to be what the tale is 'about.'"[2] Much of the critical attention to language or speech in the tale has tended to concern the court and the

An early version of a portion of this essay was presented at the Midwest British Studies Conference in Columbus, Ohio, in 2002. I wish to thank the anonymous readers of *SAC* for their thoughtful comments and suggestions on earlier drafts of this essay.

[1] For instance, Derek Pearsall argues that the Manciple maintains that language "is a form of trickery, a sham, a way men have of dressing up their acts of animal instinct in a fancy guise. The thing to do, the Manciple implies, is to learn the tricks (to learn how to call black white) and use them for one's own advantage, and not to be carried away by passion or idealism or that shibboleth called truth." Pearsall, *The Canterbury Tales* (London: Routledge, 1993), 241. Edwin D. Craun concludes that the "Manciple's parody demonstrates that, divorced from both its semiotic basis and the analysis of specific sins, general prudential discourse on restraining speech is contradictory in its very prolixity, exaggerated in its claims to govern all speech, nauseatingly self-serving, tediously admonitory, and easily reducible to disjointed babble." Craun, *Lies, Slander, and Obscenity in Medieval English Literature: Pastoral Rhetoric and the Deviant Speaker* (Cambridge: Cambridge University Press, 1997), 229. See also J. Burke Severs, "Is the 'Manciple's Tale' a Success?" *JEGP* 51 (1952): 1–16; Britton J. Harwood, "Language and the Real: Chaucer's Manciple," *ChauR* 6 (1972): 268–79; Carl Lindahl, *Earnest Games: Folkloric Patterns in the "Canterbury Tales"* (Bloomington: Indiana University Press, 1987), 153–55; Celeste A. Patton, "False 'Rekenynges': Sharp Practice and the Politics of Language in Chaucer's *Manciple's Tale*," *PQ* 71 (1992): 399–417; Helen Cooper, *Oxford Guides to Chaucer: "The Canterbury Tales,"* 2nd ed. (Oxford: Oxford University Press, 1996), 55.

[2] Louise Fradenburg, "The Manciple's Servant Tongue: Politics and Poetry in *The Canterbury Tales*," *ELH* 52 (1985): 85–118 (88). See also Marianne Børch, "Chaucer's Poetics and the *Manciple's Tale*," *SAC* 25 (2003): 287–97.

role of the poet in it. This focus on the court, however, overlooks another important setting where, as Chaucer would have known, speech needed to be guarded: the City of London. Certainly a court poet needed to be very careful about what he or she wrote.[3] But London was also a dangerous place for problematic language and incautious speech. Additionally, the Manciple's position as a London servant working in a house of lawyers compounds the potential risks to the person who cannot govern his or her tongue. His behavior and his tale demonstrate an anxiety less about language and aristocratic courts than about the sovereign power that makes the rules governing speech and which excludes individuals from the community when they have transgressed these rules.

The Manciple embodies anxiety over public utterance more than any other pilgrim, his tale revealing that his greatest fear is to be excluded or exiled from any company. He would have resided in the City, where lurked reminders of what happened when one's livelihood disappeared or was taken away: London had a large number of beggars, cast-off apprentices, and luckless poor, wretched individuals who had no way out of their poverty except through death.[4] To avoid this fate, the Manciple believes he needs to keep his masters happy and himself free from suspicion. Above all, he must not give offense in anything he says lest others more powerful than himself misconstrue his words. As a character associated with litigation and domestic service in the City, Chaucer's Manciple is the pilgrim most qualified to speak about the consequences of crimes of the tongue.[5]

The Manciple stands in contrast to the talkative Canon's Yeoman, whose entry precedes the Manciple's tale in the Ellesmere order of the *Canterbury Tales*.[6] The Canon's Yeoman talks his way out of the Canon's

[3] William Askins argues that the Manciple, as a teller, is gossiping about aristocratic depravity. The Manciple is a London gossip who "would have nothing to say were it not for chivalric decadence." Askins, "The Historical Setting of *The Manciple's Tale*," *SAC* 7 (1985): 87–105 (105).

[4] For a discussion of the poor in late medieval London, see Caroline M. Barron, *London in the Later Middle Ages: Government and People, 1200–1500* (Oxford: Oxford University Press, 2004), 273–78.

[5] For an account of the "sins of the mouth" in the theology of the period, see R. F. Yeager, "Aspects of Gluttony in Chaucer and Gower," *SP* 81 (1984): 42–55.

[6] Critics for many decades have seen a connection between the tales of the Manciple and of the Parson, who follows him. See, for instance, Wayne Shumaker, "Chaucer's *Manciple's Tale* as Part of a Canterbury Group," *UTQ* 22 (1953): 147–56; Paul G. Ruggiers, *The Art of the "Canterbury Tales"* (Madison: University of Wisconsin Press, 1965), 247–49; Trevor Whittock, *A Reading of the "Canterbury Tales"* (Cambridge: Cambridge University Press, 1968), 280–85; Harwood, "Language and the Real"; Donald R. Howard, *The Idea of the "Canterbury Tales"* (Berkeley and Los Angeles: University of

service and into membership of the pilgrim company by indicting his master's character. After his prologue and tale, the Canon's Yeoman appears to have no secrets left. This is not the case with the Manciple: both the Host and the narrator hint that the Manciple may be cheating his employers, but he is clever enough to "sette hir aller cappe."[7] Harry Bailly claims to have knowledge of the Manciple's secret in order to silence him when the Manciple rebukes the drunken Cook (IX.69–75). Since the Manciple does not want to make public what he is trying to hide, he overcompensates for any insult he may have given the Cook by offering him wine. His behavior suggests a perception that Harry's warning creates a double standard. Allowing the Canon's Yeoman to reveal all the secrets of his master while warning that the Manciple will have his own secrets revealed, Harry exposes the danger in a community where the speech codes are not exactly clear or are arbitrarily enforced and raises the question of why a sovereign power would sanction one speaker and not another.

In response to Harry's comments, the Manciple makes his tale of the crow into a cautionary fable condemning the license Harry gives the Canon's Yeoman. Both the Canon's Yeoman and the Manciple tell tales about servants who know something that will destroy their masters' reputations. The masters respond to the revelations by abandoning the servants who made them. As a consequence, the crow's future is grim, but for the Canon's Yeoman, abandonment seems a more positive development, as he is now free of the negligent Canon. Nevertheless, the Yeoman's future is potentially difficult also, as he will have no trade, friends, or money once he quits the pilgrim company. Hence by pairing these tales and tellers, Chaucer has the Manciple reveal his anxiety over exclusion in a tacit condemnation of the behavior of the Canon's Yeoman and Harry's apparent validation of this behavior. At the same time, he expresses the insecurity that London's speech codes produced for the powerless in the face of a sovereign power that seemed unpredictable and inconsistent in enforcing these codes.

The Manciple's tale poses and answers two tacit questions: Why is exclusion or exile a consequence of saying the wrong thing, and how

---

California Press, 1976), 304–6; Cooper, *Oxford Guides to Chaucer*, 391–92; John Hines, " 'For sorwe of which he brak his minstralcye': The Demise of the 'Sweete Noyse' of Verse in the *Canterbury Tales*," *SAC* 25 (2003): 299–308.

[7] *General Prologue*, I.586. Quotations from Chaucer are from *The Riverside Chaucer*, gen. ed. Larry D. Benson (Boston: Houghton-Mifflin, 1987).

does anyone know what the wrong thing is? In both questions, and for both pilgrims, what is at issue is the larger question: Who makes the rules?[8] Words permitted in one place or among one group of speakers may not be permitted elsewhere or among a different group of speakers. Similarly, speech that one regime would sanction might be considered treasonous in another.

John Gower, in his *Vox Clamantis,* provides one way of answering the Manciple's first implicit question, that of why exclusion should be the punishment for saying the wrong thing. Gower warns of a dangerous force in cities he calls *Susurrus* (or murmuring) that utters many scandals to the disgrace of the people ["Plebis in obprobrium scandala plura mouet"].[9] It is the force of all subversive speech, and consequently *Susurrus* needs to be removed from the city or the city will be destroyed (947–48). Gower's opinions on the sins of the tongue and their effect on urban spaces are, as we will see, in line with the philosophy of punishment under which London and other medieval societies worked. False speakers, troublemakers, and sowers of discord all need to be exiled for the good of the community.

The theoretical figure for this excluded or exiled individual is Giorgio Agamben's *homo sacer,* the individual who can be killed but not sacrificed. Agamben postulates that the sovereign power can create the situation for exclusion.[10] This sovereign power can be an individual, such as the figure of Phebus in *The Manciple's Tale*; it could also be a body of individuals, such as London's mayor and aldermen or one of its guilds. Agamben built his theory on Carl Schmitt's thesis that the sovereign decides on the exception to established rules.[11] If rules were enforced without exception, Schmitt argued, the result would be repetition or

---

[8] Pierre Bourdieu argues that language and power determine one another especially as they are governed by place: "This linguistic 'sense of place' governs the degree of constraint which a given field will bring to bear on the production of discourse, imposing silence or a hypercontrolled language on some people while allowing others the liberties of a language that is securely established." Bourdieu, *Language and Symbolic Power,* ed. John B. Thompson, trans. Gino Raymond and Matthew Adamson (Cambridge, Mass.: Harvard University Press, 1991), 82.

[9] *Vox Clamantis,* 5:884, in John Gower, *The Complete Works of John Gower,* ed. G. C. Macaulay, 4 vols. (Oxford: Oxford University Press, 1899–1902), vol. 4. All citations from Gower's poetry are from these volumes, and all translations are mine.

[10] Giorgio Agamben, *Homo Sacer: Sovereign Power and Bare Life,* trans. Daniel Heller-Roazen (Stanford: Stanford University Press, 1998), 15–29.

[11] Carl Schmitt, *Political Theology: Four Chapters on the Concept of Sovereignty,* trans. George Schwab (Cambridge, Mass.: MIT Press, 1985), 5.

mindless application.[12] This behavior would indicate a force that really does not have sovereignty. Consequently, the sovereign power can make laws more flexible and allow for extenuating circumstances.[13] For instance, London's beadles and constables enforced the laws of the City without exception, while the mayor and his aldermen could make exceptions in applying the law to account for specific situations.[14]

In having the power to grant exceptions to the rules, the sovereign becomes a gatekeeper for the community. Any transgressors of the rules who get no exception must be punished with separation from the community through exile or death. Once exiled or banned from the human community, a person loses all value and can be killed with impunity. For instance, killing an outlaw is not murder because the outlaw had forfeited his or her life once he or she was banished. Agamben adds that "what has been banned is delivered over to its own separateness and, at the same time, consigned to the mercy of the one who abandons it."[15] This separateness is what Gower argued for in the *Vox* when he proposed the removal of *Susurrus* from the city. Exile or separation from the general community deprives the banned individual of the protection of and identification with the community. In making his case, Agamben cites Germanic law, which states that the excluded person, "'banned from his city on pain of death must be considered as dead.'"[16] Once considered dead, the separated individual can expect no hope of return to the society that had expelled him or her. Separation, therefore, eliminates any security the person had inside the society.

In London, exclusion was particularly dangerous because the city's population was large and the kin structures that would normally form the bonds of security in the shires and market towns were not often to be found in the City. Individuals had to rely on their own reputations and the favor of others more powerful than themselves whose personal connections were based on employment, status, or charity. London's governors or its guild masters would separate individuals from their society internally through imprisonment or externally through exile. Separated or excluded individuals would lose their reputations, making it

[12] Schmitt, *Political Theology*, 15.
[13] Agamben argues that initially the state of law and exception are distinct until exceptions become the rule and everything becomes indistinct (*Homo Sacer*, 38).
[14] Barron, *London in the Later Middle Ages*, 124–25, 154–56.
[15] Agamben, *Homo Sacer*, 110.
[16] Ibid., 105.

difficult to rejoin the guild or the City from which they had been excluded. In the *Canterbury Tales,* the Canon's Yeoman fails to see the potential harm separation can bring him, while the Manciple is anxiously concerned about it.

Michel de Certeau provides an answer to the second question, that of knowing what speech is permissible. He suggests that a "person in-between" is a newcomer to a social situation. This person must use the systems imposed on him or her in order to find a means of assimilating: "Without leaving the place where he has no choice but to live and which lays down its laws for him, he establishes within it a degree of plurality and creativity. By an art of being in between, he draws unexpected results from his situation."[17] In other words, the person finds a middle ground between the systems of the place from which he or she had departed and the place where he or she now resides. As speech codes are among the most basic of integrating modes in a society, their understanding would be crucial for a person remaining in the society. De Certeau's "person in-between" never fully leaves the original society or joins the new society. He or she will make mistakes in the transition from one society to the other. The hope is that none of these mistakes will be fatal to inclusion in the new society. Consequently, finding this middle ground between these two societies involves a great deal of negotiation with the native population of the new society who would presumably know the codes that the assimilating individual does not. Also, the unexpected results de Certeau mentions may not always be positive. But the "person in-between" would be keen on learning what is acceptable behavior in order to stay in the position that he or she has created between societies. This middle position makes him or her vulnerable since he or she is neither one thing nor another.

Because of his court connections and his London background, Chaucer was a "person in-between." He created a space for himself in between both places while not entirely occupying either one. David Wallace argues that Chaucer was in fact an outsider wanting to stay inside an environment (in this case, the court) of which he was not naturally a member. His reliance on court patronage rather than his own birth made his position precarious, particularly when that patronage came into conflict with the shifting power structures that characterized

[17] Michel de Certeau, *The Practice of Everyday Life,* trans. Steven Rendall (Berkeley and Los Angeles: University of California Press, 1984), 30.

Richard II's reign. Wallace believes that Chaucer may have considered his non-noble roots as a potential hindrance to a would-be court poet. As such, Chaucer was especially vulnerable to saying the wrong thing in the presence of powerful people and being banished from court society.[18] His surviving poetry demonstrates his deftness at avoiding anything critical of the king or his policies.

But, as Gower argues, danger from incautious speech can occur in the city as well as in the court. Chaucer would have found this danger inside London more readily than inside the court. He possessed nearly a lifetime's experience of living and working in London, although he composed most of his *Tales* outside of it in Kent.[19] Also, the French-speaking court is probably not the primary audience for his *Tales*. That audience, as Paul Strohm has speculated, was instead a mixture of government bureaucrats, royal servants, and a host of Londoners.[20] Despite these contacts, Chaucer had no automatic security in either City or court; his inclusion would have involved being careful about what he said. He created a similar "person in-between" in the Manciple, a servant mingling with lawyers,[21] an outsider trying to remain part of a community while being mindful of how easy it is to be excluded from that same community.

Three different sovereign powers appear in the tales and prologues of the Canon's Yeoman and the Manciple. These powers create the rules governing permissible speech and declare the exclusions. First, London, the site of the Manciple's employment and ostensible point of departure for the Canterbury pilgrims, is a community under the sovereignty of its mayor and aldermen, who seek to keep its peace by regulating behavior (especially speech) and who have the power to ban all who transgress the City's laws. This cultural context is crucial for understanding the Manciple's anxiety. The history of the last two decades of the fourteenth century in London showed clearly that what was dangerous in speech depended on who had the sovereign power in the City.

[18] David Wallace, *Chaucerian Polity: Absolutist Lineages and Associational Forms in England and Italy* (Stanford: Stanford University Press, 1997), 249. Lindahl suggests that Chaucer "must have shared the Manciple's disgust at the deceitful rules which helped him hold his jobs" (*Earnest Games,* 155).

[19] Derek Pearsall, *The Life of Geoffrey Chaucer: A Critical Biography* (Cambridge, Mass.: Blackwell, 1992), 225.

[20] Paul Strohm, *Social Chaucer* (Cambridge, Mass.: Harvard University Press, 1989), 47–83.

[21] As Wallace suggests, Chaucer and the Manciple try to authenticate themselves "by hanging around men of law" (*Chaucerian Polity,* 249).

The same is true with the second sovereign power: the Host. Harry Bailly, as the governor of the Canterbury pilgrims, permits the Canon's Yeoman's separation from his master by sanctioning his public indictment of the Canon. The Canon's Yeoman is a "person in-between" by being literally a man between service to a master and membership in the pilgrim community. Revealing his master's secrets would have caused him to be punished in London, but Harry allows him to do so. Conversely, Harry advises the Manciple not to speak against the Cook. The apparent inconsistency in Harry's actions must serve to excite the Manciple's anxiety over licit and illicit speech, an anxiety expounded on in the digressions and moral of his tale.

This tale describes the third sovereign power, Phebus, the god of Truth, who runs his household like an absolute monarch, deciding the fates of all members therein by determining truth and falsehood. The end of the tale seems to name a fourth sovereign power, in the Manciple's mother. However, she is not a sovereign because her discourse allows for no exceptions. She demonstrates how repetition of rules without exception characterizes an absence of sovereignty. As such, she serves as a contrast to Phebus in the tale. Each of the sovereign entities enforces speech codes, maintaining power through intimidating those who wish to remain in their communities with the fear of exclusion. These factors demonstrate why the Manciple's message cautions against injudicious speech among the powerless and questions a sovereign power that would encourage such speech.

II

In late fourteenth-century London, speech was as much a commodity as wool, spices, or shoes. Its value was proportional to the status of the speaker and his or her allies. Guilds could rally around members, providing them with significant support. Alternatively, they could abandon an incautious member, exiling this person from the guild and exposing him or her to legal punishment or worse. For instance, the guild of Saint James, Garlickhithe, threatened any member who slandered the guild or who rebelled against its rules with banishment from it.[22]

Peace in London was tenuous at best in the later Middle Ages, but

[22] Toulmin Smith, *English Gilds,* EETS o.s. 40 (Oxford: Oxford University Press, 1870; rpt. 1963), 4–5.

the last four decades of the fourteenth century, as many scholars have noted, were particularly volatile, with internal and external rivalries playing out in the City's public spaces.[23] Sylvia L. Thrupp reports that the resources of the City were not adequate to police it; its leaders "were like the rulers of a nation engaged in a war for existence, who dare not throw too many controversial issues open for public discussion lest disagreements should weaken the unity that is for the moment so vital."[24] The fear of unregulated speech was similar to the fear of fire in the City. Just as a single unattended flame could get out of control and destroy the City, so a single quarrel could destroy the City if it was not silenced.[25] The responsibility of determining what was and what was not licit speech fell to the mayor, who could declare who should be punished for his or her words, and who could be granted an exception for them. Thrupp argues that "the individual's inescapable respect for authority" held him or her in check, serving as a "psychological prop," with those in power couching disobedience in such emotionally charged terms as sin.[26] This terminology in the mayor's denunciation of incautious speech extended the impact of a speaker's words to the disposition of his or her soul as well as to the body. Difficulties arose when the mayor himself caused the division he was charged with preventing. The last three decades of the fourteenth century saw this particular situation as a periodic occurrence.

King Richard II added to the insecurity of public utterance in London with his 1387 proclamation that threatened death and forfeiture of property to those who said anything against himself, his queen, or any

[23] See, for instance, Ruth Bird, *The Turbulent London of Richard II* (London: Longman, 1949); Paul Strohm, *Hochon's Arrow: The Social Imagination of Fourteenth-Century Texts* (Princeton: Princeton University Press, 1992); Pamela Nightingale, *A Medieval Mercantile Community: The Grocers' Company and the Politics and Trade of London, 1000–1485* (New Haven: Yale University Press, 1995); Wallace, *Chaucerian Polity*; Ardis Butterfield, ed., *Chaucer and the City* (Cambridge: D. S. Brewer, 2006).

[24] Sylvia L. Thrupp, *The Merchant Class in Medieval London, 1300–1500* (1948; Ann Arbor: University of Michigan Press, 1989), 99. She adds, "Having no adequate means at their disposal for insuring the orderly conduct of large public meetings or for coping with local riots, the authorities clung to policies of repression. No criticism was permitted save by action at law against a city officer" (99).

[25] See Marion Turner's discussion of what she calls "Discursive Turbulence" in London during the 1380s for an analysis of how Chaucer's *House of Fame* encapsulates the instability caused by forces inside and outside the City. Marion Turner, *Chaucerian Conflict: Languages of Antagonism in Late Fourteenth-Century London* (Oxford: Oxford University Press, 2007), 8–30.

[26] Thrupp, *The Merchant Class*, 16.

past, present, or future member of his court.[27] Marion Turner argues that his proclamation is indicative of the king's desire to control all discourse in order "to maintain his own sovereign voice as the only possible voice in London society."[28] It effectively made all comments, concerning just about any individual, illegal, particularly since it was impossible to determine who might be a future member of the king's court.

But London's government had been trying for decades before this proclamation to control public speech. It prosecuted those who spoke lies, spread scandal, fomented discord, or voiced opinions not generally thought to be prudent. Personal insults and other verbal offenses between citizens, rather than outright sedition, were the more common crimes of the tongue that led to punishment. The civic documents record cases of people convicted of using words often described in legal Latin as *contumeliosa* ["abusive"] or *maliciosa* ["malicious"]. These specific words, though, probably come from canon law. According to Gratian (who attributed the canon to the eighth-century pope Hadrian I), clerics should be whipped for malicious words ["*verba contumeliosa*"].[29] While probably not a direct influence on the development of English law for defamation, this canon is one of the earliest in Western Europe to establish a procedure for punishing slander.[30] R. H. Helmholz records that Roman law classified slander as a form of injury, considering that the damage was done to a person's reputation: "Thus, it was actionable to call another man a thief. But it was equally actionable to call him a blockhead, to say that he was of illegitimate birth, or even to call him blind, with the intent to do him harm."[31] London records demonstrate that the injury from insults, slander, and other malicious words damaged the City's peace as well as an individual reputation. As Gower cautions in the *Vox,* those individuals whose words damaged peace in the City needed to be removed from it.

---

[27] *Letter-Book H,* Corporation of London Records Office (London: Guildhall), fol. 223v.

[28] Turner, *Chaucerian Conflict,* 8–10. Turner adds, "Indeed, debates about discourse— about who has the right to speak, and what one is allowed to say, about who controls the preservation or destruction of documents, about the abuse of documentary culture, about whose voices are privileged, and how one can get one's voice heard—were central to political conflict in the late fourteenth century" (12).

[29] Gratian, *Decretum,* C. 6, q. 1, c. 1, in J.-P. Migne, ed., *Patrologiae latina, cursus completus,* vol. 187 (Paris, 1861), col. 715.

[30] R. H. Helmholz, *Select Cases on Defamation to 1600,* vol. 108 (London: Selden Society, 1985), xvi–xvii.

[31] Ibid., xix.

While the mayor usually did not exile people found guilty of using malicious words, he did exclude them from society by imprisoning them. For instance, Nicholas Bethewar, a skinner, was sent to prison in 1365 for uttering opprobrious and malicious words [*"uerba obprobria et maliciosa"*] in contempt of the mayor's court.[32] Eleven years later, another mayor committed Richard Harold to prison for calling John Baldock, the mayor's sergeant, a "babelmonger."[33] Alternatively, a mayor could sentence a spreader of lies to the pillory, often with a whetstone around the malefactor's neck. The punishment would be twofold. First, it would expose the falsity of the guilty person to public shame, thereby ruining his or her reputation. Second, the whetstone would indicate the potential for collateral harm that the person's incautious words could create. Frank Rexroth glosses the whetstone as indicating that "just as the stone was not itself capable of cutting, yet could sharpen a dagger so that it might cut, political lies were not in themselves violent, but caused people to rise up against the authorities!"[34] The whetstone also metaphorically sharpens the tongue of a malicious speaker to cause division by his or her words. Its use as a symbol of the potential serious damage resulting from the guilty person's lie presupposes a public sophisticated enough to understand how this punishment fits the crime. Chaucer's Pandarus attests to the clarity of the symbol when he advises Troilus: "A wheston is no kervyng instrument, / But yet it maketh sharppe kervyng tolis."[35] Pandarus, and people who saw the whetstone around the neck of the person in the stocks, understood it as being the means by which collateral damage can occur. Like a whetstone, words do not themselves cut, but they cause actions that do.

In sentencing people found guilty of using malicious words, the mayor needed to weigh the status of the speaker and the potential harm the words might cause. Lindahl points out that a slander case "was adjudged not by the actual damage incurred, but by its ultimate conceivable social consequences."[36] The mayor also needed to take into ac-

---

[32] "dictum in curiam maiori uerba obprobria et maliciosa in contemptu curia . . . ," *Plea and Memoranda Rolls,* Corporation of London Records Office (London Guildhall), A.10, mem.18v.

[33] A. H. Thomas, ed., *Calendar of Plea and Memoranda Rolls of the City of London Preserved Among the Archives of the City of London at the Guildhall, 1364–1381* (Cambridge: Cambridge University Press, 1929), 226.

[34] Frank Rexroth, *Deviance and Power in Late Medieval London,* trans. Pamela E. Selwyn (Cambridge: Cambridge University Press, 2007), 115.

[35] *Troilus and Criseyde,* 1.631–32.

[36] Lindahl, *Earnest Games,* 76.

count who was involved directly or indirectly. A person with a recognized dubious character, accused of using malicious words, might not garner any support for an exception to his or her punishment. Association with a person of bad character could be toxic for any supporter. For instance, John Walpole, a tailor, accused a sergeant of the City, John Bodesham (or Botlesham) of Bury, of being "a false ribald and a harlot" ["*falsum ribaldum siue harlotum*"] because in 1388, when Keeper at Ludgate prison, Bodesham had had Walpole transferred to Newgate when Walpole complained about Bodesham to the mayor. Walpole was eventually condemned because "he was and is a great disseminator of discord" in the City ["*fuit et est magnus seminator discordiarum*"].[37] Walpole was already in prison, where his potential for discord could be contained. The tailors did not come forward to defend him from this charge because Walpole had a proven record of unacceptable behavior. Using a similar defense against the possibility of civic disorder, the mayor's court punished several fullers in 1366 for uttering "malicious and contumelious words, causing a great affray and disturbance of the King's peace."[38] Here, the possibility of greater discord at the hands of a few members keeps the guild from intervening. In both cases, preserving the honorable reputation of the guild is more important than defending a member, especially if that member is breaking the City's speech codes.

However, if a guild were to support its member and this support were to have serious repercussions for the City, the mayor had to consider making an exception. As a case in point, when the tailor William Spaldyng was brought before the court of the mayor and alderman in March 1383 for "speaking evil and shameful words against Robert Croule, a tawyer," it was determined that "discord might have arisen between the two misteries of Tailors and Tawyers" because of Spaldyng's words. The mayor decided to send him to Newgate for forty days. On the day of his sentencing, however, the aldermen and the tawyers requested that Spaldyng be set free. The motivation of the tawyers in interceding for a tailor is not made clear in the record. Perhaps they hoped to prevent any subsequent reprisals from the tailors, or to heal the breach between the two guilds. In any case, the mayor freed Spal-

---

[37] *Plea and Memoranda Rolls*, A.34, mem.2r. On the term "harlot," see David Burnley, *A Guide to Chaucer's Language* (Norman: University of Oklahoma Press, 1983), 198.

[38] Thomas, ed., *Calendar of Plea and Memoranda Rolls*, 54–55; "per verba maliciosa ac contumeliosa insultum fecerunt in magnum affraium et perturbacionem pacis domini Regis . . ." (*Plea and Memoranda Rolls*, A.11, mem.3r).

dyng, warning him that he would be fined 100 marks (ca. £67) if he offended again.[39]

What differentiated Spaldyng from Bethewar and Walpole was the intervention of powerful allies. With the backing of a guild, Spaldyng was no longer a solitary troublemaker, but had protection that caused the mayor to amend his decision and create an exception for Spaldyng. Bethewar, who had no guild coming to his rescue, had to go to prison; because of his protectors, Spaldyng remained within the community.

When slander cases involved individuals of different social rank in the City, the words of the person of higher rank were accepted, regardless of whether or not they were true. In a case that provides an important precedent for Chaucer's Manciple, William Gedelyne charged his former master William de Ely with spreading a false rumor to defame Gedelyne so that he could not get a position in London but had to move to York, where his subsequent behavior showed him to have an exemplary character and Ely's remarks to have been slander. Gedelyne returned to challenge his former master's account, now with the support of four of his fellow guildsmen on oath. He even produced a document from York testifying to his good conduct there. When faced with the falseness of his accusation, Ely was found guilty and punished. However, his punishment consisted of standing on a stool in Guildhall.[40] Lindahl comments that Ely's was the "mildest act of public humiliation found in any of the records. . . . Clearly, the major effect, as well as the intent, of the actions, was to reinforce the control exercised by powerful citizens over weaker enemies."[41] Gedelyne's guilt is accepted initially without examination until he can muster support from persons with status to his defense. The damage Gedelyne suffers (exiled and unemployable) relative to what Ely endures underscores how powerless someone without support was in the City.

[39] A. H. Thomas, ed., *Calendar of Select Pleas and Memoranda of the City of London Preserved Among the Archives of the City of London at the Guildhall, 1381–1412* (Cambridge: Cambridge University Press, 1932), 40. In 1305, the Tailors and the Tawyers had had a particularly bloody conflict in London that lasted eight days and resulted in the indictment of several participants. See Ralph B. Pugh, ed., *Calendar of London Trailbaston Trials Under Commissions of 1305 and 1306* (London: HMSO, 1975), 33. Whether hostilities continued for the rest of the century is not known, but the case does illustrate how the rivalry between two trading groups in the City had the potential for volatility.

[40] Thomas, *Calendar of Plea and Memoranda Rolls 1364–1381*, 14; see also Lindahl's discussion of this case, *Earnest Games*, 78–79.

[41] Lindahl, *Earnest Games*, 79.

When a case of slander involved a Londoner and a noble or member of a noble household, however, the mayor was more interested in silencing his fellow Londoner than investigating any real basis in his or her words. Two cases illustrate how the City government acted in these situations. The first case concerns Simon Figge, who was found guilty on November 29, 1381, of spreading a lie throughout London about a murder involving a member of the earl of Northumberland's household. Figge was sentenced first to the pillory and then to prison by the mayor, who, the record proclaims, "had the King's commands to keep in peace the said City, and the suburbs thereof, so as to have no strife or affray therein." When he pronounced sentence, the mayor told Figge that if his lie reached the king, the City could be condemned and dissension might occur among the nobility.[42] The mayor's warning to Figge probably exaggerates the seriousness of his accusations, but his justification of Figge's punishment reflects the City's need to avoid at all costs possible division within itself.[43] Figge's offense comes only five months after the Peasants' Revolt. The mayor and aldermen could not afford to be lenient with someone slandering one of the most powerful men in the kingdom.[44] Putting Figge in the stocks first makes his punishment public so that anyone can see the result of slandering an aristocrat; sending him to prison afterward forces all legitimate society to abandon him.

The second case involves one of London's own officials charged with

---

[42] Henry Thomas Riley, ed., *Memorials of London and London Life in the XIII, XIV, and XV Centuries* (London: Longman's, 1868), 454; "in preceptio per dominium regem quod ipsi pacifice custodirent dicte ciuitatem et suburbes eiusdem ita quod nullum debatum nec affraium in eis fieret. Si illud mendacium auribus ipsius domini regis prouentur fuerit tota ciuitas leuiter dampnificari potuisset et etiam causa illius mendacii discordia inter magnates regni quod absit defacili euenisse potuisset" (*Letter-Book H,* fol. 138r). In another instance, a clerk of the Church of St. Peter the Little was arrested for having "spoken disrespectful and disorderly words" of John of Gaunt "to the great scandal of the said lord, and to the annoyance of all good folks of the city" ["a grant esclaundre du dit seigneur et pesantye des totes bones gentz de la cite"] (*Letter-Book H,* fol. 96v; Riley, *Memorials of London and London Life,* 425; Reginald R. Sharpe, ed., *Calendar of Letter-Books Preserved Among the Archives of the Corporation of the City of London at the Guildhall, Letter-Book H, 1375–1399* (London: John Edward Francis, 1907), 107–8.

[43] Rexroth's reading of this case argues that Northampton used Figge's case as an example to the people of London and to the king that he took seriously his charge as mayor to keep the peace especially while Parliament was in session (Rexroth, *Deviance and Power in Late Medieval London,* 144–45).

[44] To take one instance, the case against Nicholas Mollere in 1371 invokes a statute commanding that "no one shall presume to publish or spread false news, or to invent the same, whereby dissension, or tendency to dissension or scandal, may be produced between the King and the people, or other nobles of his realm, on pain of imprisonment" (Riley, *Memorials of London and London Life,* 352).

policing the City for dangerous speech. In 1388, a London beadle of the Cornhill Ward named William Asshewelle claimed that the king had arrested two aldermen and that the duke of Gloucester had broken the head of one of them with a key. Since Asshewelle's job as a beadle extended to arresting "such liars and inventors of such lies and rumors; and especially those who have reported such words or designs against the said Mayor, Sheriffs, and Aldermen," and since Gloucester was one of the Lords Appellant, Asshewelle had to lose his position because of the damage to London's liberties his words, as a City employee, could cause.[45] The City abandons Figge and Asshewelle, their status gone because of what they have said about powerful people around them. Whether what they said was true (and the accounts condemned their words emphatically as lies) was irrelevant since the mayor may not have been in the position to demand trials of Gloucester or Northumberland's man. Instead, punishing the powerless speakers of allegedly malicious words protects the City. The mayor turns each man into *homo sacer*. They are not to be killed, but the City abandons them.

The punishment of *powerful* Londoners in London, however, was more complicated. An illustration is the career of Nicholas Exton, alderman and fishmonger. Aldermen were the elite of the City, often wealthy and well connected. Under one mayoral regime, Exton became an exile; under another, he was an unjustly wronged citizen. Two different mayors made these conflicting determinations, basing their decisions (as Agamben argues the sovereign should do) on an exception to a specific rule. On August 10, 1382, Exton was arraigned in the court of the mayor of London and his aldermen for uttering "opprobrious words" against the mayor.[46] Three days later, a similar petition was lodged together with Exton's own wish to be discharged from his aldermancy. No final decision was made until a week later, when Exton was removed as alderman and Gilbert Maunfield (or Maghfeld) was chosen to take his

[45] Riley, *Memorials of London and London Life*, 507–8; "tales mentitores et talium mendacium et rumorum inuentores et precipue illos qui super dictos maiorem vicomites et aldermannos vel aliquem eorum talia verba vel consilia dixerint" (*Letter-Book H*, fol. 229r). See Barron, who reports that the beadle "was expected to ensure that there was no immorality in the ward, no peace-breaking, and no selling of goods contrary to mayoral precepts" (*London in the Later Middle Ages*, 124). See also Rexroth, *Deviance and Power in Late Medieval London*, 60–67.

[46] See Barbara A. Hanawalt's discussion on the mayor's official space that made transgressing these boundaries, such as with violent language, a crime against the dignity of the mayor. Hanawalt, *"Of Good and Ill Repute": Gender and Social Control in Medieval England* (Oxford: Oxford University Press, 1998), 20–24.

place. Exton had not appeared for the second and third reading of the petition.[47]

The mayor whom Exton slighted with his offensive words was John of Northampton. Elected for his first term in 1381, Northampton tried to break the power of Exton and his fellow fishmongers, who held a monopoly on the lucrative fish trade in London, by allowing foreigners and aliens to sell their wares at retail in direct competition with the fishmongers.[48] The fishmongers reacted strongly against the mayor, but Northampton must have planned on this response. Exton's fiery temperament played right into Northampton's hands, his words providing the mayor with a pretext to remove a political adversary from a powerful position in the City government, because slandering the mayor was a punishable offense. Later, Northampton deprived Exton of his citizenship because of these words and others he had spoken in Parliament; he also fined Exton £1,000.[49] By these actions, Northampton may have believed he had eliminated his foe, forcing Exton's friends to abandon him as too dangerous for their own association. If this was his hope, he miscalculated.

Almost two years later, a petition was sent to the mayor asking for the judgment against Exton to be reversed. The mayor by this time was Nicholas Brembre, Northampton's successor and political enemy, who had begun his mayoralty by reversing Northampton's legislation against the fishmongers.[50] He reinstated Exton, thereby garnering the support of Exton's guild. Moreover, Brembre and his aldermen ruled that Exton was deprived of his aldermancy and citizenship in error and that his fine was excessive. Exton regained his office and his citizenship.[51] The official entry record of his exile and fine is cancelled in the manuscript of the City's *Letter-Book H*.[52]

Agamben comments that the "troublemaker is precisely the one who tries to force sovereign power to translate itself into actuality."[53] In spite

---

[47] Sharpe, *Cal. Letter-Book H,* 196–97.

[48] Pamela Nightingale suggests that the fishmongers were easy targets because they controlled this food source "and could be accused of profiting at the expense of the poor" (*Medieval Mercantile Community,* 273). See also Bird, *The Turbulent London of Richard II,* 77–80.

[49] Sharpe, *Cal. Letter-Book H,* 204–5. See also Paul Strohm's entry on Exton in the *Dictionary of National Biography* (Oxford: Oxford University Press, 2004).

[50] Bird, *The Turbulent London of Richard II,* 79.

[51] Sharpe, *Cal. Letter-Book H,* 233–34.

[52] *Letter-Book H,* fol. 154r; Sharpe, *Cal. Letter-Book H,* 197 n. 1; 205 n. 1.

[53] Agamben, *Homo Sacer,* 47.

of his status and regardless of whether he was correct in the sentiments he expressed, Exton was clearly a troublemaker. Slandering the mayor challenged the sovereign power in the City, and Exton's opposition galvanized others in his trade to speak out against the mayor.[54] The *Letter-Book H* even comments that, when Exton came to Parliament on September 29, 1382, he and his companions appeared as if they were setting up a rivalry with the mayor.[55] This kind of behavior upset the delicate balance of order in the City. It also provided Northampton the opportunity to make a public example of those who would rebel against him as Northampton chose not to ignore Exton's challenge of his rule.

But the rivalry between Northampton and Brembre continued to disrupt London's civic life. In 1391, when Northampton was in exile and Brembre was dead, Mayor Adam Bamme had to issue a proclamation that no one should express opinions of either man within the City because, if something was not done about these two factions, "destruction and annihilation to [London] may readily ensue, and peril and damage to all the realm." Those who expressed these dangerous opinions were to be excluded from London society by being sent to Newgate Prison.[56] The proclamation's phrasing is legal boilerplate, evocative of other laws against unwise speech with the mayor again determining exactly what speech is permissible.

The case of Exton shows how his connections made what amounted to a rebellious attitude successively illegal, then legal. Another case, occurring at the same time though involving a person of a decidedly different social status, ended in death. Mayor Brembre executed John Constantyn, a Northampton partisan, in 1384 for "going among, counselling, comforting, and inciting the people" to rebel against the mayor. The king sanctioned Constantyn's death to strengthen the City government by "repressing and checking conspirators and contrivers of such covins and congregations, and all other misdoers through whom aught might hereafter ensue against our peace in the said city."[57] Constantyn's motivation derived in part from sympathy with Northampton; whether he was actually fomenting a rebellion is not certain. What is important

---

[54] *Letter-Book H* describes how a small group of fishmongers got into an altercation over whether to support or abandon Exton, with one of them threatening to fight the mayor himself at Horsedoune (Sharpe, *Cal. Letter-Book H,* 203).

[55] Ibid., 204.

[56] Riley, *Memorials of London and London Life,* 526–27.

[57] Ibid., 482–83.

is that a mayor of London ordered the death of one of his fellow citizens. Even though he was doing precisely what Constantyn was, Exton had connections in the City that kept Northampton from ordering his death. Conversely, Constantyn was a poor man from a powerless guild. Brembre probably thought that he could easily be killed or, to use Agamben's term, made a *homo sacer*.

Brembre himself suffered a similar fate a few years later. He found himself outside the law and abandoned by his own allies when Parliament condemned him to execution for treason in 1388. He had been loyal to Richard II; yet Richard did not have sovereign power in England at the time Brembre was tried for treason. The Lords Appellant, instead, judged that Brembre should be executed since he was not among their partisans. Now, Brembre was in Constantyn's position of not having sufficiently powerful allies to save him from the consequences of his words and deeds. Any potential supporter of Brembre in the City may have felt that coming to his aid at this moment challenged the most powerful men in the realm. This thought may have occurred to the mayor of London at the time of Brembre's trial: ironically, he was Nicholas Exton.

Exton's career illustrates how the classification of dangerous speech is a function of the support a speaker has with a sovereign power. When that power is against him, just as it was with William Gedelyne, Exton is removed from his position in society. When he has the mayor's support, he is reinstated and becomes the ultimate insider when he becomes mayor in his turn. His malicious words do him no permanent harm, while similar words earn Constantyn his death. Each mayor justified his actions by arguing that he was trying to eliminate any possibility of strife that malicious words would have caused when he separated the offender from the community. The Manciple's tale of the crow shows what happens when the sovereign removes support from the speaker who, like speakers from Exton to Northampton, speaks unwisely. Unlike Exton or Gedelyne, though, the crow cannot get reinstated.

Gower's version of the tale of the crow in Book III of the *Confessio Amantis* focuses on removing the cause of division from the community. According to Genius, this tale illustrates the sin of *cheste,* an English term for "strife." In Gower's tale, Phebus removes the crow's white feathers and its ability to speak, in punishment for its "wicke speche" (3.805). He then abandons the crow, excluding it from his household. From that time on, the bird's utterance only signals bad news: "som mishapp it signefieth" (814). Its exile removes the possibility of strife in Phebus's household because of the crow's "wicke speche." Gower's condemnation of the person whose words cause strife in the household is consistent with his condemnation in the *Vox* of the person whose words cause division in the city. These speakers need to be separated from the rest of the community.

Chaucer, in his own tale of the crow, uses not *cheste* but *janglyng,* a word he employs throughout the *Tales* to mean foolish speech. Chaucer's crow is not the purveyor of "wicke speche"; it is instead guilty of folly. Those few civic documents of the period written in English, such as the guild returns of 1389, often use the word *janglyng* to stand for incautious or even unwise speech. Chaucer's Parson defines *janglyng* as "whan a man speketh to muche biforn folk, and clappeth as a mille, and taketh no keep what he seith" (X.406).[58] A jangler is, then, a thoughtless prattler. The Pilgrim Miller is disparaged in the *General Prologue* as a "janglere and a goliardeys" (I.560). The Manciple's mother claims that a *jangler* is "to God abhomynable" and that a "litel janglyng causeth muchel reste" (IX.343, 350). The Nun's Priest's Daun Russell suggests that one should avoid *janglyng:*

> ". . . but God yeve hym meschaunce,
> That is so undiscreet of governaunce
> That jangleth whan he sholde holde his pees."
> (VII.3433–35)

In *The Manciple's Tale,* Phebus accuses the crow of *janglyng* because his own version of his wife's death bases itself not on the allegation that the wife had committed adultery, but that the crow had slandered her.[59] As such, the crow is being thoughtless rather than malicious. The words are not causing strife in Phebus's household but danger for the crow because they are unwise rather than wicked. The focus then in the Manciple's tale is on the individual rather than on the community, as Gower would maintain, because the individual's words are miscast against the

---

[58] The Parson also condemns tale-telling: "if he tale vanytees at chirche or at Goddes service, or that he be a talker of ydel wordes of folye or of vileynye, for he shal yelden acountes of it at the day of doom" (X.378).

[59] L. A. Westervelt writes that the accusation of *janglyng* fits the crow because it probably does not intend to have the wife killed, but to warn the master that his reputation is at stake. "The Mediaeval Notion of Janglery and Chaucer's *Manciple's Tale,*" *Southern Review* 14 (1981): 107–15 (112–13).

speaker. Phebus condemns the words as foolish, and the crow is power-less to correct him.

J. Burke Severs explains that *The Manciple's Tale* illustrates that "even when the informer acts from the best of motives, he still will suffer for his jangling."[60] Susan E. Phillips argues that the Manciple is a gossip or a person engaged in idle talk and, in this case, "the narrative and its moral participate in the 'janglyng' they condemn."[61] This would be the case if the Manciple's tale wasted a listener's time, as a jangler would do. Instead, as Phillips says, his "idle words are productive; they have the ability to blur boundaries not simply between vice and virtue, but between acquaintances and kin, narrative and news, idle talk and pasto-ral practice."[62] Since the crow suffered needlessly for its words, the Man-ciple's mother concludes that one should not invent tidings at all, whether they are new or old (IX.359–62). Narratives can be misinter-preted and good intentions taken the wrong way. The danger with speech is that a speaker cannot be entirely sure how his or her words will be received: "he that hath mysseyd . . . / He may by no wey clepe his word agayn" (353–54). The speaker needs to know what is, in de Certeau's words, the "linguistic 'sense of place.'" It is sound advice in the City given the court cases cited above, which show how dangerous incautious speech was.[63] The unfortunate speaker in the City suffers sep-aration for his or her words and is rendered silent by exile, prison, or death because of them. This approach to the problem of speech affects the relationships in the *Canterbury Tales'* frame-narrative as well as the Manciple and his tale.

III

Given that malicious words can lead to exclusion from civic society for most people except the very powerful because of their potential to gen-erate discord, how does Chaucer apply the anxiety over illicit speech in

---

[60] Severs, "'Manciple's Tale,'" 8.

[61] Susan E. Phillips, *Transforming Talk: The Problem with Gossip in Late Medieval En-gland* (University Park: Pennsylvania State University Press, 2007), 3.

[62] Ibid., 3.

[63] One of the complaints that the Reeve makes about the Miller's tale is that it defamed a man and his wife: "It is a synne and eek a greet folye / To apeyren any man, or hym defame, / And eek to bryngen wyves in swich fame" (I.3146–48). The Reeve explains that defamation is both a moral and an intellectual failing (sin and folly). His reading is different from the Parson's since it puts dangerous speech in the social envi-ronment of both the pilgrimage and society at large.

the context of London to the fictional trip to Canterbury? He makes Harry Bailly like London's mayor by giving him the power to determine what speech is licit or illicit. With this elevation to a higher status only for the duration of the pilgrimage and only for the pilgrim company, Harry embodies Agamben's concept of the sovereign. In his self-appointed role as governor, he outlines rules the company must follow and also grants exceptions to his rules. Unlike London's mayor, Harry cannot send any pilgrim to prison. He also cannot judge an offender as Agamben's *homo sacer*. The punishment he *can* impose is the separation of the malefactor from the company by silence. At first, he threatens to fine the pilgrims: " 'Whoso be rebel to my juggement / Shal paye for al that by the wey is spent' " (I.833–34). But as the *Tales* unfold, Harry's preferred method of punishment in practice shifts to silencing those who cause disturbances against his rule. A punished pilgrim remains in the company but ceases to participate actively in its discussions.

For instance, when the Knight interrupts the Monk, Harry sides with the Knight, validating his interruption and insulting the Monk, who has abused his position by telling more than his allotted number of tales. The Monk agrees to say nothing further when he refuses Harry's invitation to tell a tale of Harry's own choosing (VII.2805). In other words, Harry denies the Monk permission to speak any longer on his own topic, deeming it a waste of time and complaining, " 'I sholde er this han fallen doun for sleep' " (VII.2797). However, Harry gives the Miller (a noted "jangler") permission to speak so that the Miller does not follow through on his threat to leave the pilgrimage and break the fellowship (I.3133). Harry's decisions in these instances keep his people together and retain the integrity of the tale-telling game. They may, however, seem to be arbitrary to a character, such as the Manciple, wary of public utterance and surrounded by potentially dangerous speakers, janglers, and practitioners of fraud.

Silence then becomes the substitute for physical exile, just as the invitation to speak is a mark of inclusion in the company. The best example of Harry's enforcement of silence as a punishment is when he angrily responds to the Pardoner's comment that Harry "is moost envoluped in synne" (VI.943). The Pardoner's decision to remain with the pilgrimage tacitly accepts what the Manciple will make clearer: that to remain in a community, one needs to regulate one's tongue in deference to the sovereign power, or be excluded from further participation in the community. Nicholas Bethewar and John Walpole learn that they cannot remain in London society if they abuse the sovereign power or its minions with their words. While the Pardoner could leave (as the Canon will do), he chooses to stay, and no more words come from his mouth in the Ellesmere ordering of the *Tales*. The same is true for the Monk. In essence, he and the Pardoner agree to remove themselves from a group organized around the principle of talk.

In keeping the pilgrims together, Harry does not necessarily keep them peaceful. He uses his power to regulate speech in ways that appear to foment discord rather than quell it. By so doing, he allows pilgrims to insult each other without punishment. For instance, he forestalls the Reeve and the Summoner from abusing other pilgrims only to sanction their abuse when their turn comes to tell a tale. He picks a fight with the Cook (I.4344–55). He calls the Monk's tale dull (VII.2780–805) and Chaucer's *Sir Thopas* awful (919–25, 929–31). The Cook, the Monk, and Chaucer do not appear to challenge what he says. As the Pardoner's example shows, a pilgrim cannot insult Harry without punishment. Similarly, when Harry cautions the Manciple against speaking too freely after encouraging the Canon's Yeoman to do so (VIII.652–56, 697–98), he seems to be using a double standard. He seems also hypocritical in light of his own condemnation of the Cook. Harry does not silence the Manciple but warns him that the Cook may disparage the Manciple when given the chance to speak. Since the Reeve and Summoner had their chances to attack their rivals, the Manciple has good reason to believe that the Cook will be allowed to do so as well.

Harry's behavior matters for the Manciple here because it clarifies that Harry's intent is to encourage rivalry among speakers. Perhaps he thinks it will make the pilgrimage more interesting. In any case, Harry's warning that the Cook may know secrets about the Manciple does not mean that the Cook actually knows these secrets but that he will be given a turn to tell what he does know. Although the Cook and the Manciple are roughly equivalent in social level, Harry as governor is above them. He can sanction the Cook's words as he has just done for the Canon's Yeoman, a stranger allowed to betray every secret that his master possessed with Harry's encouragement. If his servant's revelations so discomfited the Canon that he exiled himself, how could an anxious Manciple fare, especially if he had something to hide?

The license given to the Canon's Yeoman to talk freely about the Canon is consistent with Harry's other invitations to offer potentially damaging information about another pilgrim. What makes this invitation different from all the others is that Harry is asking a servant to speak against his master. It is a significant exception to a cultural code that servants do not speak against their masters, especially in matters of trade. The Canon's Yeoman consents because he does have a legitimate complaint against his master, and Harry is the sovereign bidding him to speak.

The Canon and his Yeoman appear on the scene and crave membership of the pilgrim company without having followed the process whereby all the other pilgrims became members. The pilgrims have two basic rules for acceptance: all members tell tales and all members submit to Harry's authority. The Canon and his Yeoman cannot know these rules, which is why one of Harry's questions to the Canon's Yeoman about his master is, "'Can he oght telle a myrie tale or tweye, / With which he glade may this compaignye?'" (VIII.597–98). Although the Canon's Yeoman answers this question in the affirmative, he provides the requested tale after his master flees. As such, the Canon's Yeoman is the newcomer who adapts to the rules of his surroundings by breaking other rules. He shifts from what we can assume is his accustomed patter to indicting his master when it appears that the rules governing his speech are now different somehow.

At first, the Canon's Yeoman performs a system of boasts and dodges that he had presumably received from his master in peddling his master's skill (VIII.599–614, 620–26). For instance, to Harry's question whether his master is "a clerk, or noon," the Canon's Yeoman replies that "he is gretter than a clerk" (616–17), a response that does not answer the question. Only when Harry pierces this cloud of obfuscation by wondering how the sloppy appearance of the Canon accords with the Yeoman's speech does the servant change the substance of this speech and move to dissociate himself from the Canon (VIII.628–51). He agrees to reveal trade secrets, a decision that breaks any covenant he had with his master. Among other things, for instance, the Canon's Yeoman confesses that he and his master claim that "'of a pound [of gold] we koude make tweye. / Yet is it fals'" (VIII.677–78). Given his revelations, the Canon's Yeoman's return to his master (who cannot adapt and so must leave the society on which he had intruded) is unlikely.

The Canon's Yeoman's speech is dangerous for a servant, especially since the Canon accuses his Yeoman of slander (VIII.695).[64] The burden of proof should then be with the servant, as was demonstrated in the case of William Gedelyne, who suffered exile because the false opinion of William de Ely, his master, was accepted by virtue of his master's status. But Harry encourages the Canon's Yeoman to continue, bidding him to "'telle on, what so bityde. / Of al his thretyng rekke nat a myte!'" (VIII.697–98). This command seems in conflict with practice in London, which had initially condemned Gedelyne and upheld his master's opinion. However, Gedelyne was able to prove the falsity of his former master's accusation against him when he had the support of his guild. The same situation occurs here: the Canon's Yeoman has the authority of Harry urging him to speak and the pilgrims supporting this authority behind him. The Canon's status as superior to his servant, especially since he has no membership in the pilgrim community, is nullified.

Significantly, the Canon does not offer a contrary narrative to prove his charge of slander. Instead, he exiles himself from the community and presumably severs his connections with his servant forever. He is the only character in the frame narrative who chooses exclusion rather than silent participation. The narrator explains the Canon's decision to flee as deriving from the fear that "his Yeman wolde telle his pryvetee" (VIII.701). Once the Canon is gone, his Yeoman justifies that fear. The Canon may be the master of the Yeoman when he arrives, but the Canon has no status relative to the Canterbury pilgrims. Harry's decision to allow an exception in the relationship between servant and master ensures that the Canon would then have a problematic relationship with the pilgrims, who will know him to be a fraud. The Canon must be excluded. He leaves his former servant and silences himself in his exile.

The Canon's Yeoman becomes de Certeau's man in-between when he joins the pilgrims. He truly does not know the rules of this new situation. He uses the systems that appear to him and adapts to them as he sees fit. De Certeau comments that such a method of adaptation produces "unexpected results." As the Canon's Yeoman indicts his master, the Canon's Yeoman is in between his master and Harry Bailly. He is in between sales (in explaining the wonderful achievements of the Canon) and confession of their fraudulent character. He is in between employ-

[64] Hanawalt suggests that complaints about physical punishment by servants are rare in the surviving records probably because servants "expected a less sympathetic hearing from the mayor." Barbara A. Hanawalt, *Growing Up in Medieval London: The Experience of Childhood in History* (Oxford: Oxford University Press, 1993), 185.

ment with a dubious master and inclusion in the pilgrim company. Un-expectedly, the master, not the disobedient servant, is exiled from the community. But the Canon's former Yeoman does not achieve complete separation from the Canon, however, because he retains his association with his master in his name. Even after his master flees, he is still the Canon's Yeoman. He has no independent identity. His new society will not give him one. The in-between status the Canon's Yeoman now has is highly insecure. Once the pilgrimage is completed, he will have no place to go.

To a sensitive listener such as the Manciple, the Canon's Yeoman's revelations must be an unexpected result of Harry's governorship as well. Harry allows a servant to indict a master without fear of retribu-tion and to expose a fraud without evidence beyond the servant's per-sonal testimony. If the Canon feared that his "pryvetee" would be revealed, the Manciple may fear that the Cook would tell something about the Manciple's behavior that could get him dismissed from his position. Since the Manciple would need to purchase food from cooks, the pilgrim Cook might be able to reveal a trade secret, such as the Canon's Yeoman had been invited to do. The Manciple would have re-membered that Harry had exposed the shoddy work of the Cook earlier in the Prologue to the Cook's own tale. But what the Manciple would have witnessed and what he finds in his own experience when he con-demns the faults of another pilgrim in front of Harry are two different things. The unexpected result that the Manciple finds is that the rules of speech to which all the pilgrims agreed and which Harry should be regulating are not as free as the Manciple imagined them to be.

Like the Canon's Yeoman, the Manciple is also a "person in-between." He believes he has support when he condemns the Cook since Harry had done so. Harry's warning demonstrates that the Manciple is wrong in this assumption:

> "But yet, Manciple, in feith thou art to nyce,
> Thus openly repreve hym of his vice.
> Another day he wole, peraventure,
> Reclayme thee and brynge thee to lure;
> I meene, he speke wole of smale thynges,
> As for to pynchen at thy rekenynges,
> That were nat honest, if it cam to preef."
>
> (IX.69–75)

Accusing the Manciple of being too "nyce" or foolish, leaving himself open to some kind of response from the Cook, Harry is warning him against speaking openly. Harry evidently is an exception to his own rule. He can say anything, even slander, without any repercussions because he is the sovereign. The Cook does nothing when Harry alleges that the Cook practices fraud except to threaten to tell a tale about innkeepers; this threat never materializes in the surviving fragments (I.4356–63). Harry's behavior is consistent, though, with the behavior of the mayors of London, who could determine that the violent threats of Exton were illegal but, a few years later, legal. Harry's advice to the Manciple is the closest thing to a real assessment of the dangers of unguarded speech. It is also the closest thing to a demonstration of London's speech codes expressed before the Manciple begins his tale.

In his advice to the Manciple, Harry hits him exactly where the Manciple is the most vulnerable.[65] The powerless can only speak when protected by a powerful individual or group. William Spaldyng is considered a troublemaker by London's mayor until Spaldyng has the support of an entire guild to convince the mayor that a prison sentence for his malicious words would be unadvisable. William Gedelyne has a bad character until a group of his fellow guildsmen from York swears that he does not. Similarly, the Canon's Yeoman is not a troublemaking servant but a revealer of fraud once the leader of a large group of pilgrims bids him to do so. Harry's warning makes it difficult for the Manciple to know for certain what is permitted speech. It is a tacit caution that the Manciple's words do not have Harry's support, as the Canon's Yeoman's did. The Manciple speaks only as an individual without support of the company's sovereign. Consequently, the Manciple panics with the counterintuitive response of giving wine to the drunken Cook as a peace offering; this offering makes a suspicion of guilt more difficult to hide (IX.82–86).[66] He is assuredly feeling shame for speaking so unguardedly, but he deflects it by telling a tale emphasizing the Canon's Yeoman's incautious behavior and Harry's unwise decision to encourage it.

[65] Bourdieu explains that the "sense of one's own social worth . . . governs the practical relation to different markets (shyness, confidence, etc.) and, more generally, one's whole physical posture in the social world" (*Language and Symbolic Power*, 82).

[66] Scattergood argues that *The Manciple's Tale* advises care in speech, advice that is fitting for a man whose position is "responsible but dependent, in which the virtues of tact, circumspection and watchfulness would have been necessary." "The Manciple's Manner of Speaking," *EIC* 24 (1974): 124–46 (130).

The Manciple's tale of the crow responds to the confusion he experiences from this interchange with Harry and his own anxiety about speech codes. His tale critiques the ways in which a sovereign power determines licit speech. It is a cautionary tale for the Canon's Yeoman to explain why separation from one's master may not give the freedom one seeks. Like the Canon's Yeoman, the Manciple's crow also has no place to go once its association with Phebus is ended. This is the Manciple's point. As with the Canon's Yeoman, the crow has no independent identity except through its master: "Now hadde this Phebus in his hous a crowe . . . And taughte it speken, as men teche a jay" (IX.130–32). The crow, like the Canon's Yeoman, lodges with its master and is taught by him. The thing each master teaches his servant (the "knowledge" of alchemy or of speech) will be the means by which the servant will betray the master. The Manciple, though, imagines the separation between master and servant to be worse than what seems to be the Canon's Yeoman's experience.

For the Manciple, the Canon's Yeoman's decision to speak ill of the Canon and Harry's encouragement of it are unwise because the outcome is doubtful. The Manciple has Phebus encourage the crow to tell him why it is singing " 'Cokkow!' "—to which the foolish bird explains exactly what it knows about Phebus's cuckolding. The Manciple here criticizes both the sovereign for putting a servant in such a position as to betray him and the bird for agreeing to be put in that position (IX.243–61). The Manciple believes that inclusion, even if problematic, is preferable to exile. He uses the loss of the crow's livery of white feathers when Phebus exiles it (IX.304–5) as a metaphor for the loss of the security of inclusion; Phebus himself, in exiling the crow, represents the way in which sovereign power governs speech and determines silence.[67]

IV

The Manciple's anxiety over exclusion and the way in which the breaking of speech codes can cause it is the subject of both his tale and the long moral following it, placed in the mouth of his mother. The mother functions as a repeater of codes without the power to mitigate them as a sovereign can. She is presented in contrast to the third sovereign power

---

[67] Fradenburg suggests that this act marks the "ultimate subjection of the crow to the signification of the sovereign" ("The Manciple's Servant Tongue," 109).

associated with the Manciple: the character of Phebus in his tale. Phebus, like Harry Bailly, has sole control over whom or what he permits into and excludes from his society. When Phebus exiles the crow from his household, he turns the bird into a kind of *homo sacer*. He takes away the crow's voice and its white feathers in a ritual of preparation for exclusion. Each item is something Phebus has given the bird; its removal negates association with him. The removal of the white feathers negates any visual association and is analogous to removing a livery of cloth. The removal of the voice negates any aural association and eliminates any threat of the crow's countering Phebus's invented narrative account of his wife's death. The ocular proof of the denuded crow serves as a metaphor for the excluded individual. In this equation, the Canon's Yeoman is also a denuded crow because of the sovereign actions of Harry Bailly.

Liveried members of an aristocratic household stand for the person of their master. Elliot Kendall argues that the aristocratic household grew during the fourteenth century. This household relied on various kinds of exchanges for its sustenance.[68] For instance, in exchange for loyal service, a lord bestowed liveries on a servant to signify his ownership of the servant as well as the servant's membership in the lord's household. The liveried servant stood for the presence of the master. Richard II established his own livery, granting White Hart badges in the 1390s to create a band of followers who became loyal to him rather than to his government.[69] Fradenburg writes that these households or courts become "the instrument whereby the sovereign expresses the truth and magnificence of his being."[70] Servants, then, are "no more than a signifier."[71] Every servant in this court subsumes his or her individuality to the will of the sovereign.

Liveries of badges were signs of possession since they were cheap to produce and caused no visual change in status, only ownership. Liveries of cloth, however, "could designate status and rank within the household"; consequently, the wearer's own significance could change.[72] For

---

[68] Elliot Kendall, *Lordship and Literature: John Gower and the Politics of the Great Household* (Oxford: Oxford University Press, 2008), 17.

[69] See Nigel Saul's discussion on Richard's creation of a courtier-knightly class as his own personal affinity by the distribution of badges. Saul, *Richard II* (New Haven: Yale University Press, 1997), 263–69.

[70] Fradenburg, "The Manciple's Servant Tongue," 88.

[71] Ibid., 89.

[72] Kendall, *Lordship and Literature,* 191–92.

instance, Griselda in *The Clerk's Tale* undergoes such a change in status, akin to receiving a livery, when she is stripped of her peasant's clothing and clad in the costume befitting her new rank as Walter's wife (IV.377–78). This new costume stands for the visual proof of Walter's possession of her. When he sends her away from his household, this clothing is ritually removed, literally denuding her of her association with him (IV.894–96).

Like aristocratic households, guilds in medieval London also designated membership with liveries of cloth, such as the pilgrim Guildsmen wear (I.363). A person admitted to a guild and agreeing to wear its livery subsumed his or her identity into the guild, agreeing to its code of behavior in order to remain a member.[73] The guild could exclude members from wearing its livery should they break its rules, such as by betraying trade secrets as the Canon's Yeoman does. For instance, in 1360 the goldsmiths expelled John de Barton from their mystery and ordered his livery taken because of his "evil outrageous deeds which were not good, suitable nor faithful." Barton came before the whole company to beg its forgiveness, offering ten tuns of wine as a pledge of his good behavior. The guild accepted the tuns but ordered him to surrender a pipe of wine and pay twelve pence each week for the rest of the year for the support of a poor member of the guild. The tuns were forfeited to the guild if Barton resumed his evil deeds. Once he agreed to these demands, Barton could resume the livery.[74] Like Barton, the crow loses his livery because of deeds that seemed counter to the integrity of the community to which it is attached. Unlike Barton, the crow has no possibility of reinstatement.

The loss of the crow's voice strips it of the other gift Phebus has given it. Phebus keeps the crow as a pet, teaching it to speak "as men teche a jay." This trans-species meddling makes the crow into de Certeau's "person in-between": it is more than a crow but not quite a jay. The Manciple's message here is that the ability to speak does not bestow on the crow a natural understanding of what to say. Phebus did not teach that. Like the Canon's Yeoman, the crow is a "new-comer" in de Cer-

---

[73] Recognized inclusion in a guild (either attained through apprenticeship or sponsorship by another member) was a necessary precondition for enfranchisement in its society. See Reginald R. Sharpe, ed., *Calendar of Letter-Books Preserved Among the Archives of the Corporation of the City of London at the Guildhall, Letter-Book G, c. AD 1352–1374* (London: John Edward Francis, 1905), 179.

[74] Lisa Jefferson, ed., *Wardens' Accounts and Court Minute Books of the Goldsmiths' Mistery of London, 1334–1446* (Woodbridge: Boydell, 2003), 76–79.

teau's sense. It is in a place where it needs to learn the rules for inclusion. The difference is that Harry influences the Canon's Yeoman's words against his master by ranging the strength of this community against the frantic threats of the Canon. The crow, however, has no ally in its sovereign.

By stripping the crow of feathers and voice, Phebus transforms it from a speaking servant-bird into an inarticulate beast. This kind of transformation is what the *homo sacer* undergoes when he or she is exiled from the city. Agamben cites Marie de France's *Bisclavret* as a metaphor describing the state of exception for the *homo sacer*. In the lay, the were-wolf Bisclavret is a man when he has his clothes; when he strips them off, he becomes a wolf.[75] As a wolf, he is excluded from the human community and can be killed. The king's attendants urge the king to kill Bisclavret when, in his lupine form, he runs up to the king, seeming to attack him. But the wolf appears to beg mercy of the king, who then makes an exception to the law of killing wolves because the wolf seems to have human intelligence. Its demonstration of intelligence negates its bestial form, for the king and, consequently, for its ban. Bisclavret is the "person in-between" two states of existence (bestial and human), and society (forest and court). Bisclavret's story illustrates the opposite situation from that of Phebus's crow as, once the crow loses its humanlike speech, it becomes a beast that can be excluded from Phebus's household. Stripped of its "clothes," it has no status to identify itself with Phebus or his protection. In this state, the crow can be abandoned.

Individuals abandoned by families or neighborhoods were regarded with suspicion. They have no one to vouch for their character.[76] In the example of John de Barton, the prospect of being abandoned by his guild urges him to offer a high price to be reinstated. Abandonment affords him no security. Agamben writes that the abandoned being is "exposed and threatened on the threshold in which life and law, outside

---

[75] Agamben, *Homo Sacer,* 107–8.

[76] Bronislaw Geremek observes: "People on the margins of society, composed of constantly shifting elements, immigrants, and 'strangers', owed their instability to the fact of not being attached to a family. The servant or the journeyman, bound by a contract, or even the scholar lodged in a university college, found a substitute for the family tie in the guardianship of a master or a teacher; however, when this was absent, and he had left the paternal roof, he was abruptly placed outside the sphere of operation of models of behaviour, and escaped all control." Geremek, *The Margins of Society in Late Medieval Paris,* trans. Jean Birrell (Cambridge: Cambridge University Press, 1987), 276–77.

and inside, become indistinguishable."[77] Ruth Evans applies these distinctions to the tales of the Knight, the Clerk, and the Physician, in which certain characters seem to be placed outside any law and yet are still subject to a sovereign's will.[78] She suggests that Agamben's *homo sacer* enjoys an exception similar to the sovereign: "Sovereign and outlaw are reciprocally related: both are states of exception."[79] The Manciple recognizes a similar relationship: "'the tirant is of gretter myght / By force of meynee . . . / . . . the outlawe hath but smal meynee, / And may nat doon so greet an harm as he'" (IX.227–32). The presence or absence of power defined by secure support of a household, guild, or family (the "meynee") gives both tyrants and outlaws their respective statuses.[80] As we have seen, it is the principle that helps to determine whether speech in London is licit or dangerous. The Canon's Yeoman may believe he has a "meynee" on his side allowing him to speak frankly of his fraudulent master. The crow has no such thing. The Manciple's sentiment here is that betraying a master is only safe in his situation because of the associative body supporting him. But that body could change abruptly, especially if its sovereign changed his mind. The Canon's Yeoman's accusations are never tested, just as the crow's assertions are never challenged by Phebus's wife. Truth was never really at issue; what was important was the support the speaker had.

If the Canon's Yeoman's remarks concerning the Canon were true, a sovereign power, such as Harry, could accept them (as John of Northampton did with Exton's words), discount them (as with William de Ely's words against William Gedelyne), or create his own (as Phebus does). The Canon's Yeoman's testimony would then only have the veracity that Harry's agreement would give it. Similarly, Harry could accept

---

[77] Agamben, *Homo Sacer,* 28. Jean-Luc Nancy suggests that to be banished "does not amount to coming under a provision of the law, but rather to coming under the entirety of the law." Nancy, *The Birth to Presence,* trans. Brian Holmes et al. (Stanford: Stanford University Press, 1993), 44. According to Nancy, the abandoned person is not outside the law, but is subject to all the direct authority of the law.

[78] Ruth Evans, "The Production of Space in Chaucer's London," in *Chaucer and the City,* ed. Butterfield, 53–56.

[79] Ibid., 53; Agamben, *Homo Sacer,* 71–74.

[80] Sir Frederick Pollock and Frederic William Maitland, *The History of English Law Before the Time of Edward I,* 2nd ed., 2 vols. (Cambridge: Cambridge University Press, 1968), 1:476–78. According to medieval English legal justification, the outlaw was so designated when he failed to appear in court to answer charges brought against him; often the outlaw would then join or create his own criminal band. See John Bellamy, *Crime and Public Order in England in the Later Middle Ages* (London: Routledge and Kegan Paul, 1973), 69–70.

whatever the Cook said against the Manciple whether the Cook's statement is true or false. This tactic is easier for a sovereign than for a
servant because, as Schmitt argues (citing Thomas Hobbes), authority,
rather than truth, makes the laws.[81] By being the god of truth, Phebus
has the authority in the tale to make truth.[82] In fact, his power in the
tale is in determining (or in this case, inventing) truth. Consequently,
he recasts his adulterous wife as a wronged woman: "'O deere wyf! O
gemme of lustiheed! / That were to me so sad and eek so trewe'" (274–
75). His poetic lament creates a false narrative of her death. As such, it
proves the Manciple's axiom that word choice is linked with power:

> But that the gentile, in estaat above,
> She shal be cleped his lady, as in love;
> And for that oother is a povre womman,
> She shal be cleped his wenche or his lemman.
>
> (IX.217–20)

If one described Phebus's wife as she behaves, she is a "wenche" because
she chose as a lover a man who is not the god's peer: "oon of litel
reputacioun" (253). If one described her by the status she should have
by virtue of being the consort to a god, she is a lady. The Manciple's
justification, that the "word moot nede accorde with the dede" (208),
creates an important, though tacit, comment on *realpolitik*. It is appro-
priating the Host's observation about commercial fraud to the realm of
politics. Words and deeds get reinterpreted after the fact, changing their
meaning so that the only character in the Manciple's tale who did not
misbehave becomes the villain.

Phebus's rhetorical move saves his reputation by destroying his servant's reputation and security. He abuses his authority by creating his
own truth from a falsehood to satisfy no one but himself. This abuse is
a demonstration of his power. Agamben argues that "the sovereign is

---

[81] Schmitt, *Political Theology*, 33.

[82] Wallace remarks that Phebus "need not know how to persuade people to act in his
own household: he needs only to command" (*Chaucerian Polity*, 252–53). Stephanie
Trigg reads the relationship between Phebus and the crow as an example of friendship,
particularly since the crow uses the familiar "thou" when addressing its master. The
relationship changes to a hierarchical one between servant and master when Phebus
blames the crow for his wife's death. She explains: "It's a not big step from the idea
that offending someone enslaves you to them, to the idea that telling a displeasing story
has the same effect." Trigg, "Friendship, Association, and Service in *The Manciple's Tale*,"
SAC 25 (2003): 325–30 (330).

the point of indistinction between violence and law, the threshold on which violence passes over into law and law passes over into violence."[83] Phebus has the power to make violence legal. His unjust murder of his wife executes his judgment without allowing her a chance to speak in her defense. To Phebus, her behavior allows no exception if the words from the crow are to be believed. However, the wife's murder creates a dilemma for Phebus, as her death validates the crow's words and makes Phebus into a cuckold. What works best for Phebus's own fame, instead, is that the murder of his wife was a mistake based on false information provided by a troublemaking liar.[84] In essence, Phebus creates an exception for his own behavior.

Killing his wife and stripping the crow of the ability to speak ensures that Phebus's version of the story can never be countermanded by anyone who knows the truth. The man with whom Phebus's wife cuckolded Phebus is dismissed as a man of "litel reputacioun" (IX.199). His low status compared to Phebus automatically invalidates anything he said. Moreover, this man also has the wife's execution and the crow's exile as lessons for what could happen to him should he boast of his relationship with Phebus's wife. While Schmitt might believe that Phebus's actions show the strength of the sovereign, an individual or a group who can override the law or make exceptions to it based on an invented reality at the expense of those beneath them can create significant anxiety among the populace. Any guarantee of security that the law may provide is gone. The crow moves from being a loyal servant in Phebus's narrative to becoming a troublemaker who must be excluded. For its words, the crow is "slong / Unto the devel," into the hellish reality of banishment (IX.306–7). Its punishment is worse than the wife's. In the Manciple's grim vision, the bird brought on its exclusion with its ill-advised speech; it deserved what it got, as unfair as the capricious judgment may seem. With the message, messenger, and object of the message removed, the sovereign's narrative is now the unchallenged truth and order has been maintained. This is the truth that the Manciple takes from his mother's teaching.

[83] Agamben, *Homo Sacer*, 32.

[84] Eve Salisbury reminds us that when Chaucer served as Justice of the Peace for Kent, he would have been presented with the procedure for murder prosecution. *The Manciple's Tale* shows how a husband's murder of his wife in a jealous rage would have been a mitigating circumstance in a medieval English court of law: "The poet tells us that fictions surrounding private acts of violence could cleverly elude indictment and allow irate husbands to get away with murder." "Murdering Fiction: The Case of *The Manciple's Tale*," *SAC* 25 (2003): 309–16 (316).

The inclusion of the Manciple's mother in the role of providing an explicit moral to the tale is to show the voice of the powerless, resigned to accept that they have no control over their own speech in the presence of a sovereign power. While some scholars have read the mother in the context of Freudian desire,[85] another way of reading her is as a critique of sovereignty. Although a kind of authority figure to the Manciple by virtue of being his mother, she is, importantly, not a sovereign, such as Phebus, Harry Bailly, or the guild masters of London. She cannot provide any exceptions to the rules she relates. All her advice about speech to the Manciple is dogmatically negative. Improper speech will lead to exclusion. For instance, she argues that "A tonge kutteth freendshipe al a-two" (IX.342).[86] This violent metaphor stands for the severe punishment that she believes dangerous words will cause an unwise speaker. She warns that a "jangler is to God abhomynable" (IX.343), and says that because of too much talking has "many a man ben spilt" (IX.325–26). Each of these dire pronouncements implies a separation from human company, from God, and from one's life. She demonstrates Schmitt's thesis that mindless application of rules does not illustrate the power of a sovereign because, for her, punishment will come from other sources not from her. She can do nothing. The other sovereign entities associated with the Manciple (London, Harry, and Phebus) can decide on punishment and exclusion. The Manciple repeats her beliefs but with more thoughtful reflection than his crow demonstrates. This difference in reflection is his point. The crow's story is a moral lesson for a man who has been taught to believe that there are no exceptions for incautious speech.

As a result, the use of his mother here is not based on desire; she is rather the origin of his anxiety over how one's security can be lost after ill-considered words.[87] Because he does not have a group of individuals

[85] See, for instance, Peter W. Travis, "The Manciple's Phallic Matrix," *SAC* 25 (2003): 317–24.

[86] Craun observes that the mother's chief advice is not to spread tales: "'Avyse' (also X. 327 and 335) conveys looking mentally at potential utterances, prudently deliberating about what ought to be spoken. . . . Its moral opposite is 'janglyng'" (Craun, *Lies, Slander, and Obscenity in Medieval English Literature,* 205). See also Travis, "The Manciple's Phallic Matrix," 317–24.

[87] This suggests a different application of Freud to the tale, given that he explains that anxiety arises as a response to a dangerous situation. Sigmund Freud, *The Problem of Anxiety,* trans. Henry Alden Bunker (New York: W. W. Norton, 1936), 72. While the Manciple does seem to have a general suspicion of everyone around him, his anxiety is derived from what Freud describes as a situational fear. In this case, he feels anxiety where most people recognized a danger but were "accustomed to minimize the danger

on whom he can rely for security, the Manciple fixates on the exile that will come from transgressing societal rules.[88] The fate of the Manciple's crow justifies the preciseness of the anxiety. It says what it should not to whom it should not and loses everything.[89]

The message that the Manciple takes from his mother is that anything one says can cause one to be abandoned by everyone.[90] No exception will be granted to a speaker and no one should hope for a sovereign to intercede. Living in a place as prone to division and unrest as late fourteenth-century London, Chaucer's Manciple seems to believe that saying nothing at all is the best security, especially if silence can still allow inclusion, such as occurs among his fellow silenced pilgrims. However, silence does not relieve his anxiety, as his panic at the possibility of the Cook revealing the truth of his reckonings shows. He believes, as his mother cautioned, " 'Thyng that is seyd is seyd, and forth it gooth, / Though hym repente, or be hym nevere so looth' " (IX.355–56). One's words become everyone's words to be manipulated and misused. His mother saw no chance of redemption from badly chosen words. The Manciple believes this is so. If he can keep the Cook silent, he can escape

---

and not to anticipate it." Freud, *Introductory Lectures on Psychoanalysis,* trans. James Strachey (New York: W. W. Norton, 1977), 399.

[88] Additionally, the Manciple's anxiety over the crow in the tale could be what Freud might call a "screen memory," in which the associative properties of the image, rather than the content itself, are significant. In other words, the Manciple remembers the story that his mother told him because of the consequence of the crow's action rather than because of what the story actually contained. The Manciple's digressions underscore the instability of his narrative constructed by his own hazy memory of it. Sigmund Freud, *The Psychopathology of Everyday Life,* trans. Alan Tyson, ed. Angela Richards, Penguin Freud Library, vol. 5 (New York: Penguin, 1966), 83.

[89] In the case of the crow, Fradenburg comments that the "liberation from the cage of court is imagined, in the obsessional text, as mutilation and expulsion" ("The Manciple's Servant Tongue," 109).

[90] A better interpretive model for the Manciple's mother, though, is from Saint Augustine's reading of his own mother, Monica, a woman who (Augustine believed) exemplified the proper use of speech. In his *Confessions,* Augustine recalls that one of her virtues was that she did not stir up discord by repeating hateful things others said, but kept divisive things to herself. Drawing from his memory of his mother in these instances, Augustine concludes that "human decency should not cause a person to stir up enmities between people or cause them to grow through speaking evil if that person is also not willing to extinguish them with speaking good." ["cum contra homini humano parum esse debeat inimicitias hominum nec excitare nec augere male loquendo, nisi eas etiam extinguere bene loquendo studuerit."] Saint Augustine, *Confessions,* ed. James J. O'Donnell, 3 vols. (Oxford: Oxford University Press, 1992), 1:112 (my translation). What Augustine learns from Monica in this aspect of her character is how to speak well. He also captures the exception—that "speaking good" will negate "speaking evil." Monica's example teaches Augustine that speech is not always dangerous but should be moderated. The Manciple's mother sees no such possibilities except in prayer.

any punishment for whatever the Cook may say about him. He cannot apparently rely on Harry to be a mitigating force, and he wishes to avoid the fate of the Canon, who must flee out of shame for his deeds. The Manciple may be safe for the present but at the cost of not being happy.

Chaucer's last fiction reacts against the freedom of speech demonstrated by the Canon's Yeoman because a speaker cannot be assured of a fair hearing and a speaker's words can always be used against him or her. The Manciple understands better than the Canon's Yeoman does the price of ill-judged words. He acknowledges how impotent are the powerless before the political machinations of the great, even if they possess the truth. In Chaucer's London, truth also is relative to power. Sovereigns may grant license to speak, but their support is not always permanent. The "person in-between" is the most vulnerable and needs to take more care with what he or she says. One should not jangle, criticize, slander, or otherwise cause trouble. While tale-telling can be sanctioned by an authority, it risks a response or a misinterpretation from someone else that can harm the speaker.

Consequently, the Manciple, as the last secular tale-teller, maps out a dangerous landscape that any public speaker must negotiate. While the benefit may be continued inclusion in a society, the risk is silence through separation. The best way to protect one's self is not to say anything remotely controversial at all. For the Manciple and Chaucer beyond the *Tales,* speaking is to be done only when necessary; otherwise, saying nothing is preferable because both "persons in-between" know that it is better to be silent and included than silenced and alone.

Reading Codicological Form in John Gower's Trentham Manuscript

Arthur W. Bahr
Massachusetts Institute of Technology

T HE BROAD AGREEMENT THAT HAS EMERGED in recent years on the relevance of paleographical and codicological evidence to literary interpretation in medieval studies has not yielded analogous consensus on best practices for such interdisciplinary endeavors, particularly when we begin thinking about whole manuscripts rather than individual texts.[1] This dilemma stems largely from the "oscillation between the planned and the random" that the construction of medieval literary manuscripts so often seems to display.[2] On the one hand, the fact that the great majority of them were commissioned for specific purposes or patrons makes it likely that some logic would have animated their assemblage. Yet many factors, on the other, combine to make such logics extremely difficult to retrieve. Exemplar poverty rather than thematic

I am grateful to Noel Jackson, Eleanor Johnson, Steve Justice, Anne Middleton, and Bob Yeager for their consistent support and helpful comments; to the participants of the "French of England" conference held at Fordham University in the spring of 2007, where I presented preliminary thoughts on the Trentham manuscript; and to members of the 2009 MIT Women's and Gender Studies symposium where I shared thoughts on the *Cinkante Balades*. The two anonymous readers for *SAC* also offered generous and insightful suggestions from which this essay has greatly benefited.

[1] Even the agreement on the relevance of codicology to literary study is hardly absolute. Perhaps the most insistently dissident view has come from the distinguished paleographers Richard H. and Mary A. Rouse, who argue that attempts to link the realms of codicological and literary analysis "harmfully blur the distinction between what an author composed, and the physical form in which that composition is presented in any manuscript. . . . Literary creation and the physical layout of surviving manuscripts are not results of the same actions." See their "*Ordinatio* and *Compilatio* Revisited," in *Ad Litteram: Authoritative Texts and Their Medieval Readers,* ed. Mark D. Jordan and Kent Emery Jr. (Notre Dame: University of Notre Dame Press, 1992), 113–34 (124).

[2] Ralph Hanna, "Miscellaneity and Vernacularity: Conditions of Literary Production in Late Medieval England," in *The Whole Book: Cultural Perspectives on the Medieval Miscellany,* ed. Stephen G. Nichols and Siegfried Wenzel (Ann Arbor: University of Michigan Press, 1993), 37–51 (37–38).

connections may have led two texts to cohabit in a given manuscript; a short poem juxtaposed with a longer one may be there simply because it fits the space the scribe had left in the quire, and not because of the echoes of phrasing and image between the two. Literary scholars, trained to make arguments about thematic connections and formal echoes, are naturally inclined to see such ideational and aesthetic considerations at work rather than more mechanical ones, and this inescapable predisposition makes it both difficult and vital for us to grapple with the question of when it is legitimate to propose literary interpretations of manuscripts' codicological features, using those features to support readings of texts they contain.

One possible condition of legitimacy would be the personal involvement of the author in the manuscript's construction.[3] Besides valorizing authorial intention in a way that no longer commands universal support among literary scholars, however, this criterion severely limits the range of manuscripts available for analysis, excluding a great many—such as the Trentham manuscript of John Gower, which I will take up momentarily—whose construction seems interpretably purposeful, but where the historical fact of that purpose is uncertain and irrecoverable. In this tension between interpretive impulse and factual unknowability, we can see brewing another version of the conflict between form and history that has been too readily accepted by some of the many recent studies appealing for renewed attention to questions of form or aesthetics.[4] One of my main goals in this essay will be to suggest that this is a false dichotomy,[5] and to propose a notion of codicological form as one way of

[3] This level of involvement satisfies even the Rouses, who acknowledge "exceptions and qualifications" to the starkly categorical position outlined above: "some authors," they admit, "did take a lively interest in how their texts would be presented physically. And a few [they specify Hoccleve and Christine de Pizan] . . . even took steps to ensure that the physical appearance of their texts conformed to their wishes." "*Ordinatio* and *Compilatio* Revisited," 124. They imply that in such cases the manuscript situation of texts becomes part of their authorially sanctioned meaning, and equally amenable to literary interpretation.

[4] For a survey of these, see Marjorie Levinson, "What Is New Formalism?" *PMLA* 122 (2007): 558–69; Levinson remains skeptical of the coherence of any movement or methodology. See also volume 104.1 (2008) of *Representations,* devoted to explorations of form, formalism, and aesthetics; in the medievalist sphere, see also Peggy Knapp, *Chaucerian Aesthetics* (New York: Palgrave Macmillan, 2008); and volume 39.3 (2005) of *The Chaucer Review,* devoted to Chaucer and aesthetics.

[5] Many recent studies have lamented this opposition, but Samuel Otter's "An Aesthetic in All Things" (*Representations* 104 [2008]: 116–25) produces a particularly compelling reading of form with, rather than against, history. Taking up two sentences about Manila and hemp rope in *Moby Dick,* he points out that the historical fact of where these two varieties of rope were produced in the nineteenth century complicates

bringing form and history into more fruitful collaboration.[6] I take *form* here to mean both the structure or arrangement of parts (here the individual texts that make up the manuscript), and their rhetoric or "style," all the minute details and indeterminacies that invite and reward close reading.[7] Applying this second understanding of form to codicology may seem counterintuitive, but we will see that the disposition of texts in a manuscript can in fact be as richly productive of aesthetic and metaphorical meaning as "words in poetry," which Derek Pearsall, in a bracing defense of literary appreciation, regards as having "a wider range of possible meanings than they have in ordinary discourse."[8] In proposing an analogy between "words in poetry" and "texts in manuscripts," I am not claiming that manuscripts are functionally equivalent to poetry. Doubtless the great majority of medieval manuscripts do not offer "metaphorical potentialities" in their selection and arrangement of texts. But when we are faced with the appearance of interpretively meaningful design in a manuscript, we should be open to how it creates meaning not just in individual poems but in the broader concatenation of their codicological form, even when the concrete impulses behind that form remain unknowable. Codicological form, I suggest, rewards reading as both history and art.

The Trentham manuscript—London, British Library Additional MS 59495—is an attractive test case for this proposition because it merits attention in other ways, too.[9] Composed entirely of texts by Gower, it

---

the seemingly straightforward racial metaphor in the passage; historical context thus creates rather than deadens stereotypically "literary" forms of allusion and metaphorical play. (Otter's essay is also valuable for imposing some clarity on three terms that have frequently been conflated in recent discussions: *form, formalism,* and *aesthetics*.)

[6] See as an example Maura Nolan's "Lydgate's Worst Poem," in *Lydgate Matters: Poetry and Material Culture in the Fifteenth Century,* ed. Lisa H. Cooper and Andrea Denny-Brown (New York: Palgrave Macmillan, 2008), 71–87, in which the codicological situation of Lydgate's "Tretise for Lauandres" is used to argue for the poem as a metaphorically and aesthetically complex work.

[7] On the apparent tension between a concern with large-scale structure, on the one hand, and fine-grained detail, on the other, see Catherine Gallagher, "Formalism and Time," *MLQ* 60 (2000): 229–51, esp. 230–32.

[8] Derek Pearsall, "Towards a Poetic of Chaucerian Narrative," in *Drama, Narrative, and Poetry in the "Canterbury Tales,"* ed. Wendy Harding (Toulouse: Presses Universitaires du Mirail, 2003), 99–112 (99–100).

[9] Siân Echard argues that a tendency to collect shorter texts on linguistic rather than codicological grounds has marginalized the Trentham manuscript, the texts of which are dispersed into three of the four volumes of G. C. Macaulay's *Complete Works of John Gower* (Oxford: Clarendon Press, 1899–1902). See her *Printing the Middle Ages* (Philadelphia: University of Pennsylvania Press, 2008), 97–125.

includes works throughout the poet's career in all three of his literary languages, among them the only surviving copies of *In Praise of Peace* and the *Cinkante Balades*. Its opening texts, moreover, directly address a newly crowned Henry IV, while the remarkable symmetry of its arrangement of texts, and the internal connections between them, gives the impression of purposive and quite sophisticated design. This strong appearance of design, coupled with Gower's well-known and much-discussed shift to the Lancastrian cause, encourages interpretation of the whole as celebrating Henry's coronation; and indeed, from as early as the seventeenth century, the only real debate among commentators has been whether Trentham itself was given to Henry, or whether it was the plainer draft copy for a now-lost presentation manuscript.[10] Yet no external historical record justifies this certainty, and on thematic grounds, too, we will see that the manuscript's overall trajectory gradually shies away from its early texts' direct royal addresses and could thus be read as working at cross-purposes with its generally accepted goal. The material state of the manuscript further complicates the situation, for though generally well preserved, Trentham has been damaged in two key places.[11] The end of the dedication to the *Cinkante Balades* and the first poem of the sequence proper have been mangled, leaving about one and a half stanzas of each illegible; and the loss of an entire page has deprived us of the end of "Ecce patet tensus" (if that poem is in fact incomplete),[12] the first balade and a half of the subsequent *Traitié,* and

[10] The first blank leaf of the manuscript contains a note in the hand of Sir Thomas Fairfax, its owner in the seventeenth century, identifying the compendium as "Sr. John Gower's learned Poems the same booke by himself presented to kinge Edward ye fourth att his Coronation," with "Edward" subsequently corrected to "Henry" and "or before" added above "att," after which the words "att" and "or" were struck through. Macaulay doubts the authority of the claim for royal presentation and thinks Trentham more likely to be a copy written about the same time as a presentation copy. See his description of the manuscript, *Complete Works,* 1:lxxix–lxxxiii. John H. Fisher, in *John Gower: Moral Philosopher and Friend of Chaucer* (New York: New York University Press, 1964), argues by contrast that "both the script and initials appear to be up to the standard of the best Gower manuscripts" (72), but he does not actually dispute Macaulay's conclusion. R. F. Yeager concurs with Macaulay, noting that "the manuscript is plain, unlike most royal presentation copies." "John Gower's French," in *A Companion to Gower,* ed. Siân Echard (Woodbridge: D. S. Brewer, 2004), 137–51 (145).

[11] Except where otherwise attributed, these comments are based on my time working with the manuscript in the British Library in the summer of 2008; I am extremely grateful to the staff there for their help.

[12] Macaulay (*Complete Works,* 1:lxxx), argues for incompletion on the basis of the missing page, but the poem, unique to Trentham, does end grammatically, if somewhat abruptly.

whatever linking material might once have joined them. The evidence of the scribal hands is also ambiguous. With two exceptions, all of Trentham's texts were written by the Scribe 5, identified by Malcolm Parkes, who also worked extensively on a number of other Gower compilations. The exceptions are "Ecce patet tensus" and "Henrici quarti primus," which were copied by Parkes's Scribe 10, who wrote two of the final poems in Cotton Tiberius A.iv but otherwise appears in no other Gower manuscripts.[13] Both scribes added various revisions and corrections, but Parkes suggests that Scribe 10 added his texts after Scribe 5 had finished his work. We therefore cannot prove that Gower, Scribe 5, or any other identifiable agent intended the Trentham manuscript to have the codicological form that it does. The manuscript thus presents its modern readers with an interpretive quandary. Its suggestions of purpose are too numerous and fundamental to ignore, but they are sufficiently complicated by literary ambiguity and material uncertainty that we cannot extract from the manuscript a single goal, audience, or agent.

I believe this is less of a problem than it might at first seem. Ambiguity of purpose or meaning, after all, hardly disqualifies texts from literary analysis; quite the reverse. And Trentham's codicological indeterminacies can be read in aesthetic terms even if accidentally produced, for a range of recent works in medieval studies has demonstrated the potential of thus interpreting objects seemingly resistant to such readings.[14] Intention is in any event hardly a readily knowable category, even (or especially) when openly declared.[15] Maura Nolan has argued that in contexts like these we should not insist upon provable authorial or scribal intention, but instead "locate intention in the *manuscript,* where it is lodged in the interstices of the various sequences of poems that structure it." This gambit does not simply transfer the author-

---

[13] Malcolm B. Parkes, "Patterns of Scribal Activity and Revisions of the Text in Early Copies of Works by John Gower," in *New Science Out of Old Books: Studies in Manuscripts and Early Printed Books in Honour of A. I. Doyle,* ed. Richard Beadle and A. J. Piper (Aldershot: Scolar Press, 1995), 81–121 (esp. 90, 94).

[14] See, further, Christopher Cannon's "Form"—which proposes that the apparent resistance of many Middle English texts to formal analysis in fact makes this type of inquiry more rather than less essential—and Lisa H. Cooper's "The Poetics of Practicality," which takes the self-avowedly "impractical" aim of finding a meaningful poetics in even the most apparently prosaic of places. Both in Paul Strohm, ed., *Middle English: Oxford Twenty-First Century Approaches to Literature* (Oxford: Oxford University Press, 2007), 175–90, 491–505 (quotation, 492).

[15] See, further, Paul Strohm, "What Can We Know about Chaucer That He Didn't Know about Himself?" in Strohm, *Theory and the Premodern Text* (Minneapolis: University of Minnesota Press, 2000), 165–81.

function intact to an inanimate object, for both the inherently collaborative nature of manuscript production and the factual uncertainties surrounding nearly every medieval manuscript ensure that the intentions
cited by Nolan cannot be totalizing or unitary; indeed, as she goes on
to note, codicological form both inspires and anchors meanings "that
seem, at first glance, to be *unauthorized* or illicit, and to exceed the brief
of the manuscript or the words on the page."[16] History of various sorts
has a vital role to play here, both in grounding potentially fanciful interpretations and in preventing this approach as a whole from turning into
a codicological kind of New Criticism, devoted to beautiful close readings of the interplay of texts in manuscripts without reference to the
historical circumstances of either.[17] The history that will most directly
inform my analysis of Trentham is Gower's own authorial history, which
the manuscript's texts revise and reimagine at several key points. My
broader argument is not that literary ambiguities are metaphorically
interchangeable with other kinds of unknowability. Rather, it is that
choosing to read Trentham's codicological form as meaningful despite
its uncertainties allows us fuller engagement with the aesthetics of its
literary texts, and the complexity of their multiple histories.

Close examination of the Trentham manuscript's overarching structure will establish both its strong appearance of design and the interpretive problems that arise when we try to pin down that design's precise
nature. The manuscript contains the following texts:

1. Seven lines of Latin verse addressed to Henry IV ("Electus
   Christi, pie Rex Henrice");
2. 385 lines of English decasyllabic rime royal (*In Praise of Peace*);
3. Latin prose link identifying the preceding work as *carmen de pacis
   commendacione,* and naming Gower as author of both it and the
   following *epistola;*
4. Fifty-six lines of Latin verse ("Rex celi deus");

---

[16] "Lydgate's Worst Poem," 80, 82, second emphasis mine. On the importance of
collaborative models to understanding the literary nature of medieval manuscripts, see
Deborah McGrady, *Controlling Readers: Guillaume de Machaut and His Late Medieval Readers* (Toronto: University of Toronto Press, 2006); and Elizabeth J. Bryan, *Collaborative
Meaning in Scribal Culture: The Otho Laȝamon* (Ann Arbor: University of Michigan Press,
1999).

[17] Like Nolan, Samuel Otter emphasizes the role of history in helping us see the
"excess" that is a key component of the literary: he insists we remain "alert to the
humor, the *excess,* and the complexities of both history and text." "An Aesthetic in All
Things," 121–23, emphasis mine.

5. One three-stanza dedicatory *balade* in French addressing the king, followed by Latin (twelve lines of verse, two lines of prose) and a second, four-stanza French dedicatory *balade,* both of which address Henry by name;

6. Fifty-two French *balades* totaling 1,390 lines, with French incipit and Latin explicit (the *Cinkante Balades*);

7. Thirty-six lines of Latin verse ("Ecce patet tensus," possibly incomplete owing to loss of one folio);

8. The *Traitié pour essampler les amantz marietz,* here missing the first *balade* and a half owing to the loss of one folio, but in all other manuscripts consisting of eighteen *balades* totaling 385 lines of decasyllabic rime royal;

9. Seventeen lines of Latin verse on love and marriage, drawn from lines that follow the *Traitié* in all ten of its extant manuscripts;

10. Twelve lines of Latin verse referring to Henry IV ("Henrici quarti primus").

The first point to emerge from this brief résumé is the extent to which the manuscript concerns the newly crowned Henry IV, whom the opening Latin verses directly address. Of the three longest works, *In Praise of Peace* also addresses him by name, and the *Cinkante Balades* are dedicated to him. "Rex celi deus" is a prayer to God on Henry's behalf and fulsomely praises the monarch, who then reappears in the first line of the manuscript's final poem. Given their explicit links to Henry, the fact that *In Praise of Peace* and the *Cinkante Balades* are unique to Trentham heightens the sense that this particular object, or one modeled on it, was designed for him.

This impression of design is strengthened by the remarkable symmetry with which the manuscript's texts have been arranged, a pattern that this streamlined list of its contents will emphasize:

A) Brief Latin verses addressing Henry;

B) 385 lines of vernacular rime royal stanzas, followed by Latin matter (prose explicit and incipit to following text);

C) Fifty-six-line Latin poem;

D) *Cinkante Balades,* preceded by dedicatory and introductory material in French and Latin; followed by Latin explicit;

C') Thirty-six-line Latin poem (possibly incomplete);

B') 385 lines of vernacular rime royal stanzas (assuming missing ma-

terial identical to all other manuscript witnesses), followed by
Latin matter (seventeen lines of verse);

A') Brief Latin verses referring to Henry.

The symmetry is not perfect (though the identical length of *In Praise of
Peace* and the *Traitié* is remarkable), but it is marked enough to suggest
definite effort. So too is the way the Latin is woven throughout the
manuscript, framing it at the beginning and end (A and A') and recur-
ring after each major vernacular work as a kind of literary palate cleanser
(C and C'). Four of the five main poems, in turn, are further linked
by textual matter ranging from simple incipits and explicits to sets of
dedicatory verses,[18] indicating an attempt to unite the manuscript's disparate languages and genres into a coherent whole. Given Gower's history as Lancastrian supporter, and Trentham's insistent address to
Henry in its opening texts, we can imagine interpreting its multilingual
codicological symmetry as an elaborate compliment to the new king:
just as Trentham uses Gower's poetry to unite into a pleasing whole the
multiple languages set loose upon the world by human pride at Babel,
for example, so too will the manuscript's royal recipient prove able to
reunite his fractious kingdom, undoing the political chaos that Gower
so strongly associated with linguistic *divisioun*.[19]

[18] Because of the missing folio, we cannot be certain that there was ever a link between the *Traitié* and the preceding "Ecce patet tensus," though the evidence of the
rest of the texts in the manuscript would make it surprising if there wasn't. The *Cinkante
Balades* are preceded by two dedicatory balades with Latin verses and prose in between;
these verses are themselves a combination of the first eight lines of the "O recolende,
bone, pie Rex Henrice" and the brief four-line "H. aquile pullus." The link between the
Cinkante Balades and "Ecce patet tensus," by contrast, is a brief explicit: "Expliciunt
carmina Iohannis Gower, que Gallice composita Balades dicuntur." *In Praise of Peace,*
"Rex celi deus," the Latin prose that links the two poems, and the manuscript's opening,
"Electus Christi, pie Rex Henrice," are all included in Macaulay's second volume of
Gower's English works in the order that they appear in Trentham. Similarly, the Latin
verses that connect the *Traitié* and "Henrici quarti primus" are printed immediately
following the *Traitié* in his volume of Gower's French works. See *Complete Works,*
3:481–94 and 1:391. These represent two of Macaulay's relatively rare nods to codicological rather than linguistic unity.

[19] On this connection, see the chapter on Gower in Mary Catherine Davidson, *Medievalism, Multilingualism, and Chaucer* (New York: Palgrave Macmillan, 2009); Tim William Machan, "Medieval Multilingualism and Gower's Literary Practice," *SP* 103
(2006): 1–25; Diane Watt, *Amoral Gower* (Minneapolis: University of Minnesota Press,
2003), 21–37 and esp. 32–35; and Rita Copeland's discussion in *Rhetoric, Hermeneutics,
and Translation* (Cambridge: Cambridge University Press, 1991), 213–220. As Machan
puts it, "Sociolinguistically, language change and variation originated because of human
pride and in this sense testify, like all moral failures, to our fallen condition" (2).

Yet Trentham's codicological form resists such a tidy summary of its propositional content, for plenty of other texts and contexts in the manuscript work against a Henrician reading of both parts and whole. "Ecce patet tensus" takes blind Cupid to task for the destructive effects of love—Henry is not mentioned—and the *Traitié* likewise offers no explicit connection with the king. The *Traitié*'s various *exempla* demonstrate a pointed interest in royal misbehavior that might suggest admonitory content for the newly crowned Henry, but this interpretation at first seems hard to square with the manuscript's earlier praise of him. We should note, too, that references to the king become thinner and more oblique as the manuscript progresses: its three longest texts go from embedding an address to Henry in the poem itself (*In Praise of Peace*), to sequestering this address outside the text proper in dedicatory matter (*Cinkante Balades*), to, finally, simply offering up historically distant royal figures for moral assessment (*Traitié*). The considerable length of the *Cinkante Balades* means, moreover, that nearly all of the numerous direct addresses to the king take place in the first quarter or so of the manuscript. When he recurs at the very end, in "Henrici quarti primus," it is only to measure time: "It was in the first year of the reign of King Henry IV" that Gower went blind, he tells us.[20] Instead of the monarch that its early texts addressed, Trentham concludes by emphasizing the author who composed them all: "Henrici quarti primus" includes seven first-person personal pronouns and six first-person verb forms in its twelve lines, which offer an intimate farewell to writing; and the preceding *Traitié* ends with a dedication that rather grandiloquently puts Gower in conversation with the entire world rather than just his king.[21] All these facts make it difficult to sustain fully Trentham's initial invitation to read its texts in Henrician terms.

We should not conclude, however, that because Trentham's texts cannot all be equally drafted into service as part of a celebratory volume

---

[20] See R. F. Yeager's edition and translation in *John Gower: The Minor Latin Works* (Kalamazoo: TEAMS and Medieval Institute Publications, 2005), where it is included as a unique version of "Quicquid homo scribat," the first line of the poem as it appears in Oxford, All Souls College MS 98.

[21] "Al universiteé de tout le monde, / Johan Gower ceste Balade envoie . . ." (XVIII.22–23). *Traitié* and *Cinkante Balades* cited from R. F. Yeager's edition and translation, *John Gower: The French Balades* (Kalamazoo: TEAMS and Medieval Institute Publications, 2009), which he was gracious enough to allow me to consult before it went to press. My translations tend closely to track his, but they are my own throughout unless otherwise noted. I take *universiteé* as even more all-inclusive than Yeager's *community*, and so: "To the entirety of all the world / John Gower sends this balade."

for Henry, the earlier indications of purpose I have considered—its multiple addresses to him, symmetrical arrangement, and codicological threading—all add up to uninterpretable accidents. In fact, the manuscript demonstrates a clear, consistent interest in kingship, including but not limited to Henry's, for the three major texts not addressed to him explicitly—"Rex celi deus," "Ecce patet tensus," and the *Traitié*—all concern royal behavior and misbehavior. "Rex celi deus" prays to the king of its opening words, God, on behalf of the king identified in its incipit as Henry, while its text draws on a section of *Vox Clamantis* that addressed yet another king, Henry's predecessor Richard II; "Ecce patet tensus" depicts Cupid as a crowned king defined by chaotic and destructive misrule;[22] and the *Traitié* cites a host of misbehaving kings to insist on self-control in love. Underlying this pervasive focus on kingship is another suggestive, chiastic structure emphasized by Trentham's symmetrical codicological form: the poems that follow the central *Cinkante Balades* recall their structural counterparts from the first half of the manuscript, but in darker or more ambivalent terms. *In Praise of Peace* is largely laudatory, its hints of disquiet kept mostly below the surface, while its chiastic other, the *Traitié,* uses the same rime royal stanza to take a darker tone, emphasizing the dire consequences of royal malfeasance. The fulsome praise of King Henry contained in "Rex celi deus," meanwhile, contrasts sharply with the comprehensive denunciation of King Cupid's rule in its codicological mirror image, "Ecce patet tensus." Even the brief initial and concluding Latin verses suggest this pattern. The opening "Electus Christi, pie Rex Henrice" implies that Henry has inspired the poetry that follows, a suggestion that the next three texts confirm. In "Henrici quarti primus," by contrast, the first year of his reign also marks Gower's farewell to writing. At the beginning of Trentham, Henry inspires poetic production; by its conclusion, the first year of his reign marks its cessation.

My point here is that even before we engage closely with its various individual texts, the Trentham manuscript itself subtly suggests a wide range of designs but refuses to allow us to settle comfortably on any single one of them. By celebrating Henry in its first three main texts, it strongly suggests one kind of purpose; it later undercuts the impression of that *specific* design, even as its sophisticated codicological form contin-

---

[22] Cupid is described as *ipse coronatus* at line 13; text and translation in Yeager, *John Gower: The Minor Latin Works*.

ues strongly to support the impression of *some sort* of design(s). The manuscript thus plays with our expectations and perceptions, creating a shifting, complex relationship between content and form. In so doing, it enables us to apprehend it as more than just the material medium of its texts, and in fact as an aesthetically compelling work in itself. The question then becomes how, in the absence of provable audience or agent, to ground our interpretations of it, and here I will have recourse to another "history" to complement that of Trentham's codicological form: Gower's authorial history, which the manuscript frequently evokes and rewrites. Specifically, I will argue that Trentham's first two texts, those that most explicitly celebrate Henry's accession, rewrite poems from earlier in Gower's career in ways that raise cautionary doubts about that accession. These doubts become most fully legible, however, only when reconsidered in the context of the manuscript as a whole, after a reading of "Ecce patet tensus" and the *Traitié,* which are far more obviously cautionary but also far less explicitly connected with Henry. The manuscript thus crafts (at least) two different meanings for its first two poems: the largely celebratory explicit content that they would have on a first reading, and the darker resonance they might acquire only gradually and retrospectively, in conjunction with other texts and other aspects of Gower's career.

Trentham's Opening Texts: Rewriting the Past

Gower's revision and rededication of the *Confessio Amantis* to Henry, *comes Derbiae,* is only the most famous instance of the poet's lifelong penchant for rewriting earlier works.[23] A subtler form of rewriting also characterizes *In Praise of Peace* and "Rex celi deus." Frank Grady has demonstrated that the first of these returns to and reverses the opposi-

---

[23] For a revisionist argument concerning the standard "three recension" narrative of the *Confessio*'s composition, see Wim Lindeboom, "Rethinking the Recensions of the *Confessio Amantis,*" *Viator* 40 (2009): 319–48. For an acute (and slyly humorous) reading of how Gower manipulates and rewrites images of kings in boats in *Vox Clamantis* and *Confessio Amantis,* see Frank Grady, "Gower's Boat, Richard's Barge, and the True Story of the *Confessio Amantis*: Text and Gloss," in *TSLL* 44 (2002): 1–15. Other poets also inspired Gower to recast past works; on his use of *cento,* the originally classical practice of constructing a poem out of lines written by earlier famous poets, see Eve Salisbury, "Remembering Origins: Gower's Monstrous Body Poetic," in *Re-Visioning Gower,* ed. R. F. Yeager (Asheville, N.C.: Pegasus Press, 1998), 159–84; R. F. Yeager, *John Gower's Poetic: The Search for a New Arion* (Woodbridge, Suffolk: D. S. Brewer, 1990), 52–60; and Yeager, "Did Chaucer Write Cento?" in *John Gower: Recent Readings,* ed. R. F. Yeager (Kalamazoo: Medieval Institute Publications, 1989), 113–32.

tion between Solomon and Alexander found in Book VII of the *Confessio*,
where Alexander was presented as a model of philosophically enlightened governance and Solomon condemned for lustful idolatry. *In Praise
of Peace,* by contrast, distinguishes between Solomon, who "ches wisdom
unto the governynge / Of goddis folk" and thereby "gat him pees"
(31–32, 35), and Alexander, who is introduced in the next stanza with
the adversative *Bot* (36) and achieves his mythic status by war and conquest. Grady argues that Gower steps back at the last moment, and
rather than "condemning Alexander, choos[es] instead to indict the
world in which he existed, as if it deserved to be subdued and con-
quered."[24] This stark reversal of the roles they played in the *Confessio* (a
poem also ultimately dedicated, of course, to Henry of Lancaster), however, forces the reader of Trentham to think long and hard about the
ramifications not just of Gower's cautionary use of Alexander here, but
of the fact that the hero of one poem could so abruptly become the
villain of the other.

Indeed, Gower's suggestion that Alexander's pagan world deserved
conquest, in contrast with the "pite and grace" that Christians deserve
from their princes (52), somewhat exculpates Alexander, but even more
deeply it condemns Henry, should he follow such an example in his own
Christian era. The *bot* that opened the stanza introducing Alexander is
the first word of the next two stanzas as well, grammatically establishing the adversative as a central thematic in the poem as a whole, by
which any affirmative statement can be instantly qualified, withdrawn,
rewritten. The stanzas following those that introduce Alexander offer a
wealth of examples:

> It sit hem [Christian princes] wel to do pite and grace;
> *Bot* yit it mot be tempred in manere.
>
> So mai a kyng of werre the viage
> Ordeigne and take . . .
> *Bot* other wise if god himsilve wolde . . .
> Pes is the beste above alle erthely thinges.
>
> Thus stant the lawe, that a worthi knight
> Uppon his trouthe may go to the fight;
> *Bot* if so were that he myghte chese,
> Betre is the pees, of which may no man lese.
>   (52–53, 57–63, 67–70)

[24] "The Lancastrian Gower and the Limits of Exemplarity," *Speculum* 70 (1995):
552–75 (563).

These passages all allude to the fact that political idealism is subject to revision by practical realities. Grady notes the adversatives that here enact that revision, but he argues that Gower forestalls the "implicit and dangerous analogy between Macedonian conquest and Lancastrian usurpation . . . by plunging ahead on the theme of peace" and delaying the next adversative *bot* for some ten stanzas, "after the poem has safely established some momentum away from the vortex of this stanza [lines 64–70]."[25] Gower cannot, however, so readily elide the larger and more daunting reality that his early use of the word *bot* suggests: just as any clear-cut statement can be undone by a simple adversative construction, so too the contrasting examples of Solomon and Alexander in the *Confessio* and *In Praise of Peace* demonstrate that a ruler, once held up as an ideal, can be textually deposed by subsequent rewriting.

In this context, the simplistic "praise of peace" contained in the next stanzas (e.g., "The werre is modir of the wronges alle" [106]) cannot be taken at face value, because as we saw in the *bot*-infused passages cited above, Gower has begun the poem as a meditation on the tension between moral idealism and political reality, giving neither a chance to triumph completely; we can hear a similar *bot* lurking behind the clear-cut statements of lines 71–133, waiting to undo them. And sure enough, the word returns later to qualify similarly straightforward principles:

> Aboute a kyng good counseil is to preise
> Above alle other thinges most vailable;
> *Bot yit* a kyng withinne himself schal peise,
> And se the thinges that been resonable. . . .
>
> Ha, wel is him that schedde nevere blod,
> *Bot* if it were in cause of rihtwisnesse.
> (141–44, 148–49)

Later in the poem the word clusters so thickly that it threatens to undermine the explicit meaning of the text, as in the following passage:

> *Bot* if the men within himself be veine,
> The substance of the pes may noght be trewe,
> *Bot* every dai it chaungeth uppon newe.
>
> *Bot* who that is of charite parfit . . .
> (313–16)

[25] Ibid., 565.

The *bot*s of lines 313 and 315 enclose and thus highlight the pessimistic statement of line 314; and while line 316 attempts to start a new stanza with a contrast that leaves this pessimism behind, its initial *bot* connects it both to the preceding stanza and to that word's thematization of abrupt reversals and subtle qualifications of seemingly straightforward commonplaces about good governance. The cumulative effect of all this is that when *bot* shows up twice in close proximity to Henry near the end of the poem,[26] it is tinged with the ambivalence it has acquired over the course of the work as a whole.

This ambivalence is hardly overpowering. *Bot* is a sufficiently common word that it would be easy to ignore hints of deeper significance in it; the reversal of the Alexander/Solomon dichotomy, while striking, relies for its effect on the reader's familiarity with the antecedent in *Confessio Amantis*; and both these elements could easily be drowned out by the generally laudatory tone of the whole, set by the introductory Latin verses and straightforwardly celebratory opening stanzas. The cautionary undertones of *In Praise of Peace* are sufficiently subtle that they require a substantial level of active apprehension from the reader. In this they begin the Trentham manuscript's gradual construction of ambivalent patterns whose initial outlines—a fraught conjunction, a rewritten comparison—seem significant, and potentially threatening, only in retrospect. Here those outlines, if we choose to perceive them, suggest a recognition that whatever our idealistic wishes, the possibility remains that Henry's reign will slide off in the other direction: not peace but war; not ancestry or acclamation or any of the various Lancastrian claims alluded to in the poem's opening stanzas,[27] but conquest—like Alexander's—pure and simple.

The role of "Rex celi deus" in this process of gradually ambivalent rewriting is suggested by the explicit and incipit that link it with *In Praise of Peace*: "Here ends the poem about the excellence of peace, which in praise and memory of the most serene prince of God, King Henry IV, his humble orator John Gower composed. And now follows

---

[26]"*Bot* evere y hope of King Henries grace / That he it is which schal the pes embrace" (272–73); "Noght only to my king of pes y write, / *Bot* to these othre princes cristne alle . . ." (379–80).

[27]For an overview both of the various claims put forth by Lancastrians in favor of Henry's accession and of how those claims find expression in literary texts, including *In Praise of Peace,* see Paul Strohm, "Saving the Appearances: Chaucer's *Purse* and the Fabrication of the Lancastrian Claim," in *Chaucer's England: Literature in Its Historical Context,* ed. Barbara Hanawalt (Minneapolis: University of Minnesota Press, 1992), 21–40.

an epistle, in which with the highest devotion the same John entreats for the health and well-being of his said lord."[28] The incipit to "Rex celi deus" in other manuscripts fails to identify Gower as author,[29] whereas Trentham not only does so but also emphasizes the identity of the John who writes (*idem Iohannes*) and Henry being written of (*dicti domini sui*) in the two texts. These identifications of Gower and Henry, moreover, depend on the first sentence, the explicit to *In Praise of Peace* that initially identifies them. These two sentences thus present the two poems as parallel efforts, such that their strategic rewriting becomes parallel, too. "Rex celi deus," moreover, suggests a significantly more threatening binary than the Solomon/Alexander one of *In Praise of Peace*: Henry/Richard.[30] The technique is different, however, for "Rex celi deus" gains its initial force precisely by declining to rewrite: its first eight lines are exactly the same as those that open VI.xviii of the earliest version of *Vox Clamantis,* the one most kindly disposed to Richard. The praise of Henry in Trentham thus recalls the fact that Gower once prayed, for example, that "it be granted to you, O king [Richard], always to hold the honored scepter firmly in your hand during our lifetime," or that "He Who gave you [Richard] your first realms [should] give you assurance of your future realms" (VI.1175 and 1187). That these lines appear almost unchanged in "Rex celi deus" suggests the contingent nature of the poem's praise of Henry,[31] particularly since Gower expunged and substantially rewrote this entire chapter from subsequent versions of the *Vox,* replacing them with much sterner admonitions to wise rulership. What happened to Richard could, in theory, happen to Henry.

Indeed, the epistle in the *Vox* from which "Rex celi deus" derives is addressed to Richard not by name but merely as "our king now reigning

[28] "Explicit carmen de pacis commendacione, quod ad laudem et memoriam serenissimi principis domini Regis Henrici quarti suus humilis orator Iohannes Gower composuit. Et nunc sequitur epistola, in qua idem Iohannes pro statu et salute dicti domini sui apud altissimum devocius exorat." Macaulay, *Complete Works,* 2:492.

[29] Cf. the All Souls manuscript, which reads "Here follows a poem by which our magnificent King Henry, singled out by God and men with every blessing, will be glorified" ("Sequitur carmen unde magnificus rex noster Henricus prenotatus apud Deum et homines cum omni benediccione glorificetur"). See Yeager, *John Gower: The Minor Latin Works,* 42.

[30] For a fascinating exploration of how this binary works in the repeated letters, R and H, by which the two kings are known at the end of the *Cronica Tripertita,* see Robert Epstein, "Literal Opposition: Deconstruction, History, and Lancaster," *TSLL* 44 (2002): 16–33.

[31] VI.18.1159–98. Yeager makes a suggestion similar to my argument here in his *John Gower: The Minor Latin Works,* 72.

at present" (VI.viii.headnote), and "Rex celi deus," too, nowhere explicitly names Henry as the king being praised; we have to read the incipit to discover his identity. This fact further emphasizes the importance of Trentham's codicological links between texts. More broadly, the text's refusal to name the king explicitly and decision to recycle praise of an earlier, now-deposed monarch collectively emphasize both the transience of royal power and the ultimate instability of subjects' loyalty. The revised *Vox* states explicitly that "if you turn yourself strictly to your own affairs, then the people which should be yours will turn itself away" (VI.1197–98). Far from condemning such behavior as disloyal fickleness, however, Gower implies that kings who cannot maintain the people's loyalty have only themselves to blame, and by transferring praise of Richard to Henry, he suggests that similar shifts are possible in the future as well—but in that case Henry would be the dispossessed party. As with *In Praise of Peace,* this is a subtle form of ambivalence that relies on knowledge of the text being alluded to and its then addressee, so I do not claim that "Rex celi deus" demands or even encourages this interpretation on a first reading. It gains cumulative force by being juxtaposed with *In Praise of Peace,* however, and further linked to that poem by the explicit/incipit considered above.

The *Cinkante Balades* that follows "Rex celi deus" is Trentham's central and longest text, yet immediately offers interpretive challenges, not least because *forme fixe* love poetry is a genre of highly conventional topics, themes, and images. Fortunately Trentham's first two texts' understated evocations of Gower's authorial past offer a key way of grappling with the *Cinkante Balades,* which likewise rewrite the poet's authorial history as he himself has twice represented it. As early as the *Mirour de l'Omme,* Gower describes such "fols ditz d'amours" as the product of a misspent youth:

> Jadis trestout m'abandonoie
> Au foldelit et veine joye,
> Dont ma vesture desguisay
> Et les fols ditz d'amours fesoie,
> Dont en chantant je carolloie
> Mais ore je m'aviseray
> En tout cela je changeray,
> Envers dieu je supplieray
> Q'il de sa grace me convoie;

> Ma conscience accuseray,
> Un autre chançon chanteray,
> Que jadys chanter ne soloie.[32]

Once I entirely abandoned myself to foolish pleasure and vain joy, with which I adorned my appearance, and I made foolish poems of love to which I danced while singing. But now I will take counsel and change in all this; I will pray to God that He send me his grace; I will rebuke my conscience and sing a different song, which I have not in the past tended to sing.

This passage precedes the life of the Virgin that concludes the *Mirour,* so it is possible to interpret the many future-tense verbs as referring only to the current poem. But combined with Gower's later and far more famous leavetaking from love in the *Confessio* (VIII.3138–72), it suggests that whenever they were originally written, the *Balades* as presented in Trentham represent a return to the literary and personal past. In the dedication to the *Cinkante Balades,* moreover, Gower emphasizes the newness and now-ness of this gesture. After two stanzas praising the king, he writes:

> Vostre oratour et vostre humble vassal,
> Vostre Gower, q'est trestout vos soubgitz,
> Puisq'ore avetz receu le coronal,
> Vous frai service autre que je ne fis,
> Ore en balade, u sont les ditz floriz,
> Ore en vertu, u l'alme ad son corage:
> Q'en dieu se fie, il ad bel avantage.[33]

He who prays for you and is your humble vassal, / Your Gower, who is entirely your subject, / Since now you have received the crown, / I do you a service different from what I have done before, / Now in *balade,* where poetry's flower resides, / Now in virtue, where the soul has its heart: / Whoever trusts in God has the best of it.

The first two *ore*s suggest an equivalence between the newness of Henry's kingship and that of Gower's poetic effort. The allusion to present service recalls Gower's earlier dedication of the *Confessio* to Henry, so at

---

[32] *Mirour de l'Omme,* 27337–49, in Macaulay, *Complete Works,* vol. 1.
[33] Ded. Bal. I.15–21.

its most literal, this anaphoric *ore* simply analogizes the difference between King Henry and Henry *comes Derbiae,* and the difference between
the literary works addressed to each. But while it may be literally true
that Gower has never before written love poetry for Henry, line 18's
insistence that the forthcoming offering marks a break with the past
ignores the fact that within Gower's own authorial history, love poetry
is the very genre that the poet has twice foresworn. The *Cinkante Balades*
is a return to the past that presents itself as wholly new.

This is significant because it means that each of Trentham's first three
texts has an important antecedent in Gower's authorial history: reversed
exempla (*In Praise of Peace*), readdressed political praise ("Rex celi deus"),
or renewed generic activity (the love poetry of the *Cinkante Balades*).
Moreover, Gower draws attention to this contrast between past and
present elsewhere in the dedicatory balades:

> Noz coers dolentz par vous sont rejois;
> Par vous, bons Roys, nous susmes enfranchis,
> Q'ainçois sanz cause fuismes en servage. . . .
>
> Ensi le bon amour q'estre soloit
> El temps jadis de nostre ancesserie,
> Ore entre nous recomencer om doit
> Sanz mal pensier d'ascune vileinie.[34]

Our grieving hearts are rejoiced by you; / By you, good King, we are freed, /
Who before, without cause, were in servitude. . . . And so we should begin
again, between us, the good love that used to exist in the former time of our
ancestors—without a wicked thought of any villainy.

The repeated *re-* words (*rejois, recomencer*) emphasize that Henry is merely
and properly restoring the good things his subjects have recently (under
Richard) been denied. Of course this is a prudent rhetorical position to
adopt, and inasmuch as Gower's choice of genre recalls his own earlier
depictions of his authorial history, we can see the outlines of a still more
elaborate compliment: that in addition to returning his kingdom to an
idealized past of freedom and "bon amour," Henry's accession has reversed the inexorable process of age that left Gower an absurd *senex
amans* at the end of the *Confessio,* and thus enabled the poet at the dawn

---

[34] Ded. Bal. I.5–6, II.21–24.

of the fifteenth century to take up once more the poetry of his youth in order to "desporter vo noble Court roia[l]" ["To entertain your noble royal Court"].[35]

Nor are these allusions to and revisions of Gower's authorial history the only connections among Trentham's first three texts, for the dedicatory material to the *Balades* creates others. Gower's characterization of himself as the king's *oratour* in the passage considered earlier (Ded. Bal. I.15) echoes *suus humilis orator,* the term used for him in the explicit/incipit between *In Praise of Peace* and "Rex celi deus." Even Trentham's opening Latin verses are echoed by later works; their initial characterization of the king as "pie Rex" is taken up repeatedly by "Rex celi deus," where the epithet describes Henry five times in the poem's fifty-five lines.[36] These Latin poems are also thick with the *re-* verbs of renewal and rejoicing that we saw in the passages from the *Cinkante Balades* cited above.[37] Collectively these instances draw attention to the role of "minor" introductory and dedicatory texts in reinforcing the larger works that they surround and contextualize, and thus further encourage reading Trentham as a meaningfully constructed object.

What remains is to consider how, as constructed to this point, Trentham associates the seemingly dissimilar themes it treats: of politics and a Henrician restoration in *In Praise of Peace* and "Rex celi deus," and of love and *desport* in the *Cinkante Balades*. The echoes of phrasing and vocabulary that I considered above are a generalized kind of invitation to connect these two realms, but the anaphoric passage that I have already briefly considered offers a more pointed one:

> Puisq'ore avetz receu le coronal,
> Vous frai service autre que je ne fis,
> Ore en balade, u sont les ditz floriz,
> Ore en vertu, u l'alme ad son corage:

[35] Ded. Bal. II.27. Venus tells Gower after receiving his letter in the *Confessio* that he must "remembre wel hou thou art old" (VIII.2439). It is only her later production of a mirror, however, which leads to a devastatingly exhaustive anti-blason of the poet's decrepitude (VIII.2820–33), that finally convinces Gower to abandon the posture and the poetry of courtly love.

[36] Lines 10, 21, 33, 51, 55. By contrast, he is described as "rex . . . fortissime" (41) and plain "rex" (30) just once each, which makes "pie Rex" by far the poem's favorite term for Henry, whom as we saw above, the poem never addresses by name.

[37] Two of the seven lines of "Electus Christi, pie Rex Henrice" end with *re-* verbs: *restituisti* (3) and *renovata* (5); such verbs occur six times in the first twenty-eight lines alone of "Rex celi deus" (13, 15, 18, 19, 22, 28).

> Q'en dieu se fie, il ad bel avantage.
> O gentil Rois, ce que je vous escris
> Ci ensuant ert de perfit langage,
> Dont en latin ma sentence ai compris:
> Q'en dieu se fie, il ad bel avantage.[38]

He who prays for you and your humble vassal, / Your Gower, who is entirely your subject, / Since now you have received the crown, / I do you a service different from what I have done before, / Now in *balade,* where poetry's flower resides, / Now in virtue, where the soul has its heart: / Whoever trusts in God has the best of it. / Oh gentle king, this which I write for you— / What follows here uses polished language, / Whose message I have written in Latin: / Whoever trusts in God has the best of it.

The third *ore* links Henry's coronation, Gower's offering of love poetry, and a concern for virtue that echoes the themes of *In Praise of Peace* and "Rex celi deus." This connection then leads into the envoy, which draws attention to the multilingualism of the dedicatory material and thus encourages us to read the entirety of that material—French poems, Latin verses, and Latin prose—as a single authorial gesture ("ce que *je* vous escris . . . en latin *ma* sentence *ai* compris"). This is significant because the intercalated Latin material is emphatically political, and thus connects the amatory *Cinkante Balades* that it introduces with the preceding poems.[39] Like "Electus Christi, pie Rex Henrice" and "Rex celi deus," these lines address Henry as "pie Rex" (1); like *In Praise of Peace,* they urge him to seek peace ("pacem compone," 5). We see references to the deliverance from Egypt and the sacred anointing oil of Saint Thomas Becket, and prayers drawn from the Psalms that the people will "live under the rule of reason," and Henry will "moderate the powers of the crown."[40]

None of this Latin in the least suggests the elegant love poetry that follows, yet it is not just present in the manuscript, but obtrusively so, abruptly changing the language, verse form, images, and tone of the

[38] Ded. Bal. I.17–25.

[39] The Latin is an odd mixture: the first eight lines of "O recolende, bone, pie Rex Henrice," followed by the four-line "H. aquile pullus" and a two-sentence prayer, in prose, offering a further prayer for Henry's health and success. The whole is included in Yeager, *John Gower: The French Balades,* 56–59.

[40] These references are at lines 2, 11, 4 ("vivant sub racione"), and 5 ("vires moderare corone"), respectively; the quotations are from the Vulgate Psalms, 88:23 and 40:3.

first dedicatory balade, which has nevertheless not just alluded to this Latin but presented it as Gower's own speech. We then shift, equally abruptly, back to French balade form and the vocabulary of "bon amour" in the second dedicatory poem that follows. Like the Trentham manuscript as a whole, then, the codicological form of the *Cinkante Balades* and its dedication offers a strong initial impression of design while presenting discontinuities that make that design hard to pin down. Here, however, the lexicon of virtue shared by both courtly-love speech and political discourse offers an interpretively helpful tangent point. The Latin praised Henry, "than whom no one is more gracious" ("quo nunquam gracior ullus," 9), and the French likewise identifies God as having imbued "Henri le quarte . . . de grace especial" (Ded. Bal. II.2–3). The Latin's general emphasis on moral and political rectitude, combined with this sort of direct echo, enables us to read the dedicatory balades' explicit and insistent focus on virtue—long lists open the first and close the second poems[41]—as suggesting a greater relevance for the following *Cinkante Balades* than mere *desport*.

This is significant because we will see that even in the context of the poems' generic expectations of intense erotic lament over the instability of love and the sudden shifts of Fortune, the *Cinkante Balades* present striking discontinuities of tone, narrative, and persona. I suggested earlier that it is possible to read Gower's representation of his return to love poetry as a complimentary gesture to Henry and the personally rejuvenating effects of the king's *renovatio imperii*. The discontinuities in the *Cinkante Balades* proper, however, suggest another possible interpretation. If we read these fissures in the context of the dedication's concern with virtue, its normally distinct courtly and political associations blurred by that material's juxtaposition of the two discourses, their effects are reminiscent of the ambivalent authorial revisions we saw earlier with *In Praise of Peace* and "Rex celi deus"; that is, they subtly call into doubt the most purely celebratory attitude toward Henry's accession. As with Trentham's first two texts, there are plenty of reasons not to take up this darker interpretation: here, the conventionality of the genre and subject matter, which makes the interpretation of any larger significance, including the political, difficult to substantiate. My argument

---

[41] "Pité, prouesse, humblesse, honour roial" (Ded. Bal. I.1: "Mercy, prowess, humility, regal honor"), and "Honour, valour, victoire et bon esploit, / Joie et saunté, puissance et seignurie" (Ded. Bal. II.33–34: "Honor, valor, victory, and good success, / Joy and health, power and lordship").

therefore is not that this is the only or necessarily best way, then or now, of reading the *Cinkante Balades* themselves. Rather, it is that Trentham's codicological form, its juxtaposition of poems and intervening material, and the echoes among them, are gradually offering an alternate, more cautionary way of understanding poems of both political praise and courtly *desport*.

Narrative Structure in the *Cinkante Balades:*
Juxtaposition and Reversal

I have space here to discuss only a few of the many delights and complexities offered by the *Cinkante Balades,* but even this truncated analysis requires a brief résumé of the narrative arc that the sequence suggests.[42] The male lover first laments his lady's inaccessibility, then attacks the scandal-makers who are damaging her reputation. He suggests that he will absent himself from her in order to preserve her honor, and eventually does so, but then reproaches her for infidelity. She makes the same charge against him, but they are reconciled at the end of the sequence, which concludes with generalized thoughts on love and an address to the Virgin. Marked silences and discontinuities characterize this metanarrative, however, the most striking of which is the shift in the lady's tone between Balades XLIII and XLIIII: the first of these concludes a set of three poems excoriating the lover's faithlessness, which she denounces as worse even than Jason's to Medea or Aeneas's to Dido. Yet the very next poem, also written in a female voice, praises him (or some male figure, at least) as "vailant, courtois, gentil et renomée / Loyal, verrai, certain de vo promesse" ["valiant, courteous, honorable, and renowned, / Loyal, true, unwavering in your promise"].[43] The change is sufficiently abrupt as to prompt wry, antifeminist commentary by Macaulay, who explains the "startling abruptness" of her apparent mood change as "the prerogative of her sex"; R. F. Yeager suggests that a second, worthier lover has here taken the place of the first, but even if he is correct it remains a remarkably sudden shift.[44]

---

[42] Yeager has argued that *Cinkante Balades* have "a narrative unity, even a chronology, traceable through references to feast days and seasonal changes over the course of two or three years." "John Gower's French," 146. I find this metanarrative both less consistently apparent and less coherent than does Yeager, but he is nevertheless right to emphasize its general contours.

[43] Balade XLIIII.1–2.

[44] Macaulay, *Complete Works,* 1:lxvii. Yeager, *John Gower: The French Balades,* 49.

How significant we judge this and other comparable discontinuities to be to the Henrician context that Trentham's opening texts have established will depend largely on how inclined we are to read the *Cinkante Balades'* representations of erotic virtue and constancy, deceit and treachery, in social or political terms. The text's only substantive codicological feature, which occurs early in the sequence, encourages us to ponder precisely this issue of the balades' deeper significance; two marginal glosses to Balades V and VI, respectively, read:

Les balades d'amont jesques enci sont fait especialement pour ceaux q'attendont lours amours par droite mariage.

Les balades d'ici jesqes au fin du livere sont universeles a tout le monde, selonc les propretés et les condicions des Amantz, qui sont diversement travailez en la fortune d'amour.[45]

The balades from the beginning up to this point are made especially for those who wait on their loves in expectation of rightful marriage; the balades from here until the end of the book are universal, for everyone, according to the properties and conditions of Lovers who are diversely suffering the fortunes of Love.

Written in the same hand and with the same decoration as the balades themselves, the manuscript presents these glosses as integral to the poems they comment on.[46] What they suggest, however, is distinctly odd. Only the first six poems,[47] we are told, celebrate that love which looks forward to marriage for its ultimate fulfillment; the remaining, far greater number address the many vicissitudes endured by those under *la fortune d'amour*. This trajectory—away from the legally permanent

---

[45] Yeager, *John Gower: The French Balades,* 134.

[46] The initial letter of the first margin note is gold, that of the second, blue; this is the same pattern that predominates for the balades, all of which have an initial gold letter that usually (though not always, e.g., Balades XII and XXI) alternates with blue. On the importance of marginal glosses to Gower's work, and the *Confessio* in particular, see two essays by Siân Echard, "Gower's 'bokes of Latin': Language, Politics, and Poetry," *SAC* 25 (2003): 123–56; and "With Carmen's Help: Latin Authorities in the *Confessio Amantis,*" *SP* 95 (1998): 1–40; Ardis Butterfield, "Articulating the Author: Gower and the French Vernacular Codex," *YES* 33 (2003): 80–96; and Derek Pearsall, "Gower's Latin in the *Confessio Amantis,*" in *Latin and Vernacular: Studies in Late-Medieval Texts and Manuscripts,* ed. A. J. Minnis (Cambridge: D. S. Brewer, 1989), 13–25.

[47] The manuscript marks two adjacent Balades IV, so "Balade V" is actually the sixth in the sequence.

and divinely sanctioned love of marriage and into the Fortune-tossed seas of courtly wooing—contrasts sharply with the emphasis on stability, law, and virtue that we saw in the dedicatory material preceding the *Cinkante Balades*. It also runs counter to the trajectory of the manuscript as a whole, in which the courtly wooing of the *Cinkante Balades* is followed by the *Traitié*'s defense of precisely the marital love that the *Balades* begin by briefly exploring, then cast aside. Of course, for this very reason it is possible to read *that* pairing as rationalizing and minimizing the disjunction provided by these two margin notes. But in the course of reading the *Balades* sequentially—which their metanarrative and their numbering in the manuscript encourage us to do—we experience the strangeness of a movement from marriage to courtly love.

Still more important, the reference to "droite mariage" grafts onto the first six balades a significance that they themselves nowhere make explicit or even particularly suggest. To be sure, in them the narrator promises his lady constancy and loyal love, which can in theory be taken as describing the permanent and holy bonds of marriage. But these terms are equally if not more characteristic of courtly-love discourse, and the first six poems also feature plenty of the pain-as-sweetness/ sweetness-as-pain language that typifies such *forme fixe* expression and emphatically resists association with marriage:

> D'ardant desire celle amorouse peigne
> Mellé d'espoir me fait languir en joie;
> Dont par dolçour sovent jeo me compleigne
> Pour vous, ma dame, ensi com jeo soloie.[48]

This loving punishment of burning desire / Mingled with hope sickens me with joy: / Thus from sweetness often I complain / On your account, my lady—just so am I accustomed.

Although this poem's refrain, "en attendant que jeo me reconforte," does pick up the lexicon of waiting from the first marginal gloss,[49] the vocabulary of the poem as a whole is such that only the most stubbornly ascetic reader would conclude that it is marriage for which the narrator

---

[48] Bal. III.1–4.
[49] "Awaiting the time when I shall be comforted." Compare the vocabulary of the first marginal gloss: "Les balades d'amont jesques enci sont fait especialement pour ceaux q'attendont lours amours par droite mariage," emphasis mine.

is burning. The codicological form of the *Cinkante Balades'* opening, then, claims explicitly that very different interpretive contexts apply to these poems that look initially like straightforward representatives of their genre.

The second marginal gloss attempts to shut down this disconnect between apparent and deeper significance by reassuring us that the remaining, substantial majority of the balades are, in fact, just what they appear: poems about the travails of lovers and the fortunes of love. But the first gloss's introduction of extratextual meaning is not so easily forgotten, since the supposed "marriage-balades" do not sound markedly different from those that follow. The effect of these glosses, I think, is to make us read the *Cinkante Balades* as a whole more actively and more skeptically than the conventionality of their theme and expression might otherwise encourage. After all, if we are told that the opening poems of courtly *desport* actually signify something quite different, yet they seem broadly similar to those the manuscript insists are, in fact, just what they appear, then the arbitrariness of the distinction between them, and the initial encouragement to read for more than outward content, is likely to make us suspect the later poems, too, of containing some other or deeper meaning. In this spirit I read three of the most arresting moments in the sequence: the reappearance of one line from the dedicatory balades as the refrain to Balade XXI; the bizarre about-face of the lady toward her courtly lover alluded to earlier; and the concluding poems' attempts to define love, which raise again the glosses' contrast of "amours par droite mariage" and "la fortune d'amour."

But first, another instance of Gower's penchant for self-echoing: "Sanz mal pens(i)er d'ascune vileinie" ["Without a wicked thought of any villainy"] is both the refrain of Balade XXI and the twenty-fourth line of the second dedicatory balade.[50] Gower's lover-persona is thus

---

[50] Ded. Bal. II.24 and Bal. XXI.refrain. Yeager adds variation to the refrain in his translation by rendering *vileinie* variously as vulgarity, wickedness, deceit, and degradation, but the word remains the same throughout in the original (as of course it must, being part of a refrain). He also translates *penser* in Balade XXI as a noun ("without wicked thought of any *vileinie*"), and *pensier* in the dedicatory poem as a verb ("without thinking *vileinie* of any"). But *pensier* can just as easily be a noun (the orthographical difference between *penser* and *pensier* is not lexically significant), and it works better understood as such. For one thing, this allows *ascune* to be an adjective modifying *vileinie* (as in Balade XXI), instead of a substantive that *vileinie* must look backward to—a considerably more awkward option. It is also thoroughly typical of Gower's career-long penchant for strategic revising and self-echoing, which we have already seen Trentham exploit in its first two texts.

making the same address to his courtly lady that earlier, as poet, he made to his sovereign. In itself, the echo is not so surprising, since as we have seen the discourses of politics and courtly love share a lexicon of virtue (e.g., *mal pensier, vileinie*), but it does invite us to link the *Balades* themselves and their dedication, whose French-Latin-French structure conjoined political with amatory discourse, and which also linked the *Cinkante Balades* to the explicitly political *In Praise of Peace* and "Rex celi deus." If we take up this invitation to look outward for the *Balades'* significance, an invitation first made by the marginal glosses just considered, then we find other similarities between the dedication and Balade XXI, as this comparison suggests:

Vostre oratour et vostre humble vassal,	Au solail, **qe les herbes eslumine**
Vostre Gower, q'est *trestout vos soubgitz,*	**Et fait florir,** jeo fai comparisoun
Puisq'ore avetz receu le coronal,	De celle q'ad dessoutz sa discipline
Vous frai service autre que je ne fis,	Mon coer, mon corps, mes sens, et ma resoun
Ore en balade, **u sont les ditz floriz,**	Par fin amour *trestout a sa bandoun*:
Ore en vertu, u l'alme ad son corage:	*Et servirai* de bon entencioun,
Q'en dieu se fie, il ad bel avantage.	Sanz mal penser d'ascune vileinie.[51]

He who prays for you and is your humble vassal, / Your Gower, who is entirely your subject, / Since now you have received the crown, / I do you a service different from what I have done before, / Now in *balade,* where poetry's flower resides, / Now in virtue, where the soul has its heart: / Whoever trusts in God has the best of it.

To the sunshine that shines on the plants / And makes them flower, I compare / The one who has under her control / My heart, my body, my sense and my reason. / Because of the pure love entirely in her power— / By that I shall live a joyful life. / And serve with good intention, / Without bad thought of any vulgarity.

These and other, comparable similarities of phrasing and image that I could quote are sufficiently conventional that individually they do not support much interpretive weight. Collectively, however—in the con-

---

[51] Ded. Bal. I.15–21; Bal. XXI.1–7.

text of the repeated "Sanz mal penser" line, Trentham's insistent focus on politics generally and Henry specifically to this point, and the marginal glosses' initial invitation to read the balades in terms of other, essentially extratextual interpretive programs—they suggest that the "bon amour" promised by the *Cinkante Balades* in some way reflects the political harmony that Lancastrian partisans hoped would result from Henry's accession.

Balade XXI particularly engages the reader's attention, moreover, because it reverses with striking suddenness the images and tones of the preceding Balade XX. That poem laments Fortune's unceasing hostility to the narrator, which he claims belies the adage that Fortune's wheel is always turning (XX.1–4). This perverse constancy is in conflict with the natural processes of change that he observes elsewhere:

> Apres la guerre om voit venir la pes,
> Apres l'ivern est l'estée beal flori,
> Mais mon estat ne voi changer jammes.[52]

After war one sees peace arrive, / After winter the beautiful foliage of spring; / But never do I see my situation change.

This image of flowers following winter looks forward to the opening lines of the next balade, quoted earlier, where the narrator's constant torment has abruptly eased. The parallel, juxtaposed war-peace/winter-summer comparisons, meanwhile, further suggest a political resonance for these amatory poems, since both *In Praise of Peace* and the Latin dedication to the *Cinkante Balades* exhorted Henry to choose peace rather than war; and this context is sharpened by Balade XX's references to figures from the Trojan War.[53]

This conflict conjoined the political and the amatory not just in the celebrated judgment and abduction that precipitated it, but also in its aftermath (Agamemnon murdered by Clytemnestra), and in the way that Troilus's erotic fortune and ultimate fall paralleled those of his city. This is a theme with which Gower was intimately familiar, and not just as co-dedicatee of Chaucer's *Troilus and Criseyde*; he had earlier used London's associations with Troy in *Vox Clamantis* to inveigh against the

---

[52] Bal. XX.9–11.
[53] See Bal. XX.17–24, where Diomedes, Agamemnon, Troilus, and Calchas are all mentioned.

rebels of the 1381 Rising and, with increasing harshness, Richard II as well.[54] As we have seen, Gower's use of material from the *Vox* for Trentham's "Rex celi deus" implied that similar rewritings could occur to Henry, and Balade XX's Trojan references likewise allude to sudden and unforeseen reversals, though here in the realm of love: Fortune saw to Diomedes' happiness by changing Criseyde's affections (XX.19–21), for example, and though Gower does not allude to it here, we know what sort of welcome Agamemnon was to receive from Clytemnestra upon returning home from Troy. (If by chance we *are* ignorant of that episode, we will be educated by Balade VI of the *Traitié* at the end of Trentham.)

To this point the *Cinkante Balades* have given only brief hints of the metanarrative that makes the sequence more than a loosely juxtaposed set of *forme-fixe* lyrics, which minimizes the importance of psychological plausibility as a way of accounting for the narrator's sudden shift from abject despair to reverent joy in Balades XX–XXI. But this larger issue of abrupt shifts in tone, and what if anything they suggest, returns dramatically when the lovers respond to one another in Balades XL–XLVI, by which time the initially fitful metanarrative has been much more firmly established. The preceding Balade XXXIX is one of the most ecstatic in the set: the envoy concludes by sending many thousands of greetings ("Mil et Mil et Mil et Mil salutz," XXXIX.27) to one the lover hails as full of goodness (XXXIX.3). In the next poem, however, he abruptly accuses his lady of inconstancy, calling her a Helen to his forsaken Menelaus (XL.5–6). This prompts a response of three increasingly furious balades (XLI–XLIII), in which she lobs back both the charge of faithlessness and the classical references: the lover is "au matin un et autre au soir" ("one person in the morning and another at night," XLI.25); a serial traitor to women (XLII.5) worse even than Jason or Aeneas (XLIII.1–5); and a lecher who beds his victims with greater haste than Hector displayed in arming himself at Troy (XLIII.9–11). And yet Balade XLIIII, also in the lady's voice, fulsomely praises the lover with long lists of his virtues and the refrain that "au tiel ami jeo vuil bien estre amie" ["To such a friend/beloved I greatly wish to be a friend/beloved"].

What on earth has happened? Even if the lover who graciously answers her in Balade XLV, and whose love she happily accepts in Balade

---

[54] On Gower's use of Troy in *Vox Clamantis* (and indeed throughout his career), see Sylvia Federico, *New Troy: Fantasies of Empire in the Late Middle Ages* (Minneapolis: University of Minnesota Press, 2003), 1–28.

XLVI, is, as Yeager suggests, a different person from the lover of Balades I–XL, the effect is exceptionally disorienting, and while Yeager's proposition of a love triangle may restore some semblance of psychological plausibility, it does so at the expense of narrative coherence, for there have been only brief and tiny hints of a third party.[55] In any event, no interpretation can remove either the initial, highly destabilizing effect of the multiple quick shifts in tone or the suspicion that something more is at issue than a lover's quarrel. The allusions to Paris and Helen, Menelaus and Hector, return us to the Trojan context initiated in Balade XX and to that conflict's melding of the political and the erotic. The lady's most elaborate classical reference is also the most striking:

> Unqes Ector, q'ama Pantasilée,
> En tiele haste a Troie ne s'armoit,
> Qe tu tout nud n'es deinz le lit couché . . .[56]

Never did Hector, whom Penthesilea loved, / Arm himself in such haste at Troy, / As you fully naked have lain down in bed . . .

The counterintuitive nature of this comparison—Hector's presumably laudable eagerness to defend Troy is similar to but exceeded by the lover's despicably quick-acting lust—emphasizes by its strangeness the link between erotic vice and a great city's ultimate downfall, and, by extension, the vocabulary of love and politics.

Balade XLVI suggests a context for interpreting both these wild shifts in tone and the Trojan references that underlie them. Its opening stanza reads:

> En resemblance d'aigle, qui surmonte
> Toute autre oisel pour voler au dessure,
> Tresdouls amis, vostre amour tant amonte

---

[55] The only evidence I could find is in the lover's repeated assertion in Balade XL that the lady has responded to another lover's suit: she has taken a Paris and abandoned his Menelaus (5–6), and her "affection is not solely to one alone, / But rather to two" (21–22). We could interpret this third figure as the lover she addresses in Balade XLIIII, and who responds in the following poem. It is a slight indication, however, and must be balanced against the lady's denials and counter-accusations, which are far more passionate than the lover's initial complaint.

[56] Bal. XLIII.9–11. The reference to Penthesilea, the Amazon queen who for love of Hector fights for Troy, also suggests the connection between love and battle. Gower tells her story in *Confessio Amantis* IV.2135–82.

> Sur toutz amantz, par quoi jeo vous assure
> De bien amer, sauf toutdis la mesure
> De mon honour, le quell jeo guarderai:
> Si parler n'ose, ades jeo penserai.[57]

Just like the eagle, which surpasses / All other birds for flying up above, / Very sweet friend, your love ascends so / Above all lovers, for which I assure you / Of true love, saving always the measure / Of my honor, which I shall protect: / If I dare not speak, I shall think unceasingly.

This is the final poem in the *Cinkante Balades'* narrative sequence—Balades XLVII–L offer general thoughts on love, and Balade LI is a concluding address to the Virgin—so its opening image of a soaring, noble eagle deserves special consideration, particularly since it echoes the four-line poem "H. aquile pullus," which concludes the poetic part of the Latin dedication to the *Cinkante Balades* and is included in a number of other Gower manuscripts as a self-standing poem:

> H. son of the eagle, than whom no one is ever more graceful,
> Has broken his enemies, and subjugated tyrannical necks.
> H. the eagle has captured the oil, by which he has received the rule
>   of the realm;
> Thus the new stock returns, anointed and joined to the old stem.[58]

Prompted by this imagistic echo to look back to the dedication, we find further connections: the lady repeatedly praises this lover's *prouesce* (9), *valour* (11, 23), and *honour* (12, 22)—all virtues attributed to Henry by the dedicatory balades that frame the Latin verses cited above.[59]

What are we to do, interpretively, with the abrupt tonal shifts, narrative discontinuities, and outward-looking allusions and references dis-

---

[57] Bal. XLVI.1–7.

[58] See Yeager, *John Gower: The Minor Latin Works,* 46–47. In addition to Trentham, the poem survives in five other manuscripts; in three of these, it follows the *Cronica Tripertita* that narrates the downfall of Richard II. Yeager writes further (78): "The reference is to the 'Prophecy of the Eagle,' a thirteenth-century offshoot of the Merlin prophecies . . . which among Lancastrian supporters associated Henry IV with an eaglet (*pullus aquilae*) who comes from across the sea to depose a white king (*rex albus*—i.e., Richard, whose badge was a white hart). Henry was supposed the eagle because the symbol of John the Evangelist, namesake of his father, John of Gaunt, was an eagle, and because the badge of Edward III, his grandfather, was an eagle also—little notice was given to Edward's status as Richard's grandfather also."

[59] See Ded. Bal. I.1 and II.33.

played by this sequence of poems? By this point, we have received a wide range of invitations from both the *Cinkante Balades* and the manuscript as a whole to read them as more than merely conventional reverses. The narrative sequence ends with the joy and devotion expressed in Balades XLIIII–XLVI, and given the last poem's reference to the lover as a soaring eagle, we might interpret this happy ending as an optimistic comment on the prospects for "bon amour," and the hosts of virtues associated with it by the dedication, under the ascendance of "H. aquile pullus." But Balade XLVI's emphasis on silence, discretion, and thoughtfulness encourages greater reflection in the reader,[60] too, on the broader arc of the lovers' dialogue: the abrupt revelation of amatory discord in Balade XL, its equally sudden disappearance just four poems later, and its politically charged allusions to classical and especially Trojan history. Even leaving aside the potential for disruptive love triangles,[61] this sequence that concludes the *Balades'* narrative portion scarcely performs that seamless continuity emphasized by the last line of "H. aquile pullus." Instead, the juxtaposed performance of irreconcilable extremes of emotion presses us to consider more critically what these poems might suggest or represent.

Any hope that the last poems in the sequence might resolve these contradictions quickly evaporates, for the more gnomic tone of Balades XLVII–L raises its own set of problems. Each poem's refrain makes a claim about love:

> N'est pas oiceus sil qui bien amera.

> En toutz errours amour se justifie.

> Lors est amour d'onour la droite meire.

> Amour s'acorde a nature et resoun.
> (Balades XLVII–L, refrains)

---

[60] The refrain line quoted above emphasizes silence and thoughtfulness; other verbs of protection (*guarderai*, 6) and discretion (*m'aviserai*, 13) pepper the poem.

[61] I do not think that the *Cinkante Balades* encourages us to insist upon precise and stable referents for the various figures of the metanarrative, but it is worth remembering that if, as Yeager suggests, the lover of Balades XLIIII–XLVI is *not* the same as that of Balades I–XL, then much the greatest part of the *Cinkante Balades* as a whole has been devoted to his predecessor in the lady's good graces; if he *is* one and the same, then he stands accused of vile conduct that the lady's subsequent about-face does not resolve and, indeed, in its abruptness manages to highlight.

He who will love well is not lazy; In all errors love justifies itself; Then love is the rightful mother to honor; Love accords itself with nature and reason.

The autonomous, amoral, self-justifying love described in Balade XLVIII is antithetical both to the love of the following two poems (where love is mother of Honor and handmaid of Reason) and to the "bon amour" promised in the dedication. Yet by using the same word in each case—we cannot instantly distinguish as between *caritas* and *cupiditas*—these poems collectively recall the early marginal glosses' challenge to distinguish between celebrations of courtly as opposed to marital love. Indeed, Balade XLVIII takes the impossibility of defining love as its opening theme: "Amour est une chose merveilouse, / Dont nulls porra savoir le droit certain" ["Love is a marvelous thing / Of which no one is able to know the true certainty"].[62] The rest of this poem consists largely of oxymora, which both characterize love itself ("odible et graciouse" [17], serf and sovereign [24]) and which love in turn creates in whatever it touches: under its influence, "le riche est povere et le courtois vilein, / L'espine est molle et la rose est urtie" ["the rich man is poor and the courteous man a knave, / The thorn is soft and the rose is a nettle"], and so on.[63] This is a radically destabilizing poem to include at this point, after Gower has so self-consciously if heavy-handedly re-solved the lover's spat of Balades XL–XLV. In their exuberantly contradictory definitions of love, Balades XLVII–L codicologically perform, as a sequence, a version of the oxymora that according to Balade XLVIII constitute love's chief characteristic. In this sense, that sole dissenting poem has the last word, effectively trumping the other balades' individually performed insistence upon love's socially and ethically reinforcing power.

The sequence's final poem acknowledges these contradictions and attempts simply to define them away:

> Amour de soi est bon en toute guise,
> Si resoun le governe et justifie;
> Mais autrement, s'il naist de fole emprise,
> N'est pas amour, ainz serra dit sotie.[64]

[62] Bal. XLVIII.1–2.
[63] Bal. XLVIII.5–6.
[64] Bal. LI.1–4.

Love in itself is good in every guise, / If reason governs and justifies it; / But otherwise, it is but a foolish enterprise, / It is not love, but will be called madness.

And so we are told, finally, that the socially disruptive contradictions of Balade XLVIII were not love at all, but rather madness. Yet the echoes between the two balades make it hard to forget the assertion of love's disruptive qualities made by the earlier poem, which included the same "amour de soi" formula we see above (XLVIII.3) and similar language of justification in its refrain ("en toutz errours amour se *justifie*"). Its envoy, moreover, defined love in terms of that very *sotie* that this later balade insists is wholly different from it: "N'est qui d'amour poet dire la sotie" ["There is no one who is able to describe the folly of love"] [65] Balade LI's earnest protestations thus recall and draw attention to precisely the poem whose unsettling assertions it is attempting to shut down. This gambit is comparable to others we have seen in the *Cinkante Balades*: the early marginal glosses' initial demand that we read for more than the poems' apparent *desport,* only then to insist on the fundamental difference of later poems that look very much the same; and the abrupt, forced resolution of a lovers' spat that was itself an abrupt shift from the narrator's tone to that point. This final instance of this pattern that we just considered, however, is especially striking because its very existence, *after* Gower has supposedly shut the lid on troublesome kinds of love by imposing a happy ending to the lovers' quarrel, suggests the ultimate futility of all such moves. Whatever their intention, all these moments elicit a more careful, skeptical mode of reading than either the poems' genre or the dedication's emphasis on *desport* might otherwise suggest.

Earlier I raised but did not answer the question of what a Henrician context might suggest about how to interpret both these discontinuities and the efforts apparent in the manuscript to resolve them. The *Cinkante Balades*' final stanza gives new urgency to this issue by naming Henry explicitly, and both recalling and rewriting elements of the dedication:

> O gentile Engleterre, a toi j'escrits,
> Pour *remembrer* ta joie q'est novelle,
> Qe te survient du noble Roi Henri,
> Par qui dieus ad *redrescé* ta querele:

[65] Bal. XLVIII.23.

> A dieu purceo prient et cil et celle,
> Q'il de sa grace au fort Roi coroné
> Doignt peas, honour, joie et prosperité.[66]

Oh gentle England, I write for you, / In *remembrance* of your new joy, / Which comes to you from the noble King Henry, / By whom God has *redressed* your quarrel: / Let one and all therefore pray to God, / That He may graciously give to the strong, crowned King / Peace, honor, joy, and prosperity.

The final list of virtues echoes those that open the first dedicatory balade and close the second;[67] the *re-* verbs italicized above recall the profusion of such verbs in the dedication and earlier in the manuscript; and the reference to Henry as "Roi coroné" evokes the "ore avetz receu le coronal" line discussed above (Ded. Bal. I.17). Gower's claim to be writing to England (*a toi j'escrits*) recalls the phrase with which he addressed Henry earlier (*ce que je vous escris,* Ded. Bal. I.22), though this echo reinforces the fact that Henry is only being referred to here, not addressed. The most striking thing about this stanza, however, is its explicit reference to discord—the *querele* of line 28—that the dedication would allude to only obliquely.[68] Within this stanza, the most obvious referent for such conflict would seem to be that which led to Richard II's deposition and Henry's elevation as king. But in the context of the *Cinkante Balades,* it seems equally likely to recall the quarrel between the lovers in Balades XL–XLIIII, and thus continues the subtle connection of the political and amatory realms that the sequence as a whole has gradually suggested.

In so doing, moreover, this *querele* suggests a cautious perspective on Henry's accession, for although this stanza in isolation is straightforwardly laudatory, the idea of redressed quarrels reminds readers of the fact that earlier narrative discord (between the lovers) and thematic discontinuity (on just what love really is) were more papered over than resolved. This ambivalence is thoroughly consonant with what we have seen in *In Praise of Peace* and "Rex celi deus," where authorial revisions

[66] Bal. LI.25–31, emphasis mine.

[67] "Pité, prouesse, humblesse, honour roial" (Ded. Bal. I.1: "Mercy, prowess, humility, regal honor"), and "Honour, valour, victoire et bon esploit, / Joie et saunté, puissance et seignurie" (Ded. Bal. II.33–34: "Honor, valor, victory, and good success, / Joy and health, power and lordship").

[68] For example, the references to "our former servitude" (Ded. Bal. I.6), or to beginning again the "bon amour" that used to exist in former times (Ded. Bal. II.21–24).

suggested ambiguity at odds with those poems' outwardly celebratory tone and content. These suggestions gather force cumulatively, and any one of them might be declined, so my goal here is less to argue for a specific interpretation of the *Cinkante Balades* than it is to emphasize that all these poems are most compellingly complex when analyzed in the context of form and history alike: the codicological form of the Trentham manuscript, which includes multiple invitations to read its poems as building upon and commenting upon one another, and its intervening material (incipits, explicits, dedications) as significant; and the authorial history of Gower himself, which makes many of these invitations legible and significant in the context of a broader history of Lancastrian power.

Blind Cupid, Libidinous Kings, and an Author's Farewell

The next work in the manuscript, the Latin poem "Ecce patet tensus," amply demonstrates the impossibility of simply defining away the dangerous, disruptive side of love as mere *sotie,* as the concluding Balade LI has just attempted to do. This poem, which is unique to Trentham, opens with the declaration that "love conquers all" (3), and depicts a lord Cupid whose reign is terrifyingly absolute in its destructive chaos.[69] The blind god "knows not whither his trail will lead" (4), and his blindness is matched only by his power: "everyone obeys his precepts" (12), for "he is the crowned king" (13), who "subdues everything that Nature has created" (15). The description of Cupid as *coronatus*—emphasized by the fact that a crown is not a universal attribute for him—recalls the *Cinkante Balades'* initial address to Henry and concluding reference to him.[70] It is hard to read this resemblance as other than admonitory, given the amatory subject matter of the *Cinkante Balades* and the fact that several moments in "Ecce patet tensus" look even further back in the manuscript, to *In Praise of Peace*:

---

[69] Elliot Kendall has recently proposed that Cupid in the *Confessio Amantis* embodies a "magnificent lordship" that alienates and objectifies the servitor, as contrasted with the more productive "reciprocalist lordship" offered by Venus; this interpretation is consonant with my reading of Cupid in "Ecce patet tensus." See his *Lordship and Literature: John Gower and the Politics of the Great Household* (Oxford: Oxford University Press, 2008), 109–31.

[70] Cf. Ded. Bal. I.17: "ore avetz receu *le coronal*" ("you who have now received *the crown*"); Bal. LI.30: "fort Roi coroné" ("strong *crowned* king"), emphases mine.

Vulnerat omne genus, nec sibi vulnus habet.
Non manet in terris qui prelia vincit amoris,
Nec sibi quis firme federa pacis habet.

He [Cupid] wounds every nation, but receives no wound himself.
In the wars of Love there is no victor on earth,
Nor has anyone concluded with him a firm treaty of peace.

(18–20)

Trentham's first long poem admonished Henry to be a peacemaker, so, at its most basic, "Ecce patet tensus" holds up Cupid as an antimodel for the new king. But a set of four couplets apostrophizing human nature hints at the difficulty of avoiding completely the competing model of kingship that Cupid embodies:

O natura viri, poterit quam tollere nemo,
    Nec tamen excusat quod facit ipsa malum!
O natura viri, que naturatur eodem
    Quod vitare nequit nec licet illud agi!
O natura viri, duo que contraria mixta
    Continet, amborum nec licet acta sequi!
O natura viri, que semper habet sibi bellum
    Corporis ac anime, que sua iura petunt!

O human nature, which no one can abolish,
    Nor yet excuse the evils it does!
O human nature, irresistibly disposed
    To that unlawful thing which it cannot shun!
O human nature, that contains two mixed contraries
    But is not allowed to follow the deeds of both!
O human nature, which always has war within itself
    Of body and soul, both seeking the same authority!

(23–30)

This passage emphasizes that every person must somehow cope with two antithetical and competing impulses, the "two mixed contraries" of human nature: "body and soul," each seeking to be ruler of the self. The couplets' anaphora distances this message from Henry by universalizing its relevance. But Trentham has been full of competing dualities that threaten to morph into one another: the Alexander/Solomon and

Alexander/Henry binaries of *In Praise of Peace*; the Henry praised by "Rex celi deus," competing with the spectral presence of Richard from the lines' earlier existence in *Vox Clamantis*; and the "bon amour" to which the *Cinkante Balades* exhort the king, which dissolved into charges of treachery only hastily and somewhat artificially resolved at the end of the sequence. "Ecce patet tensus" presents yet another: a lord who competes with Henry, and whose *amor* differs radically from the "bon amour" that Henry was earlier imagined promoting.

These broad structural and thematic connections between "Ecce patet tensus" and other works in Trentham are reinforced by more local echoes, too. A reference to Solomon in "Ecce patet tensus," for example, recalls his role in *In Praise of Peace,* where he served as an exemplary figure for Henry, the one who (unlike Alexander) "ches wisdom unto the governynge / Of goddis folk" and thereby "gat him pees" (31–32, 35). But as the later Latin poem would have it, even "the intelligence of Solomon" can boast of "nothing praiseworthy" when faced with the all-consuming destructiveness of Love (22). This line not only casts retrospective doubt on the exemplary status he enjoyed earlier in the manuscript, but recalls in its terms his characterization in the *Confessio,* where his voracious sexual appetite prompted his descent into idolatry (VII.4469–573). But the Alexandrine model, exemplary in the *Confessio* and abruptly reversed in *In Praise of Peace,* is no more acceptable here than that of Solomon. Not just Solomon's wisdom but Samson's strength and David's sword are powerless in the face of love (21), and the image of Cupid as an indiscriminate conqueror who refuses to make peace takes the negative depiction of the conquering Alexander initiated in Trentham's first poem to an almost nightmarish extreme. All of this broader significance, however, is intelligible only in the context of Trentham's codicological form, and in that sense "Ecce patet tensus" offers its own form of duality: interpreted as I have suggested, it is the most cautionary of any of Trentham's texts about Henry's accession, but it also includes the fewest explicit indications—none, in fact—that it should be read in this way; such an interpretation depends on our willingness to see Trentham's larger codicological form as meaningful. "Ecce patet tensus" thus allows itself to be read as a conventionally homiletic text whose universally applicable admonitions neither threaten nor particularly speak to Henry; or as a serious warning to right behavior that has gained cumulative force by building upon the images and associations of the manuscript as a whole. My larger point is that by prompting us to ponder the issue, Trentham's codicological form gives its texts deeper aesthetic resonance than they have if analyzed in isolation.

Trentham's final major text, the *Traitié pour essampler les amantz marietz,* opens by continuing the project of distinguishing between the love-as-*sotie* of Balade XLVIII and "Ecce patet tensus," and a more wholesome love, restrained by the body's recognition that reason must be its constable.[71] Balades I–V hail marriage as God's instrument for promoting this second, nobler love, and in that sense the "Ecce patet tensus"/*Traitié* pairing appears to be playing a similar role to the *Confessio*/*Traitié* pairing in the Fairfax manuscript that gives the poem its modern title.[72] Together, these two poems finally subdivide the category of love, whose dangerous slipperiness we saw amply displayed in the *Cinkante Balades,* into the bad ("Ecce patet tensus") and the good (*Traitié*). Indeed, the Trentham copy of the *Traitié* appears particularly eager to avoid love's contradictions, for it omits the Latin poem "Est amor," which follows the balade sequence in all other manuscripts and consists of oxymoronic definitions of love akin to those of Balade XLVIII in the *Cinkante Balades.*[73] Read in this way, we could see the *Traitié* as attempting to shut down not just these definitional ambiguities but others that I have considered in Trentham: those of *In Praise of Peace* and "Rex celi deus," where authorial rewriting hinted at warnings for their royal addressee; or of the *Cinkante Balades,* whose dedication implied a

[71] Due to the missing folio, the first balade and a half of the *Traitié* has been lost. Since the textual witnesses to the *Traitié* are quite consistent, I have assumed for the purposes of my argument that the *Traitié* as it originally appeared in Trentham was essentially equivalent to the versions in Fairfax 3, Glasgow Hunterian T.2.17, and Bodley 294, the three surviving witnesses to the *Traitié's* opening. (The All Souls manuscript also includes the *Traitié,* but it lacks the first two poems and the first three lines of the third.)

[72] Oxford, Bodleian Library, MS Fairfax 3 includes the following link between *Confessio Amantis* and the *Traitié:* "Puisqu'il ad dit ci devant en Englois par voie d'essample la sotie de cellui qui par amours aime par especial, dirra ore apres en François a tout le monde en general un traitié selonc les auctour pour essampler les amantz marietz, au fin q'ils la foi de lour seintes espousailes pourront par fine loialté guarder, et al honour de dieu salvement tenir." ("Because the preceding poem in English was by way of example of the foolishness of those in particular who love in a courtly manner, now the subsequent treatise will be in French, for all the world generally, following the authorities, as an example for married lovers, in order that they might be able to protect the promise of their sacred spousal through perfect loyalty, and truly hold fast to the honor of God.") Quoted in Yeager, *John Gower: The French Balades,* 34.

[73] For "Est Amor," see Yeager, *John Gower: The Minor Latin Works,* 32–33 and 67–69. Claims that love is "warlike peace" (*pax bellica,* 1), "a peaceful fight" (*pugna quietosa,* 3), and "a joyful death" (*mors leta,* 7) typify the poem.

larger relevance for the "bon amour" it imagined Henry promoting, but that the sequence's metanarrative only imperfectly displayed. Indeed, the *Traitié* declines clear opportunities to emphasize the Henrician context that the manuscript's early texts established. It nowhere addresses or refers to the king, and the poem's final moves instead highlight Gower: the envoy that concludes the *Traitié* (the only one in the sequence) puts him in direct address to the entire world ("Al université de tout le monde / Johan Gower ceste Balade envoie"),[74] while the Latin verses adjoined to the sequence's conclusion first universalize the audience of the *Traitié* as all who have undertaken "the sacred order of marriage," then retreat into another mention of Gower, and the fact that he himself, "old in years . . . / Safely approach[es] the marriage bed in the order of husbands."[75]

Yet the *Traitié* is still crucially informed by other poems in the manuscript, particularly in its choice of verse form and *exempla*. Like the *Cinkante Balades,* of course, it is a balade sequence. But its uniformly rime royal stanzas, as opposed to the *Cinkante Balades'* varied stanza structures, look back to *In Praise of Peace,* which aside from the letter to Venus at the end of the *Confessio* (VIII.2217–2300) is Gower's only use of rime royal in English. These two poems are thematically linked as well. *In Praise of Peace* considered how the examples of two celebrated antecedents, Alexander and Solomon, might inform the reign of the newly crowned Henry IV. The *Traitié,* meanwhile, uses kings for most of its *exempla* on the dire consequences that await adulterers: Nectanabus and Ulysses, Jason and Agamemnon, Tarquin and Albinus, Tereus and Pharaoh are all duly punished for their adulterous behavior.[76] This adultery, moreover, is typically framed as violence or conquest, from Nectanabus's rape of Olimpeas (VI.4) or Hercules' conquest of Deianira (VII.5–6: "en armes *conquestoit* / La belle Deianire par *bataile,*" emphasis mine), to Albinus's marriage of his defeated enemy's daughter (XI.3–45) or Pharaoh's *ravine* of Abraham's wife Sarrai (XIII.9). This association of love and war recalls not just the depiction of Cupid as a rapacious warlord in "Ecce patet tensus," but also the Trojan references in the

[74] Bal. XVIII.22–23.

[75] See Yeager, *John Gower: The Minor Latin Works,* 33.

[76] On what this might suggest about the dating and intended audience of the *Traitié,* see Cathy Hume, "Why Did Gower Write the *Traitié?*" in *John Gower, Trilingual Poet: Language, Translation, and Tradition,* ed. Elizabeth Dutton with John Hines and R. F. Yeager (London: D. S. Brewer, 2010), 263–75.

Cinkante Balades and *In Praise of Peace*'s more general admonition to avoid conquest. The emphasis on royal figures in these *exempla,* moreover, means that while Trentham ends by moving away from the specifically Henrician context that its initial texts suggested, it continues and even strengthens the focus on kingship more generally that we have seen in each of the main texts so far: the first three dedicated to or addressing Henry directly, the final two presenting counter-models of royal misbehavior, from Cupid's in "Ecce patet tensus" to that of legendary adulterous kings in the *Traitié*.

This makes the *Traitié*'s final *exemplum,* the only positive one in the sequence, particularly important. Balade XVI tells of how the Roman emperor Valentinian lived to a miraculously old age by maintaining his chastity. He denied meriting any praise for "the kinges and the londes / To his subjeccion put under,"[77] however, accepting accolades only for his victory over fleshly desire. He thus not only becomes the antithesis of Cupid as presented in "Ecce patet tensus," but also presents a model of spiritual might that could redeem the negative associations of earthly conquest from *In Praise of Peace.* The only problem with this positive interpretation of Valentinian is that he seems curiously at odds with the *Traitié*'s focus on marriage, since he achieved his heroic conquest of the flesh without the help of matrimony. The strangeness of this *exemplum* will be most apparent to readers of Trentham with a detailed knowledge of Gowerian antecedents, since Gower's other two treatments of him are more explicit about the fact that Valentinian never married.[78] Even here, however, the *Traitié* cites him as an example of one of those few who "guarderont chaste lour condicion" ["Guard their chaste condition"],[79] before pivoting to assert near the end of the poem that "en mariage est la perfeccioun" ["In marriage is perfection"].[80] The *Traitié*'s only positively depicted figure thus turns out actually to have rejected the institution that the sequence as a whole supposedly praises. We should recognize here a gambit we have seen throughout Trentham: a piece of praise or a positive *exemplum* that reveals darker significance

[77] *Confessio Amantis,* V.6408–409. The story of Valentinian is also told in *Confessio* (V.6395–417) and *Mirour de l'Omme* (17089–100).

[78] He comes up in *Mirour de l'Omme* in the encomium on virginity (16825–17136), not the subsequent discussion of matrimony (17137–748), and in the *Confessio* is introduced as "withoute Mariage" (V.6401).

[79] Bal. XVI.4.

[80] Bal. XVI.19.

when apprehended in the context of the manuscript, and Gower's career, as a whole.

Trentham's final text, "Henrici quarti primus," puts this issue of Gower's career squarely before us; it is brief enough to quote in its entirety:

> Henrici quarti primus regni fuit annus
> Quo michi defecit visus ad acta mea.
> Omnia tempus habent; finem natura ministrat,
> Quem virtute sua frangere nemo potest.
> Ultra posse nichil, quamvis michi velle remansit;
> Amplius ut scribam non michi posse manet.
> Dum potui scripsi, set nunc quia curua senectus
> Turbavit sensus, scripta relinquo scolis.
> Scribat qui veniet post me discrecior alter,
> Ammodo namque manus et mea penna silent.
> Hoc tamen, in fine verborum queso meorum,
> Prospera quod statuat regna futura Deus. Amen.

> It was in the first year of the reign of King Henry IV
> When my sight failed for my deeds.
> All things have their time; nature applies a limit,
> Which no man can break by his own power.
> I can do nothing beyond what is possible, though my will has remained;
> My ability to write more has not stayed.
> While I was able I wrote, but now because stooped old age
> Has troubled my senses, I leave writing to the schools.
> Let someone else more discreet who comes after me write,
> For from this time forth my hand and pen will be silent.
> Nevertheless I ask this one final thing, the last of my words:
> That God make our kingdoms prosperous in the future. Amen.[81]

Two other, apparently later versions of this poem assert a simple physical causation ("I stopped writing, because I am blind," and "I am unable to write any longer, because I am blind") for the poet's farewell to writing, instead of the circumlocutions used here: "my sight failed for my deeds" and "stooped old age has troubled my senses."[82] Compared to

---

[81] Yeager, *John Gower: The Minor Latin Works*, 47.

[82] "Henrici quarti primus" is unique to Trentham. A slightly longer, fifteen-line version, "Henrici regis annus," appears in the Cotton, Harley, and Glasgow manuscripts, while the All Souls manuscript version opens "Quicquid homo scribat" and consists of

the later two versions, which specify "writing" both at that point and almost obsessively throughout, these are curiously allusive formulations.[83] And that makes another line in the Trentham version stand out: Gower's desire in line 9 that "someone else more discreet who comes after me" should write in his stead, a prayer that the final All Souls version omits. What deeds has Gower failed at in Trentham that a more discreet, more prudent, wiser man will have to take up? The poem is legible in completely conventional and therefore nonthreatening terms by a Lancastrian audience, but I wonder if it might also represent a private acknowledgment that the Gower compilation it rounds out is not as fully laudatory as discretion and prudence might dictate; and that the safest course, not just the one prompted by physical disability, might be to retire from writing altogether?

This is a biographically inflected reading of Trentham's final poem. The poem itself, with its insistently repeated first-person verbs and pronouns, encourages such interpretations even as the manuscript, as we saw early on, makes itself difficult to pin down historically or paleographically as precisely intended by anyone, scribe(s) or author. In my explorations of such paradoxes throughout this essay, I hope to have demonstrated that the Trentham manuscript's codicological form works together with its individual texts and their multiple evocations of Gower's authorial history to create that excess, that refusal to submit to clear messages or single meanings, which in their various ways we saw Maura Nolan, Samuel Otter, and Derek Pearsall all propose as one key component of the literary and aesthetic. Thus far I have emphasized the ways in which Trentham creates meaning through juxtaposition and accretion, but it is worth remembering in conclusion that fragmentariness is the necessary corollary of such assemblage; every collection, examined closely, reveals destabilizing fissures, evidence of its status as a con-

---

seventeen lines. For all three, see Yeager, *John Gower: The Minor Latin Works,* 47–50. The parenthetical quotations about blindness are from lines 2 and 4 of "Henrici regis annus" and "Quicquid homo scribat," respectively.

[83] I should acknowledge first that "Henrici quarti primus" appears to be the earliest of the three versions, since it references the first year of Henry's reign, while "Henrici regis annus" mentions the second; "Quicquid homo scribat" incorporates phrases from both versions and thus appears to be the latest. This means that we can resort to the simplest explanation for the different vocabularies of blindness: that when Trentham was being compiled, Gower merely suffered from failing eyesight, and it wasn't until a year later that he actually went blind and felt compelled to describe himself as such. This is quite possible of course, maybe even probable, but in any event does not preclude the metaphorical interpretation of the poem I suggest above.

structed object that is imperfect like every other. I have suggested that
Trentham thematizes those fissures, allowing us to see disjunctions between the most obvious, explicit content of its texts and the significance
that they might have if examined in the context of other (codicological)
forms and (authorial and political) histories. Much of that significance
seems to me cautionary: Trentham's early texts, laudatory and Henrician, seem more ambivalent when read in the context of Gower's authorial history and the manuscript's later, darker poems; those texts'
relevance to the king, however, is far from clear unless we elect to read
them in the context of the manuscript as a whole.[84]

My larger argument about Trentham, however, is not that it conveys
a specific "message," or is "about" a specific figure. It is an artfully
constructed meditation on the multiple natures and implications of
kingship, and the very complexity of its construction serves to acknowledge both the visceral pleasure of using aesthetic modes to grapple with
such vitally important questions and the impossibility of creating clear-
cut "propositional content" as answers to them. And this is the sense in
which we can understand Trentham's literal, physical fragmentariness,
alluded to briefly at the beginning of this essay, as complementing key
elements of its texts' meanings even as it occludes others. Any of the
manuscript's missing pieces—the fragmentary stanzas of the second
dedicatory balade and first poem of the *Cinkante Balades* proper, the end
(perhaps) of the (perhaps) incomplete "Ecce patet tensus," and whatever
linking material might once have joined it to the *Traitié*—might have
provided the key to a certain kind of understanding of the manuscript
that we now will never have. But the tidy meaning such a key might
have made available to us might in turn have compromised the manuscript's aesthetic excess, by pinning down the range of shifting meanings
offered by Trentham's texts and form, meaning and excess, that I have
explored in this essay. Trentham's physical lacunae are as much a part

[84] Although I have used forms and histories both medieval and modern to argue for
such a reading, it is worth acknowledging in conclusion the inescapability of idiosyncratic, personal response inherent to any such "election to read." Academia's continuing
affinity for the deconstructive, and especially for imagining that artists and writers
ought properly to be skeptical of political establishments, must inflect to some degree
my arguments here, as must the ongoing attempts (justified, I believe) by many scholars
to suggest that Gower was in fact a less blindly slavish Lancastrian than an earlier
generation of critics tended to suppose. To acknowledge thus much, however, is, I believe, not to undermine the arguments I have made but rather more fully to historicize
them.

of its texts' meaning as are its many attempts to stitch those texts together into a coherent and unified whole. The manuscript thus becomes much more than a gift to Henry IV, or a warning to him, or a book of poems about kingship, or a collection of Gower's verse. It is a reminder of why we grapple with literary texts in the first place: the fact that their delights and their frustrations, their significances and their silences, are all—literally—bound up together.

A Holograph Copy of Thomas Hoccleve's *Regiment of Princes*

Linne R. Mooney
University of York

THE FOCUS OF THIS ARTICLE is the British Library manuscript Royal 17 D.XVIII, a copy of Thomas Hoccleve's *Regiment of Princes*. I here argue first, on paleographic, codicological, and linguistic grounds, that this manuscript is written by the hand of the author Thomas Hoccleve; second, that the text of the *Regiment* in this manuscript represents a revised version of the poem written in 1412–13, in which the author had made alterations reflecting the changed circumstances of himself, of his dedicatee, Henry of Derby, and of the country a year or two after the completion and first dissemination of the poem; and third, that this manuscript was in fact the copy given to John of Lancaster, later duke of Bedford, to whom a balade written at the end may be addressed.

British Library, Royal 17 D.XVIII: A Hoccleve Holograph

We have more identified examples of Thomas Hoccleve's handwriting than of any other vernacular English medieval writer: three manuscripts of his own literary works, two and a half leaves of a copy of John Gower's *Confessio Amantis,* documents written in his daily work as a Clerk of the Office of the Privy Seal, and a formulary he wrote for that office.[1] The

Research for this article was partly funded by a major research grant from the Arts and Humanities Research Council of the UK.

[1] For identification of the holographs and the portion of the *Confessio Amantis* manuscript, see A. I. Doyle and M. B. Parkes, "The Production of Copies of the *Canterbury Tales* and the *Confessio Amantis* in the Early Fifteenth Century," in *Medieval Scribes, Manuscripts, and Libraries: Essays Presented to N. R. Ker,* ed. M. B. Parkes and A. G. Watson (London: Scolar Press, 1978), 163–210, esp. 182–85; rpt. M. B. Parkes, *Scribes, Scripts, and Readers: Studies in the Communication, Presentation, and Dissemination of Medieval Texts* (London: Hambledon Press, 1991), 201–48, esp. 220–23; hereafter cited with both sets of page numbers.

formulary survives as British Library, Additional 24062, a volume of 201 parchment leaves, mostly written by Hoccleve in an informal, loose cursive version of his hand but also, as I shall argue below, containing one quire that includes examples of his neater, more formal, hand.[2] The manuscripts of his literary work, recently published in a facsimile by the Early English Text Society, are Durham University Library, Cosin V.iii.9, folios 13–95, and Henry E. Huntington Library MSS 111 and 744, folios 25–68v.[3] Ian Doyle and Malcolm Parkes identified Hoccleve as one of the five scribes who wrote the Cambridge, Trinity College R.3.2, copy of John Gower's *Confessio Amantis* (his contribution, folios 82r–84r);[4] and more tentatively as one of the correctors for Adam Pinkhurst's copy of Chaucer's *Canterbury Tales* in the National Library of Wales, Peniarth 392D, the so-called Hengwrt manuscript (his corrections on folios 83v, 138v, and 150), besides a number of documents written in the course of his work as a Clerk of the Office of the Privy Seal.[5] I recently published a list of Privy Seal documents written by Hoccleve's hand, ranging from his earliest years in that office until a time within a year of his death in 1426.[6] In the introduction to the facsimile of Hoccleve's holograph literary works, John Burrow and Ian Doyle comment that the three manuscripts reproduced in the facsimile contain "all the poems currently attributed to him . . . [w]ith the important exception of Hoccleve's major work *The Regiment of Princes,* of which no holograph copy is known."[7] I here put forward an argument that a holograph of the *Regiment* does survive, British Library, Royal 17 D.XVIII, which has not previously been recognized as being written by Hoccleve's hand.[8]

[2] The formulary was transcribed by Elna-Jean Young Bentley, "The Formulary of Thomas Hoccleve" (Ph.D. diss., Emory University, 1965).

[3] Reproduced in facsimile with an introduction by J. A. Burrow and A. I. Doyle, *Thomas Hoccleve: A Facsimile of the Autograph Verse Manuscripts,* EETS s.s. 19 (2002).

[4] Doyle and Parkes, "The Production of Copies," 182–85, 220–23.

[5] For corrections to the Hengwrt manuscript, see A. I. Doyle and M. B. Parkes, "Palaeographical Introduction," in *The Canterbury Tales: A Facsimile and Transcription of the Hengwrt Manuscript, with Variants from the Ellesmere Manuscript,* ed. Paul G. Ruggiers (Norman: University of Oklahoma Press, 1979), xix–xlix; for documents identified by Doyle and Parkes, see "Production of Copies," 82, 222.

[6] Linne R. Mooney, "Some New Light on Thomas Hoccleve," *SAC* 29 (2007): 293–340, esp. appendix B, 322–40.

[7] Burrow and Doyle, "Introduction" to *Facsimile,* xi.

[8] Others have pointed out the closeness of this manuscript to Hoccleve's original but have shied away from claims that it is written in his own hand. See Mary Ruth Pryor, "Thomas Hoccleve's Series: An Edition of MS Durham Cosin V.iii.9" (Ph.D. diss., University of California, Los Angeles, 1968), "Introduction"; and Marcia Smith Marzec, "The Latin Marginalia of the *Regiment of Princes* as an Aid to Stemmatic Analysis," *Text: An Interdisciplinary Annual of Textual Studies* 3 (1987): 269–84; both are cited by Charles

The manuscript Royal 17 D.XVIII has been overlooked by scholars for a number of reasons: first, it and most manuscripts of the *Regiment* have remained in the shadow of the two sumptuously prepared manuscripts of the poem generally agreed to be original presentation copies, British Library MSS Arundel 38 and Harley 4866; second, it was dated to the quarter-century after Hoccleve's death by J. A. Burrow in his 1994 biography of Hoccleve;[9] third, the hand of this manuscript differs somewhat in general aspect from that of the accepted Hoccleve holographs, as I will discuss further below.

The identification of Hoccleve's hand in Royal 17 D.XVIII depends upon many factors: paleographical, codicological, and linguistic. Appendix A below lists and illustrates the characteristics of Hoccleve's handwriting that have been identified in manuscripts already attributed to him: the holograph manuscripts, the formulary, and his two-and-a-half-folio stint in Trinity College R.3.2. These characteristic letter forms also occur in the newly identified holograph manuscript of the *Regiment,* Royal 17 D.XVIII, as illustrated below.

Burrow and Doyle offer the most recent description of Hoccleve's hand in the introduction to their facsimile of the holograph literary manuscripts Huntington Library HM 111 and 744 and Durham University Library, Cosin V.iii.9.[10] The section on dating the manuscripts establishes that the three holographs were written between 1422 and 1426, and the formulary in this same period; in other words, all of the examples of his handwriting that they analyze, with the exception of five sides in Cambridge, Trinity College R.3.2, were written during the

---

Blyth in the introduction to his edition of *The Regiment of Princes* (Kalamazoo: Western Michigan University, 1999), 16. Blyth writes, "There is evidence that another Royal manuscript, British Library MS Royal 17 D.xviii, derives ultimately from a copy written in Hoccleve's hand. . . . More than any other scribal copy, it preserves some of Hoccleve's characteristic spellings, and as a manuscript not closely related to the family of manuscripts of which Arundel and Harley are the best examples, this Royal manuscript often serves as a relatively independent witness confirming their readings" (16–17).

[9] J. A. Burrow, *Thomas Hoccleve,* Authors of the Middle Ages, vol. 4 (Aldershot: Variorum, 1994), 51. The British Library Harley catalogue did not date the manuscript: see George F. Warner and Julius P. Gilson, *Catalogue of the Western Manuscripts in the Old Royal and King's Collection,* 4 vols. (London: British Museum, 1921), 2:256. Neither did M. C. Seymour assign it a date in his "The Manuscripts of Hoccleve's *Regiment of Princes,*" *Edinburgh Bibliographical Society Transactions* 4.7 (1974): 253–97 (this manuscript described on 273). F. J. Furnivall, in his *Hoccleve's Works: The Regement of Princes and Fourteen Minor Poems,* EETS e.s. 72 (1897), did not even include a list, let alone description, of the manuscripts.

[10] Burrow and Doyle, "Introduction" to *Facsimile,* xxxiv–xxxvii.

last four years of the poet's life. They note that even if we take the earliest date, 1408, for Trinity College R.3.2, they have not analyzed "any specimen of his handwriting that can be assigned certainly to a date before 1408 or 1413 (that is after he had been working for the Privy Seal for more than twenty years)."[11] By the time of writing of the holograph literary manuscripts and formulary, Hoccleve's control of handwriting and ability to see what he was writing had obviously suffered from his many years as a full-time clerk; and he tells us in his writings as early as 1415 that his eyesight had deteriorated but that he was too vain to wear spectacles.[12]

Hoccleve was a professional writer, so it seems entirely reasonable that in his younger days he should have been capable of writing in neat and attractive script for copying documents going out over the king's Privy Seal, as well as writing in less formal script for documents intended only for internal use within government (such as the E 404 documents I identified as written by his hand in my recent article)[13] and within the Office of the Privy Seal itself (such as the formulary). We are so accustomed to examining the texts of his holograph manuscripts at Durham and the Huntington Library that we lose sight of the fact that his hand appears much different in other manuscripts accepted as being written by him, like the Trinity Gower or the documents of the Privy Seal. The more formal hand of his stint in Trinity College R.3.2 shows us that in his younger days Hoccleve was also capable of writing in a smaller script and more neatly than he does in the three later holographs.

Although many scholars have written about the formulary, there is no agreement about which portions are written by Hoccleve and which by others.[14] The formulary is mostly written in Hoccleve's handwriting, with a few entries in the first half by another hand, and more frequent entries by this and other hands intermixed with Hoccleve's in

---

[11] Ibid., xxxiv.

[12] In his "Balade to the Duke of York," which Burrow (*Thomas Hoccleve,* 23) dates to before the death of Edward, Duke of York, at Agincourt in 1415, Hoccleve wrote that "pryde is un-to me so greet a fo / Þᵗ the spectacle forbedith he me / And hath y-doon of tyme yore ago" (Huntington HM 111, folios 32v–34r for the whole poem, these lines 56–58 from folio 33v); and he also complains of poor eyesight in the envoy to John of Lancaster, as discussed and quoted above.

[13] Mooney, "Some New Light."

[14] Even experts like Burrow and Doyle have not been entirely clear on this issue: see their "Introduction" to *Facsimile,* xxxvi n. 1. I am currently preparing an article in which I shall set out which folios are written by Hoccleve and which by other contemporary or later scribes.

the second half. For the most part, Hoccleve's entries in the formulary date from the latter years of his life: these are written in a swift and informal cursive script because here he was writing only for fellow clerks of the office, and so only for legibility. However, the formulary also contains a sample of his formal, neat document hand on folios 105–108v, such as he must have used to copy the official charters or grants awarded by the king over the Privy Seal. These folios preserve samples of letters patent, that is, legal documents by which the monarch personally made a grant to an individual or group, including rights to land or privileges, titles, exemptions, and so forth. The collection of samples in Hoccleve's formal hand may have been a separate booklet into which he copied forms earlier in his lifetime, keeping a booklet of sample letters patent for his own or other clerks' consultation just as he later created the complete formulary. The material on these leaves, Bentley's items 573–603, dates from the reigns of Edward III, Richard II, and Henry IV, with the latest whose date can be determined being from 1413.[15] In the formulary, then, we have examples of two types of Hoccleve's handwriting. Figure 1 shows us the hand that is typical in most of the formulary, large and sprawling and less controlled than we find in his stint in the Trinity Gower; but this hand is nevertheless recognizable as Hoccleve's by the characteristic

---

[15] For those that can be dated, see Bentley, "The Formulary of Thomas Hoccleve," items 573–603. Bentley shows these as occurring on folios 109–112v, but her foliation numbers are off by four at this point in the manuscript: the manuscript had not been refoliated when she was working with it, and the older foliation did not count blank leaves. These folios (marked in bold) form the core of a quire of 14, now (by the newer foliation) folios 103, 104, **105, 106, 107, 108,** 109, 110, 111, 112, 113, blank, blank, blank. The blanks are unfoliated, and only the first of them is ruled. Thus Hoccleve's original booklet of sample letters patent would have consisted of eight to ten leaves, of which he had written only the first four; and to which he later added two bifolia as an outer wrapper containing further texts at the beginning but being blank at the end. The earliest of the sample letters patent on folios 105–108 is dated 1378 and all the rest date from before 1406 with the sole exception of item 581, datable to April 1413. Folio 102v, immediately preceding this quire, marks the end of the first portion of Hoccleve's formulary, where he instructs the reader to skip over the intervening pages and begin again at folio 120. What is now folio 102r he foliated Cvj and what is now folio 120v he also foliates Cvj; then 121r he foliates Cvij. At the bottom of folio 102r, Hoccleve wrote, "Passe over th'acente of leves betwixt this and the begynnynge of O*mn*egadriu*m* at fol. Cvj[m] in the latter syde of the same leef / & thanne looke the markynges folwynge." It appears that the texts written in a formal version of Hoccleve's hand on folios 105–108 were the core of a quire inserted as Hoccleve assembled the formulary, but that he later decided to instruct his readers to look beyond this quire for a continuation of the organization of documents in the formulary: he had perhaps decided after the fact that letters patent did not belong in this place in the order.

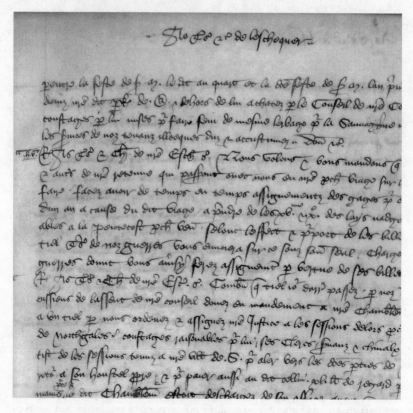

Fig. 1. British Library, Add. 24062, fol. 49, extract. Reproduced with permission of the British Library.

flat-topped **A** ("As" in title and line 5), coat-hanger **g** ("assignementz" in line 7), the **y** whose descender rises alongside or through the letter to curl at the top as the tick above the letter ("ainsy" in line 11), **h** with shoulder lower than minim height ("dehors" and "achatez" in line 2), pointing and flat-bottomed return for ascender of **d** ("don" near end of line 4), and two-stroke **N** with distinct feet at the base of each stroke ("Nous" in line 5), among others. (For these characteristics of Hoccleve's hand, see Appendix A.)

This loose, informal hand is recognizably the same as the least formal portions of the holograph literary manuscripts, such as the leaf from Huntington Library HM 744 illustrated in Figure 2.

Illustrating his neater, more controlled, more formal hand from the

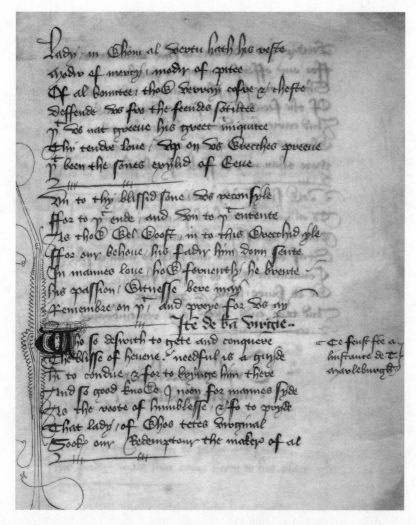

Fig. 2. San Marino, California, Henry E. Huntington Library, MS HM 744, fol. 36 (extract), reproduced with permission of the Huntington Library.

letters patent quire of the formulary, Figure 3 offers samples of his self-dotting y ("y," line 6, "Royne," line 4), h with low shoulder ("hous-teux," line 11), the round-topped version of A ("A," line 20), his angli-cana w with distinct feet at the base of the main strokes ("Weidantz," line 18), pointed and flattened d ("dengleterre," line 21), and initial v

269

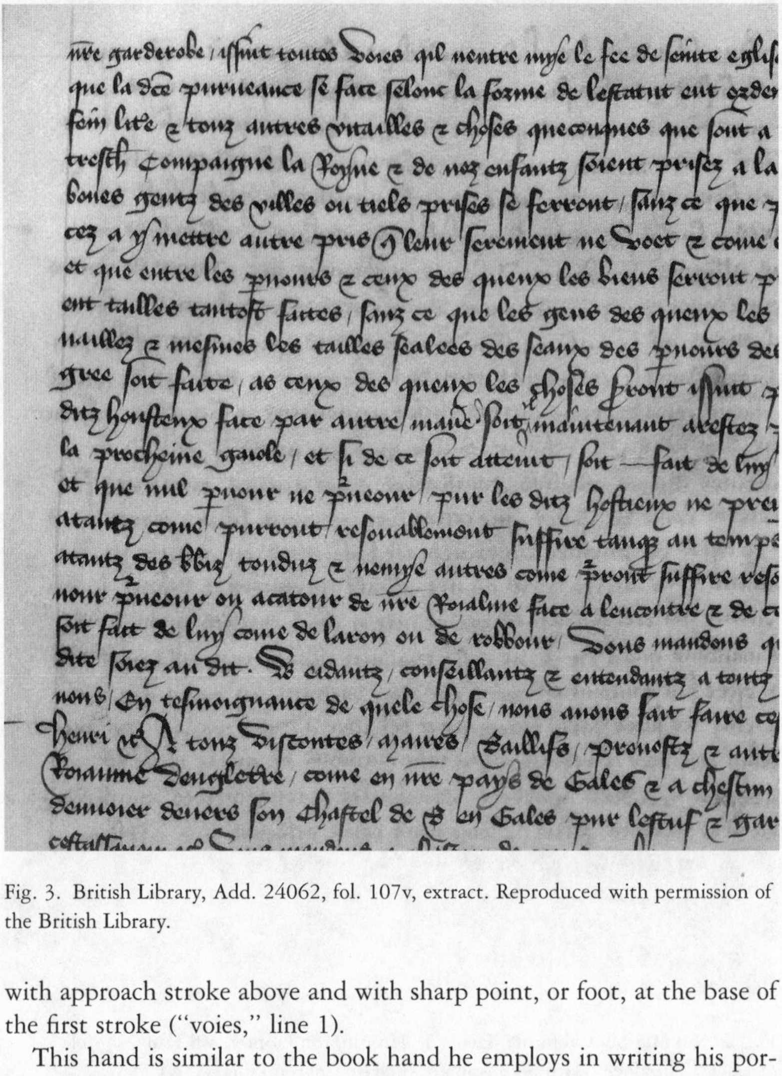

Fig. 3. British Library, Add. 24062, fol. 107v, extract. Reproduced with permission of the British Library.

with approach stroke above and with sharp point, or foot, at the base of the first stroke ("voies," line 1).

This hand is similar to the book hand he employs in writing his portion of Gower's *Confessio Amantis* copied by five scribes, now Cambridge, Trinity College, MS R.3.2. This script is neater and more formal than that of the three late holographs.[16]

The copy of Hoccleve's *Regiment of Princes* in Royal 17 D.XVIII is a

[16] Doyle and Parkes also comment on the "tighter, more upright and deliberate manner" of Hoccleve's script in MS R.3.2. "The Production of Copies," 182, 220.

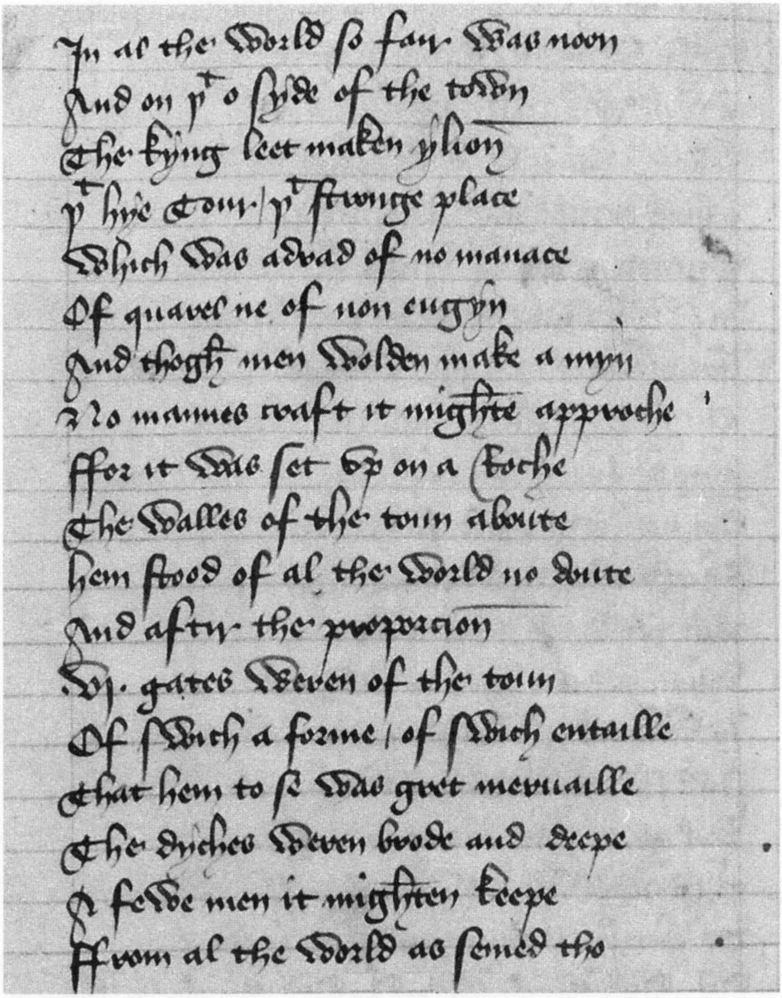
In al the world so fayr was noon
And on þt o syde of the toun
The kyng leet maken ylion
þt hye tour / þt stronge place
Which was adrad of no manace
Of quarel ne of non engyn
And thogh men wolden make a myn
No mannes craft it mighte approche
ffor it was set up on a roche
The walles of the toun aboute
hem stood of al the world no doute
And after the proporcion
vj. gates weren of the toun
Of swich a forme / of swich entaille
That hem to se was gret mervaille
The dyches weren brode and depe
A fewe men it mighten kepe
ffrom al the world as semed tho

Fig. 4. Cambridge, Trinity College, MS R.3.2, fol. 82vb (extract).[17] Reproduced with the permission of the Master and Fellows of Trinity College, Cambridge.

[17] Burrow and Doyle assign the folio number 82v to their Figure 2 on page xxxv of the EETS *Facsimile* volume, but they in fact illustrate folio 83v there.

complete copy of the poem to which is appended a balade addressed to a member of the royal family to whom he is presenting this copy of the *Regiment,* on folio 100.[18] In this sample of his handwriting, Hoccleve employs a script somewhere between that of the Trinity College MS R.3.2 of Gower's *Confessio Amantis* and the later holographs.

With the exception of a few graphs illustrating varying preferences in his scribal career, all letter forms of the hand of Royal MS 17 D.XVIII match exactly Hoccleve's idiosyncratic letter forms (see Appendix A). Folio 73v (Fig. 5) illustrates the square-topped uppercase **A** ("And," beginning of line 23), the y whose descender rises through the letter and curls back to form the dot, or tick, over the letter ("restreyne" line 5 and "ioynt" line 7), the uppercase **T** ("Ther" line 3, "Than" line 19, etc.), the **d** whose ascender points to the left and has a straight lower portion of the looped ascender ("due" line 6), and the **h** with low shoulder ("moche" line 16). These distinctive idiosyncratic forms are to be found in the Trinity College, Cambridge, manuscript R.3.2, illustrated in Figure 4, or in the later holograph manuscripts, for example, Huntington Library HM 744 (Fig. 2).

The most striking differences of letter forms from the later holographs are the forms of **w** and **g**, final **e**, and thorn, but these are earlier graphetic preferences of the poet that (except for thorn) are found also in his stint in the Trinity Gower and in the Privy Seal documents written by his hand in the first half of his career. The anglicana form of **w** lacks the distinct sharp turnings, or feet, at the base (Fig. 5, line 1, "Whan" and "wit"), but such forms with rounded bases can be found in his copying in the Trinity Gower, as illustrated above (Fig. 4, line 5, "was") and in some of his Privy Seal documents, like National Archives E 404/40/162, written in 1423 (see Fig. 6 below, "Westm*inster*" in the last line).

The upper lobe of secretary **g** in the Royal manuscript of the *Regiment* does not have the straight top, nor does the descender form the coat-hanger shape that is distinctive in Hoccleve's handwriting: it merely curls under the letter, sometimes closing the lower lobe by joining where the upper lobe meets the stalk (Fig. 5, line 2, "to-gider"). But this form,

---

[18] For a brief description of the manuscript, see Seymour, "The Manuscripts of Hoccleve's *Regiment of Princes,*" 273. Seymour's descriptions are not without errors, some of which are noted by Richard Firth Green, "Notes on Some Manuscripts of Hoccleve's *Regiment of Princes,*" *British Library Journal* 4 (1978): 37–41, and J. A. Burrow, *Thomas Hoccleve,* 50–55; and additional manuscripts noted by A. S. G. Edwards, "Hoccleve's *Regiment of Princes:* A Further Manuscript," *Edinburgh Bibliographical Society Transactions* 5.1 (1978): 32. See below for further discussion of the dedicatee.

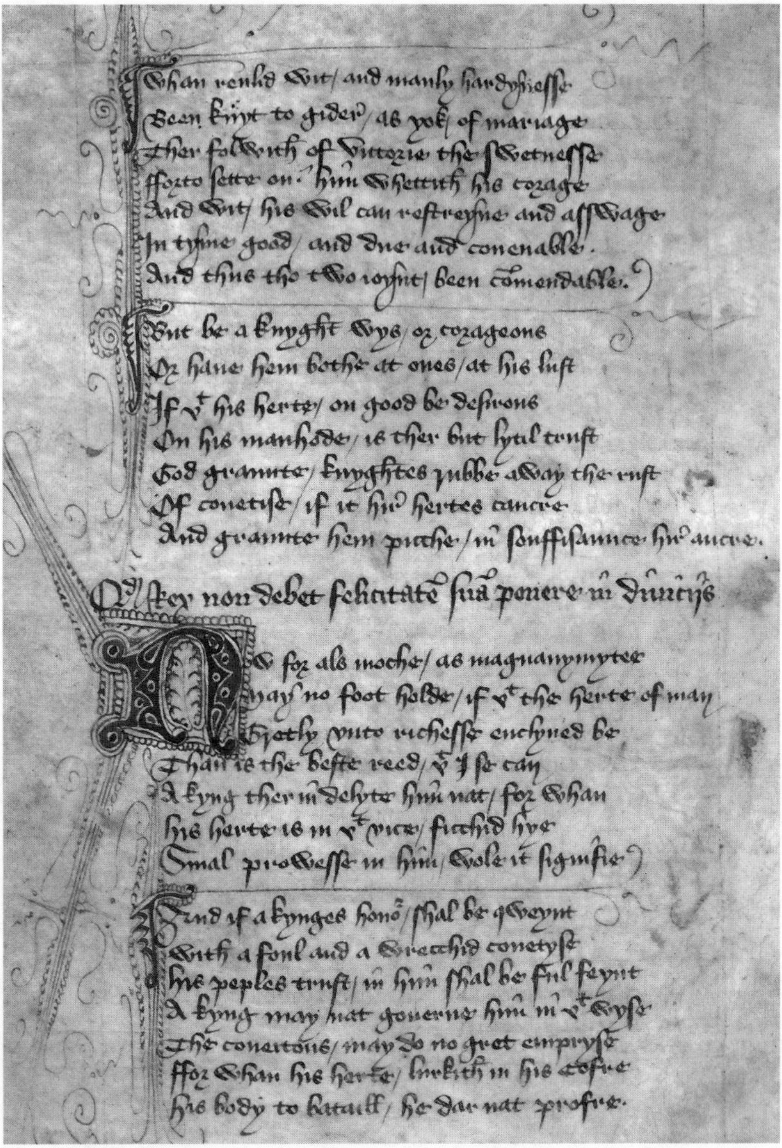

Whan renk wit/ and manly hardynesse
Been knyt togider/ as yok of mariage
Ther folleth of victorie the swetnesse
ffor to sette on hym whettith his corage
And whan his wil can restreyne and asswage
In tyme good/ and due and convenable
And thus tho two ioynt/ been comendable

But be a knyght wys/ or corageous
Or haue hem bothe at ones/ at his lust
If yt his hertes/ on good be desirous
On his manhode/ is ther but lytil trust
God graunte/ knyghtes rubbe away the rust
Of couetise/ if it his hertes ancre
And graunte hem prowesse/ in souffisaunce sw ancre

Rex non debet felicitate sua ponere in diuicijs

As for als moche/ as magnanymytee
May no foot holde/ if yt the herte of man
Wrothly vnto richesse enchyned be
Than is the beste reed/ yt I se can
A kyng ther in delyte hym nat/ for whan
his herte is in yt pyce/ fixhid hye
Smal prowesse in hym/ wole it signifie

And if a kynges honour/ shal be qweynt
With a foul and a wrecchid coneityse
his peples trust/ in hym shal be ful feynt
A kyng may nat gouerne hym in yt wyse
The coueitous/ may do no gret empryse
ffor whan his herte/ lurketh in his cofre
his body to bataill/ he dar nat profre.

Fig. 5. British Library MS Royal 17 D.XVIII, fol. 73v, reproduced with permission of the British Library.

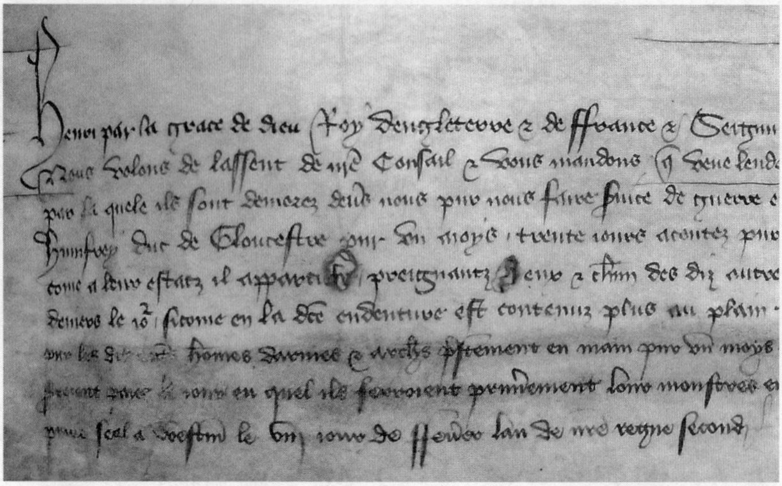

Fig. 6. Kew, National Archives E 404/40/162. Warrant for payments to John Shilley and Thomas Denney, Esquires, who are fighting in France with Humphrey, Duke of Gloucester, dated 8 February, 2 Henry VI, or 1423. Reproduced with permission of The National Archives.

too, can be found in his copying of the formulary (Fig. 1, line 3, "ler-bage," and line 14, "assignez") and the Trinity Gower (Fig. 4, line 13, "gates"); and Doyle and Parkes also commented on this "**g** form with a pointed head" in Hoccleve's stint in Trinity R.3.2.[19] As a professional scribe, Hoccleve would have been careful to write distinctive graphs for legibility, and I suggest that he would use this simplified graph for **g** more in copying English than Latin or French, since English would contain few samples of **q** with which the simplified **g** could be confused: in French and Latin copying, his graph for **q** has this same simple pointed lobe at the top, but its descender is straight (e.g., Fig. 1, line 1, "quart"). Another letter perhaps not associated with Hoccleve is the final **e** with tongue, as seen in Figure 5, the final letters of each line in the first stanza; but this form, too, can be seen in the Trinity Gower (Fig. 4, the final **e** of the word "the" in each of lines 1, 3, and 13). The final

[19] Doyle and Parkes, "The Production of Copies," 182, 220. Note that while this form of **g** does not occur in the holographs or formulary, they had no hesitation in assigning the stint in Trinity College R.3.2 to Hoccleve, presumably accepting that the scribe's preferences for letter forms vary with time or with the requirements of the piece he is copying—just the argument I am applying here.

graph that differs in the Royal MS of the *Regiment* is the thorn: in the later holographs, its stalk extends well below the line, whereas in the Royal MS its stalk is very short and positioned at an oblique angle (Fig. 5, line 10, "þᵗ"). In Hoccleve's short stint in Gower's *Confessio Amantis,* the thorn sometimes has a long and straight stalk but also sometimes has a shorter, curved, and partly oblique stalk (as in "þᵗ" of Fig. 4, line 2), and sometimes an oblique upper stalk bending to a straight vertical lower stalk (as in "þᵗ" of Fig. 4, line 4). Since the Privy Seal documents and the formulary's sample texts contain no examples of thorn, being written in French or Latin, we have no other samples of Hoccleve's earlier writing in which to find possible changing preferences for the form of thorn in his writing. As in the other holographs, Hoccleve avoids the use of thorn in Royal 17 D.XVIII, usually preferring "th," except in the abbreviated thorn with superscript "t" for "þat." Again I believe this demonstrates Hoccleve's care to write graphs that could not be confused with one another. In his day-to-day writing in Latin and French, he would not use thorn, so when he was copying this English text he was very careful to use a form that could not be confused with **p**. When copying the Trinity College *Confessio Amantis,* he usually used a more straight-stalked form, perhaps to conform to graphs used by other scribes in this manuscript, and this straight form reappears in his later holographs. While it is not matched exactly by any identified piece of Hoccleve's handwriting, this graph alone marks a difference from his known preferred or occasional graphs. Although it is difficult to explain the distinctive form of this one letter in this manuscript, nevertheless, taken together, the number of his most distinctive forms found together in Royal 17 D.XVIII offers clear paleographic evidence that Thomas Hoccleve was the copyist for this manuscript of the *Regiment.*

In layout, the Royal 17 D.XVIII manuscript also matches Hoccleve's practice. Here as in the later holographs, Hoccleve employs an enlarged anglicana formata script for headings (Fig. 5, line 15). As in the other holographs, the writing surface is ruled for a specific number of stanzas per page (for the *Regiment,* generally four 7-line stanzas), with frame and ruling drawn in brownish plummet, very faintly. The ruling above and below the top and bottom lines of text extends across the gutter to serve both openings as in the other Hoccleve holographs (see Fig. 7).

Hoccleve's punctuation of the *Regiment* in Royal 17 D.XVIII is also comparable to that of the other holographs. In these, Burrow and Doyle comment on Hoccleve's use of paraphs for specific signals, usually in-

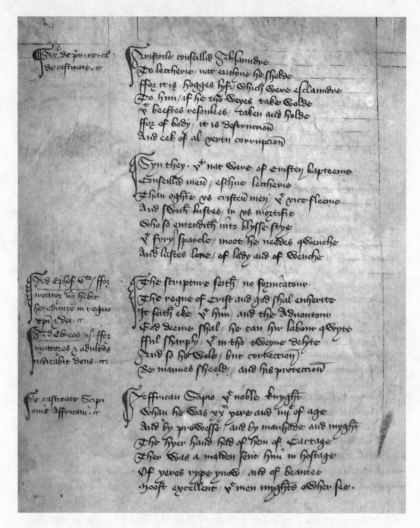

Fig. 7. British Library MS Royal 17 D.XVIII, fol. 67v, reproduced with permission of the British Library.

serted in the form of scribal **cc** but sometimes more clearly as paraphs, to guide the decorator in the Durham manuscript. In the Royal manuscript of the *Regiment,* as in the other holographs, Hoccleve did not mark paraphs for beginnings of stanzas, but the decorator inserted them anyway in the margins beside each stanza. Hoccleve indicated that paraphs were needed to set off marginal glosses by adding a scribal cc form (as he had used in the Huntington holographs) at the end of each gloss (see marginal glosses in Fig. 7).

Burrow and Doyle note Hoccleve's light touch in punctuation: he allows the line end to serve as a pause instead of punctuation, and appears to use the *punctus* only rarely and for specific purposes, as, for instance, to set off numbers in a text. The virgules, they note, are used to represent medial pauses in lines of prose as well as in verse, where they do not occur as frequently as in "some other copies of the time" but "do play a significant part in articulating the rhythm of the lines in which they occur."[20] Virgules appear more frequently in this holograph copy of the *Regiment* than Burrow and Doyle describe for the HM 111 copy of the *Male Regle,* but their function seems the same, and their frequency is similar to that in some of the other texts of the later holographs.[21] The second form of punctuation Burrow and Doyle describe is the *punctus elevatus,* which in Hoccleve's later holographs takes the form of either a *punctus,* or dot, with an s-shaped stroke above or the s-shaped stroke standing alone. This too is found in the holograph *Regiment,* either as the punctus with s-shape above or sometimes with the s-shaped stroke in an abbreviated and more angular form, as illustrated below in Figure 8. Hoccleve inserts a *punctus elevatus,* with dot and s-shape form,

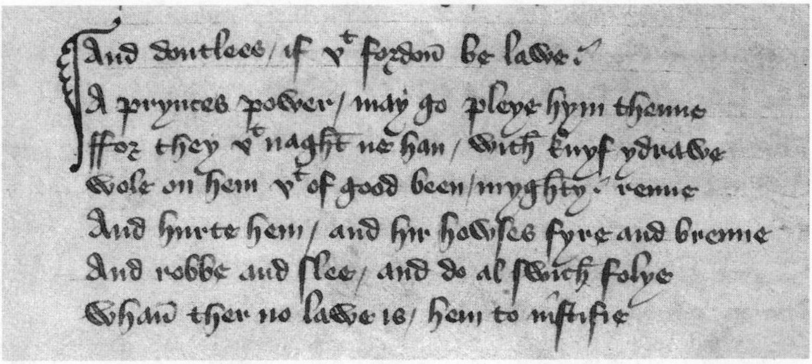
And doutlees/ if þt forbode be lawe.
A prynces power/ may go pleye hym thenne
ffor they þt naght ne han/ with knyf ydrawe
wole on hem þt of good been/ myghty. renne
And hurte hem/ and hir houses fyre and brenne
And robbe and slee/ and do al swich folye
Whan ther no lawe is/ hem to iustifie

Fig. 8. British Library MS Royal 17 D.XVIII, fol. 51v, lines 7 to 14. Reproduced with permission of the British Library.

[20] Burrow and Doyle, "Introduction" to *Facsimile,* xxxix.

[21] For instance, there are thirteen virgules in the twenty-one lines illustrated in Figure 2, an extract from folio 36r of Huntington HM 744, as compared with sixteen virgules in the top twenty-one lines of Figure 7, folio 67v of Royal 17 D.XVIII.

at the end of the first line of this stanza, and another in the variant form near the end of the fourth line, after "myghty." This second form is the unusual one, being a hasty writing of the first, the bottom of the s-shaped stroke lost and the top written so hastily as to form a sharp corner at the top of the s.

Finally, the language of the *Regiment* in Royal 17 D.XVIII also matches Hoccleve's usage in the known holographs. The spellings of this manuscript have often been remarked upon as following Hoccleve's usage in the holographs. For instance, Blyth comments that "more than any other scribal copy, it preserves some of Hoccleve's characteristic spellings."[22] Table 1, following, illustrates the match of some distinctive spellings in Royal 17 D.XVIII and the later holographs, represented by Huntington HM 744. Significant are "sy" as the past form of "to see," "naght" for "nought," "nat" for "not," "swich(e)" for "such," doubling of vowels, and exact matches for other key words such as "thurgh."[23]

One spelling that Hoccleve appears to have changed over his career is that for the second-person pronoun, "you"; he prefers the spelling "you" in Royal 17 D.XVIII, with only a smattering of "yow" spellings (7 instances as opposed to 94 of "you"), whereas by the time of writing the later holographs his preference has shifted to "yow."[24]

J. A. Burrow describes Hoccleve's orthography and morphology in the introduction to his recent Early English Text Society edition of Hoccleve's *Complaint* and *Dialogue*.[25] The Royal 17 D.XVIII copy of *Regiment* reveals preferences exactly matching those Burrow describes. Examples are the spelling <aa> where /a:/ precedes a single final consonant, in *maad,* and for a long vowel before consonant clusters, in *chaast(e), haath;* spellings with <ee> regardless of whether /e:/ or /ɜ:/, except in rhyming position, as *needes, deeme, sheeld, meet, eete,* but also *freend, feend, heest,* and *kneewe;* final <e> indicated by suspension only after <r> and

---

[22] Blyth, ed., *Regiment of Princes,* 16–17.

[23] The only spellings of a word "not" are for the contraction "ne wot"; there are three instances of "such(e)" as against 140 instances spelled "swich(e)".

[24] In his stint of writing in Trinity College R.3.2, Hoccleve also uses the spelling "yow" in the few instances of the word in those leaves. Together with the shift of shape for his graph of thorn, this might suggest that R.3.2 postdates Royal. R.3.2 has been dated to any year between Gower's death in 1408 (because of the phrase "dum vixit" in the short Latin poem, "Unusquisque," following the *Confessio* in the manuscript) and Hoccleve's death in 1426.

[25] J. A. Burrow, ed., *Thomas Hoccleve's "Complaint" and "Dialogue,"* EETS o.s. 313 (1999), "Introduction," l–liii.

Table 1. Corresponding spellings in Royal MS 17 D.XVIII of Hoccleve's *Regiment of Princes* and the Huntington HM 744 manuscript of Hoccleve's minor works.

	Royal 17 D.XVIII	Huntington HM 744
SAW	sy	sy
NOUGHT	naght	naght
OUGHT	oght(e)	oght(e) (aghte)
THOUGHT	thoght	thoght
THROUGH	thurgh	thurgh
WILL	wole	wole
THEIR	hir(e)	hir(e)
SHE	she, shee	she, shee
ARE, BEEN	been	been
MUST	moot	moot
SHOULD	sholde	sholde
HELD	heeld	heeld
DOTH	dooth	dooth
NOT	nat	nat
SUCH	swich(e) (such)	swich(e)

<ll>; short /i/ spelled <i> except before <m> and <n>, where <y> is the preferred form, e.g., *sikir* and *with* but *kynge, prynces, hym*; both /o:/ and /ə/ represented by <oo> except that they are distinguished in rhyming position, thus *dooth, moost, moot*. I have already noted that Hoccleve normally uses thorn only in the abbreviated form of "þᵗ" as Burrow also states. Burrow and Doyle noted a shift in Hoccleve's preferred usage in writing the first-person pronoun over the course of copying the Durham holograph manuscript. They show that Hoccleve represented the pronoun by <I> at the beginnings of verse lines and <y> at the ends of lines; in the middle of lines, he used <I> in the three manuscripts, except that in the course of copying the Durham manuscript his preference changed from representing the mid-line first-person pronoun by <I> to representing it by <y>. In the Royal 17 D.XVIII manuscript, Hoccleve uses <I> consistently for the first-person pronoun both initially and in mid-line positions, with <y> at the ends, suggesting that Royal, like the Huntington

holographs, precedes the Durham manuscript.[26] One could argue that these language matches result from a scribe copying *literatim* from a good exemplar using Hoccleve's spellings, but the coincidence of language, idiosyncratic letter forms, layout, and punctuation seem to me too weighty for any other conclusion than that this manuscript is another Hoccleve holograph.

Authorial Revisions in Royal 17 D.XVIII

In this section, I argue that the Royal manuscript records authorial revisions made by Hoccleve one to two years after the original completion and dissemination of the *Regiment*.

Marcia Smith Marzec concluded from a trial collation of forty-three *Regiment* manuscripts based on 829 lines of the text that Royal 17 D.XVIII and Bodleian Library, Dugdale 45 constituted a separate branch of the stemma, "a distinct and quite early stage in the transmission of the *Regiment* texts."[27] Not only do these two texts uniquely append a balade presenting the text to a royal patron, but they also make significant changes to the text that are distinct from all other extant copies of the *Regiment*. One of these changes shows that this second recension of the text was written a year later than the first, principal version of the *Regiment*. In the Royal 17 D.XVIII manuscript of the poem, at lines 804–5, Hoccleve tells us that he will have lived in the hostel of the Office of the Privy Seal for twenty-five years come Easter, as contrasted with twenty-four years in manuscripts of the principal recension, Arundel 38 and Harley 4866:

> ". . . Wher dwellist thow?" "ffadir, withowten dreede,
> In thoffice of the privee seel I wone
> And write—there is my custume and wone
> Vnto the seel, and have xxᵗⁱ yeere
> And vᵉ come Estren, and þat is neer."
> (Royal 17 D.XVIII, lines 801–5)

At line 1023, he confirms this writing one year later when he tells us that he has been writing for the Office for more than twenty-four years,

---

[26] See Burrow and Doyle, "Introduction" to *Facsimile,* xx–xxi, for this change over the three holograph manuscripts reproduced there.

[27] Smith Marzec, "Latin Marginalia," quoted from 271; for the stemma, see 279. Seymour also includes Bodleian, Rawlinson poet. 10, in this family of *Regiment* manuscripts: see "The Manuscripts of Hoccleve's *Regiment of Princes*," 263.

as contrasted with twenty-three years in the principal manuscripts of the earlier recension:

> "What man þat xxiiii^ti yeer and more
> In wrytynge hath contynued, as have I,
> I dar wel seyn, it smertith him ful sore
> In euery veyne and place of his body; . . ."
> (Royal 17 D.XVIII, lines 1023–26)

Hoccleve must have written the *Regiment* between March 1410, the date of the burning of the Lollard John Badby to which he refers in the poem (lines 281–329), and the death of Henry IV in March 1413, when Prince Henry, to whom the *Regiment* is dedicated, became King Henry V. Dates of 1410–11 or 1411–12 have been proposed for the completion of composition and the production of the earliest copies, including British Library MSS Arundel 38 and Harley 4866; so the second recension represented by Royal 17 D.XVIII and Dugdale 45 must date from 1412–13.

Other changes reflect Hoccleve's or Henry's changed circumstances in the period between first composition and second recension. One argument for dating the composition to 1411 is Hoccleve's frequent reminder about how hard it is to live when annuities are not being paid. One such reminder occurs around line 1877, where the Old Man suggests that since it is impossible to receive payment from the Exchequer ("'Syn þou maist nat be paied in thescheqer,'" Harley 4866, line 1877),[28] Hoccleve should ask the prince to be paid out of the Hanaper instead. This has been changed in Royal 17 D.XVIII to "'Syn it is hard be payed in thescheqer,'" reflecting the better times, since payments received on July 8, 1411 (payment for half a year through Michaelmas 1410) and February 26, 1412 (for the whole year up to Michaelmas 1411) had been made: both might have been received since writing of the first recension before Easter 1411, when Hoccleve's payments were a year overdue.[29] Similarly, lines 4383–85, which in Harley 4866 read,

---

[28] This and all further quotations from the Harley 4866 copy of the *Regiment* are taken from Furnivall, ed., *Hoccleve's Works,* which uses Harley as its base text.

[29] Payments of Hoccleve's annuity occurred as follows in these years: May 23, 1409, for the half-year to Easter 1409 (on time), November 22, 1409, for the half-year to Michaelmas 1409 (on time), July 17, 1410, for the half-year to Easter 1410 (three months late), July 7, 1411, for the half-year to Michaelmas 1410 (nine months late), February 26, 1412, for the whole year to Michaelmas 1411 (one payment eleven months late, the other five months late), and then no more until the accession of Henry V with the September 28, 1413, confirmation of the annuity stating that the arrears have been

"'My yeerly guerdoun, myn annuite, / That was me graunted for my long labour, / Is al behynde, I may naght payed be,'" have been changed in Royal 17 D.XVIII so that the last line, 4835, reads instead, "'No sikir paiement beheetith me.'"

Two other small changes suggest a date one year after the first composition by noting Henry's changed position at court. Hoccleve wrote the *Regiment* in 1410 and 1411, when the prince, as head of the King's Council, was in control of government, but the king took back the reins at the meeting of Parliament in the autumn of 1411. For the last fifteen months of Henry IV's reign, according to Christopher Allmand, "the Prince and most of his former associates were excluded from the exercise of power."[30] Yet the king's illness was still limiting his power and movement, and it was clear that he could not live long. In the first, principal copy of the *Regiment,* with the prince in full power, Hoccleve wrote of the greater good to the people that would come when he succeeded to the throne: at lines 2161–63, Hoccleve urges Henry to pray God that when he is king "Swych gouernance men may feele and se / In yow, as may ben vn–to his plesance, / Profet to vs, and your good loos avance" (Harley 4866, lines 2161–63). Composed under changed conditions in the spring of 1412, the second recension witnessed in Royal 17 D.XVIII urges Henry to ask God that his kingship will instead bring honor to himself and enhance his profit: "Swich gouernance men may in you see / And feele as may been vnto his plesance / Honur to you and your profyt enhaunce" (Royal 17 D.XVIII, lines 2161–63). In another change, Hoccleve apparently sees Henry's accession as so near that he is recommending Henry's *kingly* behavior: at line 4834, where the manuscripts of the first or principal recension ask with regard to overspending on a lavish lifestyle, "Is it knyghtly lyue on rapyne? nay!" (Harley 4866, line 4834), the second recension asks, "Is it kyngly lyue on rapyne? nay!" (Royal 17 D.XVIII, line 4834).

Hoccleve retains the pleas for peace at the end of the poem, but makes some subtle changes to reflect the means for this that Henry had been contemplating in 1411. In September 1411, in pursuing an alliance with the duke of Burgundy, Prince Henry had sent English forces to assist Burgundy's army, which had contributed to their victory at

---

paid directly to Hoccleve (perhaps for the whole year Michaelmas 1411 to Michaelmas 1412), December 1, 1413, for a whole year to Michaelmas 1412 (one payment seven to eight months late, the other almost on time).

[30] Christopher Allmand, *Henry V* (London: Methuen, 1992), 53.

St. Cloud.[31] Part of the prince's negotiations with Burgundy involved solidifying this alliance through marriage with Anne, the Duke of Burgundy's daughter;[32] so Hoccleve's original stanza at lines 5398–404, concluding his plea for peace, urged this policy of peace through marriage:

> Now syn þe wey is open, as ye see,
> How pees to gete in vertuous manere,
> ffor loue of him þat dide vppon þe tree,
> And of Mary, his blysful modir dere,
> ffolweþ þat way, and your strif leye on bere;
> Purchaseth pees by wey of mariage,
> And ye þerinne schul fynden auauntage.
> (Harley 4866, lines 5398–404)

By the spring of 1412, the king had put a stop to these proposals and led England to support the Armagnac side, against the Burgundians, so Hoccleve could only urge Henry to make peace with France and then look to form his Burgundian alliance through marriage if and when he could:

> Syn pees is soules helthe, as men may see,
> Conformeth you therto in al maneere,
> ffor loue of him þat starf vp on the three,
> And of Marie, his blessid Modir deere,
> You[r] stryf and your debat leyeth on beere;
> Of pees and reste entreth now thusage
> And whan yee may knytte vp swich mariage.
> (Royal 17 D.XVIII, lines 5398–404).[33]

Hoccleve also appears to have taken the opportunity that this second writing allowed to make some corrections to his text, perhaps to correct errors of scribes from whose copies the two earliest extant manuscripts of the *Regiment* were made. One correction occurs at line 4500, where the text of the two principal manuscripts of the first version refer to

---

[31] Ibid., 52–53.

[32] Ibid., 54.

[33] Many other alterations suggest Hoccleve's awareness of the changed circumstances of the prince; e.g., he also changes lines 2463–64 to suggest that now Righteousness has been banished from the land.

Isaiah, whereas the actual source of the allusion is Saint Jerome, as correctly referenced in the Latin marginal note; the second recension as witnessed in Royal 17 D.XVIII corrects the reference in the text to "Ieromie."[34] Another correction occurs at line 4578, where some scribes of the first recension had misplaced the stanza meant to follow this line by moving it five stanzas later, to appear as lines 4607–13. In fact, Harley 4866 and Arundel 38 use the same order as this holograph Royal manuscript—lines up to 4578 followed by 4607–13, followed by 4579–606, 4614 and onward—but the other Royal manuscript of the *Regiment*, Royal 17 D.VI, puts these lines in the order we use for editions of *Regiment* following Furnivall's emendation. It is easy to see why the scribe of Royal 17 D.VI and others misplaced it: not only might their eyes skip from one stanza ending with the words "fool largesse" (4578) to another at the same place on the next page ending "fool largesse of two" (4606), but they might also think that "fool largesse" having been introduced at 4578, the following stanza should continue with this theme, beginning "Fool largesse" as does line 4579. The misplaced stanza is virtually the same in Royal as in Harley 4866, reading in Royal,

> The Phelosophre preeueth auarice
> Wel werse than is Prodigalitee.
> By thre causes he halt it gretter vice:
> Ffirst, he seith, better it is seke forto be
> Of seeknesse or an infirmite
> Of which a man may have rekeuerynge
> Than of swich on as ther is non helynge.
> (Royal 17 D.XVIII, after line 4578;
> almost exactly the same as Harley
> 4866, lines 4607–13)

The stanza introduces three reasons why Avarice is worse than Prodigality, and introduces the first reason as being that it is better to be sick of an infirmity from which one could hope to be cured (Prodigality) than from an incurable one (Avarice). But in Royal 17 D.VI and the edited texts altered to agree with it, this is not further explained, and the text goes on immediately to introduce the second reason at line 4616, whereas by resituating this stanza five places earlier, the following four

---

[34] See Smith Marzec, "Latin Marginalia," 272, who notes that many other manuscripts also make this correction, and Blyth, ed., *Regiment of Princes*, note to line 4500.

stanzas, beginning with 4579–85, elucidate this argument about incurable vices; it continues after the stanza just quoted:

> ffool largesse is a seeknesse curable
> Outhir of indigence or elles age.
> He þat fool large in youthe is, is ful able
> In elde to abate it and asswage;
> ffor agid folk been moore in the seruage
> Of auarice than been folk in youthe,
> And what I shall eek seyn herkneth wel nouthe.
>
> But auarice, he seith, incurable is;
> ffor ay the moore a man therin proceedith
> And wexith old, so mochil moore ywys
> He auaricious is; in him nat breedith
> But thoght and wo, for ay his hert dreedith
> His good to leese; and more for to hepe,
> His thoghtes stirten heer and theer and lepe.
>
> Now if the heed of al a Regioun,
> By whom þat al governed is and gyed,
> Be of so seekly a condicioun
> þat it may by no cure be maistried,
> Than is he to the werse part applied,
> And, as the Philosophre seith vs to,
> The lesse wikke is fool largesse of two.
> (these lines from Royal 17 D.XVIII
> are equivalent to Harley 4866,
> lines 4579–606)

Lines 4605–606 sum up the argument regarding the first reason, stating that the Philosopher shows fool largesse is the less wicked of the two vices: it makes much more sense for lines 4607–13 to have occurred before these lines, setting forth the Philosopher's three reasons, than that the Philosopher's three reasons should follow them. After the misplaced stanza in Royal 17 D.VI, the next stanza begins, "The seconde cause is, Prodigalitee / Is more ny to vertu many del / Than auarice, and why yee shul wel see" (lines 4614–17), and this second reason is elucidated over three stanzas before the third is introduced at line 4635. The placement of the stanza between 4578 and 4579, as in Harley 4866, Arundel 38, and this holograph Royal manuscript, gives us an introduction of the three reasons with three and a half stanzas dedicated to the first, three stanzas dedicated to the second, and one stanza dedicated to the third. Furnivall offers no explanation for his alteration of Harley's order, and Blyth simply follows him in moving this stanza to placement as in Royal 17 D.VI:[35] that the author ordered the stanzas here in accord with Harley 4866 and Arundel 38 confirms that this was the authorial ordering.

Thus the second recension shows us a revised version of the *Regiment* incorporating changes relevant to Hoccleve's receipt of his annuity and to Henry's changed position as heir, and it corrects errors a few scribes had made in copying manuscripts of the first recension. These are changes an author would make to his text and that a scribe would be less likely to make.

The Manuscript Royal 17 D.XVIII: A Gift to John of Lancaster

As mentioned above, the copy of the *Regiment* in Royal 17 D.XVIII has appended an additional balade addressed to a "royal Eagle," who will receive this copy of the poem. This balade is appended to only one other copy of the *Regiment,* Dugdale 45, which, as Smith Marzec discovered by collation, is textually the closest manuscript to Royal 17 D.XVIII.[36] This balade also appears separately in Hoccleve's holograph manuscript, Huntington Library HM 111.[37] In the balade, Hoccleve apologizes for the poor quality of the writing of the text to which it is appended, both in rhetorical terms and in terms of the handwriting, attributing the latter defects to overwork and the weakness of his eyes.[38] He also addresses a "Maister Massy," who will presumably receive the manuscript on behalf of the member of the royal family to whom it will be given. A heading squeezed into the upper margin of folio 37v of HM 111

---

[35] "H[arley 4866] wrongly puts st. 659 here, before sts. 655–8. R[oyal 17 D.VI] puts st. 659 in its right place." Furnivall, ed. *Hoccleve's Works,* 165, note to line 4578. Blyth, ed., *Regiment of Princes,* incorrectly describes Arundel's order when he attaches the textual note to line 4571 instead of 4578: "Arundel mistakenly places the stanza containing lines 4607–13 after this line, as do some other MSS including Harley. The correct order is given below" (244).

[36] Smith Marzec, "Latin Marginalia." Bodleian Library, Dugdale 45, can be dated to the mid-fifteenth century or latter part of the second quarter of the fifteenth century (see Stephen Partridge, "A Newly Identified Manuscript of the Scribe of the New College *Canterbury Tales,*" *EMS* 6 (1997): 229–36, esp. 233).

[37] Henry E. Huntington Library, HM 111, folios 37v–38r.

[38] Ibid., reproduced in the EETS *Facsimile,* and commented upon by Burrow and Doyle, "Introduction" to *Facsimile,* xi.

reveals that the balade was placed ("mys") in the book of Monsieur John, recently named Regent of France and Duke of Bedford. Because of its importance to my argument, I reproduce the text of this balade from Huntington Library HM 111 here:[39]

Ce feust mys en le livre de mons*ieu***r** Johan lors nomez ore Regent de France & Duc de Bedford

> Un to the rial egles excellence
> I humble Clerc, with al hertes humblesse,
> This book presente & of your reuerence
> Byseeche I pardon and foryeuenesse
> Þat of myn ignorance & lewdenesse
> Nat haue I write it in so goodly wyse
> As þat me oghte vn to your worthynesse:
> Myn yen hath custumed bysynesse
> So daswed þat I may no bet souffyse.
>
> I dreede lest þat my maistir Massy,
> Þat is of fructuous intelligence,
> Whan he beholdith how vnconnyngly
> My book is metrid, how raw my sentence,
> How feeble eek been my colours, his prudence
> Shal sore encombrid been of my folie;
> But yit truste I þat his beneuolence
> Compleyne wole myn insipience
> Secreetly & what is mis rectifie.
>
> Thow book, by licence of my lordes grace
> To thee speke I, and this I to thee seye:
> I charge thee, go shewe thow thy face
> Beforn my seid Maistir & to him preye
> On my behalue þat he peise and weye
> What myn entente is þat I speke in thee;
> For rethorik hath hid fro me the keye
> Of his tresor, nat deyneth hir nobleye
> Dele with noon so ignorant as me.
> Cest tout.

[39] This transcription is taken from HM 111, folios 37v–38. I have regularized upper-case "F" and substituted modern punctuation for the scribe's.

Because the balade is appended to the *Regiment* in two manuscripts of that poem and appears nowhere else except in this stand-alone context in HM 111, it is generally assumed that the balade was written into a copy of the *Regiment of Princes* given to John, Duke of Bedford, and he is consequently named as one of the royal recipients of copies of the poem.[40] One could argue that neither the heading nor the text in HM 111 refers to the *Regiment* as the text to which the balade was appended in John's book, and that the balade in Royal 17 D.XVIII makes no mention of John: it is appended after the usual dedication to Henry as prince, which concludes with three stanzas (lines 5440–463) on folio 99v followed by "finis"; the balade begins at the top of folio 100r without any heading and is followed at the bottom of folio 100r by Hoccleve's usual colophon, "Cest tout." However, it is difficult to explain why the balade would be appended to two copies of the *Regiment* and to no other Hoccleve manuscripts if this were not the text to which it was to be added. Furthermore, the address to "Maister Massy," whom Thorlac Turville-Petre has shown was John of Lancaster's receiver-general, does not make sense unless the royal eagle to whom the balade was addressed is John.[41] It seems likely, then, that the balade was intended to be attached to a copy of the *Regiment,* and that Royal 17 D.XVIII is the holograph manuscript referred to in the balade heading, and thus the manuscript given to John of Lancaster, later Duke of Bedford and Regent of France.

Like the holograph manuscripts now in the Huntington Library, the production of Royal 17 D.XVIII is relatively inexpensive: it contains

---

[40] Warner and Gilson, *Catalogue of the Western Manuscripts,* treat it as a certainty that the balade in Royal 17 D.XVIII is the one addressed to John, Duke of Bedford, so they make clear the connection between the balade and the *Regiment* (2:256). M. C. Seymour, ed., *Selections from Hoccleve* (Oxford: Clarendon Press, 1981), 127, suggests Harley 4866 as a possible candidate for the volume presented to John of Lancaster, to which Ethan Knapp responds that Harley could not have been the manuscript dedicated to John because the balade makes clear that *that* copy of the *Regiment* was written in Hoccleve's hand: see Ethan Knapp, *The Bureaucratic Muse: Thomas Hoccleve and the Literature of Late Medieval England* (University Park: Pennsylvania State University Press, 2001), 81 and n. 12. Smith Marzec counts Bedford as the recipient of one of "five . . . patronic copies [of the *Regiment*]" ("Latin Marginalia," 270–71). See also Nicholas Perkins, *Hoccleve's "Regiment of Princes": Counsel and Constraint* (Cambridge: D. S. Brewer, 2001), 171.

[41] Thorlac Turville-Petre, "Maister Massy," in Thorlac Turville-Petre and Edward Wilson, "Hoccleve, 'Maister Massy,' and the *Pearl* Poet: Two Notes," *RES,* n.s. 26, no. 102 (1975): 129–43, esp. 129.

only flourished initials in blue, red, and purple;[42] it is written in a slightly informal script such as was used for the other holographs; and the quality of its vellum is not high, this last characteristic perhaps reflecting the poverty of which Hoccleve complains in so many of his verses.[43] It seems an unlikely candidate for presentation to so great a person as John of Lancaster, Duke of Bedford. It is certainly inferior to the two early presentation manuscripts of the *Regiment* that survive, British Library, MSS Arundel 38 and Harley 4866. Harley 4866 includes the Chaucer portrait next to lines 4992–98 of the *Regiment,* but it lacks both first and last folios where the recipient might be identified. Neither of these manuscripts is believed to be the presentation copy for Henry V. Arundel 38 was for a time considered the likely candidate for the original presentation copy for Henry V, but Kate Harris has shown that the coats of arms in this manuscript are those of John Mowbray, Duke of Norfolk.[44] Scholars have asked whether Harley or Arundel might therefore have been the copy intended for John, Duke of Bedford, but have ruled them out based on the balade's claim that Hoccleve had written that manuscript in his own hand.

Because of its inferior quality, one might argue that the Royal 17 D.XVIII manuscript could not be a presentation copy, but rather served as the *exemplar,* for use by another professional as the basis for an illuminated presentation copy for the duke. However, the balade clearly states that Hoccleve himself wrote the copy of the *Regiment* for John to which it was appended, and furthermore states that Hoccleve felt that he had to apologize for his poor handwriting. Unless we assume that he wrote another, grander copy of the *Regiment* to present to John, still apologizing for his handwriting, and wrote this lesser copy for someone else, still appending the balade addressed to John, we must assume that this manuscript, being both written by Hoccleve's hand and containing a

[42] An anonymous reader for *SAC* commented that the flourishing is unusual for London literary manuscripts, and I would agree. Perhaps it was done by someone trained outside that London literary tradition, or perhaps it was added later: the flourishing was certainly added after the quires were assembled, since the color is offset from folio 88v to the facing folio 89r, across a quire boundary: the manuscript is collated 1–12⁸ 13⁴.

[43] See, for instance, Burrow and Doyle's comments on the vellum of the Durham holograph, Cosin V.iii.9, as "not of high quality" in their introduction to *Facsimile,* xxviii.

[44] Kate Harris, "The Patron of British Library MS Arundel 38," *N&Q* 229 (1984): 462–63.

balade apologizing for his handwriting, is the one referred to in the balade copied here and in HM 111.[45]

Besides its inferior quality, another reason for scholars having not considered Royal 17 D.XVIII as a possible candidate for the manuscript presented to John of Lancaster is the assumption that because of its substantial textual variance from the principal early manuscripts—indeed the rest of the manuscript tradition for this work—the family represented by Royal 17 D.XVIII and Dugdale 45 could not date from Hoccleve's lifetime. Indeed Seymour and others have assumed that only Arundel 38 and Harley 4866 were written before Hoccleve's death in 1426.[46] There is no internal evidence in the manuscript or text to suggest a later date—in fact the text points to a date for this version of the poem to ca. 1412, as discussed above—and there is nothing in the style of the script to argue against a date in the second decade of the fifteenth century.

Marcia Smith Marzec's stemma of the manuscripts shows a manuscript not known to survive that she posits as the original, Hoccleve-written manuscript given to John, Duke of Lancaster, the earliest of what she calls the *gamma* family of manuscripts of the *Regiment,* and serving as the common exemplar for Royal 17 D.XVIII and Bodleian Library, Dugdale 45.[47] She argued for the existence of a common exemplar, rather than the manuscripts being copied one from the other, because of a substantial passage that appears in Royal and not in Dugdale:

Du [Dugdale 45] f. 89 lacks ll. 4978–5012, probably owing to the loss of one leaf in the exemplar, the leaf where the Chaucer portrait appears in the manuscripts which are illuminated—an illumination which seems from the very beginning to have been prized more highly than the Hoccleve text itself and, therefore, excised from some copies. Moreover, the fact that only Du and Ry[3] append to the Envoy the three dedicatory stanzas to John, Duke of Bedford,

---

[45] As noted above, the balade is also appended to the copy in Bodleian Library, Dugdale 45.

[46] Seymour does not assign a date—as he does not for any of the manuscripts—nor do Warner and Gilson in *Catalogue of the Western Manuscripts,* 2:256. Blyth writes that "Harley is one of only two [manuscripts of the *Regiment*] to date from the time of the poem's completion in 1411" and "to the demonstrable excellence of these two manuscripts [Harley 4866 and Arundel 38] is added the strong probability that they were executed with some degree of supervision by Hoccleve himself." Blyth, ed., *Regiment of Princes,* 15, 16.

[47] Smith Marzec, "Latin Marginalia," 269–84. Stemma on 279 and discussion of these two manuscripts on 271.

suggests that the *gamma* manuscript may itself have been that patronic copy, with Ry[3] copied before the excision and Du after.[48]

However, this explanation does not account for the number of missing stanzas in Dugdale, since lines 4978–5012 account for only five missing stanzas. For this to represent an excised folio in a presentation manuscript, one would have to assume a three-quarter-page miniature as the portrait of Chaucer, since Dugdale, like most manuscripts of the *Regiment,* contains four stanzas per page. The early manuscript that contains the Chaucer portrait, British Library Harley 4866, folio 88r, shows the form that this Chaucer portrait took in the presentation manuscripts, that is, a marginal image of the poet pointing to lines 4995–96, ". . . I haue heere his lyknesse / Do make . . ." The other early manuscript, British Library Arundel 38, is lacking *eight* stanzas where a leaf with the Chaucer portrait was excised after folio 90, showing that there, too, the Chaucer portrait was marginal, allowing for all eight stanzas to be copied on the excised leaf, four per side. Thus unless we imagine that the presentation manuscript for John contained a three-quarter-page miniature while other, earlier presentation copies contained only a marginal portrait, we cannot account for the missing five stanzas in Dugdale as resulting from copying from a *gamma* exemplar after excision of a leaf with the portrait. Instead, the omission of these five stanzas *can* be accounted for as resulting from a scribe's deliberately omitting them. Not only Dugdale 45 but also the unrelated manuscript, Cambridge University Library Gg.VI.17, has omitted these five stanzas, and since it, too, is laid out four stanzas to a side, the same argument regarding the missing leaf applies. The five stanzas missing from Dugdale exactly cover the references to the portrait of Chaucer, discussion of images, and prayers for his soul. Therefore a scribe might deliberately omit them from a manuscript to which the portrait of Chaucer would not be added, so as not to draw attention to the omission of the portrait itself. By contrast, deliberate omission might also result from scribal or patronal disagreement in principle with Hoccleve's views on images:

> The ymages þat in the chirches been
> Maken folk thynke [o]n god and on his seyntes
> Whan the ymages they beholden and seen,

[48] Ibid., 271.

> Wher ofte vnsighte of hem causith restreyntes
> Of thoghtes goode. Whan a thynge depeynt is
> Or entaillid, if men take of it heede,
> Thoght of the liknesse it wole in hem breede.
>
> Yit sum folk holde oppynyoun and seye
> That non ymages sholde makid be.
> They erren fowle and gon out of the weye;
> Of trouthe han they scant sensibilitee.
>
> (Royal 17 D.XVIII, lines 4999–5010)

Either way, Smith Marzec's argument for a lost *gamma* manuscript's being the holograph presentation to John, rather than Royal 17 D.XVIII, because of the lack of these five stanzas in Dugdale, does not hold up to scrutiny. Thus we have the possibility that Royal 17 D.XVIII itself is the holograph presentation copy and that Dugdale was copied from it by a scribe who deliberately omitted lines 4978–5012.

Now the remaining impediment to Royal's having itself been the manuscript presented to John of Lancaster is its inferior quality. First of all, one could compare it with the Durham holograph, Cosin V.iii.9, intended for Joan Beaufort, Duchess of Westmoreland, a manuscript whose parchment is of similar (inferior) quality and whose decoration is only marginally better than Royal's, with illuminated champ initials in the portion that survives, though it perhaps had an illuminated initial and border with coat of arms at the beginning, now lost. Since Hoccleve often complained of the state of his finances, perhaps he could not afford higher-quality productions even for presentations to noble and royal patrons.[49]

Second, the inferior quality of this manuscript might relate to its date. John of Lancaster was not raised to the honor of Duke of Bedford until 1414, after his brother's accession, and he was not named Regent of France until 1422, on the death of Henry V—which Hoccleve tells us had recently occurred when he wrote the copy of the balade into HM 111, folio 37v.[50] If written in 1412, as Hoccleve's changed references to

[49] If the quality of this manuscript and that of the Durham one dedicated to Joan Beaufort illustrate what Hoccleve could afford, this might argue that Henry of Derby paid for the manuscripts Arundel 38 and Harley 4866, which were to be given to his supporters.

[50] Burrow and Doyle, "Introduction" to *Facsimile,* xx, note that because the heading to the balade in HM 111 "speaks of John, Duke of Bedford, as 'now' Regent of France, [this implies] a date not long after the duke took up that office, in September 1422." At the same time as he was named Regent of France, John had been named Protector

his years at the Privy Seal suggest, this presentation copy to John of Lancaster would have been addressed to him as Henry IV's third son, still in his early twenties (he was born in June 1389) and not yet risen to power. In that spring, he was just taking his place at court, having been chosen to accompany his uncle's expedition to France. The prince (the future Henry V), to whom Hoccleve had dedicated his work, was out of favor with the king and his brother John was *in* favor, so Hoccleve may have decided to cast his net a bit wider in hopes of finding an influential patron in the newly elevated John.[51] If he had not already made this copy on purpose to present to the young prince, then the brief period available to him to make this presentation before John went abroad might be a reason to use a copy of the poem he had already made for a less exalted purpose and append to it, on its last, blank, folio, a presentation balade apologizing for the handwriting.[52]

The balade makes reference to a "Maistir Massy," to whose greater knowledge of rhetoric Hoccleve defers, who will apparently receive the *Regiment* as intermediary between Hoccleve and John, and (Hoccleve humbly suggests) might make corrections to it before it comes beneath the princely gaze.[53] Thorlac Turville-Petre identified "Maistir Massy" as William Massy, who served as attorney and receiver-general for John of

---

of England, though his brother Humphrey, Duke of Gloucester, was deputized to keep the kingdom when John was absent in France. Bedford was created *"regni Anglie et ecclesie Anglicane protector et defensor ac consiliarius principalis domini regis"* on December 5, 1422. Humphrey was to hold these same titles and powers whenever John was absent from the country. The titles lapsed on November 5, 1429, at the time of Henry VI's coronation. See *Handbook of British Chronology,* ed. F. Maurice Powicke and E. B. Fryde, 2nd ed. (London: Royal Historical Society, 1961), 37.

[51] See Derek Pearsall, "Hoccleve's *Regement of Princes:* The Poetics of Royal Self-Representation," *Speculum* 69 (1994): 386–410, esp. 387–88 and 410, among others, for the suggestion that Hoccleve addressed the *Regiment* to Henry V in part in hopes to assure the regular payment of his annuity.

[52] This second possible scenario would depend upon Hoccleve's already having written a changed version of the poem a year after the first for some other less exalted purpose and having left the last leaf of its final quire blank, for the ink color and script to have been identical from 99v to 100r even though the copy up to 99v had been made before its purpose was devised, and for the decoration to be added after the balade was appended.

[53] Pearsall, "Hoccleve's *Regement of Princes,"* 395, describes Massy and a man called John Picard who is named in Hoccleve's address to Edward, Duke of York, as "the kind of people Hoccleve would get to know, and who provided him with an appropriate means of access to the persons of these great dukes: they were men of comparable, if higher, rank and could be referred to in a plausibly familiar and self-deprecating manner as Hoccleve's intermediaries, higher rungs on the ladder to ducal eminence." On Picard, see Turville-Petre, "Maister Massy," 132–33.

Lancaster from at least 1415 until his death within a few years after 1426.[54] According to the biographical details gathered by Turville-Petre, Massy had served Sir Hugh Waterton, a "loyal and favoured retainer of John's father," Henry IV, and had "looked after three of his children" during Henry's exile in 1397–99.[55] Thus it appears that John acquired this steward, attorney, and receiver-general, William Massy, from his father's affinity, and although he first appears in the records as Lancaster's receiver-general in May 1415, he may well have been taken on earlier, perhaps in 1412, to manage his estate because John was intending to leave the country.[56]

Conclusion

The team that conceived the Blyth edition of Hoccleve's *Regiment,* and Blyth himself, argued for introducing spelling changes to the text of Arundel 38 in their edition because they believed no holograph copy of Hoccleve's *Regiment* survived; and because holographs survived of all other known poems by Hoccleve, they thought this was the best way artificially to create a holograph-like version of the poem.[57] As I have just argued, Arundel 38 and Harley 4866 still present the best readings for the earliest version of Hoccleve's *Regiment,* but the Royal manuscript, being written by Hoccleve's own hand, will present authorial readings from the text as revised by the author a year after completing the poem. Royal 17 D.XVIII has been recognized as having spellings comparable to Hoccleve's, but because it was assumed to be written by another scribe after Hoccleve's death, neither Blyth nor any previous editors of the *Regiment* had considered the Royal manuscript as a base text for an edition. The more splendid manuscripts, Arundel 38 and Harley 4866, alone had been considered to have been written in Hoccleve's lifetime,

---

[54] Ibid., 131–32. Turville-Petre explains that we have certain records referring to William Massy in 1425 and 1426, and another, a "writ of *diem clausit extremum* . . . issued in 1428 after the death of a William Massy esquire, who is probably the same man" (132).

[55] Ibid., 131.

[56] According to the documents gathered by Turville-Petre, Massy was serving as Waterton's financial officer in or before 1403, and his first appearance in the records as John's retainer is in May 1415: see "Maistir Massy," 131. Turville-Petre either misrepresents the 1403 document on page 131—". . . Sir Hugh Waterton, whose finances he was handling in or before July 1403 (*C.P.R. 1401–5,* 242)"—or misreads it in summing up on page 132, where he writes that "Massy was John of Lancaster's Receiver-general in 1403."

[57] Blyth, ed., *Regiment of Princes,* "Introduction," 16–27.

because they were grand enough to have been prepared and given as presentation copies. In this respect, the lowly Royal 17 D.XVIII is somewhat similar to the Hengwrt manuscript of Chaucer's *Canterbury Tales,* misdated and ignored until Tatlock pointed out that it was written by the same scribe as the grander Ellesmere manuscript, and, predating it, might offer as good a text or better of Chaucer's greatest work.[58] I hope this argument that Royal 17 D.XVIII was written in Hoccleve's own hand will mark a change in scholarly attitudes toward it as well, and that future editors of the *Regiment* will take account of the authorial readings from this manuscript written by the poet himself.

Appendix A: Characteristics of Hoccleve's Handwriting

Characteristics of Hoccleve's hand[59] include a flat-topped **A** with large loop at lower left; this sometimes occurs with a rounded top, sometimes more pointed as well. He tends to drag the pen along from the descender of **y** such that a hairline stroke runs through or to the right of the letter and curls back above the letter to dot it. He writes both anglicana and secretary forms of **g**; the secretary form often has a straight top with sides of the lobe extending slightly above the straight top, and the descender sometimes curls first to the right and then to the left, forming a coat-hanger shape. This descender can also sometimes curl to the right; and he also wrote a form without the straight line at the top of the lobe, with a point at the top similar to his secretary **a** with a tail. He clearly wrote the rounded or oval form of **w** most of the time, especially in writing drafts or lesser documents, but he also wrote an anglicana form as seen in his stint

[58] J. S. P. Tatlock, "The *Canterbury Tales* in 1400," *PMLA* 50 (1935): 100–139, esp. 128.

[59] Many of these have been enumerated and illustrated before; see Doyle and Parkes, "Production of Copies," 182–84, 220–23; Burrow and Doyle, "Introduction" to *Facsimile,* xxiv–xxxvii.

in Trinity College R.3.2, occasionally in his holographs, and in some documents in the formulary. This anglicana form of **w** often has a distinct point at the foot of the left stalk and sometimes at the foot of both stalks; but these bases of the stalks can also be rounded when he is writing more quickly. Similarly, the graph of **v** used initially often has a large approach stroke forming an arch or loop above the letter and a

distinct point at the foot of the down-stroke at lower left. The shoulder of **h** is often slightly lower than minim height, and he some-

times tucked the descender of **h** awkwardly under the letter. At

other times, the descender curls up and to the right. Initial **H** is sometimes set well below the line at the base of the other letters in the word: Hoccleve may have done this unconsciously since he so often wrote a display uppercase **H** beginning "Henri par la grace de dieu" in Privy Seal documents. Uppercase **T** is the simple form, with the crossing at the top seamlessly connected to a convex arc along the left side of the letter, curling under the letter to rise again through the center and finish

at the cross-stroke at top in what appears to be a single stroke.

Ascenders of **s** and **f** sometimes flatten out to form a "roof" projecting

over the following letters. Uppercase **N** is two strokes, each with

very distinct feet at the bottom. Uppercase **D** has a long looping ascender whose return, or lower, side is straight rather than curved; the

lobe of this letter may be rounded or pointed toward the left. All of these sample images have been extracted from two leaves accepted as being written by Hoccleve: Trinity College R.3.2, folio 82v and Huntington Library HM 744, folio 36r.

REVIEWS

ELIZABETH ARCHIBALD and AD PUTTER, eds. *The Cambridge Companion to the Arthurian Legend*. Cambridge: Cambridge University Press, 2009. Pp. xix, 261. £55.00; $90.00, cloth. £18.99; $28.99, paper.

The sheer scope of the Arthurian legend, medieval to modern, as well as the number of existing handbooks, means that any new companion needs to be more than typically creative and scholarly to stand out. Elizabeth Archibald and Ad Putter are aware of this, since they take pains in their introduction to situate the *Cambridge Companion* against two of its most obvious rivals, Derek Pearsall's 2003 *Arthurian Romance* and Alan Lupack's 2005 *Oxford Guide to Arthurian Literature and Legend:* the first (it is said) overly selective, and the second overly descriptive. These are perhaps unfair criticisms, but Archibald and Putter's goal is "to strike a balance between" coverage and analysis, offering "an overview of the evolution of the legend in the dominant traditions": Latin, French, and English in the Middle Ages, and primarily Anglophone materials in the modern tradition (2–3). German and Dutch materials do get occasional mention, but since these traditions were less influential both within and beyond the Middle Ages, Archibald and Putter utilize a laudable and practical aim, one that editors and contributors ably fulfill, thus rendering necessity a virtue. The editors' next solution to the problem of coverage and rivalry is again to adopt a middle way. The *Cambridge Companion* is divided into two halves: the chronological Part I focuses on the "Evolution" of the legend, while Part II analyses sundry crucial "Themes," usually with each chapter making use of both medieval and postmedieval materials.

The "Evolution" section begins with Ronald Hutton's overview of the problems and possibilities surrounding the historical, mythic, and folkloric "early Arthur." Hutton clearly shares some of David Dumville's skepticism about the validity of the *Historia Brittonum,* but in general he offers an evenhanded account of the principal texts and issues. Ad Putter begins Chapter 2 by observing that "King Arthur came into his own in the twelfth century" (36), outlines the pan-European "traces of a vanished [Arthurian] tradition," and then offers an outstandingly cogent, learned, and occasionally witty overview of and commentary on the principal Welsh, Latin, French, and English texts of "the twelfth-century Arthur." In her account of French verse and prose romance, including the Continuations, Vulgate and Post-Vulgate Cycles, some German and Dutch romances, and Gauvain romances, Jane H. M. Taylor focuses on what she considers the thirteenth-century penchant for (one or more of) grails, deferred endings, and all-encompassing quasi-historical cycles. In the fourteenth century, says J. A. Burrow at the outset of Chapter 4, Arthur still belonged as much to the historical-political world of chronicle as to romance. Hence poems like the alliterative *Morte Arthure*. This is especially true of England, where, in contrast to France and Germany, romance enjoyed a relatively late flowering, including *Ywain and Gawain*, "the most writerly of all the English Arthurian metrical romances" (74), as well as *Sir Gawain and the Green Knight*. Barry Windeatt treads equally widely and perceptively in his survey of "the fifteenth-century Arthur," but he uses Malory's dominant and "discerning" *Morte Darthur* as the touchstone of his analysis (84). In Chapter 6, Rob Gossedge and Stephen Knight have the unenviable task of accounting for "the Arthur of the sixteenth to nineteenth centuries," a period in which, in England as opposed to Scotland or Wales, Arthur was long the subject of irony, political "propaganda," or "popular culture" (105). Tennyson reestablished Arthur as serious art, even if successors like Mark Twain still subjected Arthur to irony. In the final chapter of the "Evolution" section, Norris J. Lacy manages to survey "the Arthur of the twentieth and twenty-first centuries." Although he does close with a brief account of non-English Arthuriana, Lacy introduces the Anglophone nature of his materials by observing that "just over 80 per cent of all Arthurian works in English date from the twentieth century," particularly the 1980s and 1990s (121). Despite such a daunting subject, Lacy—as one would expect—successfully highlights key themes and styles of modern Arthuriana, identifying in the process lesser-known authors as well as those who have thus far proven most influential or popular.

Elizabeth Archibald opens the "Themes" section with a characteristically fine study, "Questioning Arthurian Ideals," from the twelfth century onward. Jane Gilbert then turns to the construction (or absence) of an "Arthurian ethics" across a wide range of medieval and postmedieval materials, including generic conventions about when and whom to smite, kiss, interrogate, or grant mercy to. This witty generic characterization is nonetheless problematized by Gilbert's overarching premise that "Arthurian chivalry *always* lies in a past discontinuous from the present" (155; my emphasis). Andrew Lynch in Chapter 10 analyzes the conception and presentation of Arthurian imperialism in the Middle Ages, the "covert" but still morally sanctioned imperialism of the Victorian Arthur (178), and the antiwar views of T. H. White and the Pythons. Peggy McCracken's essay, "Love and Adultery," looks not so much at Guinevere's adultery—"a central element of most medieval versions" (189)—but rather Arthur's own transgressions and their familial and political consequences. Some of Arthur's affairs are instigated by his lover's use of magic, an apt preface to Corinne Saunders's study, "Religion and Magic," twinned themes that "are crucial to the Arthurian legend" (201). Magic, says Saunders, takes many forms, both secular and sacred. The chronicle tradition tends to use magic to endorse Arthur as a great—and fundamentally Christian—king. Romance magic often takes the form of "marvellous adventure" (205), but it can also be used to generate suspense and test heroic identity. Malory, meanwhile, is characteristically diverse in his presentation of the supernatural. In the final chapter, "Arthurian Geography," Robert Allen Rouse and Cory James Rushton examine not merely where things are (or might be) in the legend, but the political and cultural uses medieval kings and even modern tourist industries make of Arthurian topography. At first glance this may seem a curious chapter, far removed from the literary themes or evolutions of the remainder of the *Companion*. Yet the mythical and political aspects of Arthurian geography implicitly echo many concerns and themes from elsewhere in the book, thereby rendering Rouse and Rushton's argument a fitting conclusion.

The Cambridge Companion series is erratic: some of the books, such as the *Companion to Greek Tragedy,* are extremely good; others are much less valuable. *The Cambridge Companion to the Arthurian Legend* is excellent. A lot of the legend is left out, as are a lot of languages and a good many nonliterary examples—but as noted above, the editors admit this at the outset. Further, the brevity of my review necessarily does only partial justice to the wide range of important material that *is* present, including some film, the Modena archivolt, a chronology, and a full index. There are numerous helpful cross-references, and the major texts and authors are mentioned repeatedly throughout the *Companion,* meaning that readers will come away with a clear sense or reminder of the key texts and issues. It is also worth remembering that the much larger and more comprehensive *New Arthurian Encyclopaedia* cannot be as analytical, and must regularly be updated to manage adequate coverage of the ongoing spate of modern Arthuriana. Archibald, Putter, and their contributors are, within the limits of the genre, remarkably thorough and often remarkably insightful in providing a *Companion* to the most important Latin, French, and English examples of the Arthurian legend from the Middle Ages to today. The *Companion* is, moreover, a text that students can use to their benefit, that will not scare them away, and that could actually be assigned to a course given the paperback price. If I may close with a phrase from Malory, who appears often throughout the *Companion,* Archibald and Putter have thus admirably and success-fully "taken the adventure."

K. S. WHETTER
Acadia University

KATHARINE BREEN. *Imagining an English Reading Public, 1150–1400.* Cambridge: Cambridge University Press, 2010. Pp. x, 289. £55.00; $95.00.

In this fascinating and deeply learned book, Katharine Breen argues that, beginning in the late twelfth century, English writers began to imagine a lay readership. They did so by experimenting with ways in which laypeople could participate in a clerical *habitus,* by which Breen means the ingrained habits formed by study or rule, and, more specifi-cally, a life ordered from childhood by Latin grammar. As Breen argues, for medieval writers, a clerical *habitus,* underwritten by *grammatica,* was an inherently virtuous activity, in which readers, disciplined in the rules of a grammar not their own, could habituate themselves to an ethical life. By the end of the fourteenth century, and most spectacularly with *Piers Plowman,* writers schooled in Latin grammar began to figure out ways of conferring a clerical *habitus* onto lay readers, an ethical frame-work accessible through vernacular texts and translations. Langland, Breen argues, responding to a "spiritual public health crisis" (174), took it upon himself to invent a new discourse capable of inculcating a "virtu-ous vernacular *habitus*" (175).

According to Breen, however, this imagined lay reader of fourteenth-century England was anticipated by earlier writers. For centuries, the idea of *habitus* had been central to a well-ordered clerical life and something potentially communicable to the laity through pastoral care. For example, the *Ormulum,* a twelfth-century English biblical commentary with an idiosyncratic spelling system, offered a "form of the vernacular that substitutes for the moral and grammatical regularity of Latin" (83); at the beginning of the next century, the *Ancrene Wisse* portrayed female enclosure as a kind of disciplined reading and an alternative to Latin grammar; in the mid-thirteenth century, the historian Matthew Paris created a visually enterprising world map, which posits crusading in the Holy Land as a grammar for laypeople (a cartographical *habitus*).

For the last two decades, medievalists have debated the ideological functions of the vernacular, the exclusions performed by clerical Latinity, and the competing versions of piety that writing in English supported (more recently, scholars have introduced French and Welsh into discussions of medieval language culture). Breen offers a fresh approach to these debates by showing that the project of imagining a lay English readership depended on Latinate models of the relationship between order and virtue. Breen also successfully bypasses the critical narrative in which the Fourth Lateran Council, with its stipulation about annual confession, becomes the pivotal event in the history of English letters, leading ultimately to the Wycliffite Bible and the Reformation. By contrast, Breen analyzes several loosely connected projects, the motivation for which was not so much the appropriation of cultural authority from Latin for the vernacular, as the transference of a virtuous self-ordering (i.e., *habitus*). As Breen cogently shows moreover, the nature of that ethical transfer is dispositional rather than propositional: it has to do not with what one learns but about how one goes about self-consciously acquiring and internalizing something external to oneself. This virtuous acquisition is, importantly, physical, even vigorous: it involves the body, whether in the form of a costume, in the case of a professional religious, or a position in space, as when one uses a map to reorient one's position toward the world. As Breen argues, material textuality works as an extreme case in which non-Latinity meets the ethical requirements of *grammatica* by privileging disposition over proposition and arrangement and use over content.

Breen's approach is very compelling and the examples she gives are generally persuasive. Some readers, however, will find this a difficult book to navigate. For one thing, although the book is long, it seems to be missing chapters. I noticed the absence, for example, of any sustained discussion of Lollard writing, which would benefit from Breen's approach. I would like to have read more about the relationship between traditional Christian notions of *habitus* (for example, taking the monastic habit and reordering oneself to a heaven-bound life) and the very different Aristotelian model of *habitus,* in which noble young men bound for public life can be virtuously instructed because they already possess the "raw material." As Breen knows, the Aristotelian *habitus* is significant to fourteenth-century political and ethical philosophy, and for the education of secular princes, a subject that Breen has written about elsewhere. A chapter dedicated to an Aristotelian work would have helped bridge the twelfth-century and late fourteenth-century materials. For another thing, the book takes a while to get started. Chapters 1–3, though they contain some interesting case studies, read like three alternative introductions to the book: Chapter 1 lays out a diachronic view of *habitus,* how the word developed over time and was appropriated by vernacular writers; Chapter 2 traces the range of meanings of *habitus* across medieval discourses (e.g., monastic *vitae,* scholastic philosophy); and Chapter 3 deals with grammar theory. Perhaps this imbalance reflects an organizational compromise in the book between two arguments: first, that late fourteenth-century English writers faced a crisis about vernacular translation, at the heart of which was a crisis about *habitus*; and second, that medieval writers, both insular and Continental, were always aware that the inculcation of virtue through study was available to the laity in some form.

In my opinion, however, this is a book that repays careful reading, and its readers, whether they agree or disagree with Breen's thesis, will find it difficult to get it out of their heads. Recently, my undergraduate Old English class read Ælfric's *Colloquy on the Occupations,* a Latin dialogue for schoolboys learning grammar, which was later translated into Old English. After reading *Imagining an English Reading Public,* Ælfric's text seemed like the perfect occasion to have the students reflect on how formal grammar education instills virtue (or doesn't), and how the performance of language study, and the translation of Latin grammar into Old English (and into modern English), change the nature of that disciplinary *habitus.*

EMILY STEINER
University of Pennsylvania

ARDIS BUTTERFIELD. *The Familiar Enemy: Chaucer, Language, and Nation in the Hundred Years War*. Oxford: Oxford University Press, 2009. Pp. xxx, 444. £60.00; $99.00.

The last twenty years have borne witness to a major shift in the scholarship of medieval insular texts, particularly narratives, with a much greater appreciation of the multilingual context of medieval England. A growing interest in working across linguistic divides and a resistance to the disciplinary divisions of academia have been seen in the thriving biennial conferences on romance in medieval England, which attract specialists in different linguistic cultures, and in the publication of a few studies that bring together a combination of English, French, and Latin material. (See, for example, Laura Ashe, *Fiction and History in England, 1066–1200* [2007]; Neil Cartlidge, ed., *Boundaries in Medieval Romance* [2008]; and Keith Busby and Christopher Kleinhenz, eds., *Medieval Multilingualism: The Francophone World and Its Neighbours* [2010]). Ardis Butterfield's wide-ranging and erudite analysis of the background and context of Chaucer's work is thus very timely.

This ambitious study is informed by Derrida and by postcolonial theory, but the theory never overwhelms the textual analysis. The title itself is heavy with meaning and allusion, punning on "familiar," recalling the family links between the textual communities of France and England, while at the same time alluding to the concept of familiar alterity (Lacanian *extimité*). Chaucer is referred to in the subtitle, and yet Butterfield challenges what she calls our "Chaucer-centred" view that pushes other important authors to the margins. While it cannot be reduced to a simple point, the main thesis of this study is that the French of England and the English vernacular cannot be considered in isolation from each other. This perspective is very welcome. On occasion it may seem that Butterfield is slightly overstating her case and suggesting that French and English are scarcely separate languages (e.g., 99). This renders significant the minor typographical error of footnote 61 in Chapter 1, where we read that Caxton translated a work by Christine de Pisan into (rather than out of) French. It is clear, however, that French must be considered as an insular vernacular alongside and interacting with English.

Part I focuses on the background to the period of conflict between France and England up to 1300 and examines the concept of nation and the relationship between nation and language. While there has been a growing awareness of a medieval Francophonia among French scholars, there is still a tendency, almost inevitable in our period of "post-nation" states, to consider French literature as belonging to France. Yet for much of this period, French literature was not only read outside the borders of modern France, but it was produced outside modern France. For someone who, like Chaucer, was based in London or the royal court, French was not alien or foreign but part of the local culture. All this is clear in Butterfield's analysis in which she draws upon the work of major historians as well as literary scholars in a truly interdisciplinary approach. She begins in Chapter 1 with two francophone writers from outside continental France in different periods: Wace and Victor Hugo, the former a "Norman" from Jersey, the latter a Frenchman exiled to Jersey and then Guernsey, illustrating the ambiguity of linguistic identity. The Channel both divides and connects. The analysis of the whole of Part I demonstrates the linguistic awareness of many writers from both sides of the Channel and in both vernaculars. This section also includes an excellent review of recent work on the use of Anglo-Norman (56–57). Butterfield does question whether Anglo-French can be considered properly a dialect, though given that she is writing here about the early period it is difficult to know how the French of England could be considered as anything other than a "dialect" of French, in the same way as "francien" was a dialect of French. What is evident is that the period of the Hundred Years War was preceded by one in which linguistic exchange between England and France, English and French, was both tense and fruitful.

In Part II, the study moves into the period of open hostility between England and France in the fourteenth century. Chapter 4 looks at the production of linguistic invective. Space is given for detailed textual analysis of specific Deschamps *ballades,* with a particularly nuanced interpretation of Deschamps's famous *ballade* addressed to Chaucer (143–51). This is read in the context of the less-studied antagonistic exchange between Jean de le Mote and Philippe de Vitry. The focus of much of this central section is on lyric rather than narrative poetry. In Chapter 5, *The Knight's Tale* and *Troilus and Criseyde* are read in the context of negotiation. *Troilus and Criseyde* is also read as a lyric sequence in a study that traces the development of the *ballade* form. This chapter casts more light on the international nature of literary culture at the time, with Italian as well as French and English taking its part in poetic dialogue, and it leads into a discussion of linguistic exchange in a mercantile context. Chapter 6, "Trading Languages," is focused particularly on London, beginning with a consideration of what it meant to be a "stranger" in London. The exploration of how vernaculars were used in the urban context informs the reading of Chaucer's Merchant and his tale and *The Shipman's Tale*. Again it is clear that even when writing in English, Chaucer is not drawing upon French as on a "foreign" language. Diplomatic as well as courtly language contributes to our understanding of Chaucer and our appreciation is enriched as we see wordplay working across two languages (228–29).

The juxtaposition of Chapter 6, which demonstrates hostility as well as exchange in trading links, with the chapter "The International Language of Love" itself suggests Butterfield's challenge to the binary opposition of town and court. It also reminds the reader that the poetry of love is written against this complex background and must not, as Butterfield puts it, "be read as an expression of naïve sentimentality" (109). The lyric poetry of Machaut, Froissart, Chaucer, Gower, and Graunson comes under discussion with a considerable amount of space given to Gower, whose French poetry is sadly understudied by French specialists. The examination of specific poetic exchanges between poets highlights the need not to reduce any intertextual approach to medieval literature to a study of sources, for these texts are interdependent. We are challenged, too, to consider how we understand the concept of "translation." Again we see fluidity in the borders between French and English, with Chaucer "using the same stylistic language but in another language" (264), the analysis itself here depending on the French sense of *langage*.

The last chapters of the book focus more specifically on English emerging as a medium for vernacular literary culture from the fourteenth century on, yet this is English functioning in a still complex linguistic environment. The first chapter of Part III begins with Gower and ends with Charles d'Orleans, the Frenchman who also wrote poetry in English. As anglicists increasingly take into account the French literary culture of these poets, so should scholars of French lyric poetry take the English works into account.

The Familiar Enemy makes a major contribution to our awareness of multilingual and interlingual literary production in medieval England. One would like to think that it will no longer be possible to work on either of the main insular vernaculars without at least an awareness of the other. If this is so, Butterfield must take a significant portion of the credit.

MARIANNE AILES
University of Bristol

ANDREW COLE and D. VANCE SMITH, eds. *The Legitimacy of the Middle Ages: On the Unwritten History of Theory.* Durham: Duke University Press, 2010. Pp. 288. $84.95 cloth, $23.95 paper.

The chief concerns of this volume are the history of "theory's" attachment to the Middle Ages and the related question of whether and how (our constructions of) the past are present in (our constructions of) the present. Given its focus, however, *The Legitimacy of the Middle Ages* (*LMA*) does little in the way of assessing its own temporality. *LMA*'s Introduction says it "intends to compete" with Hans Blumenberg's *The Legitimacy of the Modern Age* (2), with which indeed it fences, in a doughty if somewhat quixotic way. But why should we worry about Blumenberg's futurism in the first place? And who would "we" be? Enter Heidegger and the "phenomenological orientation to history"—for example, Heidegger's "insistence that the Middle Ages lacks a world picture," and his characterization of medieval metaphysics as "thematic." It turns out that Heidegger vitiates his own position by also assigning "thematic metaphysics" to philosophers from Thales to "Hegel and beyond." Nonetheless, this un-Blumenbergian ahistoricism doesn't stop Heidegger from similarly repudiating scholasticism (10–11). Okay, whatever. But *quo vādimus?* What is the burning question this windy excursus is meant to address? A number of *LMA*'s essays (Davis, Cole, Knapp, Blanton) also focus on German writers (Hegel, Marx, Heidegger, Koselleck, Adorno). Why, in the first decade of the twenty-first century, are *die deutschen Düden* rolling in again? True, *LMA*'s range is wider than this formulation might suggest: women, and the French, make occasional (and rewarding) appearances. But, the editors say, our work will not be "worthwhile" if we fail to study Hegel and Heidegger. What of the "revolutionary" contexts (and southern disappointments) that cultured American medievalisms, particularly those of the mid-Atlantic academies that cultured so many of *LMA*'s authors? In short, for some readers, *The Legitimacy of the Middle Ages: On the Unwritten History of Theory* will seem a misleadingly ambitious and overgeneral title. Why *these* theories *now*?

To be sure, it is inspiring to see a group of medievalists display so much acuity and erudition. *LMA* is a volume of rare quality and deserves our serious attention. Unfortunately, medievalists who are not theory-prone may have trouble appreciating, for example, Ethan Knapp's painstaking discussion of the relationship between early and late Heidegger and Kittredge, or Blanton's claim that "nominalist turn[s]" in history are "symptoms" of underlying transformations of value (Ockham meets Adorno), or Andrew Cole's analysis of Hegel's and Marx's medievalism (the Eucharist meets the commodity form), or Erin Labbie's and Michael Uebel's vision of Schreber's memoir as "a textbook for how . . . to interpret religious, scientific and poetic relays between the medieval and the modern" (128). But even the minimally adventurous will find admirable scholarship and brainy twists and turns throughout *LMA*. The responses by Michael Hardt, Jed Rasula, and Fredric Jameson are leavening, for irony, patient clarity, and love of poems and stories. Labbie's and Uebel's "We Have Never Been Schreber," the most original and thought-provoking essay in the collection, reminds us that "theory" has many mansions: the Providence whose demotion Kathleen Davis seems to lament looks different to a paranoiac who experiences God's interventions in human time as erotized crucifixion. And there are other airs—Charles D. Blanton's dazzling range of motion, and Bruce Holsinger's stylish report on contemporary (disavowals of) apocalypticism. These are all exemplary essays in the history of thought, rational or otherwise. *LMA* joins Labbie's *Lacan's Medievalism,* and the work of scholars like John Ganim, Amy Hollywood, and Holsinger, in confirming the legitimacy of writing history by reading theory for the circulations of medieval signifiers.

Still, at times one feels like Alice in Wonderland when reading *LMA,* as the adults dash about on errands of obscure urgency. It is not always clear why previous critiques of postmedieval self-congratulation will not do, or how *LMA*'s critiques mean to intervene in them. Davis deals a familiar blow to "the familiar Enlightenment 'triumphalist' narrative of secularization," whose "underside is the history of colonialism, empire and slavery" (40); but how does the triumphalist narrative of Christendom, such as Augustine's interpretation of forced conversion as *caritas,* differ, and from what? Are we simply scorning the notion that secularization redeems us from triumphalism, colonialism, empire, and slavery? (This is a truth not yet tired with iteration, admittedly.) Yes, the imaginary is always with us; but secularization at least acquaints us with a few alternatives (the open systems of the symbolic order, Jane Bennett's vibrant matter, field theory). What a relief to encounter Jameson's citation of Sade to the effect that God is the only unforgivable human invention, or Hardt's gentle reminder that, while the Eucharist and the commodity form have a lot in common, they also differ in very important ways. At times *LMA* seems to be resurrecting the old habit of legitimizing Christian piety for modernity by dressing it up as cultural analysis/critical theory. The harder task of understanding the transformative interactions of complexity seems always waiting to be done.

LMA's title is itself a puzzler. Seriously, *"legitimacy"*? Does Blumenberg's title deserve repeating, even in the form of riposte? I would have preferred "Now gods, stand up for bastards!" True, things did not work out too well for Gloucester's Edmund—perhaps a little better for Yorick's "multi-coloured generations," as they appear at the end of Salman Rushdie's genealogical disseminations in *East-West Stories*. The impious among us, filial or otherwise, do enjoy judging books by their covers. *LMA* faces us with the "portrait" of Saint Thomas Aquinas usually attributed to Botticelli, which eerily resembles the mien of the late J. Edgar Hoover. Likewise does *LMA,* too often for my taste, put away its culprits without due process: "No critico-temporal project, nor any form of postmodern medievalism, would be worthwhile if it disavowed or occluded the texts and traditions that go into the making of modernity—or, for that matter, of modernism—in order to affirm the novelty of this or that new methodology," as, apparently, did Stephen J. Nichols and the "New Philology" (22). Affirming affinities between postmodernity and medieval textuality (authorship *sous rature,* scribal "variation") is admittedly a murky proceeding. Scribal variation is not a critique *avant le fait* of the early modern desire for perfectly unadulterated transmission. And, yes, any break with modernism will be implicated (not necessarily shamefacedly) in modernism's own autogenetic modes of enjoyment. But what is meant by "worthwhile"? Who is disavowing and occluding *merely* "in order to affirm . . . novelty"? The new philology shook up the editorial notion of manuscript "authority"; textual variants could be treated not as impediments but as aspects of (inter)textual meaning; the lives of manuscripts and their readers became salient. I don't think "new" is an arrogant term for this approach—though it has a certain poignancy now that the new philology is almost old enough to drink (the *Speculum* issue on "The New Philology" appeared in 1991).

Again, why are *these* the arguments with which we must be jousting? Why Nichols, Zumthor, et al.? The Introduction relegates to footnotes influential contemporary work on its topics of interest (Haidu, Cohen, Dinshaw, etc.). Said footnotes are quite chunky but cannot offer scope for serious discussion of, say, an oeuvre like Dinshaw's (35 n. 94). *LMA* exhorts us not to "elide" the "theoretical precedents" of German modernism but itself elides the theoretical precedents of contemporary American medievalism. We are told that "modernity and postmodernity have defined themselves *toward* the Middle Ages and they will never let it go" (24), a statement (of no great seismic power) meant to "challenge" Blumenberg and "revise" Nichols; but neither has a strong grip on current thinking about temporality. Where is the *corpus delicti*? Even worse than eliding, or using the wrong preposition, would be "*to suggest that thinking within multiple time frames is a particularly new project, or only a queer one*" (my emphasis, 24). *Only* a queer one? Given the generous reach of contemporary uses of the term "queer," I must cavil at this minoritizing phrase—and ask, instead, what mode of enjoyment is at stake in the "exposure" (Holsinger's term) of all these neophiles? Once again, incorrigible eliders, disavowers, and ignorers such as myself are being scolded *für ihre vermeintlichen Unzulänglichkeiten*. Will these chidings never end? A short while ago we were insufficiently diachronic; now we need to straighten out.

Or, at least, *LMA*'s editors want us to stop arrogating to ourselves ideas to which we have no legitimate title. That should actually be easy enough. When the project of queering history was getting under way, the goal was *not* to impound the idea of multiple temporalities, but to question the periodization of acts vs. identities inspired by Michel Foucault's *History of Sexuality: Volume 1* and renegotiated by Foucault himself in volumes 2 and 3. [N.b.: this periodicity had most certainly not been conceived by a "straight guy" (35 n. 91)]. In *The Order of Things*, Foucault had called for a ceaseless rethinking (not jettisoning) of periodicity; by the mid-1990s, it was time to take a look at queer history's own investments in modernity. Previous to that, throughout the 1980s, alternatives to linearity and periodicity were sought by those attempting to critique the notion that our "own" world(s) have nothing in common whatsoever with medieval ones. Especially in its Princetonian form, this radical alteritism was a way of policing the precincts; how could feminist or psychoanalytic theory possibly raise any interesting questions about a historical period that knew them not? Never mind that discontinuist historicism was equally unexampled in the deliberations of medieval intellectuals (32 n. 68). These tendentious uses of historicism deserved what they got. If we have managed to move on, so much the better. If we have not—as the neophobes might have it—let us by all means redouble our efforts. But do let us understand our own history, too. (The epistemological question of how, if medieval worlds were completely different from ours, we could claim to understand anything [objective] about them, hangs in the air to this day.)

Holsinger also takes aim at all the trendy talk about alternative temporalities: it seems that "cyclical history" (*Bitte!*) and the return of the repressed aren't nearly so new as some might like to believe. Let's concede, for the sake of argument (though the claim is far from proven), that the idea of multiple temporalities is not *schpanking* new; is the idea then vitiated just because it is not new? Further, does or does not the idea make a difference to the linearities and/or periodicities it sought to complicate, even if Pythagoras, or Ibn Khaldun, or Nietzsche *via* Benjamin, got us started? In Holsinger's mind, nothing seems to be interestingly different from anything else. Some of our contemporaries, he notes, ascribe medievalness to radical Islam, for example, Walter Newell's remarkable conflation of Heidegger's "foggy, medieval, blood-and-soil collectivism" with Osama bin Laden, Paris '68, and American academic postmodernism (98)! But Holsinger in turn conflates academic critiques of periodicity with such ascriptions: "The 9/11 premodern radically situates our own field's longstanding and ongoing critical work on the ideological stakes of temporality . . . by exposing the guiding axioms of this work—that the past inhabits the present, that any argument over the past is at heart a political claim on the present, that collective memory and trauma complicate linear models of temporality . . . —as symptomatic of the globalizing rhetoric of modernity." Describing "critical work on the ideological stakes of temporality" as a "symptom" of "globalizing rhetoric" is fuzzy and dismissive. Do signifiers not travel? Do they not take on many different functions and meanings along the way? And how would we distinguish Holsinger's own homogenizing impulses from those of Newell (for Holsinger, postmodern work on temporality is a symptom of globalizing rhetoric; for Newell, it's a symptom of Bin Laden-ism)? How should we read the figure of totalization in the globalizing rhetoric of modernity?

All of *LMA*'s essays, including Holsinger's, are beautifully produced; as a consideration of modernism's use of the Middle Ages to define itself, the volume is a tour de force. *LMA* is most solid and thoughtful when writing intellectual biography and genealogy. Happily, that remains a "worthwhile" achievement. But the book's analyses of contemporary "critical work on the ideological stakes of temporality" are sometimes more attitudinal than achieved; and for a volume so committed to the historicity of thought, it is strangely uninterested in its own.

L. O. ARANYE FRADENBURG
University of California, Santa Barbara

HELEN COOPER. *Shakespeare and the Medieval World*. London: Arden Shakespeare, 2010. Pp. 272. £55.00; $100.00.

The melancholy Jaques of *As You Like It* has made the ancient metaphor of the "world" as "stage" a familiar one, although it is no less potent for this familiarity. Reading Helen Cooper's magnificent book from my perspective as a medieval theater historian, I find myself wanting to take up the world/stage reciprocity and rename her work "Shakespeare and the Medieval Stage." This title could be less appealing to a general readership, but I contemplate it as a means of paying grateful homage to Cooper for what will stand as one of her major achievements in this publication: the rehabilitation not just of the "Medieval World" but also of the "Medieval Stage."

Many fine studies of medieval theater have been published over the past half a century, but Cooper's book must surely take the prize for the most significant contribution to the appreciation of this drama since V. A. Kolve's work, *The Play Called Corpus Christi* (1966), opened up the field for serious attention. Cooper provides new starting points for reading Shakespeare, and, using the very plays that others have presented as benchmarks against which the earlier drama must be seen as inferior, has exploded the myth of that inferiority. She has shown that far from being a "foreign country," the Middle Ages was a place with which Shakespeare was totally familiar in terms of the built environment in

311

which he moved, the literary and dramatic conventions that he and his audience understood, and even the religious culture that had crossed the divide of the Reformation.

Readers will find an elegant coherence to this book in which Cooper deftly returns to familiar ground throughout, reminding us of the "Englishness" of Shakespeare's output and of the grounding of that quality in pre-1500 literature and culture. The influence of the classical world is not dismissed, but it takes second place to the medieval. Even *The Comedy of Errors,* often studied productively alongside Plautus's *Menaechmi,* is shown to be indebted to John Gower's "Apollonius of Tyre" in his *Confessio Amantis*; while in *Pericles,* which returns to Gower and "Apollonius," we can see Shakespeare's medievalism at its most overt, his appreciation of the Middle Ages most fully articulated.

Chapter 1 argues that those living in "Shakespeare's Medieval World" could recall the physical past, even when it had given way to the present. Attitudes to life and death were largely unchanged, and print made medieval literature widely available to the Renaissance readership, ensuring that the language and verse forms, particularly those employed by Chaucer, provided models for Shakespeare and his contemporaries. In "Total Theatre," we learn how the audience for Shakespeare's plays had been trained by their experience of medieval theater to use "imagination" in the ways that are enjoined by the Prologue of *Henry V.* Far from being classical in inspiration, the conventions of Shakespeare's theater are both native and medieval, with the well-known Towneley *Second Shepherds' Play* offering the first surviving example of a subplot being used in English drama. Cooper speculates persuasively, albeit on circumstantial evidence only, that Shakespeare was familiar with the cycle plays of towns like Coventry. He alluded to them frequently, not just through the rude mechanicals of *A Midsummer Night's Dream* and the reference to out-Heroding Herod in *Hamlet* so often cited by other modern scholars, but also in plays such as *3 Henry VI, Titus Andronicus,* and *King Lear.*

"Staging the Unstageable" takes the notion of the imagination further to consider the staging of the invisible, such as supernatural beings and nonterrestrial places, and of illusions of stage violence, both of which are inherited from the earlier religious theater. Cooper compares the use of monologues and expositor figures in medieval drama with similar techniques that Shakespeare used to prompt the audience to engage inwardly with the world of the play. Again, the staging tricks of

English medieval theater in the plays of the saints and in the mystery plays, rather than those of classical theater, provide appropriate and recognizable models. Imagining "place" and reimagining the same space as a different "place" also stems from the open-air staging of medieval plays, both the mysteries in the streets on wagon stages and the in-the-round performance of moralities such as the *Castle of Perseverance*. So too, imagining "time" as a staged present that extends over lengthy periods comes from medieval practice; while Shakespeare's sequences of history plays are likened to the multiple episodes of the medieval mysteries.

"The Little World of Man" focuses on the earlier morality play tradition. Cooper raises again the notion of "staging the invisible" when she considers how morality conventions inform the writing of plays such as Marlowe's *Dr. Faustus,* closest to the older-style moral plays, and a number of Shakespeare's texts, including *Richard III, Macbeth, King Lear,* and *Othello*. The use of allegory and "types" (kings, shepherds, and fools), although perhaps more obvious in the earlier tradition, informs these later plays in a way that is more thoroughgoing than previously recognized.

"The World of Fortune" explains how the medieval concept of Fortune, through the work of Chaucer, rather than the idea of Fate in classical theater, shapes Shakespeare's tragedies and histories. In this chapter, Cooper questions the validity of modern categorizations of Shakespeare's plays. Using the example of the "Richard" plays, she argues that Shakespeare regarded them as "tragedies" rather than "histories." She also reminds us that while he was capitalizing on medieval conventions, Shakespeare was also questioning both these conventions and those of the classical stage and diverging from them to create something unique. "Romance, Women, and the Providential World" deals with Shakespeare's "comedies" and "romances," linking them to the popular English medieval romances in which love leads to marriage and the heroine is allowed some measure of "self-realization." Elements in this chapter dealing with magic and the supernatural revisit and consolidate the issue of "staging the unstageable" discussed in Chapter 3, while Shakespeare's "last plays," *Pericles, The Winter's Tale,* and *The Tempest,* are given more extensive consideration than has been possible elsewhere in relation to other plays.

Appropriately, the last chapter, "Shakespeare's Chaucer," engages with Shakespeare's last surviving play (along with *Henry VIII*), *The Two*

Noble Kinsmen, written in collaboration with John Fletcher. Acknowledging that Shakespeare and his contemporaries also admired Gower and Lydgate, Cooper concentrates on the most Chaucerian of Shakespeare's plays: *A Midsummer Night's Dream, Troilus and Cressida,* and the *Kinsmen.* She claims that none of them could have been written without Chaucer and that the *Kinsmen,* which closely follows its source, *The Knight's Tale,* is actually engaged in a "debate" with it.

By concluding with the idea of debate between Shakespeare and the medieval world, suggesting succinctly that there are ways of reading difference as well as overlap, Cooper generously and challengingly throws the matter open to her readers and encourages them to it take up where she has left off.

MARGARET ROGERSON
University of Sydney

RITA COPELAND and INEKE SLUITER, eds. *Medieval Grammar and Rhetoric: Language Arts and Literary Theory, AD 300–1475.* Oxford: Oxford University Press, 2009. Pp. xii, 972. £95.00; $175.00.

The student who approaches the history of literary theory from existing sourcebooks could be excused for seeing the Middle Ages as dark. To take only one example, the latest (2005) edition of Hazzard Adams and Leroy Searle's *Critical Theory since Plato* finds space for Strabo and Plotinus among the ancients and Ludovico Castelvetro among the moderns, but includes no author between Boethius in the sixth century and Aquinas in the thirteenth. This willful erasure of seven centuries of thought seems to require explanation. In part, surely, it betrays the persistence of a Renaissance view of intellectual history, in which after a thousand years of arid scholasticism the insights of Horace and Pseudo-Longinus were revivified by Boccaccio and Sidney. But it probably also reflects the recalcitrant nature of the medieval material. Foundational authors like Servius, Priscian, and Isidore deal with the minutiae of Latin etymology and semantics. Reading them in English is a bit like reading a French version of Fowler's *Modern English Usage* or Strunk and White's *Elements of Style.* Much medieval theory is embedded in commentaries and glosses, often anonymous and hard to date. Many of these still lack a reliable modern edition. So do some important freestanding texts like Alexander Neckam's *Corrogationes Promethei*.

Rita Copeland and Ineke Sluiter have set out to do something about this. What they offer us is a massive sourcebook focused on grammar and rhetoric, which they refer to collectively as "language arts." This is not a medieval term, at least in this sense. (*Artes sermocinales* typically designates the trivium as a whole, not just these two members of it.) But its vagueness is useful here. It embraces something that is not quite literary criticism, not quite (or not solely) poetics. It overlaps linguistics without being coextensive with it. It embraces both the interpretation of existing texts and the generation of new ones. It is instantiated in the educational curriculum but not confined to it. One thing it notably does *not* include, for Copeland and Sluiter, is logic or dialectic. There is some justification for this. Dialectic does seem to have been subsidiary to the other two legs of the trivium, at least in the early Middle Ages. The editors have excluded on principle the speculative "modist" grammar of the thirteenth and fourteenth centuries, which draws heavily on logic but which they regard as belonging rather to the history of philosophy. Even so, there is a sense at times that one is reading the liberal arts equivalent of *The Two Musketeers*.

The readings are divided into various sections: early medieval approaches (late antique grammarians through Alcuin); twelfth-century speculation (John of Salisbury, Alan of Lille, and the like); the handbooks and poetic *artes* of the late twelfth and thirteenth centuries (Matthew of Vendôme, Geoffrey of Vinsauf, and others); new thirteenth-century developments (scholasticism, civic rhetoric, and *dictamen*). Each section is preceded, like the individual selections, by an able and lucid introduction. A final section on "reception" focuses primarily on English texts, including selections from Lydgate, Gower, the general prologue to the Wycliffite Bible, and a Middle English text on the liberal arts based on Grosseteste. The diachronic sequence is varied by "dossiers" on two sample topics: etymology and the ablative absolute.

To their credit, the editors have not confined themselves to prefaces or other programmatic passages. They give us a real sense of what it is like to read Priscian or Servius *in extenso*. Given the size of the volume and the range of texts represented, a few omissions are noteworthy. Augustine's *De Doctrina Christiana* is absent because easily available elsewhere (though some of it is paraphrased in the prologue to the Wycliffite Bible). Room might have been found for Fulgentius's short but influential interpretation of the nine muses as sequential stages of literary composition (*Mitologiae* 1.15). Hugh of St. Victor's *Didascalicon* crops up in the introductions and notes to other texts but is not itself excerpted. Brunetto Latini is here, but not Dante. Also missing is Boccaccio, though his *De casibus illustrium virorum* underlies the excerpts from Lydgate. Allegorical interpretation appears only incidentally, a useful reminder that most medieval reading was (or at least aimed to be) literal reading. Overall, however, most of the texts one would expect to find here are represented, and even seasoned medievalists will encounter some that are new to them.

The editors draw on existing English renderings where available, sometimes with slight changes and usually with added annotation. The remaining translations—well over half—are their own. Those I have checked in detail are basically sound but not always quite as accurate or elegant as one might wish. Some of the verse texts (Terentianus Maurus, Alexander of Villa Dei) seem particularly unhappy, and the renderings of Servius and Osbern of Gloucester contain a number of errors. The editors were evidently not aware of the standard edition of Osbern's *Derivationes* by Paola Busdraghi et al. (Spoleto, 1996), or that of Hugutio of Pisa by Enzo Cecchini et al. (Florence, 2004). Technical terminology is sometimes missed. In Servius, for example, *latenter defendit* means "defends by implication" (not "in secret"), while *bene addidit* means "he did well to add" (not "it is good of him"). There are some odd slips. We meet with an Etruscan divinity named "Taga" (read "Tages") and a biblical commentator named "Lyre" (as if this were Nicholas of Lyra's surname). And the English is occasionally questionable ("lest he seemed"; "like Virgil himself does").

The material covered is vast and various, from the nymph Carmentis (inventor of the alphabet) to the nature of metaphor, from debates over the vocative of *ego* to a Middle English treatment of vowel phonology. The selections attest to both continuity and change. Priscian was clearly central at all periods; indeed, I have often thought that one could write a history of European culture from 500 to 1500 just from Marina Passalacqua's inventory of the extant manuscripts. Other texts waxed and waned in popularity. A recurrent feature is the medieval obsession with categorization. Excerpts are full of the five stages of this, the three branches of that, the four types of something else. At the micro level, this often strikes a modern reader as fussy and pedantic. But what is at issue here, from a medieval perspective, is nothing less than the ordering of the world and its reflection in human knowledge.

Readers of this journal might be tempted to look for the book's payoff in the final section. Does awareness of a "language arts" tradition (or traditions) help us better understand late medieval literature? The answer, I think, is yes—Copeland and Sluiter make a compelling case, at any rate, for Gower and Lydgate. At the same time, I should stress how much the anthology benefits from being read complete and in chronological sequence. Readers who make it through the almost nine hundred pages of text will emerge with insight into a good many smaller questions (such as why there are so many fourteenth- and fifteenth-century manuscripts of the *Rhetorica ad Herennium*). They will also be provoked to think about some larger issues, like the relationship of pedagogical theory to classroom practice, and of literary theory to composition. Above all, they will have begun to feel at home in a discourse and praxis that had some effect on almost every medieval author.

GREGORY HAYS
University of Virginia

EDWIN D. CRAUN. *Ethics and Power in Medieval English Reformist Writing.* Cambridge: Cambridge University Press, 2010. Pp. viii, 217. £50.00; $85.00.

J. ALLAN MITCHELL. *Ethics and Eventfulness in Middle English Literature.* New York: Palgrave Macmillan, 2009. Pp. 187. $90.00.

Poetica ethicae subponitur quia de moribus tractat: as Judson Allen noted almost thirty years ago in *The Ethical Poetic of the Later Middle Ages,* it was a particularly medieval notion that poetry should be "classified as ethics because it deals with behaviour" (9). But as the durable ethicist tradition in literary criticism shows, it is not a dead one. Ethics and poetry continue to cohabit fruitfully both in medievalist criticism and in literary study in general. A recent resurgence of interest in ethics does not so much portend the onset of "ethical chic" (as J. Allan Mitchell notes glancingly in his introduction) as point to the long-standing centrality of such concerns, both within texts and about them, especially for medievalists.

Edwin Craun's *Ethics and Power in Medieval English Reformist Writing* focuses tightly on the subject of *correctio fraterna,* "fraternal correction of sin," as the ethical duty "of admonishing others charitably for their evil conduct in order to reform them" (1). This was both a clerical and laical responsibility, biblically sanctioned and prelatically endorsed. The first two chapters of Craun's book establish the conceptual background of fraternal correction in scriptural, patristic, and canonical sources, as well as the complexities of its ethical demands. Fraternal correction is "a matter of precept divinely ordained and therefore obligatory" (24); it is a practice both moral and ethical and, when done compassionately and privately, charitable; and it is uniquely available to clergy and laity alike, to both women and men, as an authoritative disciplinary practice. It also presents challenges and potential contradictions. The injunction to correct sin runs up against the equally strong precept against ethical judgment ("Judge not and you shall not be judged"), and it opens the door to hypocrisy, raising the thorny issue of when, and to what extent, sinners may admonish other sinners, as well as the question of what marks the ethical boundary between virtuous correction and vicious or slanderous reproof. From these concerns there developed a fascinating body of clerical discourse on the practice of fraternal correction that was equal parts biblical exegesis, moral theology, pastoral training, and rhetorical theory. Craun's explication of it is clear and quite engaging.

In the four following chapters, the practices and implications of fraternal correction are mapped onto *Piers Plowman,* Wycliffite theology, and the "Lancastrian reformist lives" of *Mum and the Sothsegger* and the *Book of Margery Kempe.* A central development during this period was the shift from an exclusive focus on the pastoral correction of individuals to the ideological and political critique of groups: *correctio fraterna* was invoked as a framework for the clerically sanctioned remonstration of the clerisy itself as a class. Analyses of the characters of Meed, Clergy, Lewte, and Will, and a particularly fine close reading of *Piers Plowman* B.11, show how Langland adroitly manipulates the "ethos of the corrector" for public reformist purposes (65, 71–79). Chapters 4 and 5 on Wyclif deepen this analysis, showing how the renegade theologian "transformed fraternal correction into a disciplinary process" necessitating both admonition and punishment "not only for the soul of the cleric, but also for the common good of the church" (88). Fraternal correction offered a license for Wyclif's radical critique of the clergy and for advocating disendowment, both to be enforced by corrective secular power (91–92). Thus it emerged in Wycliffite discourse as an individual ethical duty and as a public communal tool "to redistribute power in institutional life" (97). This was especially so in the polemical agenda of later Wycliffism, which dropped many of the meliorating requirements of prelatically sanctioned *correctio*. Little surprise, then, that the early fifteenth century seems to have brought a retreat from the more daring speculations on fraternal correction, even as figures such as the beleaguered truth-teller of *Mum and the Sothsegger* and the ever-bold Margery Kempe embodied the vibrant dynamic between orthodox and "deviant" correction in contemporary reformist discourse. Craun concludes with the now-familiar observation that such texts founded their calls for clerical reform "on the discourse of pastoral reform itself" (146), with the added insight that the positioning of correctors drew specifically from this fraternal ethics, even when correction was a *de facto* call to revolution.

If Craun's analysis centers on a medieval and pastoral ethical framework, Mitchell's is correlatively modern and theoretical. *Ethics and Eventfulness in Middle English Literature* approaches the hoary topic of Fortune from the category of "the event"/*l'évènement,* the existential notion of the radical contingency of "something genuinely singular" (4) as the ground and enabling condition of ethical possibility itself. An awareness of "eventfulness" calls for a bracketing or *epoche* of sorts for the *casus,* one appropriate to a more nuanced understanding of Fortune not as a category of ineluctable fate nor as some sort of true-pattern-in-apparent-randomness (the "Wheel" of Fortune), but as the unforeseen, "futural," and hence radically contingent—in some senses precisely the opposite to what Fortune has traditionally been held to be. Mitchell reads through the philosophical catena from Boethian Fortune to Scotian nominalist *haecceitas* to the Heideggerian "scoteity" of *das Ereignis* to (in Chapter 2) a Levinasian understanding of eventuality, which, Mitchell contends, bears "a particular formal relationship" to the ethical challenges of literature (26). The givenness of things, as events, eludes cognitive mastery; and so the real possibility of ethics arises not in deontological or casuistical reflection but in the adventure of encountering precisely what one has not prepared for or foreseen. In this sense, ethics is neither a program nor a prescription, but a form of awareness in the constitutive temporality of historical events: "there is no ethics *of* the event, but instead only ever *an emergency here and now that demands ethics"* (24; italics in original).

This paradigmatic revision of the Boethian touchstone is borne across Chaucer's *Troilus and Criseyde,* Usk's *Testament of Love* (and the anonymous *Chanse of the Dyse*), Gower's *Confessio Amantis,* Lydgate's *Fall of Princes,* and Malory's *Le Morte Darthur.* This is a big group for a small book. But what the analyses sometimes lack in depth they compensate with density and suggestiveness. Most rewarding is the reading of *Troilus and Criseyde* through Levinas's recuperation of courtly love (over and against both Lacan and Deleuze and Guattari) as subjection to *l'évènement* in the figure of *l'arrivant,* the one who presents herself or himself in the foundational ethical encounter: the other whose arrival teaches the subject, for the first time, that "one is not free from the otherness of the world" (46). The courtly lover is thrown to love always unexpectedly and with an ambiguous will (like Troilus and like Criseyde), but not "nonetheless" ethically. Rather, by this very fact the lover comes to ethical awareness—which is to say true volitional selfhood—in the demands of the other, demands that *l'arrivant* never cannot make. Thus in the event itself, amatory fortune—not despite its determined relation but because of it—represents not the negation but rather the "gift" of ethics (42), as ethical love, in the adventitious relation of self to other, is always fundamentally adventurous. This is a challenging re-vision on several levels. Lack of agency—that famous sticking point of the *Troilus*—is neither virtuous nor vitiating. It is, simply, the condition of events prior to the abstractions of morality, what calls ethics into being. A similar dynamic operates in Usk's *Testament* and *The Chanse of the Dyse,* two Troilan texts of aleatory "vernacular ethics," and more distantly in the contingent ethics of Gower's *Confessio,* the analysis of which in Chapter 4 largely builds on Mitchell's previous work.

The broader sense in which we are never free from the demands of the other, nor free from the chances of the event, also animates the analysis of Lydgate, but here matters of politics and patronage further complicate matters. The last chapter, "Moral Luck in Malory," similarly reads several opening episodes of the *Morte* in the light of the eventfulness of its sequences, particularly the narratives of Gawain and Balin. These later chapters are somewhat less successful only insofar as such large and complex texts must be read so deeply in such a small space. They are nonetheless suggestive and they reward close study. Mitchell's theoretical acumen, as well as his cogent and clear prose, invites both assent and argument in all the best ways.

In both books, the artistic representations of ethical behavior animate really lively investigation. It is interesting to reflect that five to fifteen years ago, their titles almost certainly would have had the word "authority" in them; now it's about ethics. This signals perhaps a salutary loosening of the well-worn Foucauldian framework of power/knowledge-authority/discourse-subversion/containment. There is, for the most part, a happy lack of constructed subjects in these books. What we get instead (or additionally) is well-warranted investigation into the conditions of both subjective experience and intersubjective responsibility that is ever a concern of ethical literature, in terms drawn from both the medieval period and from modern times.

MATTHEW GIANCARLO
University of Kentucky

HOLLY A. CROCKER. *Chaucer's Visions of Manhood*. New York: Palgrave Macmillan, 2007. Pp. xiii, 250. $80.00.

The obstacle in the path of any historical study of men and masculinity is the same as that in the path of women's studies: masculine universality. Textual studies of *medieval* masculinity must also negotiate a number of other impediments. As is well known, the use of masculine pronouns as a default, along with the lack of gendered inflections in Middle English, and the frequent anonymity of texts in manuscript cultures, all too regularly obscure the roles that we know women must have played in their worlds. It also, however, naturalizes men, causing them to recede as an object of study. So that when scholars turn to focus on men, they can, bafflingly, evade observation precisely through a masculine covering of feminine influence and agency, of gender difference. As Thelma Fenster pithily observed, in the introduction to one of the earliest publications on medieval masculinities: "Although the subjects of traditional historical discourse were for the most part men, that discourse was still not precisely about men" (*Medieval Masculinities,* ed. Lees, 1994). But it is apparent, too, that straightforwardly rewriting the grand narratives of history as, more specifically, the history of men will not do. This is because those narratives do not reliably get the Middle Ages right, so that the histories of masculinity that are predicated on them, however inadvertently, describe medieval masculinity as primitive and uncomplicated, as a nonsubject. Masculinity is both everywhere and nowhere and medieval masculinity seems especially adept at slipping in and out of view; the problem of how scholarship should approach something that is both dominant *and* decentered has never been resolved.

Holly A. Crocker's *Chaucer's Visions of Manhood* skillfully circumnavigates this obstacle, transforming the problems of study into its research object. The "Visions" of Crocker's title is used in its most specific senses; this is a study of seeing, both with the bodily and the mind's eye. This enables a head-on assessment of how gender—whether masculinity or femininity—can be looked at both in its own time and in modern scholarship. What emerges is an account not only of the past but also our relation to it, of what *can* be seen, studied, and said about gender in the Middle Ages. Chapter 1 opens with an account of medieval theories of optics, settling on Baconian intromission as a way to refuse easy equations between seeing and agency, between passivity and the object. The subsequent readings of Chaucer then connect up a number of different themes relating to the visible and the invisible, treating, for example, the absent author, secrecy, privacy, coverture, images, passing and the mundane. Chaucer himself, according to Crocker, is the ultimate invisible man, covering himself with personae and *retraccioun*. "Chaucer refuses to own, inhabit, or animate his works in a fully visible fashion," she concludes (151). At the end of the book, the Ovidian tale of Ceyx and Alcyone, which Chaucer embeds in *The Book of the Duchess,* is ingeniously offered as a synecdoche for the ways in which later manuscript compilers and readers, responding to Chaucer's absence in his verse, reanimated the Chaucerian corpus, presenting a vision that is at turns recognizable and unrecognizable as Chaucer.

The themes of sight and visibility are discovered across a number of Chaucer's texts and not those that one might expect. In Chaucer's oeuvre, the idea of the gaze has been most thoroughly explored in relation to *Troilus and Criseyde,* by Sarah Stanbury and others, and this study sensibly chooses some territory less traveled. While *The Wife of Bath's Prologue* is to be expected in a gender study of Chaucer, Crocker otherwise makes some surprising choices: the enigmatic *Tale of Melibee, The Physician's Tale, The Shipman's Tale,* and *The Book of the Duchess.* Her last chapter looks at the place of Chaucer in British Library, Harley MS

7333, a mid-fifteenth-century poetry anthology, which contains a copy of the *Canterbury Tales*. But Crocker's analysis of that manuscript mostly considers the Chauceriana attributed to "Impingham" in a refreshing turn to Chaucer's fifteenth-century reception. Indeed, part of the question that the book raises, notably in the readings of *Melibee, The Physician's Tale,* and Harley 7333, is about the difficulty of regarding disesteemed work, of finding the subject in "boring" universalizing texts, of including the dispersed Chaucer of the manuscripts in our studies. Thus Crocker points openly at some of the bits of Chaucer that scholars find it hard to look at—because they are too plain, bizarre, banal, or multiple—asking what it is we see when we do.

This study is relational, considering men and women together, indeed saying as much about women as men. Crocker's engaged feminism shows that studies of masculinity are not competitors but contributors to women's history. It is the relationship *between* the sexes that is investigated here. These texts are case studies in that investigation, affording an opportunity to look at gender relations as if *in vitro,* in stylized accounts of families and marriages. While giving readings of specific Chaucerian texts, Crocker uses them to expose the workings of gender more broadly within the culture in which those texts were written. Crocker asks how and why it is that female agency constructs masculine public identity, effecting its own effacement in these texts. In this way she complicates the picture of masculine ubiquity, crediting medieval women with intelligence and influence even when they are seemingly disappeared or demoted. This book suggests that these texts offer some answers to the question of what investment medieval women might have had in, or what uses they made of, their own invisibility. Crocker manages this even when she looks at the depressing subject of male violence against women, a thread that runs through the book and that features particularly in its readings of *The Tale of Melibee, The Physician's Tale,* and *The Wife of Bath's Prologue.* Here the question shifts to observe how, in Chaucer's equivocal verse, violence publicizes and makes visible the limits of masculine control.

This book is an important contribution not just to the study of gender in the past but also to current theory, offering a combination of psychoanalysis and historicism. Its use of Roger Bacon, to consider the question of male and female mutuality, even intersubjectivity, is compelling in that it engages in theoretical debates with historical sensitivity. The end effect is a full account of the medieval contribution to the construction of the male universal, finding out some of the early ways that gendered vanishing acts were designed and performed. In this way *Chaucer's Visions of Manhood* shows that medieval relics clutter up our cultural assumptions, just as surely as their material counterparts have collected in the treasuries of Gothic cathedrals. Crocker's book is a crucial and intelligent addition to the subject, and a credit to the interesting New Middle Ages series at Palgrave.

ISABEL DAVIS
Birkbeck College, University of London

BRIAN CUMMINGS and JAMES SIMPSON, eds. *Cultural Reformations: Medieval and Renaissance in Literary History.* Oxford: Oxford University Press, 2010. Pp. 540. £85.00; $160.00.

The argument of *Cultural Reformations* is that the religious transformations in English Protestantism concomitantly transformed culture as a whole. Thirty-three contributors consider the impact of the English, Protestant, religion on what the editors categorize as histories, "spatialities," doctrines, legalities, "outside the law," literature, communities, labor, and selfhood. The book largely treads familiar ground as it considers the ways the long and evolving religious changes, ranging from the fifteenth to eighteenth centuries, may have directly reformed other aspects of life. While it transcends a narrow definition of literature, it pays little attention to voyages of discovery, diplomacy, and trade, or even travel writing; or other religious writing such as Bible translation, polemic, sermons, and homilies (though they round up the usual mystics); or international book history and the reprint culture in which translation played such a crucial role. The asymmetries of status, gender, or age, as might be found in domestic writing such as letters, cookery, and health manuals, do not appear, though Colin Burrow on "households" is one of the book's outstanding essays. Nor do Scotland, Ireland, and Wales make much of an appearance, and neither does the flowering of long poems and national histories (Ardis Butterfield's chapter of that name is about diversity). There is a distinct lack of sex and an almost complete failure of merriment.

As one would anticipate, there are some very good essays in the collection. Some of the best are at an angle to literature, such as the chapters on medical writing about childbirth or the survey of London bookselling, buying, and reading. Tim Machan's analysis of semantic and morphological change in the English language is an overview that manages to explain the language, the ambitions of the grammarians, and the bedrock nationalism of their defense and demonstration of English grammar, though it is not clear that the changes he describes can be due to an evolving Protestantism. The chapter titled "Idleness" ranges beyond its key word, and, incidentally, contains the book's best subtopic: "the rise and rise of the sturdy beggar." Room should always be made for good work only loosely connected to a book's subject: the final chapter is a history of Continental readings of Augustine's *Confessions,* not broadly about autobiography at all, as is evidenced by its innocence of the long bibliography on life writing from Georg Misch via psychoanalytically-oriented medieval analyses of writers and artists to the Annales school.

Pride of place goes to the chapters that rehearse key concepts in Western religious culture, such as ideas about saints or the Eucharist. These chapters have a similarly angular relationship to the ambitions of the book's intended scope. They do, however, point to the most striking aspect of *Cultural Reformations*: the editors' unwillingness to examine presuppositions and received ideas about the triumph of an innate, Insular Protestantism, to consider the jagged nature of "reform's" eventual victory, or indeed what ended up being victorious. This is a book with an apparent grand narrative about cultural change in one country, and largely in one vernacular, that ignores the secular incursions of globalism into everyday life: trade, exploration, migration, as well as the unprecedented expansion of learning through books imported and translated. That is, the book seems to endorse the reformers' claim to reestablish an originary dispensation, rather than looking around and forward to arguably equally influential changes. Many of its determinedly theological contributors take for granted the often-repeated assumption that knowledge was always moral, despite the fact that really, often, it was not. Rome is the site of contestation; but that Thomas More should be the book's central figure (and central Latinist) is an instance of the contradictions inherent in its orientation. One might argue that this is a plus.

This volume appears in a new series, in which the publishers insist that they "mean to provoke rather than reassure, to challenge rather than codify. Instead of summarizing existing knowledge, scholars work-ing in the field aim at opening fresh discussion; instead of emphasizing settled consensus, they direct their readers to areas of enlivened and unresolved debate." Well, maybe. Even if one does not summarize exist-ing knowledge, it is crucial to know what that knowledge is. When we move away from our specialist boundaries, we always risk missing the contexts and specialist assessments of what we read, with the result that we depend upon famous, but outdated, even superseded, work. The weakest essays in the collection are startling: an underinformed and pos-itivist "Historiography"; a prosodically cloth-eared interpretation of scansion in three poets to argue about "Style." In many instances there is evident a desire to reach to the present as if to suggest contemporary relevance, or perhaps just resonance.

Even in the best essays, there are sentences such as this: "The Middle Ages, however, understood neither spatial nor historical distance" (28). This is followed by several quotations from Erwin Panofsky, as if no one had written since, or everyone agreed with Peter Burke's long-super-seded *Renaissance Sense of the Past*. Or this: "the desire to locate nation in a particular historical moment is a modernist activity, in any period" (35), without any historical analysis of "modern" or distinction between "nation" and "nation-state," or consideration that Benedict Anderson's pathbreaking work is located in its own Marxian-inflected historical mo-ment. Of course, when we reach back in search of ancestors or the ances-tral rupture, we will find them. About Wyatt's conservative English version of an anticourt Aesopic fable: "Wyatt's Kent stands in a wholly adversarial relationship with Christendom" (95), a view quietly cor-rected by Burrow (464). The chapter titled "Communities" seems inno-cent of the points made in the chapter titled "Anachronism."

Of course authors are well advised to focus on a small number of examples to illustrate a point. The power of such restricted illustrations depends upon their convincing readings of the detail against an equally convincing summary of the context. It is always a difficult balancing act, and carries most weight when the author speaks with the authority of someone who has dealt with the subject in greater detail elsewhere. This can work well even if one has reservations. Seth Lerer begins by examining the concept of "Literary History" through occurrences in the *OED,* then examines how some sixteenth-century readers and writers might have understood their national past, by arguing for a moment in which the retrieval and construction of a national literature was filtered through its polemical relationship to religious change. Lerer confines himself to one powerful example: an idea of Love's and Religion's martyrs, though the interplay of such suffering is as old as interpretation of the Song of Songs, as commentators—but probably not the Song's authors—recognized the semantic interplay between the intensities of human desires for love and Love. By contrast, Andrew Hadfield's "new historical" and eccentric choice of two utterly different pilgrims, two centuries apart, to stand for "Travel" is less convincing.

Lorna Hutson addresses recent discussions of sacramentalism in drama, and how far changes in London theatrical practice might diverge from the participatory theology of the Mystery Plays, by considering what she calls a neo-classical orientation, what is sometimes identified as the use of rhetorical practice in education. Her essay offers a fine counter-example through an analysis of *Gammer Gurton's Needle*. Perhaps, though, the best response to the huge claims that medieval drama was incarnational and penitential would be to begin by reconsidering just how many kinds of "playing" existed, over how long a time, and in what different spaces and circumstances: public, popular, private, school, university, professional, for what audiences. The jump from the Mysteries to Marston regularly skips two or three generations of schoolboy practice intended to train future elites through eloquence. By contrast, texts exist, such as *Everyman,* in the form of a moral play for private reading, encouraged by the international book trade's imports of dramatic works, classical and Continental. Hutson's eye to laughter offers a partial corrective, but by and large these arguments strike me as being remarkably innocent of what happens in performance, as if unified audiences all only experienced one thing. The determined emphasis on theology is almost undermined by Greg Walker on Folly, where he remembers that Thomas More was a man of witty malice. Vincent Gillespie's attention to the range of writing about monasticism is another of the book's successes because it attends to long-lived and international habits of satire as well as repeated reforms; so, similarly, Helen Cooper uses the history of reading, imitating, and invoking Chaucer, that well of English undefiled, to think about "Fame" in its guises of secular, poetic, national and literary renown.

The other outstanding essay is by Thomas Betteridge, who realized in the course of writing a chapter on "mystics" that that old term would no longer do. He sets out a clear exposition of the problems in cross-century comparisons and acknowledges that the same word hides not only semantic change but also the context of social change. This chapter, by addressing its author's puzzlement, gives a fine example of how research sometimes enlightens by bringing its own terms into doubt. By contrast to Hadfield's Margery Kempe, this is a serious attempt to grapple with the risks and rewards of the soul's search for union with its god before philosophy and physiology made brain dysfunction central to our understanding of the visionary experience. *Quis custodiet,* we might ask: societies that policed claimants to revelation had little power to guard their guardians. Before Big Brother met Big Pharma, there was no way to police the inner life, beyond sequestration or the stake. Ostensible reform had no quarrel with that.

RUTH MORSE
Université Paris–Diderot

KATHLEEN DAVIS and NADIA ALTSCHUL, eds. *Medievalisms in the Postcolonial World: The Idea of "the Middle Ages" Outside Europe*. Baltimore: Johns Hopkins University Press, 2009. Pp. vi, 444. $70.00.

The first generation of publications on the intersection of medieval studies and postcolonial theory—from the seminal collection of essays edited by Jeffrey Jerome Cohen, *The Postcolonial Middle Ages* (2000), to Lisa Lampert-Weissig's recent survey, *Medieval Literature and Postcolonial Studies* (2010)—has come to a close. In *Medievalisms in the Postcolonial World,* Kathleen Davis and Nadia Altschul lay the foundations for the second generation of such studies, in which an informed self-awareness of the stakes of an investment in the medieval past is of crucial importance. The essays collected here address a broad span of topics with a diverse chronological and geographical range, and establish new parameters for evaluating the various uses of the medieval past: in this respect, Davis and Altschul's collection has its peers in Karla Mallette's *European Modernity and the Arab Mediterranean: Toward a New Philology and a Counter-Orientalism* (2010) and Michelle R. Warren's *Creole Medievalism: Colonial France and Joseph Bédier's Middle Ages* (2010). Like the studies of Mallette and Warren, the essays collected by Davis and Altschul have a common aim: that is, to analyze the strategic deployment of a "Middle

Ages" in the service of modern political agendas, from the nineteenth through the twenty-first centuries.

Perhaps the most striking feature of Davis and Altschul's collection is their organizing principle: each of the four sections of the volume is composed of a sequence of three essays, each of which presents a different perspective on the section's theme, followed by a "response" that points out areas of convergence and divergence among the preceding cluster of essays, leading to possible future research questions. This structure creates a greater sense of continuity and common purpose in the volume as a whole than one might have thought possible, given the widely disparate areas of research—in terms of field of study, methodological approach, and theoretical orientation—on the part of the volume's contributors. In two of the four sections, Davis and Altschul themselves have written the response essays; in the other two sections, responses are written by outstanding theorists in the field of postcolonial studies, Dipesh Chakrabarty and Simon Gikandi. In addition, greater cohesiveness across the volume is achieved by anchoring three of the four sections of the volume with an essay centered on the field of Latin American studies: this counterintuitive approach inverts the conventional scenario of medieval studies, situating Latinity in the New World setting rather than in the superannuated institutions of the European Middle Ages.

In their introduction, Davis and Altschul make explicit their aim to address "medievalism in spaces outside Europe, particularly colonies and former colonies that did not have their 'own' medieval period, and where the concept of a Middle Ages came as a function of European colonization" (1). This approach raises fascinating questions about the role of periodization, especially what it might mean to call a period "medieval," and what kinds of power—and what kinds of inadequacies—are implied by such a designation. Davis and Altschul suggest that the medieval is at once a "spatiotemporal concept," "part of a temporal grid" and "part of a spatial imaginary" (1). By investigating how "colonial medievalisms contribute *both* to medieval studies *and* to postcolonial theory," Davis and Altschul hope to "bring medievalist and postcolonial scholars into conversation about the shared histories of their fields and the potential of their mutual endeavor" (3). In some ways, this trail has been blazed already by Lampert-Weissig and, earlier, by Bruce Holsinger in *The Premodern Condition: Medievalism and the Making of Theory* (2005). Here, however, the movement toward dialogue is truly innovative, building upon the preliminary effort in this direction found in Ananya Kabir and Deanne Williams's *Postcolonial Approaches to the European Middle Ages* (2005) but widening the temporal and geographical frame very substantially.

The first section, "Locations of History and Theory," begins with José Rabasa's "Decolonizing Medieval Mexico," which places the history of Spanish colonization of the New World at the beginning of a genealogy of modern imperial history. This initiative is taken up in a very strong essay by Ananya Kabir on the reception of Tacitus's *Germania* in British India, which explores the ways in which fantasies about Germanic national character informed English rule in Southeast Asia; this aggressive imperialist impulse is countered by the fantasy of a pacific, deeply Franciscan Middle Ages that informs Louise D'Arcens's study of the "resistant practice" (81) of the Australian medievalist George Arnold Wood. In his response to this sequence of essays, Dipesh Chakrabarty highlights the role of temporality in the negotiation of the medieval past, noting the "duality of distance and proximity" that "haunts" efforts to pick apart the "medieval/modern binary" (112) and suggesting that, far from being a liability, this "back and forth movement" is a "symptom" of the postmodern global perspective.

"Repositioning Orientalism," the second cluster of *Medievalisms in the Postcolonial World,* is perhaps the most exciting and provocative of all, opening with Hernán Taboada's reconsideration of the fraught question of the nature of "convivencia" in "three religion Spain." Taboada's account of "Spanish Orientalism" (123) is followed by Haruko Momma's fascinating account of Japanese novelist Natsume Soseki's "appropriation of western medievalism" coupled with an adaptation of "Orientalist mode[s] of representation" (166), and by Hamid Bahri and Francesca Canadé Sautman's study of Lebanese exile Amin Maalouf's "uses of the 'medieval'" (174). Bahri and Sautman illustrate how Maalouf's writings, ranging from his widely read historical compilation, *The Crusades Through Arab Eyes* (1983), through his avant-garde operatic libretto, *L'Amour de Loin* (2001), participate in a "linguistic nomadism" (177) that confronts a "postcolonial Arab world" in which "the past remains very much part of the present, and the West can no longer own it exclusively" (185). Kathleen Davis's response is a highlight of the volume, drawing together the ways in which each essay illustrates how a community's "identification *as* a people is never a matter of an 'origin,'" but instead emerges "from the very history of their displacement" (212).

The third cluster of essays, "Nation and Foundations," offers a series of explorations of the crucial role of periodization in the invention of national identity, including Altschul's study of the role of Andrés Bello in the foundation of a Spanish "national philology," Elizabeth Emery's survey of neo-Gothic cathedrals in the United States, and Heather Blurton's provocative account of historian Charles Homer Haskins's role at the Paris Peace Conference of 1918 and his resistance to the pervasive "fundamentally nostalgic" attitude toward the Middle Ages (276). Michelle Warren's response highlights the foundational role of epic in "ethnic nationalism," as texts were edited, read, and taught in such a way as to " 'create' national peoples" (289). The volume's final cluster, "Geography and Temporality," is centered on Africa and the Caribbean colonies that were largely populated by enslaved Africans: these essays include Sylvie Kandé's study of Ahmadou Kourouma, Kofi Campbell's account of Wilson Harris, and Victor Houliston's striking survey of medieval studies in South Africa's apartheid and postapartheid state. In his response, Simon Gikandi points out the crucial element that links all these sites of colonization in terms of their engagement with the European "Middle Ages": namely, the effort to "use the existence of an African Middle Ages as a gateway to history—specifically, European notions of historical time—and at the same time reject its instrumental use by powerful political interests with dynastic ties to the past" (377–78). In this remarkable collection, Davis and Altschul have made a significant contribution to the next phase of postcolonial medieval studies, in which the responses of the postcolony come to the fore and periodization is increasingly shown to be among the most powerful weapons in the European canon.

SUZANNE CONKLIN AKBARI
University of Toronto

SIÂN ECHARD. *Printing the Middle Ages.* Philadelphia: University of Pennsylvania Press, 2008. Pp. xvi, 314. $65.00.

"Printing the Middle Ages" is a sweeping title, but readers alarmed at the prospect of a wide-ranging concept-based analysis of how mechanized communication might have reformatted medieval themes and images will be relieved to know that most of this book is rigorously undertheorized, even undercontextualized. Its detailed and well-illustrated discussion of the use of Anglo-Saxon letters in early replica publishing is, for example, quite innocent of the notion of "The Norman Yoke," or that the term and idea "Saxon" bore (however improbably) overtones of egalitarian justice that encouraged timid English liberals. The overview absences are compensated locally: in the first chapter, Anglo-Saxon letters are given detailed description and reproduction (the whole volume is finely illustrated). Then an inherently disconnected sequence provides chapters on the transmission of the stories of Sir Guy of Warwick and Sir Bevis of Hampton, in specific texts rather than historicized overview; the handling and valuing of Gower manuscripts, including by Lord Gower; juvenile Chaucer texts of the nineteenth century; the varying treatment of Froissart and his texts; and finally a "Coda" on modern electronic textualities.

Through this series, the intricate research on manuscript contents is full, gathering elusive data from libraries around the world, but reporting it rather than seeing cultural or political patterns. Some of the data are Eng Lit classical, like the *Beowulf* manuscripts, transcripts, and print facsimiles, but Echard also communicates cultural-studies detail from her own university's holdings of the Mary Haweis materials in a chapter on nineteenth-century juvenile Chaucers that deserves a title less offhand than "Bedtime Chaucer."

The ambition of the book is limited. A central methodological move, signaled in the introduction, is toward reified book history, not full-text meaning: Echard speaks about how "sober scholarly editions and cleaned-up school texts of the post-war era certainly suggest a deliberate (if temporary and of course illusory) cultivation of text over the thingness of the book" (xv). Fetishizing-ness may seem part of the thing-ness implied, and this limitedly material approach has in fact already been avowed: "Each chapter has a particular text-object at its core" (xi).

This book-history limitation is itself limited. As we hear about the Trentham Gower transcript, or the Haweis children's Chaucers, we do not find the politically meaningful connections book history has shown itself capable of making since Benedict Anderson linked printing to nationalism. Rather, we share the object-focus that led aristocrats to treasure these objects. The post-William Morris interest in script and illumination is called a "nostalgic nod to handwork" (59). Actually it signified a resistance to dehumanized manufacturing processes and the exile of craft values. Other opportunities to read texts in their formative contexts are missed. In a long and often well-detailed chapter on the varying reception of Froissart, we do hear, if briefly, about "medievaliz-ing nationalism" in Scott (164) and, potentially more interestingly, in the American Sidney Lanier (193), but while Henry Newbolt's interest in this mode is noted, his major impact on the English curriculum and the turn-of-the-century English national myth seems quite unknown (195).

This text-as-object approach, where context is largely limited to peri-text, induces some misreadings. Thomas Warton, the breakthrough his-toricizing medievalizer, is taken as the erroneous bore that the splenetic Joseph Ritson declared him in defense of his own insistent textualism. More misleadingly, the interest that Warton and (cited here only in the Sir Guy of Warwick connection) Thomas Percy had in the idea of the Gothic Germanic north as free from serfdom, Catholicism, and imperial-ism, lasting through Germanophile writers like Coleridge and George Eliot as an icon of European liberalism, is here belittled as "Chaucer as Teuton" and traduced as "Aryan" in 1940s terms (161).

This mix of a form of consumerist fetishization and a very limited reading of the political contexts is at best a way of transmitting to more illuminating analysts a set of sometimes intriguing details about texts and their receptions. By only having this potential use-value, most of this book is essentially a modern if bibliographically rich parallel to what Echard calls "self-interested aristocratic antiquarianism" (118). Early in the lengthy chapter about the transmission of *Guy of Warwick* and *Bevis of Hampton* (which never explains their disappearance, but then Tenny-son's Arthurian impact on the medievalizing canon is not a topic here, just mentioned on page 127 as not being Chaucerian), Echard mocks the late eighteenth-century antiquarian John Nichols, at best "eclectic" and "avid," but in terms of scholarly professionalism a purveyor of what Frederic Madden called "egregious nonsense" (62). Yet Nichols's obses-sion with the artifacts under his scrutiny, his lack of any real filiations of connecting analysis from one to the other and out to their contexts, is not unlike the undertone of much of this book itself.

All the stranger then to find that the last chapter of *Printing the Mid-dle Ages* suddenly snaps into focus as an astute and self-aware critique of hypermodernity. In a "Coda," a tail that wags this book, or should do, Echard gives a well-thought-out account of the recent adventures of medievalists into electronicity. Beginning by noting how the new technologic primarily celebrates itself (201–2)—fair enough, but overlooking the pre-Raphaelites' parallel mix of hyperrealism and sentimental subjectivity—she moves on through the first, and long-awaited use of the term "fetishization" (202) to describe how the electronicists objectify texts. The observation might have been shared with the tradition-transmitters discussed in previous chapters, but she notes well that modern objectification is in the service of the market, and that, ironically, these innovative versions go rapidly out of technological date and so, without new cost, usability—while the old books are still up for reading.

With this heightened awareness of what material texts can actually mean and do, Echard does not miss the manipulative "Britishness" (210) of the much-relished Sherborne Missal in the hands of the postcolonial but still financially imperial British Library, and there is neat comment on the factitiously political localization the machines permit to what is called the St. Chad Gospels by the middle Englanders of Lichfield and the Llandeilo Gospels by the Welsh it last saw a thousand years ago. As a final touch to this fine piece of writing, Echard deploys the concept of the Freudian "uncanny" to account for both the ghostly consolation on the screen and the real presence repressed by hypermodern medievalizing forces.

It is indeed strange that such a sharp, well-targeted piece of writing should both conclude and seemingly contradict a book that before this is only usefully read against the grain for its potentially intriguing but underanalyzed data. *Printing the Middle Ages* is ultimately a palimpsest, but unlike a treasured object it is the modern element that claims attention, not the limited-value underlay that it both superscribes and overcomes.

STEPHEN KNIGHT
Cardiff University

JENNIFER FELLOWS and IVANA DJORDJEVIĆ, eds. *"Sir Bevis of Hampton" in Literary Tradition.* Cambridge: D. S. Brewer, 2008. Pp. xii, 207. £50.00; $95.00.

Sir Bevis of Hampton is a familiar presence in romance studies, acting since *Sir Thopas* as a representative Middle English romance. It is also, as this new collection makes clear, one of the most enigmatic, problematic, and difficult to place whether textually or ideologically. The geographical and chronological expanse of the Bevis story outlined in the introduction to this volume is remarkable: from the eleventh to the nineteenth centuries, from its earliest appearances in Anglo-Norman and Middle English through French and Italian to Yiddish and Russian, with traces in folklore and oral tradition. The title of this collection establishes that it is concerned with the literary tradition, but it is also the case that apart from one welcome discussion of the Old Norse version, this book is confined to the British Isles—to the Bevis known to readers of Anglo-Norman, English, Welsh, and Irish.

The Anglo-Norman *Boeve de Haumtone* is the subject of the first two papers. Marianne Ailes examines the question of genre surrounding a "romance" written in *chanson de geste* form. From the perspective of Continental tradition, *Boeve* is a characteristically insular development combining *chanson* discourse with the scholarly rhetoric of the schools. It is useful to be reminded at the start that this apparently direct narrative is a carefully constructed literary artifact. Judith Weiss focuses on Boeve's mentor Sabaoth, who departs in several vital ways from similar figures in other insular romances, and indeed in contemporary society. Her conclusion, that Sabaoth is a figure whose role and name evoke the pre-Conquest past and link the D'Albini family with English history, gives a new weight to the reading of *Boeve* as foundational history.

The other languages of insular literature give the Welsh and Irish prose Bevis narratives considered by Erich Poppe and Regine Recke. The thirteenth-century Welsh *Bown* does not depart from the plot or narrative intention of its Anglo-Norman original, but does adapt its style to native convention. As with the fifteenth-century Irish reworking of the Middle English *Bevis,* this means the excising of the narratorial presence that features so strongly in the earlier versions. The Irish redactor, probably Uilliam Mac an Leagha, adopts the florid Irish style and this later version does modernize some of the material dealing with honor and morality. The Old Norse *Bevers saga,* studied by Christopher Sanders, survives in eighteen copies. He argues for a clerical author producing a narrative of historical prose, less fictional and less humorous than its Anglo-Norman source. In line with later developments in English, it is also more emphatically Christian and anti-Islamic. Ivana Djordjević provides a close examination of the translation of formulae from Anglo-Norman to Middle English and the often unconventional, even playful, use the translator makes of a common generic repertoire. These three contributions, drawing on expertise across five languages and underpinned by reference to translation theory, provide valuable material for the ongoing study of the freedoms and strategies of medieval translation.

The second part of the volume, dealing with the English-language versions of *Bevis,* begins with a clear exposition by Jennifer Fellows of the complex interrelation of the manuscript and printed versions from the fourteenth century to the eighteenth. The Auchinleck manuscript does not deserve the authority it is often given, as she demonstrates from analysis of the clear traces of *Boeve* or the original Middle English to be found in later manuscripts and the printed tradition. The English versions position Bevis as Christian hero, even martyr, drawing on the Saint George legend, while at the same time developing Josiane as a strong romance heroine. An appendix to this chapter provides a detailed descriptive list of the surviving manuscripts and printed editions from the 1330s to 1711.

The chronological range of the reworkings of *Bevis* causes tensions and inconsistencies that provide a common theme for the following essays. Robert Rouse analyzes the conflicting identities that make up the figure of Bevis—"a strange and unsettling example of an English knight" apparently more at home in the East (116). Anxieties about hybridity and the perils of acculturation cluster around Bevis's actions abroad, while in England he represents a regional identity at odds with both the king and the alien society of London. Rouse suggests that the romance past can create a space for an inclusive fantasy of Englishness, but the evidence here, together with that of the following contributions, indicates that tensions remain unresolved. Siobhain Bly Calkin traces the changes in Bevis's role as a Christian knight, from the earlier version in which Saracens play an important and positive role in Bevis's upbringing and career to the increasingly intolerant attitudes that culminate in fifteenth-century talk of burning unbelievers. By the end of the Middle Ages, tensions within Christendom demand a demonized enemy to encourage unity. Melissa Furrow analyzes the problematic figure of the Saracen giant, Ascopard, showing that the inconsistencies in this figure go back to the continuator of the second part of *Boeve.* Later versions find different strategies to explain his sudden betrayal of Bevis and present him as grotesque pagan or as comically childlike, manipulating various Saracen stereotypes. The disruption of stereotypes is also the subject of Corinne Saunders's study of gender and wisdom in the

Auchinleck text. Josiane acts both as a contrast to Bevis's evil mother, an unusual and shocking figure for romance, and as a foil to Bevis's development as a Christian hero. She becomes a figure of active virtue, wise in natural magic, in contrast to Bevis's patient suffering, a substantial adjustment of gender expectations.

The Bevis material through the Renaissance to the seventeenth century is examined by Andrew King. Mentioned as a byword for childish fantasy in *Henry VIII, Bevis* brings into sharp focus the problems a Protestant readership had with "monkish" literature. The rereading of the medieval literary past by Spenser presents a Calvinist pattern of human history and salvation in which noble birth symbolizes election. In the following century, Bevis again merges with Saint George to give a figure of patriotic, muscular Christianity. For Bunyan, *Bevis* is still a valid point of reference for the romances that must be renegotiated to become Christian narratives of pilgrimage. This thoughtful essay rounds off the survey of the cultural tensions and changes evident in the Bevis material.

Each contribution to *"Sir Bevis of Hampton" in Literary Tradition* provides a fresh, thoroughly referenced discussion across the range of versions and approaches to the insular Bevis story. The volume as a whole demonstrates both the secret of *Bevis's* appeal across the centuries and the problems the story and its imperfect hero present to those who would rework it for their own times. *Bevis* is a prime example of the protean nature of romance and its ability to adapt to changing cultural climates. This volume will be essential for those looking for expert views on *Bevis* and the textual and cultural questions it raises. With its detailed information on manuscripts and printed editions and a comprehensive bibliography of *Bevis* scholarship, it is a valuable resource and likely to stimulate further research into one of the most significant of insular romances.

ROSALIND FIELD
Royal Holloway, University of London

LAURIE A. FINKE and MARTIN B. SHICHTMAN. *Cinematic Illuminations: The Middle Ages on Film*. Baltimore: Johns Hopkins University Press, 2010. 445 pp. $60.00 cloth; $30.00 paper.

Since the 1990s, the subfield of the study of the depiction of the Middle Ages in film (also known as "medieval film," "cinematic medievalism," or similar) has garnered a large amount of academic attention and activity. The monographs and collections released in this subfield generally take one of two approaches: either they address a small subset of the large corpus of medieval films distinguished by topic (examples include *Hollywood in the Holy Land* [ed. Haydock and Risden, 2009] or *Cinema Arthuriana* [ed. Harty, 2002]), or, less often, they attempt to address the entirety of medieval film through a particular theoretical perspective (for example, *Movie Medievalism* [Haydock, 2008], or *Medieval Film* [ed. Bernau and Bildhauer, 2010]). *Cinematic Illuminations: The Middle Ages on Film* is, as its name implies, of the latter type, and remarkable in the breadth and scope of its ambition and accomplishment.

The monograph is split roughly into three parts. Part I (Chapters 1–3) presents a broad exploration of the theory and the methods of cinematic medievalism. Its introductory chapter lays out many of the core issues central to the study of the medieval film today: in particular, the interaction between medieval past and medievalist present, and between fantasy and history. Chapter 2 presents what the authors call a "sociological stylistics" of the medieval film, regarding many aspects of "the cinematic codes that have developed over the last century for representing the Middle Ages" (24). Particularly interesting is their Barthesian semiological "mythology" of the medieval film, addressing the genres, formulae, and conventions that filmmakers use to indicate "the Middle Ages." Chapter 3 addresses the vexed question of historical accuracy in medieval film through the lens of postmodern deconstruction.

Part II more closely examines examples of medieval film in light of their sociopolitical contexts and messages. Chapter 4 focuses on the representation of medieval political authority, from the complex antiestablishment messages of *Monty Python and the Holy Grail* (a favorite of the authors), to conservative, nationalist, or dynastic discourses in *Excalibur, Becket,* and *The Lion in Winter.* Chapter 5 considers three Joan of Arc films, particularly the "shifting and unstable" (109) interpretation of her life (and associated myth) that constantly remakes Joan as a saint for all times, places, and political ideologies. Chapter 6 then addresses the projection of modern politics into a medieval setting: *Camelot* is seen as a nostalgic American bourgeois fantasy, *Braveheart* as an instance of the real political impact of medieval film. Chapter 7 examines three films that depict the Crusades within the context of the politics of the times in which they were made. Each film uses the past to argue, through allegory, the hope that peace may yet be achievable in our time, to "stare down the apocalypse with wishful thinking" (241).

Part III addresses films that grapple with anxieties of modernity: consumerism, commodification, and the failure of signification. Chapter 8 examines three films that demythologize the familiar Arthurian legends, which dismiss and lay bare "our desire for origin, for truth, for stability, for history" (286). Chapter 9 examines Ingmar Bergman's *The Seventh Seal* and *The Virgin Spring* and New Zealander Vincent Ward's *The Navigator: A Mediaeval Odyssey* as reflections on the breakdown of society when faced with nuclear or ecological apocalypse. The final chapter addresses the most recent wave of cinematic medievalisms: big-budget Hollywood extravaganzas that use the Middle Ages to promote capitalist, materialist desires in young people.

As should be obvious, the scope of this monograph is impressive, covering both a geographically and temporally wide swath of films. Finke and Shichtman bring to bear a range of methods for examining their subjects, giving due attention to the aesthetic and political, to audience reception and cultural context. However, as a result of this scope, the book at times feels unfocused. In reading it, I found many enjoyable and well-considered passages, such as their analysis of knight-as-rockstar in *A Knight's Tale* privileging surface over substance in Chapter 10, or of Luc Besson's rendering of Joan of Arc in the context of post-Vatican II neofundamentalism in Chapter 5. Upon reflection, however, I often found it difficult to link these close examinations with an overarching thesis or a broader context, making the book feel more like a collection of essays than a monograph. Perhaps that is the difficulty of writing on a body of work so diverse as medieval film. This becomes especially evident in a monograph that attempts to examine the whole corpus with an array of theories, as this one does.

Cinematic Illuminations is occasionally encumbered—particularly in Part I—by the overly dense language and theoretical jargon that has become an unfortunate mainstay in many discussions of medieval film. Take, for example, the following sentence: "Embedded within a diachronic matrix (in the sense of an interconnecting network or system) of paradigmatic and syntagmatic relations, these signs combine to produce utterances, always in dialogue with other utterances" (39). The point is simple, the language needlessly complex. This problem is compounded by the variety of complex theory that Finke and Shichtman choose to employ. On the one hand, this is quite impressive, but, on the other, it can be dizzying for the reader, particularly when it seems that the authors do not always explain why they are employing all of the theories they do. This both contributes to, and is something of a victim of, the larger issue of the book's lack of focus and central argument.

When Finke and Shichtman engage in close analyses of specific films, their prose is enjoyable, accessible, and scholarly. But when relating those analyses to one of the many theories they employ, the verbiage can become frustratingly difficult, as above. In many ways, this is not their doing; film theory generally employs jargon-laden language and it is difficult for the film theorist not to follow suit. Additionally, this language has crept into analyses of medieval films possibly because the subject appears "soft" to certain medievalists. But it is regrettable that this restrictive language is the dominant way in which we have come to discuss what is by definition an accessible medium. As a result, I would hesitate to recommend this book to undergraduates or postgraduates interested in medieval film without recommending that first they become conversant with a variety of film and critical theories.

Those criticisms aside, *Cinematic Illuminations* is an impressive achievement that contextualizes a large range of medieval film with acumen and rigor. Overall, it engages well with the difficult task of finding commonalities in all the myriad ways that the Middle Ages have been rendered compatible with the format and the political, cultural, and aesthetic functions of the big screen over the course of the twentieth century.

PAUL STURTEVANT
University of Leeds

JOHN BLOCK FRIEDMAN. *Brueghel's Heavy Dancers: Transgressive Clothing, Class, and Culture in the Late Middle Ages.* Syracuse: Syracuse University Press, 2010. Pp. xxv, 361. $45.00.

Many recent scholarly monographs on representations of clothing in medieval literature have examined the intersection between aristocratic attire and courtly identities. John Block Friedman's study contributes to this critical conversation by shifting its focus to depictions of peasant dress and behaviors. The scope of the book is admirable in its breadth.

Drawing from northern French lyric *pastourelles,* their *bergerie* variants, Spanish *serranillas,* antipeasant German satires, two of Chaucer's *fabliaux,* and the portrait of the Squire's Yeoman in the *Prologue* to the *Canterbury Tales, Brueghel's Heavy Dancers* surveys what Friedman finds to be the "realistic treatment" of "clothing, accessories, and even related behaviors that formed part of the bourgeois and aristocratic views of rustics" (xiv). Such careful attention to rustic dress ultimately reveals, according to Friedman, bourgeois anxiety about peasants encroaching on urban social space.

Brueghel's Heavy Dancers takes the artist's *Peasant Dance* and *Wedding Dance* as points of departure for a study in medieval clothing, class, and culture. For Friedman, these sixteenth-century paintings featuring offensive sartorial and sexual behaviors observed by a solitary bourgeois figure emblematize upper-class discomfort with lower-class deportment that also appears in a variety of late medieval literature. Chapters 1 and 2 consider the *pastourelle* and its subgenre, the *bergerie,* as two forms that convey one of the book's central ideas: that a peasant's excessive sexuality as represented through dress or behavior could threaten noble status.

Where the first two chapters demonstrate that protagonists in the *pastourelles* wear dress inappropriate to social status, Chapter 3 considers clothing along with other forms of transgression, namely, physical ugliness and the inverted sexual roles of mountain women in Iberian *serranillas* by Juan Ruiz (ca. 1298–1350), Iñigo López de Mondoza, Marqués de Santillana (1398–1458), and Carvajal (fl. 1457–60). In a lengthy section on the rhetorical trope, *effictio,* Friedman presents head-to-toe descriptions of ugliness in Iberian poetry as influenced by poetic conventions of unattractive women in French and Italian literature. The conclusions reached in this chapter repeat those of the earlier ones: Spanish poets, like their French counterparts, dress their female protagonists in "transgressive" courtly attire so as to indicate peasant desire for social advancement while simultaneously appealing to an elite readership curious about rustic life. Strangely absent, given Friedman's assertions, is evidence of the circulation of the poetic works or mention of manuscript contexts, which might address the ways in which medieval readers experienced this literature.

Chapter 4 examines German variants of the *pastourelle* as a bridge between the French form and the English fabliaux of Chaucer. Building upon scholarship that positions German antipeasant satires as some of the most gross and comic representations of rural excesses, Friedman

341

focuses less on dress than on physical ugliness, a woman's desire to dominate her male suitor, and sexual insatiability in the works of late medieval German writers Neidhart (fl. 1215–40), Oswald von Wolkenstein (1377–1455), and Hermann von Sachsenheim (1366–1458). These writers provide examples of "peasant and female transgressivity not seen in the romance-language poems" (133).

Chapters 5 and 6 turn to "villagers" in Chaucer's fabliaux and the *General Prologue.* Reading against Helen Cooper's reminder that Chaucer portrays individuals rather than groups in the *General Prologue,* Friedman finds Chaucer describing "a social milieu that more or less corresponded to the way such people actually lived during the poet's lifetime" (171). In Chapter 5, "Chaucer's Miller and Alison," realism correlates so closely with "transgressivity" that it becomes an expression of it: "Surely the more threatening and antihierarchical a character is, the more concretely—realistically—that character will be portrayed" (171). Friedman then treats the pilgrim Miller, and Symkin, the corrupt Miller of *The Reeve's Tale,* as interchangeable figures: "Both characters are halves of the same 'village portrait,'" a point that Friedman believes Chaucerians have "generally agreed upon," although there is no citation that outlines precedent for this claim (175). The portrait of Robin in the *General Prologue* provides one of two clothing details that mark him as "class transgressive," namely, the sword and buckler worn by *"arrivistes* in French fabliaux" (176–77). The second article is the red hose worn by Symkin in *The Reeve's Tale.* Friedman consequently collapses distinctions between Robin and Symkin and reads the aggregate "Miller" as "a social climber . . . extremely insecure in his role of yeoman, as his ill-considered collection of weapons shows" (181).

The second half of Chapter 5 asserts that Alison's "transgressive attire" in *The Miller's Tale* reflects a difference between bourgeois city dwellers and peasants living in the country. Noting that Alison's filet accentuates her broad forehead, Friedman examines Alison's hairline and eyebrows, which, he concedes, have not prompted discussion with respect to fashion but physiognomy. We should instead reread Alison's eyebrows and hairline as elements of aristocratic fashion, he suggests. Finally, in a deductive move that is by this time symptomatic of the study, Friedman associates Alison's "country clothing" with that of the *pastourelle* heroine. He concludes that Alison's *effictio* offers "an upper-class view of the villager's extravagant social reach and the limitations of her taste" (196).

In Chapter 6, "Chaucer's Yeoman and the Social Context of Archery," Friedman analyzes the Squire's Yeoman's costume accessories in the *General Prologue* as social signifiers. Few scholars have noted the Yeoman's ostentation with his peacock-fletched arrows, dagger, armguard, and brooch, and none until Friedman have concluded that the portrait of the Squire's Yeoman is "another instance of Chaucer's view of transgressivity" (200). As with the Miller of Chapter 5, Friedman understands the Yeoman as "a showy, *parvenu* character who represents a class somewhere between the land and the town striving for emblematic recognition through attire and heraldic bearings" (199). He then establishes a literary and social context for archery (the latter drawn from evidence of Continental practices with the crossbow instead of English use of the longbow) that ties the sport to rustic desires for social mobility parodied in the *pastourelle*.

The final chapter, "Clothing and German Antipeasant Satire," returns to peasant sartorial details as threats to elite social status in Neidhart's poetry and Heinrich Wittenwiler's *Ring*. Friedman posits Wittenwiler as a near-contemporary of Chaucer's who shares not only his cultural and class milieu but also his penchant for particular plot motifs, namely, the use of bagpiping (played as the Canterbury pilgrims depart on pilgrimage and in the background in the *Ring*) and misplaced kisses and falls from roofs (as in *The Miller's Tale*). From these similarities, Friedman concludes that the author and readership of the German poems were bourgeois and that they "look[ed] down at those immediately below them, which corresponds in some particulars to portions of the audience for the *Canterbury Tales*" (263).

Brueghel's Heavy Dancers is valuable for its comprehensive cataloguing of peasant attire and uncouth behaviors in late medieval pastoral and satiric poetry of Western Europe. That said, Friedman's editors have done him something of a disservice by insisting neither on consistency in translation nor thoroughness in proofreading. Translations are not always provided for foreign-language texts, especially titles of poems and lengthy prose excerpts, and sometimes only English translations of poems appear. Several typographical errors persist throughout the book (27, 105, 135, 170, 197). Despite these minor shortcomings, John Block Friedman's study is refreshing for its attention to the sartorial tastes of a social group that has largely been overlooked by literary scholars interested in medieval dress.

NICOLE D. SMITH
University of North Texas

RALPH HANNA, ed. *Speculum Vitae: A Reading Edition*. EETS o.s. 331, 332. Oxford: Oxford University Press, 2008. Pp. xcvi, 674. £74.00; $150.00.

The landscape of Middle English literature has changed. For many years, literary histories treated medieval England as a locally undifferentiated place that produced, simply, English literature. Or they treated it as a place synonymous with London and its court poetry, from which poets in literally marginal places might take their models and inspiration. No more, however. Scholars of Chester, Norfolk, Scotland, and the Welsh border area (to name just four examples) have all recently shown the late medieval literary landscape to be both less coherent and less focused on London than once imagined. With his work on Yorkshire as well as London, Ralph Hanna has been among the boldest of these new geographers, and his edition of the *Speculum Vitae* will take its place as a crucial contribution to this emergent mapping of the literary landscape.

Previously unedited, the anonymous *Speculum* is a late fourteenth-century northern verse translation of the *Somme le roi* by Lorens of Orléans. It is a translation, however, in the way that many late medieval works are translations—a work indebted to a source for its ideas, structure, and much of its language but also to an array of ancillary works that can be incorporated to amplify what the translator understood to be the source's essential meaning. In this case, these ancillary works are distinctively northern, including anonymous lyrics, Rolle's "Form of Living," and the *Cursor Mundi*. Extant in forty-five manuscripts that vary from fragments to documents containing more than sixteen thousand lines of text, the *Speculum* offers a fairly complete catechism by way of meditations on topics like the *Pater Noster,* the seven virtues, and the seven vices. Structurally, it is at once rigid in its reliance on listing and subdividing and also casual in its expansiveness. While no one would

ever consider it a must read—Hanna well describes one of the translator's rearrangements as "awkward, but . . . at least clever" (lxxii)—it is
not without its occasional charms, as in a comparison between the allure
of false speech for sinners and honey for bears:

> Þai enoynt with swete hony
> Þe way to helle for þam namely,
> Forþi þat þai suld hardylyer ga
> By þat way þat enoynte es swa,
> Als men does þat þa beere taas.
>
> (13763–67)

Ultimately, though, the greatest contribution of the *Speculum* to the literary landscape is conceptual. In its length, methods, and number of
extant manuscripts, the poem attests to a thriving Yorkshire literary
culture that looked inward for its texts and methods rather than outward to the court and society of London. Like *Cursor Mundi,* the *Speculum*
opens with warnings to readers to avoid minstrelsy and romances like
Ysumbras, and, like Rolle's "Form of Living," it stipulates that sins of
thought, word, and deed are joined by those of omission: "Þe synnes of
leuynge of gode vndone" (5592).

Hanna subtitles his text a "reading edition" because it is understand-
ably based on collation of only a selection of manuscripts—the five best
ones, as he sees them, along with two copies from another of the poem's
textual traditions and sporadic collation from other manuscripts. He
describes editorial capitalization and punctuation as "heavier than customary, since I have tried to disambiguate complex grammatical sequences and to mark the poet's abiding interest in Vices and Virtues"
(lxxxvii). Variants are located at the bottom of the page, and the second
volume concludes with notes and a glossary. In the introduction, Hanna
provides characteristically thorough descriptions of the manuscripts
along with discussions of authorship, date, dialect, sources, and meter.
While thoroughly informed and informative, this material sometimes
seems to reflect the enthusiasm that long work on an obscure text can
produce. Hanna grants, for instance, that deducing phonology from the
Speculum and then reading it against *LALME* is problematic (lxvi), but
then does this very thing. And the discussion of metrics in particular
raises concerns, maintaining as it does that the poem is written not
in octosyllabics but in a four-stress pattern. The "poem's graphemic

presentation," Hanna suggests, differs from its "likely metrical performance" (lxxv). While traditionally textual-critical, such disjunction between manuscript witnesses and some underlying deep structure seems
difficult to maintain for a poem as sprawling and adaptable as the *Speculum*. The notion that in the late fourteenth century in the north, inflec-
tional *-e* can optionally appear for metrical reasons, one of the means by
which "metrical performance" is demonstrated, likewise gives pause, as
does a claim that in a poem like this emendations might be based on
the grounds that a word or syllable can ever be "metrically otiose" (546,
passim). Looked at another way, one might say that the many three-
and even two-stress lines in the poem poorly justify claims for a predom-
inant four-stress metrical pattern.

While works like the *Speculum* clarify late medieval England's literary
geography, they also raise additional questions. If literary culture proceeded at times in regional rather than national directions, for example,
to what extent were regional cultures self-aware and to what extent
simply matters of convenience? That is, did the author of the *Speculum*
intrude material from Rolle because he wished for the production of a
distinctly regional Yorkshire literature or simply because, being in the
north, he had easy access to Rolle's works? And in another vein, precisely how did works like the *Speculum,* the *Cursor,* and the *Northern English Homily Cycle* contribute to literary culture? Each is lengthy, shows
signs of revision and therefore ongoing interest, and survives in numerous manuscripts. All dynamically coexist with lyrics that either supplement or are extracted from them. In measurable ways like these, all
three might be regarded as having more medieval vitality than *Troilus
and Criseyde,* and yet the title of this journal remains *Studies in the Age of
Chaucer,* not *Studies in the Age of Rolle.* As we sort through such issues of
medieval literary geography, volumes like Hanna's careful and thorough
edition of the *Speculum* will become all the more necessary.

TIM WILLIAM MACHAN
Marquette University

JUDITH JEFFERSON and AD PUTTER, eds. *Approaches to the Metres of Alliterative Verse*. Leeds: Leeds Texts and Monographs, New Series 17,
2009. Pp. 311. £40.00; $65.00 paper.

It is difficult to make a completely satisfying book from a set of conference papers, and the editors' choice of title for this collection (emanating

from a 2005 conference in Bristol) highlights the differences of perspective in the thirteen essays; they do not even claim that the contributors are discussing a single meter, though they have provided a unified bibliography (but not an index). So, although a significant number of essays take as their starting point the existence of "rules" for the composition of the alliterative long line, following Hoyt Duggan and others, and attempt further definition of the patterns of lifts and dips, the constraints that operate in the two half-lines, the presence or absence of pronounced final -e, the hierarchies of allowable alliterating words, and so on, usually by subjecting chunks of poetic text to statistical processes, others return to basic questions about linguistic history and how alliteration works, and to the consideration of individual poems.

In my youth, before computers, I served a two-year apprenticeship to the scholarly alliterative trade by analyzing the syntax of every sentence of *Sir Gawain and the Green Knight,* and from close study of J. P. Oakden's monumental *Alliterative Poetry in Middle English* developed, alongside interest in the subject, a fair dose of skepticism about the rum-ram-ruffery of it all. How did discussion of alliterative meter get stuck in "lifts and dips" when the ear tells us that strong stresses go down, not up? Why not hops and skips, thumps and flutters, landings and scurries? Noriko Inoue takes the nine manuscript versions of *The Siege of Jerusalem* as the coal-face from which to chisel evidence that preference for *for to* + infinitive over *to* + infinitive is always a metrically determined choice in *b*-verses and that, therefore, its use in *a*-verses is proof that the requirement for a long medial dip is stricter than the need to observe the aa/ax pattern. But I cannot help wondering why one should trust in matters metrical a poet who is such an indifferent performer in matters narrative. Working alongside are Nikolay Yakovlev, who challenges the view that final -e had disappeared in northern dialects by the end of the fourteenth century by examining all the *b*-verses in *Sir Gawain*; Donka Minkova, who uses the *b*-verses of *Winner and Waster* and *The Parliament of the Three Ages* to demonstrate constraints on metricality with an impressive display of statistics, tables and code words; Geoffrey Russom, who compares *Beowulf* and *Sir Gawain* in terms of the classes of words that may bear alliteration, to demonstrate patterns of alliterative usage and the contrasts between *a*-verses and *b*-verses; and Gilbert Youmans, who examines syntactic inversions in the alliterative *Morte Arthure* in order to rank the poet's metrical principles in order of strictness, with observance of the ax pattern in the *b*-verse scoring highest, followed by the avoidance of unstressed words at the line ending. All these bear witness to a good deal of meticulous labor and are within the boundaries of the modern orthodoxies of rules and constraints; yet they have a quaint look about their methodology—Youmans almost made me nostalgic for my own unreadable M.A. thesis of fifty years ago by using some familiar examples of noun/adjective inversion such as "on a stede ryche."

It is refreshing to find some essays that step outside the world of the alliterative long line, as Thomas Cable does in examining the alliterative lyrics from the Harley manuscript in terms of Duggan's theory of alliterative meter and asking whether a native or foreign model lies behind them. His conclusion that there is no single alliterative meter but various meters that use alliteration "as a cue to metrically stressed syllables, which in turn establish a rhythm" opens a door to the broader discussion of alliteration as a metrical phenomenon. Allan Gaylord, in a close reading of *Pearl,* considers its "peculiar metric," resisting the idea that alliteration is merely decorative, seeing it rather as "a kind of oral italics." Although he stresses the expressiveness of the verse, he does not confront Duggan's claim (in *The Companion to the Gawain-Poet*) that "*Pearl* is an alliterative poem in only trivial senses of the term." Jeremy Smith contrasts Old English, where the alternation of stress/unstress defines the half-line, and where alliteration is a technique of cohesion, and Middle English, where alliteration, not the stress/unstress pattern, seems to define a genre. The key to the difference is the change from the basically trochaic rhythm of Old English (stem + inflexion) to the iambic rhythm of Middle English (article + noun, etc.); where the former naturally emphasizes openings, the latter naturally shifts to end-rhyme. Smith argues that what we are witnessing in Middle English alliterative poetry is experimentation in a period of linguistic change; old material, such as a liking for alliteration, mingled with new. Equally broadly, Elizabeth Solopova identifies the prosodic features that contributed to the development of alliterative verse in Old English and sees what happens to them in Middle English. Romance borrowings, consequent variations in stress patterns, uses of elision, the development of syllabic-accentual meters, all created conditions less favorable to alliterative verse, or, as Solopova suggestively restates it, conditions less favorable for structural alliterative meters but more favorable for varied mixtures, both within the alliterative long line and in the construction of new hybrid types of line and stanza. One of the problems from *Sir Gawain* that Myra Stokes uses to discuss "Metre and Emendation" illustrates the point about elision: line 660 is clarified by identification of alliteration on *n* ("Withouten [n]ende at any noke") which helps one to see that the disputed reading of the *b*-verse ("I oquere fynde" in Tolkien and Gordon, rev. Davis) should be emended to include the word "noquere," though I think "I noquere fynde" better than Stokes's longer version.

Ron Waldron sticks to the alliterative long line, but thinks of how it is heard rather than how composed. He argues persuasively that, as with iambic pentameter, it is full of variation, with two tiers perceived simultaneously: the underlying metrical scheme and the individual poetic line's modulations of it. Such interplay is the theme in Hoyt Duggan's own contribution as he steps nimbly across the minefield of Langland's metrics. He has substantially revised his 1987 view that Langland adhered to the same rules that governed the other poets of the period and is now thinking that Skeat was right in 1886 when he said that "Langland considered metre of much less importance than the sense." Actually that is not quite what Duggan demonstrates. His illustrations of the ways in which a poet could ignore the defining features of his meter do not undermine the role the meter plays.

So where does the collection leave us? If one believes that alliterative poetry was a matter of rules perhaps recoverable by closer and closer analysis of surviving examples, then it may enable editors to use the rules to reconstruct lost texts, as Judith Jefferson and Ad Putter argue interventionist editing could do with the seventeenth-century text of *Death and Life*. If, however, the written texts are merely conventionalized representations of varying experiments in rhythm and sound, perhaps the most that may be achieved is a definition of alliterative poetry that includes not only the metronomically regular aa/ax lines of *The Destruction of Troy* but also *Pearl, Piers Plowman,* and Harley lyrics such as "Annot and John."

W. A. DAVENPORT
Royal Holloway, University of London

•

EILEEN A. JOY and MYRA SEAMAN, eds. *Postmedieval: A Journal of Medieval Cultural Studies.* Vol 1.1/2 (Spring/Summer 2010): "When Did We Become Post/human?" ed. Eileen A. Joy and Craig Dionne. New York: Palgrave Macmillan. Pp. 289.

It is a sign of a discipline's good health that it is not only generating, at accelerating speed, a raft of high-quality monographs and essay collections, but that it has also spawned a new, strongly credentialized journal that aims not only to add to the store of knowledge but to reflect on the field's critical directions, and to foster its participation in debates beyond its disciplinary borders. *Postmedieval: A Journal of Medieval Cultural Studies* is just such a journal. Of course, it is not the only journal devoted to medievalism, which has long been served by *Studies in Medievalism* and *The Year's Work in Medievalism,* the major strength of which has been their showcasing over many years of significant and diverse case studies of the postmedieval afterlife of the Middle Ages. More recently, these have been joined by *Medievally Speaking,* which reviews texts relating to medievalism. *Postmedieval* complements these journals by taking a more avowedly theoretical angle that aims, as its website (www.palgrave-journals.com/pmed/) states, to "bring the medieval and modern into productive critical relation."

Postmedieval enters the scene with a hefty double issue, "When Did We Become Post/human?" It comprises twenty-nine short essays, three brief response essays, and a review essay. The journal's interest in multitemporality is announced in the evocative cover photograph of Birmingham's built environment in which the futuristic exterior of Selfridges department store is shadowed by the nearby neo-Gothic spire of the church of St. Martin in the Bullring, which was itself built over a demolished thirteenth-century forerunner. "When Did We Become Post/human?" offers a series of medievalist engagements with the critical dismantling of the liberal humanist subject, but it also reflects the journal's stated interest in those "deep historical structures—mental, linguistic, social, cultural, aesthetic, religious, political, sexual, and the like—that underlie contemporary thought and life."

It is only possible here to offer a sketch of the many angles from which the essays in this collection interrogate the complexity, and the instability, of medieval and early modern formulations of the "the human." Among the categories that these essays argue have placed pressure on premodern perceptions of human subjectivity are the animal (Scott Maisano and Karl Steel), the mineral (Jeffrey Jerome Cohen), the ecological (John Moreland), the dead (Bettina Bildhauer), waste (Susan Signe Morrison), the disabled (Julie Singer), and prehistoric humanity (Daniel Lord Smail). A number of authors (E. R. Truitt and Scott Lightsey, just to name two) speak to questions of unique human volition and morality, or to questions of human embodiment (among these are Jen Boyle, Karmen McKendrick, and David Gary Shaw), while others, such as Ruth Evans, offer arguments for how medieval practices created "cyborg" relations in which the architecture of the human mind was altered by its interaction with what can be regarded as assistive technologies. These essays unite in challenging the idea that notions of "posthumanism" must always point toward futurity—to emerging biotechnologies, cybernetic and information cultures, and so on. In offering a panoramic historical corrective to this assumption, *Postmedieval*'s inaugural issue responds to the journal's fundamental brief of "demonstrat[ing] the important value of medieval studies . . . to the ongoing development of contemporary critical and cultural theories that remain under-historicized."

One occasionally encounters what seems like a certain belatedness of critical idiom in some of the essays, in that the theoretical vocabulary and some of the key works being addressed (Avital Ronell's *Telephone Book,* Bruno Latour's *We Have Never Been Modern,* Katherine Hayles's *How We Became Posthuman,* as well as Deleuze and Guattari in translation) arguably enjoyed their greatest currency within the Anglophone academy some years back. But to criticize these essays on this basis would be ungenerous, and would miss one of the central points of this collection, which is, as mentioned above, that the conversation on posthumanism has been going on for too many years without the historical disciplines being invited to contribute, and thus without the enriching dimension that an analysis of "premodern posthumanism" can bring to our understanding of the parameters of what has constituted the "human" across time. To signal their revisitation of the question of the posthuman, these essays have necessarily taken up the familiar terminology found in conversations conducted in other fields. Where this terminology is brought into direct contact with sensitive and original interpretations of medieval and early modern sources, the results are compelling. It is here, armed with the more traditional skills of their scholarly training, that the authors of the essays in *Postmedieval* offer solid proof that the interrogation of the parameters of the category "human" has an undeniable and multifaceted long history.

That this is a long overdue intervention is conveyed by the very large number of essays included in this volume. The decision to include so many contributions runs the risk of overwhelming the reader; but this is offset somewhat by the use of the short essay, which is a good format for offering a snapshot to orient the reader and suggest future areas for investigation. It is not an easy format for scholars accustomed to the more expansive format of the long essay, but the essays here are, on the whole, characterized by a careful balance between general comments that signal the potential of their area of study and well-chosen moments of close analysis. Some contributions, such as the final essay, "Continuous R(E)volutions: Thermodynamic Processes, Analog Hybridizations, Transversal Becomings, and the Post-human" by "zooz" (Bryan Reynolds and James Intriligator), which argues "in the spirit of transversal poetics" (235) and "Individuation: This Stupidity" by Nicola Masciandaro, which uses some of the techniques of ficto-criticism, could be jarring for readers more comfortable with the academic essay form. But in a collection of this size that pits itself against modes of academic exclusion, it would be stranger *not* to encounter stylistic and methodological experimentation.

The theoretical unanimity that occasionally threatens this collection is diffused by the inclusion of a forceful dissenting perspective. Crystal Bartolovich's "Is the Posthuman the Post in Postmedieval?" cautions against the social and political dangers of too readily dispensing with periodization and the category of the human, a sentiment that is echoed in Kate Soper's response essay. Soper's is one of three excellent response essays—the others are by Andy Mousley and N. Katherine Hayles—that round out the collection, drawing out the implications, benefits, and potential pitfalls of the research undertaken through the preceding essays. Their quite different, but equally thoughtful, summaries give premodern and early modern scholars much to chew over for their future forays into posthuman studies.

For an issue dedicated to the contestation of exclusions, it is difficult not to notice the fact that extremely few of the contributions come from scholars outside the North American academy, and those that do are all from Britain. One of the most welcome elements of medieval cultural studies over the past decade is the number of scholars from non-transatlantic and non-northern hemisphere contexts whose work has attended specifically to the journal's remit of highlighting "the question of the relation of the medieval to the modern (and vice versa) in different times and places," so one might have expected to see this reflected in the issue's range of contributors. To take just one example, the valid point raised in Smail's essay on medieval studies' tension with Deep Historical perspectives—what can be called its antiquarian competition with prehistoric archaeology—has been discussed by scholars working on the discipline's unfolding in colonial environments, who could have added an international perspective. Looking ahead to forthcoming issues of *Postmedieval,* however, which offer a broader representation of the field's global reach, this potential for a closed loop of exchange appears to have been short-circuited early. This is important, because the expansion, and thus lasting health, of any area of inquiry depends on not having its vital questions posed and answered by the same people. To that end, its suggestive short-essay format ensures that the inaugural issue of *Postmedieval* offers an array of leads that other scholars working across the medieval period and in different academic contexts can take up in distinctive ways. *Postmedieval* is an energizing new addition to the adjacent fields of medieval and medievalism studies, and it will be fascinating to follow its development.

LOUISE D'ARCENS
University of Wollongong

KATHRYN KERBY-FULTON, ed. *Women and the Divine in Literature Before 1700: Essays in Memory of Margot Louis.* Victoria: ELS Editions, 2010. Pp. xi, 279. $30.00 paper.

Although I did not have the privilege of knowing Margot Louis, the contributors to this collection of essays present her as a woman of keen intellect, wide learning, and great pedagogical skill. This volume is therefore a fitting memorial, because every contribution is of exceptional quality and the territory the essays cover is large indeed. In spite of this wide scope, the essays speak intelligently to one another and the collection coheres quite well.

In her introductory essay, Kathryn Kerby-Fulton tackles two "interconnected problems" central to studying medieval female spirituality: the problem of male scribal filtering of female religious experience, and the problem of understanding how medieval people felt about visionary experiences. She makes a compelling case for the complexity of medieval attitudes toward visionary experiences. Because of the seriousness with which visions and their *probatio* were taken, male scribes relating the lives of visionary women faced daunting choices. Kerby-Fulton analyzes ways in which male scribes accordingly muted the voices of Saint Perpetua and Christina of Markyate to overcome doubts about visions. In contrast, she argues that the Benedictine and English Cardinal Adam Easton, who wrote the *Defensorium Sanctae Birgittae* for Saint Birgitta's canonization process, sees the saint's visions as "theological problems to be solved" (15), and he finds the solutions in scholastic philosophy.

In her contribution, Linda Olson first examines the portrayal of Monica in Saint Augustine's own writings, noting that "the mother he presents is not perfect" (21). Olson then turns to medieval writers' and artists' representations of Monica. She considers the interest in Monica's weeping and prayers for her son, and she discusses the frequency of Monica's appearance in the visual tradition associated with Augustinian hermit friars. She also examines visual depictions of Monica's prophetic dream as well as textual treatments of Monica that emphasize her wisdom and ability to interpret this revelation.

Thea Todd also concerns herself with the ways in which a holy woman is presented textually. She argues that the anonymous St. Albans monk who wrote or redacted Christina of Markyate's *Life* interpreted Christina's struggles with her family concerning her marriage and her private vow of virginity (events that occurred between about 1115 and 1118) in light of "much later developments of ecclesiastical thought on marriage" (49). Christina's *Life* was composed during the 1140s, and Todd argues that Gratian's *Decretum,* produced around the same time, established ecclesiastical views on the necessity of the woman's consent in marriage, and on ecclesiastical control of marriage, that shape the *Life*'s presentation of these key events in Christina's career as a holy woman.

Julianne Bruneau's contribution centers on a fascinating, sophisticated close reading of Alan of Lille's wordplay in *De planctu naturae*. In particular, she focuses on the poem's well-known concerns with sexual deviations and grammatical errors. Bruneau argues that "linguistic and sexual intercourse are of equal importance to the literal and metaphorical work of the text and reflect multiple aims" (66). Alan's wordplay is a vehicle for wrestling with the "problem of marrying truth and expression" (83) and it is in a sense performative, since *De planctu* demonstrates the "use of poetry to express philosophy" (66).

Adrienne Williams Boyarin also considers, in a sense, the work that words do and the ways in which they do it. Her essay treats the motif of feminine flesh as text in the life of Saint Margaret that composes part of the Katherine Group. She argues that Saint Margaret's body in this version of her life is neither wholly physical nor entirely spiritual. Instead, "it sits somewhere in between, as a textual body" (87). In particular, Saint Margaret's body becomes first a legal text authorized by Christ, then a book, and finally a relic. These categories, though, are not fully stable; the boundaries demarcating them are porous.

Maidie Hilmo again picks up the theme of the visual representations of female spirituality. Her contribution examines the visual depictions of the Prioress and the Second Nun in the Ellesmere manuscript and in Caxton's 1483 *Canterbury Tales*. She compares the Ellesmere illustration of the Prioress to the illustrated analogue of *The Prioress's Tale* in the Vernon manuscript, and she compares the Ellesmere depiction of the Second Nun to the illustrations of Saint Cecilia's life on the Uffizi altarpiece and in an illuminated Carmelite missal (British Library MS Additional 29704–29705). Her argument focuses on the ways in which illustrations of the *Canterbury Tales* effect a shift "from narrative to narrator," so affecting the reading process (108).

Heather Reid undertakes a comparative reading of a relatively little studied Middle English text, *The Storie of Asneth*. The late twelfth-century Hellenic Jewish text *Asneth,* which recounts the events surrounding the marriage of Potiphar's daughter to Joseph the Patriarch, was translated from Greek into Latin, probably at Canterbury. Then, an early fifteenth-century aristocratic woman commissioned a vernacular translation. Reid explores the resonances of this Middle English text with female initiation rites in antiquity, particularly in Greek mythology. She then considers the ways in which medieval female monastic profession, as well as female mystical experiences, resonates with antique female initiation rites as well as with *Asneth*.

Johanne Paquette's contribution undertakes an original, highly informative analysis of a male reader's annotations of *The Book of Margery Kempe,* focusing on "the red-ink annotator's effort to prepare the text for his readers" (155). Paquette views the *Book* as a tool that the Carthusians may have used to minister to the emerging mercantile class. The annotations correspondingly seek to guide the reader to an understanding of "Margery as a mirror reflecting divine grace" (159), even as the annotator steers readers away from potentially alarming interpretations.

Jonathan Juilfs's contribution treats Margery Kempe's contemporary and interlocutor Julian of Norwich's *A Revelation of Love*. Like Paquette, Juilfs is not interested primarily in the text produced by the later medieval holy woman, but rather in the textual history of the holy woman's work. He examines the ways in which Julian's Long Text is "packaged" in the *Norton Anthology of English Literature,* 1993 edition (the first edition of the Norton in which the *Revelation* appeared). He argues that the editorial concerns revealed by the packaging mirror "the same kinds of editorial concerns that much earlier 'packagers' . . . share" (173). In particular, Juilfs discusses "packaging" evident in the versions of the

Revelation included in the Amherst manuscript and in the Westminster manuscript. He then turns his attention to Serenus Cressy's 1670 printed edition, exploring Cressy's efforts to "monasticize" Julian and his assertions of Julian's simplicity as aspects of Cressy's efforts to control the text's reception.

Jennifer Morrish's tripartite contribution first presents the life and career of Susanna Elisabeth Prasch, considering in particular the role she played in the creation of her husband's neo-Latin novel *Psyche Cretica*. The second and third sections examine the genre of the neo-Latin novel, recount the plot and themes of *Psyche Cretica,* and present an analysis of its female characters. Morrish argues that these female characters "demonstrate the rational, social, and loving nature of human beings" (201).

The collection closes with Rosalynn Voaden's epilogue, "A Catena of Women." The brief, meditative piece considers Margot Louis as a link in a chain of female scholars and argues for the importance of thinking about the ways in which medieval holy women were "helped, supported, and inspired by other women" (203). The epilogue is a fitting way to draw the volume to a close, since the essays themselves form such a fascinating, well-crafted catena of arguments.

Nancy Bradley Warren
Texas A & M University

Lee Patterson. *Temporal Circumstances: Form and History in the "Canterbury Tales."* New York: Palgrave, 2006. Pp. xi, 288. $80.00.

Lee Patterson. *Acts of Recognition: Essays on Medieval Culture.* Notre Dame: University of Notre Dame Press, 2010. Pp. xii, 356. $38.00 paper.

Lee Patterson has written some of the very best Chaucer criticism of the past generation, a fact that whets our appetite for these two collections of essays. *Acts of Recognition* and *Temporal Circumstances* consist almost entirely of previously published material, with the exception of a chapter on *Troilus and Criseyde* in *Acts of Recognition* and the introduction to *Temporal Circumstances*. Part memoir and part manifesto, this introduction details Patterson's thoughts on "Historicism and Postmodernism," somewhat revising the opinions he formulated in "On the Margin: Postmodernism, Ironic History, and Medieval Studies" (*Speculum* 65 [1990]: 87–108). The first of these two collections, *Temporal Circumstances,* reprints the Matthews Lectures on the Wife of Bath, which Patterson gave at Birkbeck College, London, as the first two chapters; there are two essays originally published in *SAC*: one on Chaucer's tales of *Thopas* and *Melibee,* the other on *The Canon's Yeoman's Tale*; these appear alongside his well-known *Speculum* essay on *The Pardoner's Tale,* an essay from *JMEMS* on *The Prioress's Tale,* and an essay on *The Clerk's Tale* originally published in a festschrift for Elizabeth Kirk. The more recent volume, *Acts of Recognition,* offers no introduction or contextualization for its collection of more eclectic materials. Here Patterson reprints an often-cited chapter of *Negotiating the Past* on Historical Criticism and its relation to Exegetics; a pedagogy essay first published in *Exemplaria*; two essays on Hoccleve, one of which first appeared in *SAC*; essays on Lydgate, Clanvowe, Chaucer and the complaint, the gaze, the heroic laconic style, and, finally, an essay on Franciscanism and the natural world. Most of these essays originally appeared in collections of one kind or another. Space does not permit me to summarize these eighteen chapters, nor to give each its due attention, but it is possible to provide an assessment of the cumulative weight of these materials.

Temporal Circumstances's introduction situates the historicism Patterson has consistently practiced in a long history of Chaucerian interpretation. Such command of the field is one of Patterson's strengths as a scholar, and it makes reading his books a pleasure. His prose is striking and his argument engaging. But his version of history can also be a source of frustration for its willful and at times stubborn prejudices (a mounting animosity to feminism, psychoanalysis, and most poststructuralist thinking—even that from which he benefits). Thankfully, and somewhat self-consciously, Patterson makes these prejudices clear by laying out the lines of his thought. His definition of the historicism to which he adheres is nicely put in his pedagogy essay from *Acts of Recognition*: "Historicism wants to understand nothing less than what Chaucer meant when he wrote his poems, what the poems meant to the society within which they circulated, and—at a higher level of abstraction— how the poems connect not just to the self-aware intentions of the poet and the explicit expectations of his audience but to larger patterns of social practice and ideology" ("Disenchanted Classroom," 46). Such articulation makes Patterson's reliance on empiricism and his often positivistic proclivities clear; not that there's anything wrong with that. But he is also far less patient with critics who are after different textual effects: "for the new-fangled multiculturalist or feminist or queer theorist or postcolonialist, [art] is valuable because it provides a privileged vehicle for the appreciation of culturally determined identities" (*Temporal Circumstances,* 8). Thus while he calls for a most sophisticated and subtle form of historicism, he positions everything else as simpleminded and mere fashion.

One might be tempted to read *Temporal Circumstances* as a continuation of *Chaucer and the Subject of History* (1991), surely Patterson's best and most influential book. *Subject of History* set an entire generation of scholars to a historicist and self-consciously political mode of reading Chaucer. *Temporal Circumstances* takes up the ways Chaucer's poetry engages with history—even when his poetry tries to disengage itself from its historical entanglements, such as may be claimed for *Troilus and Criseyde*. Much of the new book concerns tales not treated in *Subject of History*. And as in that former volume, Patterson is at his best when talking about the details of a literary text, rather than the historical documents that subtend his arguments or the Marxist theory that underwrites his attention to material culture. While both books contain lengthy chapters on the Wife and the Pardoner, *Temporal Circumstances* picks up, as it were, where the other left off, treating tales from the Clerk's to the Canon's Yeoman's. By way of its extended treatment of the *Tales, Temporal Circumstances* does complete *Subject of History*.

And yet, the chapters covering an overlapping duo of tales in these two books—one on the Wife and one on the Pardoner—tell an interesting story of revision and refocusing. Indeed another way of looking at the essays collected in *Temporal Circumstances* would be to see them as a reissuing of those arguments that Patterson feels have been neglected, especially his Birkbeck College lectures and the antipsychoanalysis rant wedged into the pages of *Speculum*. One understands the desire to have the Birkbeck lectures better circulated perhaps, but the rest of the book is quite easily accessible. *Speculum, JMEMS,* and now *SAC* are all available full-text online from various databases. The chapter on *The Clerk's Tale* was produced simultaneously with *Temporal Circumstances* in the aforementioned Kirk festschrift also published by Palgrave (*Mindful Spirits in Late Medieval Literature* [2006]), which raises questions about its reprinting here. On a generous reading of the situation, that simultaneous publication argues that the *Clerk's Tale* chapter works to make

Temporal Circumstances a "real" book. The chapter lends some chronological cohesion to Patterson's study of the *Canterbury Tales* and thus it "needed" to be here.

When other circumstances urge us to consider (and forgive) the temporal location of the original essays, we might wonder at the arrangement of these essays. The chapters in *Temporal Circumstances* do not follow the chronological order of their making (thus they trace no development in Patterson's historicist practices or his more abstract musings on the nature of historicism) but instead roughly trace the order of the Ellesmere manuscript: Wife of Bath, Clerk, Pardoner, *Thopas,* Prioress, Canon's Yeoman. Patterson's quiet reliance on the Ellesmere order (discussed explicitly as his means of organization in *Subject of History,* 41–45) implies a continuity of argument about, or at least a treatment of, these later Canterbury stories and silently dispenses with any problems of the historicity of the essays/chapters themselves, their location in critical temporal circumstances. But as anyone who reads Chaucer in the editions that follow Ellesmere (and that would be most of them) knows, the Pardoner is sorely out of place in this order. Patterson has moved the Pardoner forward (he should follow the Prioress) to occupy the center of his book, in an essay that shows Patterson at his most rebarbative. He calls this essay "the most controversial part of this book" (*Temporal Circumstances,* 36), but it is also the one many have decided out of politeness to ignore. (For a cogent, and quite generous, rebuttal to Patterson, see Mark Miller's *Philosophical Chaucer* [2005]: 141–44.) In toto, while continuing a line of historical interpretation begun in *Subject of History, Temporal Circumstances* does not work as well as that earlier book in offering a coherent reading of the *Canterbury Tales*.

Alternately, *Acts of Recognition* offers us Patterson's non-Canterbury, often non-Chaucerian, essays. A preface acknowledges the volume's noncohesive state. While its opening chapter from *Negotiating the Past* (Wisconsin, 1987) appears because that book is now out of print and the essay widely cited, the others are more of a hodge-podge. Speaking so much of history and the contours of the critical field as he does, Patterson prompts us to ask about the politics of republication, and in particular the temporal arrest of critical discussion that comes with this territory. What does the book propose to offer us in 2010–11, both in terms of its ongoing usefulness and its representation of the history of scholarship? These are, for the most part, essays situated in their critical day, even though we are being asked to read them as a book in the now.

This is where such collections hope to have it both ways, demanding some patience at being merely a set of reprints (and offering minimal-to-no updating of bibliography or resituating of argument) and simultaneously wanting our time and money. Collecting and reprinting pretends to be about accessibility, but I think it is both more and less than that. Such volumes ask for us to read essays in their original contexts but to use them now, a practice that leads all too easily into slighting what was written in the interim.

These final comments provoke me to more general concerns about reprinting and republication than I can lay at Patterson's feet, even though it is the second of his volumes (as well as its very secondness) that leads me to this point. This is a new trend in self-festschriftizing that we see with academic presses and their shrinking medieval lists. Patterson's *Recognitions* is not the only "retirement book" out there, nor is it likely to be the last. I find this trend disturbing for the pressure it exerts (and reflects) in the larger academic market. Patterson belongs to a generation of critics who did not have to write a monograph for tenure, and one wonders why he feels impelled to retire with half his output freshly anthologized, effectively doubling the number of book titles under his signature. If this urge can be explained as an expression of human vanity, it is harder to justify institutionally. Why do presses cooperate with this impulse? Adding an important name to a list is understandable from a short-term perspective. But it is a poor investment in the future. We could expect presses like Notre Dame to take chances on new authors in the field. Younger scholars would be likely to have learned from, and be ready to build upon, the foundations for the historical study of Chaucer and his medieval culture that Patterson himself laid.

ELIZABETH SCALA
University of Texas at Austin

CURTIS PERRY and JOHN WATKINS, eds. *Shakespeare and the Middle Ages.* Oxford: Oxford University Press, 2009. Pp. xiv, 295. £56.00; $99.00.

Writing twenty years ago, Brian Stock argued that "the Renaissance invented the Middle Ages in order to define itself" (*Listening for the Text*

[1990], 69). *Shakespeare and the Middle Ages* is predicated on two related premises: that Shakespeare invented the Middle Ages, and that he was invented by the Middle Ages. Moreover, since Shakespeare "has become a frequent stand in for the modernity of the early modern" (5), the volume seeks to approach broader questions about early modern modernity and interrogate critical narratives about the relationship of the medieval to the early modern. As such, *Shakespeare and the Middle Ages* contributes to a growing body of recent collections that seek to refigure accepted period designations.

Drawing together the work of a multidisciplinary group of scholars, the collection is arranged in three parts. The first, "Texts in Transition," which includes essays by Sarah Beckwith, Elizabeth Fowler, John Watkins, and Christopher Warley, questions narratives about the transition from the medieval to the early modern as a shift from feudalism to capitalism, Catholicism to Protestantism, and dynastic to national identity. While at least one of the aims of this section is to dismantle some aspects of the sharp division between the medieval and the early modern, "the historiographic attractions of a rigid opposition," (13) though playfully explored, are not always so successfully resisted. For instance, in his essay "Shakespeare's Fickle Fee-Simple: *A Lover's Complaint,* Nostalgia, and the Transition from Feudalism to Capitalism," Warley argues that by combining the genre of the female complaint with the language of feudalism, *A Lover's Complaint* participates in the creation of a new, commodified system of social interaction. However, by ignoring medieval texts, like *Piers Plowman,* which similarly contribute to the emergence of commodification through a longing for originary value, his essay ultimately confirms rather than challenges conventional wisdom about periodization.

The second section, "Medievalism in Shakespearean England," which features essays by Patrick Cheney, William Kuskin, Brian Walsh, and Curtis Perry, is concerned with the potency of the medieval past as an early modern construct. Here, attempts to challenge the linear progression from the medieval to the early modern are perhaps more successful, and nowhere more so than in Kuskin's subtle work titled "Recursive Origins: Print History and Shakespeare's *2 Henry VI.*" Resisting the kind of critical work that reads Chaucer as the dawn-star of the Renaissance, Kuskin recuperates such fifteenth-century authors as Lydgate, Malory, Skelton, and Caxton as powerful precedents for sixteenth-century literature. And, by attending to the ways that Shakespeare's first printed play, *The First Part of the Contention Betwixt the Two Famous Houses of York and Lancaster* (1594), both appropriates and subordinates the fifteenth century, he presents the compelling argument that Shakespeare's innovation is better understood as a process of "repeated return" (129).

The three essays by Michael O'Connell, Karen Sawyer Marsalek, and Rebecca Krug that make up the final section, "Shakespeare and the Resources of Medieval Culture," similarly argue against Shakespeare's unique genius, here by tracing the continuities between various medieval traditions (morality plays, mystery plays, and religious exemplum) and his plays. In attending to the recurrence of motifs (the summons of death, the resurrection of the Antichrist, the debate between the four daughters of God, the bond story, and the casket story) across the medieval/early modern divide, these essays are concerned more with tracing patterns than they are with identifying sources. In the case of O'Connell's essay, "*King Lear* and the Summons of Death," this leads to the useful conclusion that medieval drama is more properly adjacent than anterior to early modern theater. But elsewhere, as in Sawyer Marsalek's reading of the resurrected Falstaff in *1 Henry IV* as a type of Antichrist, the lack of historical specificity can make some of the arguments in this section seem forced.

While the collection's broad aim to interrogate critical narratives about the Otherness of the medieval past might not be as groundbreaking as the editors would have us believe (and dutiful references to articles by Lee Patterson and David Aers point to the fact that these lines of inquiry are at least twenty years old), one of this book's strengths lies in the range of perspectives offered from across the confessional spectrum, with energetic contributions from medievalists, early modernists, and scholars working in both fields. Unlike a literary history, a collection of essays will never offer a smooth, conjoined narrative, but in many ways this lack of joined-up thinking is one of this collection's virtues. As Kuskin argues, "Texts do not emerge simply by linear means, and so a literary history premised on linearity, however modified by notions of reform or revolution, fails to capture the essentially self-referential nature of literary reproduction" (129–30). Individually then, the essays in this collection challenge the reader to reassess Shakespeare's relationship to the Middle Ages and to look again at specific moments of continuity and discontinuity between the medieval and the early modern. However, all too often, potentially fruitful interactions between essays are overlooked and the collection never quite becomes a real conversation. How, for instance, might Kuskin's ideas about "recursive origins" refine Brian Walsh's sense of the Reformation, the advent of the printing press, and the dawn of professional theater as "developments that undeniably mark major breaks from the world of the early fifteenth century" (152)? For Walsh, as for other contributors to this collection, the medieval past is very much a foreign country, and so, despite the editors' enticing claim that Shakespeare is as much the creation as creator of the Middle Ages, when taken as a whole this collection more readily subscribes to, rather than problematizes, well-worn arguments about Shakespeare and the emergence of modernity.

TAMARA ATKIN
Queen Mary, University of London

HELEN PHILLIPS, ed. *Chaucer and Religion*. Cambridge: D. S. Brewer, 2010. Pp. xix, 216. £55.00; $95.00.

An understanding of how Chaucer the man related to the religious culture of his day is something we are never likely to attain: his personal stance in this area seems beyond reach. The title of this book therefore proves to be something of a tease. That Chaucer was born into a culture routinely aware of and alive to the pulse of Christian tradition and its obligations is self-evident, and Helen Cooper, in a masterly overview of the topic and introduction to the essays that follow, makes a similar point. So what remains if the ostensible topic of the book is in fact elusive? What we have here is largely a series of individual approaches to different aspects of late medieval Christianity and piety as these are refracted in Chaucer's poetry.

While each study in *Chaucer and Religion* is coherent within its own terms, cumulatively the essays seem nevertheless to amount to an eclectic mix. The final impression conveyed by the volume is that its insights—and there are many for which to be grateful—arise locally but are not orchestrated as an integrated ensemble. This being so, they too give the lie to the book's title to the extent that this may be taken to suggest that the promised account of Chaucer and religion will be a fully coordinated one. Thus, since the volume has no overarching argument, little injustice will be done to it by listing its contributions serially here, although limitations on space necessarily mean that some will unjustly receive too short a shrift.

Alcuin Blamires considers the topic of love, marriage, sex, and gender in Chaucer's writing, and restores to our present-day comprehension of these things an awareness of the values with which they came freighted in the later fourteenth century. This is a useful essay and impeccably informed. Like a number of others in the volume, its scope is broad, its examples selected from anywhere within the Chaucerian corpus. Unfortunately, the next essay, by Graham D. Caie, does not sustain the initial promise and interest of Blamires. Caie writes on the topic of Chaucer and the Bible, rehearsing conventional knowledge about the currency of biblical versions in Chaucer's day. When he cites the essay that follows his own, that by Frances M. McCormack on the subject of Chaucer and Lollardy, it appears that he has not actually read it closely, for contrary to Caie (25), there *is* evidence that Chaucer knew the Wycliffite Bible translation, nor is McCormack unaware of it (37). Her own essay, well informed though very brief, leaves the reader wanting to hear more on this important topic. Stephen Knight comes next with the first of two chapters that he has contributed, this one on Chaucer's treatment of the Church and churls, while Anthony Bale follows with an account of what the terms "Jew" and "Muslim" meant within the *Canterbury Tales*.

Like Knight, the editor of the volume, Helen Phillips, has also contributed two chapters, and both show a critic working at the height of her powers. The first considers the "matter" of Chaucer, his thematic preoccupations and their intersections with Christianity. It ranges effortlessly in search of supporting examples throughout the oeuvre. Next, Sherry Reames writes well on the cult of the saints in Chaucer, and shows him to have resisted the tendency of the hagiographic genre to simplify complex moral and theological issues. Carl Phelpstead treats questions of death and judgment in Chaucer, and is followed by Laurel Broughton, who adds further thoughts on the topic of Chaucer and the saints. Dee Dyas writes on medieval notions of pilgrimage. In his second chapter for the volume, Stephen Knight illustrates what he perceives to be a complex tension in Chaucer's dream poems between the predominantly classical and secular domain of their subject matter and an offstage Christian voice that repeatedly questions that subject matter. The second chapter of Helen Phillips concludes the series of studies proper, and is as impressive as was her first. This time her concern is how morality is constructed in a number of Chaucer's works, generally concluding that he located moral certainties beyond this world's grasp.

The declared aim of the series in which the volume has appeared is that some space should be devoted to a consideration of pedagogical issues. Four essays of this sort complete the volume. The first is by Roger Dalrymple, who usefully illustrates the benefits of an inquiry-based learning approach to the study of Chaucer in the classroom. D. Thomas Hanks follows with some considerations on how to address profitably the challenge posed by students' lack of familiarity with the Christian tradition and the negative impact of this upon their understanding of Chaucer. David Raybin reflects on his experience teaching teachers about Chaucer, and the last essay, by Gillian Rudd, offers her thoughts on teaching Chaucer and religion in the context of *The Nun's Priest's Tale* and *The Man of Law's Tale*.

Even the all-too-brief account provided in this review ought to be sufficient to alert readers to what they might in reality expect from this volume. It is about Chaucer and religion in a somewhat uncoordinated and scattered fashion. For the most part worthwhile, and also in a number of places powerfully compelling (for this reviewer, Blamires, Cooper, and Phillips were egregious), it nevertheless leaves us feeling that the book that the title seems to promise remains yet to be written. Perhaps many of the essays contained here will constitute indispensable reading when some future author lifts the pen to attempt precisely that.

ALAN J. FLETCHER
University College Dublin

S. H. RIGBY. *Wisdom and Chivalry: Chaucer's Knight's Tale and Medieval Political Theory.* Leiden: Brill, 2009. Pp. xvi, 329. €119.00; $169.00.

Wisdom and Chivalry is a deeply researched and closely argued piece of historical criticism. Stephen Rigby chooses as his analytical tool for *The Knight's Tale* Giles of Rome's *De Regimine Principum,* a mirror for princes composed circa 1280 for the future Philip IV of France. Giles, a student of Aquinas, synthesizes the political/religious ideas of his—and Chaucer's—day with respect to the personal and public qualities a ruler ought to possess, and demonstrate. The *De Regimine,* which shows the influence of Aristotle and Plato, Cicero and Seneca, survives in some 350 manuscripts, mostly Latin, some vernacular. John Trevisa translated it into English; Thomas of Gloucester, Richard II's uncle, possessed a Latin copy. It is, then, an appropriate touchstone for a study of this sort. Indeed, a reader/listener who had internalized Giles's ideas might well find that "in idealizing Duke Theseus . . . *The Knight's Tale* seeks to offer a confirmation of the 'dominant' ideology of late medieval England" (285) and that "Duke Theseus embodies the virtue which political theorists demanded a ruler should possess as an individual, as the head of a household, and as a sovereign ruler" (276).

Rigby structures his analysis in terms of this tripartite division: Part I ("Ethics: The Good Rule of the Self") deals with Theseus's personal ethics; Part II ("Economics and Politics: The Good Rule of Others") shows these personal ethics in public action; Part III ("The First Mover and the Good Rule of the Cosmos") views Theseus's rule of self and others in the wider context of Jupiter's/the Christian God's dominion over the universe.

Rigby, then, evaluates Theseus's conduct from the microcosmic-personal to the macrocosmic-universal. There is no ambiguity here. By every measure, and in all circumstances, Theseus comports himself as Giles, and political theorists roughly contemporary with Chaucer—Dante, Boccaccio, John Gower—think an ideal ruler should. We learn, for example, that the duke had every right to send Palamon and Arcite to prison *forte et dure* and set the "pilours" on the fallen Thebans; he had shown his banner on the march against Creon, and this gesture counted to Chaucer's contemporaries not only as a formal declaration of war but also as an indication that little, or no, quarter need be expected. Later we discover that Saturn, whose intervention concludes the strife in heaven, can be understood as representing the wisdom of old age. We are also told that Theseus's First Mover lecture is informed not only by Boethius but by current ideas of the Christian God's control of the universe and everything in it. There are numerous such interpretations, all positive; Rigby consistently sees the duke's actions as ideal and exemplary. But this need not necessarily be so, even for a reader steeped in the *De Regimine*.

A Gilesian reader might recognize Theseus's right to conduct himself as he does on the Theban battlefield, but yet question the charity of his so doing. Given the dynamics of the poem, such a reader might well find it odd that Jupiter, who attempts to resolve the contention in heaven—"Juppiter was bisy it to stente" (2442)—signally fails. If our Gilesian could trace the semantic range of "bisy" and "stente," he would find, perhaps, the terms suggesting that Jupiter worked for a solution over a significant period of time and became worried and distressed when he did not succeed. Saturn's malevolent self-characterization embodies the worst violence depicted on the walls of the temples of Mars, Venus, and Diana. Our Gilesian reader might find an *in bono* interpretation here a very large order indeed, and discover little in the text to warrant an assertion that "the agency of Saturn, in resolving the conflict between Mars and Venus, can actually be seen as an instrument of Jupiter's power" (269). Again, our Gilesian might recall Saturn's activity when Theseus runs his First Mover speech, and might agree that Jupiter is usually a positive and all-powerful deity, but might be moved to offer the caveat: not in *The Knight's Tale*. Finally, our Gilesian might wonder about Theseus's preparations for Arcite's funeral, which entail the destruction of the grove—for the second time, the grove having been razed previously for the amphitheater—and the displacement of its terrified inhabitants, the "nymphes, fawnes and amadrides" who dwelt in this little space "in reste and peace" (2928, 2927).

Rigby's is not a source study, but he does refer often to Boccaccio's *Teseida*. It is fair to mention, then, that the first two instances I note above—Palamon and Arcite doing hard time, and the intervention of Saturn—are changes Chaucer introduces to his source. What would our Gilesian reader make of the fact, were he able to know it, that Teseo treats his prisoners reasonably well and sends in the medics to tend to the fallen Thebans; he, and we, already know what Theseus in fact does. And what is our Gilesian to understand of the Saturn business? This displacement of heavenly authority and the strife that is a part of it are not of course recognized by the "human" inhabitants of the artistic frame, surely not by Duke Theseus, Jupiter's human reflection. But we, the readers, see it.

Rigby's study shines an intensely bright but narrowly focused beam on *The Knight's Tale*. In terms of one of the author's declared purposes, the book is successful: a reader who accepts Giles's political theology might read the poem as Rigby suggests. But, then again, he or she would be missing just those things that speak to doubts rather than certitudes. I am not convinced that the monograph provides a rejoinder to those who see one of the prime functions of this piece of literary art as asking questions rather than providing answers.

Finally, I am distressed by the number of typesetting errors in the book. They range from dropped commas, to dropped or added words, inverted phrases, footnotes that occasionally send the reader to "note 000 above" (19 n. 68; 200 n. 143), and to this curiosity: "the mastery of Thebes by Athens is equated with the rightful victory of vice over virtue . . ." (197). Rigby's arguments and the scholarship he deploys to explicate and defend them—to say nothing of the book's price—deserve a cleaner text.

ROBERT EMMETT FINNEGAN
The University of Manitoba

WILLIAM T. ROSSITER. *Chaucer and Petrarch*. Cambridge: D. S. Brewer, 2010. Pp. xi, 235. £50.00; $95.00.

Assessment of Chaucer's reception of Petrarch has always pivoted about the question of how well the English poet knew the Italian poet's vernacular and Latin works. Chaucer translated one sonnet from the *Canzoniere*: "S'amor non è" (*RFV* 132). Did he encounter the poem alone, or did he read it in a florilegium? If the latter, was it in a gathering of various works by mixed, probably unnamed writers, or a version of the *Rerum vulgarium fragmenta*? In either case, why did he single out this particular poem? If Chaucer knew other lyrics from Petrarch's cycle, why does he not recall them? Did Chaucer know, or know of, the *Africa,* the unfinished epic about Scipio, for which Petrarch was crowned "lauriat poete"? The only work in prose that Chaucer read was Petrarch's "Griselda," which was part of the third of the four letters to Boccaccio that comprise the seventeenth book of the *Epistolae seniles*. Did Chaucer have the full letter? Was he able to read the other three? Could he have intuited from them the nature and scope of what we have come to call Petrarch's humanist project?

These questions, and others like them, suggest that any account of these poets will want to factor what Chaucer did not know about Petrarch and Italy into what he did. William Rossiter navigates the gaps in Chaucer's (and in our) knowledge by conceptualizing the poets' relations as forms of translation. The plural is important. For Rossiter, translation is both linguistic and cultural; he wants to attend to poetic practice and to the historical concerns that connect and differentiate each man's work. In his introductory chapter, Rossiter therefore rehearses ancient, medieval, and modern theories of inter- and intralingual translation; he argues that, in essence, all ideas about translation are attempts to adjudicate the competing logical, rhetorical, and hermeneutic claims of letter and spirit. Though his survey mostly paraphrases well-known work, and his conclusion is pedestrian, Rossiter is able to assemble the critical principles of the "translative aesthetics" that inform his study. Among these principles are the appropriative force of translation, its multiplicity, and its paraphrastic nature. For Petrarch and Chaucer, translation simultaneously defers to and displaces the authority of its source, blends many sources into "a oneness that is unlike them all," and rejects word for word rendering.

These ideas underwrite Rossiter's imaginative conceit that Chaucer "met" Petrarch, not in person but intertextually, through his experience of Italy and his reading of Dante and Boccaccio. Rossiter positions himself between David Wallace, whose Chaucer readily understood Italy, and me, whose Chaucer found it at once familiar and strange. Rossiter would smile on both of us; I, for one, was disappointed by his paraphrase of my argument, which washes every nuance from it; he simplifies Wallace's position as well. What, then, were the points of contact that Rossiter claims enabled Chaucer to meet and translate Petrarch? Foremost is the Petrarchan voice of exile; the fragmented self who laments the fragmentation of Italy into warring city-states served to configure the English poet's grasp of Italian politics. Rossiter does not explain how Chaucer came to know this voice—are we to suppose he intuited it from the one sonnet he translated? But even if he was aware of it, Chaucer surely measured it against the great exilic voice we know he knew, Dante's. Instead of investigating the intersection and divergences between sightlines—Rossiter discusses "Italia mia" (*RFV* 128) but not "Ahi serva Italia" (*Purg.* 6)—and then comparing Chaucer's own representation of political matters, Rossiter simply juxtaposes common interests. The *Canzoniere* is an accretive work; it mixes and reformulates elements from many traditions. Chaucer would have found the collection congenial, since he was also a poet who worked by accretion. Petrarch and Chaucer both experienced court culture; both decried clerical abuse.

Rossiter is more responsive to the complexities of cross-cultural translation in his next chapter. Here he proposes that Chaucer was able to incorporate the "Canticus Troili" into the *Troilus* without disrupting the narrative because he had adopted, without knowing it, Boccaccio's inversion of various Petrarchan topoi. Rossiter embeds this argument in a distracting discussion about the anxiety of influence. More germane is his reevaluation of Petrarch's knotty response to Dante, and Boccaccio's deference to Petrarch. Rossiter then argues persuasively that Boccaccio did incorporate some of Petrarch's poems into the *Filostrato*—a claim that has been doubted. He concludes by showing that a number of Boccaccio's inversions appear in Chaucer; by replacing the amorous narrator of the *Filostrato* with the love-naif of the *Troilus,* however, Chaucer attempted to remove Boccaccio's voice. The deletion is only partial, but it enabled Chaucer to "inherit potential traces of the 'Petrarchan' voice" (107).

Rossiter then turns to "S'amor non è" and argues that Chaucer's refashioning of it "enacts the reflexive, dynamic 'becoming' of the writer through translation" (110). Following a discussion of the place the poem holds in the *Canzoniere* and the conversation it conducts with Provençal conventions and Dante's "Tutti li miei pensier," Rossiter examines Chaucer's additions and omissions to determine the "legitimate ratio" (112) he created between the sonnet and rhyme-royal stanza. This goal requires preparatory excurses on the origin of each form; Rossiter then argues that Chaucer's expansion of two seven-line blocks (the way the sonnet appears in manuscripts of the *Canzoniere)* into three rhyme-royal stanzas translates Petrarch in the manner Petrarch himself recommended. Through subtraction, concurrence, and supplement, Chaucer makes lyric and narrative companionable and the "Canticus Troili" the first English sonnet.

Rossiter's final chapters are devoted to the tale of Griselda. In the first he considers her progress from Boccaccio to Petrarch. Rossiter's thesis is that the folkloric/mythological motifs that underlie Boccaccio's novella invest it with the semantic potential to be read allegorically. Petrarch certainly read it this way; by realizing its figural possibilities, his retelling became as polysemous as Boccaccio's. Petrarch's translation, in fact, represents "the hermeneutic process [of translation] itself"; it is "an allegory of its own translative existence" (135). To support these hypotheses, Rossiter discusses allegory as extended metaphor and figurative speech and translation as a "metaphorical turning." To translate, he concludes, is to engage in a sort of allegoresis, to allegorize is to practice a kind of translation. There is much to ponder here; in the end, however, I think Rossiter underestimates the allegorical inclination of

Boccaccio's Griselda and mischaracterizes Petrarch's. Dioneo explicitly invites the *brigata* to apply his tale to themselves when he says the events and people he will speak about are not too removed from his companions' experience. That Boccaccio also short-circuits any such reading only adds an exclamation point to the reciprocal interrogation of irony and allegory that the *Decameron,* otherwise called *Prencipe Galeotto,* has explored from its co-titles on. As for Petrarch's allegoresis, Rossiter looks at the proem, which turns Dioneo's Saluzzo into an Eden. Petrarch's geography, I think, is more pertinent than this. Mount Viso, majestic and unmovable, seems a natural proxy for Gualterius; the humble streamlet that issues from its side, but grows, after passing through spots of rough turbulence, to become the kingly Po, anticipates Griselda's itinerary. Petrarch's exordium quite brilliantly reworks the implications of Dioneo's suggestion that his friends consider their behavior in light of Griselda's stoic acceptance of the plagues Gualtieri visits on her.

When he turns to *The Clerk's Tale,* Rossiter rejects, rightly I think, the notion that Chaucer saw Petrarch's Griselda as a sexist, tyrant-supporting monument to monologism, to which he restored verbal heteroglossia and communal ideals. The fusion of classical and Christian elements, its mixture of genres, all assure the multivocality of Petrarch's retelling. Chaucer's translation thus provides a glimpse of his "understanding of Petrarch's socio-political landscape" (176): by concentrating on issues of gender and power, Rossiter examines the values the two poets shared and the ways in which they disagree.

Here, too, there is much to commend and much that will raise some eyebrows. As the first book-length study of these poets, Rossiter's *Chaucer and Petrarch* provides a wealth of information and many intriguing readings. His study fulfills his hope for it: he has laid the groundwork, and laid it well, for future work on the first English translation of Italian humanism.

Warren Ginsberg
University of Oregon

Peter W. Travis. *Disseminal Chaucer: Rereading the "Nun's Priest's Tale."* Notre Dame: University of Notre Dame Press, 2010. Pp. xii, 443. $40.00 paper.

Peter Travis has spent his career rereading Chaucer to great effect, as anyone with this journal in hand knows. His papers and many articles

have helped define the state of contemporary Chaucer studies. And now
we have *Disseminal Chaucer,* a sustained rereading, or rather set of re-
readings, of *The Nun's Priest's Tale* that will teach and delight its readers
boundlessly and open up much territory for new exploration. The book
is organized in seven chapters and a brief epilogue, aptly titled "Moralitas." The chapters each take on a fundamental question about *The Nun's
Priest's Tale,* ranging from the tale's genre, about which no consensus
has developed over the course of many years of admired reading, to the
great problem of its general intelligibility—what, in the last analysis, is
this tale all about, or to use Chaucer's own terms, what is its *sentence?*
What is the *fruit* that the reader is encouraged to take from the tale?
And even, who *is* the reader of this tale—both the reader implied by
the fiction and the actual historically possible reader—and what might
the relation of that historically or aesthetically determinable reader be
to the contemporary critical rereader who writes *Disseminal Chaucer?* To
approach such questions, each chapter engages the Chaucerian text in
an act of extremely close and attentive reading, what Travis calls a kind
of microanalysis of a very particular moment in the tale. Very often
these close analyses have been manifestly stimulated by Travis's extremely attentive readings in the history of Chaucer criticism and in the
work of his contemporaries. Travis fully engages these other minds in
explicit dialogue. Nowhere will one find the author shoving aside other
writers in order to clear a space for his own point; rather, the contributions of others are embraced with wide-open arms, so that one of the
many joys of this book is its evocation of a real community of learning
and critical acumen.

While focusing tightly on very specific aspects of the text, Travis's
method of close reading also opens out into a vastly erudite consideration of the intellectual context of *The Nun's Priest's Tale.* As he sees it,
this context is a creation of the medieval system of education, a cultural
possession held in common by Chaucer and any of his conceivable contemporary readers. And Travis argues that since the educational system
is, by way of parody, a central preoccupation of the text itself, this intellectual context is also a fundamental component of the text's content.
We access the world "outside" the text through the textual operations
themselves, not the least significant implication of Derrida's usually
misunderstood assertion, "il n'y a pas de hors-texte." And Travis's discussion of this material is immensely learned, detailed, clear, thorough,
and smart.

Travis first of all proposes that *The Nun's Priest's Tale* is Chaucer's *ars poetica*—a sustained meditation on the process of poetry and its intellectual and cultural setting within the institution of the curriculum of the *artes*. Thus *The Nun's Priest's Tale* also provides its readers a gateway to the *Canterbury Tales* taken as a whole, and indeed to the fundamentals of Chaucer's creative artistry. Its genre is menippean satire most broadly construed. Such a generic identification, as Travis argues convincingly, allies *The Nun's Priest's Tale* with examples as far distant from it and from each other in style and aim as *The Satyricon, The Anatomy of Melancholy,* and *Candide*. In this definition, "satire" possesses its etymological meaning, from *satura,* of a stew of wildly different things—indeed, in the more narrow definition, the mixture in question is merely that of prose and verse, as in *The Consolation of Philosophy*. To avoid confusion, Travis rejects "satire" out of hand, preferring to call the genre in question "menippean parody," where the object of imitation is not necessarily the target of satiric exposure. And since the medieval and late antique examples of this genre—*De Cosmographia, The Complaint of Nature, The Marriage of Mercury and Philology, The Consolation of Philosophy*—all involve education and its institution quite explicitly, Travis underlines its didactic, or rather its didascalic, function.

The discussion of genre and its educational function leads then quite directly to Travis's engagement with elements of the curriculum. Travis approaches this through the literary properties of the text. Thus the concern with metaphor in the Heliotropes chapter (much of which previously appeared in *Speculum*) leads to a long discussion of the meaning of the figures of thought in rhetorical discourse. Logic, and the vexed boundaries it shares in medieval theory with rhetoric and grammar, is seriously investigated throughout many of Travis's readings. Many readers, though, will single out the investigation of the Cretan Liar Paradox and other forms of *insolubilia* that constitute the spine of Chapter 7, "The Parodistic Episteme." This is a stunning tour de force that for many, I am sure, will be worth the whole book. Others will note rather the unusual concern, for a literary scholar, with the quadrivium in Travis's scrupulously detailed discussion of telling time and its mechanization in Chapter 6, "Chaucerian Horologics and the Confounded Reader."

Travis finally sees *The Nun's Priest's Tale* as celebrating an ideal of open narrative inviting a creative response from the reader. The moralitas is finally that there can be no single moralitas, let alone one posed by appending a new discursive event onto the tale in such a way that a bare truth adequately translates a fiction. Rather, meaning in fiction is labile. It proliferates, disseminates, and indeed inseminates as genera- tions of readers are provoked into new responses by the ever-unfolding layers of meaning generated by the text. And Travis himself fully parti- cipates in this vision of openness: unlike those critics who, as Walter Benjamin once perspicaciously said, want their judgment to be a last judgment, Travis's readings desire to be a new word in an ever-continuing conversation and to provoke an unexpected response. His close readings are deeply informed by his engagement with medieval grammatical, rhetorical, and dialectical theory. They are also deeply informed by his creative engagement with late twentieth-century deconstruction. Like many of the critics once associated with Yale—especially J. Hillis Miller and Paul de Man—Travis does not so much approach the Chaucerian text armed with the tenets of deconstructive interrogation; rather, he sees the text as itself an actively self-consuming artifact, if I may borrow this apt phrase, engaged in its own self-questioning, parodying its own operations of meaningfulness even as it makes the search for meaning- fulness a profoundly human possibility. The result is an exhilarating ride that no Chaucerian should miss.

ROBERT M. STEIN
Purchase College and Columbia University

MALTE URBAN, ed. *John Gower: Manuscripts, Readers, Contexts*. Turnhout: Brepols, 2009. Pp. xii, 242. €60.00; $87.00.

It is a measure of Gower studies today that this excellent volume can come out and not be a gathering of the usual suspects. The list of con- tributors is distinguished, and graced with scholars who have done sub- stantial work on the poet John Gower; yet this collection contributes to a conversation with a much larger group of voices than we could find even ten years ago, the product of what Diane Watt in her preface to this book calls a "renaissance" in Gower studies (xii). Heady days for a figure burdened for so long by the sobriquet of "moral" poet and still barely taught to undergraduates.

Despite inevitable disjunctions in such a collection, two sets of paired chapters on the *Confessio Amantis* strike sparks within and across the volume. Russell Peck and Andrew Galloway have worked together on a recent edition of the *Confessio,* and their opening essays interact on the image of Gower as a *compilator.* Peck's essay, "John Gower: Reader, Editor, and Geometrician 'for Engelondes sake,'" positively fizzes with the energy of big ideas. This is one of those essays where some of the action takes place in footnotes to support reader-response theories from Todorov to Bloom to Bleich that assert the *Confessio* "is essentially an exercise in the phenomenology of reading as cultural therapy" (18); or to argue Gower's place as the "first humanist in English" (20). Consequently this article resists summary, but it does succeed in fusing Gower's fascination with experimental science to Amans's function as an exemplary reader.

Galloway has earned the right to characterize the "dogged dullness" (50) of Gower's glosses after translating them all for his edition with Peck, in "Gower's *Confessio Amantis,* the *Pricke of Conscience,* and the History of the Latin Gloss in Early English Literature." The sheer scope of this title uncovers aspirations at least as large as Peck's, and the essay takes an important step in our halting recovery of Latin glossing in literary manuscripts. Galloway proposes that we see the Latin summaries in the *Confessio* as the primary text and the English poem as an extended gloss on that dull authority. The two *Pricke* manuscripts Galloway presents do provide useful parallels, though more context has to accrete through further scholarship before we can get a full sense of Gower's play with polyvocality in the *Confessio* or his other glossed poems, *Cronica Tripertita* and *Traitié.* Still, both Peck and Galloway have much new to say on the *Confessio*'s construction of late medieval reading.

The other pair of essays, by J. Allan Mitchell and Georgiana Donavin, highlights rhetorical structures. "Gower's *Confessio Amantis,* Natural Morality, and Vernacular Ethics" finds Mitchell arguing that Gower developed an ethical philosophy outside of scholastic models—again, a vernacular response to the traditions of Latin authority—and beyond the familiar mirrors for princes. As Peck begins with geometry, Mitchell begins with Nature *tout court,* and he sees Gower developing vernacular morality as heightened consciousness that does not require a psychic crossing into the supernatural. Donavin is, like Galloway, more focused on particulars in "Rhetorical Gower: Aristotelianism in the *Confessio Amantis*'s Treatment of 'Rethorique.'" She associates Gower's revision of Aristotelian categories in Book VII of the *Confessio* with the *Commentary* of Giles of Rome on Aristotle's *Rhetoric,* and proposes a "rhetorical psychomachia" in the dialogue between Genius and Amans that ultimately coalesces into the Gowerian narrator emerging in Book VIII (169).

One other topic, Gower and women, links three essays here. Martha Driver extends an earlier study to argue yet more convincingly in "Women Readers and Pierpont Morgan MS M. 126" that this deluxe *Confessio* manuscript was written by the scribe Ricardus Franciscus for Elizabeth Woodville, wife of Edward IV. This manuscript has a hugely ambitious, and rare, program of miniatures for the *Confessio.* Driver points out the striking representations of women in these miniatures as more heroic and dominant than their accompanying males; implicit in this analysis is the observation that Gower's tales offer a remarkable range and number of powerful women. María Bullón-Fernández develops this observation further in "Translating Women, Translating Texts: Gower's 'Tale of Tereus' and the Castilian and Portuguese Translations of the *Confessio Amantis.*" Bullón-Fernández explores these little-known translations as probable products of the marriage of John of Gaunt's two daughters, Philippa and Catherine of Lancaster, to João I of Portugal and Enrique III of Castile, respectively. No simple source study here: the "Tale of Tereus" becomes the tragic ground for an examination of the exchange of women as commodities in the power games of royalty. Finally, Eve Salisbury considers the identities projected onto Agnes Groundolf, whose marriage to Gower in his final years happened under special license in Gower's chambers at St. Mary Overeys. "Promiscuous Contexts: Gower's Wife, Prostitution, and the *Confessio Amantis*" reads only one tale from the *Confessio,* "The Tale of Thaise." That reading, however, brings up provocative parallels between Gower's Thaise and the story of Saint Agnes that might shed light on Gower's Agnes. Among the images scholars have conjured with no direct evidence for Agnes Groundolf are Flemish origin and a career in the stews of Southwark as background for the job of nursemaid/wife to an old invalid. Salisbury instead offers the possibility that John and Agnes Gower had undertaken a spiritual marriage, devoted to good works rather than carnal matters of sex or approaching death.

Two other essays stake out more independent grounds. Malte Urban, the volume's editor, plunges into "Past and Present: Gower's Use of Old Books in *Vox Clamantis.*" Urban quotes to excellent effect a famous passage from Walter Benjamin on the Angel of History facing the past, seeing the events that the world calls progress smash at his feet. Parallels with the Statue of the Ages of Man from Nebuchadnezzar's dream prompt Urban to look at the less familiar version in *Vox* to consider the fragmentary nature of what history we can see, along with the embedded fragments of past and present in Gower's use of *cento*—lines taken from Latin poets interwoven with his own. Craig Bertolet takes a noticeably historicist tack in " 'The slyest of alle': The Lombard Problem in John Gower's London." Bertolet is convincing in arguing that Gower's writings on "Lombards" (a term that covered a variety of Italians) suggest that he supported the business interests of the City merchants over the international policies of the royals, and this point is an important corrective to the lazy characterization of Gower as royalist through and through. However, Bertolet whets the appetite for some more substantial discussion of Gower's apparent alignment with the City, possibly into the period around 1392, when Richard II was at once in a state of profound conflict with those same players and apparently commissioning a major poem from Gower himself.

John Gower's engagement with polyvocality, his transformation of Ovidian narrative and scholastic moralizing, his vexed relations with the turbulent political world of revolt, revolving kings, and rebranded queens all prompt probing discussions in this volume. We can hope we are approaching critical mass in our conversations about Gower. This collection at least anticipates that happy state. The lack of an index and a fair number of misprints undercut the effect a bit, but it is a handsome and useful book.

Joel Fredell
Southeastern Louisiana University

Nila Vázquez, ed. *"The Tale of Gamelyn" of the Canterbury Tales: An Annotated Edition*. Lewiston, N. Y.: Edwin Mellen Press, 2009. Pp. 466. $175.30.

The Middle English romance of *Gamelyn* (902 lines in couplets in its fullest form) survives in twenty-seven manuscripts, far more than for any other such romance. Its survival seems less an indication of its popularity than of the company it keeps: it appears only in manuscripts of the *Canterbury Tales,* generally as a continuation of *The Cook's Tale.* No critical edition has ever been published based on the evidence of all the manuscripts.

Nila Vázquez's edition does not fill this gap. It contains two main elements. There is what is termed a "Critical Edition" of *Gamelyn* (294–332), together with an "Apparatus Criticus" (332–79). This is preceded by a series of what are termed "diplomatic editions" of ten manuscripts. These are the basis for what is termed a "Synoptic Edition," which, she explains, "is conformed by [*sic*] the different diplomatic editions of the manuscripts in which the text appears" (37).

Vázquez goes on to describe the reasons for the choice of these manuscripts:

The manuscripts to be collated against the base text [Corpus] were selected taking into account a combination of significant criteria. On the one hand, their nature as old (i.e. closer to Chaucer's lifetime) and valuable manuscripts. On the other hand, their representativeness within the general classification in the textual tradition of the *Canterbury Tales*. . . . Bearing all these criteria in mind, a first group of manuscripts, comprising [Harley 7334, Lansdowne 851 and Petworth] was selected. . . . A second group of manuscripts includes [CUL Mm.II.5, Lichfield Cathedral and BL Royal 18.C.II], which together with [Petworth], are some of the best representatives of type *d*. . . . Thirdly, [Fitzwilliam McClean 181] and [*sic*] exemplify type *d* with some variations. Finally [Christ Church 152] was selected on account of its classification as another worthy manuscript and its close relation with the oldest exemplars. (36)

Several aspects of these statements of method may be unclear to many students of Middle English manuscripts. What is a "synoptic edition"? Does it differ from a critical edition? Such questions do not receive answers. What is clear is that the grounds on which the majority of surviving manuscripts of *Gamelyn* are ignored are wholly unsound. The assumption that only "old" manuscripts should be of concern to the editor is wholly without justification. Age does not provide a criterion for ignoring the majority of the manuscripts of *Gamelyn*: there is no reason why later manuscripts should not preserve forms of the text, or particular readings, that need to be considered by the editor. And to choose to select manuscripts for scrutiny on criteria that may have no bearing on the text of *Gamelyn* ("some of the best representatives of type *d*" of the *Canterbury Tales* and "another 'worthy' manuscript") is simply nonsensical. The only responsible way the textual tradition for *Gamelyn* can be established is through collation of all manuscripts and analysis of the evidence from such a collation.

These fundamental confusions about method extend into the form of this edition. Why are ten "diplomatic" transcripts of manuscripts actually presented in this volume? Especially since Vázquez has no clear understanding of what a diplomatic transcript is: in hers, the expansion of contractions is silent; and at times (e.g., 262, line 547; 266, line 711), they are not expanded at all; seemingly otiose terminal flourishes are, however, regularly recorded. What is gained by providing "diplomatic" transcriptions of a number of manuscripts rather than collating all of them? No answer presents itself to this question. But what comparison of these transcripts with the "Apparatus Criticus" reveals is that, far from actually recording "all the details regarding different manuscript occurrences" (294), there are a number of substantive readings occurring in the "diplomatic transcripts" that do not appear in this "apparatus." Space permits only examples from Lansdowne 851 (L) and Harley 7334 (H), lines 1–20; Vázquez's text provides the lemma:

1. Lithen and lesteneth}
L And þerefore
listeneþ & herkeneþ;
aright} L þis tale ariht
3. his} H his right
8. ate} H L att þe
15. among} H amonges
16. hadde} L miht haue
19. blyue} L belyue

(Occasional readings are recorded that are not substantive, for example, 19. hyȝe} hie.) I suspect this list of omitted readings could be greatly extended. But those noted above may stand as typical of the general competence in the recording of variants.

There is also a series of "Notes to the Text," the chief aim of which is seemingly to provide explanatory notes. These notes are not generally helpful. We are told that this poem is "an oral-like romance" (line 1), but not what this term means. If it is intended to convey the presence of recurrent stock formulaic phrases in the poem, these are not noted (for example, "mote I thee," lines 379, 413, 448, 577, 720, 833). Middle English proverbial phrases are not recorded; for example: "stille as a stoon" (263, 395) = Whiting S772; "He moste needes walke in woode that may not walke in towne" (672) = Whiting 559. Capitalization is inconsistent: "Sire Ote" (753), but "sire Ote" (759); "abbots and priours monk and Chanoun" (781; note also the lack of punctuation here). The seeming fitt-divisions of the romance (at 169, 341, 551, 769), themselves formulaic, excite no comment. Assertions are made without any supporting documentation; for example: "In medieval times, it was considered sacrilege to draw blood from a churchman" (316, n. on 524).

At a very basic level, inaccuracy abounds: for example, the (otiose) list of *Canterbury Tales* manuscripts (6–9) includes "Arundel Castle 140" (for BL Arundel 140); "Univ. of Texas Humanities Research Centre 43" (for 143); "Harley 2551" (for 2251); "Magdalen College Pepys 2006" (for Magdalene College). The English is not infrequently eccentric or incorrect, and important modern studies of *Gamelyn* manuscripts (for example, by Stephen Partridge and Jacob Thaisen) are not cited.

It is not possible here to give more than a general sense of the inadequacies of this edition. Its confusions of thought and execution render it of very limited value. Vázquez has clearly been very badly advised by her supervisor and her publisher, both of whom ought to have been alert to deficiencies in this work. A full critical edition of *Gamelyn* is still a desideratum of Middle English scholarship.

A. S. G. EDWARDS
De Montfort University

EDWARD WHEATLEY. *Stumbling Blocks Before the Blind: Medieval Constructions of a Disability.* Ann Arbor: University of Michigan Press, 2010. Pp. xii, 284. $70.00.

The key question in this survey of medieval texts about blindness is why medieval French literature was "cruel toward and satirical about blind characters while English literature was much less so" (4). In order to formulate some answers to this question, Edward Wheatley brings together an impressive array of sources. These include a number of widely known and widely studied works, such as Langland's *Piers Plowman* and Froissart's *Chroniques,* but he nonetheless succeeds in offering readers new perspectives on these familiar texts. In reaching his conclusions about the position of the blind in England and in France, Wheatley takes the reader through some fascinating customs and stories, such as the French entertainment involving blind men chasing a pig with cudgels and the horrific tales of children being deliberately blinded in order that they might be put to work as beggars.

Wheatley's approach is strongly informed by modern disability theory, an area that over the past decade has come to be of increasing interest to medievalists. Like scholars such as Irina Metzler (*Disability in Medieval Europe* [2006]), Wheatley seeks to adapt theoretical models of disability to the medieval context. In order to do this, he posits a " 'religious' model of disability" (x), which parallels the modern medical model in seeing the discourse of disability as institutionally controlled and dominated. In the medieval period, however, the controlling institution is the church rather than the medical profession. The role of organized religion in controlling the epistemological categorization of disability has of course been discussed by a number of theorists in sociology and other disciplines, and Wheatley builds on this scholarly background to make a persuasive argument for the particular centrality of religion to medieval constructions of disability.

Like most modern theorists writing about disability, Wheatley examines the distinction between "disabled" and "impaired," a distinction that is highlighted and promoted by the social model of disability. Simply put, impairment is a biological category, which refers to a difference from the physical norm, whereas disability is considered to be a social category and refers to the external barriers faced by people with impairments. However, although Wheatley affirms the utility of this distinction in the discussion of the medieval evidence, his discussion seems to use the two terms interchangeably, referring to "impaired people" and "disabled people" without any apparent rationale behind the choice of term in each case. Because of the tendency in general discourse to refer to what the social model calls "impairments" as "disabilities," it is not surprising to find writers on the subject falling into the trap of using "disabled" in its general sense, but it is nonetheless rather confusing for the reader. Despite this, Wheatley's employment of disability theory is nuanced and considered, providing an innovative way into his material.

This theoretical discussion comprises Chapter 1 of the study. The following chapters move neatly and persuasively from the general to the particular. The second chapter gives the reader an overview of the historical context of blinding, comparing the role of blinding in medieval

French judicial and political processes with the general absence of this kind of mutilation in medieval England. Wheatley also discusses the institutionalization of blindness through the creation of hospices, again comparing the far greater prominence of blind people in France with their apparent neglect in England. This chapter provides a solid historical foundation upon which the following textual discussions can be based.

In the third chapter, Wheatley examines the common trope of the spiritual blindness of the Jews, and the way in which this association of blindness with discourses of Jewish evil and sinfulness had the concomitant effect of implying that the blind were themselves sinful and deserving of distrust and marginalization. Following this, the fourth and fifth chapters consider the humiliation of the blind through their role in comedy and their association with sexual transgression. Wheatley discusses the genres of fabliau, drama, and romance, with a particularly interesting discussion of Chaucer's *Man of Law's Tale* and *Merchant's Tale* in Chapter 5. The sixth chapter deals with the hagiographic evidence and the role of the miracle in disabling the blind by suggesting that those who were not cured were too sinful to be deserving of cure. Finally, the seventh chapter provides close studies of three figures: Jean l'Aveugle, king of Bohemia; the Picard poet Gilles Le Muisit; and the English poet John Audelay. Wheatley marshals medieval medical and scientific writings on blindness to elucidate the lives of these men, all of whom were visually impaired. The comparison between Le Muisit and Audelay is particularly interesting: whereas Le Muisit was cured of his cataracts, and wrote both before and after his "miraculous" cure, Audelay appears to have experienced no such relief. The differences in the ways the two men engaged with their impairment gives us a fascinating insight into the ways the blind and the cured understood their roles within society and the religious discourse of their day.

Wheatley has produced a varied and stimulating analysis of medieval blindness. He makes a persuasive argument for the reasons behind the differences between French and English attitudes, and the effects these attitudes had on the real lives of blind people. In the third chapter on the trope of Jewish spiritual blindness, it was somewhat surprising not to find any engagement with Andrew P. Scheil's 2004 study, *The Footsteps of Israel,* which discusses a number of the same passages as Wheatley does. Indeed, this seems symptomatic of a more general issue with Wheatley's handling of Anglo-Saxon evidence, which is easily the least thoroughly researched aspect of this book. Nowhere, for example, does he mention King Alfred the Great's fear that blindness would make him useless and contemptible to his people, or the numerous discussions of spiritual blindness in the writings of Ælfric. As a result, the references to Anglo-Saxon literature in this study give the impression of being somewhat cursory, and are rather a disappointment in comparison with Wheatley's impressive discussions of later French and English texts. Nonetheless, this is otherwise an excellent book, which will appeal to disability theorists, medievalists, and religious scholars alike.

BETHAN TOVEY
Oxford English Dictionary

Books Received

Bale, Anthony. *Feeling Persecuted: Christians, Jews, and Images of Violence in the Middle Ages*. London: Reaktion Books, 2010. Pp. 254. £29.00; $45.00.

Bate, Jonathan. *English Literature: A Very Short Introduction*. Oxford: Oxford University Press, 2010. Pp. xii, 179. £7.99; $11.95.

Beidler, Peter G. *Chaucer's Canterbury Comedies: Origins and Originality*. Seattle: Coffeetown Press, 2011. Pp. xvii, 308. $18.95 paper.

Bildhauer, Bettina. *Filming the Middle Ages*. London: Reaktion Books, 2011. Pp. 264. £25.00; $40.00.

Burrow, John A., and Hoyt N. Duggan, eds. *Medieval Alliterative Poetry: Essays in Honour of Thorlac Turville-Petre*. Dublin: Four Courts Press, 2010. Pp. 229. €55.00; $78.00.

Campbell, Kristy. *The Call to Read: Reginald Pecock's Books and Textual Communities*. Notre Dame: University of Notre Dame Press, 2010. Pp. xi, 310. $38.00 paper.

Copeland, Rita, and Peter T. Struck, eds. *The Cambridge Companion to Allegory*. Cambridge: Cambridge University Press, 2010. Pp. xxiii, 295. £55.00, $95.00 cloth; £18.99, $29.00 paper.

Crassons, Kate. *The Claims of Poverty: Literature, Culture, and Ideology in Late Medieval England*. Notre Dame: University of Notre Dame Press, 2010. Pp. xi, 389. $40.00 paper.

Da Rold, Orietta, and Elaine Treharne, eds. *Textual Cultures: Cultural Texts*. Essays and Studies 2010. Woodbridge: D. S. Brewer, 2010. Pp. xi, 221. £30.00; $48.00.

Davidson, Mary Catherine. *Medievalism, Multilingualism, and Chaucer*. New York: Palgrave Macmillan, 2010. Pp. xi, 211. $95.00.

Donavin, Georgiana, and Anita Obermeier. *Romance and Rhetoric: Essays in Honour of Dhira B. Mahoney.* Turnhout: Brepols, 2010. Pp. viii, 281. €60.00; $85.00.

Dutton, Elizabeth, John Hines, and R. F. Yeager, eds. *John Gower, Trilingual Poet: Language, Translation, and Tradition.* Woodbridge: D. S. Brewer, 2010. Pp. xi, 358. £60.00; $99.00.

Epstein, Robert, and William Robins, eds. *Sacred and Profane in Chaucer and Late Medieval Literature: Essays in Honour of John V. Fleming.* Toronto: University of Toronto Press, 2010. Pp. vii, 238. $60.00.

Fichte, Joerg O. *From Camelot to Obamalot: Essays on Medieval and Modern Arthurian Literature.* Trier: Wissenschaftlicher Verlag, 2010. €24.50; $35.00 paper.

Fumo, Jamie C. *The Legacy of Apollo: Antiquity, Authority, and Chaucerian Poetics.* Toronto: University of Toronto Press, 2010. Pp. xvi, 351. $70.00.

Gayk, Shannon. *Image, Text, and Religious Reform in Fifteenth-Century England.* Cambridge: Cambridge University Press, 2010. Pp. viii, 254. £55.00; $95.00.

Hanning, Robert W. *Serious Play: Desire and Authority in the Poetry of Ovid, Chaucer, and Ariosto.* New York: Columbia University Press, 2010. Pp. xviii, 286. $45.00.

Janes, Dominic, and Gary Waller, eds. *Walsingham in Literature and Culture from the Middle Ages to Modernity.* Farnham: Ashgate, 2010. Pp. xvi, 251. £55.00; $90.00.

Kelly, Henry Ansgar. *Law and Religion in Chaucer's England.* Farnham: Ashgate Variorum, 2010. Pp. xiv, 400. £75.00; $120.00.

Krummel, Miriamne Ara. *Crafting Jewishness in Medieval England: Legally Absent, Virtually Present.* New York: Palgrave Macmillan, 2011. Pp. xix, 243. $85.00.

Lawrence-Mathers, Anne, and Phillipa Hardman, eds. *Women and Writing, c. 1340–c. 1650*. Woodbridge: York Medieval Press, 2010. Pp. ix, 238. £50.00; $95.00.

Ní Chuilleanáin, Eiléan, and John Flood, eds. *Heresy and Orthodoxy in Early English Literature, 1350–1680*. Dublin: Four Courts Press, 2010. Pp. 174. €55.00; $78.00.

Niayesh, Ladan, ed. *A Knight's Legacy: Mandeville and Mandevillian Lore in Early Modern England*. Manchester: Manchester University Press, 2011. Pp. xi, 216. £55.00; $75.00.

Oswald, Dana M. *Monsters, Gender, and Sexuality in Medieval English Literature*. Woodbridge: D. S. Brewer, 2010. Pp. viii, 227. £50.00; $90.00.

The "Piers Plowman" Electronic Archive. Vols. 1–6. Ann Arbor: University of Michigan Press; and Woodbridge: D. S. Brewer, 2000–2008. £30.00; $50.00 per volume.

Powell, Susan, ed. *John Mirk's "Festial,"* vol. 1. EETS o.s. 334. Oxford: Oxford University Press, 2009. Pp. cxlv, 188. £70.00; $130.00.

Rosenfeld, Jessica. *Ethics and Enjoyment in Late Medieval Poetry: Love after Aristotle*. Cambridge: Cambridge University Press, 2011. Pp. vii, 245. £55.00; $90.00.

Saunders, Corinne, ed. *A Companion to Medieval Poetry*. Oxford: Blackwell, 2010. Pp. xvii, 683. £110.00; $209.95.

Scattergood, John. *Occasions for Writing: Essays on Medieval and Renaissance Literature, Politics, and Society*. Dublin: Four Courts Press, 2010. Pp. 272. €55.00; £78.00.

Simpson, James. *Under the Hammer: Iconoclasm in the Anglo-American Tradition*. Oxford: Oxford University Press, 2010. Pp. xiii, 222. £25.00; $45.00.

Tambling, Jeremy. *Dante in Purgatory: States of Affect*. Turnhout: Brepols, 2010. Pp. ix, 292. €60.00; $86.00.

Tinkle, Theresa. *Gender and Power in Medieval Exegesis*. New York: Palgrave Macmillan, 2010. Pp. xvi, 196. $80.00.

Warner, Lawrence. *The Lost History of "Piers Plowman": The Earliest Transmission of Langland's Work*. Philadelphia: University of Pennsylvania Press, 2010. Pp. xviii, 117. $49.95.

Woods, Marjorie Curry. *Classroom Commentaries: Teaching the "Poetria nova" across Medieval and Renaissance Europe*. Columbus: Ohio State University Press, 2010. Pp. xlii, 367. $59.95.

An Annotated Chaucer Bibliography, 2009

Compiled and edited by Mark Allen and Bege K. Bowers

Regular contributors:

Anne Thornton, *Abbot Public Library* (Marblehead, Massachusetts)
Stephen Jones, *Ball State University* (Indiana)
George Nicholas, *Benedictine College* (Kansas)
Debra Best, *California State University at Dominguez Hills*
Gregory M. Sadlek, *Cleveland State University* (Ohio)
David Sprunger, *Concordia College* (Minnesota)
Winthrop Wetherbee, *Cornell University* (New York)
Elaine Whitaker, *Georgia College & State University*
Michelle Allen, *Grand Valley State University* (Michigan)
Elizabeth Dobbs, *Grinnell College* (Iowa)
Andrew James Johnston, *Humboldt-Universität zu Berlin*
Wim Lindeboom, *Independent Scholar* (Netherlands)
Teresa P. Reed, *Jacksonville State University* (Alabama)
William Snell, *Keio University* (Japan)
Denise Stodola, *Kettering University* (Michigan)
Brian A. Shaw, *London, Ontario*
William Schipper, *Memorial University* (Newfoundland, Canada)
Martha Rust, *New York University*
Warren S. Moore III, *Newberry College* (South Carolina)
Cindy L. Vitto, *Rowan College of New Jersey*
Brother Anthony (Sonjae An), *Sogang University* (South Korea)
Stephanie Amsel, *Southern Methodist University* (Texas)
Ana Saez Hidalgo, *Universidad de Valladolid* (Spain)
Stefania D'Agata D'Ottavi, *Università per Stranieri di Siena* (Italy)
Martine Yvernault, *Université de Limoges* (France)
Cynthia Ho, *University of North Carolina, Asheville*
Margaret Connolly, *University of St. Andrews* (Scotland)
Rebecca Beal, *University of Scranton* (Pennsylvania)

Mark Allen, *University of Texas at San Antonio*
John M. Crafton, *West Georgia College*
Bege K. Bowers, *Youngstown State University* (Ohio)

Ad hoc contributions were made by several contributors: by Philipp Hinz and Elisabeth Kempf at the Freie Universität Berlin, by Stephen H. Rigby of the University of Manchester, and by Laurel Boshoff of the University of Texas at San Antonio. The bibliographers acknowledge with gratitude the MLA typesimulation provided by the Center for Bibliographical Services of the Modern Language Association; postage from the University of Texas at San Antonio Department of English; and assistance from the library staff, especially Susan McCray, at the University of Texas at San Antonio.

This bibliography continues the bibliographies published since 1975 in previous volumes of *Studies in the Age of Chaucer*. Bibliographic information up to 1975 can be found in Eleanor P. Hammond, *Chaucer: A Bibliographic Manual* (1908; reprint, New York: Peter Smith, 1933); D. D. Griffith, *Bibliography of Chaucer, 1908–1953* (Seattle: University of Washington Press, 1955); William R. Crawford, *Bibliography of Chaucer, 1954–63* (Seattle: University of Washington Press, 1967); and Lorrayne Y. Baird, *Bibliography of Chaucer, 1964–1973* (Boston: G. K. Hall, 1977). See also Lorrayne Y. Baird-Lange and Hildegard Schnuttgen, *Bibliography of Chaucer, 1974–1985* (Hamden, Conn.: Shoe String Press, 1988); and Bege K. Bowers and Mark Allen, eds., *Annotated Chaucer Bibliography, 1986–1996* (Notre Dame, Ind.: University of Notre Dame Press, 2002).

Additions and corrections to this bibliography should be sent to Mark Allen, Bibliographic Division, The New Chaucer Society, Department of English, University of Texas at San Antonio 78249-0643 (Fax: 210-458-5366; e-mail: mark.allen@utsa.edu). An electronic version of this bibliography (1975–2009) is available via The New Chaucer Society Web page at http://artsci.wustl.edu/~chaucer/ or directly at http://uchaucer.utsa.edu. Authors are urged to send annotations for articles, reviews, and books that have been or might be overlooked.

Classifications

Abbreviations of Chaucer's Works

ABC	*An ABC*
Adam	*Adam Scriveyn*
Anel	*Anelida and Arcite*
Astr	*A Treatise on the Astrolabe*
Bal Compl	*A Balade of Complaint*
BD	*The Book of the Duchess*
Bo	*Boece*
Buk	*The Envoy to Bukton*
CkT, CkP, Rv–CkL	*The Cook's Tale, The Cook's Prologue, Reeve–Cook Link*
ClT, ClP, Cl–MerL	*The Clerk's Tale, The Clerk's Prologue, Clerk–Merchant Link*
Compl d'Am	*Complaynt d'Amours*
CT	*The Canterbury Tales*
CYT, CYP	*The Canon's Yeoman's Tale, The Canon's Yeoman's Prologue*
Equat	*The Equatorie of the Planetis*
For	*Fortune*
Form Age	*The Former Age*
FranT, FranP	*The Franklin's Tale, The Franklin's Prologue*
FrT, FrP, Fr–SumL	*The Friar's Tale, The Friar's Prologue, Friar–Summoner Link*
Gent	*Gentilesse*
GP	*The General Prologue*
HF	*The House of Fame*
KnT, Kn–MilL	*The Knight's Tale, Knight–Miller Link*
Lady	*A Complaint to His Lady*
LGW, LGWP	*The Legend of Good Women, The Legend of Good Women Prologue*
ManT, ManP	*The Manciple's Tale, The Manciple's Prologue*
Mars	*The Complaint of Mars*
Mel, Mel–MkL	*The Tale of Melibee, Melibee–Monk Link*
MercB	*Merciles Beaute*
MerT, MerE–SqH	*The Merchant's Tale, Merchant Endlink–Squire Headlink*

MilT, MilP, Mil–RvL	*The Miller's Tale, The Miller's Prologue, Miller–Reeve Link*
MkT, MkP, Mk–NPL	*The Monk's Tale, The Monk's Prologue, Monk–Nun's Priest Link*
MLT, MLH, MLP, MLE	*The Man of Law's Tale, Man of Law Headlink, The Man of Law's Prologue, Man of Law Endlink*
NPT, NPP, NPE	*The Nun's Priest's Tale, The Nun's Priest's Prologue, Nun's Priest's Endlink*
PardT, PardP	*The Pardoner's Tale, The Pardoner's Prologue*
ParsT, ParsP	*The Parson's Tale, The Parson's Prologue*
PF	*The Parliament of Fowls*
PhyT, Phy–PardL	*The Physician's Tale, Physician–Pardoner Link*
Pity	*The Complaint unto Pity*
Prov	*Proverbs*
PrT, PrP, Pr–ThL	*The Prioress's Tale, The Prioress's Prologue, Prioress–Thopas Link*
Purse	*The Complaint of Chaucer to His Purse*
Ret	*Chaucer's Retraction {Retractation}*
Rom	*The Romaunt of the Rose*
Ros	*To Rosemounde*
RvT, RvP	*The Reeve's Tale, The Reeve's Prologue*
Scog	*The Envoy to Scogan*
ShT, Sh–PrL	*The Shipman's Tale, Shipman–Prioress Link*
SNT, SNP, SN–CYL	*The Second Nun's Tale, The Second Nun's Prologue, Second Nun–Canon's Yeoman Link*
SqT, SqH, Sq–FranL	*The Squire's Tale, Squire Headlink, Squire–Franklin Link*
Sted	*Lak of Stedfastnesse*
SumT, SumP	*The Summoner's Tale, The Summoner's Prologue*
TC	*Troilus and Criseyde*
Th, Th–MelL	*The Tale of Sir Thopas, Sir Thopas–Melibee Link*
Truth	*Truth*
Ven	*The Complaint of Venus*

WBT, WBP, WB–FrL	*The Wife of Bath's Tale, The Wife of Bath's Prologue, Wife of Bath–Friar Link*
Wom Nob	*Womanly Noblesse*
Wom Unc	*Against Women Unconstant*

Periodical Abbreviations

AdI	Annali d'Italianistica
Anglia	Anglia: Zeitschrift für Englische Philologie
Anglistik	Anglistik: Mitteilungen des Verbandes deutscher Anglisten
AnLM	Anuario de Letras Modernas
ANQ	ANQ: A Quarterly Journal of Short Articles, Notes, and Reviews
Archiv	Archiv für das Studium der Neueren Sprachen und Literaturen
Arthuriana	Arthuriana
Atlantis	Atlantis: Revista de la Asociacion Española de Estudios Anglo-Norteamericanos
AUMLA	AUMLA: Journal of the Australasian Universities Language and Literature Association
BAM	Bulletin des Anglicistes Médiévistes
BJRL	Bulletin of the John Rylands University Library of Manchester
C&L	Christianity and Literature
CarmP	Carmina Philosophiae: Journal of the International Boethius Society
CE	College English
ChauR	The Chaucer Review
CL	Comparative Literature (Eugene, Ore.)
Clio	CLIO: A Journal of Literature, History, and the Philosophy of History
CLS	Comparative Literature Studies
CML	Classical and Modern Literature: A Quarterly (Columbia, Mo.)
CollL	College Literature
Comitatus	Comitatus: A Journal of Medieval and Renaissance Studies
CRCL	Canadian Review of Comparative Literature/Revue Canadienne de Littérature Comparée
DAI	Dissertation Abstracts International

DR	*Dalhousie Review*
ÉA	*Études Anglaises: Grand-Bretagne, États-Unis*
EHR	*English Historical Review*
EIC	*Essays in Criticism: A Quarterly Journal of Literary Criticism*
EJ	*English Journal*
ELH	*ELH: English Literary History*
ELN	*English Language Notes*
ELR	*English Literary Renaissance*
EMS	*English Manuscript Studies, 1100–1700*
EMSt	*Essays in Medieval Studies*
Encomia	*Encomia: Bibliographical Bulletin of the International Courtly Literature Society*
English	*English: The Journal of the English Association*
Envoi	*Envoi: A Review Journal of Medieval Literature*
ES	*English Studies*
ESC	*English Studies in Canada*
Exemplaria	*Exemplaria: A Journal of Theory in Medieval and Renaissance Studies*
Expl	*Explicator*
FCS	*Fifteenth-Century Studies*
Florilegium	*Florilegium: Carleton University Papers on Late Antiquity and the Middle Ages*
FMLS	*Forum for Modern Language Studies*
Genre	*Genre: Forms of Discourse and Culture*
H-Albion	*H-Albion: The H-Net Discussion Network for British and Irish History, H-Net Reviews in the Humanities and Social Sciences* http://www.h-net.org/reviews/home.php
H-German	*H-German: The Discussion Group for Historians of German Around the World, H-Net Reviews in the Humanities and Social Sciences* http://www.h-net.org/~german/
H-HRE	*H-HRE: The Discussion Group for the History and Culture of the Holy Roman Empire, H-Net Reviews in the Humanities and Social Sciences* http://www.h-net.org/~hre/
HLQ	*Huntington Library Quarterly: Studies in English and American History and Literature* (San Marino, Calif.)

Hortulus	*Hortulus: The Online Graduate Journal of Medieval Studies* http://www.hortulus.net/
IJES	*International Journal of English Studies*
JAIS	*Journal of Anglo-Italian Studies*
JBSt	*Journal of British Studies*
JEBS	*Journal of the Early Book Society*
JEGP	*Journal of English and Germanic Philology*
JELL	*Journal of English Language and Literature* (Korea)
JEngL	*Journal of English Linguistics*
JGN	*John Gower Newsletter*
JHiP	*Journal of Historical Pragmatics*
JMEMSt	*Journal of Medieval and Early Modern Studies*
JMH	*Journal of Medieval History*
JML	*Journal of Modern Literature*
JNT	*Journal of Narrative Theory*
JRMMRA	*Quidditas: Journal of the Rocky Mountain Medieval and Renaissance Association*
L&LC	*Literary and Linguistic Computing: Journal of the Association for Literary and Linguistic Computing*
L&P	*Literature and Psychology*
L&T	*Literature and Theology: An International Journal of Religion, Theory, and Culture*
Lang&Lit	*Language and Literature: Journal of the Poetics and Linguistics Association*
Lang&S	*Language and Style: An International Journal*
LeedsSE	*Leeds Studies in English*
Library	*The Library: The Transactions of the Bibliographical Society*
LitComp	*Literature Compass* http://www.literaturecompass.com/
MA	*Le Moyen Age: Revue d'Histoire et de Philologie* (Brussels, Belgium)
MÆ	*Medium Ævum*
M&H	*Medievalia et Humanistica: Studies in Medieval and Renaissance Culture*
Manuscripta	*Manuscripta* (St. Louis, Mo.)
Marginalia	*Marginalia: The Journal of the Medieval Reading Group at the University of Cambridge* http://www.marginalia.co.uk/journal/
Mediaevalia	*Mediaevalia: An Interdisciplinary Journal of Medieval Studies Worldwide*

MedievalF	*Medieval Forum* http://www.sfsu.edu/~medieval /index.html
MedPers	*Medieval Perspectives*
MES	*Medieval and Early Modern English Studies*
MFF	*Medieval Feminist Forum*
MichA	*Michigan Academician* (Ann Arbor, Mich.)
MLQ	*Modern Language Quarterly: A Journal of Literary History*
MLR	*The Modern Language Review*
MP	*Modern Philology: A Journal Devoted to Research in Medieval and Modern Literature*
N&Q	*Notes and Queries*
Neophil	*Neophilologus* (Dordrecht, Netherlands)
NLH	*New Literary History: A Journal of Theory and Interpretation*
NM	*Neuphilologische Mitteilungen: Bulletin of the Modern Language Society*
NML	*New Medieval Literatures*
NMS	*Nottingham Medieval Studies*
NOWELE	*NOWELE: North-Western European Language Evolution*
Parergon	*Parergon: Bulletin of the Australian and New Zealand Association for Medieval and Early Modern Studies*
PBA	*Proceedings of the British Academy*
PBSA	*Papers of the Bibliographical Society of America*
PLL	*Papers on Language and Literature: A Journal for Scholars and Critics of Language and Literature*
PMAM	*Publications of the Medieval Association of the Midwest*
PMLA	*Publications of the Modern Language Association of America*
PoeticaT	*Poetica: An International Journal of Linguistic Literary Studies*
PQ	*Philological Quarterly*
RCEI	*Revista Canaria de Estudios Ingleses*
RenQ	*Renaissance Quarterly*
RES	*Review of English Studies*
RMRev	*Reading Medieval Reviews* http://www.rdg.ac.uk /AcaDepts/ln/Medieval/rmr.htm

RMSt	*Reading Medieval Studies*
SAC	*Studies in the Age of Chaucer*
SAP	*Studia Anglica Posnaniensia: An International Review of English*
SAQ	*South Atlantic Quarterly*
SB	*Studies in Bibliography: Papers of the Bibliographical Society of the University of Virginia*
SCJ	*The Sixteenth-Century Journal: Journal of Early Modern Studies* (Kirksville, Mo.)
SEL	*SEL: Studies in English Literature, 1500–1900*
SELIM	*SELIM: Journal of the Spanish Society for Medieval English Language and Literature*
ShakS	*Shakespeare Studies*
SIcon	*Studies in Iconography*
SiM	*Studies in Medievalism*
SIMELL	*Studies in Medieval English Language and Literature*
SMART	*Studies in Medieval and Renaissance Teaching*
SN	*Studia Neophilologica: A Journal of Germanic and Romance Languages and Literatures*
SoAR	*South Atlantic Review*
SP	*Studies in Philology*
Speculum	*Speculum: A Journal of Medieval Studies*
SSF	*Studies in Short Fiction*
SSt	*Spenser Studies: A Renaissance Poetry Annual*
TCBS	*Transactions of the Cambridge Bibliographical Society*
Text	*Text: Transactions of the Society for Textual Scholarship*
TLS	*Times Literary Supplement* (London, England)
TMR	*The Medieval Review* http://www.hti.umich.edu/t /tmr/
Tr&Lit	*Translation and Literature*
TSLL	*Texas Studies in Literature and Language*
UTQ	*University of Toronto Quarterly: A Canadian Journal of the Humanities*
Viator	*Viator: Medieval and Renaissance Studies*
WS	*Women's Studies: An Interdisciplinary Journal*
YES	*Yearbook of English Studies*
YLS	*The Yearbook of Langland Studies*
YWES	*Year's Work in English Studies*

Bibliographical Citations and Annotations

Bibliographies, Reports, and Reference

1. Allen, Mark, and Bege K. Bowers. "An Annotated Chaucer Bibliography, 2007." *SAC* 31 (2009): 399–497. Continuation of *SAC* annual annotated bibliography (since 1975); based on contributions from an international bibliographic team, independent research, and *MLA Bibliography* listings. 302 items, plus listing of reviews for 90 books. Includes an author index.

2. Allen, Valerie, and Margaret Connolly. "Later Medieval: Chaucer." *YWES* 88 (2009): 280–319. A discursive bibliography of Chaucer studies for 2007, divided into four subcategories: general, *CT, TC,* and other works.

3. Goodall, Peter, ed. *Chaucer's "Monk's Tale" and "Nun's Priest's Tale": An Annotated Bibliography, 1900–2000.* The Chaucer Bibliographies, [no. 8]. Buffalo, N.Y.: University of Toronto Press, 2009. xlviii, 338 pp. A comprehensive annotated bibliography of scholarly and critical discussion of *MkT* and *NPT,* subdivided into the following categories: editions and translations; bibliographies, handbooks, and indices; manuscripts and textual studies; prosody, linguistics, and lexical studies; sources, analogues, and allusions; the Monk and Nun's Priest considered as characters; *MkT* and *NPT* considered together; and *MkT* and *NPT* considered separately. The items in each category are arranged by date of publication and cross-listed. Includes an index and a summary of critical trends.

Recordings and Films

4. Edmondson, George. "Naked Chaucer." In Elizabeth Scala and Sylvia Federico, eds. *The Post-Historical Middle Ages* (*SAC* 33 [2011], no. 88), pp. 139–60. The appearance of naked "Geoff" Chaucer in Brian Helgeland's *A Knight's Tale* "challenges the logic of the present . . . assumed by presentism," even while reminding us that historical periods exist, "each one haunted by the moment of its diachronic foundation." In a Lacanian sense and by means of an "allegorized sexuality," "Geoff"

is a reminder of the uncanny presence of the past in the present. Edmondson compares moments in the film to *KnT* and to the prologue to *Th*.

5. Prendergast, Thomas, and Stephanie Trigg. "The Negative Erotics of Medievalism." In Elizabeth Scala and Sylvia Federico, eds. *The Post-Historical Middle Ages* (*SAC* 33 [2011], no. 88), pp. 117–37. The authors contemplate the relationship of medievalism to medieval studies, considering several (re)constructions of the Middle Ages, including Brian Helgeland's *A Knight's Tale* and various critics' efforts to gloss *queynte*. Such considerations reveal more about the desires of the present than about the nature of the past.

6. Spearing, Anthony, reader. *The Canterbury Tales: The Knight's Tale*. Tokyo: Senshu University, 2009. 2 audio discs; 141 min. Middle English reading of *KnT*, preceded by lines 1–78 of *GP*. Recorded by Spearing, with the assistance of Hiroshi Miura.

See also nos. 35, 81.

Chaucer's Life

7. Pan Sánchez, María Rosa. "Navarra y la literatura inglesa: El juglar taillefer y la presencia en Navarra de John Chandos y de Geoffrey Chaucer." *Notas y Estudios Filológicos* 10 (1995): 111–24. Gauges the influence of Navarra on English literature at two crucial junctures: the Norman Conquest and during the march of Edward, the Black Prince, when both Chaucer and John Chandos were involved. Reproduces several archival documents and includes an abstract in English.

8. Weir, Alison. *Mistress of the Monarchy: The Life of Katherine Swynford, Duchess of Lancaster*. New York: Ballantine Books, 2009. xxii, 392 pp. Biography of Katherine Swynford, emphasizing the love she shared with John of Gaunt. Includes color illustrations, notes, index, bibliography, and several appendices (including a genealogical table of the Chaucer family). Numerous brief references to Geoffrey and Philippa Chaucer, their marriage, and their children and descendants. Also comments on Chaucer's works, especially *BD*.

See also nos. 14, 37, 73, 81, 147.

Facsimiles, Editions, and Translations

9. Ackroyd, Peter, trans. *The Canterbury Tales—Geoffrey Chaucer: A Retelling by Peter Ackroyd*. London: Penguin; New York: Viking, 2009.

xii, 436 pp., [11] b&w illus. by Nick Bantock. Primarily a prose modernization of *CT* (*Th* in verse; *Mel* and *ParsT* excluded) that emulates Chaucer's shifts in register and idiom. Includes a translator's note and an introduction on Chaucer's life and works. See also nos. 56 and 206.

10. Boenig, Robert, and Andrew Taylor, eds. *"The Canterbury Tales": A Selection.* Buffalo, N.Y.: Broadview Press, 2009. lviii, 400 pp., [11] b&w illus. Selections from Boenig and Taylor's 2008 edition of *CT* (*SAC* 32 [2010], no. 16), including *GP, KnT, MilPT, RvPT, WBPT, SumPT, ClPT, SqE, FranPT, PardPT, PrPT, NPPT,* and *Ret.* Also contains an introduction (pp. ix–lviii), brief bibliography, and fifteen "background documents" that include selections from sources and historical records. Glosses to the Middle English are included in the margins to the text, with brief notes at the bottom of the page.

11. Connolly, Margaret. "'Dr Furnivall and Mother like the same old books': Mary Haweis and the Experience of Reading Chaucer in the Nineteenth Century." Supplement, *Philologie im Netz* 4 (2009): 5–20. Describes how Mary Haweis's 1877 publication of *Chaucer for Children: A Golden Key* brought Chaucer's stories to the domestic realm of women and children as a tool for organization and education. Connolly suggests that Haweis authored later books such as *Chaucer for Schools* (1881) and *Tales of Chaucer* (1887) with the aim of commoditizing Chaucer and her texts.

12. Edwards, A. S. G. "W. W. Greg and Medieval English Literature." *Textual Cultures: Texts, Contexts, Interpretation* 4.2 (2009): 54–62. Surveys Greg's publications that address medieval English literature, including his commentary on early printed editions of Chaucer.

13. Klitgård, Ebbe. "Translation as Transformation: Two Translators of Chaucer in 19th-Century Denmark." *Perspectives: Studies in Translatology* 16.3–4 (2009): 133–41. Klitgård assesses the translation practices of two Danish translations of Chaucer: T. C. Bruun's 1823 translation *The Wife of Slagelse: After Pope's "The Wife of Bath,"* which follows the modernizations of Dryden and Pope; and Charlotte Louise Westergaard's 1853 booklet, which places Chaucer as the first British author.

14. Lauer, Christopher, trans. *The Canterbury Tales.* Richmond, Surrey: Oneworld Classics, 2009. 517 pp. Verse modernization of most of *CT* (except *CkT, Mel,* and *ParsT*), based on the 1963 edition of A. C. Baugh; meter and verse forms parallel Chaucer's. Additional material includes brief notes (pp. 484–502), a summary of Chaucer's life, and comments on translating the work.

15. Snell, William. "A Woman Medievalist Much Maligned: A Note in Defense of Edith Rickert (1871–1938)." Supplement, *Philologie im Netz* 4 (2009): 41–54. Clarifies Edith Rickert's role in her collaborative work with John Matthews Manly—i.e., *Chaucer Life-Records* and *Text of the "Canterbury Tales"*—arguing that people need to study the background of Rickert to see her as an important female medievalist and scholar.

See also nos. 3, 97, 127, 128, 162, 169, 188, 203, 205.

Manuscripts and Textual Studies

16. Horobin, Simon. "The Criteria for Scribal Attribution: Dublin, Trinity College MS 244 Reconsidered." *RES* 60 (2009): 371–81. Reconsideration of Alan J. Fletcher's evidence (*RES* 58 [2007]: 597–632) does not support the claim that Adam Pynkhurst is the scribe of Dublin, Trinity College MS 244.

17. Merrill, Darin A. "A Comparative Analysis of the Text of the Hengwrt and Ellesmere Manuscripts of the 'Canterbury Tales,' based on the Hengwrt Digital Edition, Estelle Stubbs, Ed." *DAI* A70.05 (2009): n.p. Analysis of the two fundamental *CT* manuscripts indicates that "the organization and theme of the individual tales affected" copy quality; for example, scribes copied moral tales more conscientiously than they copied bawdy ones, and prose tales were less "carefully" copied than poetic tales.

18. Pearsall, Derek. "Beyond Fidelity: The Illustration of Late Medieval English Literary Texts." In Marlene Villalobos Hennessy, ed. *Tributes to Kathleen L. Scott. English Medieval Manuscripts: Readers, Makers, and Illuminators* (*SAC* 33 [2011], no. 76), pp. 197–220, 29 b&w illus. Distinguishes between the modern "expressive" function of book illustration and various medieval practices. Modern practice is evident in W. Russell Flint's 1928 illustrations to *CT,* while the Ellesmere illustrations evince efforts to "restore social and cultural norms" that the poem undermines. Pearsall comments on the horses and costumes of the Ellesmere illustrations and those in Cambridge University Library MS Gg.4.27. He discusses medieval practices exemplified in manuscripts of Gower's *Confessio Amantis* and of *Piers Plowman*.

19. Thaisen, Jacob. "Overlooked Variants in the Orthography of British Library, Additional MS 35286." *JEBS* 11 (2008): 121–43.

Thaisen illustrates how a distribution of orthographical variants can be an "internal standard of reference," using as an example the Ad³ manuscript of *CT*. He comments on the order of tales in the manuscript and on various features of the manuscript's *ordinatio,* stemmatic relations, planning, and transmission. Tabulating orthographical variants and aligning them with available dialectical information, Thaisen maintains that the manuscript was "copied consecutively" from *GP* to *ParsT,* "based on a single exemplar."

20. ———. "Statistical Comparison of Middle English Texts: An Interim Report." *Kwartalnik Neofilologiczny* 56.3 (2009): 205–21. Using available electronic transcriptions of manuscripts of *WBP* and *MilT* tests the reliability of a statistical model ("interpolated, modified Kneser-Ney smoothed 3-gram backoff model") for determining various linguistic and scribal features of the manuscripts. Thaisen compares statistical data with results from more traditional methods to call for further investigation of the use of statistics and electronic transcriptions in manuscript study.

21. Weldon, James. "The Naples Manuscript and the Case for a Female Readership." *Neophil* 93 (2009): 703–25. The intended audience of the Naples manuscript was secular females, evidenced by its internal style and content of four romances and inclusion of medical recipes. The advice to wives in *ClT* points to the instruction of women—and thus to the intended audience.

See also nos. 71, 179, 188, 203.

Sources, Analogues, and Literary Relations

22. Albritton, Benjamin L. "Citation and Allusion in the Lays of Guillaume de Machaut." *DAI* A70.04 (2009): n.p. Considers Machaut's allusions to earlier works in his lays (e.g., *Roman de Fauvel* and *Remede de Fortune*) and gauges Machaut's impact on English court poetry, using Chaucer and Froissart as examples.

23. Breeze, Andrew. "Jean de Meun and Dafydd ap Gwilym." *National Library of Wales Journal* 34 (2008): 311–21. Like Chaucer, the fourteenth-century Welsh poet Dafydd ap Gwilym borrowed from Jean de Meun, using *Le Roman de la Rose* as the source for *Y Gwynt* ("The Wind"). Breeze notes sixteen motifs common to both poems and con-

trasts the Welsh poet's method of imitation with Chaucer's preference for direct translation.

24. Gutiérrez Arranz, José M. *The Cycle of Troy in Geoffrey Chaucer: Tradition and "Moralitee."* Newcastle upon Tyne: Cambridge Scholars, 2009. xiii, 135 pp. Commenting on medieval literary renditions of the story of Troy, Gutiérrez Arranz identifies places where Chaucer refers or alludes to this material, focusing on Chaucer's references to specific characters.

25. Heffernan, Carol Falvo. *Comedy in Chaucer and Boccaccio.* Chaucer Studies, no. 40. Cambridge: D. S. Brewer, 2009. ix, 151 pp. Exploring the question "When is Chaucer known in Italy?" Heffernan surveys other scholars who have examined Chaucer's writings within the Italian tradition and focuses on shared comedic themes in the works of Boccaccio and Chaucer. She reviews the historical background of Chaucer's two trips to Italy in 1373 and 1378 and argues that the trips offered Chaucer a chance for literary exchange, which heavily influenced his fabliaux. Heffernan examines parallel comic tales in the *Decameron* and *CT*; Chaucer's comedy "is not so much derivative of Boccaccio's as part of a common European comic tradition that both poets inherited and revived" (129).

26. Ingham, Patricia Clare. "Amorous Dispossessions: Knowledge, Desire, and the Poet's Dead Body." In Elizabeth Scala and Sylvia Federico, eds. *The Post-Historical Middle Ages* (*SAC* 33 [2011], no. 88), pp. 13–35. Ingham considers evidence from the exhumation of Petrarch's skull and from Chaucer studies to demonstrate the role of "amorous dispossessions" in historicist pursuits. Lacan's comments on courtly love theorize such dispossessions and complicate notions of truth and knowledge. The author discusses the "problem" that Chaucer's knowledge of Petrarch causes for claims about historical periods and explores aspects of global study of Chaucer.

27. Kamath, Stephanie A. Viereck Gibbs. "The *Roman de la Rose* and Middle English Poetry." *LitComp* 6 (2009): 1109–26. Kamath surveys scholarly discussion of the influence of the *Roman de la Rose* on Middle English literature, with special attention to Chaucer's works, including *Rom,* as well as to those of his contemporaries and descendants.

28. Linder, Amnon. "The Knowledge of John of Salisbury in the Late Middle Ages." *Studi Medievali,* 3rd ser., 18 (1977): 315–55. Surveys the availability of manuscripts of John of Salisbury's *Policraticus* and allusions to this work among theologians, jurists, and political writers

of the twelfth through the fifteenth centuries. Comments on uses of the text by various vernacular writers in Europe, including brief mention of Chaucer's uses.

29. Long, Lynne. "The European Lending Library: Borrowing, Translating, and Returning Texts." In Ashley Chantler and Carla Dente, eds. *Translation Practices: Through Language to Culture*. New York and Amsterdam: Rodopi, 2009, pp. 17–29. Long assesses medieval translation practice through modern translation theory, exploring techniques of translation and the impact of translation on vernacular literatures. Includes sustained, comparative attention to Jean de Mean and Chaucer, with comments on *Bo* and *TC*.

30. Urban, Malte. *Fragments: Past and Present in Chaucer and Gower*. New York: Peter Lang, 2009. 248 pp. Studying how Chaucer's and Gower's uses of their sources reflect their understandings of history and their political agendas, Urban invites readers to consider parallels between the poets' uses of sources and historicist criticism. Uses various theoretical approaches to compare and contrast the poets' treatments of rebellion and vision in *Vox Clamantis* and *NPT* (with discussion of *HF* and *PF*), their depictions of Troy in *TC* and several sections of *Confessio Amantis*, their mirrors for princes in *Mel* and *Confessio Amantis* VII, and their concern with the violated body in their tales of Virginia. Generally, Gower seeks to resolve into admonitory unity the splintered idealism of the past, while dialogic interaction typifies Chaucer's engagements with the past and with politics.

31. Wallace, David. "Griselde Before Chaucer: Love Between Men, Women, and Farewell Art." In Andrew Galloway and R. F. Yeager, eds. *Through a Classical Eye: Transcultural and Transhistorical Visions in Medieval English, Italian, and Latin Literature in Honour of Winthrop Wetherbee* (*SAC* 33 [2011], no. 69), pp. 207–22. Wallace reviews letters between Boccaccio and Petrarch, suggesting that it is not unreasonable to "consider Petrarch and Boccaccio toiling, sparring, and loving one another in bonds suggestive of matrimony" (210). Aligns events of the Griselda tales with events discussed in Petrarch's *Seniles* XVII and XVIII; "Chaucer found his truest imaginative kinship with poets outside of England" (215).

See also nos. 3, 7, 51, 74, 77, 93, 99, 107, 114, 116, 119–21, 133, 137, 141, 149, 153, 157–60, 172, 173, 175, 180, 186, 191, 193, 195.

Chaucer's Influence and Later Allusion

32. Bishop, Louise M. "A Touch of Chaucer in *The Winter's Tale*." In Martha W. Driver and Sid Ray, eds. *Shakespeare and the Middle Ages: Essays on the Performance and Adaptation of the Plays with Medieval Sources or Settings* (*SAC* 33 [2011], no. 39), pp. 232–44. Bishop argues that Paulina's "female eloquence" reflects the influence of Chaucer's *Mel* on Shakespeare's *The Winter's Tale*, commenting on the fact that the folio editions of Chaucer present *Mel* as "The Tale of Chaucer" and observing how Richard Greene's comments on Chaucer and Gower in *Greene's Vision* may also have influenced Shakespeare's characterization.

33. Briggs, Julia Ruth. "'Chaucer . . . the Story Gives': *Troilus and Cressida* and *The Two Noble Kinsmen*." In Martha W. Driver and Sid Ray, eds. *Shakespeare and the Middle Ages: Essays on the Performance and Adaptation of the Plays with Medieval Sources or Settings* (*SAC* 33 [2011], no. 39), pp. 161–77. Briggs describes Shakespeare's "emendation and expansion" of his medieval sources in *Troilus and Cressida* and *The Two Noble Kinsmen*, assessing the importance of *KnT* and *TC* in Shakespearean work. Also explores how the various medieval influences tend to be muted in modern performances.

34. Cheney, Patrick. "The Voice of the Author in 'The Phoenix and Turtle': Chaucer, Shakespeare, Spenser." In Curtis Perry and John Watkins, eds. *Shakespeare and the Middle Ages*. New York: Oxford University Press, 2009, pp. 103–25. Cheney examines how Shakespeare's "The Phoenix and Turtle" echoes *PF*, particularly as "a poem about the politics of authorship." As a "great poet of self-crowning," Spenser responds to Chaucer's self-effacing pursuit of fame. Shakespeare sets these two poses in opposition in his poem and comments on how poetry engages political crisis.

35. Curtis, Carl C. III. "Powell and Pressburger's *A Canterbury Tale*: New Pilgrims, Old Pilgrimage." *Literature/Film Quarterly* 36.1 (2008): 68–77. Curtis summarizes the 1944 movie *A Canterbury Tale*, gauging its successes and failures and commenting on the extent to which its sensibilities might be called "Chaucerian."

36. Davis, Paul. *Translation and the Poet's Life: The Ethics of Translating in English Culture, 1646–1726*. New York: Oxford University Press, 2009. xii, 324 pp. Davis surveys the aesthetics and politics of works by "Augustan poet-translators," including a description of William Cartwright's comments on Francis Kynaston's translation of *TC* into Latin

and an analysis of the modernizations and adaptations of Chaucer in John Dryden's *Fables*. The modernizations and adaptations exemplify Dryden's late-career turn to an "Ovidian understanding of translation as self-indulgent play."

37. Driver, Martha W. "Mapping Chaucer: John Speed and the Later Portraits." *ChauR* 36 (2002): 228–49. Driver examines John Speed's portrait of Chaucer (first printed version, Speght 1598) as a representation of "Elizabethan nationalism" and an emblem of Chaucer's reception. She also discusses Speed's career as a cartographer and historian and comments on the impact of his portrait of Chaucer.

38. ———. "Reading *A Midsummer Night's Dream* Through Middle English Romance." In Martha W. Driver and Sid Ray, eds. *Shakespeare and the Middle Ages: Essays on the Performance and Adaptation of the Plays with Medieval Sources or Settings* (*SAC* 33 [2011], no. 39), pp. 140–60. Focusing on Oberon and the mechanicals, Driver explores how medieval romances influenced Shakespeare's *A Midsummer Night's Dream* and twentieth-century adaptations of it, observing the influences of *KnT, Th,* and other romances.

39. ———, and Sid Ray, eds. *Shakespeare and the Middle Ages: Essays on the Performance and Adaptation of the Plays with Medieval Sources or Settings*. Jefferson, N.C.: McFarland, 2009. vii, 276 pp. Thirteen essays, plus several introductory commentaries, gauge Shakespeare's uses of medieval materials and how those materials are reflected in modern stage and film adaptations. Shakespeare's "medievalism" shapes modern notions of the Middle Ages. Three essays pertain to Chaucer; see nos. 32, 33, and 38.

40. Fitzgerald, Jill. "A 'Clerkes Compleinte': Tolkien and the Division of Lit. and Lang." [*sic*]. *Tolkien Studies* 6 (2009): 41–57. Fitzgerald places Tolkien's essay on *RvT* (1934) in its intellectual and professional context. She explores the role of Chaucer in Tolkien's scholarship and creative works, including the allusions to Chaucer's works that appear in Tolkien's satiric poem "The Clerkes Compleinte."

41. McCabe. Richard. "Spenser, Plato, and the Poetics of State." *SSt* 24 (2009): 433–52. McCabe views Spenser's alleged completion of Chaucer in *The Legend of Friendship* as a move to represent himself as a "Bonfont" rather than a "Malfont" poet.

42. Moll, Richard J. "'O Lady Fortune': An Unknown Lyric in British Library Ms Harley 2169." *N&Q* 254 (2008): 192–94. An eight-line poem reminiscent of Chaucer's *For* in both theme and word choices

survives in three copies (transcribed here), each in a different hand, written upside down on the final folio of this heraldic manuscript.

See also nos. 51, 65, 127, 153, 165, 170, 175, 198.

Style and Versification

43. Ahl, Frederick. "Chaucer's Englishing of Latin Wordplay." In Andrew Galloway and R. F. Yeager, eds. *Through a Classical Eye: Transcultural and Transhistorical Visions in Medieval English, Italian, and Latin Literature in Honour of Winthrop Wetherbee* (*SAC* 33 [2011], no. 69), pp. 267–86. Citing rhymes, wordplay, puns, and anagrams, Ahl proposes that Chaucer produces the "kind of wordplay found in classical Latin poets." Ahl compares Chaucer's uses with examples from Shakespeare and Milton, showing that such wordplay in Chaucer is not limited to comedy and farce.

44. Burrow, J. A. "Vituperations in Chaucer's Poetry." *EIC* 59 (2009): 22–36. *Laus* (praise) and *vituperatio* (rendered by Chaucer as *sklaunder*) find their way into medieval *ars poetriae*. Using the "idiom of odium" (e.g., traditionally disreputable animals and bodily functions), Chaucer focuses on reporting angry speech. *HF, PF, LGW, TC,* and *CT* provide examples of the theme.

45. Dane, Joseph A. "Toward a Description of Chaucer's Verse Forms." *SN* 81 (2009): 45–52. Outlines a method for describing Chaucer's verse forms as syllabic, with accent overlaid secondarily on this base. Dane argues that this method is more simple than descriptions that give priority to accent and the iamb, as well as more useful in distinguishing Chaucer's verse from that of his sources and of other Middle English poets.

46. Holton, Amanda. "Chaucer and *Pronominatio*." *RMSt* 33 (2007): 69–86. Holton argues that Chaucer generally prefers direct naming techniques, but he recurrently uses *pronominatio* (i.e., epithets and related circumlocutions) when relying on Virgil as a source in *HF* and *LGW*. Also shows how Chaucer exploits the negative possibilities of *pronominatio* in *TC* and *PrT*.

47. Kumamoto, Sadahiro. "The Poetic Technique of Enjambment in Chaucer's Poems: The Case of Five Sentence Elements (S, Aux, V, O, C)." In Masahiro Hori, Tomoji Tabata, and Sadahiro Kumamoto, eds. *Stylistic Studies of Literature: In Honour of Professor Hiroyuki Ito.* New York

and Frankfurt am Main: Peter Lang, 2009, pp. 71–92. Kumamoto examines eleven syntactical patterns used in conjunction with poetic enjambment. Chaucer's poetry contains more enjambment than do three anonymous romances included for comparison—and Chaucer uses enjambment more in his early poetry (*BD, HF, PF*) than in *KnT, MilT,* and *RvT.*

48. Maíz Arévalo, Carmen. "'What sholde I make a lenger tale of this?' Linguistic and Stylistic Analysis of Rhetorical Questions in the *Canterbury Tales.*" *SELIM* 15 (2008): 39–60. Maíz Arévalo describes the functions of rhetorical questions and assesses their uses in *CT,* where the device is linked to "heigh style" (Harry Bailey's term) and specific genres. Rhetorical questions are used to express and elicit emotion, to suspend action, and to reinforce climactic moments.

See also nos. 143, 180, 192.

Language and Word Studies

49. Berrozpe Peralta, Carlos. *Estudio lingüístico del Inglés Medio (Middle English) a través de obras de Geoffrey Chaucer y William Shakespeare.* [Albacete, Spain]: C. Berrozpe, 2006. 112 pp. Includes a diachronic linguistic analysis—phonetic, orthographical, morphological, syntactical, lexical, and stylistic—of the description of the Reeve from *GP.* Traces elements backward to Old English and forward to Modern English.

50. Butterfield, Ardis. "Chaucerian Vernaculars." *SAC* 31 (2009): 25–51. The Biennial Chaucer Lecture, The New Chaucer Society, Sixteenth International Congress, 17–22 July 2008, Swansea University. Considers the relations among French, Anglo-French, and English in the linguistic and cultural conditions of Chaucer's time. Calls for a new sensitivity to translation as process, proposes more subtle awareness of interdependent etymologies (e.g., *frank* and *fraunchise*), and encourages a more sensitive array of source studies. Butterfield explores uses of *forein* in *Bo*; the diplomatic and poetic functions of *envoy* in Chaucer's five Boethian *ballades*; Criseyde's second letter in *TC* as diplomatic exchange; and *ManT* as a "quasi-*envoy.*"

51. ———. *The Familiar Enemy: Chaucer, Language, and Nation in the Hundred Years War.* New York: Oxford University Press, 2009. xxx, 444 pp. 10 b&w figs.; 3 maps. Explores the political, linguistic, and cultural

relations between "France" and "England" before the stabilization of the areas' geographical boundaries. Interdependence between the two areas challenges modern notions of nationality, linguistic priority, and cultural identity, especially as reflected and refracted in diplomacy, invective, and literary exchange. Butterfield focuses on Chaucer as a central case in these reciprocal exchanges and comments on a wide variety of Chaucer's contemporaries on either side of the Channel, especially Deschamps, Froissart, and Gower. Includes sustained commentary on *KnT* and *TC* (diplomatic language), *ShT* and *MerT* (mercantile language), *BD* and *TC* (vernacular self-consciousness), and the Deschamps *ballade* to Chaucer. The discussion extends forward to Pisan, Caxton, and Shakespeare.

52. Vennemann, Theo. "Celtic Influence in English? Yes and No." *English Language and Linguistics* 13.2 (2009): 309–34. Traces idiomatic usage of *yes* and *no* in responses to questions in the English language, comparing it with German usage to illustrate the influence of the Celtic, Brittonic language. Concludes by exploring roots of the English method of response in linguistic developments between Chaucer and Shakespeare resulting from increased contact between Anglo-Saxon and Brittonic.

53. Watts, William. "*Verray Felicitee Parfit* and the Development of Chaucer's Philosophical Language." *ChauR* 43 (2009): 260–81. Chaucer's uses of *verray felicitee parfit* and *verray parfit* evince his engagement with Boethius's concern with "the true and everlasting good, the *summum bonum*" in the *Consolation of Philosophy*. Whether meant ironically or used in the spirit of their original contexts, these phrases signal a relevance of the topic at hand to the larger philosophical question. Watts comments on usage in *MerT, TC,* and especially *GP* (Franklin).

54. Wentersdorf, Karl P. "The 'Viritoot' Crux in Chaucer's *Miller's Tale*." *ChauR* 44 (2009): 110–13. The clear erotic context of the blacksmith's response to Absolon's late-night visit supports a gloss of *viritoot* as a derivation of "the Latin ablative *cum virtute*," meaning "with manly ardor."

55. Wogan-Browne, Jocelyn, et al., eds. *Language and Culture in Medieval Britain: The French of England, c.1100–c.1500*. Woodbridge and Rochester, N.Y.: York Medieval Press, 2009. xxii, 533 pp. Thirty-four essays by various authors (and an introduction by the editor) on a variety of linguistic and literary topics. Essays are arranged in four categories: (1) Language and Socio-Linguistics; (2) Crossing the Conquest: New

Linguistic and Literary Histories; (3) After Lateran IV: Francophone Devotions and Histories; and (4) England and France in the Late Fourteenth and Fifteenth Centuries. The volume includes extensive notes, bibliography, and several indices, including an Index of Primary Authors with fifteen references to Chaucer. For an essay that pertains to Chaucer, see no. 166. See also no. 286.

See also nos. 5, 48, 84, 124, 147, 150, 178.

Background and General Criticism

56. Acocella, Joan. "All England: *The Canterbury Tales* Retold." *New Yorker,* December 21 and 28, 2009, pp. 140–45. Appreciative criticism of Chaucer's art and reputation; includes a review of Peter Ackroyd's 2009 translation of *CT* (*SAC* 33 [2011], no. 9).

57. Amtower, Laurel, and Jacqueline Vanhoutte, eds. *A Companion to Chaucer and His Contemporaries: Texts and Contexts.* Buffalo, N.Y.: Broadview Press, 2009. 480 pp. Readings in social and cultural history for classroom purposes, arranged in eight sections: politics and ideology, social structures, daily life, religious life and prayer, knighthood and war, reading and education, sciences and medicine, and international influences and exchanges. Each section includes a general introduction, followed by ten to fifteen texts and documents (usually excerpted), introduced individually and in Modern English translation. Throughout, the introductions link the texts and documents to details of Chaucer's works, with reference to those of his contemporaries.

58. Archibald, Elizabeth. "Questioning Arthurian Ideals." In Elizabeth Archibald and Ad Putter, eds. *The Cambridge Companion to the Arthurian Legend.* Cambridge and New York: Cambridge University Press, 2009, pp. 139–53. Archibald surveys subversions and satires of Arthurian literature, commenting that Chaucer "seems to be fairly hostile to the Arthurian world," even if implicitly so.

59. Astell, Ann W., and J. A. Jackson, eds. *Levinas and Medieval Literature: The "Difficult Reading" of English and Rabbinic Texts.* Pittsburgh: Duquesne University Press, 2009. x, 374 pp. Twelve essays by various authors, plus an introduction by the editors, consider interactions among Christian allegory, talmudic hermeneutics, and the interpretive theory of Emmanuel Levinas. Three essays pertain to Chaucer; see nos. 140, 152, and 197.

60. Bankert, Dabney A. "Teaching the Middle Ages Through Travel in a Semester Residential Program." *SMART* 16.1 (2009): 39–61. Pedagogy, syllabus, sample assignments, and itineraries for a semester-long, London-based excursion course on English medieval literature, including Chaucer.

61. Cavill, Paul, and Heather Ward. *The Christian Tradition in English Literature: Poetry, Plays, and Shorter Prose*. Grand Rapids, Mich.: Zondervan, 2007. 512 pp. Summaries of literary works, plus study questions designed for self-teaching, ranging from works of Bede and Caedmon to those of Philip Larkin and Edna O'Brien, with a summary of biblical plots, Christian history, hymns, and a glossary of terms. Two sections pertain to Chaucer: (1) a comparison of *NPT* with the fable of Marie de France and Henryson's *The Cock and the Fox* (pp. 44–48); and (2) a commentary on Christian religion in *GP* and in *PardPT* (pp. 56–61).

62. Classen, Albrecht, ed. *Urban Space in the Middle Ages and the Early Modern Age*. New York: Walter de Gruyter, 2009. vii, 757 pp. Twenty-three essays on literary and historical topics ranging from ideas of Rome to medieval European waste, including two essays that pertain to Chaucer. See nos. 111 and 126.

63. Collette, Carolyn P., and Nancy Mason Bradbury. "Time, Measure, and Value in Chaucer's Art and Chaucer's World." *ChauR* 43 (2009): 347–50. The essays in this special issue (43.4) of the *The Chaucer Review* open new perspectives on Chaucer's works, placing them in the context of the "new impulses toward quantification and measurement" in and beyond late medieval England.

64. D'Arcens, Louise. "'She ensample was by good techynge': Hermiene Ulrich and Chaucer under Capricorn." Supplement, *Philologie im Netz* 4 (2009): 21–40. Focusing on the role of Hermiene Ulrich in formulating the modern-language curriculum at Queensland in 1911, D'Arcens notes the "frustrating" historical pattern of exclusion of women scholars from medieval studies, particularly Chaucer studies.

65. Di Rocco, Emilia. "'Le bellissime avventure di re Artù' in Inghilterra: Da Chaucer a Malory." In Michelangelo Picone, ed. *La letteratura cavalleresca dalle "Chansons de Geste" alla "Gerusalemme Liberata."* Atti del II Convegno Internazionale di Studi, Certaldo Alto, Giugno 21–23, 2007. Pisa: Pacini, 2008, pp. 191–205. Di Rocco explores the role of Chaucer's works in the development of romance in England, commenting on the poet's fusion of classical material and romance in *KnT* and

TC, the concern with *gentilesse* and *trouthe* in *WBT* and *FranT,* and the reference to Sir Gawain in *SqT.* Also discusses *Sir Gawain and the Green Knight,* the alliterative *Morte Arthure,* and Malory's *Morte Darthure.*

66. Dor, Juliette. "Caroline Spurgeon (1869–1942) and the Institutionalisation of English Studies as a Scholarly Discipline." Supplement, *Philologie im Netz* 4 (2009): 55–66. Dor examines Caroline Spurgeon's impact on England's postwar reconstruction of the education system through the reestablishment of English studies and her involvement in founding the International Federation of University Women, which protected and lobbied for women's involvement in universities.

67. Forgeng, Jeffrey L., and Will McLean. *Daily Life in Chaucer's England.* 2nd ed. Daily Life Through History Series. Westport, Conn.; and London: Greenwood, 2009. xviii, 302 pp. Updates and expands the first edition (1995—see *SAC* 19 [1997], no. 124), adding "primary source sidebars in all chapters" and a guide to digital resources. This social history of late medieval England has as its goal the creative re-creation of the period, providing a wide-ranging commentary on history, society, household practice, time-keeping, clothing, costume, entertainment, food and drink, festivities, etc.

68. Galloway, Andrew. "The Economy of Need in Late Medieval English Literature." *Viator* 40.1 (2009): 309–31. Production, consumption, and profit have helped to define individuals in more recent eras; however, an "economy of need" was an aspect of late medieval identity. Galloway traces the economy of need in sermons and prose writing and comments on its presence in works of Gower, Langland, and Chaucer. Chaucer explores "what we might call psychological and psycho-social dimensions" of the economy of need in *TC, PardT,* and *ClT.*

69. ———, and R. F. Yeager, eds. *Through a Classical Eye: Transcultural and Transhistorical Visions in Medieval English, Italian, and Latin Literature in Honour of Winthrop Wetherbee.* Toronto: University of Toronto Press, 2009. vii, 436 pp. Nineteen essays by students, friends, and colleagues of Winthrop (Pete) Wetherbee, along with an introduction by Galloway and a laudatory afterword by Robert Morgan. For seven essays that pertain to Chaucer, see nos. 31, 43, 108, 121, 133, 139, and 154.

70. Ganim, John M. "Cosmopolitan Chaucer, or, The Uses of Local Culture." *SAC* 31 (2009): 3–21. The Presidential Address, The New Chaucer Society, Sixteenth International Congress, July 17–22, 2008, Swansea University. Ganim contemplates relationships between "cosmopolitanism" and "communitarianism" as they intersect in Chaucer

studies and in medieval studies more generally, commenting recurrently on the perspectives of Erich Auerbach and reactions to him by Edward Said. The "cosmopolitan and the local are restlessly in tension in Chaucer (and Chaucer studies)," although Chaucer studies need to be more global and sensitive to technological change.

71. Gibbons, Victoria Louise. "The Manuscript Titles of *Truth*: Titology and the Medieval Gap." *JEBS* 11 (2008): 198–206. Modern notions and theory of literary titles ("titology") cannot be applied readily to medieval works. Gibbons comments on the titles of several of Chaucer's poems as an aspect of the *ordinatio* of their manuscripts. Medieval titles, especially those of brief works, are "structural signs" indicating where individual works begin and end.

72. Gray, Douglas. "Middle English Literature." In Alan Deyermond, ed. *A Century of British Medieval Studies*. Oxford: Oxford University Press for the British Academy, 2007, pp. 383–426. Gray surveys the study of Middle English literature from the founding of the British Academy until the early twenty-first century, commenting on accomplishments of individual scholars up to World War II. He describes critical trends and how they reflect changes in social concerns, technology, advances in other fields, etc. Recurrent references to Chaucer and Chaucerians.

73. Gust, Geoffrey W. *Constructing Chaucer: Author and Autofiction in the Critical Tradition*. The New Middle Ages. New York: Palgrave Macmillan, 2009. xiv, 286 pp. Gust seeks to "reenergize persona theory" for future Chaucer scholarship, arguing that Chaucer's "autofictional" persona should be regarded as the central topic not only of Chaucer's works but also of studies of his reception and literary history at large. Comments on the personae throughout Chaucer's corpus and on his reception history, focusing on biographical criticism from the fifteenth century to the present, several lyrics (*Scog, Buk, Adam, Sted, Purse*), *Ret, WBPT, PardPT,* and *Th–MelL*. Homosocial concerns in these works challenge critics to read Chaucer's persona in *CT* as queer, although not necessarily homosexual.

74. Gutiérrez Arranz, José M. "El mito de Hércules en las obras de Geoffrey Chaucer." *Estudios clasicos* 48 (2006): 47–64. Surveys references to Hercules in Chaucer's corpus, commenting on sources, their adaptations in Chaucerian contexts, and the merging of traditions.

75. Hazell, Dinah. *Poverty in Late Middle English Literature*. Dublin: Four Courts Press, 2009. 233 pp. Describes various kinds of poverty

in England in the second half of the fourteenth century, summarizing economic and social factors and assessing their representation in various works of literature in English and Latin across a range of genres. Hazell considers four broad categories of poverty (aristocratic, urban, rural, and apostolic), plus the charitable responsibilities of the Church, the state, and individuals. Examines *PrT* among depictions of urban poverty; *ClT* and *NPT,* among those of rural poverty. Also comments on the Monk, Nun's Priest, and Parson in the discussion of apostolic poverty and on the Plowman as a figure of "moral integrity and social responsibility." Other tales are mentioned throughout.

76. Hennessy, Marlene Villalobos, ed. *Tributes to Kathleen L. Scott. English Medieval Manuscripts: Readers, Makers and Illuminators.* London: Harvey Miller, 2009. 292 pp., b&w and color illus. Fifteen essays on topics related to sacred and secular English manuscripts of the late Middle Ages. For two essays that pertain to Chaucer, see nos. 18 and 173.

77. Kennedy, Kathleen E. *Maintenance, Meed, and Marriage in Middle English Literature.* The New Middle Ages. New York: Palgrave Macmillan, 2009. 185 pp. Examines a variety of medieval social relations as forms of "maintenance," i.e., "being provided or providing the wherewithal to live." Lord-retainer, master-servant, and husband-wife relations are analogous forms of maintenance that inform one another as depicted in late medieval English literature, including letters and historical records. Kennedy's literary topics focus on works by Chaucer, Gower, Langland, Lydgate, and Hoccleve. She discusses concerns with coverture and rape in *FranT* and in *WBT* and its analogue, *The Weddynge of Sir Gawain and Dame Ragnell.*

78. Knutson, Karla. "Reflections on Studying the Middle Ages Abroad: A Former Student's Thoughts and Suggestions." *SMART* 16.1 (2009): 63–70. Comments on experiences as a student visiting London, Canterbury, and Greece.

79. Kowaleski, Maryanne, and P. J. P. Goldberg, eds. *Medieval Domesticity: Home, Housing, and Household in Medieval England.* Cambridge: Cambridge University Press, 2008. xiv, 317 pp. Eleven essays by various authors (and an introduction by the editors) address a range of topics: domestic and monastic spaces, attitudes toward living alone, various literary and historical depictions of homes and households, etc. The collection cites Chaucer's works throughout, with one essay focusing on *ClT*; see no. 138.

80. Lewis, James R., and Evelyn Dorothy Oliver. *The Dream Encyclo-*

pedia. 2nd ed. Detroit: Visible Ink, 2009. xxi, 410 pp. A popular hand-book to dream psychology, dream lore, the history of interpretations of dreams, and dreaming in various cultures, with an entry on Chaucer (pp. 38–40) that comments on his biography and his dream-vision poetry. First published in 1995.

81. Malir, Gerry, featuring Terry Jones. *Chaucer and "The Canterbury Tales."* [n.p.]: Artsmagic, 2009. DVD; VHS. Ca. 120 min. Introduction to late medieval social and literary history, focusing on Chaucer. Illustrated with modern footage and reproductions from medieval life and narrated by Peter Morgan Jones. Interspersed with portions of an interview with Terry Jones that emphasizes Chaucer's biography and the possibility that Chaucer was executed in 1402 by direction of Archbishop Arundel.

82. Mann, Jill. *From Aesop to Reynard: Beast Literature in Medieval Britain.* New York: Oxford University Press, 2009. xii, 380 pp. Examines "how animals mean" in beast fable, beast epic, and related literature in classical and medieval traditions, focusing on the uses of animals in Marie de France, Nigel of Longchamp, *The Owl and the Nightingale,* the Reynard tradition, Chaucer, and Robert Henryson. The power of nature and the "superfluity" of language recur as themes throughout. Chaucer focuses on how nature constrains social hierarchy and sexuality in *PF.* Sexuality is also a concern in *SqT, NPT,* and *ManT,* but each of these *Tale*s also explores the limits and potential of language and signification, deeply inflected by comic awareness that humans are beasts who talk and laugh.

83. Pugh, Tison. " 'For to be sworne bretheren til they deye': Satirizing Queer Brotherhood in the Chaucerian Corpus." *ChauR* 43 (2009): 282–310. Despite abundant evidence of their being held in high regard by contemporary society, male oaths of friendship are consistently "satirized, broken, and/or ridiculed" in Chaucer's works, suggesting "an overarching distrust of such relationships" on Chaucer's part. Pugh assesses such oaths in *HF, KnT, FrT, PardT,* and *ShT.*

84. Ransom, Daniel J. "Imprecise Chaucer." *ChauR* 43 (2009): 376–99. An examination of Chaucer's use of temporal terminology—from references to "eternity and perpetuity" to references to seconds and moments, including seasons, days, nights, and hours—suggests that he uses such terminology with a modicum of "nonchalance." This inexact use of temporal vocabulary "subordinates science to literary aims."

85. Rigby, Stephen H. "England: Literature and Society." In Stephen

H. Rigby, ed. *A Companion to Britain in the Later Middle Ages*. Oxford: Blackwell, 2003, pp. 497–520. Rigby explores how a variety of Middle English texts reflect and reinforce the normative ideologies of class and gender in late medieval England. Contempt for the world helped to assert social hierarchies, justify inequalities, and quell tensions. Cites several works by Chaucer, with recurrent references to *ParsT*.

86. Sauer, Michelle M. "'Where Are All the Lesbians in Chaucer?' Lack, Opportunity, and Female Homoeroticism in Medieval Studies Today." *Journal of Lesbian Studies* 11 (2007): 331–45. Sauer describes the "inadequacy of lesbian criticism in today's Medieval Literary Studies" and suggests some opportunities for developing such studies, including opportunities in Chaucer studies.

87. Scala, Elizabeth. "The Gender of Historicism." In Elizabeth Scala and Sylvia Federico, eds. *The Post-Historical Middle Ages* (*SAC* 33 [2011], no. 88), pp. 191–214. Indicts the "patrilineal logic by which the [masculine] gender of historicism is perpetuated and reproduced," surveying how recent publications in medieval studies (especially Chaucer studies) embody the structures of the "patriarchal family."

88. ———, and Sylvia Federico, eds. *The Post-Historical Middle Ages*. The New Middle Ages. New York: Palgrave Macmillan, 2009. [xi], 237 pp. Nine essays by various authors and an introduction by the editors "look beyond the absolute horizon of Marxist historicism in ways that display concern with *how* we know, with the limits of our knowledge, and with ourselves as presumably knowing subjects." Recurrent topics include psychoanalytic approaches, gender studies, new ways of reading historically, and seeking a (re)new(ed) respect for medieval studies. For five essays that pertain to Chaucer directly, see nos. 4, 5, 26, 87, and 190.

89. Scanlon, Larry. "Geoffrey Chaucer." In Larry Scanlon, ed., *The Cambridge Companion to Medieval English Literature, 1100–1500*. Cambridge: Cambridge University Press, 2009, pp. 165–78. Scanlon introduces Chaucer as the "most monumental of English poets," summarizes Chaucer's biography, surveys his works and their reception, and comments on the difficulties of dealing with his legacy: especially in *CT*, Chaucer is "eager to disavow" the authority that critical tradition attributes to him.

90. Sidhu, Nicole Nolan. "Love in a Cold Climate: The Future of Feminism and Gender Studies in Middle English Scholarship." *LitComp* 6 (2009): 864–85. Sidhu surveys recent attention to gender in medieval

studies and assesses the "continuing marginalization" of gender studies. Recurrent references to Chaucer studies.

91. Smith, Nathanial B. "Dreams of Influence: Embodied Reading in Late Medieval and Renaissance English Literature." *DAI* A69.10 (2009): n.p. Considers dream visions in the works of Chaucer and his successors (Hoccleve, Lydgate, Skelton, and Spenser), arguing that these dreams break down "binary" notions, including those of body/mind, gender, and text/reader.

92. Urban, Misty Rae. "Monstrous Women in Middle English Romance." *DAI* A69.12 (2009): n.p. Using figures from Middle English literature (including Chaucer's Constance and Medea), Urban argues that the literature both dramatizes and "interrogate[s] the prevailing gender ideology."

93. Whitehead, Christiania. "Geoffrey Chaucer." In Rebecca Lemon, ed. *The Blackwell Companion to the Bible in English Literature*. Malden, Mass.: Wiley-Blackwell, 2009, pp. 134–51. Whitehead surveys Chaucer's engagement with the Bible and biblical texts in *CT* and suggests a parallel between the poem's dialogic structure and the fourteenth-century debate over Wycliffite ideology. While parts of *CT* may corroborate certain reformist doctrines, the text as a whole registers ambivalence about lay interpretation of Scripture. A similar ambivalence can be found in *HF*.

94. Yu, Wesley Chihyung. "Romance Logic: The Argument of Vernacular Verse in the Scholastic Middle Ages." *DAI* A70.03 (2009): n.p. Yu examines the changing roles of literary rhetoric and dialectic, poesy and logic, from the twelfth to the fourteenth centuries. Chaucer is cited as a writer whose use of irony reflects changes in the understanding of logic.

The Canterbury Tales—General

95. Baron, F. Xavier. "Children and Violence in Chaucer's *Canterbury Tales*." *Journal of Psychohistory* 7.1 (1979): 77–103. Because Chaucer's "children's tales" deal with "extreme violence which the children suffer as innocent victims," these narratives "tend toward despair." Yet they provoke compassion and thereby suggest that compassion is the proper response to innocent suffering. Baron discusses *MLT, PrT, ClT, PhyT, Mel,* and the Hugolino story in *MkT*.

96. Bloom, Harold, ed. *Geoffrey Chaucer's "The Canterbury Tales."*

Bloom's Guides. New York: Bloom's Literary Criticism, 2008. 118 pp. A summary/introduction to the pilgrims and plots (Part 7 excepted) of *CT*, with brief excerpts from fourteen critical commentaries written between 1956 and 2007; annotations of twenty-one book-length studies; and an index.

97. *The Canterbury Tales, by Geoffrey Chaucer*. No Fear Literature Series. New York: SparkNotes, 2009. xvi, 397 pp. Facing-page translation of selections from *CT* into informal, colloquial modern prose. A brief introduction characterizes the pilgrims and the characters in selected tales; selections include *GP, KnT, MilT, WBPT, PardPT, Th*, and *NPT*.

98. Chen, Hsiaojane Anna. "Kinship Lessons: The Cultural Uses of Childhood in Late Medieval England." *DAI* A70.06 (2009): n.p. Considers *Astr* and *CT* within a larger analysis of the formation of intra- and extrafamilial kinship bonds. Such bonds are rooted in education and common experiences.

99. Davis, Isabel. "Expressing the Middle Ages." *LitComp* 6 (2009): 842–63. Davis assesses late medieval, first-person narration in English literature as a rhetorical and allegorical device and as an autobiographical stance. She comments on the influence of Augustine and Boethius and explores a range of Middle English authors, including Chaucer, particularly his "diminution of the narrator" in *CT*.

100. Knutson, Karla. "Innocence and Innocents in Middle English Literature and Its Reception." *DAI* A70.06 (2009): n.p. Knutson examines medieval ideas of innocence associated with penitential forgiveness in *CT, Pearl*, and medieval pageants, suggesting that a later concept of innocence—a lack of "knowledge or experience"—shaped William Godwin's and Mary Eliza Haweis's representations of Chaucer as an innocent primitive with "authoritative" talent.

101. Murnighan, Jack. "Geoffrey Chaucer (1340–1400): *The Canterbury Tales* (1400)." In Jack Murnighan. *"Beowulf" on the Beach: What to Love and What to Skip in Literature's 50 Greatest Hits*. New York: Three Rivers Press, 2009, pp. 86–97. Encourages approaching Chaucer as "both funny and a little racy," giving advice on how to read with understanding, opinions on what is "sexy" in *CT*, and suggestions of what to skip in the work (*CkPT, MLT, SqT, FranT, PhyT, PrT, Th, Mel, MkT, NPT, SNT, CYT*, and *ParsT*). Then briefly summarizes the remaining prologues and tales.

102. Nakley, Susan Marie. "'From every shires ende': Chaucer and Forms of Nationhood." *DAI* A70.03 (2009): n.p. Nakley uses postcolo-

nial theory to consider a Chaucerian dialogue with ideas of "nationhood," examining *GP, KnT, WBP, WBT,* and *MLT* en route to arguing that *CT* presents England as nation, "community," and "homeland."

103. O'Hear, Anthony. "Chaucer: *The Canterbury Tales.*" In Anthony O'Hear. *The Great Books: A Journey Through 2,500 Years of the West's Classic Literature.* Wilmington, Del.: ISI [Intercollegiate Studies Institute] Books, 2009), pp. 177–95. Description of *CT* that comments on Chaucer's social range and authenticating detail, arranges the Pilgrims into social classes, and comments on the plot of each of the *Tale*s.

104. Sancery, Arlette. "Canterbury, la cathédrale où Chaucer n'arrive jamais . . . Mais est-ce bien sûr?" *BAM* 76 (2009): 97–107. Explores implications of the fact that the pilgrims never arrive at their destination in *CT,* commenting on late medieval travel and pilgrimage.

105. Scala, Elizabeth. "The Women in Chaucer's 'Marriage Group.'" *MFF* 16.2 (2009): 50–56. Clarifies the foundational role of Eleanor Prescott Hammond in identifying and labeling Chaucer's "marriage group" in *CT*.

See also nos. 9, 10, 14, 17–19, 44, 48, 73, 93, 100.

CT—The General Prologue

See nos. 6, 53, 61, 75, 102, 112.

CT—The Knight and His Tale

106. Bell, Adrian R. "The Fourteenth-Century Soldier: More Chaucer's Knight or Medieval Career?" In John France, ed. *Mercenaries and Paid Men: The Mercenary Identity in the Middle Ages. Proceedings of a Conference Held at University of Wales, Swansea, 7th–9th July 2005.* Smithsonian History of Warfare, no. 47. Leiden: Brill, 2008, pp. 301–15. Bell analyzes the military record of 5,600 soldiers from Chaucer's lifetime to discover how many had records of military service similar to the experience of Chaucer's Knight. It was not uncommon for English soldiers to serve as mercenaries in locales such as Italy and Prussia. Most surprising is that the Knight is not credited with service in the Hundred Years' War, an omission that was "very unusual" for a soldier of this time. See also no. 228.

107. Finnegan, Robert Emmett. "A Curious Condition of Being: The

City and the Grove in Chaucer's *Knight's Tale*." *SP* 106 (2009): 285–98. Focuses on the city of Thebes, the Athenian grove, and Theseus's First Mover speech in *KnT* to define and explore implications of the "elastic ontology" of *KnT*. Unlike the city in Boccaccio's *Teseida,* in *KnT* Thebes is mysteriously whole after having been razed, while the grove is inexplicably razed twice. The unstable hierarchical relationship between Saturn and Jupiter in *KnT* underlies its concern with human inability to know the contradictions of the universe.

108. Gambera, Disa. "Windows and Wounds in Fragment I of the *Canterbury Tales*." In Andrew Galloway and R. F. Yeager, eds. *Through a Classical Eye: Transcultural and Transhistorical Visions in Medieval English, Italian, and Latin Literature in Honour of Winthrop Wetherbee* (*SAC* 33 [2011], no. 69), pp. 316–38. Connections among figurative wounds, literal wounds, and architectural "apertures" in Fragment 1 teach us "to notice the narrative dissonance of bodies and spaces" in *CT* (334).

109. Greenwood, Maria K. S. "Chaucer's Knight in Lithuania: British and Polish Critical Assessments." *BAM* 75 (2009): 1–22. Considers Chaucer criticism rather than praise of the Knight in *CT*.

110. Heyworth, Gregory. *Desiring Bodies: Ovidian Romance and the Cult of Form*. South Bend, Ind.: University of Notre Dame Press, 2009. xvii, 357 pp. Six studies on literature ranging from Marie de France to Milton. In the chapter on Chaucer, Heyworth examines medieval cultural values and suggests that Chaucer complicates those values, particularly marriage. *KnT* and *FranT* depict the social institution of marriage as a hybrid between genuine love and a desire for power over one's spouse.

111. Jost, Jean. "Urban and Liminal Space in Chaucer's *Knight's Tale*: Perilous or Protective?" In Albrecht Classen, ed. *Urban Space in the Middle Ages and the Early Modern Age* (*SAC* 33 [2011], no. 62), pp. 373–94. In *KnT,* space within a city constitutes more than just a physical context; it also provides identity for the individual protagonists.

112. Morgan, Gerald. "The Worthiness of Chaucer's Worthy Knight." *ChauR* 44 (2009): 115–58. Ironic readings of the *GP* portrait of the Knight are undermined by an understanding of the medieval ideals of "honor," "prudence," and "moral goodness" and by recognition of their signs in the Knight's portrait. An understanding of the medieval "rhetoric of praise" should prompt unalloyed "admiration for so excellent a man."

113. Rigby, Stephen H. "Ideology and Utopia: Prudence and Mag-

nificence, Kingship and Tyranny in Chaucer's *Knight's Tale.*" In Matthew Davies and Andrew Prescott, eds. *London and the Kingdom: Essays in Honour of Caroline M. Barron.* Proceedings of the 2004 Harlaxton Symposium. Harlaxton Medieval Studies, no. 16. Donington, England: Shaun Tyas, 2008, pp. 316–34. Orthodox notions of royal prudence and magnificence underlie the idealized figure of Theseus in *KnT*. Theseus embodies the traits that Richard II was accused of lacking.

114. ———. *Wisdom and Chivalry: Chaucer's "Knight's Tale" and Medieval Political Theory.* Medieval and Renaissance Authors and Texts, no. 4. Boston: Brill, 2009. xvi, 329 pp. Rigby reads *KnT* as a mirror for princes, comparing it with Giles of Rome's *De regimine principum* and finding Theseus of *KnT* to be an ideal ruler by this standard. Theseus's personal ethics, his treatment of his household, his political and military activities, and his philosophical outlook are consistent with the ideals expressed in Giles's text and in other medieval political treatises of the Aristotelian tradition. Recurrent attention to Chaucer's use and adaptation of Boccaccio's *Teseida* and Boethius's *Consolation.*

115. Szell, Timea. "Teaching Unstable Animal Identities in Medieval Narrative." *ELN* 47.1 (2009): 147–57. Pedagogical report on how to study animal and human identity in Hebrew Scripture, Ovid, and medieval narrative to acquire the interpretive skills to understand postmodern texts and culture. Animals in the imagery and narrative of *KnT* enable readers to question categories of the human as unique and to understand the text's "containing and shaping impulses."

116. Vander Elst, Stefan. " 'Tu es pélerin en la sainte cité': Chaucer's Knight and Philippe de Mézières." *SP* 106 (2009): 379–401. Vander Elst argues that the "life and writings of the French soldier and statesman Philippe de Mézières" inspired "almost every line" of Chaucer's description of the Knight in *GP*. This inspiration evinces the circulation of Philippe's works in Chaucer's milieu, indicates that the *GP* description is both realistic and idealistic, and suggests that Chaucer supported Philippe's efforts to encourage reconciliation between England and France.

117. Wheatley, Edward. "Murderous Sows in Chaucer's *Knight's Tale* and Late Fourteenth-Century France." *ChauR* 44 (2009): 224–26. Chaucer's reference to a sow eating a baby "right in the cradle" (*CT* I.2019) may evince Chaucer's knowledge of "just such an occurrence in the Norman town of Falaise" in 1385, later memorialized in paint on

the walls of a Falaise church. This detail may help to date versions of *KnT*.

118. Withers, Jeremy. "The Ecology of War in Late Medieval Chivalric Culture." *DAI* A69.08 (2009): n.p. Withers examines medieval writers' interest in the effect of medieval warfare, tactics, and technology on "the natural world," arguing that several works (including Lydgate's *Siege of Thebes,* the Alliterative *Morte,* and *KnT*) paid significant attention to these concerns.

See also nos. 4, 6, 33, 38, 51, 65, 83, 102.

CT—The Miller and His Tale

119. Biggs, Frederick M. "A Bared Bottom and a Basket: A New Analogue and a New Source for the *Miller's Tale*." *N&Q* 254 (2009): 340–41. Among the four fabliaux in London, British Library Harley MS 2253, "La gageure," featuring the "misdirected kiss" motif, is an analogue of *MilT,* while "Le chevalier e la corbeille" is a possible source, providing not only a container that forces "the lovers' antagonist" into a punishing fall but also an architectural setting with the verticality necessary for such a descent.

120. ————. "The *Miller's Tale* and *Decameron* 3.4." *JEGP* 108 (2009): 59–80. Biggs argues that *Decameron* 3.4 is a source for *MilT,* inspiring the latter's density of detail, its religious sentiment, and many of its narrative features, particularly the Flood story. *MilP* also echoes Boccaccio's "Conclusione dell'autore" and its concern with religious rather than rational judgment.

121. Nolcken, Christina von. "Another 'Lollere in the wynd'? The Miller, the Bible, and the Destruction of Doors." In Andrew Galloway and R. F. Yeager, eds. *Through a Classical Eye: Transcultural and Transhistorical Visions in Medieval English, Italian, and Latin Literature in Honour of Winthrop Wetherbee* (*SAC* 33 [2011], no. 69), pp. 239–66. Assesses the Miller in the historical context of clerical responsibilities and the Wycliffite translation of the Bible. *MilT* is comic, but its narrator is "deadly serious about furthering the cause of lay intellectualism and the Wycliffites' contribution to this"; Chaucer explores this discrepancy between comedy and seriousness.

122. Scott, Anne. "Come Hell or High Water: Aqueous Moments in Medieval Epic, Romance, Allegory, and Fabliau." In Cynthia Kosso and

Anne Scott, eds. *The Nature and Function of Water, Baths, Bathing, and Hygiene from Antiquity Through the Renaissance.* Boston: Brill, 2009, pp. 407–26. Scott addresses use of water imagery in medieval narratives. In *MilT,* flood imagery affects all classes of society and provides a common experience through which the satire of each individual class can occur. See also no. 242.

123. Walts, Dawn Simmons. "Tricks of Time in the *Miller's Tale.*" *ChauR* 43 (2009): 400–413. In *MilT,* Nicholas's real and reputed knowledge of astrology convinces John of the upcoming Flood, evidence that he has spent his time well in learning the science of reckoning time. Indeed, in contrast to the carpenter, the educated clerk has the power "to direct the actions of the other characters in the tale and establish the timeline for the narrative."

See also nos. 54, 108.

CT—The Reeve and His Tale

124. Breeze, Andrew. "Chaucer's Strother and Berwickshire." *N&Q* 254 (2009): 21–23. For both linguistic and political reasons, the town in *RvT* from which John and Aleyn hail may be identified as Westruther in Berwickshire, making Chaucer's rendition of their speech "the first imitation of Scots dialect in English literature."

125. Delasanta, Rodney. "The Mill in Chaucer's *Reeve's Tale.*" *ChauR* 36 (2002): 270–76. The mill in *RvT* is a setting that carries sexual and "eschatological" resonances.

See also nos. 40, 49, 108.

CT—The Cook and His Tale

126. Pigg, Daniel F. "Imagining Urban Life and Its Discontents: Chaucer's *Cook's Tale* and Masculine Identity." In Albrecht Classen, ed. *Urban Space in the Middle Ages and the Early Modern Age* (*SAC* 33 [2011], no. 62), pp. 395–408. *CkT* presents merriment at ribaldry, as well as social anxiety over the monetary waste of degenerate apprentices.

CT—The Man of Law and His Tale

See nos. 92, 95, 102, 132.

CT—The Wife of Bath and Her Tale

127. Barrington, Candace. "Retelling Chaucer's *Wife of Bath* for Modern Children: Picture Books and Evolving Feminism." In Karen A. Ritzenhoff and Katherine A. Hermes, eds. *Sex and Sexuality in a Feminist World*. Newcastle upon Tyne: Cambridge Scholars Press, 2009, pp. 26–51. Modern adapters of Chaucer interfere with the transmission of Chaucer by infusing their own values. In each era, the versions written for children bear witness to what aspects of feminism have reached popular culture.

128. Harbus, Antonina. "Interpreting *The Wife of Bath's Prologue* and *Tale* in a Contemporary Note to Thynne's 1532 Edition." *ANQ* 22.3 (2009): 3–11. An inscription at the end of *ParsT* in a copy of Thynne's edition in the Beinecke Library, Osborn Collection, Yale University, reveals something of the general reception of the Wife of Bath.

129. McIntyre, Ruth Anne Summar. "Memory, Place, and Desire in Late Medieval British Pilgrimage Narratives." *DAI* A69.08 (2009): n.p. Examines the uses of memory and place to develop authoritative "ethos" in John Mandeville's *Travels,* Margery Kempe's *Book, WBP,* and *WBT.* The Wife relies on medieval commonplace texts and essentially turns her own experience into such a text.

See also nos. 13, 58, 65, 73, 77, 102, 136, 139.

CT—The Friar and His Tale

See no. 83.

CT—The Summoner and His Tale

130. Allen, Valerie. *On Farting: Language and Laughter in the Middle Ages.* New York: Palgrave Macmillan, 2007. xii, 239 pp., 7 b&w illus. Considers the imagery and implications of flatulence, wind, excrement, and refuse in medieval culture, considering anecdotes, visual imagery,

religious commentary, and other literature. Occasional mention of Chaucer's work, with focused attention to *SumT,* commenting on its puns, associations of excrement with gold, and alignment of flatulence with inspiration.

131. Olson, Glending. "Measuring the Immeasurable: Farting, Geometry, and Theology in the *Summoner's Tale.*" *ChauR* 43 (2009): 414–27. By framing his "Pentecostal parody" within a parody of fourteenth-century English academics' preoccupation with measuring "both physical and metaphysical realities," Chaucer registers "a cautious but not gloomy attitude" regarding the spectrum of reality that may be conducive to human measurement.

CT—The Clerk and His Tale

132. Florschuetz, Angela. "'A Mooder He Hath, but Fader Hath He Noon': Constructions of Genealogy in the *Clerk's Tale* and the *Man of Law's Tale.*" *ChauR* 44 (2009): 25–60. *ClT* and *MLT* dramatize contemporary uncertainties concerning the extent of a mother's genetic "influence" on her offspring, even as they critique the "fantasy of an autonomous male line." Given that disputes regarding monarchal succession formed the crux of the Hundred Years' War, these two portions of *CT* also critique the French tendency to deny maternal transmission of royal blood.

133. Ginsberg, Warren. "From Simile to Prologue: Geography as Link in Dante, Petrarch, Chaucer." In Andrew Galloway and R. F. Yeager, eds. *Through a Classical Eye: Transcultural and Transhistorical Visions in Medieval English, Italian, and Latin Literature in Honour of Winthrop Wetherbee* (*SAC* 33 [2011], no. 69), pp. 145–64. Ginsberg compares Dante's, Petrarch's, and Chaucer's descriptions of geography in their poems: Dante relied on the landscape of Italy to establish a geographical base; Petrarch allegorized Dante's geography; and Chaucer then "translated Petrarch's revisions," particularly in *ClT.* Ginsberg examines Dante's "psychological and discursive" extended simile in the *Inferno* and then focuses on how Petrarch used the geographical simile and how Chaucer translated it to different effect.

134. Hodges, Laura F. "Reading Griselda's Smocks in the *Clerk's Tale.*" *ChauR* 44 (2009): 84–109. Hodges "reads" Griselda's "sartorial transformation[s]" in light of detailed knowledge of fourteenth-century material culture. For instance, the fact that a smock could be made of

plain linen or embroidered silk, or that it was the innermost of many layers of noblewomen's apparel, heightens drama and underscores symbolism.

135. Odierno, Alfred. "Chaucer Knows Best." *Momentum* (Washington, D.C.) 38.2 (2007): 6–7. Editorial commentary on the joys of teaching, using as a touchstone Chaucer's Clerk—one who would "gladly" teach.

136. Scala, Elizabeth. "Desire in the *Canterbury Tales*: Sovereignty and Mastery Between the Wife and Clerk." *SAC* 31 (2009): 81–108. In Lacanian terms, *WBT* and *ClT* reveal "what each speaker seems most desperate to deny." Ideas of sovereignty ("self-determination"), mastery ("control over another"), and the desires they help to constitute are parallel in the *Tales*. So are the representations of the "powerful mobility" of the loathly lady and Griselda, evident in their transformations. The endings of *WBT* and *ClT* (including the "Envoy" to *ClT*) reveal how the narrators "recoil" from their *Tales* and from the "structure of desire underwriting them."

137. Shutters, Lynn. "Griselda's Pagan Virtue." *ChauR* 44 (2009): 61–83. Chaucer modifies his sources for *ClT* in a way that emphasizes Griselda's virtue as specifically "feminine" and exclusively "wifely." The reflections of her wifely virtue in the pagan wives of *LGW,* who "view devotion to their husbands as their highest ideal," provoke a consideration of "the degree to which a married woman can and should be fully devoted to her husband."

138. Sidhu, Nicole Nolan. "Weeping for the Virtuous Wife: Laymen, Affective Piety, and Chaucer's 'Clerk's Tale.'" In Maryanne Kowaleski and P. J. P. Goldberg, eds. *Medieval Domesticity: Home, Housing, and Household in Medieval England* (*SAC* 33 [2011], no. 79), pp. 177–208. Adaptations of its sources shape *ClT* in ways that encourage male, bourgeois readers to imagine themselves as Griselda's protectors. Infused with a sense of moral and patriarchal responsibility and driven by religious devotion, such readers also respond to the assertion of male authority in the *Tale*.

139. Stillinger, Thomas C. "New Science, Old Dance: The Clerk and the Wife of Bath at Philology." In Andrew Galloway and R. F. Yeager, eds. *Through a Classical Eye: Transcultural and Transhistorical Visions in Medieval English, Italian, and Latin Literature in Honour of Winthrop Wetherbee* (*SAC* 33 [2011], no. 69), pp. 223–38. Observing that threshold between the Wife of Bath and the Clerk and between their tales, Stil-

linger explores how Chaucer stands at the "threshold between the Middle Ages and the Renaissance" (224): "If the Clerk imports the new science of the Renaissance" into *CT,* the Wife of Bath "seems to stand for the old dance of the Middle Ages" (232).

140. Yager, Susan. "Levinas, Allegory, and Chaucer's *Clerk's Tale.*" In Ann W. Astell and J. A. Jackson, eds. *Levinas and Medieval Literature: The "Difficult Reading" of English and Rabbinic Texts* (*SAC* 33 [2011], no. 59), pp. 35–56. Examines parallels between Levinas's writing and medieval allegory. Yager reads *ClT* in a Levinasian mode to generate an open-ended reading or "an exercise in *ifs.*" *ClT* can be read as an ethical allegory; Chaucer, as an ethical allegorist. Yager discusses similarities between Griselda and the ethical other.

141. Yvernault, Martine. "Le personnage de Grisildis dans *The Clerk's Tale* de Chaucer: Un discours sur l'effacement." *Clio* (Toulouse) 30 (2009): 137–52. Yvernault assesses Chaucer's ambiguous uses and rewriting of Boccaccio in *ClT,* especially in his treatment of Griselda.

See also nos. 21, 68, 75, 95, 166.

CT—The Merchant and His Tale

142. Kolve, V. A. *Telling Images: Chaucer and the Imagery of Narrative II.* Stanford: Stanford University Press, 2009. xxxiii, 368 pp., b&w illus. Reprints six of Kolve's essays on visual imagery and iconography in Chaucer and medieval literature and adds two new ones—both on *MerT*: "Of Calendars and Cuckoldry (1): January and May in *The Merchant's Tale*" (pp. 93–122) and "Of Calendars and Cuckoldry (2): The Sun in Gemini and *The Merchant's Tale*" (pp. 123–70). In the two new essays, Kolve provides visual background for January and May and for the pear-tree episode of *MerT* from medieval and early modern calendar traditions. He argues that these traditions underlie the characterizations in *MerT* and affirm the fabliau erotics of the conclusion, despite countervailing concerns with the Fall of Man. About forty-five black-and-white illustrations accompany the two essays. See also no. 241.

See also nos. 51, 53, 189.

CT—The Squire and His Tale

143. Benton, Andrea Gronstal. "Telling Description: Convention, Coherence, and the Making of the Self in Middle English Romance."

DAI A69.09 (2009): n.p. Benton contrasts *SqT* and the work of the *Gawain*-poet with popular romances as a way of understanding how romances employ descriptive passages as an essential "formal and conceptual" element.

144. Ingham, Patricia Clare. "Little Nothings: *The Squire's Tale* and the Ambition of Gadgets." *SAC* 31 (2009): 53–80. Reads *SqT* as Chaucer's exploration of the "double-face of newness." Cambyuskan's encounter with the brass steed is counterpointed by Canacee's communication with the eagle, posing an ambiguous pairing of "creative rationality" and "enchanted desire." This ambiguity reflects the more fundamental fascination of Western medieval romance with understandings of "oriental" Arabia.

145. Kordecki, Lesley. "Chaucer's *Squire's Tale*: Animal Discourse, Women, and Subjectivity." *ChauR* 36 (2002): 277–97. Various concepts of "otherness" in *SqT*—oriental setting, magic, nonhuman speech, female centrality—reflect Chaucer's "reshaping" of Ovidian "transformation" myth. His efforts to enter "into feminized animal subjectivity . . . intertwine with magic." Yet "the experiment must inevitably fail." Kordecki also comments on *ManT* and *NPT*.

See also nos. 65, 82, 177.

CT—The Franklin and His Tale

146. Furrow, Melissa. *Expectations of Romance: The Reception of a Genre in Medieval England*. Cambridge: D. S. Brewer, 2009. viii, 264 pp. Setting out to establish what medieval readers thought about romances and what they labeled romances, Furrow concentrates on a wide range of romances from the twelfth to the fifteenth centuries. Her discussion of romance and truth includes analysis of *FranT* as a reflection of Chaucer's concern with reader reception of romance. Particularly if *FranT* is read without irony, it "undercuts happy adherence to the genre's expectations" and may even be seen as "an attack on belief in the truth of romances" (208).

147. Hersh, Cara. "'Knowledge of the Files': Subverting Bureaucratic Legibility in the *Franklin's Tale*." *ChauR* 43 (2009): 428–54. As knight, sheriff, and "contour" (I.359), the Franklin is the quintessential late medieval county "bureaucrat," whose duties provided incentives both to disclose and to hide the financial information to which he was

privy. From its "dramatic irony" to its frequent use of the "highly equivocal" adjective *certein*, *FranT* dramatizes an administrator's skill—perhaps Chaucer's own—with finding a strategic balance between textual transparency and ambiguity.

148. Jost, Jean. "What Kind of Words Are These? Courtly and Marital Words of Love in the *Franklin's Tale* and *Sir Gawain and the Green Knight*." In Albrecht Classen, ed. *Words of Love and Love of Words in the Middle Ages and the Renaissance*. Tempe: Arizona Center for Medieval and Renaissance Studies, 2008, pp. 395–420. Courtly literature is an intellectual battleground in which reversals of gender and social positions clash. The men's rhetorical competition in *FranT* shows a courtly love of words.

149. Pearcy, Roy J. "*Epreuves d'amour* and Chaucer's *Franklin's Tale*." *ChauR* 44 (2009): 159–85. A study of works featuring the test-of-love motif argues for including *FranT* among them rather than among narratives employing the motif of the "maiden's rash promise." However, by devising a "test" for Dorigen's suitor that expresses her concern for her husband's safety, Chaucer twists this staple of the courtly love genre, thereby pointing out that "the reconciliation of romantic love and Christian marriage is a fragile fantasy."

150. Sayers, William. "*Tregetours* in 'The Franklin's Tale': Stage Magic and Siege Machines." *N&Q* 254 (2009): 341–46. Glossed in *The Riverside Chaucer* as "illusionists, magicians," *tregetours* cause their subjects to experience "a fall from cognitive certitude to amazement and bafflement," a result that is captured in the "associational field" that includes both Middle English *tregetour* and *trepeget,* a siege machine. The two terms arise, respectively, from Old French *tresjeter,* "to throw over," and *trebuchier,* "to cast down."

See also nos. 53, 65, 77, 110.

CT—The Physician and His Tale

151. Skerpan, Elizabeth Penley. "Chaucer's Physicians: Their Texts, Contexts, and the *Canterbury Tales*." *JRMMRA* 5 (1984): 41–54. Explores Chaucer's depictions of physicians, focusing on how they exemplify the tension between *medici corporals* (bodily medicine) and *spirituals* (spiritual medicine). None of Chaucer's physicians exhibits an ideal balance; Chaucer explores a contemporary debate without seeking to re-

solve it. Skerpan considers the Physician, the Pardoner, and the physicians of *Mel*.

See also nos. 30, 95.

CT—The Pardoner and His Tale

152. Astell, Ann W. "When Pardon Is Impossible: Two Talmudic Tales, Chaucer's *Pardoner's Tale,* and Levinas." In Ann W. Astell and J. A. Jackson, eds. *Levinas and Medieval Literature: The "Difficult Reading" of English and Rabbinic Texts* (*SAC* 33 [2011], no. 59), pp. 255–80. Two Talmudic tales interpreted by Levinas complement *PardT* in "uncanny ways." While Chaucer explores the impossibility of forgiveness from the perspective of the offender, the Talmudic tales explore the impossibility of forgiveness from the perspective of the offended. *ParsT* informs a reading of *PardT* just as the sayings of the Rabbis inform the tales of Rab. Astell explores the concept of time in relation to forgiveness and comments on Chaucer's petition for forgiveness in *Ret*.

153. Goth, Maik. *From Chaucer's Pardoner to Shakespeare's Iago: Aspects of Intermediality in the History of the Vice*. Frankfurt am Main: Peter Lang, 2009. 143 pp. Reconsiders Harold Bloom's argument that Shakespeare, when creating Iago, was influenced by Chaucer's Pardoner. Goth explores the "dramatic" nature of the Pardoner's character and his relations with Vice figures from late medieval drama as well as Faus Semblant from the *Roman de la Rose*. Common features of Iago and the Pardoner, the book suggests, derive independently from the Vice tradition.

154. Minnis, Alastair. "Once More into the Breech: The Pardoner's Prize 'Relyk.'" In Andrew Galloway and R. F. Yeager, eds. *Through a Classical Eye: Transcultural and Transhistorical Visions in Medieval English, Italian, and Latin Literature in Honour of Winthrop Wetherbee* (*SAC* 33 [2011], no. 69), pp. 287–315. Exploring the "cultural sources and significance of the humor which Chaucer brings into play" in *PardT* (288), Minnis examines medieval relics, shrines, and cures and suggests that if we understand more about these practices, "we may gain a better understanding of the comic discourse surrounding Chaucer's Pardoner and his ridiculous relics—and measure the extent to which they were ridiculous" (306).

155. ———. *Translations of Authority in Medieval English Literature:*

Valuing the Vernacular. New York: Cambridge University Press, 2009. xvi, 272 pp. Six studies by Minnis on the relationships among the vernacular, demotic attitudes, and Lollard concerns. One study pertains to Chaucer: chapter 6, "Chaucer and the Relics of Vernacular Religion" (pp. 130–62), reads the Pardoner's involvement with relics and his altercation with the Host at the end of *PardT* in light of various late medieval attitudes toward the veneration (and kissing) of relics. Minnis discloses the comedy of the Host's "put-down of the Pardoner" and exemplifies how to discover non-elite attitudes within "high-culture texts."

156. Swan, Richard. *The Pardoner's Prologue and Tale*. AS/A-Level Student Text Guide. Deddington, Oxfordshire: Phillip Allan Updates, 2009. 90 pp. Study guide to *PardPT,* with discussion of themes, genre, verse, and characterization. Includes running commentary on the poem and various pedagogical tools for teachers and students, keyed to the UK exam board specifications and assessment objectives.

157. Twombly, Robert G. "*The Pardoner's Tale* and Dominican Meditation." *ChauR* 36 (2002): 250–69. Examines the rioters' encounter with the Old Man in *PardT* in light of Dominican meditation on death as a form of "affective psychology," exemplified in Henry Suso's *The Little Book of Eternal Wisdom*. In this genre, "meeting" Death is a means to spiritual enlightenment; it clashes with other scenarios of facing death to generate the complicated "ambiguities" of Chaucer's scene.

See also nos. 61, 68, 73, 83, 151.

CT—The Shipman and His Tale

158. Beidler, Peter G. "Medieval Children Witness Their Mothers' Indiscretions: The Maid Child in Chaucer's *Shipman's Tale*." *ChauR* 44 (2009): 186–204. Reading *ShT* in the context of fabliaux in which children witness their mothers' infidelity, Beidler recalls that the *Tale* was originally intended for the Wife of Bath. He argues that the placement of a prepubescent girl on the scene of another wife's "illicit" extramarital activities may be understood as a case of the wife's fulfilling a responsibility to teach her daughter by example "the ways a woman can get what she needs in the world."

See also nos. 51, 83.

CT—The Prioress and Her Tale

159. Birenbaum, Maija. "Affective Vengeance in *Titus and Vespasian*." *ChauR* 43 (2009): 330–44. Its fierce anti-Semitism notwithstanding, *Titus and Vespasian* is an important document of cultural uses of the "fall-of-Jerusalem narrative" and of attitudes toward Jews and Judaism in late medieval England. Thus it deserves scholarly attention alongside works such as the *Siege of Jerusalem* and *PrT*.

160. Dahood, Roger. "English Historical Narratives of Jewish Child-Murder, Chaucer's *Prioress's Tale,* and the Date of Chaucer's Unknown Source." *SAC* 31 (2009): 125–40. Dahood attributes several features of the plot of *PrT* to "non-Marian, historical English narratives of Jews crucifying English Christian boys" and explores how and when these features became attached to narratives of a chorister murdered by Jews. The tradition was influenced by tales of Hugh of Lincoln, the building of a shrine to him, and the development of a "Lincoln sub-group" of analogous tales (*PrT* and the Spanish version known as C9).

161. Delany, Sheila. "La Priora de Chaucer, los Judíos y los Mussulmanes." *Indaga: Revista Internacional de Ciencias Sociales y Humanas* 4 (2006): 223–42. Spanish translation of Delany's essay entitled "Chaucer's Prioress, the Jews, and the Muslims" (see *SAC* 23 [2001], no. 194).

162. Hilmo, Maidie. "Iconic Representations of Chaucer's Two Nuns and Their Tales from Manuscript to Print." In Kathryn Kerby-Fulton, ed. *Women and the Divine in Literature Before 1700: Essays in Memory of Margot Louis*. Victoria, Canada: ELS Editions, 2009, pp. 107–35, 9 b&w figs. Hilmo explores the iconography of representations of the Prioress, the Second Nun, and their *Tale*s, commenting on the Ellesmere illustrations of the tellers, the Vernon manuscript depiction of *PrT,* two manuscript depictions of Saint Cecilia, and the woodcuts used by Caxton, de Worde, and Pynson.

163. Weissberger, Barbara F. "Motherhood and Ritual Murder in Medieval Spain and England." *JMEMSt* 93 (2009): 703–25. Contrasts *PrT* with Damián de Vegas's *Memoria del Santo Niño de La Guardia* (1544), exploring mother figures in the works and arguing that the latter work (like Spanish tradition more generally) reflects the influence of the *converso,* a hybrid figure who blurs Christian/Jewish boundaries.

See also nos. 46, 75, 95.

CT—The Tale of Sir Thopas

164. Pugh, Tison. "Teaching the Genders of Medieval Romance with Parodies: A Case Study Featuring Guerin's 'Long-Assed Berenger,' Chaucer's 'Tale of Sir Thopas,' and *Monty Python and the Holy Grail*." *SMART* 16.2 (2009): 111–25. Pugh explores opportunities for defining gender conventions of romance by examining parodies: knightly masculinity in Guerin's "Long-Assed Berenger" and in *Th* and gender construction in episodes from *Monty Python and the Holy Grail*.

165. Rushton, Cory. James. "Modern and Academic Reception of the Popular Romance." In Raluca L. Radulescu and Cory James Rushton, eds. *A Companion to Medieval Popular Romance*. Cambridge: D. S. Brewer, 2009, pp. 165–79. Rushton suggests that *Th* and *Sir Gawain and the Green Knight* may be accountable for the lack of sustained academic focus on medieval popular romance. Modern popular fiction, games, and films have, by contrast, embraced many features of the popular romance. Comments particularly on Thomas Chestre's *Sir Launfal* in light of *Th*. See also no. 267.

See also nos. 4, 38, 73.

CT—The Tale of Melibee

166. Collette, Carolyn. "Aristotle, Translation, and the Mean: Shaping the Vernacular in Late Medieval Anglo-French Culture." In Jocelyn Wogan-Browne et al., eds. *Language and Culture in Medieval Britain: The French of England, c. 1100–c. 1500* (*SAC* 31 [2011], no. 55), pp. 373–85. Collette explores interest in "mediation and moderation" in vernacular texts, commenting on the vernacular as a way to make learning more broadly available, on "the mean" in such texts as Nicole Oresme's translations of Aristotle, and on Chaucer's use of ideas of moderation in *ClT, ParsT,* and, especially, *Mel*.

See also nos. 30, 32, 95, 151.

CT—The Monk and His Tale

167. Lindeboom, Wim. "Zenobia in Chaucers *Canterbury Tales*." *Armada* (Amsterdam) 14/53 (2008): 36–44 (in Dutch). Lindeboom dis-

cusses how Zenobia in *MkT* helps to characterize the Monk and his spiritual condition.

See also nos. 3, 75, 95.

CT—The Nun's Priest and His Tale

168. Bradbury, Nancy Mason, and Carolyn P. Collette. "Changing Times: The Mechanical Clock in Late Medieval Literature." *ChauR* 43 (2009): 351–75. Bradbury and Collette survey historical records and literary representations of clocks in works by Jean Froissart, Henry Suso, Philippe de Mézières, and Christine de Pizan. The article counters the notion that the mechanical clock caused a sudden shift from "qualitative" to "quantitative" time, showing instead that the clock was a figure for personal and political regulation. Multiple kinds of time in *NPT* invite readers to consider "the extent to which Chaucer genuinely adheres to traditional ideas of qualitative time."

169. Coote, Stephen. *Chaucer: The Nun's Priest's Tale*. Penguin Masterstudies. New York: Penguin, 1985. 152 pp. Middle English text of *NPPT* (with the Croesus account from *MkT*), accompanied by facing-page notes, a glossary (pp. 147–52), and an introduction (pp. 7–94) that surveys Chaucer's life and works; the sources of *NPT*; the characterization of the Nun's Priest, Chauntecleer, Pertelote, Russell, and the widow; and uses of rhetoric and comic wisdom in the *Tale*.

170. Flavin, Louise. "The Similar Dramatic Function of Prophetic Dreams: Eve's Dream Compared to Chauntecleer's." *Milton Quarterly* 17 (1983): 132–38. Flavin argues that Milton may have been influenced by Chaucer: like Chauntecleer in *NPT,* Milton's Eve ignores her prophetic dream and falls victim to flattery. Milton's Adam is also similar to Chauntecleer in passionate submission to beauty.

171. Fulwiler, Lavon. "*Babe*: A Twentieth-Century *Nun's Priest's Tale?*" *CCTE* (Conference of College Teachers of English) *Studies* 61 (1996): 93–101. Fulwiler looks at how *Babe* and *NPT* use the genre of animal fable and prosopopoeia to create moral tales. *Sentence* and *solaas* combine in *Babe,* as in Chaucer, to intrigue the audience into deeper exploration of the story. Via structure, setting, characterization, and typology, *Babe* and Chaucer exhibit a world where both humans and animals are capable of Christian goodness.

See also nos. 3, 30, 61, 75, 82, 145, 190.

CT—The Second Nun and Her Tale

172. Grossi, Joseph L., Jr. "The Unhidden Piety of Chaucer's 'Seint Cecilie.'" *ChauR* 36 (2002): 298–309. Grossi compares details of *SNT* with Jacob of Voragine's version in the *Golden Legend* and the Franciscan "abridgement" of the life of Saint Cecilia, arguing that Chaucer "sought to widen the intellectual divide between Roman paganism and primitive Christianity" that he found in his sources.

See also no. 162.

CT—The Canon's Yeoman and His Tale

173. Friedman, John B. "The *Merda Philosophorum*: An English Problem." In Marlene Villalobos Hennessy, ed. *Tributes to Kathleen L. Scott. English Medieval Manuscripts: Readers, Makers, and Illuminators* (*SAC* 33 [2011], no. 76), pp. 83–100. *CYPT* shares details and concerns found in other late medieval and early modern English alchemical treatises, part of the genre of "alchemical autobiography." Like *CYPT* in considering the function of organic material (especially excrement) in alchemical transformation, other treatises, however, are less satiric than Chaucer's work: Thomas Norton's *Ordinal of Alchemy,* Bernard of Trévisan's *Livre,* George Ripley's *Compound of Alchemy,* and others.

See also no. 180.

CT—The Manciple and His Tale

See nos. 50, 82, 145, 177.

CT—The Parson and His Tale

174. McCann, Christine. "Fertility Control and Society in Medieval Europe." *Comitatus* 40 (2009): 45–62. The warnings in *ParsT* against contraceptive methods are literary evidence that women successfully limited fertility in the late Middle Ages.

175. Winstead, Karen A. "Chaucer's *Parson's Tale* and the Contours of Orthodoxy." *ChauR* 43 (2009): 239–59. By assigning his English translation of Raymund of Pennaforte's "orthodox" yet "contritionist"

Summa de poenitentia to the Parson, Chaucer subtly resists the emphasis on oral confession to priests that characterized the doctrine of penance in his day. In this way, he began a trend followed by fifteenth-century writers such as Julian of Norwich, Eleanor Hull, Margery Kempe, and Thomas Hoccleve.

See also nos. 75, 85, 152, 166.

CT—Chaucer's Retraction

176. Herman, Jason Michael. "Intention, Utility, and Chaucer's Retraction." *DAI* A70.04 (2009): n.p. Suggests that *Ret* should be considered as a rhetorical appeal for the prayers of readers, who are encouraged to reflect on their own readings of *CT* and to engage in the self-scrutiny that *Ret* exemplifies.

See also nos. 73, 152.

Anelida and Arcite

177. Patterson, Lee. "'Thirled with the Poynt of Remembraunce': Memory and Modernity in Chaucer's Poetry." In Brigitte Cazelles and Charles Méla, eds. *Modernité au Moyen Âge: Le défi du passé*. Recherches et rencontres, no. 1. Geneva: Droz, 1990, pp. 113–51. Chaucer's *Anel* explores the "dilemma of the modern poet in the late Middle Ages." The "Thebanness" of the text engages its Boethianism as a competing and fatalistic view of memory and history. Allusions to Statius, Corinna, Virgil, Ovid, Dante, and others reflect Chaucer's anxieties about literary origins and history. Patterson also comments on *SqT, ManT,* and *Mars.*

A Treatise on the Astrolabe

178. Banks, David. "Your Very First ESP Text (Wherein Chaucer Explaineth the Astrolabe)." *ASp {Anglais de spécialité}: La revue du GERAS* 15–18 (1997): 451–60. Banks gauges the place of *Astr* in the development of English scientific prose, tabulating grammatical metaphors, verbal nouns (ending with *-ing*), passive voice, personal pronouns, and instructional syntax (an infinitive clause followed by an imperative

clause). Treats *Astr* as a "how-it-works" manual, comparing it with modern examples.

179. Horobin, Simon. "The Scribe of Bodleian Library MS Bodley 619 and the Circulation of Chaucer's *Treatise on the Astrolabe*." *SAC* 31 (2009): 109–24. Paleographical analysis of the text of *Astr* in Bodley MS 619 reveals that it was produced not by a professional astronomer but by Stephen Dodesham, a professional scribe who became a Carthusian monk. Other features of the manuscript encourage suggestions about its production and the audience of the text.

See also no. 98.

Boece

180. Johnson, Eleanor. "Chaucer and the Consolation of *Prosimetrum*." *ChauR* 43 (2009): 455–72. Boethius's *prosimetrum* lets readers experience the "consolation of temporality" that Philosophy offers. In *Bo*, Chaucer demonstrates his understanding of this consolation by highlighting Philosophy's references to time; however, by rendering the work entirely in prose, Chaucer leaves a metrical "aestheticization" of time for another work: *CYT* is a work of "verse alchemy," in which Chaucer "writes his own consolation," though one of "poetry, rather than . . . *prosimetrum*."

See also nos. 29, 198.

The Book of the Duchess

181. An, Li. " 'Nature' in Chaucer's *Book of the Duchess*." *Foreign Literature Studies* 138 (2009): 45–54 (in Chinese). Explores the meaning of "nature" in *BD*, focusing on the alignment of love and natural law.

182. Ciccone, Nancy. "The Chamber, the Man in Black, and the Structure of Chaucer's *Book of the Duchess*." *ChauR* 44 (2009): 205–23. In its evocations of a *locus amoenus, fin' amors*, and Aeneas, the dream chamber in *BD* serves as a "structural analogue" to the Man in Black's autobiography, which narrates an idyllic youth, describes falling in love, and refers to the duties of leadership. In turn, this analogue puts Chaucer's early poetic "craft" on display as "an investigation into the relationship between art and life."

183. Floyd, Jennifer Eileen. "Writing on the Wall: John Lydgate's Architectural Verse." *DAI* A69.10 (2009): n.p. In discussing Lydgate's "architectural-decorative" verses, the dissertation reflects on connections between literary and physical spaces in *BD*.

184. Huber, Emily Rebekah. "'For Y am sorwe, and sorwe ys Y': Melancholy, Despair, and Pathology in Middle English Literature." *DAI* A69.08 (2009): n.p. Huber uses *BD* as a case study in a larger examination of depression and self-scrutiny (especially as embodied in confession) in Middle English texts.

185. Lettau, Lisa. "Conscious Constructions of Self: Dreams and Visions in the Middle Ages." *DAI* A69.09 (2009): n.p. As part of an exploration of medieval efforts to understand a physical/spiritual dichotomy, the dissertation sets *BD* in conversation with Margery Kempe, with an eye toward development of a "unified selfhood."

186. Treacy, Anne-Marie. *"Et pour la joie que j'avoie ce rondelet fis*: The Emotional Use of Song in Chaucer's *Book of the Duchess*." In Karl Kügle and Lorenz Welker, eds. *Borderline Areas in Fourteenth- and Fifteenth-Century Music*. Middleton, Wis.: American Institute of Musicology, 2009, pp. 221–29. Comments on the influence of *Roman de la Rose* and Machaut's *Remede de Fortune* and *Jugement du Roy de Behaigne* on *BD*, suggesting that Chaucer reinvents the "French fashion for lyric interpolation" to "suit the needs of the grieving Black Knight."

See also nos. 8, 51, 190.

The Equatorie of the Planetis

[No entries]

The House of Fame

187. Meecham-Jones, Simon. "'Englyssh Gaufride' and British Chaucer? Chaucerian Allusions to the Condition of Wales in the *House of Fame*." *ChauR* 44 (2009): 1–24. Chaucer's sensitivity to the "cultural survival" of Wales is suggested in three moments in *HF*: the insinuation that Wales is near the river of forgetfulness through a visual pun on "Cymerie" (73); the citation of an unknown and hence implicitly forgotten Welsh bard, "Bret Glascurion" (1208); and the reference to the Welsh Geoffrey of Monmouth as "Englyssh" (1470).

See also nos. 30, 44, 46, 83, 93, 190.

The Legend of Good Women

188. Dane, Joseph A. *Abstractions of Evidence in the Study of Manuscripts and Early Printed Books.* Burlington, Vt.: Ashgate, 2008. 176 pp. Includes a study that details the bibliographical and physical instability of two variants of the 1542 Chaucer edition—the Reynes imprint and the Bonham imprint—as they exist in the Hoe, the Chew, and the Hagen-Clark copies, paying particular attention to the title pages. Dane argues, with George Kane and against Skeat and Robinson, that the Cambridge MS Gg.4.27 *LGWP* is a variant of the F version, rather than an authorial revision. Unlike Kane, Dane attributes radical textual variation to catastrophic manuscript damage rather than to ordinary scribal practice.

See also nos. 44, 46, 92, 137.

The Parliament of Fowls

189. Escobedo, Andrew. "The Sincerity of Rapture." *SSt* 24 (2009): 185–208. Escobedo treats Chaucer as a link between Spenser and Plato and considers choice a crucial value in *PF*. Also notes that *MerT* shows that "mastery cannot compel love" (196).

190. Fradenburg, Aranye. "(Dis)continuity: A History of Dreaming." In Elizabeth Scala and Sylvia Federico, eds. *The Post-Historical Middle Ages* (*SAC* 33 [2011], no. 88), pp. 87–115. Fradenburg contemplates similarities between Freud's *Interpretation of Dreams* and medieval dream theory (especially Chaucer's in *PF, BD,* and *NPT*) as a way to explore the continuities of history and human psychology.

See also nos. 30, 34, 44, 82.

The Romaunt of the Rose

191. Campbell, Laura J. "Reinterpretation and Resignification: A Study of the English Translation of *Le Roman de la Rose*." *Neophil* 93 (2009): 325–38. James Holmes's "mapping technique" applied to *Rom* reveals a systematic reinterpretation of the French text's ambiguous language.

192. Fitzmaurice, Susan M., and Donka Minkova, eds. *Studies in the*

History of the English Language IV: Empirical and Analytical Advances in the Study of English Language Change. New York: Mouton de Gruyter, 2008. ix, 433 pp. Nineteen studies, including position papers, responses, and counter-responses. A set of exchanges pertains to Chaucer: In "Metrical Evidence: Did Chaucer Translate *The Romaunt of the Rose?*" (pp. 155–79), Xingzhong Li affirms on metrical grounds that Chaucer translated Fragment A of *Rom,* did not translate Fragment B, and probably did translate Fragment C. Thomas Cable, in "The Elusive Progress of Prosodical Study" (pp. 101–19), critiques Li for emphasising meter while ignoring "beat." In "Trochees in an Iambic Meter: Assumptions or Evidence?" (pp. 181–85), Li argues that statistical evidence better supports his own claims than it does Cable's critique.

See also nos. 23, 27.

Troilus and Criseyde

193. Anastasopoulos, Alexandra. "Inherent Meaning from Homer, to Benoît, to Chaucer." *Meeting of Minds XVII* 11 (2009): 199–203. Anastasopoulos argues for mediated influence of Benoît's *Le Roman de Troie* on characterization, didactic message, and acknowledgment of sources in *TC.*

194. Carney, Clíodhna. "Chaucer's 'litel bok,' Desire, Plotinus, and the Ending of *Troilus and Criseyde.*" *Neophil* 93 (2009): 357–68. Carney considers the two-stanza envoy to *TC* "in the light of Plotinus' Neoplatonic scheme of *exitus* and *reditus*" (ending and return).

195. Kaylor, Noel Harold, Jr. "The Shape of Chaucerian Tragedy." In Marcin Krygier and Liliana Sikorska, eds. *Þe Laurer of Oure Englische Tonge.* Medieval English Mirror, no. 5. Frankfurt am Main: Peter Lang, 2009, pp. 93–105. The five-book structure of *TC* is informed both by Dante's *Divine Comedy* and by Boethius's *Consolatio,* a combination that adds to the text's ambiguity. Chaucer extends Dante's three-step journey from Inferno to Heaven by adding Troilus's downward movement, thus completing Fortune's turn. At the same time, Troilus's five books parallel the steps in Boethius's epistemology of knowledge: *sensing* (Book I), *imagining* (Book II), *reasoning* (Books III and IV), and *knowing* (Book V).

196. Lim, Gary. "'Thus Gan He Make a Mirour of His Mynde': Fragmented Memories and Anxious Desire in *Troilus and Criseyde.*" *Neo-*

phil 93 (2009): 339–56. Lim traces "anxiety [as] the definitive characteristic of Troilus's desire" in *TC*.

197. Mitchell, J. Allan. "Criseyde's Chances: Courtly Love and Ethics About to Come." In Ann W. Astell and J. A. Jackson, eds. *Levinas and Medieval Literature: The "Difficult Reading" of English and Rabbinic Texts* (*SAC* 33 [2011], no. 59), pp. 185–206. Reads courtly love in *TC* through a Levinasian lens: courtly desire is ethical because it is never satisfied. Yet Criseyde's case disallows a direct application of Levinasian ethical theory. Mitchell comments on the role of fortune in *TC,* the exchange of Criseyde, and the possibility of her becoming a moral subject. Also comments on gender differences in relation to the question of ethics and erotic love in *TC*.

198. ———. *Ethics and Eventfulness in Middle English Literature*. The New Middle Ages. New York: Palgrave Macmillan, 2009. xiv, 187 pp. Mitchell explores the relationships among fortune, ethics, and validity in *TC* and other late medieval writings: Usk's *Testament of Love, The Chaunce of the Dyse,* Gower's *Confessio Amantis,* Lydgate's *Fall of Princes,* and Malory's *Morte Darthure*. Examines *Bo* and the Boethian concepts of love, fortune, and freedom in *TC* and how these concerns are manifest in related ways in Usk's work and *The Chaunce of the Dyse*.

199. Rossiter, William. "The Chaucerian Sonnet." *Interculturality and Translation* (Universidad de León) 2 (2006): 177–99. Analyzes Chaucer's use and adaptation of Petrarch's sonnet as the "canticus Troili" in *TC,* exploring prosodic and contextual features in light of R. A. Shoaf's description of translation as either rape or marriage.

200. Smith, Kendra O'Neal. "Untimely Translatio in Fourteenth-Century British Literature." *DAI* A70.06 (2009): n.p. Smith posits feminine and masculine modes of the transmission of power and culture from the ancients to the medieval, using *Sir Gawain and the Green Knight,* the *Alliterative Morte Arthure,* and *TC* to demonstrate the existence of "a feminine means of transferring identity and authority."

201. Webb, Diana. *Privacy and Solitude in the Middle Ages*. New York: Hambledon Continuum, 2007. xvii, 266 pp. Surveys medieval notions and representations of privacy in relation to various religious and devotional practices, study, gardening, social spaces, and the demise of community. Comments recurrently on Chaucer's depictions of solitude, focusing on his "acute sense of place and interior space" in *TC*. See also no. 280.

See also nos. 29, 30, 33, 36, 44, 46, 50, 51, 53, 65, 68.

Lyrics and Short Poems

See nos. 50, 71, 73, 199.

Adam Scriveyn

See no. 73.

The Complaint of Chaucer to His Purse

See no. 73.

The Complaint of Mars

See no. 177.

The Envoy to Bukton

See no. 73.

The Envoy to Scogan

See no. 73.

Fortune

See no. 42.

Chaucerian Apocrypha

202. Higl, Andrew. "Joining the *Canterbury Tales*: The Interactivity of Its Reception and Transmission." *JEBS* 12 (2009): 29–49. Reads continuations of *CT* in light of new-media theory, treating the apocryphal tales as textual interactions invited by the storytelling frame.

203. Vázquez, Nila. *The "Tale of Gamelyn" of the "Canterbury Tales": An Annotated Edition.* Lewiston, Maine: Mellen, 2009. vi, 466 pp. Edition of the *Tale of Gamelyn,* including a description of manuscripts, diplomatic transcriptions of ten manuscripts, a critical edition with collated

variants, and critical apparatus. Also includes a Modern English translation of *Gamelyn* and a glossary of the Middle English text.

204. Vázquez González, Nila. "The *Tale of Gamelyn*: A New Critical
Edition." PhD diss., University of Santiago de Compostela, 2006. 720
pp. Edition of the *Tale of Gamelyn,* including a description of manuscripts, illustrations from diplomatic transcriptions of ten manuscripts,
a critical edition with collated variants, and critical apparatus. Also includes a Modern English translation of *Gamelyn* and a glossary of the
Middle English text.

205. Wimsatt, James I. *Chaucer and the Poems of "Ch."* Rev. ed.
TEAMS Middle English Texts Series. Kalamazoo: Medieval Institute
Publications, Western Michigan University, 2009. vii, 162 pp. Revised,
reformatted version of 1982 edition (see *SAC* 8 [1984], no. 14) of the
poems signed "Ch" in University of Pennsylvania Manuscript 15. Includes an updated, expanded introduction; revised commentary on the
poems and Chaucer's relations with his French contemporaries; and a
newly introduced numbering system for the edited poetry. See also no.
285.

Book Reviews

206. Ackroyd, Peter, trans. *The Canterbury Tales—Geoffrey Chaucer: A
Retelling by Peter Akroyd* (*SAC* 33 [2011], no. 9). Rev. Joan Acocella, *New
Yorker,* December 21 and 28, 2009, pp. 140–45; Germaine Greer,
http://www.ft.com [*Financial Times*], April 20, 2009, n.p.; Carolyne Larrington, *TLS,* July 10, 2009, p. 7; Phoebe Pettingell, *The New Leader*
92.6 (November/December 2009): 30–32.

207. Alexander, Michael. *Medievalism: The Middle Ages in Modern England* (*SAC* 31 [2009], no. 48). Rev. Helen Brookman, *Marginalia* 9
(2009): n.p.; Roger Simpson, *Arthuriana* 18.3 (2008): 75–76; Angela
Jane Weisl, *Historian* 71 (2008): 400–401.

208. Amodio, Mark C., ed. *New Directions in Oral Theory* (*SAC* 29
[2007], no. 301). Rev. Elissa R. Henkin, *Western Folklore* 68.1 (2009):
122–23.

209. Anderson, Judith H. *Reading the Allegorical Intertext: Chaucer,
Spenser, Shakespeare, Milton* (*SAC* 32 [2010], no. 46). Rev. Andrew Es-
cobedo, *Shakespeare Quarterly* 60.3 (2009): 369–72; Clare R. Kinney,
RenQ 62 (2009): 621–23.

210. Barrington, Candace. *American Chaucers* (*SAC* 31 [2009], no. 50). Rev. David Watt, *TMR* 09.11.14, n.p.

211. Bliss, Jane. *Naming and Namelessness in Medieval Romance* (*SAC* 32 [2010], no. 99). Rev. Mary Flannery, *Arthuriana* 19.3 (2009): 136–37; Paul Vincent Rockwell, *Encomia* 31 (2009): 21–23.

212. Bowers, John M. *Chaucer and Langland: The Antagonistic Tradition* (*SAC* 31 [2009], no. 37). Rev. A. V. C. Schmidt, *MÆ* 78.2 (2009): 336–37.

213. Bullón-Fernández, María, ed. *England and Iberia in the Middle Ages, 12th–15th Century: Cultural, Literary, and Political Exchanges* (*SAC* 31 [2009], no. 15). Rev. Kathleen Ashley, *SCJ* 40 (2009): 585–86; Simon Doubleday, *JBSt* 48 (2009): 743–44.

214. Burrow, J. A. *The Poetry of Praise* (*SAC* 32 [2010], no. 63). Rev. Linda Bates, *Marginalia* 9 (2009): n.p.; Nicholas Perkins, *SAC* 31 (2009): 311–13; James Simpson, *N&Q* 254 (2009): 278–80; Matthew Woodcock, *RES* 60 (2009): 477–79.

215. Butterfield, Ardis, ed. *Chaucer and the City* (*SAC* 30 [2008], no. 108). Rev. Míceál F. Vaughan, *JEGP* 108 (2009): 114–17.

216. Chaganti, Seeta. *The Medieval Poetics of the Reliquary: Enshrinement, Inscription, Performance* (*SAC* 32 [2010], no. 240). Rev. Robyn Malo, *TMR* 09.11.15, n.p.

217. Cohen, Jeffrey Jerome. *Of Giants: Sex, Monsters, and the Middle Ages* (*SAC* 23 [2001], no. 199). Rev. Melissa Ridley-Elmes, *Hortulus* 5.1 (2009): n.p.

218. ———, ed. *The Postcolonial Middle Ages* (*SAC* 24 [2002], no. 145). Rev. Simon Gaunt, *CL* 61.2 (2009): 160–76.

219. Cole, Andrew. *Literature and Heresy in the Age of Chaucer* (*SAC* 32 [2010], no. 107). Rev. Ian Forrest, *Journal of Ecclesiastical History* 60 (2009): 808–9; John M. Ganim, *TMR* 09.05.05, n.p.; Kantik Ghosh, *SAC* 31 (2009): 318–21; Margaret Harvey, *Journal of Theological Studies* 60 (2009): 741; J. Patrick Hornbeck II, *Church History* 78 (2009): 678–80; Seth Lerer, *TLS,* January 30, 2009, p. 23; Emily Steiner, *Religion and Literature* 41.1 (2009): 156–60; Karen A. Winstead, *RES* 60 (2009): 479–80; Simon Yarrow, *History Today* 59.6 (2009): 61.

220. Condren, Edward L. *Chaucer from Prentice to Poet: The Metaphor of Love in Dream Visions and "Troilus and Criseyde"* (*SAC* 32 [2010], no. 299). Rev. Helen Phillips, *H-Albion* (March 2009): n.p.; Willam A. Quinn, *Arthuriana* 19.4 (2009): 71–72; Barry Windeatt, *SAC* 31 (2009): 321–24.

221. Considine, John. *Dictionaries in Early Modern Europe: Lexicography and the Making of Heritage* (*SAC* 32 [2010], no. 70). Rev. Adam Smyth, *TLS,* June 29, 2009, p. 32.

222. Cooper, Lisa H., and Andrea Denny-Brown, eds. *Lydgate Matters: Poetry and Material Culture in the Fifteenth Century* (*SAC* 32 [2010], no. 108). Rev. Scott-Morgan Straker, *SAC* 31 (2009): 324–27.

223. Davis, Isabel. *Writing Masculinity in the Later Middle Ages* (*SAC* 31 [2009], no. 271). Rev. Mike Rodman Jones, *SAC* 31 (2009): 327–30.

224. Desmond, Marilynn. *Ovid's Art and the Wife of Bath: The Ethics of Erotic Violence* (*SAC* 30 [2008], no. 199). Rev. Jane Chance, *International Journal of the Classical Tradition* 15 (2008): 683–87; Nunzio N. d'Alessio, *GLQ: A Journal of Gay and Lesbian Studies* 15.3 (2009): 522–25; Susan J. Dudash, *SIcon* 30 (2009): 258–60; Laura Gowing, *Journal of Women's History* 21.2 (2009): 146–52; L. A. J. R. Houwen, *Scriptorium* 61 (2007): 180.

225. Echard, Siân. *Printing the Middle Ages* (*SAC* 32 [2010], no. 20). Rev. Joel Fredell, *Textual Cultures* 4.1 (2009): 160–63; Anat Gueta, *Parergon* 26.2 (2009): 168–69; Helen McManus, *Comitatus* 40 (2009): 283–84.

226. Ellis, Steve, ed. *Chaucer: An Oxford Guide* (*SAC* 29 [2007], no. 108). Rev. Alexandra Gillespie, *N&Q* 254 (2009): 100–101.

227. Evans, Ruth, Helen Fulton, and David Matthews, eds. *Medieval Cultural Studies: Essays in Honour of Stephen Knight* (*SAC* 30 [2008], no. 115). Rev. *FMLS* 45 (2009): 227–28.

228. France, John, ed. *Mercenaries and Paid Men: The Mercenary Identity in the Middle Ages* (*SAC* 33 [2011], no. 106). Rev. James Hester, *SCJ* 40 (2009): 1214–15; William Urban, *H-HRE* (May 2009): n.p.

229. Fyler, John M. *Language and the Declining World in Chaucer, Dante, and Jean de Meun* (*SAC* 31 [2009], no. 101). Rev. Helen Cooper, *EIC* 59 (2009): 59–65; William Sayers, *AdI* 27 (2009): 445–46.

230. Giancarlo, Matthew. *Parliament and Literature in Late Medieval England* (*SAC* 31 [2009], no. 103). Rev. Sarah Peverley, *TMR* 09.04.11, n.p.; Clare Sponsler, *Historian* 48 (2009): 187–89; Lynn Staley, *SAC* 31 (2009): 337–40; Marion Turner, *RES* 60 (2009): 299–301.

231. Gillespie, Alexandra. *Print Culture and the Medieval Author: Chaucer, Lydgate, and Their Books, 1473–1557* (*SAC* 30 [2008], no. 23). Rev. Tamara Atkin, *N&Q* 254 (2009): 1109–10; Paul Dean, *ES* 90 (2009): 245–47; Alex Devine, *Marginalia* 9 (2009): n.p.; Jordi Sánchez-Martí, *Atlantis* 31 (2009): 151–56.

232. Gray, Douglas. *Later Medieval English Literature* (*SAC* 32 [2010], no. 53). Rev. Julia Boffey, *SAC* 31 (2009): 340–42; J. A. Burrow, *N&Q* 254 (2009): 644–45.

233. Green, D. H. *Women Readers in the Middle Ages* (*SAC* 31 [2009], no. 104). Rev. Jennifer N. Brown, *JBSt* 48 (2009): 182–83; Nicola McDonald, *SAC* 31 (2009): 343–45.

234. Hass, Andrew, David Jasper, and Elisabeth Jay, eds. *The Oxford Handbook of English Literature and Theology* (*SAC* 31 [2009], no. 168). Rev. Mark Harris, *N&Q* 254 (2009): 473–75.

235. Heng, Geraldine. *Empire of Magic: Medieval Romance and the Politics of Cultural Fantasy* (*SAC* 28 [2006], no. 127). Rev. Simon Gaunt, *CL* 61.2 (2009): 160–76.

236. Holton, Amanda. *The Sources of Chaucer's Poetics* (*SAC* 32 [2010], no. 68). Rev. John M. Bowers, *RES* 60 (2009): 481–82; Thomas J. Farrell, *SAC* 31 (2009): 345–48.

237. Hopkins, Amanda, and Cory James Rushton, eds. *The Erotic in the Literature of Medieval Britain* (*SAC* 31 [2009], no. 110). Rev. Tison Pugh, *ESC* 34 (2008): 271–74.

238. Ingham, Patricia Clare, and Michelle R. Warren, eds. *Postcolonial Moves: Medieval Through Modern* (*SAC* 29 [2007], no. 190). Rev. Simon Gaunt, *CL* 61.2 (2009): 160–76.

239. Kabir, Ananya Jahanara, and Deanne Williams, eds. *Postcolonial Approaches to the European Middle Ages: Translating Cultures* (*SAC* 29 [2007], no. 52). Rev. Simon Gaunt, *CL* 61.2 (2009): 160–76.

240. Knapp, Peggy A. *Chaucerian Aesthetics* (*SAC* 32 [2010], no. 121). Rev. Virginia Langum, *Marginalia* 9 (2009): n.p.

241. Kolve, V. A. *Telling Images: Chaucer and the Imagery of Narrative II* (*SAC* 33 [2011], no. 142). Rev. Don Fry, *Virginia Quarterly Review* 85.4 (2009): 213.

242. Kosso, Cynthia, and Anne Scott, eds. *The Nature and Function of Water, Baths, Bathing, and Hygiene from Antiquity Through the Renaissance* (*SAC* 33 [2011], no. 122). Rev. Paolo Squatriti, *TMR* 09.12.17, n.p.

243. Kuskin, William. *Symbolic Caxton: Literary Culture and Print Capitalism* (*SAC* 32 [2010], no. 24). Rev. Anne Laskaya, *TMR* 09.03.02, n.p.; Daniel Wakelin, *SAC* 31 (2009): 348–51.

244. Léglu, Catherine E., and Stephen J. Milner, eds. *The Erotics of Consolation: Desire and Distance in the Late Middle Ages* (*SAC* 32 [2010], no. 124). Rev. Sherry Roush, *Speculum* 84 (2009): 746–47.

245. Lerer, Seth, ed. *The Yale Companion to Chaucer* (*SAC* 30 [2008], no. 131). Rev. James H. Morey, *TMR* 09.10.20, n.p.

246. Lightsey, Scott. *Manmade Marvels in Medieval Culture and Literature* (*SAC* 31 [2009], no. 118). Rev. Michael Calabrese, *YLS* 23 (2009): 292–96; Laura L. Howes, *JBSt* 48 (2009): 183–84.

247. Lindeboom, B. W. *Venus' Owne Clerk: Chaucer's Debt to the "Confessio Amantis"* (*SAC* 31 [2009], no. 158). Rev. Jonathan Hsy, *JEGP* 108 (2009): 261–63.

248. Little, Katherine C. *Confession and Resistance: Defining the Self in Late Medieval England* (*SAC* 30 [2008], no. 245). Rev. Jane Bishop, *Historian* 70 (2008): 373–74.

249. Machan, Tim William, ed. *Chaucer's "Boece": A Critical Edition Based on Cambridge University Library, MS Ii.3.21, ff. 9ʳ–180ᵛ* (*SAC* 32 [2010], no. 287). Rev. Simon Horobin, *SAC* 31 (2009): 351–53.

250. Masciandaro, Nicola. *The Voice of the Hammer: The Meaning of Work in Middle English Literature* (*SAC* 31 [2009], no. 121). Rev. Martine Yvernault, *MA* 115 (2009): 388–89.

251. McMullan, Gordon, and David Matthews, eds. *Reading the Medieval in Early Modern England* (*SAC* 31 [2009], no. 56). Rev. Randy P. Schiff, *JBSt* 48 (2009): 194–95.

252. McSheffrey, Shannon. *Marriage, Sex, and Civic Culture in Late Medieval London* (*SAC* 30 [2008], no. 133). Rev. Karen Bollermann, *SMART* 16.1 (2009): 145–51.

253. Meyer-Lee, Robert J. *Poets and Power from Chaucer to Wyatt* (*SAC* 31 [2009], no. 57). Rev. Paul Strohm, *N&Q* 254 (2009): 646–47; Greg Walker, *JEGP* 108 (2009): 263–65.

254. Meyerson, Mark D., Daniel Thiery, and Oren Falk, eds. *"A Great Effusion of Blood"? Interpreting Medieval Violence* (*SAC* 28 [2006], no. 138). Rev. Laura Jose, *N&Q* 254 (2009): 281–82.

255. Mieszkowski, Gretchen. *Medieval Go-Betweens and Chaucer's Pandarus* (*SAC* 30 [2008], no. 285). Rev. Holly A. Crocker, *Arthuriana* 18.3 (2008): 83–84.

256. Minnis, Alastair. *Fallible Authors: Chaucer's Pardoner and Wife of Bath* (*SAC* 32 [2010], no. 247). Rev. Dominique Battles, *TMR* 09.03.17, n.p.; Andrew Galloway, *SAC* 31 (2009): 353–57; Jennifer A. T. Smith, *Comitatus* 40 (2009): 317–18.

257. Momma, Haruko, and Michael Matto, eds. *A Companion to the History of the English Language* (*SAC* 32 [2010], no. 80). Rev. Jack Lynch, *TLS,* May 1, 2009, p. 22.

258. Morgan, Gerald. *The Tragic Argument of "Troilus and Criseyde"* (*SAC* 30 [2008], no. 286). Rev. Nicolas Jacobs, *MÆ* 78 (2009): 134–36.

259. Morrison, Susan Signe. *Excrement in the Late Middle Ages: Sacred Filth and Chaucer's Fecopoetics* (*SAC* 32 [2010], no. 152). Rev. Valerie Allen, *TMR* 09.03.08, n.p.; Virginia Langum, *Marginalia* 10 (2008–9): n.p.; Peter J. Smith, *Times Higher Education Supplement,* January 15, 2009, p. 52.

260. Neal, Derek G. *The Masculine Self in Late Medieval England* (*SAC* 32 [2010], no. 129). Rev. Bettina Bildhauer, *TLS,* August 7, 2009, p. 31; Isabel Davis, *H-Albion* (September 2009): n.p.

261. Norris, Ralph. *Malory's Library: The Sources of the "Morte Darthur"* (*SAC* 32 [2010], no. 58). Rev. Michael N. Salda, *Arthuriana* 18.4 (2009): 92–93.

262. Phillips, Susan E. *Transforming Talk: The Problem with Gossip in Late Medieval England* (*SAC* 31 [2009], no. 123). Rev. Theresa Coletti, *SCJ* 40 (2009): 1310–11; Karla Taylor, *Speculum* 84 (2009): 205–6.

263. Pugh, Tison. *Sexuality and Its Queer Discontents in Middle English Literature* (*SAC* 32 [2010], no. 132). Rev. Gary Lim, *Arthuriana* 18.3 (2008): 87–88; Robert Mills, *SAC* 31 (2009): 361–64.

264. ———, and Marcia Smith Marzec, eds. *Men and Masculinities in Chaucer's "Troilus and Criseyde"* (*SAC* 32 [2010], no. 319). Rev. A. J. DeLong, *TMR* 09.03.04, n.p.; Amanda Hopkins, *SAC* 31 (2009): 364–67; Adrienne J. Odasso, *SCJ* 40 (2009): 1203–4.

265. Purdie, Rhiannon. *Anglicising Romance: Tail-Rhyme and Genre in Medieval English Literature* (*SAC* 32 [2010], no. 265). Rev. Kathleen M. Blumreich, *Encomia* 31 (2009): 56–58.

266. Quinn, Esther Casier. *Geoffrey Chaucer and the Poetics of Disguise* (*SAC* 32 [2010], no. 133). Rev. Michael Calabrese, *TMR* 09.10.10, n.p.

267. Radulescu, Raluca L., and Cory James Rushton, eds. *A Companion to Medieval Popular Romance* (*SAC* 33 [2011], no. 165). Rev. Megan Leitch, *Marginalia* 10 (2008–9): n.p.

268. Raffel, Burton, trans. *The Canterbury Tales* (*SAC* 32 [2010], no. 36). Rev. Joseph Bottum, *First Things* 191 (2009): 49–51.

269. Rayner, Samantha. *Images of Kingship in Chaucer and His Ricardian Contemporaries* (*SAC* 32 [2010], no. 135). Rev. Robert W. Barrett Jr., *Encomia* 31 (2009): 58–60; Rebecca Davis, *YLS* 23 (2009): 310–15; Siân Echard, *RES* 60 (2009): 483–84; Don Hoffman, *Arthuriana* 19.3 (2009): 148–49; Robert J. Meyer-Lee, *TMR* 09.06.17, n.p.

270. Scase, Wendy. *Literature and Complaint in England, 1272–1553*

(*SAC* 31 [2009], no. 127). Rev. Ethan Knapp, *SAC* 31 (2009): 3367–70; Gregory L. Laing, *Prolepsis* n.v. (2009): n.p.; T. Turville-Petre, *TMR* 09.05.12, n.p.

271. Schoff, Rebecca L. *Reformations: Three Medieval Authors in Manuscript and Movable Type* (*SAC* 31 [2009], no. 128). Rev. Bryan P. Davis, *JEBS* 12 (2009): 307–9.

272. Stanbury, Sarah. *The Visual Object of Desire in Late Medieval England* (*SAC* 32 [2010], no. 141). Rev. Mary C. Olson, *SCJ* 40 (2009): 1363–64; Sarah Salih, *RES* 60 (2009): 639–40; Elizabeth Scala, *TMR* 09.03.06, n.p.; Veronica Sekules, *Speculum* 84 (2009): 779–81; Karen Winstead, *SAC* 31 (2009): 378–81.

273. Strohm, Paul, ed. *Middle English* (*SAC* 31 [2009], no. 133). Rev. Jamie Taylor, *SAC* 31 (2009): 381–84.

274. Summit, Jennifer. *Memory's Library: Medieval Books in Early Modern England* (*SAC* 32 [2010], no. 28). Rev. Alexandra Gillespie, *SAC* 31 (2009): 384–87.

275. Swanson, R. N., ed. *Promissory Notes on the Treasury of Merits: Indulgences in Late Medieval Europe* (*SAC* [2009], no. 135). Rev. John T. Slotemaker, *SCJ* 40 (2009): 1220–21; Jennifer L. Welsh, *H-German* (April 2009): n.p.

276. Thomas, Alfred. *A Blessed Shore: England and Bohemia from Chaucer to Shakespeare* (*SAC* 31 [2009], no. 137). Rev. Ian Forrest, *International History Review* 30 (2008): 823–24; Deanne Williams, *RenQ* 61 (2008): 659–60.

277. Turner, Marion. *Chaucerian Conflict: Languages of Antagonism in Late Fourteenth-Century London* (*SAC* 31 [2009], no. 138). Rev. Tamara Atkin, *N&Q* 254 (2009): 109–11.

278. Wakelin, Daniel. *Humanism, Reading, and English Literature, 1430–1530* (*SAC* 32 [2010], no. 289). Rev. Tamara Atkin, *N&Q* 254 (2009): 107–8; David Rundle, *EHR* 124 (2009): 145–47; Wendy Scase, *SAC* 31 (2009): 388–91.

279. Wallace, David. *Premodern Places: Calais to Surinam, Chaucer to Aphra Behn* (*SAC* 28 [2006], no. 92). Rev. Simon Gaunt, *CL* 61.2 (2009): 160–76.

280. Webb, Diana. *Privacy and Solitude in the Middle Ages* (*SAC* 33 [2011], no. 201). Rev. Sarah Stanbury, *SMART* 16.2 (2009): 131–34.

281. Wheeler, Bonnie, ed. *Mindful Spirit in Late Medieval Literature: Essays in Honor of Elizabeth D. Kirk* (*SAC* 30 [2008], no. 154). Rev. Nancy Bradley Warren, *YLS* 23 (2009): 308–10.

282. Whetter, K. S. *Understanding Genre and Medieval Romance* (*SAC* 32 [2010], no. 267). Rev. Yin Liu, *TMR* 09.11.11, n.p.

283. Wilcockson, Colin. *"The Canterbury Tales": A Selection* (*SAC* 32 [2010), no. 30). Rev. Carolyne Larrington, *TLS*, July 10, 2009, p. 7.

284. Williams, Deanne. *The French Fetish from Chaucer to Shakespeare* (*SAC* 28 [2006], no. 94). Rev. Alexandre Leupin, *SMART* 16.2 (2009): 127–30.

285. Wimsatt, James I. *Chaucer and the Poems of "Ch."* Rev. ed. (*SAC* 33 [2011], no. 205). Rev. George Keiser, *TMR* 09.11.26, n.p.

286. Wogan-Browne, Jocelyn, et al., eds. *Language and Culture in Medieval Britain: The French of England, c. 1100–c. 1500* (*SAC* 33 [2011], no. 55). Rev. Elizabeth Dearnley, *Marginalia* 10 (2008–9): n.p.

287. Woods, William F. *Chaucerian Spaces: Spatial Poetics in Chaucer's Opening Tales* (*SAC* 32 [2010], no. 160). Rev. John H. Ganim, *RES* 60 (2009): 297–99.

288. Zieman, Katherine. *Singing the New Song: Literacy and Liturgy in Late Medieval England* (*SAC* 32 [2010], no. 263). Rev. Sam Barrett, *SAC* 31 (2009): 392–94; Kevin Teo Kia-Choong, *Comitatus* 40 (2009): 344–45; Michael Kuczynski, *TMR* 09.06.11, n.p.; Malcolm Richardson, *Religion and Literature* 41 (2009): 159–61; Ann Sadedin, *Parergon* 26.2 (2009): 216–17.

Author Index—Bibliography

The New Chaucer Society
Seventeenth International Congress
July 15–19, 2010
Università per Stranieri di Siena

WEDNESDAY, JULY 14

13:00–19:00 **Early Registration**

11:00 **Trustees' Meeting**

13:00–19:30 **Graduate Workshop**
13:00–14:00 Opening and students' presentations on their research

14:00–14:30 Elaine Treharne, Florida State University, on manuscript descriptions

14:30–15:00 **Break**

15:00–16:30 Orietta Da Rold, University of Leicester, on materials, Alexandra Gillespie, University of Toronto, on bindings, and Jessica Brantley, Yale University, on illuminations

16:30–17:00 **Afternoon Tea**

17:00–18:30 Simon Horobin, Magdalen College, Oxford, on scribal hands, Kathryn A. Lowe, University of Glasgow, on language, Toshiyuki Takamiya, Keio University, on collecting manuscripts

18:00–19:30 Roundtable discussion

THURSDAY, JULY 15

8:00–13:00 **Registration**

9:00–10:30 **Concurrent Sessions, Group 1 (1–6)**

Session 1: Chaucer and the Traditions of Medieval Authorship (Thread C)
Session Organizer and Chair: Robert R. Edwards, Pennsylvania State University
- "Authorial Arrogance: Criseyde, the Miller, and Chaucerian *Sprezzatura*," Wolfram R. Keller, Humboldt-Universität zu Berlin

- "Hagiography and the Invention of the Author," Jennifer L. Sisk, University of Vermont
- "Revisionary Poetics, Problematic Bodies, and the Body of Literature," Robert M. Stein, Purchase College and Columbia University

Session 2: Common Languages: Linguistic Hierarchies in the Fifth Century (Thread I)
Session Organizer and Chair: Ardis Butterfield, University College London
- "Chaucer and the Claims of Language," Tim Machan, Marquette University
- "Code-Switching in the Linguistic Hierarchy: Three Bureaucrats and Their Texts," Rebecca Fields, Exeter College, Oxford
- "Lending Authority? Reconsidering the Latin Marginal Glosses in Hoccleve's *Regiment of Princes,*" Elisabeth Kempf, Freie Universität Berlin
- "Words and War in Accounts of the Conflict Between England and France, 1337–1453," Joanna Bellis, Pembroke College, Cambridge

Session 3: How to Talk About God (Thread R)
Session Organizer and Chair: Sarah Beckwith, Duke University
- "Faith and Conversion in the *Second Nun's Tale,*" Kate Crassons, Lehigh University
- "Julian of Norwich and Boethius," Eleanor Johnson, Columbia University
- "Faith in Chaucer: The Friar, the Prioress, the Experts," Claire M. Waters, University of California Davis

Session 4: Bodily Boldness in Women (Thread B)
Session Organizer and Chair: Alcuin Blamires, Goldsmiths College, University of London
- "Mulier Ludens," Nicola McDonald, University of York
- " 'What, may I nat stonden here?' The Heroine's Body in *Troilus and Criseyde* and *The Testament of Cresseid,*" J. Seth Lee, University of Kentucky
- "Bold Bodies and Emergent Minds: Narrating Suicide and Chaucer's Lucrece," Corinne Saunders, University of Durham
- "The Touch of Class: What Nice Girls Don't Do in Chaucer," Sheila Fisher, Trinity College, Hartford

466

Session 5: Animals and the Human Social Order (Thread A)

Session Organizer: Lisa Kiser, Ohio State University
Chair: Gillian Rudd, Liverpool University

- " 'Grete kyndenes ys in howndys': The Ways of Dogs and Men in Three Middle English Romances," Harriet Hudson, Indiana State University
- "Judicial Violence, Biopolitics, and the Bare Life of Animals," Robert Mills, King's College London
- "Animal Debates: Chaucer's *Parliament of Fowls* and Lydgate's *The Horse, The Goose, and The Sheep*," Wendy Matlock, Kansas State University
- "Uxor Noe and Animal Inventory," Sarah Elliott Novacich, Yale University

Session 6: The Materials of Manuscript Production (Thread D)

Session Organizer and Chair: Alexandra Gillespie, University of Toronto

- "Rethinking the Fascicle: Booklet 3 of the Auchinleck Manuscript as Fragment and Assemblage," Arthur W. Bahr, Massachusetts Institute of Technology
- "From Treasured Text to Binder's Scrap: The Fragmentary Survival of Medieval Literature," Ann Higgins, Westfield State College
- "Paper Chaucer Manuscripts: What Can the Physical Evidence Tell Us and Why Should That Be Important?" Daniel W. Mosser, Virginia Tech
- "Analyzing the Material Structure of Manuscripts," Estelle Stubbs, University of Sheffield

10:30–11:00 **Morning Tea**

11:00–12:30 **Concurrent Sessions, Group 2 (7–12)**

Session 7: Chaucer and Adaptation (Thread M)

Session Organizers: Carolyn Dinshaw, New York University, and Bruce Holsinger, University of Virginia
Chair: Dana Symons, Buffalo State College

- "Chaucer in Danish: Adapting an Adaptation," Ebbe Klitgård, Roskilde University
- "Chaucer on Dickens's Hearth," David Raybin, Eastern Illinois University
- "Pornographic Chaucer," George Shuffleton, Carleton College

Session 8: Mare Nostrum and the Archipelago 1 (Thread T)

Session Organizer: Suzanne Conklin Akbari, University of Toronto
Chair: Candace Barrington, Central Connecticut State University

- "Archipelagic Ursula," Catherine Sanok, University of Michigan, Ann Arbor
- "Britannia est omnis divisa in partes tres: Remapping Wales and Scotland in Late Medieval England," Matthew Fisher, University of California, Los Angeles
- "The Archipelagic Otherworld: Geography and Identity in Medieval Ireland and Britain," Aisling Byrne, St. John's College, Cambridge
- "A Distinction of Poetic Form: What Happened to Rhyme Royal in Scotland?" James Goldstein, Auburn University

Session 9: Conflict Resolution in the Canterbury Tales (Thread P)

Session Organizer: Jerome Mandel, Tel Aviv University
Chair: Frances Beer, York University

- "Chaucer's Pardoner and Prioress: Managing Interfaith Conflicts," Catherine S. Cox, University of Pittsburgh
- "Recognition and Misrecognition in *The Clerk's Tale*," Michael Raby, University of Toronto
- " 'The same I seye: ther is no difference': Distinguishing Sovereign and Outlaw in the *Manciple's Tale*," Valerie B. Johnson, University of Rochester
- "Conflict Resolution in the *Wife of Bath's Prologue* and *Tale*," Jerome Mandel, Tel Aviv University

Session 10: Sense and Cognition (Thread S)

Session Organizer and Chair: Charles Archer, University of York

- "Sensing Chaucer: Articulating Perception in the *Canterbury Tales*," Richard Newhauser, Arizona State University
- "The Gendered Gaze in *Troilus and Criseyde*: Visual and Tactile Pleasures," Robert Sturges, Arizona State University
- "Moving Horses, Imagination, and *The Squire's Tale*," Michelle Karnes, Stanford University
- Respondent: Elizabeth Robertson, University of Glasgow

Session 11: Language and Learning in Late Medieval Europe (Thread I)

Session Organizers: Susie Phillips, Northwestern University, Claire M. Waters,

University of California Davis, and Michael Calabrese, California State University, Los Angeles
Chair: Claire M. Waters, University of California Davis
- "Huntington Library, Manuscript 128: *Piers Plowman* as a Medieval Book About Grammar," Michael Calabrese, California State University, Los Angeles
- "The Difficult Vernacular: Translation and Grammar Instruction in Chaucer's *Boece*," Kara Gaston, University of Pennsylvania

Session 12: Honor in Chaucer: For Derek Brewer
Session Organizer and Chair: Richard Firth Green, Ohio State University
- "Shame, Honour, and Individuality," Alcuin Blamires, Goldsmiths, University of London
- "Dishonorable Spooning," Stephanie Viereck Gibbs Kamath, University of Massachusetts, Boston
- " 'Oure Lady for to honoure': Worship of the Virgin in 'The Prioress's Tale,' " Laurel Broughton, University of Vermont

12:30–13:30 **Lunch**

1:30–14:30 **Business Meeting**
Presider: David Lawton, Washington University, Saint Louis

14:30–16:00 **Concurrent Sessions, Group 3 (13–18)**

Session 13: Revisionary Chronologies and the Chaucer Canon (Thread C)
Session Organizer and Chair: Kathryn Lynch, Wellesley College
- "Chronology as History: Chaucer, Langland, Shakespeare," Louise Bishop, University of Oregon
- "Talking Through Gower's Recensions: Speech and Politics in the *Confessio Amantis*," David Coley, Simon Fraser University
- "Chaucer's Childhood: William Godwin's Revisionary Biography," Karla Knutson, Concordia College
- "Chaucer and Astronomy: A Chronology," Edgar Laird, Texas State University
- "Did Chaucer Retire? Reading the 'Envoy to Scogan' After Pinkhurst," Stephen Partridge, University of British Columbia
- " 'The First Testimony of Chaucer's Genius': Chronology, Canonicity,

469

and the Middle English *Romaunt of the Rose,*" Liv Robinson, St. Hilda's College, Oxford

- "Dating Chaucer, Dating Langland: Toward Textual Historicism," Lawrence Warner, University of Sydney

Session 14: Common Languages: Vernacular Identity and Genre (Thread I)

Session Organizer: Ardis Butterfield, University College London
Chair: Andrew Taylor, University of Ottawa

- "Vernacularity and Sexuality," Larry Scanlon, Rutgers
- "Lyricizing the Vernacular: Richard Rolle's Isolationist Aesthetic," Gabriel Haley, University of Virginia
- "Vernacular Romance Manuscripts of Thirteenth- and Fourteenth-Century England," Elizabeth Watkins, University of Toronto

Session 15: Image Trouble, 1380–1538: The Secular Image (Thread V)

Session Organizer and Chair: Jessica Brantley, Yale University

- "Image Trouble in Vernacular Commentary: The Glossing of Evrart de Conty and Francesco da Barberino," Alastair Minnis, Yale University
- "An Iconography of the Secular in *Der Welscher Gast,*" Kathryn Starkey, University of North Carolina, Chapel Hill
- "René of Anjou and the Heart's Two Quests," Barbara Newman, Northwestern University

Session 16: Animal Speech (Thread A)

Session organizer: Susan Crane, Columbia University
Chair: Karl Steel, City University of New York

- "Singing the Other into Existence: Animals and Lyric in Chaucer," Emma Gorst, University of Toronto
- "Dreams, Domestication, and the Fable of Animal Speech in Chaucer's *Nun's Priest's Tale,*" Lesley Kordecki, De Paul University
- "Chaucer's Chauntecleer: Speech Fowl and Fair," Megan Palmer Browne, University of California, Santa Barbara
- "The Signifying Bird," Carolynn Van Dyke, Lafayette College

Session 17: Chaucer, Langland, and Ethics (Thread S)

Session Organizers and Chairs: J. Allan Mitchell, University of Victoria, and Jessica Rosenfeld, Washington University

- "Chaucer, Langland, and Pastoral Ethics," Edwin D. Craun, Washington and Lee University
- "Literary Ethics and the Tropological Sense," Ryan McDermott, University of Virginia
- "The Aristotelian Clerk: Thought, Perception, and Imagination in the *Clerk's Tale*," Amy Goodwin, Randolph Macon College

Session 18: Before Chaucer: From Anglo-Norman to English
Session Organizer and Chair: Helen Cooper, Magdalene College, Cambridge
- "Chaucer's Philosophical Use of an Anglo-Norman Text: *The Man of Law's Tale*," John Hirsh, Georgetown University
- " 'Is constancy such a disloyal thing?' Chaucer's Retellings of the Unchanging Self," Laura Ashe, Worcester College, Oxford
- " 'Wose is onwis': Competing Ideologies in *Dame Sirith*," Gabriel Ford, Pennsylvania State University

16:00–16:30 **Afternoon Tea**

16:30–17:45 **Biennial Chaucer Lecture**
Chair: Richard Firth Green, The Ohio State University
L. O. Aranye Fradenburg, University of California, Santa Barbara
"Living Chaucer"

18:30–19:30 **Civic Reception**
Palazzo Pubblico, Cortile del Podestà

FRIDAY, JULY 16

9:00–10:30 **Concurrent Sessions, Group 4 (19–24)**

Session 19: "Whilom": Medieval Medievalisms (Thread M)
Session Organizers: Carolyn Dinshaw, New York University, and Bruce Holsinger, University of Virginia
Chair: Bruce Holsinger, University of Virginia
- "Chaucer and the New Nostalgia," Marisa Libbon, UC-Berkeley
- " 'Whilom': Troy," Kathryn McKinley, University of Maryland–Baltimore County
- "Chaucer as a Language Historian: Multilingualism and Tolkien's

'Chaucer as a Philologist,'" Mary Catherine Davidson, Glendon College–York University
- "Spatializing Time: Chaucer's Multiple Temporalities in the *Man of Law's Tale*," Andrew James Johnston, Freie Universität Berlin

Session 20: Borders and Centers (Thread F)
Session Organizer: Warren Ginsberg, University of Oregon
Chair: Brenda Schildgen, University of California, Davis
- "Chaucer, Boccaccio, and the Medieval World System," John Ganim, University of California, Riverside
- "Paradisal Ethnography in Dante and Chaucer," Mark Sherman, Rhode Island School of Design
- "When Borders Become Centers in Petrarch and Chaucer," Lenny Koff, University of California, Los Angeles

Session 21: Transnational French (Thread T)
Session Organizer: Suzanne Conklin Akbari, University of Toronto
Chair: David Matthews, University of Manchester
- "French on Land and Sea: Anglo-Flemish Trade, Gilbert Maghfield, and the *Shipman's Tale*," Jonathan Hsy, George Washington University
- "Literary Identities in Chaucerian England: The English Translations of the Romance *Partonopeu de Blois*," Sif Rikhardsdottir, University of Iceland
- "'Sailing Between Scylla and Charybdis': Philippe de Mézières, the Order of the Passion, and Negotiations for an Anglo-French Peace," Sara V. Torres, University of California, Los Angeles
- "Virtue and the Vernacular: Brunetto Latini, Chaucer, and Christine de Pizan," Suzanne Akbari, University of Toronto

Session 22: Gendered Bodies: Class, Violence, Pity, and the Erotic (Thread B)
Session Organizer: Ruth Evans, Saint Louis University
Chair: Holly Crocker, University of South Carolina
- "Female Muscle: Violence and the Working Woman's Body in Fifteenth-Century Texts," Nicole Nolan Sidhu, East Carolina University
- "Augustine's and Chaucer's Dido: *Pudor* and Eroticized Pity in the 'Legend of Dido,'" Matt Irvin, Sewanee University

- "Shaved Pussy? Alison's Beard and the Semiotics of Medieval Female Pubic Depilation," Ruth Evans, Saint Louis University

Session 23: Manuscripts Before and After Chaucer (Thread D)
Session Organizers: Daniel Wakelin, University of Cambridge, and William Robins, University of Toronto
Chair: William Robins, University of Toronto
- "The English Language and 'Literature' Before Chaucer," Emily Butler, University of Toronto
- "Literary Codicologies: Bookish Form and Formal Play in the *Canterbury Tales*," Helen Marshall, University of Toronto
- "Compiling Chaucer in the Sixteenth Century," Simon Horobin, Magdalen College, Oxford

Session 24: Before Chaucer: Latin and English
Session Organizer: Helen Cooper, Magdalene College, Cambridge
Chair: Robert M. Stein, Purchase College and Columbia University
- "Chaucer and the Late Fourteenth-Century Renaissance of Anglo-Latin Rhetoric," Martin Camargo, University of Illinois
- "Macaronic Poetry Before Chaucer," Elizabeth Archibald, University of Bristol
- "Predecessors of Chaucer's Prosody," Thomas Cable, University of Texas, Austin
- "Middle English Marvels: Magic, Spectacle, and Morality from *Sir Orfeo* to *The Wife of Bath's Tale*," Tara Williams, Oregon State University

10:30–11:00 **Morning Tea**

11:00–12:30 **Concurrent Sessions, Group 5 (25–30)**

Session 25: The Place of Medievalism (Thread M)
Session Organizers: Carolyn Dinshaw, New York University, and Bruce Holsinger, University of Virginia
Chair: Carolyn Dinshaw, New York University
- " 'The Wife of Brittany' and the Civil War Veteran: Remaking *The Franklin's Tale* for the Vanquished South," Candace Barrington, Central Connecticut State University
- "From Rock Creek to Chartres: Revisiting Henry Adams's Medievalism," Amy Hollywood, Harvard Divinity School

473

- "Place and the Invitation to Medievalism," Thomas Prendergast, College of Wooster

Session 26: Italian Encounters: Forms and Venues of Literary and Cultural Exchange, 1350–1430 (Thread F)
Session Organizer: Carolyn Collette, Mount Holyoke College
Chair: Peter W. Travis, Dartmouth College
- "An English Reader of Dante in Papal Avignon," N. R. Havely, York University
- "Did Chaucer Meet Sercambi?" William Robins, University of Toronto
- "Richard de Bury, Petrarch, and Avignon," Carolyn Collette, Mount Holyoke College

Session 27: Image Trouble, 1380–1538: The Sacred Image (Thread V)
Session Organizer and Chair: James Simpson, Harvard University
- "'Marioles,' 'babouins' and 'fyoles': Eustache Deschamps' Opposition to Painted Religious Statues," Laura Kendrick, Université de Versailles
- "John Capgrave's Material Memorials," Shannon Gayk, Indiana University
- "Confessing Your Things in Guillaume de Digulleville," Nicolette Zeeman, Cambridge University

Session 28: Bodily Boldness in Women (Thread B)
Session Organizer: Alcuin Blamires, Goldsmiths, University of London
Chair: Robert Rouse, University of British Columbia, Vancouver
- "'Do wey thy boldnesse': Cecile and Her Body in the *Second Nun's Tale*," John F. Plummer, Vanderbilt University
- "Erotic (Subject) Positions in Chaucer's Fabliaux," Amy S. Kaufman, Wesleyan College
- "The Wife of Bath's 'walkynge out,'" Kenneth Bleeth, Connecticut College

Session 29: Diplomatics and Poetics (Thread P)
Session Organizers: Wendy Scase, University of Birmingham, and Matthew Giancarlo, University of Kentucky
Chair: Matthew Giancarlo, University of Kentucky

- "A Tale of Royal (Dis)Continuity: The Preamble to the New Statutes of England," Rosemarie McGerr, Indiana University
- "Voicing the King: Edward II, the 1311 Ordinances, and Regal Poetics," David Matthews, University of Manchester
- "The Petition of Nicholas Lassy of Chester, c. 1443, and *The Libelle of English Policy*," Michael Bennett, University of Tasmania

Session 30: Ethics: A Roundtable (Thread S)
Session Organizers and Chairs: Jessica Rosenfeld, Washington University, and J. Allan Mitchell, University of Victoria
- "Beyond Moral Demand," Mark Miller, University of Chicago
- "The Ethics of Form," Valerie Allen, John Jay College of Criminal Justice
- "Green Ethics," Jill Rudd, University of Liverpool
- "Ethics and Economics," Elizabeth Edwards, University of King's College

12:30–14:00 **Lunch**

14:00–15:30 **Plenary Session**
David Wallace, University of Pennsylvania
Miri Rubin, Queen Mary, University of London
"Chaucer's Mary, Queen of Siena"

15:30–16:00 **Afternoon Tea**

16:00–17:30 **Concurrent Sessions, Group 6 (31–36)**

Session 31: Remediating Chaucer: Roundtable on Modern Chaucer, Medievalisms, and Multimedias (Thread M)
Session Organizers: Laurie Finke, Kenyon College, and Kevin Harty, LaSalle University
Roundtable Chair: Laurie Finke, Kenyon College
- "The BBC Remediates *The Man of Law's Tale*," Kevin Harty, LaSalle University
- "Marketing Chaucer," Martin B. Shichtman, Eastern Michigan University
- "Incontrovertible Facts? We Don't Need No Stinkin' Incontrovert-

ible Facts! Terry Jones as Historian," Roberta Davidson, Whitman College

- "Chaucer at the Fringe: Staging the *Canterbury Tales*," Christine Neufeld, Eastern Michigan University
- "The Sacrilegious Pleasures of Chaucer Rap," Kathleen Coyne Kelly, Northeastern University
- "Murder, He Wrote: Chaucerian Mystery Novels," Susan Aronstein, University of Wyoming
- "Sites of Resistance: Chaucer, Medievalism, Media," Elizabeth Sklar, Wayne State University

Session 32: Diplomacy and Diplomats, 1 (Threads F and P)
Session Organizer: Warren Ginsberg, University of Oregon
Chair: Candace Barrington, Central Connecticut State University
- "Divine Diplomacy and Audience Responsibility in *Troilus and Criseyde* and the *Canterbury Tales*," Elizabeth Capdevielle, University of Wisconsin–Madison
- "Chaucer's Affective Vocabulary," Susan Yager, Iowa State University
- "*Translator studii*: Nicholas Trivet and the Reinvention of Senecan Tragedy in Chaucer and Lydgate," John T. Sebastian, Loyola University New Orleans

Session 33: Chaucer's World and the Global Middle Ages (Thread T)
Session Organizer: Geraldine Heng, University of Texas, Austin
Chair: Bonnie Wheeler, Southern Methodist University
- "The African Queen: Chaucer's Dido and Her Avatars," Thomas Hahn, University of Rochester
- "Chaucer in Bohemia," Peter Brown, University of Kent
- "The World Is an Oyster: Prester John of 'India,' the Fifth Crusade, and the Relations Between Islam and the West," Chris Taylor, University of Texas
- "Politics of Wonder and Displacement: Domesticating the Tartars in Chaucer's *Squire's Tale* and *The King of Tars*," Leila K. Norako, University of Rochester

Session 34: Illuminated Manuscripts and International Commerce in Fourteenth-Century Europe (Thread V)
Session Organizer: Michael Hanly, Washington State University

Chair: Eugene Green, Boston University
- "Jacopo Rapondi of Lucca and the Illuminated Book in Late Medieval European Commerce," Michael Hanly, Washington State University
- "'Ther was nowher swich another man': The Great Khan and His Court in Fifteenth-Century Illuminated Manuscripts," Anamaria Gellert, University of Pisa
- "Sensing the Italian Manuscript in a European Context," Elaine Treharne, Florida State University

Session 35: Liturgy, Sacraments, Ecclesiology (Thread R)
Session Organizer: Sarah Beckwith, Duke University
Chair: Rosalind Field
- "Unlocking and Locking the Lay Imagination: Some Benedictine English Vernacular Projects at the Turn of the Fourteenth Century," Alan Fletcher, University College Dublin
- "Chaucer, the Church, and the Truth of Religion," Jim Rhodes, Southern Connecticut State University
- "Seeing Is Believing: Exploring and Communicating the Visual Experience of Medieval Parishioners in Research and Teaching," Dee Dyas, University of York

Session 36: Princepleasing (Thread P)
Session Organizer and Chair: Susanna Fein, Kent State University
- "Trevisa's Index," Emily Steiner, University of Pennsylvania
- "Treason and Silence: Froissart and His English Patrons in 1395," Andrew Taylor, University of Ottawa
- "Cawing Truths to Power in *The Manciple's Tale*," Nancy Mason Bradbury, Smith College
- Respondent: Richard Firth Green, Ohio State University

19:00–20:15 **Concert of I Madrigalisti Senesi**
Chiesa di San Francesco–Piazza s. Francesco-Siena

SATURDAY, JULY 17

9:00–10:30 **Concurrent Sessions, Group 7 (37–42)**

Session 37: Touching the Past (Thread C)
Session Organizer: Jeffrey J. Cohen, George Washington University
Chair: George Edmundson, Dartmouth College

- "The Surfaces of Emelye's Body," Jaime A. Friedman, Cornell University
- "Ekphrasis and Polytemporality in *Pearl*," Claire Barbetti, Duquesne University
- "The Touch of Happenstance or a Staged Encounter? Mel Gibson's *The Passion of the Christ* Reenacts the York Mystery Cycle," Miriamne Krummel, University of Dayton

Session 38: Latin and Its Rivals, 1: The Limits of Official Culture (Thread I)
Session Organizer and Chair: Thomas Hahn, University of Rochester
- "English Latinity and the London Court of Husting Rolls, 1350–1485," Eileen Kim, University of Toronto
- "Wives and Property in Chaucer's London: Latin and English Terminology," Henry Ansgar Kelly, University of California, Los Angeles
- "English, French, or Latin? The Use—and Disuse—of Language in the Records of English Central Government, c. 1400–1470," Gwilym Dodd, University of Nottingham

Session 39: Conduct Literature and Performative Reading: Rereading a Genre (Thread B)
Session Organizers: Glenn Burger, Queens College, CUNY, and Christine Rose, Portland State University
Chair: Christine Rose, Portland State University
- "Domesticity and Sovereignty in York's 'Christ Before Pilate I,'" Emma Lipton, University of Missouri
- "Conducting Intercession in *The Prick of Conscience*," Rosemary O'Neill, University of Pennsylvania
- "Conduct Dreams: Agency and the Chaucerian Critique of Exemplarity in Hoccleve's *Regiment of Princes*," Nathanial B. Smith, Central Michigan University

Session 40: Animal Figures (Thread A)
Session Organizer and Chair: Sarah Stanbury, College of the Holy Cross
- "Looking at Animals in Chaucer and Langland," Rebecca Davis, University of California, Irvine
- "Lover as Parrot," Sarah Kay, Princeton University
- "A Horsly Horse: Mechanical Animals in *The Squire's Tale* and Else-

where," Monika Otter, Dartmouth College [read by Sarah Stanbury in Monika Otter's absence]

Session 41: The Politics of Melibee (Thread P)
Session Organizer and Chair: Marion Turner, Jesus College, Oxford
- " 'The Trouthe of Thynges and Profit': Prudent Resolutions and Resistant Grief in the *Tale of Melibee*," Suzanne Edwards, Lehigh University
- "Werre: The Structure of Medieval Feud in the *Melibee*," Howell Chickering, Amherst College
- "Poets, Princepleasers, and Power: Identification with Female Counselors in Chaucer and Gower," Misty Schieberle, University of Kansas
- "Chaucer's *Melibee* and Political Reconciliation," John M. Hill, U.S. Naval Academy

Session 42: Annotating Chaucer and Shakespeare (Thread D)
Session Organizers and Chairs: A. S. G. Edwards, De Montfort University, and C. Jansohn, Universität Bamberg
- "Annotating the Chaucerian, Inventing Chaucer: Authority and Authorship in *The Ploughmans Tale* (1606)," Megan Cook, University of Pennsylvania
- "Reading Geoffrey Chaucer in (and out of) John Dryden's *Fables Ancient and Modern*," Simran Thadani, University of Pennsylvania
- " 'How mean you, sir?' Annotating Shakespeare's Texts," Barbara Mowatt, Folger Shakespeare Library
- "The Rationale for Apparatus in Shakespeare Editions," John Jowett, University of Birmingham
- Respondent: Jill Mann, University of Notre Dame

10:30–11:00 **Morning Tea**

11:00–12:30 **Presidential Lecture**
Chair: Carolyn Dinshaw, New York University
Richard Firth Green, Ohio State University
"Griselda in Siena"

12:30–14:00 **Lunch**

14:00–15:30 **Concurrent Sessions, Group 8 (43–48)**

Session 43: Diplomacy and Diplomats, 2 (Threads F and P)
Session Organizer: Warren Ginsberg, University of Oregon
Chair: Marilynn Desmond, Binghamton University
E-session, with responses and expansions to papers from Session 32:
- "Heir to Innocence: Gender and *The Legend of Good Women*," Lynn Arner, Brock University
- "The Diplomatic Context of *The Franklin's Tale*," William Askins, Community College of Philadelphia
- "Attempting Diplomacy in *The Legend of Good Women*," Elizabeth Martin, University of Maryland

Session 44: Mare Nostrum and the Archipelago 2 (Thread T)
Session Organizer: Suzanne Conklin Akbari, University of Toronto
Chair: Cynthia Ho, University of North Carolina, Asheville
- "Is There a Chaucerian Cosmopolitanism?" Shayne Aaron Legassie, University of North Carolina Chapel Hill
- "Isolation, Reticulation, Dissolution: Insularity in Middle English Literature," Matthew Goldie, Rider University
- "Margaret of Teschen's Czech Prayer: Transnationalism and Female Literacy in the Later Middle Ages," Alfred Thomas, University of Illinois, Chicago

Session 45: Animal Theories and Methodologies (Thread A)
Session Organizer and Chair: Susan Crane, Columbia University
- "Membrane Aesthetics," Bruce Holsinger, University of Virginia
- "Talking Bird / Gentle Heart: Bonding Between Women and Across Species in *The Squire's Tale*," Sara Schotland, Georgetown University
- "Derrida's Cat," Sarah Stanbury, College of the Holy Cross
- "It's Not Easy Being Green," Carolyn Dinshaw, New York University

Session 46: Conduct Literature and Performative Reading: Individualizing Conduct Within Manuscript Culture (Thread B)
Session Organizers: Glenn Burger, Queens College, CUNY, and Christine Rose, Portland State University
Chair: Glenn Burger, Queens College, CUNY
- "Room for Improvement: Modes of Conduct in Late Middle English Household Manuscripts," Myra Seaman, College of Charleston
- "The Game of Life in *Le Ménagier de Paris*: Performing the Exemplum in Bruyant's Poem," Christine Rose, Portland State University

- "Conduct Becoming a Man: Circulating the Masculine Social Self in Conduct Poetry," Christina M. Fitzgerald, University of Toledo
- "Reading the Ethics of Sleep in Courtesy Books and Cotton Nero A.x," Megan Leitch, St. John's College, Cambridge

Session 47: Chaucerian Humanism and *The House of Fame*
Session Organizer: Helen Fulton, Swansea University
Chair: Helen Phillips, University of Cardiff
- "The Myth of Daedalus and the House of Rumor in Chaucer's *House of Fame*," Colin Fewer, Purdue University
- "Urban Humanism and Chaucer's *House of Fame*," Helen Fulton, Swansea University
- "'Let us now praise famous men': Rumor, Writing, and Immortality in the *House of Fame*," Simon Meecham-Jones, Cambridge University and Swansea University

Session 48: Speech, Writing, and Venues for the Vernacular in Late Medieval England (Thread I)
Session Organizer: NCS Program Committee
Chair: Peter Brown, University of Kent
- "'The voyce of the pepille is cleped vox dei': Listening for the (Political) Text," Roger Nicholson, University of Auckland
- "Franciscanism and *Dives and Pauper*," Elizabeth Harper, University of North Carolina, Chapel Hill
- "Catherine of Siena in English Miscellanies," Jennifer Brown, Marymount Manhattan College
- "Access, Authority, and Chaucerian Vernacularity," Derrick Pitard, Slippery Rock University

15:30–16:00 **Afternoon Tea**

16:00–17:30 **Concurrent Sessions, Group 9 (49–54)**

Session 49: Authorship and Authority in Italy and England (Thread F)
Session Organizer and Chair: Warren Ginsberg, University of Oregon
- "'Encress' and Authority in Gower and Chaucer," Karla Taylor, University of Michigan

- "The End of Authorship: Chaucer's Shadow," Tom Stillinger, University of Utah
- "From Subaltern to Self-Actualization: Redefining Medieval Female Authorship and Authority in Italy and England," Stephanie A. Amsel, University of Texas, San Antonio
- "Dante, Boccaccio, and the Claims of Authority," Teresa A. Kennedy, University of Mary Washington
- "The Poetics of Fraud: False-Seeming Authors in Dante and Chaucer," Brendan O'Connell, Trinity College Dublin
- "Translating Formal 'Equivalence': The Mystery of Chaucer's 'Monk's Stanza,'" William A. Quinn, University of Arkansas

Session 50: Border Patrol: Race, Gender, and Religion (Thread T)
Session Organizer and Chair: Sylvia Tomasch, City University of New York
- "Borders, Blackness, and Global Christianity in *The Three Kings of Cologne*," Cord J. Whitaker, University of New Hampshire
- "On Firm Carthaginian Ground: Ethnic Boundary Fluidity in *The Legend of Women*," Randy Schiff, State University of New York, Buffalo
- "The Prioress's Boundaries and Bury St. Edmunds," Michael Widner, University of Texas, Austin
- "Chaucer's Cleopatra and the Color Line," Donna Crawford, Virginia State University

Session 51: Latin and Its Rivals, 2: Chroniclers in the Age of Chaucer (Thread I)
Session Organizer: Sylvia Federico, Bates College
Chair: Lynn Staley, Colgate University
- "The Audience of the Monastic Chronicler in Late Medieval England," James G. Clark, University of Bristol
- "Thomas Walsingham and the Peasants' Revolt," Andrew Prescott, University of Glasgow
- "The Author of the *Continuatio* of the *Eulogium Historiarum*," George B. Stow, LaSalle University
- "Walsingham's Dictys in Ricardian New Troy," Sylvia Federico, Bates College

Session 52: Conduct Literature and Performative Reading: Toward a Corporeal Ethics (Thread B)
Session Organizers: Glenn Burger, Queens College, CUNY, and Christine Rose, Portland State University
Chair: Ruth Evans, Saint Louis University

- "Virtues of Performance? Chaucer's Ruined Heroines and Late Medieval Conduct Literature," Holly A. Crocker, University of South Carolina
- "Memorable Conduct," Anke Bernau, University of Manchester
- "Jephtha's Daughter as Model of Conduct," David Wallace, University of Pennsylvania

Session 53: Experience and the Body (Thread S)
Session Organizer and Chair: Kellie Robertson, University of Wisconsin–Madison
- "Experience, Physik, and Self-Preservation in the *Canterbury Tales*," Virginia Langum, Magdalene College, Cambridge
- "Experience, Ethics, and Form in *Troilus and Criseyde*," Andreea D. Boboc, University of the Pacific
- "Transforming Troilus: Technological Metaphor in *Troilus and Criseyde*," Joel Nebres, University of Connecticut

Session 54: Editing the Works of Chaucer: Reopening the Debate (Thread D)
Session Organizer and Chair: Orietta Da Rold, University of Leicester
- "Editing Chaucer and the Chaucer Canon," Anthony Edwards, De Montfort University
- "The Text and Canon of Chaucer's Lyrics," Julia Boffey, Queen Mary, University of London
- "The Blake Editions of the *Canterbury Tales*," Michael Pidd, University of Sheffield
- "Offline Text, Online Notes: The Next Chaucer Edition?" Mark Allen, University of Texas, San Antonio
- "Editing Chaucer's *Legend*," Helen Phillips, University of Cardiff

7.00 **Dinner at the Enoteca Italiana**

SUNDAY, JULY 18

8:30–9:00 **Registration**

9:00–10:30 **Concurrent Sessions, Group 10 (55–60)**

Session 55: The French of Italy

Session Organizers: Marilynn Desmond, Binghamton University, and Karen Gross, Lewis & Clark College
Chair: Jane Gilbert, University College London

- "French and the Literary Market in the Mediterranean," William Burgwinkle, King's College, Cambridge
- "Angevin Naples: A French Kingdom in Southern Italy," Charmaine Lee, Università di Salerno
- "Troy and the Francophone Court of Robert of Anjou, King of Naples," Marilynn Desmond, Binghamton University
- Respondent: "Chaucer and the French of Italy," Karen Gross, Lewis & Clark College

Session 56: Illuminating Authors (Thread V)

Session Organizer: Joyce Coleman, University of Oklahoma
Chair: Elizabeth J. Bryan, Brown University

- "'Me thynketh it acordaunt to resoun / To telle yow al the condicioun / Of ech of hem': The Politics of the Pilgrim Portraits," Aditi Nafde, Keble College, Oxford
- "Where Chaucer Got His Pulpit: Audience and Intervisuality in the *Troilus and Criseyde* Frontispiece," Joyce Coleman, University of Oklahoma
- "The Embodied Mandeville of BL Harley MS 3954," Sarah Salih, King's College London

Session 57: Italian Matters: Rhetoric, Civic Culture, and Literary Writing (Threads F and P)

Session Organizer: Michaela Paasche Grudin, Lewis & Clark College
Chair: Rebecca S. Beal, University of Scranton

- "Brunetto's 'Rettorica': From Ciceronian Tension to Boccaccian Subversion," Michaela Paasche Grudin, Lewis & Clark College
- "Chaucer and Italian Matter in Scotland: The *Tale of Melibee*, Humanist Rhetoric, and Political Thought in John Ireland's *Meroure of Wysdome*," Lee Manion, Stern College for Women/Yeshiva University
- "Brunetto Latino, 'più sommo maestro in retorica,'" Julia Bolton Holloway, Mediatheca "Fioretta Mazzei," "English" Cemetery

Session 58: Cognitive Alterities 1. Chaucer and the Visionary Mind

Session Organizer and Chair: Jane Chance, Rice University

- "Thinking About Thinking, Then and Now," Peggy A. Knapp, Carnegie-Mellon University
- "The Neuroplastic Aesthetics of Chaucer's *House of Fame*," Ashby Kinch, University of Montana
- "Feelers: Touch, Cognition, and Identity," Lara Farina, West Virginia University

Session 59: Religion and Reading: Hermeneutics and Subjectivity (Thread R)

Session Organizers: Sarah Beckwith, Duke University, and Jim Rhodes, Southern Connecticut State University
Chair: Jim Rhodes, Southern Connecticut State University

- "Exegesis as Autobiography," Steven Kruger, Queens College and Graduate Center, CUNY
- "Sixteenth-Century Fundamentalism and the Specter of Ambiguity, or the Literal Sense Is Always a Fiction," James Simpson, Harvard University
- "Rolle and His Reader/Performers," Katherine Zieman, University of Notre Dame

Session 60: Blogging, Virtual Communities, and Medieval Studies (Thread M)

Session Organizer: Stephanie Trigg, University of Melbourne
Chair: John Ganim, University of California, Riverside

- "Blogging Past, Present, and Askew," Jeffrey J. Cohen, George Washington University
- "Blogging on the Margins: *Got Medieval,* Medieval Blogging, and Mainstream Readership," Carl S. Pyrdum III, Independent Scholar
- "How Do You Find the Time? Work, Pleasure, Time, and Blogging," Stephanie Trigg, University of Melbourne
- "An Englishman's Blog Is His Castle: Names, Freedom, and Control in Medievalist Blogging," Jonathan Jarrett, Fitzwilliam Museum, Cambridge
- Respondent: David Lawton, Washington University, Saint Louis

10:30–11:00 **Morning Tea**

11:00–12:30 **Plenary Session**
Chair: Thomas Hahn, University of Rochester

Warren Ginsberg, University of Oregon
"Found in Translation: Chaucer and Italy"

12:30–13:30 **Lunch**

13:30–18:30 **Half-day Excursion to San Gimignano or to San Galgano**

MONDAY, JULY 19

8:30–9:00 **Registration**

9:00–10:30 **Concurrent Sessions, Group 11 (61–66)**

Session 61: Cognitive Alterities, 2. Medieval Drama and Mysticism: Body in Mind
Session Organizer: Jane Chance, Rice University
Chair: Juliette Dor, University of Liège
- "Minding the Passion," Kerstin Pfeiffer, University of Stirling
- "Mirroring Christ as a Meme," Mayumi Taguchi, Osaka Sangyo University
- Respondent: Anthony D. Passaro, University of Texas–Health Science Center, Houston

Session 62: Touching the Past (Thread C)
Session Organizer and Chair: Jeffrey J. Cohen, George Washington University
- "Chaucer's Anglo-Saxons," Mary Kate Hurley, Columbia University
- "No Longer Quarantined in Private Vacuums: Chaucer's Griselda and Lars von Trier's Bess McNeill," Eileen Joy, Southern Illinois University, Edwardsville
- "Weeping with Erkenwald, or Complicit with Grace," Karl Tobias Steel, CUNY Brooklyn

Session 63: Doxa and Its Discontents (Thread R)
Session Organizer: Sarah Beckwith, Duke University
Chair: Peggy A. Knapp, Carnegie-Mellon University
- "St. Catherine of Siena and Chaucer's Preaching Nun," Gail Gibson, Davidson College

486

- "Social Contingency and Religious Context for the English *Elucidarium*," Sarah James, University of Kent
- "Traitors in Sanctuary: Eleanor Cobham and the Rhetoric of Religion," Elizabeth Allen, University of California, Irvine

Session 64: Defining the "Medieval" in Films of the Middle Ages (Thread M)

Session Organizer and Chair: Arthur Lindley, University of Birmingham

- "Everything New Is Old Again: Feminism and Antifeminism in Two Modern Versions of *The Wife of Bath* and Her *Tale*," Alan Baragona, Virginia Military Institute
- "Defining the Medieval in *A Canterbury Tale* and Beyond: Time, Visuality, and the Human," Bettina Bildhauer, University of St. Andrews
- "Camelot Redefined: Merlin as a Non-Othering Text of the Middle Ages," Züleyha Çetiner-Öktem, Ege University

Session 65: Italy and England: Learned Traditions and Vernacular Articulations (Thread F)

Session Organizer: NCS Program Committee
Chair: Stefania D'Agata D'Ottavi, Università per Stranieri di Siena

- "William Flete's *Remedies Against Temptations*: A Stylistic Appraisal," Gabriella Del Lungo Camiciotti, University of Florence
- "Chaucer and Filippo Ceffi, Again," Kenneth P. Clarke, Pembroke College, Cambridge University
- "Friars' Discourse: Fourteenth-Century Raymundina," Krista Sue-Lo Twu, University of Minnesota, Duluth
- "Poetic Authority and Political Factionalism in Chaucer and the Anonymous Genoese," Joseph Grossi, University of Victoria

Session 66: Women's Work in Women's Writing

Session Organizer: NCS Program Committee
Chair: Fiona Tolhurst, University of Geneva

- "Material Girls? Middle English Female Scribes and Their Secular Groupies," Kenna Olsen, Mount Royal College
- "Observance and Heterodoxy Meet: Anna Eybin's Books," Sara S. Poor, Princeton University
- "Anxious *Auctoritas*: Chaucer's Narrative Strategies in *The Legend of Good Women*," Deborah Strickland, Indiana University

- " 'Namoore to seye': Conflict and the Silenced Woman," Cathy Hume, University of Leeds

10:30–11:00 **Morning Tea**

11:00–12:30 **Concurrent Sessions, Group 12 (67–72)**

Session 67: Animal Interactions (Thread A)
Session Organizer: Sandy Feinstein, Penn State Berks
Chair: L. O. Aranye Fradenburg, University of California, Santa Barbara
- "Sir Gowther's Saintly Greyhounds," Emily Huber, Franklin and Marshall College
- "Shrews, Polecats, and Rats: The Smell of Death in *The Pardoner's Tale*," Sandy Feinstein, Penn State Berks, and Neal Woodman, USGS & National Museum of Natural History, Smithsonian
- "Knight and Horse," Susan Crane, Columbia University

Session 68: The Friar's Discourse (Thread R)
Session Organizer: Sarah Beckwith, Duke University
Chair: Derrick Pitard, Slippery Rock University
- "Understanding the Theological Basis for Wyclif's Anti-fraternalism," Stephen Lahey, University of Nebraska
- " 'The sovereynte of all heremytes': Augustinian Fraternalism in Osbern Bokenham's *Legenda Aurea*," Cynthia Turner Camp, University of Georgia
- "Bodies and Buildings: The Friars and Their Lay Patrons," Caroline Bruzelius, Duke University

Session 69: Multilanguage Use in Late Medieval England (Thread I)
Session Organizer: Thomas Hahn, University of Rochester
Chair: Richard Newhauser, Arizona State University
- "Charles d'Orléans as Lyric Author: Practices of Poetic Compilation in BN MS f.fr 25458 and BL MS Harley 682," Mariana Neilly, Queen's University Belfast
- "Rough Translation: Lydgate, Hoccleve, and Charles d'Orléans," Ardis Butterfield, University College London
- "Latin Poets in Chaucer's London: Gower and Others," R. F. Yeager, University of West Florida

Session 70: What Is the Place of Theory in Manuscript Studies? (Thread D)

Session Organizers: Christina M. Fitzgerald, University of Toledo, Ohio, and Holly A. Crocker, University of South Carolina
Chair: Christina M. Fitzgerald, University of Toledo, Ohio

- "Performative Reading and Manuscript Studies," Glenn Burger, Queens College, CUNY
- "Reader Response Theory and the Challenges of Anonymity," Siobhain Bly Calkin, Carleton University
- "Barthes, Foucault, Cerquiglini, and the Discipline of Textual Criticism," Erick Kelemen, Fordham University
- "Framing Gender in the Hours of Mary of Burgundy and the Ellesmere Manuscript," Dorothy Kim, Vassar College
- "Manuscript versus Play Text: Performance Studies and the *Canterbury Tales,*" Robert J. Meyer-Lee, Indiana University, South Bend
- "The Signifier of Desire," Elizabeth Scala, University of Texas

Session 71: Seeing Is Believing: Sin, Violence, and the Godhead in Visual Culture (Thread V)

Session Organizer: NCS Program Committee
Chair: Patricia Clare Ingham, Indiana University

- "Strike a Pose: Fashion, Sin, and Pleasure in Pastoral Care," Nicole Smith, University of North Texas
- "The Role of the Image in the Medieval Gallant Tradition in England," Emily Rozier, University of Birmingham
- "The Apophatic Image and the Pearl of Greatest Price," Kerilyn Harkaway, University of Indiana

Session 72: Responses and Inventions: Literary Currents in the Fifteenth Century

Session Organizer: NCS Program Committee
Chair: Alastair Minnis, Yale University

- "Lydgate Flatters: Patronage and Praise in *The Fall of Princes,*" Amanda Walling, Amherst College
- "Saddening the Body of a Boy: Heat, the Cold, and Coming of Age in Middle English Romance," Katie L. Walter, Ruhr-Universität Bochum
- "Fifteenth-Century Reception of Chaucer: Evidence from John Shirley's Glosses," Roberta Magnani, University of Cardiff

12:30–14:00 **Lunch**

14:00–15:30 **Concurrent Sessions, Group 13 (73–78)**

Session 73: Disability (Thread B)
Session Organizer and Chair: Edward Wheatley, Loyola University
- "How to Kiss a Leper," Julie Orlemanski, Harvard University
- "Blinded by Lust: 'Re-Visioning' Gerald of Aurillac," Michelle M. Sauer, University of North Dakota
- "Textual Prosthesis: The Use of Disability in Reader-Produced Additions to Chaucer's Corpus," Andrew Higl, Winona State University

Session 74: Guild Cultures (Thread P)
Session Organizer and Chair: Jonathan Hsy, George Washington University
- "Petitionary Writing and Guild Identities," Robert Ellis, Queen Mary, University of London
- "'Kenne Me By Some Craft to Knowe the False': Guilds and Scientific Knowledge in London in the Later Middle Ages," Cristina Pangilinan, University of Pennsylvania
- "Guild Labors and Humoral Typologies," Kellie Robertson, University of Wisconsin, Madison
- "The London Skinners' Bibliography," Michelle Warren, Dartmouth College

Session 75: The Literary, Horticultural, and Historical Garden Traditions Behind Chaucer's Poetry (Thread V)
Session Organizers: Susan K. Hagen, Birmingham-Southern College, and Teresa P. Reed, Jacksonville State University
Chair: Teresa P. Reed, Jacksonville State University
- "In Terra and in Text: Gardens in Chaucer's Time," Susan K. Hagen, Birmingham-Southern College
- "Gardens Chaucer Knew, Revisited," Laura Howes, University of Tennessee
- "The Medieval Garden and the Aesthetics of Pleasure," Jane Avner, Université de Paris–Nord XIII

Session 76: Religion and Reading: Devotional Literacy (Thread R)
Session Organizers: Sarah Beckwith, Duke University, and Jim Rhodes, Southern Connecticut State University

Chair: Theresa Coletti, University of Maryland
- "Reading and Scripting the Immanent Textuality of Life: Religion and the Practice of the Letter," Patricia Dailey, Columbia University
- "Thynke on God," Ryan Perry, Queen's University Belfast, and Stephen Kelly, Queen's University Belfast
- "'This is the Englysshe': Devout Reading and Approved Women at Syon Abbey," Paul J. Patterson, Saint Joseph's University

Session 77: Experience and Alchemy (Thread S)
Session Organizer: Kellie Robertson, University of Wisconsin
Chair: Steven Kruger, Queens College and Graduate Center, CUNY
- "Alchemical Chaucer," Erin Labbie, Bowling Green State University
- "Transcendental Empiricism in *The Canon's Yeoman's Tale*," Peter W. Travis, Dartmouth College
- "Of 'Elvyssch Lore': Alchemy and the Secret of Novel Experiences," Patricia Clare Ingham, Indiana University

Session 78: Textual and Material Histories
Session Organizer: NCS Program Committee
Chair: David Wallace, University of Pennsylvania
- "Pulp Fiction, Torn Hearts: Romances on Paper in Middle English Verse Love Epistles," Martha Dana Rust, New York University
- "Textual Discoveries from the Collation of the Hengwrt and Ellesmere Manuscripts," Yoshiyuki Nakao, Akiyuki Jimura, and Masatsugu Matsuo, University of Hiroshima
- "Ancient and Ever-Living: Richard Brathwaite's Commentaries and the Humanist's Chaucer," Sean Pollack, Portland State University
- "Between Titology and Titling Practice: Negotiating Theory and Materiality in the Study of Manuscript Titles," Victoria Gibbons, University of Cardiff
- "What Is the Role of Theory in Manuscript Studies? A Reorientation," David Watt, University of Manitoba

16:00 "To knytte up all this feeste, and make an ende": Disciplinary Perspectives and the Single-Author Conference
Chair: David Lawton, Washington University, Saint Louis
Sarah Kay, Professor and Chair, Department of French and Italian, Princeton University

Andrew Prescott, Director of Research, Humanities Advanced Technology and Information Institute, University of Glasgow
Amy Hollywood, Elizabeth H. Monrad Professor of Christian Studies, Harvard Divinity School
William Burgwinkle, Reader in Medieval French and Occitan, Head of the Department of French, Cambridge University
Sara S. Poor, Professor of German, Princeton University
Short responses followed by an inclusive discussion.

18:30 **Congress Dinner**
Tenuta di Monaciano—Siena

TUESDAY, JULY 20

9:00–18:00 **All-day Excursion to the Clay Hills or to the Chianti Countryside**

Within the Program, sessions associated with a particular Thread are identified by the following codes:

A Animal Discourses, General Organizer, Susan Crane, Columbia University
B Bodies, General Organizer, Ruth Evans, Saint Louis University
C Chaucerian Temporalities, General Organizer, Jennifer Summit, Stanford University
D Manuscripts and Printed Books, General Organizer, Orietta Da Rold, Leicester University
F Found in Translation: Italy and England in the Age of Chaucer, General Organizer, Warren Ginsberg, University of Oregon
I Insular Multilingualisms, General Organizer, Thomas Hahn, University of Rochester
M Medievalisms, General Organizers, Carolyn Dinshaw, New York University, and Bruce Holsinger, University of Virginia
P Political Languages, General Organizer, Marion Turner, Jesus College, Oxford
R Religious Practice, Institutions, and Theology: Chaucerian Contexts, General Organizer, Sarah Beckwith, Duke University

S   Philosophy and Science, General Organizer, Michelle Karnes, Stanford University

T   Transnationalism, General Organizer, Suzanne Conklin Akbari, University of Toronto

V   Visual Cultures, General Organizer, Jessica Brantley, Yale University

INDEX

Page numbers of illustrations are indicated in the index by *italics*.